PRAISE FOR *The Fifth Wave*

"In a perfect world, we would clone Michael Crow, so every university would have the same advantage as Arizona State University. Until that happens, *The Fifth Wave* is our next best option." —**Malcolm Gladwell**

"The modern American university is a fountainhead of knowledge, a privileged gatekeeper, and an exorbitant money sink. Updating this vital institution for the twenty-first century is a major challenge, and no one is better placed to show us the way than Michael Crow and William Dabars. Crow is a magician who exploded conventional tradeoffs and made his university both intellectually stellar and inspiringly inclusive." —**Steven Pinker**, Johnstone Family Professor, Harvard University, and author of *Enlightenment Now: The Case for Reason, Science, Humanism, and Progress*

"As social and technological complexity accelerates, progress and adaptation are driven by waves of change in all sectors. The advent of the interconnected estate empowers citizens but has brought the imperative for broad access to scientific and technological literacy. The Fifth Wave envisioned by Michael Crow tackles this challenge and assumes responsibility not only for knowledge production but societal well-being. In this compelling assessment of the prospects for evolution in American higher education, Crow and William Dabars delineate the parameters of a league of colleges and universities that will scale advanced learning to maximize innovation and societal impact." —**Eric Schmidt**, Technical Advisor, Alphabet Inc.

"Widely admired, always discussed, Michael Crow is the most radical practitioner in American higher education. To see him lead Arizona State University is to see a pinch of genius and a pound of courage. It is theater and it is purpose. It is, at present, higher education's "greatest show on earth." Mikhail Baryshnikov said of Fred Astaire: "We are dancing, but he is doing something else." In higher education, this is Michael Crow. In *The Fifth Wave*, he and William Dabars write a blueprint for building out a research-grade higher education infrastructure proportionate to the task of educating every academically qualified applicant in America. Their ambition is to "democratize intelligence." Radically redesigned, these schools would be purpose-built to educate the next generation, by the millions, at "socially meaningful scale." An impossible ambition, save Crow already has the working prototype in his own Arizona State University." —**David G. Bradley**, Chairman, Atlantic Media

"*The Fifth Wave* recognizes the urgent need for our public universities to get off the sidelines and engage seriously with the world, from increasing access to the transformative opportunities provided by higher education to taking on the profound challenges our world faces. Michael Crow and William Dabars make a powerful case for the unique and powerful good that universities can accomplish if academia is bold enough to reconsider how its unique strengths can contribute to a more equitable, sustainable, and informed future." —**Ana Mari Cauce**, President, University of Washington

"Michael Crow and William Dabars propose a new model for American universities. Their delineation of the history and evolution of American colleges and universities and their discussion of issues facing these institutions highlight the significance and gravity of these issues as well as the substantial contributions that research universities make to society." —**Robert J. Zimmer**, President, University of Chicago

"Provocative, encompassing, and grounded—a blueprint for learning and creating that is authentic to the twenty-first century—an age, perhaps, better characterized as the age of entanglement rather than the age of enlightenment. This calls for going beyond transdisciplinarity and Pasteur's Quadrant to create new forms of institutional and disciplinary architectures better attuned to learning in action with others. Unique to this blueprint is the proposition of the Fifth Wave University as a network of practices and institutions not bounded geographically or politically. Reading this incredible book made us think John Dewey would be smiling to see how his ideas, including democracy, have evolved for this new age of entanglement." —**John Seely Brown**, former Chief Scientist, Xerox Corp., and Director of Xerox Palo Alto Research Center (PARC), and Ann Pendleton-Jullian, former director, Knowlton School of Architecture, Ohio State University and professor of design, Pardee RAND Graduate School, coauthors of *Design Unbound: Designing for Emergence in a White Water World*

"Michael Crow and William Dabars argue persuasively that a league of universities committed to broad access to world-class knowledge production can deliver both success for individuals and the economic competitiveness of our nation. This is recommended reading for those interested in preparing for the complexities that lie ahead." —**Steve Case**, Chairman and CEO, Revolution, and author of *The Third Wave: An Entrepreneur's Vision of the Future*

"Michael Crow is redefining the way research universities engage with society. In *The Fifth Wave*, Crow and William Dabars call upon us to imagine a new era in American higher education where accessible institutions are dedicated to solving global problems through technological innovation, social entrepreneurship, and world-class knowledge production. All those with a stake in the future of higher education would benefit greatly from reading this book." —**Arthur C. Brooks**, Center for Public Leadership, Harvard Kennedy School, author of *The Conservative Heart: How to Build a Fairer, Happier, and More Prosperous America*

"Michael M. Crow is one of a handful of the most creative and able presidents of any American university. I consider any new book that he produces to be an important event. *The Fifth Wave* should be read by academic, business, and governmental leaders, especially those who have a stake in the continued preeminence of the great research universities— and their future structures—in the United States." —**Jonathan R. Cole**, Columbia University, author of *The Great American University: Its Rise to Preeminence, Its Indispensable National Role, Why It Must Be Protected*

# THE FIFTH WAVE

# THE FIFTH WAVE

## THE EVOLUTION OF AMERICAN HIGHER EDUCATION

### MICHAEL M. CROW
#### AND
### WILLIAM B. DABARS

JOHNS HOPKINS UNIVERSITY PRESS

*Baltimore*

Johns Hopkins University Press
2715 North Charles Street
Baltimore, Maryland 21218-4363
www.press.jhu.edu

Library of Congress Cataloging-in-Publication Data

Names: Crow, Michael M., author. | Dabars, William B., author.
Title: The fifth wave : the evolution of American higher education /
    Michael M. Crow and William B. Dabars.
Description: Baltimore : Johns Hopkins University Press, [2020] |
    Includes bibliographical references and index.
Identifiers: LCCN 2019036586 | ISBN 9781421438023 (hardcover) |
    ISBN 9781421438030 (ebook)
Subjects: LCSH: Education, Higher—Aims and objectives—United
    States. | Universities and colleges—United States—Administration.
Classification: LCC LA227.4 .C76 2020 | DDC 378.73—dc23
LC record available at https://lccn.loc.gov/2019036586

A catalog record for this book is available from the British Library.

*Special discounts are available for bulk purchases of this book. For more
information, please contact Special Sales at specialsales@press.jhu.edu.*

# CONTENTS

Our national discussion on higher education has been dominated by concerns with workplace relevance and skyrocketing costs, but to anyone who worries about growing inequality in America, the larger concern should be with broad accessibility to the sort of world-class learning environments now generally available only to more privileged applicants. In the globalized knowledge economy, both personal success and our collective social and economic prosperity are tied to advanced levels of educational attainment. But our leading colleges and universities admit only a fraction of academically qualified students. Even at our top public research universities, the majority of students do not reflect the socioeconomic diversity of our nation. The demands of both equity and prosperity argue that society needs to expand its capacity to produce millions of additional graduates during the next several decades capable of both catalyzing and benefiting from an economy increasingly based on the generation and application of useful knowledge. Moreover, the capacity of these institutions to produce world-leading discovery, creativity, and innovative solutions should be a matter of national concern. This will require epistemic, pedagogical, and institutional innovation, including the creative use of learning technologies and, in many cases, cooperation rather than competition among institutions as well as strategic partnerships among universities, business and industry, government agencies, and organizations in civil society.

Lack of accessibility to knowledge is a principal factor in exacerbating social inequality and diminishing our national potential for innovation, economic adaptability, and socioeconomic mobility. Readers familiar with the arguments of our previous book will find in this volume further elaboration regarding the imperative for a new and complementary model for the American research university that integrates broad accessibility to world-class knowledge production with societal impact. These are among the fundamental tenets of the new model for large-scale public research universities developed during the reconceptualization of

Arizona State University and serve as the basis for our proposal that a subset of these institutions similarly commit to expand accessibility at a socially meaningful scale, which is to say, accessibility to a demographic representative of the socioeconomic and intellectual diversity of the nation.

The transformation of Arizona State University during the past seventeen years demonstrates that research excellence and broad accessibility need not be mutually exclusive. ASU is committed to offering admission to all students qualified to undertake university-level coursework regardless of financial need. In so doing, the university seeks to advance socioeconomic mobility as well as prepare students for competitiveness in the global knowledge economy. ASU has succeeded in advancing both the academic rigor and diversity of the student body, which increasingly includes more and more students from socioeconomically disadvantaged and underrepresented backgrounds, including a significant percentage of first-generation college applicants. Through research learning and pedagogical innovation, students become adaptive master learners across a range of transdisciplinary fields, prepared to succeed in the continuously changing workforce of the knowledge-based economy. The successful implementation of the New American University model at Arizona State University suggests the potential for a subset of large-scale public research universities to similarly commit to expanding educational accessibility while facilitating discovery and innovation in the public interest.

Because this book proposes profound changes to complex organizations, we have drawn ideas from an array of research from within higher education and beyond. This includes scholarship on design, economics, public policy, organizational theory, science and technology studies, sociology, and, even to some extent, cognitive psychology and epistemology. Our hope is that this book will be of interest to anyone concerned with the future of higher education in our society and its potential to contribute to the success of our democracy in the twenty-first century.

A word regarding our respective roles: As president of Arizona State University, a science and technology policy scholar, and the designer of complex large-scale interdisciplinary research collaborations conceived to address real-world problems, Michael Crow conceptualized the New

American University and Fifth Wave models and spearheaded the design process that led to the reconceptualization of ASU as the foundational prototype for the New American University. William Dabars is a historian whose research focuses on the American research university and the organizational context of knowledge production. As an associate research professor in the School for the Future of Innovation in Society and senior director of research for the New American University in the Office of the President, he brings historical and theoretical perspective to bear on this effort to understand the evolution of American higher education and orient it toward more equitable and egalitarian outcomes.

## ACKNOWLEDGMENTS

We wish to express our appreciation to the many colleagues and scholars whose insight and expertise in diverse fields inspire and inform these chapters. Any effort to recognize their contributions threatens to run aground because inspiration and ideas circulate so freely amid the collective wisdom of collaboration. In addition to the more obvious intellectual debt to academic leaders acknowledged in our earlier work, including James J. Duderstadt, Vartan Gregorian, and Frank H. T. Rhodes, readers will discover the extent to which this book has been informed by the voluminous scholarship on the American research university and the respective oeuvres of scholars whose differing approaches brilliantly elucidate these infinitely complex institutions. We are especially grateful to those who reviewed our first volume and sometimes brought novel and unexpected perspectives to its arguments.

A number of faculty colleagues have devoted considerable cognitive toil to the effort to define the New American University and now, more recently, the Fifth Wave. Derrick M. Anderson has grappled extensively with the conceptualization of these models as well as the nuts and bolts of the execution of projects that inform this volume. Craig Calhoun, David Guston, and Daniel Sarewitz have commented on various chapters and contributed to the explication of the problematics of the various claims and arguments of the book. The project has benefited inestimably from discussions with faculty colleagues too numerous to acknowledge individually—although we attempt to express our gratitude in the notes—and with scholars from across the nation and around the globe. Nevertheless, from within our own academic community we would especially like to express our appreciation to Sasha Barab, Steven Beschloss, Erik Fisher, Margaret Hinrichs, Erik Johnston, Manfred Laubichler, Andrew Maynard, Clark A. Miller, Wellington ("Duke") Reiter, Deborah Strumsky, Luke Tate, David White, and Gregg Zachary, some of whom have also commented on drafts of various passages. From further afield we especially wish to thank Jonathan R. Cole, whose expertise and insights informed this project from the outset and who subsequently commented on an earlier draft of the manuscript. Invaluable perspective was similarly forthcoming from Philip G. Altbach, Christopher Newfield, and Lorne Whitehead.

Among colleagues in administration who have brought expertise to bear on the case study we wish to express our appreciation to Sheila Ainlay, Morgan R. Olsen, Sethuraman ("Panch") Panchanathan, Peter Schlosser, Mark Searle, Richard H. Stanley, and Steven Tepper. For substantive contributions to research and policy analysis we are especially indebted to Kevin T. Dwyer, along with Drew Callow and Kyle Whitman, and for research associated with the discussion of comparative institutional systems, Justin W. Sprague. For quantitative acumen and institutional expertise brought to bear on the case study chapter, we are indebted to Mary Carrillo, Melinda Gebel, Hansa Magee, and George Raudenbush. And once again, we wish to express appreciation to Greg Britton, editorial director of Johns Hopkins University Press, and his colleagues Catherine Goldstead and Kyle P. Gipson for continued astute editorial guidance. Finally, as is customary and would here be especially appropriate, we wish to offer the standard formulation to the effect that whatever merit readers may discover in these chapters owes much to the efforts and insights of others, whereas we assume responsibility for gaffes and blunders and errors of omission.

Various chapters in this book elaborate on or even substantially recapitulate arguments from our first coauthored book, *Designing the New American University* (Baltimore: Johns Hopkins University Press, 2015). As we explain in the first chapter, recapitulation is inevitable because, in a phrase, the Fifth Wave is the New American University writ large. To the extent that we recapitulate the arguments of the first book, the present volume could almost be characterized as a second edition of our earlier work. As a consequence, portions of some chapters bear a close relation to corresponding discussions in the first book without explicit citation, which effort would needlessly encumber this volume with excessive quotation and bibliographic apparatus. Chapter 2 especially presents a revised and updated case study of Arizona State University, which constituted chapter 7 in the previous volume. Our revised case study once again draws substantially from institutional reports and presentations that were often the product of primarily unattributed collaborative authorship. In all such cases, we wish to acknowledge the contributions of the respective participants, especially those referred to in the first volume as the University Design Team.

Interspersed throughout various chapters are revised reconfigurations of discussions that appeared previously in articles and book chapters we have either coauthored or authored singly. The more substantive of these are cited in the notes. Otherwise, readers will find a full account of source material that informed our first book on pages xi–xiii in the acknowledgments section of that volume. The recapitulation of arguments from our first book that here informs the first chapter is derived from our coauthored article "A New Model for the American Research University," which appeared in *Issues in Science and Technology* 31, no. 3 (Spring 2015). Among other such discussions, revised sections from our coauthored book chapter "Interdisciplinarity and the Institutional Context of Knowledge in the American Research University," which appeared in *The Oxford Handbook of Interdisciplinarity*, 2nd edition, edited by Robert Frodeman, Julie Thompson Klein, and Roberto Carlos Dos Santos Pacheco (Oxford: Oxford University Press, 2017), parallel our explication of transdisciplinarity in chapter 6. We wish to express our appreciation to respective editors and publishers for permission to interpolate revised variants of these various excerpts into the present volume.

# Toward New Models for American Colleges and Universities

Building on the arguments of our previous foray into this topic,[1] this book envisions the emergence of the Fifth Wave in American higher education—a league of colleges and universities, spearheaded initially by a subset of large-scale public research universities, unified in their resolve to accelerate positive social outcomes through the seamless integration of world-class knowledge production with cutting-edge technological innovation and institutional cultures dedicated to the advancement of accessibility to the broadest possible demographic representative of the socioeconomic and intellectual diversity of our nation. The Fifth Wave primarily augments and complements the set of American research universities, which, for reasons that will readily become apparent, we term the Fourth Wave, but will also comprise networks of heterogeneous colleges and universities whose frameworks are underpinned by discovery and knowledge production, and institutional actors from business and industry, government agencies and laboratories, and organizations in civil society.

The American research university represents a uniquely successful model that combines undergraduate and graduate education with knowledge production and research and development. Our society increasingly depends on the educated citizens and ideas, products, and processes this set of institutions produces. Their integrated frameworks of research, development, and education contribute to the discovery, creativity, and innovation that drive our economic competitiveness and determine our standard of living and quality of life. But the model for the American research university is limited by design, and the imperative for the evolution of new models that insist upon and leverage the complementarities and synergies between discovery and accessibility becomes obvious. The global preeminence of our leading institutions, moreover, does not correlate with overall excellence in American higher education. The nation has outgrown the existing infrastructure of research-grade academic platforms—colleges and universities whose academic frameworks are underpinned by discovery and knowledge production—and needs to expand its capacity to produce millions of additional graduates during the next several decades capable of both catalyzing and benefiting from an economy increasingly based on the generation and application of useful knowledge.

The admissions policies of our leading institutions exclude the majority of academically qualified applicants, even as the demographic trends shaping our nation militate against the success of students from socioeconomically disadvantaged and historically underrepresented backgrounds. As de facto national policy, excluding the majority of academically qualified students from the excellence of a research-grade education is counterproductive and ethically unacceptable. If our society is to continue to prosper, our leading colleges and universities must be augmented by a league of institutions that draw from the broader talent pool of socioeconomic and intellectual diversity and integrate the production and distribution of knowledge at socially meaningful scale. Despite diminished public support, our nation's research-grade colleges and universities must begin in earnest to expand enrollment capacity and build a higher education infrastructure proportionate to the task of educating to competitive levels of achievement one-third or more of traditional cohorts of academically qualified students representative of the socioeconomic and intellectual diversity of our society. Through universal learning frameworks, they must also provide opportunities for lifelong learning to more than half the population of the nation. A universal learning framework would serve any learner from any socioeconomic background at any stage of work and learning through education, training, and skills-building opportunities.

In chapter 1, we assess the imperative for the emergence of the Fifth Wave. In this context, the chapter considers the limited prospects of gifted, creative, and academically qualified students—from middle-class families as well as the socioeconomically disadvantaged—for admission to top-tier research-grade institutions. Public outcry over inequality in

American society remains unequivocal, but there is an open secret among the academic intelligentsia that should give pause to any parent who hopes to send a child to college someday—and to anybody who worries about growing inequality in America. The greatest predictor of academic success is not a student's grades or SAT scores but rather family income and zip code. Half of our population does not exceed a 16 percent rate of bachelor's degree attainment—a key determinant of social mobility and economic well-being—and students from families in the top income quartile are five times more likely to graduate from college with a bachelor's degree than their peers from the bottom quartile.[2]

Even our nation's leading public research universities now routinely exclude the majority of academically qualified applicants, a longstanding trend further exacerbated by consistent public disinvestment. Admissions practices that perpetuate the reproduction of privilege, moreover, dovetail with institutional policies that maintain enrollment levels disproportionate to workforce projections that have indicated a shortfall of up to three million highly educated workers.[3] But the national conversation about equality and opportunity must not focus simply on the production of more college graduates. Mere access to standardized forms of instruction decoupled from discovery and knowledge production will not deliver desired societal outcomes. It is essential that millions more individuals, including but not limited to the socioeconomically disadvantaged and historically underrepresented, realize access to research-pedagogic academic platforms that integrate comprehensive liberal arts curricula with the cutting-edge knowledge essential to the workforce of the global knowledge economy. But the imperative for the formation of the Fifth Wave is not exclusively an argument about whether the admissions policies of research-grade institutions are equitable or whether their enrollment capacities are commensurate with demand or appropriate in scale to the population growth of the nation. The Fifth Wave seeks to extend the transformational achievements of the major research universities that constitute the Fourth Wave to advance knowledge production and innovation that serve the public interest and contribute to societal well-being.

The envisioned formation of a league of Fifth Wave institutions builds most proximately on the foundations of the New American University model operationalized at Arizona State University. Chapter 2 considers the comprehensive reconceptualization undertaken by ASU, which has produced an institution with sufficient scope and scale to offer broad accessibility to an academic platform of world-class knowledge production focused on societal outcomes. As a foundational prototype for the transition of a late-stage Fourth Wave institution into the early stages of the Fifth Wave, ASU demonstrates that research excellence and broad accessibility need not be mutually exclusive. ASU has succeeded in advancing both the academic rigor and diversity of its student body, which increasingly includes more and more students from socioeconomically disadvantaged and historically underrepresented backgrounds, including a significant proportion of first-generation college applicants. The university is committed to offering admission to all students deemed qualified to undertake university-level coursework regardless of financial need and thus maintaining the admissions standards of the leading public research universities at midcentury. The case study looks more closely at the multiple strategies that have guided the university's efforts to provide a world-class educational experience, excel in its research portfolio, and maximize societal impact.

Among the chief limitations of historical institutional models are incommensurabilities between the scale of institutions and enrollment demand, which among highly selective institutions produce what we term "boutique production strategies." Scale and accessibility are by no means the sole challenges confronting these institutions, nor are they the exclusive dimension to the New American University model operationalized in Arizona. But inasmuch as access to knowledge underpins the societal objectives of a pluralistic democracy, scalability and thus accessibility must be at the core of evolving institutional models. In chapter 3 we consider the scale of research-grade higher education in the United States and the implications of the transition from the elite to the mass to the universal phases of higher education described by sociologist Martin Trow.[4] We assess various theories of growth and expansion in higher education and conclude with an explication of scale and scalability that pertains to research-grade higher education.

Building on the historical discussion in chapter 1, chapter 4 provides further perspective on the proposition that it is imperative that a subset of large-scale public research universities constitute the vanguard of an effort to effect a structural transformation in American higher education that reconciles broad accessibility and academic excellence. Beginning with the establishment of Harvard College in 1636, the four preceding waves in American higher education may be represented in a rough schema by the (1) colonial colleges; (2) state-chartered colleges and universities of the early American republic; (3) land-grant colleges and universities that were established as a consequence of the Morrill Act, which was enacted during the Civil War; and (4) the set of major research universities that emerged in the final decades of the nineteenth century. With few exceptions, most major research universities, both public and private, are evolutionary products of institutions that transitioned from preceding waves. All of these institutional types flourish in the present day and continue to operate in parallel and evolve within their respective design frameworks. The chapter also considers the relevance of the national university envisioned by the leaders of the founding generation of our nation.

Chapter 5 considers various theoretical and conceptual approaches to the Fifth Wave, beginning with an assessment of the concept of complex adaptive knowledge enterprises. This discussion is followed by considerations of the relevance of concepts such as Mode 2 knowledge production, sociotechnical integration, responsible innovation, and sustainable development. In chapter 6 we contextualize theoretical and conceptual approaches to the reflexive relationship between institutional design and knowledge production. The concept of design is integral to the emergence of the Fifth Wave university, especially with regard to its role in the organization of research and the implementation of transdisciplinarity.

In the globalized knowledge economy, awareness of the correlation between knowledge production, technological innovation, and economic growth has brought higher education to the forefront of policy discussions throughout the world. But initiatives to advance institutional innovation in research-grade higher education in various national contexts are beset with challenges, some of which we briefly survey in chapter 7. In many emerging economies the transition from the elite to the mass to the universal phases of higher education and the imperative to accommodate the hyperexpansion of student cohorts inevitably compete with intentions to develop sets of world-class research universities to advance innovation and promote economic growth. We briefly consider parallels and discrepancies between those initiatives and the envisioned Fifth Wave.

Any model for a public university is necessarily defined by its alignment with public values as well as service to the public interest. The concluding chapter thus briefly considers the role of American academe in sustaining our democracy and the relevance of public value in the formation of the differentiated institutional models that constitute the Fifth Wave. Because the success of a deliberative democracy depends on the collective decisions of those governed, the quality of the overall system of education, and especially public higher education, is critical. Inasmuch as access to knowledge underpins the societal objectives of a pluralistic democracy, accessibility to academic milieus underpinned by knowledge production and innovation must be at the core of evolving institutional models.

## Notes

1. Michael M. Crow and William B. Dabars, *Designing the New American University* (Baltimore: Johns Hopkins University Press, 2015).

2. Margaret Cahalan et al., *Indicators of Higher Education Equity in the United States: Historical Trend Report* (Washington, DC: Pell Institute for the Study of Opportunity in Higher Education, 2018), 99.

3. Anthony P. Carnevale, Nicole Smith, and Jeff Strohl, "Help Wanted: Projections of Jobs and Education Requirements through 2018" (Washington, DC: Georgetown University Center on Education and the Workforce, June 2010), 18; executive summary, 4.

4. Martin Trow, "Problems in the Transition from Elite to Mass Higher Education" (Berkeley: Carnegie Commission on Higher Education, 1973); Trow, "Reflections on the Transition from Mass to Universal Higher Education," *Daedalus* 99, no. 1 (1970): 1–42.

# ONE

# The Emergence of the Fifth Wave in American Higher Education

The Fifth Wave in American higher education may be envisioned as an emerging league of colleges and universities unified in their resolve to accelerate positive social outcomes through the seamless integration of world-class knowledge production with cutting-edge technological innovation and institutional cultures dedicated to the advancement of accessibility to the broadest possible demographic representative of the socioeconomic and intellectual diversity of our nation. Spearheaded initially by a subset of large-scale public research universities aligned in their intent to enlarge on the public purposes of the American research university, the Fifth Wave will seek to expand on the transformational achievements of this set of institutions and accelerate the processes of discovery, creativity, and innovation that have characterized this institutional type since its inception in the late nineteenth century. As sociotechnically integrated, scalable, and reflexive complex adaptive knowledge enterprises, Fifth Wave universities will be designed to complement the various institutional types of colleges and universities that constitute American higher education, all of which will continue to operate in parallel and evolve within their respective design frameworks. Although large-scale public research universities will represent the vanguard of this new model, the Fifth Wave will ultimately encompass a network of public and private research universities and liberal arts colleges linked with business and industry, government agencies and laboratories, and organizations in civil society—a plurality of differentiated institutional actors from throughout the national innovation system aligned through academic enterprise, transdisciplinary collaboration, and public purpose. This coalition or league of knowledge enterprises will be transnational as well as transinstitutional, leveraging socially robust knowledge production and innovation from throughout the world.

"For all its deficiencies," writes Jonathan Cole, provost emeritus of Columbia University, the set of American research universities comprises nothing less than the "greatest system of knowledge production and higher learning that the world has ever known."[1] We concur with this assessment but in so doing are confronted with the imperative to evaluate the deficiencies as well as the merits of the present model for what we term the Fourth Wave, especially as inherent design constraints impede the transformative potential of this set of institutions. Among their limitations are organizational frameworks that lack the capacity to reconcile the scale of accessibility essential to societal well-being with the scale of the "knowledge infrastructure" essential to world-leading knowledge production and innovation.[2] Scale may refer to the enrollment of an institution or the productivity of its research enterprise or alternatively to its impact, which often but not inevitably correlates with one or both of the former. Sufficient scale of enrollment in a context of knowledge production permits colleges and universities to educate to internationally competitive levels of achievement the broadest possible demographic representative of the socioeconomic and intellectual diversity of our nation. By world-leading knowledge production we refer to the sort of discovery, creativity, and innovation that flourishes in our nation's major research universities and leading liberal arts colleges. Although we term these colleges and universities research-grade because their academic frameworks are underpinned by discovery and knowledge production, it may be more meaningful to characterize their knowledge-intensive academic environments as "research pedagogic." The essential point is that mere access to standardized forms of instruction decoupled from discovery and knowledge production will not deliver desired societal outcomes.

The Fifth Wave builds on the foundation of the Fourth Wave, which set the academic gold standard and has served as the dynamic and entrepreneurial institutional matrix for the knowledge production and innovation that has brought widespread prosperity to millions and consolidated American leadership in the knowledge economy.[3] The integrated and complementary research, development, and education functions of these institutions, both public and private, advance not only teaching and learning but also scientific discovery that has transformed our understanding of the universe and technological innovation that has vastly improved human well-being and contributed incalculably to economic growth, which is to say nothing of their generative role in the arts, humanities, social sciences, and fields of professional endeavor.[4] But for the present, the contemporary research university remains captive to a set of entrenched design constraints retained from the organization and practices of the handful of institutions that consolidated the model for the American research university during the emergence of this institutional type in the latter quarter of the nineteenth century. It has been an immensely successful model, but one that no longer adequately aligns with the changing needs of contemporary society.

Among the central arguments on behalf of the formation of the Fifth Wave is that our nation has outgrown the existing infrastructure of research-grade academic platforms and needs to develop new and complementary institutional models committed equally to accessibility and innovation. Among the chief structural and functional limitations in historical institutional models are incommensurabilities between the scale of institutions and enrollment demand, which among highly selective institutions produce what might be termed "boutique production strategies," referring to the sort of small-scale artisanal production processes characteristic of the pre-industrial era. Scale and accessibility are by no means the sole challenges confronting these institutions nor are they the exclusive dimensions to the emerging Fifth Wave. But inasmuch as access to knowledge underpins the societal objectives of a pluralistic democracy, scalability and thus accessibility must be at the core of evolving institutional models.

The envisioned formation of a league of Fifth Wave institutions builds most proximately on the foundations of the New American University model operationalized by Arizona State University. This new model for the American research university represents its reconceptualization as a complex and adaptive comprehensive knowledge enterprise committed to discovery, creativity, and innovation, an institution accessible to the broadest possible demographic representative of the socioeconomic and intellectual diversity of our nation.[5] The transition to the Fifth Wave begins with the emergence of a league of such large-scale public research-grade universities distinguished by their capacity to integrate broad accessibility commensurate with the scale of population growth and enrollment demand with academic frameworks structured to advance knowledge production and innovation that serves the public interest and contributes to societal well-being. With its egalitarian tenets and explicit commitment to reinvigorate the public dimension of the American research university, the Fifth Wave is the New American University writ large.

The primary focus of this critique, then, is the potential for the further evolution of the Fourth Wave and the formation of the Fifth Wave, which in its inception will comprise a league of large-scale public research universities committed to expanding accessibility while facilitating discovery and innovation and the impact of knowledge in the public interest. Through the integration of cutting-edge technological innovation with institutional cultures dedicated to the advancement of public value through academic enterprise, Fifth Wave universities will deliberately aspire to effect a shift in social outcomes toward equity and equality and assume a mandate to serve as frameworks for responsible innovation and sustainable development.[6] Building on the accomplishments of institutional antecedents, Fifth Wave universities will endeavor to lend further purpose and capacity to the artistic creativity, humanistic and social scientific insight, and the scientific discoveries and technological innovations that our pluralistic democracy will need to draw on as the global community negotiates the encroaching challenges of the twenty-first century. At issue is not the education of students who graduate from the top 5 or 10 percent of their high school classes but rather the imperative to educate to internationally competitive levels of achievement the top quarter or third of respective age cohorts and through frameworks of universal learning to provide opportunities for lifelong learning to more than half the population of the United States.

## Some Preliminary Historical Perspective on the Fifth Wave

Because we propose that the Fifth Wave represents a new phase in the evolution of American higher education, a historical framework and taxonomy of antecedent institutional types is essential to subsequent discussion. But in contrast to standard historical accounts,[7] our assessment focuses on the dominant institutional types of colleges and universities in each period and seeks to develop new insight into the dynamics of their structures and functions. Such an analysis is thus at once morphological as well as typological, with the concept of morphology referring to the structural attributes of organizations and institutions.[8] In this view the institutional types are organizational structures adopted for advancing given approaches to higher education. And whereas our typology comprises five waves, more elaborate periodization from a different perspective has been proposed by Roger Geiger, who identifies ten generations in American higher education over the course of which the character of the endeavor has "perceptibly shifted in each generation, or approximately every thirty years."[9] Our intent is not to contribute to the voluminous literature on the history of American higher education, but to analyze a new and emerging institutional type, which presumes a more restricted focus on university design. We contrast this new institutional type to four preceding models, each of which emerged in a different historical context and continue to flourish to the present day. Thus we construct what the German sociologist Max Weber called ideal types—abstractions that help to identify patterns in empirical reality.[10] Each of the first four waves yields an ideal type of institution with distinctive attributes. And we attempt to identify the new ideal type as the Fifth Wave.

Since the seventeenth century, increasingly complex and still-evolving institutional models in American higher education have emerged in response to the critical cultural, economic, political, and social challenges that confront society. The emergence of each wave correlates with successive historical periods, beginning with the First Wave, which was inaugurated with the founding of Harvard College in 1636. The first four waves may be represented in a rough schema by the (1) colonial colleges; (2) state-chartered colleges and universities of the early American republic; (3) land-grant colleges and universities that were established as a consequence of the Morrill Act, which was enacted during the Civil War; and (4) set of major research universities that emerged in the final decades of the nineteenth century. With only a few notable exceptions, major research universities, both public and private, are evolutionary products of institutions that transitioned from preceding waves. All of these institutional types flourish in the present day and continue to

operate in parallel and evolve within their respective design frameworks. Undoubtedly this sort of institutional evolution will continue
indefinitely into the centuries ahead as our knowledge enterprises adapt
to meet new challenges.

A thumbnail sketch of the first four waves would look something like
this: What we term the First Wave in American higher education initially comprised a handful of what were then denominationally affiliated institutions chartered before the founding of the republic. Nine
colonial colleges, beginning with Harvard (1636), William and Mary
(1693), Yale (1701), and the schools that would become Princeton (1746),
Columbia (1754), Penn (1755), Brown (1764), Rutgers (1766), and Dartmouth (1769), were established to transmit a classical curriculum suitable for young gentlemen from propertied families preparing to enter the
ministry or the professions.[11] The colonial colleges and subsequent cohort of colleges founded during the early republic—schools like Williams (1791), Bowdoin (1794), and Middlebury (1800)—established the
prototype for highly selective residential liberal arts colleges that to the
present day retain the relative scale of enrollment and scope of societal
engagement of the eighteenth century. The establishment of new First
Wave schools during the twentieth century, including Reed College
(1908), Bennington College (1932), Harvey Mudd College (1955), and College of the Atlantic (1969), attests to the continued relevance of this institutional model.

Toward the end of the nineteenth century some First Wave colleges—
Harvard, Princeton, and Columbia, among them—evolved into major
research universities and thus, in the terms of our proposed idiom, transitioned directly from the First Wave to the Fourth Wave, albeit effectively retaining a First Wave undergraduate residential liberal arts
college at the core of the expanded institution.[12] A number of leading
institutions from the Second Wave and Third Wave similarly evolved
into major research universities and thus transitioned to the Fourth
Wave as well. Seven of the nine colonial colleges, along with Cornell University (1865), would come to form the Ivy League, which was officially
established as an athletic conference in 1954. Both William and Mary
and Rutgers became public universities, in 1906 and 1945, respectively.
Lest the typology of the five waves lapse into anachronism, it is essential
to differentiate between the historical and contemporary instantiations

of these institutions—and institutional types. Harvard College in the seventeenth century is a vastly different proposition than the Harvard University of the Fourth Wave.

Although First Wave schools that transitioned to the Fourth Wave are products of innovation and evolution from relatively simple to increasingly complex institutional forms, these schools in a sense paralleled a pattern that would be realized without institutional antecedent with the formation of Johns Hopkins University, which was founded in 1876 and represents the prototype for the American research university. The establishment of Stanford University (1885) and the University of Chicago (1892) as research universities without institutional antecedents, following the example of Johns Hopkins, represents the singular variation to the generalized evolutionary pattern. And whereas we speak of innovation and evolution from relatively simple to increasingly complex institutional forms as the mechanism that impels transition from one wave to the next—from the First Wave to the Fourth Wave, as in the case of Harvard University, for example, or from the Third Wave to the Fourth Wave, as in the case of Cornell or the campuses of the University of California system—innovation and evolution have been intrinsic ongoing processes within each of the waves. Not all innovation and evolution signals inevitable transition to successive waves.

The heterogeneous array of nonsectarian public and private denominational colleges and state-chartered universities founded beginning in the late eighteenth and early nineteenth centuries constitutes the Second Wave. The most prominent among these schools became the flagship public universities of their respective states. The University of Georgia and University of North Carolina, for example, chartered, respectively, in 1785 and 1789, along with the University of Virginia, founded by Thomas Jefferson in 1819, represent Second Wave institutions that, like their First Wave counterparts, evolved into Fourth Wave major research universities. With research expenditures approaching $1.5 billion in FY 2017, the University of Michigan, established in 1817, epitomizes the transition from the Second Wave to the Fourth Wave. In addition to new public nonsectarian colleges, many new private denominational schools were also established in the early nineteenth century. Most of the regional colleges and some state universities, however, remain dedicated primarily to teaching and continue to operate in Second

Wave mode. In our typology, community colleges represent a late-stage iteration of a Second Wave public regional college with a restricted curricular focus.

With the Third Wave, we see the first stirrings of applied research in an academic setting, albeit closely tied to agriculture and the needs of local industry, and largely confined to what has been termed "hands-on problem-solving."[13] The land-grant colleges and universities that were established as a consequence of the Morrill Act of 1862 operationalized this expansion of scope and scale. Of the fifteen institutions singled out by Roger Geiger as foundational to the formation of the American research university, six are land-grant institutions, both public and private: California, Cornell, Illinois, Minnesota, MIT, and Wisconsin.[14] The Third Wave proved critical to the emergence of the Fourth Wave, which between 1876 and roughly 1915 consolidated the institutional type of the American research university. As per the preceding caveat regarding anachronism in the First Wave, Cornell University, for example, could be considered as a land-grant school representative of the Third Wave during its first several decades or as a constituent of the Fourth Wave as it had evolved by the end of the nineteenth century.

By wide consensus, Johns Hopkins University is regarded as the prototype for the American research university, a hybrid of the British and German academic models, which integrates undergraduate education with advanced scientific research and graduate education. This model set the course for the formation of what would eventually become the set of roughly one hundred research-extensive and one hundred further research-intensive institutions, both public and private, that constitute the Fourth Wave, which in the twentieth century assumed global preeminence in knowledge production and innovation. It would not be hyperbole to characterize them as the most complex and heterogeneous knowledge enterprises that have ever evolved in the course of civilization. Our society depends increasingly on the educated citizens and ideas, products, and processes these institutions produce as their integrated platforms of teaching and research contribute to the discovery, creativity, and innovation that drive our economic and global competitiveness as well as our standard of living and quality of life. Yet, as we argue throughout these chapters, the model for the American research university is limited by design, and the imperative for the evolution of a subset of public research universities committed to broad accessibility to world-class knowledge production becomes obvious.

In all, according to Geiger, fifteen institutions ultimately consolidated the model for the American research university during the final quarter of the nineteenth century and first decade of the twentieth century: five colonial colleges chartered before the American Revolution (Harvard, Yale, Pennsylvania, Princeton, and Columbia); five state universities (Michigan, Wisconsin, Minnesota, Illinois, and California); and five private institutions conceived from their inception as research universities (MIT, Cornell, Johns Hopkins, Stanford, and Chicago). Geiger specifies that these institutions may be characterized by their interrelationships, both competitive and cooperative; capacity to institutionalize and organize specialized knowledge into academic disciplines; success at leveraging burgeoning financial resources and academic infrastructure derived from growth; and commitment to research as a complement to the traditional function of teaching.[15] These fifteen universities collectively determined the model whose potential and limitations we assess from the aspirational perspective of the Fifth Wave.

Once consolidated, the model for the Fourth Wave became increasingly resistant to change. Without recourse to any explicit theoretical appreciation of isomorphism—the paradoxical tendency for organizations and institutions operating within given sectors to emulate one another and become increasingly homogeneous but not necessarily more efficient[16]—historian Laurence Veysey eloquently delineates the early entrenchment of the model beginning even in the first quarter-century following its consolidation. "Before 1890 there had been room for decided choice about paths of action," he observed. "Harvard, Johns Hopkins, Cornell, and in their own way, Yale and Princeton had stood for distinct educational alternatives." Beginning with the final decade of the nineteenth century, however, success for the leading research universities meant conformity with the "standard structural pattern in all basic respects—no matter how one might trumpet a few particular embellishments . . . . Henceforth initiative had to display itself within the lines laid down by the given system."[17]

There is no single codified model for the American research university, strictly speaking, of course, and considerable variation among these schools is evident in scope and scale, from small private institutions with a scientific and technological focus such as the California Institute of Technology (Caltech) and MIT to comprehensive public universities epitomized by Ohio State and the University of Michigan, Ann Arbor. But for the purposes of the present organizational typology, these institutions bear a sufficiently striking family resemblance, the commonalities of which, as we subsequently explain, warrant their inclusion as representative of a unified institutional type. Despite fundamental morphological transformation during the twentieth century in response to enrollment patterns, demographic shifts, and the advent of the knowledge economy, the evolution of these institutions has in some respects been merely incremental. To an alarming extent the model for the American research university remains captive to a set of design constraints that no longer aligns with the changing needs of our society. Absent differentiation and diversification through the evolution of this institutional model, their preponderant commitment to discovery and innovation carried out largely in isolation from the socioeconomic challenges faced by most Americans threatens to impede the capacity of these institutions to contribute decisively and consistently to the collective good.

The formation of a league of institutions committed to collaboration on behalf of the public interest recalls the purposes behind proposals by various leaders of the founding generation to charter a national university. In our previous book we contended that our nation's leading public research universities could be said collectively to constitute a de facto national university,[18] referring to the envisioned federally chartered center for scientific research and scholarship in the national interest championed by James Madison at the Constitutional Convention in Philadelphia in 1787.[19] Of course, while it is possible to invoke the vision of a national university rhetorically in this context to summon public resolve to advance discovery and innovation conceived in the national interest, we underscore that failure to enact the legislation, which may have inspired the concurrent formation of a federal ministry of higher education, would in retrospect fortuitously yield extraordinary outcomes, setting the course for the decentralized—and highly competitive—configuration of American higher education.[20] "If we compare American universities with those of continental Europe, a conspicuous feature is that American universities are decentralized and highly autonomous," economist Nathan Rosenberg explains. "There has never been a federal ministry of education that bears responsibility for determining the size of university budgets, how the budgets ought to be allocated, or the intellectual priorities they ought to observe."[21] Moreover, higher education in the United States arose propitiously in a setting "where the market was strong, the state was weak, and the church was divided," David Labaree points out. "Under these circumstances, neither church nor state could establish dominion over this emerging institution, and the market gave it the ability to operate on its own."[22] The evolution of these institutions was an organic and distributed process rather than the outcome of central planning or deliberate coordination. Although competition has been a major driving force spurring research and development in our nation's research universities, in the twenty-first century cooperation as well as competition between colleges and universities will be essential if discovery, creativity, and innovation are to serve the needs of the nation. Leagues connote competition—one thinks of the Hanseatic League, for example, or the American League—but an academic league committed to the national interest and public good has the potential to maximize the scale of public benefit through teaching and research intended to maximize consequential societal impact.

Fifth Wave universities could thus alternatively be termed national *service* universities. Our usage of this term is not intended to limit the sense of "national service" to what Mitchell Stevens and Benjamin Gebre-Medhin term the "hard work of nation building," which has included "winning wars, rewarding military service, bulwarking the national labor market, and providing technical and social intelligence for the exertion of US interests in world affairs." As assessed in the sociological literature, this sense of higher education as a "vehicle of national service" underscores the extent to which our nation's universities became the recipients of substantial government investment for research in the decades following World War II but also such programs as the Servicemen's Readjustment Act of 1944, more commonly termed the GI Bill, and the two most prominent Cold War initiatives in this context, the National Defense Education Act (NDEA) of 1958 and the Higher Education Act of 1965.[23] Nor is our usage intended to evoke comparisons to the national service academies, for example, the United States Military Academy, in West Point, New York, or the United States Naval Academy, in Annapolis, Maryland. Nor is it intended to posit equivalence between the Fifth

Wave and the land-grant colleges and universities that we term the Third Wave despite their historic service orientation.[24] Most major research universities, both public and private, characterize their missions in terms of the triumvirate of teaching, research, and public service, but the concept of universities committed to national service is intended to interrelate and augment the service component associated with the Third Wave and the research orientation associated with the Fourth Wave. The subset of national service universities could be envisioned as comprising differentiated institutional models but all characterized by common design elements including scalability, sociotechnical integration, and societal impact. National service universities would operate with a commitment to maximize the scale of public benefit, integrate technology seamlessly into their operational cores, advance teaching and research intended to maximize societal impact, and commit to the production of useful knowledge. A heterogeneous subset of such differentiated institutions—a league of national service universities—inspired with a twenty-first-century vision of egalitarian access and engaged in collaboration with other colleges and universities, business and industry, government agencies and laboratories, and organizations in civil society could thus be said to constitute the emerging Fifth Wave in American higher education.

Each wave in American higher education has been initiated by one or more institutional progenitors, beginning with Harvard College, which set the pattern for the First Wave. The University of Georgia and University of North Carolina contest the claim to be the first state-chartered university[25] but the University of Virginia, with its explicit embrace of Enlightenment secularism and innovative curriculum that introduced the elective system into American higher education, arguably deserves recognition as the institutional progenitor of the Second Wave. Although the terms of the Morrill Act would lead to the establishment of more than seventy colleges and universities, including the subsequent conferral of land-grant status to dozens of schools that had been founded during the Second Wave, Cornell University most deliberately and explicitly embraced the tenets of the legislation and thus in our estimation deserves recognition as the institutional progenitor of the Third Wave. As the prototype for the American research university, Johns Hopkins University defined the contours of the Fourth Wave. Our list of institutional progenitors corresponds to the four American institutions Frank Rhodes, president emeritus of Cornell University, identifies as universities that "mark the path by which the modern American university came into being: . . . Harvard, Virginia, Cornell, and Johns Hopkins."[26]

Because the Fifth Wave in its initial phase represents an augmentation of or complement to the set of major research universities, a number of Fourth Wave institutions may be perceived already to be in transition to the Fifth Wave. As the vanguard of a potential cohort of peer institutions positioned to negotiate the demands of broad accessibility and academic excellence, we propose that Arizona State University be regarded the institutional progenitor of the Fifth Wave. Inasmuch as attributes of the Fifth Wave include a willingness to scale both on campus and online, a refusal to arbitrarily ratchet up admissions standards, and a mission of either maintaining or developing a world-class research profile, potential institutional peers in transition to the Fifth Wave could include Purdue University, Pennsylvania State University, and the University System of Maryland (figure 1).

## The Fifth Wave as a League of National Service Universities

Inspired by America's rich history of using education as an engine for social progress, empowered by emerging technologies, and committed to continuous innovation, the formation of a subset of large-scale public research universities has the potential to realize the vision of America's founders by acting collectively as a de facto comprehensive national university system. As a network or league of national service universities, these Fifth Wave institutions would serve our nation's interests by facilitating college access to all academically qualified American students and advancing research and workforce development to promote innovation and global competitiveness. Our society could create this network by leveraging the existing capabilities of innovative and forward-thinking colleges and universities, establishing a physical footprint across a network of campuses, and utilizing their assets in both on-campus immersion and online educational delivery to extend its reach to every corner of the nation. The network would consist of institutions that are already driving the transformation of American higher education by

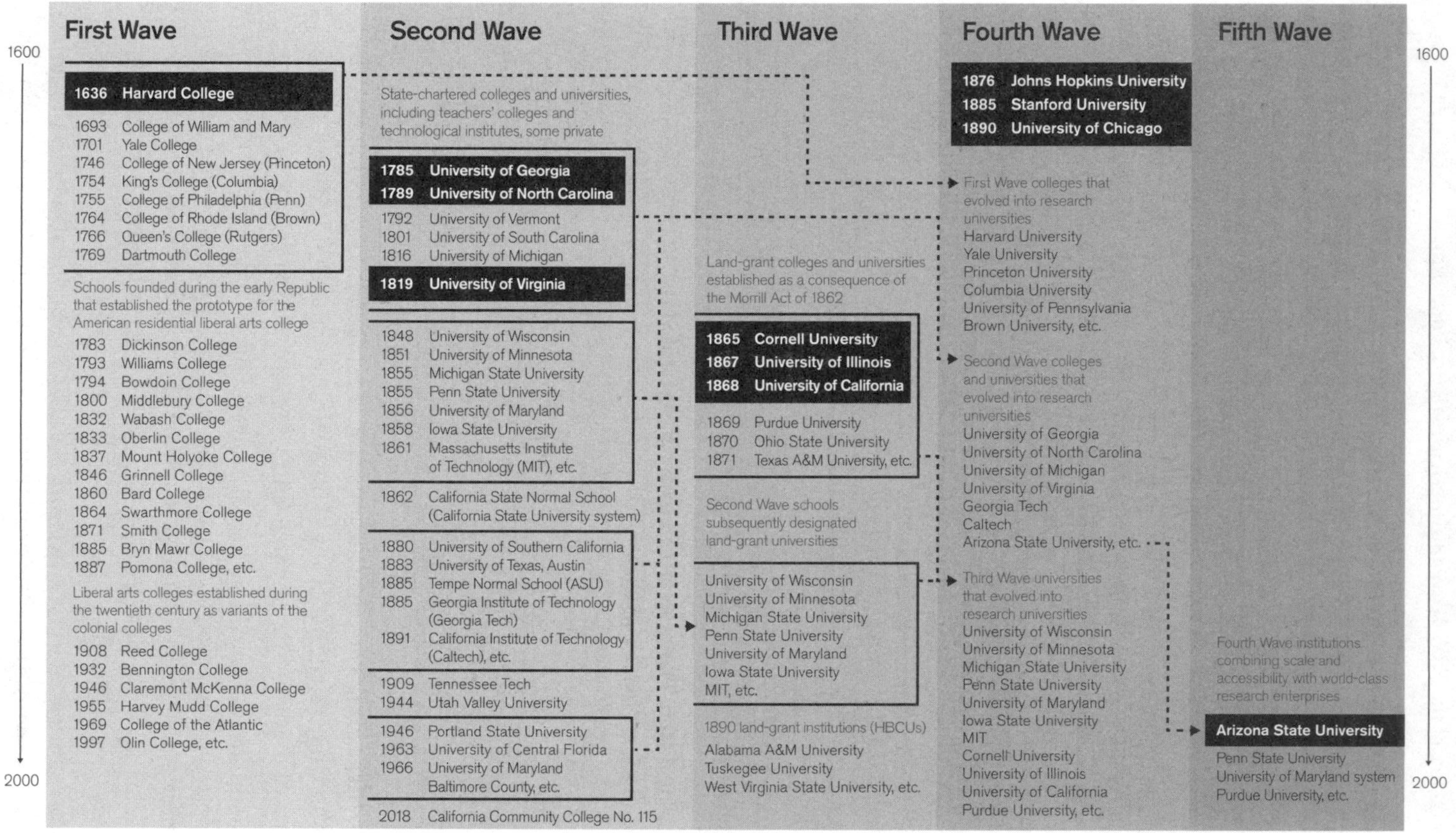

# First Wave

**1636 Harvard College**

1693 College of William and Mary
1701 Yale College
1746 College of New Jersey (Princeton)
1754 King's College (Columbia)
1755 College of Philadelphia (Penn)
1764 College of Rhode Island (Brown)
1766 Queen's College (Rutgers)
1769 Dartmouth College

Schools founded during the early Republic that established the prototype for the American residential liberal arts college

1783 Dickinson College
1793 Williams College
1794 Bowdoin College
1800 Middlebury College
1832 Wabash College
1833 Oberlin College
1837 Mount Holyoke College
1846 Grinnell College
1860 Bard College
1864 Swarthmore College
1871 Smith College
1885 Bryn Mawr College
1887 Pomona College, etc.

Liberal arts colleges established during the twentieth century as variants of the colonial colleges

1908 Reed College
1932 Bennington College
1946 Claremont McKenna College
1955 Harvey Mudd College
1969 College of the Atlantic
1997 Olin College, etc.

# Second Wave

State-chartered colleges and universities, including teachers' colleges and technological institutes, some private

**1785 University of Georgia**
**1789 University of North Carolina**
1792 University of Vermont
1801 University of South Carolina
1816 University of Michigan

**1819 University of Virginia**

1848 University of Wisconsin
1851 University of Minnesota
1855 Michigan State University
1855 Penn State University
1856 University of Maryland
1858 Iowa State University
1861 Massachusetts Institute of Technology (MIT), etc.

1862 California State Normal School (California State University system)

1880 University of Southern California
1883 University of Texas, Austin
1885 Tempe Normal School (ASU)
1885 Georgia Institute of Technology (Georgia Tech)
1891 California Institute of Technology (Caltech), etc.

1909 Tennessee Tech
1944 Utah Valley University

1946 Portland State University
1963 University of Central Florida
1966 University of Maryland Baltimore County, etc.

2018 California Community College No. 115

# Third Wave

Land-grant colleges and universities established as a consequence of the Morrill Act of 1862

**1865 Cornell University**
**1867 University of Illinois**
**1868 University of California**

1869 Purdue University
1870 Ohio State University
1871 Texas A&M University, etc.

Second Wave schools subsequently designated land-grant universities

University of Wisconsin
University of Minnesota
Michigan State University
Penn State University
University of Maryland
Iowa State University
MIT, etc.

1890 land-grant institutions (HBCUs)
Alabama A&M University
Tuskegee University
West Virginia State University, etc.

# Fourth Wave

**1876 Johns Hopkins University**
**1885 Stanford University**
**1890 University of Chicago**

First Wave colleges that evolved into research universities
Harvard University
Yale University
Princeton University
Columbia University
University of Pennsylvania
Brown University, etc.

Second Wave colleges and universities that evolved into research universities
University of Georgia
University of North Carolina
University of Michigan
University of Virginia
Georgia Tech
Caltech
Arizona State University, etc.

Third Wave universities that evolved into research universities
University of Wisconsin
University of Minnesota
Michigan State University
Penn State University
University of Maryland
Iowa State University
MIT
Cornell University
University of Illinois
University of California
Purdue University, etc.

# Fifth Wave

**Arizona State University**

Fourth Wave institutions combining scale and accessibility with world-class research enterprises
Penn State University
University of Maryland system
Purdue University, etc.

1600

2000

FIGURE 1. Representative colleges and universities of the five waves in American higher education with institutional progenitors for each wave high-lighted and indications of general evolutionary trajectories of the various institutional types.

providing educational access at scale, especially for underserved students, and their combined capabilities could be tapped to provide yet further educational pathways for Americans of every economic background; develop and deliver a constantly evolving, future-proofed curriculum relevant to U.S. competitiveness and security; and support industrial growth and economic prosperity by producing large numbers of highly skilled graduates.[27]

With an understanding of how universities have driven social and technological progress throughout the past several centuries and a deep commitment to addressing the inequities that remain unresolved in higher education, our society possesses the potential to usher in a new era defined by the fusion of the pursuit of knowledge and the desideratum of social progress. As fundamentally new types of institution, Fifth Wave universities can address many of the core educational challenges faced by American higher education in the twenty-first century. Fifth Wave universities will take responsibility for the success of each student and, by dramatically reconfiguring the delivery of content, will be able to scale to include twice as many students as are currently enrolled, produce three to five times as many graduates, and serve more than ten times the number of engaged learners. This sort of scale will be realized by augmenting traditional full-immersion research-pedagogical learning on campuses with personalized adaptive and hybrid approaches as well as massive-scale online learning and other technology-enabled methods. This effort will fulfill the commitments already made by the federal government and numerous state governments to increase educational access for underserved populations and improve outcomes for disadvantaged students. Being comprised of leading research universities, the network of Fifth Wave institutions will simultaneously conduct research and development to drive economic growth that fosters prosperity, social transformation, and the global competitiveness of the nation.

Fifth Wave universities will develop new institutional frameworks (design innovation) that support both novel approaches to discovery and knowledge production (epistemic innovation) and teaching and learning (pedagogical innovation) in order to simultaneously advance knowledge and facilitate social progress. Fifth Wave universities will represent innovative design in higher education through four aspirational imperatives, being (1) student-focused, (2) solutions-oriented, (3) connected to market needs, and (4) built to maximize public value. This approach is consistent with the recommendations of a report from the New America Foundation that sought to envision "The Next Generation University." Its authors reached four key conclusions: "An intentional student-focused vision matters; bigger can be good; it is possible to enroll and educate large numbers of unevenly prepared students well without diminishing quality; and it is possible for institutions of higher education to innovate fast and at scale."[28]

As with other periods of rapid social change, this new era of human enterprise invites us to reconsider our social values and aspirations, which inform how we go about designing, managing, and evaluating organizations and institutions. In this context, we propose universal learning as an aspiration for the Fifth Wave. Whereas Fifth Wave universities seek to realize organizational frameworks that combine academic excellence with broad accessibility, which throughout these chapters we liken to coupling within single institutions the world-class research excellence of the University of California system with the accessibility offered by the Cal State system, the introduction of the desideratum of universal learning intensifies the social commitment and embeddedness of these institutions. Accordingly, universal learning frameworks will be institutions (including organizations and networks of organizations) or designated units within institutions that rely on new institutional models to carefully integrate emerging new approaches to discovery and knowledge production and learning. For some readers the term may evoke associations of the Open University in the United Kingdom or the raft of continuing education programs offered by numerous American universities. But the concept should be approached from an epistemic or pedagogical as well as programmatic perspective. It is no less about theories of learning than the design of learning programs. This said, because universal learning operationalized through the Fifth Wave would bring the research-pedagogic resources of major research universities to curricula typically associated with community colleges and technical schools, courses would be undergirded by academic rigor as well as workforce relevance. Frameworks for universal learning would permit individuals, regardless of socioeconomic status or life situation, to gain the knowledge and skills essential to thrive and be empowered to freely shape intellectual development and self-determined creative and professional pursuits. As frameworks for universal learning, Fifth Wave universities would seek to serve any learner from any socioeconomic background at any stage of work and learning through broad accessibility to world-class knowledge production.[29]

Nearly all contemporary universities and colleges, whether public, private, or for-profit, claim to be student-focused. Were this in fact the case, we would have no need to deliberate regarding college access, affordability, or completion, and our higher education system would be indisputably equitable and efficacious in meeting the needs of learners from every socioeconomic background. Although some public universities have made strides in promoting greater educational access, most still fall short at making college affordable for all, and especially at ensuring that students continue on to complete a degree. Fifth Wave universities will focus on students beginning with a commitment to radical access, which is to say, these schools will accommodate any academically qualified learner regardless of socioeconomic background or life situation. In practice this could mean a commitment to admit all students deemed qualified to undertake university-level coursework. This also means that students will never be asked to pay more than they are able to afford and will not be saddled with debt that is infeasible to pay off following graduation. Most importantly, this means that lacking financial resources or being a first-generation student, foster child, or having learning disabilities need not constitute a barrier to pursuing postsecondary studies. Second, through comprehensive flexibility, Fifth Wave universities will accommodate the exigencies of the lives of individual students by offering the options to start, pause from, and continue studies in accordance with life circumstances. Illnesses in the family, financial insecurity, the birth of a child, or the requirements of full-time employment should not disqualify students from completing a college degree. Finally, consistent with the aspiration of universal learning as requisite to full participation in the contemporary knowledge-based economy, Fifth Wave universities will serve as perpetual resources for continuing education, retraining, and upskilling for learners at any career phase and in any season of life.

Fifth Wave universities will moreover enable significant discoveries in basic and applied—or better still, transdisciplinary and integrative—research distinctively oriented toward finding solutions to the great social, economic, environmental, and development challenges of our time. An orientation toward solutions means effectively responding to the research and programmatic priorities of federal, industry, and philanthropic funders (demand pull) but also eventually helping to shape and define funding agendas based on emerging research and cutting-edge capabilities (supply push). Whereas traditional research universities create degree and research programs around historic and current research and development areas, Fifth Wave universities will proactively anticipate future developments in innovation and market trends. Working collaboratively with industry and government and serving as a nexus for public-private interaction, Fifth Wave universities will adapt their capabilities to contribute to industrial innovation and constantly reshape curricula to prepare students with foundational skills beyond what is essential for success on graduation day, and in so doing empower graduates to thrive in an evolving economy.

Fifth Wave universities, moreover, will be designed to maximize public value. All public research universities use public funds, but not all are mission-oriented toward serving the public. Fifth Wave universities will set a new standard for how the academic sector serves the public by using the maximization of public value as the lodestar that guides their actions. To fulfill these mission prerogatives, Fifth Wave universities will be designed around very different operational logics than Fourth Wave institutions. The operations of contemporary universities are often hampered by bureaucratic inertia that is counterproductive to their missions and raises costs for stakeholders, including students and taxpayers who fund research and student financial aid. As new organizations unfettered by entrenched academic bureaucracies, Fifth Wave universities will capitalize on an operational blank slate. Ensuring their success requires the application of five design innovations: (1) economies of scale; (2) lean operations; (3) financial engineering for accessibility; (4) networked operations; and (5) technologically intensive operations.

Although innovations in online educational delivery have allowed institutions to reach large audiences at lower cost, few universities aspire to or have come close to achieving the massive-scale operations required to achieve true economies of scale. Fifth Wave universities will leverage technology and organizational design to drive the cost of serving additional learners down as the numbers served increases, simultaneously decreasing the cost of research operations while boosting returns on investment in research. With few legacy operations to create a drag on organizational speed and effectiveness, Fifth Wave universities will be able to run lean and focused operations. By centralizing and sharing core administrative functions and decentralizing others, Fifth Wave operations will maximize value while minimizing waste and avoid cost-spiraling and bloated administrative structures common to traditional universities. Forward-thinking public universities such as the institutions of the University Innovation Alliance, which we assess in chapter 2, have demonstrated that simultaneous increases in the quality of teaching and learning need not trade off with reduced accessibility but, to the contrary, can reinforce efforts to make education more affordable for disadvantaged students. These institutions have proven that expanding access is a question of institutional will and operational acumen rather than financial feasibility. Drawing on these successes, Fifth Wave universities will develop financial models that ensure that every academically qualified prospective student, regardless of socioeconomic status, is able to pursue an education.

American higher education institutions have long been blighted by isomorphism—an inclination to replicate one another rather than pursue new and innovative missions. As a result, universities waste millions of dollars competing with each other instead of cooperating as well as frivolously attempting to build capabilities in areas where they have no foundational strengths. In contrast, Fifth Wave universities will achieve greater efficiency and impact by sharing the technological, administrative, and infrastructural resources of their partner institutions. Because they will be built with the contributed capabilities of leading public research universities, Fifth Wave universities will be able to draw on partners to mobilize capabilities and achieve complementarities and synergies, which will drive down the cost of teaching, learning, and research while increasing the effectiveness of these activities. These institutions will be able to serve hundreds of thousands of learners at scale while driving research collaboration by integrating already available technological systems. Nothing new needs to be developed to make the vision of a Fifth Wave network a reality: All of the software and systems for managing students and personnel, tracking research productivity, managing facilities and finances, and teaching online at high scale already exist. These resources need only be networked and integrated to support the operations of Fifth Wave institutions individually and as a network.

Because knowledge production is a core function of universities, discovery, creativity, and innovation are foundational and precede and undergird all other functions associated with the academic enterprise. Great universities excel at supporting the work of researchers who explore fundamental questions in various domains of inquiry and find ways to disseminate knowledge and innovation into the broader social and economic fabric. As distinct from mere increases in research productivity, Fifth Wave universities will redefine knowledge production in three fundamental and related ways, creating a new paradigm for epistemic innovation. First, Fifth Wave universities will leverage their individual and shared intellectual capital to seek to develop knowledge-based solutions to the challenges that confront humanity. In an ever-smaller globalized world beset by challenges that know no borders, discovery for the sake of creating tangible progress must be prioritized over discovery for its own sake. Recognizing this reality, federal funding agencies such as the National Institutes of Health are increasingly focusing their priorities on research that translates into impact. Fifth Wave universities will drive basic and applied research that solves grand global challenges, taking responsibility for addressing issues such as poverty, climate change, sustainable economic growth, gender inequality, citizen security, and educational access.

Second, Fifth Wave universities will realize this aspiration by organizing for interdisciplinary research, as contemporary problems transcend the limits of traditional domains of knowledge. To solve grand challenges, Fifth Wave universities will motivate faculty to conduct high-impact research beyond the limits of their fields and encourage the exploration of new and emerging disciplines and tools. For example, recent developments in artificial intelligence, machine learning, and quantum computing offer new research capabilities that can be applied to addressing discipline-spanning and multidomain complex systems and wicked problems. Finally, with the recognition that knowledge production does not dictate the solutions to problems nor lead inevitably to public benefit, Fifth Wave universities can act as epistemic innovators by identifying ways to maximize the impact of research. This involves bringing new stakeholders to the discovery process such as lay researchers, citizens, and undergraduates and creating effective mechanisms to broadly disseminate research outputs. Epistemic innovation also requires partnership and collaboration between universities and the private sector, governments and funding agencies, and communities in which research-based interventions can be tested and scaled. Fifth Wave universities can act as leaders in driving relevant impact-oriented research and build on the historical legacy of traditional universities by embracing social progress, economic growth, and human flourishing as the rightful and primary objectives of discovery and knowledge production.

Design innovations that empower massive-scale learning will make research more inclusive, drawing on the capabilities of stakeholders that have been traditionally excluded from research—including undergraduates, minorities, and women as well as practitioners who are not engaged in the historically stratified faculty-driven academic workflow. At Arizona State University, for example, the research enterprise has been reconfigured for use-inspired research that translates into beneficial social, economic, and environmental impacts, and academic departments reorganized around solving emergent global challenges rather than hewing to traditional disciplines. Academic units have created research opportunities to engage undergraduates, nontraditional students, and experts and practitioners who bring skill and acumen but do not fit the typical mold of graduate students, postdoctoral researchers, and tenure-track professors. Epistemic innovation also creates novel channels for the translation of research into social impact. Accordingly, ASU has developed an array of mechanisms to ensure that research makes a meaningful impact through commercialization, public and private sector uptake, and direct application in the field—in our own community and even the developing world.

Fifth Wave universities can also function as pedagogical innovators by redesigning teaching and learning to meet contemporary needs for accessible high-quality education through technologically enabled massive-scale delivery. Historically, the small-scale liberal arts college model associated with the First Wave has been most representative of the university's role in transmitting knowledge. Large public universities, beginning with the Second Wave, adapted this approach to support their mission of expanding access to education to broader segments of society, but even this more expansive approach has reached its limits. In the years ahead, pedagogical innovation will require massive-scale teaching and learning to meet increasing demands for education. Building on emergent capabilities in online teaching and learning methodologies, Fifth Wave universities will test, refine, and deploy new educational platforms to reach larger populations without spiraling costs.

Universities facilitated the birth of alternative learning platforms such as massive open online courses (MOOCs) by developing and validating their instructional methods and supplying their content. Degree-granting online platforms take this approach much further, advancing the design and scalable delivery of digital education and incorporating adaptive learning methodologies to personalize the online experience for potentially tens and hundreds of thousands of students. Adaptive learning and artificial intelligence technologies have turned online learning into a fully personalized experience that tracks the pace of individual students. These tools can power teaching and learning across the entire network of national service universities. These and other new online education methodologies are supported by research-based advances in the theory and practice of teaching, driven by innovative colleges of education, which integrate these findings into new technologies and approaches that are tested in the field through partnerships with school systems. As pedagogical innovators, Fifth Wave universities will diffuse these approaches to every corner of society by making their offerings accessible to wider audiences at low or no cost, often with the capability to reach learners remotely. By deploying these technologies at scale to serve students across the United States, the national service universities of the Fifth Wave can transform the practice of teaching and fundamentally change the way that students learn throughout their academic lives.

## The Fifth Wave and the New American University

The Fifth Wave embraces a heterogeneous set of institutional actors spanning academia, business and industry, government agencies and laboratories, and organizations in civil society, both nationally and internationally, and thus comprises a plurality of differentiated institutional models. But because of their leading role in knowledge production and dissemination, public research universities inevitably represent key nodes in the Fifth Wave network. Even more than their Fourth Wave counterparts, Fifth Wave research universities can vary widely in their institutional models, as well as in their scope and scale, and thus circumvent the isomorphic pressures that normally impel institutions toward homogenization. Among the new models emerging in the Fifth Wave is the New American University. Indeed, the term New American University could refer collectively to the set of Fifth Wave research universities, and the Fifth Wave could be conceptualized as a league of New American Universities. As we said at the outset of this chapter, the Fifth Wave is simply the New American University writ large. And the prototype for both is Arizona State University.

The New American University model reconceptualizes the American research university as a complex and adaptive comprehensive knowledge enterprise committed to discovery, creativity, and innovation, accessible to the demographically broadest possible student body, socioeconomically as well as intellectually, and directly responsive to the needs of the nation and society more broadly. The model combines accessibility to an academic platform underpinned by a pedagogical foundation of knowledge production, inclusiveness to a broad demographic representative of the socioeconomic diversity of the region and nation, and, through its breadth of activities and functions, an institutional commitment to maximizing societal impact commensurate with the scale of enrollment demand and the needs of our nation. The objective of the new model is to produce not only knowledge and innovation but also adaptive master learners empowered to integrate a broad array of interrelated disciplines and negotiate over their lifetimes the changing workforce demands and shifts in the knowledge economy driven by continual innovation.

The comprehensive reconceptualization of Arizona State University constitutes the prototype for the New American University model. The reconceptualization was motivated by an overarching concern with accessibility to academic excellence, especially in response to the demographic trends described in chapter 2. To restore the social compact implicit in American public higher education, ASU revived the intentions and aspirations of the historical public research university model, which, building on the ideals of the Morrill Act, sought to provide broad accessibility as well as engagement with society. By some estimates the public research universities of our nation taken together have produced more than 70 percent of all baccalaureate degree recipients and conducted two-thirds of all funded research.[30] The new institutional model builds on this legacy and thus expands enrollment capacity, promotes diversity, and offers accessibility to an academic milieu of world-class knowledge production to a diverse and heterogeneous student body representative of the demographic profile of the state, which includes a significant proportion of students from socioeconomically diverse and underrepresented backgrounds, as well as a preponderant share of first-generation college applicants.

Consistent with the tenets of the Fifth Wave, ASU is determined to be of ever-greater service to the nation and the world through its research enterprise, advancing innovation on all fronts with research that imparts broadly egalitarian benefits across the entirety of society. Its most prominent research initiatives are in alignment with critical national goals in such strategic areas as earth and space exploration, sustainability and renewable energy, advanced materials, flexible electronics, healthcare, national security, urban systems design, and STEM education. Through research-based learning and new approaches to pedagogy, students become adaptive master learners across a range of transdisciplinary fields, prepared for the vicissitudes of the continuously changing workforce of the knowledge-based economy. Moreover, through strategic organizational streamlining designed to cut costs while preserving the quality of the academic core, ASU has become one of the nation's most efficient producers of both college graduates and high-impact, socially meaningful research.

The reconceptualization demonstrates that broad accessibility and excellence in knowledge production are not mutually exclusive but in fact synergistic. As a consequence of the new model, soaring enrollment growth has been accompanied by unprecedented increases in freshman persistence, degree production, minority enrollment, and academic success. Corollary achievements include growth in research infrastructure and sponsored expenditures, which since 2004 have made ASU the fastest-growing research enterprise in the United States; unparalleled academic accomplishment for both scholars and students; and the transdisciplinary reconfiguration of academic organization around broad societal challenges rather than historically entrenched disciplines. The case study in chapter 2 looks more closely at the multiple strategies that have guided the university's efforts to provide a world-class educational experience, excel in its research portfolio, and maximize societal impact.

The New American University model is intended to provide an alternative to the conventional model of major research universities and is only one among many possible variants on this institutional type. Thus, we sometimes use the somewhat infelicitous term "academic platform" to suggest that there are many unexplored and unexploited institutional models for higher education—especially those that can provide an excellent education while advancing knowledge and innovation at the scale and timeframe necessary to progress toward desired social, environmental, and economic outcomes. Inasmuch as the comprehensive reconceptualization of the institution represents a prototype for the transition of a late-stage Fourth Wave research university into the early stages of the Fifth Wave, an assessment of the New American University model and the updated case study of ASU found in chapter 2 remain relevant. Some of the tenets of the process are generalizable and thus may be adapted by other colleges and universities, both public and private. Accordingly, the account of the reconceptualization of a single institution may be construed as representative of any such effort, and the potential for collaborative transinstitutional alliances abounds. The predication of the new model, however, comes with the caveat that institutions seeking reconceptualization must not succumb to a new form of isomorphism in attempting to embrace the foundational prototype. This is to say that, although our intention is to describe an approach to institutional design that may be globally applicable among large-scale public universities, efforts must be locally adapted.

## Some Preliminary Theoretical Perspective on the Fifth Wave

This book propounds an argument, but it may justifiably be regarded as a manifesto. The model it expounds may moreover be regarded as a *heuristic*, which the *Oxford English Dictionary* defines as a "process or method for problem-solving, decision-making, or discovery; a rule or piece of information used in such a process," and, when used as an adjective, "Of, relating to, or enabling discovery or problem-solving, esp. through relatively unstructured methods such as experimentation, evaluation, trial and error, etc." The term is etymologically related to the exclamation Eureka![31] Our approach is at once descriptive, explanatory, and normative, and because the envisioned Fifth Wave operationalized at a scale commensurate to the needs of society remains at present both conjecture and desideratum, our stance toward its status varies both conceptually, with inconsistent reference to its incipience, emergence, and evolution, and temporally, with reference to its past, present, and future.

Inasmuch as the Fifth Wave is an offshoot and complement of the Fourth Wave, analysis and critique of the latter will figure largely throughout these chapters. We reiterate that in contrast to standard historical accounts, our assessment focuses on the dominant institutional types of colleges and universities and seeks to develop new insight into their structures and functions. And although throughout these chapters we consistently refer to the *evolution* of the American research university, we use the term loosely and do not intend to limit our conception only to the sense of "planned incremental improvement on what already exists," as sociologists John Padgett and Walter Powell characterize conventional notions of organizational change. Instead we propose that the potential for the "production of genuine novelty" in organizational structure and function is inherent in the Fifth Wave. This then is to posit the emergence of a new institutional type—the Fifth Wave public research university—and moreover, the formation of a network or league of Fifth Wave institutions. Nevertheless, organizational change in complex institutions must be understood as the synthesis of evolutionary processes—which sometimes simply means change that is largely reactive or at best only incremental improvement on the status quo—and planned and deliberate intervention, which we term institutional *design*.[32]

Because our account is morphological, we refer to the succession of waves in American higher education in terms of structural transformation. A morphological assessment moreover has the potential to pinpoint fundamental determinants of function such as scalability in terms of enrollment capacity as a portion of the contemporaneous population, academic organization conducive to transdisciplinary knowledge production, and adaptation to social context in terms of public value. To the extent that the book underscores the teleonomic limitations of these institutions—*teleonomy* referring to apparent purpose in the structure and function of living organisms[33]—our assessment might more appropriately be characterized as a morphological and typological analysis of the dominant institutional models in American higher education.

For some readers, allusion to structural transformation will evoke the usage of the term by Jürgen Habermas in his celebrated analysis of the development of the public sphere in the eighteenth and nineteenth centuries.[34] But our usage was suggested by its application to transformation in American universities in the late nineteenth century by the sociologist Craig Calhoun, who refers to borrowing the term from Habermas because of certain parallels between the public sphere and higher education. As Calhoun explains, Habermas contends that whereas greater openness and more abundant rational-critical discourse in the public sphere would have appeared to advance democracy, their dynamic instead provoked tension: "As the public sphere expanded in scale, the quality of its discourse was debased." Moreover, Calhoun perceives the dilemma as analogous to the tension between excellence and accessibility in academe.[35] We explore his elucidation of that dilemma subsequently in this chapter.

Our usage of the concept of *waves*—which we equate with the category of *types*—corresponds to the methodology of the "ideal type" (*Idealtypus*) proposed by Max Weber. The ideal type is simply an abstraction or construct that generalizes from the varied instantiations of some category of objects or phenomena for heuristic purposes.[36] Weberian ideal types are "abstracted from empirical reality and emphasize the functional relationships among the several components of an institutional system . . . rather than the unique characteristics of any one."[37] The wave model, in other words, is a heuristic device that allows stakeholders and policymakers to frame insights, arguments, and recommendations concerning the past, present, and future of the "organized anarchies" that are universities. Thus characterized by Michael Cohen, James March, and Johan Olsen, universities are "collections of choices looking for problems, issues and feelings looking for decision situations in which they might be aired, solutions looking for issues to which they might be an answer, and decision makers looking for work."[38] Although we acknowledge the contradictions suggested by this characterization, we discern persistent wave-like patterns within this organized anarchy. The patterns are arranged in what we call waves that emerge as actors and conditions change at universities and within the environments in which they operate. The goal is to accelerate the evaluation and resolution of the problems that confront the academy and the discovery of satisfactory responses acceptable to all constituents by consensus.

The issue of design for universities is not generally historicized, in the sense that institutional types are not typically considered as stages or phases in an evolutionary process leading from relatively simple to increasingly complex academic organizations. But as philosopher Peter Caws points out, any discussion of the constituent components of academic operations cannot evade the "problems of designing an institution to embody them." Caws historicizes the matter and implicitly corroborates both our contention that a historical perspective is essential because American higher education comprises the evolution of increasingly complex institutional types and that knowledge production is contingent on its institutional context:

> Only about a hundred years ago there were no universities in the United States. The institutions that now bear that title, but claim a longer pedigree, started out [as] colleges, seminaries, and the like. They grew into universities by adopting some functions and abandoning others, and this happened piecemeal, so that in most cases the question of the integral character of the institution was never raised explicitly. Within the last hundred years, large numbers of new institutions calling themselves universities have come into being, but with rare exceptions they have taken their form from established universities either in this country or elsewhere and have not set out to confront the question of what one would create if one could really start from scratch and redesign the educational system as a whole.[39]

The evolutionary processes leading from relatively simple to increasingly complex institutions correlate with the proliferation of knowledge but also with growth in scale and expansion in scope, which is to say, in terms of both structure and function. Sociologist Neil Smelser characterizes the processes of growth and expansion in universities as *structural accretion*, which he defines as the "incorporation of new functions over time without, however, shedding existing ones (deletion) or splitting into separate organizations."[40] The significance of structural accretion—the processes of expansion, specialization, and proliferation epitomized in universities—for institutional design in the transition from the Fourth Wave to the Fifth Wave is taken up more fully in subsequent chapters.

But because our account is more morphological and typological than historical, we underscore that the institutional types that correspond with the succession of waves may best be understood as ideal types, per the methodology proposed by Weber. The ideal type, again, is simply an abstraction or construct that generalizes from the varied instantiations of some category of objects or phenomena for heuristic purposes.[41]

Fifth Wave universities emerge out of the limitations and problematics of the Fourth Wave. The increasingly complex and still evolving institutional models in American higher education that have emerged since the seventeenth century manifest in terms of exponential rates of growth accompanied by structural accretion. In a sense, moreover, as Jonathan Cole puts the matter, the seeds of each new wave grow in the belly or womb of the previous wave. For each institutional type, the existing structure imposes inherent limitations in function and social dynamics, which become constraints as well as the impetus for evolution. To this extent, the transition from one wave to the next may be conceived as analogous to the paradigm shifts delineated by Thomas Kuhn in *The Structure of Scientific Revolutions*. In other words, the birth of the new model—or paradigm—is a consequence of anomalies that emerge from the operations of "normal science" conducted in the older model or paradigm.[42] Analogous to Kuhn's characterization of the physical sciences, we maintain that the various waves are constituted by paradigms as well as defined by social contingencies. Although this exercise is inevitably provisional and inexact, we propose that it yields insights into the inflexible and anomalous structures in American higher education.

For readers unfamiliar with *Structure*, philosopher Ian Hacking provides the following concise synopsis of the dynamic that Kuhn delineated to describe the structure of scientific revolutions: "Normal science with a paradigm and a dedication to solving puzzles; followed by a series of anomalies, which lead to a crisis; and finally resolution of the crisis by a new paradigm."[43] Extending Kuhn's notion of normal science, we contend that the set of "normal" research universities that constitute the Fourth Wave are stuck in developmental patterns consolidated in the late nineteenth century by Johns Hopkins, the prototype of the American research university. These institutions are the crown jewels of American higher education but have not moved sufficiently to address emerging threats and opportunities due in part to factors such as isomorphism and filiopietism, reinforced by what one might term "Harvardization" and "Berkeley-envy." The evolution of the American research university has stalled in a path-dependent cycle in which higher education has been "normalized" in ways that do not necessarily serve the majority of academically qualified students, who are often either rejected outright by our leading public research universities or, when admitted, sometimes encouraged to produce knowledge in a predictable or even rote manner.

"Perhaps the most striking feature of the normal research problems we have just encountered is how little they aim to produce major novelties, conceptual or phenomenal," Kuhn posited.[44] He proposed that the operations of normal science are not directed to discovery but to "determination of significant facts; matching of facts with theory; and articulation of theory."[45] He likens these operations to solving puzzles. In terms of academic administration, one might say that the puzzle-solving activities of Fourth Wave universities are dedicated to reproducing their own structures. Knowledge production constrained by isomorphic academic organization and homologous institutional structures is moreover less likely to produce the variation and diversity essential to addressing the complexity and uncertainty that characterize contemporary society. At issue is the character and quality of knowledge production itself, which is inevitably shaped by its administrative and social contexts. In turn, Fourth Wave universities predictably produce satisfactory outcomes for a select group of privileged students whose socioeconomic status ensures stellar academic preparation. Fourth Wave universities as presently constituted do not expect or produce needed innovation at the rate that society or the economy requires and to some extent arguably stifle educational novelty and reforms by enforcing the status quo.

Alert defenders of Kuhn may interpose any number of objections to our imprecise application of his concepts to the organized anarchy of higher education. For instance, whereas we contend that all five waves will operate in parallel and continue to serve their respective niches, Kuhn maintained that paradigms are incommensurate and that the switch from one paradigm to another is tantamount to a change of worldview. According to Kuhn, practitioners inculcated in the precepts of older paradigms simply cannot see the dawning new world of the emerging paradigm. But then again: "At times of revolution, when the normal-scientific tradition changes, the scientist's perception of his environment must be re-educated—in some familiar situations he must learn to see a new gestalt."[46] Robert Donmoyer quotes the philosopher Richard Bernstein to the effect that "incommensurability is not the same thing as logical incompatibility." Although Kuhn proposed that scientists do not generally summon the resilience to switch from one paradigm to another, there is no logical prohibition preventing the existence of more than one paradigm. Accordingly, "One could conceivably employ different paradigms in different circumstances and/or to accomplish different goals." Thus, "Even cutting-edge nuclear physicists, who long ago rejected the Newtonian vision of a mechanistic, cause-and-effect universe, normally think in causal terms when they leave their linear accelerators and put their feet on the accelerators of their cars."[47] Whereas Kuhn insisted that scientific fields operate according to single paradigms, the philosopher Imre Lakatos offers an alternative conceptualization relevant in this context.[48] Lakatos proposed the concept of the "research program," which, as Peter Godfrey-Smith explains, is roughly similar to a paradigm except that more than one program may operate in parallel and compete with others at any given point. In other words, the "large-scale processes of scientific change should be understood as competition between research programs."[49]

## Boutique Production Strategies and the Public Interest

Announcements each spring in recent years proclaiming that roughly 5 percent of applicants have been admitted to the respective freshman classes of schools such as Harvard and Stanford have by now become routine. Stanford no longer announces its rate of admissions, but last year it was 4.3 percent. For the Class of 2023, Harvard and Yale came in at 4.6 and 5.9 percent, respectively. The longstanding selectivity of our nation's top private research universities no longer surprises anyone. Admission to these elite institutions typically correlates more with the zip code of the family home than a student's grade point average or set of SAT scores,[50] laudable efforts by selective schools to recruit socioeconomically disadvantaged and historically underrepresented students notwithstanding. Of course, given that most academically qualified applicants are turned away, one could readily substitute the term *elitist* or even *exclusionary* for *elite* in this context. But admissions practices that as de facto policy flatly exclude the majority of academically qualified applicants are by no means unique to private institutions. Despite growing enrollment demand and projected deficits of college-educated workers, our leading public research universities have correspondingly become more and more selective as well, which is to say exclusionary, even as state funding for higher education has taken a nosedive.[51] Of course, students rejected by one or more top-tier schools are frequently welcomed at other institutions of equivalent or nearly equivalent merit—but this is not always the case and, as we will argue, not necessarily an alternative for the rank and file of academically qualified applicants whose life circumstances may preclude them from considering other options. Moreover, as we consider in chapter 3, this objection embodies and perpetuates the conventional focus on the evaluation of individual schools and individual students rather than the de facto system of American higher education. It is essential instead to look at how the system as a whole functions to realize the values of our society.

If the United States is to retain its leadership and competitiveness in the globalized knowledge economy—and if individuals are to succeed in an era when knowledge correlates with prosperity and well-being—it is imperative for policymakers and the general public to recognize that millions more Americans will need access to research-grade, or what we also term *research-pedagogic*, learning environments. This is to say that the academic infrastructure of our nation must reconcile the demands of accessibility with the potential of world-class knowledge production and innovation. But, as we assess throughout these chapters, whether by design or default, our nation's leading major research universities have failed to scale-up enrollment capacities commensurate with demand or proportionate to the growth of the population. Both the elite private and public research universities opt instead to raise thresholds for admission. Limited accessibility to research-grade academic platforms may appear to represent a nominal threat given that during the past quarter-century educational attainment has steadily increased, with roughly one-third of Americans now holding four-year degrees,[52] but academic quality and educational and socioeconomic outcomes vary drastically according to institutional type. Expansion of enrollment capacity in our nation's major research universities, to the extent that any even occurs, has been merely incremental. Enrollment growth is invariably seen primarily in less selective second-tier institutions explicitly committed to accessibility. This sort of stratification is a function of the hierarchy of institutional categories, which has been termed *vertical institutional segmentation*. The implications of stratification for the development of human capital and the economic competitiveness of our nation are assessed subsequently.[53] To reiterate the point: mere access to standardized forms of instruction decoupled from discovery and knowledge production will not deliver desired societal outcomes.

Although America's leading research universities, both public and private, consistently dominate global rankings, our nation's success in establishing and maintaining world-class levels of academic excellence in a relative handful of institutions is insufficient to ensure the broad and equitable distribution of the benefits of research-grade educational attainment, nor does it sufficiently correlate with the production of graduates with the advanced competencies and skills essential to sustain our continued national competitiveness. As nations worldwide invest strategically to educate broader segments of their citizenry for the knowledge economy, America's leading research universities generally maintain modest enrollment levels that have remained virtually unchanged since the mid-twentieth century.[54]

This is not to say that even some of the elite private research universities have not grown in size appreciably over the past four or five decades as a percentage of their enrollment levels in preceding decades. But they have grown off of a small base, as Jonathan Cole points out.[55] Leading Fourth Wave institutions characteristically maintain nominal or at best moderate enrollment levels, which in terms of degree production could well be characterized as "boutique production strategies." Prestige may seem an intangible asset, but in academic culture it correlates with profit in the corporate sector.[56] To the extent that Fourth Wave institutions define their excellence through admissions practices based on the exclusion of the majority of academically qualified applicants, enrollment growth is perceived to come at the expense of reputation and competitive standing. "Universities are not ranked on what they actually do once the students get to them; instead, they are rated on who attends the schools and how many people are excluded from attending," observes higher education policy scholar Robert Samuels. "Universities and colleges thus have a perverse incentive to recruit students so that they can reject them and thus raise their school's selectivity rating." Samuels underscores the perversity of the process: "Even the universities that reject the vast majority of interested students spend lavishly on trying to attract more students so they can reject more students."[57]

"Even Americans unfamiliar with the word embrace *meritocracy* as if it were a birthright," observes Joseph Soares in his account of the prerogatives of privilege in American higher education.[58] And indeed, the admissions policies of our top-tier institutions purport to be meritocratic—Jerome Karabel refers to the "quasi-meritocratic" processes of recent decades as a distinct improvement over the "more overtly discriminatory and hereditary system of the past."[59] But meritocratic aspirations obtain at the expense of egalitarian practices. As Christopher Newfield points out with reference to conventional rank-ordered hierarchies, "The whole point of meritocratic evaluation is to assess in order to rank, sort the great from the good, and create a pecking order. It would be a more functional pecking order than an aristocracy of birth, but would be just as rigorously and persistently stratified."[60] The designation of merit moreover obscures the exercise of advantage in power relations. As Karabel observes: "Those who are able to define merit will almost invariably possess more of it, and those with greater resources—cultural, economic, and social—will generally be able to ensure that the educational system will deem their children more meritorious."[61] Meritocratic aspirations notwithstanding, the exclusionary practices of leading colleges and universities may be interpreted as a defensive posture that correlates with the abdication of implicit responsibility. But the accessibility to a broader demographic at meaningful scale characteristic of the Fifth Wave has the potential to surpass in aggregate impact remedies to redress inequities in college admissions through meritocratic evaluation or even affirmative action policies. The Fifth Wave moreover embraces a more expansive vision of meritocracy, which, as Newfield explains, recognizes that "intelligence is spread widely rather than narrowly in human societies." He cites Christopher Lasch in this context, who referred to this ideal as the "democratization of intelligence."[62]

The intent of the Fifth Wave to democratize intelligence begins with the precept that the objective of the model is not only to engender knowledge and spur innovation but also to produce graduates better prepared through a research-pedagogical academic culture to assume the responsibilities of global citizenship and participation in our American ex-periment in democracy. Through an evolving model intended to advance universal learning frameworks, curricular and pedagogical innovation throughout the Fifth Wave will seek to produce adaptive master learn-ers empowered to integrate a broad array of interrelated and interdepen-dent disciplines sufficient to negotiate the vicissitudes and workforce demands of a knowledge economy driven by perpetual innovation. The imperative to educate to world-class levels of academic achievement not only the conventionally measured top 5 or 10 percent but at the very least the most capable quarter of academically qualified students representa-tive of the socioeconomic and intellectual diversity of our society would require a significant expansion of the infrastructure of public higher ed-ucation. As we evaluate in the following chapters, this desideratum could even more appropriately be expressed as the imperative to provide research-pedagogic education to the top third of students in traditional age cohorts, for example, eighteen to twenty-four-year olds, and oppor-tunities for lifelong learning to half of all Americans over the course of their lifetimes. Research-grade education is the basis for the intellectual or knowledge infrastructure of our nation, and the American Academy of Arts and Sciences calls on state and federal policymakers to recognize it as equivalent in significance to the nation as its physical infrastruc-ture.[63] This is a modest claim, inasmuch as the survival of humanity may well depend on our knowledge infrastructure. Thus, if many of the institutions of the Fourth Wave deem it appropriate to maintain limited enrollments while excluding the majority of applicants, other research-grade academic platforms must emerge that offer accessibility to greater numbers of students representative of the intellectual and socioeconomic diversity of our society.

## The Fifth Wave Reinvigorates the Social Contract Implicit in Public Higher Education

As economists Claudia Goldin and Lawrence Katz have shown, pub-lic higher education in the United States produced world-leading levels of educational attainment during the first three quarters of the twenti-eth century and served for countless millions as a springboard to inter-generational socioeconomic mobility. Science-based technological in-novation in our nation's research universities in the decades following

World War II spurred innovation and economic competitiveness. Through a confluence of economic, political, and social currents, these accomplishments laid the foundations for an increasingly widely shared prosperity built on the rapidly rising productivity enabled by an educated and innovative society.[64] This economic growth and widely shared prosperity are both products of the social contract implicit in public higher education.[65] As aptly summarized by Newfield: "During the 1945–1975 period, universities took for granted a social contract in which regular smart people would expend effort and forego full-time work income to attend college, thereby developing knowledge and know-how that increased their productivity. When they entered the workforce, their increased productivity would be recognized with rising wages." But, despite the success of the model, a confluence of determinants marked an inflection point. "This bargain held for thirty years, but in the mid-1970s began to fall apart."[66] Public disinvestment, especially beginning in the wake of the Great Recession, exacerbated the incommensurabilities of enrollment demand and the limited supply of places available in our nation's leading universities.[67] Such disinvestment is just one of many factors stemming the momentum of increased accessibility to our nation's colleges and universities. As a result, many of the students who would most benefit from this most obvious avenue of upward mobility—those typically categorized as socioeconomically disadvantaged or historically underrepresented—cannot gain admission to a research-grade university.

Goldin and Katz find that stagnation or decline in the proportion of college graduates beginning in the 1970s accompanied lagging productivity and increasing inequality in our society. They identify this slackening in the growth of educational attainment since 1980 as the single most important factor in the rising college wage premium, which has exacerbated inequality and contributed to trends that over the intervening decades have left the United States with the "most unequal income and wage distributions of any high-income nation."[68] Estimates of income inequality and wealth inequality in the United States vary, but more recent analysis corroborates that both have increased sharply since the late 1970s. Over the past four decades, stratification by wealth has moreover increasingly replaced income differentiation as a determinant of inequality in our society.[69] But, consistent with the arguments for the Fifth Wave, economist Thomas Piketty finds that the "principal mechanism for convergence," by which he means the reduction of inequalities in wealth and income, is the diffusion of knowledge: "In other words, the poor catch up with the rich to the extent that they achieve the same level of technological know-how, skill, and education."[70] The problem, of course, is that the socioeconomically disadvantaged—and the middle class as well—are increasingly denied access to research-pedagogic academic milieus that would impart the know-how, skill, and education to meaningfully facilitate socioeconomic mobility.

The recognition that knowledge is a public good is widely conceded.[71] Major research universities advance not only the discovery and science-based technological innovation that catalyzes industrial application and economic growth—producing what the economic historian Joel Mokyr terms the "gifts of Athena"[72]—but also knowledge production in the arts, humanities, social sciences, and professional fields that pervasively suffuses every sector of society. Frank Rhodes corroborates this point in the following terms: "Unlike other assets, whose utilization and investment are constrained by the law of diminishing returns, knowledge is autocatalytic, enlarging in the hands of its users; expanding in the range of its usefulness, even as it is applied; growing in scope, even as it is shared, increasing in refinement, even as it is questioned, challenged, and contested." Indeed, he observes, "Knowledge has become the prime mover."[73] Mathematician Alan Wilson, a fellow of the British Academy and Royal Society, moreover observes that knowledge in our contemporary society is its principal capital and social resource, which "empowers people in a knowledge-based economy . . . and underpins any kind of critical thinking."[74] Knowledge is the source of human capital, of course, a concept that in its most general sense refers to the measure of the value of the stock of knowledge, skills, and creativity that may be acquired through investment in education and training.[75]

The public value of higher education has been amply documented in numerous assessments of economic outcomes—for the individual in terms of the income gains associated with the college wage premium, and for society by the correlation between growth in overall educational attainment and the rate of growth in the economy. Among the important private and social benefits of higher education are direct and indirect effects, both market and nonmarket, that contribute to the prosperity and well-being of democratic societies. But as economist Walter McMahon explains, it is nearly impossible to estimate the private and social benefits of fields in which short-term monetary returns cannot be readily quantified. He thus proposes a human capital approach that "emphasizes the nature, measurement, and valuation of the private and social benefits of higher education—with special attention to the non-market private and social benefits, direct and indirect effects, and short- and long-term effects—all in relation to the total investment costs."[76]

Leaving aside consideration of the intrinsic value of higher education, well-documented correlates for the individual begin with substantial economic returns and significantly increased prospects for intergenerational socioeconomic mobility.[77] According to a report from the U.S. Department of Treasury, opportunities for individuals are "starkly different" depending on whether one completes a bachelor's degree.[78] (A digression here, but it would be a fallacy, of course, to infer from such assessments that all bachelor's degrees may be taken to be equivalent—a point to which we subsequently return.) Nevertheless, among the manifold correlates of educational attainment that accrue to the collective are the aggregate economic returns from larger pools of human capital and increased levels of civic engagement.[79] A more educated workforce generates greater tax revenues and influences quality-of-place policymaking. Economist Enrico Moretti estimates that all wage earners in a local workforce benefit from an increase in the proportion of baccalaureate degree holders. The rise in wages is greater for those with less education, meaning that high school graduates or even dropouts benefit more from the spillover related to a highly educated workforce than college graduates.[80] In addition to increased opportunities for more meaningful employment, higher education influences lifestyle choices that correlate with better health and greater civic participation. David Brooks offers the following synopsis of behavioral differences and social norms associated with educational attainment: "Divorce rates for college grads are plummeting, but . . . the divorce rate for high school grads is now twice as high as that of college grads. . . . High school grads are twice as likely to smoke as college grads. They are much less likely to exercise. College grads are nearly twice as likely to vote. They are more than twice as likely to do voluntary work. They are much more likely to give blood."[81]

Any coordinated effort to undertake the expansion of a subset of public research universities to integrate accessibility and academic excellence in an era when both policymakers and the general public are increasingly skeptical of the presumption that higher education serves the public interest shifts the burden of responsibility to institutions and stakeholders. Absent the effort, however, the nation will eventually have to confront the consequences of the inevitable decline of one its most essential assets. As political scientist Suzanne Mettler puts the implications: "We are squandering one of our finest accomplishments and historic legacies, a system of higher education that was long characterized by excellence and wide accessibility to what seemed to be an ever wider and more diverse group of citizens."[82] Research-grade academic infrastructure in the United States still largely retains the scale of the mid-twentieth century, with some institutions expanding only nominally in recent decades despite surging enrollment demand and projections of shortfalls of highly educated participants in the workforce. "The United States has been underproducing college-going workers since 1980," observe Anthony Carnevale and Stephen Rose at the Center on Education and the Workforce at Georgetown University. "Supply has failed to keep pace with growing demand, and as a result, income inequality has grown precipitously."[83] As a consequence, as Mettler aptly summarizes, "We are producing too few highly educated workers to provide the innovation and creativity the economy requires; our international competitiveness is fading; the ranks of those who participate intensely in the political process are growing more unequal; and the American dream is increasingly out of reach for most citizens."[84] As Brooks has observed, "We once had a society stratified by bloodlines, in which the Protestant Establishment was in one class, immigrants were in another, and African Americans were in another. But now we live in a society stratified by education." He cautions: "A social chasm is opening up between those in educated society and those in non-educated society."[85] That chasm is at least in part a function of lack of accessibility to research-grade higher education.

What distinguishes the Fifth Wave model is its capacity to catalyze innovative knowledge production as well as its dissemination to an increasing proportion of citizens. Although the Fifth Wave will in its initial phase comprise primarily large-scale public research universities, the category will also encompass a plurality of institutional actors linked through transdisciplinary collaboration and public purpose. Fourth

Wave research universities constitute key nodes in the national innovation system,[86] but Fifth Wave institutions will further leverage their interrelations with government agencies and federal laboratories, business and industry, other academic institutions, and the many knowledge networks throughout the world to advance discovery and innovation. Moreover, Fifth Wave institutional innovation is the outcome of autonomous self-determination at the local level. This said, evidence points to the imperative for such efforts to be undertaken within the context of an integrated national innovation system steered by government, perennial debate regarding the appropriate role of the latter notwithstanding.[87] Through interaction and collaboration across sectors, Fifth Wave institutions are likely to become increasingly heterogeneous, varied, and differentiated. Accordingly, conjecture regarding a unified Fifth Wave model should be construed primarily as heuristic, although for the present referring primarily to the transitional phase of the evolution of a subset of reconstituted large-scale public research universities.

## Building on the Bedrock of the Fourth Wave

Media coverage of American higher education tends to generalize when it comes to distinctions among different types of colleges and universities. Between accounts of skyrocketing tuition costs and allegations of misguided political correctness, few assessments differentiate among institutional types of vastly different mission, scale, and scope that constitute a heterogeneous and competitive academic marketplace.[88] From among the roughly 5,000 degree-granting postsecondary institutions in the United States, only 115, both public and private, conduct sufficient sponsored research to be categorized as research-extensive, with approximately 100 additional universities with less extensive research portfolios constituting a secondary research-grade cohort.[89] As Jason Owen-Smith points out, major research universities account for fewer than 3 percent of American colleges and universities but conduct nearly 90 percent of all academic research and development.[90] Deficiencies notwithstanding, American research universities consistently occupy seventeen of the top twenty slots in the assessment conducted by the Institute of Higher Education, Shanghai Jiao Tong University, and fourteen of the top twenty in the most recent edition of the *Times Higher Education World University Rankings*.[91] The number of international students seeking enrollment at American colleges and universities attests to the perception that these institutions offer opportunities found nowhere else. Apart from their role in the formation of successive generations of scholars, scientists, artists, policymakers, professionals, and practitioners in every sphere of endeavor, these institutions serve as the primary source of the scientific discovery and technological innovation that fosters economic growth and social development across the global knowledge economy. No less important is their role as the institutional matrix of scholarship in the humanities and social and behavioral sciences and of creative endeavor in the arts that too often escapes notice precisely because their influence so fully informs our intellectual culture.[92]

While the global preeminence of our leading institutions may well lead Americans to infer that on the whole our nation has the best colleges and universities in the world, the metrics used to establish the unrivaled status of these institutions—the research performance of an array of world-class universities—does not correlate with overall excellence in American higher education.[93] Whereas the top tier of research-grade institutions dominates knowledge production and dissemination, most colleges and universities are restricted in scope and offer little more than standardized instruction. However critical to the organizational ecology of American higher education, schools restricted to teaching are peripheral to the leading centers of knowledge production and dissemination. "Peripheral universities are, in the large majority, basically distributors of knowledge," Philip Altbach explains.[94] The magnitude of the disparity between our nation's leading colleges and universities and the vast majority is aptly captured in the observation quoted by economist Charles Clotfelter to the effect that the "crazy quilt" of American higher education includes "fifty of the best universities in the world and five hundred of the worst."[95] Within this "strikingly hierarchical" system, as Newfield characterizes American higher education, with its "ever-richer small elite and an ever-poorer large majority," educational outcomes are drastically uneven. "Less selective universities have lower status but does that mean that they are inferior educationally?" Newfield asks rhetorically, and is compelled to conclude, "Unfortunately, it does. They are inferior . . . because they are unable to deliver solid academic outcomes" despite the best efforts of motivated students, faculty, staff, and administrators.[96]

The exponential growth of knowledge witnessed during the past century, including but certainly not limited to the scientific discovery and technological innovation of the postwar era, has to a remarkable extent been the product of the integrated research, development, and education efforts of the set of Fourth Wave research universities. Despite the limitations of the institutional model we assess in the following chapters, the importance of the set of major research universities to societal prosperity and well-being cannot be overstated. As Cole succinctly puts it:

> Although the transmission of knowledge is a core mission of our universities, it is not what makes them the best institutions of higher learning in the world. We are the greatest because our finest universities are able to produce a very high proportion of the most important fundamental knowledge and practical research discoveries in the world. It is the quality of the research produced, and the system that invests in and trains young people to be leading scientists and scholars, that distinguishes them and makes them the envy of the world.[97]

The envisioned Fifth Wave thus builds from the bedrock of a highly successful and influential model that defines contemporary academic culture. Craig Calhoun offers a succinct and useful definition of the research university that encapsulates the parameters of the Fourth Wave: "The full model of a research university unites freedom of intellectual inquiry (for both students and professors) with the creation of new knowledge through research, the nurturance of a scholarly community integrating disparate fields, open public communication, and the effort to make knowledge widely available as a public good." Whereas in our assessment large-scale public research universities will constitute the vanguard of the Fifth Wave, Calhoun points out that distinctions between public and private are often simplistic: "Private universities often pursue public goods, starting with the preservation and sharing of knowledge and continuing through research that addresses public needs and problems."[98] Distinctions between public and private in this context generally hinge on sources of funding but should vary according to whether one chooses to observe an economic or political definition of the terms. The economic definition hinges on the distinction between non-market and market activities, Simon Marginson explains, observing the distinction delineated by Paul Samuelson. The political definition, which he derives from John Dewey, differentiates between state and non-state control.[99]

Cole posits twelve core values foundational to academic culture that will inevitably endure and define the Fifth Wave: universalism ("the belief that new truth claims and assertions of fact are to be evaluated using established impersonal criteria, not based upon the personal or social attributes of the person making the claim"); organized skepticism ("a skeptical view of almost anything proposed as fact or dogma, applying appropriately rigorous methodological criteria to claims of discovery or truth"); creation of new knowledge (discovery "leading to critical contributions to the welfare of people around the world"); free and open communication of ideas ("knowledge becomes common property, placed freely in the marketplace of ideas for examination, criticism, correction, and further development"); disinterestedness ("prescribes that individuals at universities should not profit from their ideas directly"); free inquiry and academic freedom ("sets universities apart from most other institutions, where political, religious, or social constraints can more easily restrict the introduction of new ideas"); international communities ("the resulting intellectual firepower—the intellectual capital produced—has been enormous"); peer review ("lies at the heart of academic freedom and is essential to its continuance"); working for the common good ("producing knowledge that can benefit the larger society"); governance by authority ("a 'company of equals' model in which the faculty has significant governance responsibilities"); intellectual progeny ("the core value of teaching"); and the intellectual vitality of the academic community ("the essential goal . . . to make both incremental and revolutionary advances in knowledge"). The flux of these democratic and dynamic values, he points out, contrasts markedly with the more hierarchical conceptions of authority and governance inherent to European universities.[100]

The core foundational values that Cole posits are an elaboration of the so-called Mertonian norms, referring to the codification of the ethos of scientific culture proposed by the pioneering sociologist of science Robert K. Merton. In an influential 1942 essay, Merton asserts that the scientific ethos—"norms expressed in the form of prescriptions, proscriptions, preferences, and permissions . . . legitimatized in terms of institutional values"—is defined by "four sets of institutional imperatives": communalism, universalism, disinterestedness, and organized skepticism, which subsequently came to be known as the CUDOS norms. Communalism expresses the conviction that the "substantive findings of science are a product of social collaboration and are assigned to the community." Although "esteem accrues to the producer," scientific knowledge "constitutes a common heritage." Universalism is equated with objectivity and free access to the pursuit of knowledge, which Merton terms a functional imperative. Truth claims must be "subjected to preestablished impersonal criteria," which must transcend "ethnocentric particularism." Because universalism is implicit in a democratic society, "democratization is tantamount to the progressive elimination of restraints upon the exercise and development of socially valued capacities." Merton distinguishes disinterestedness from both self-interest and altruism but locates its motivation in part to rigorous institutional control: "The translation of the norm of disinterestedness into practice is effectively supported by the ultimate accountability of scientists to their compeers." Finally, organized skepticism—"both a methodological and institutional mandate""—refers primarily to the "detached scrutiny of beliefs in terms of empirical and logical criteria" so thoroughgoing that discovery transcends the "cleavage between the sacred and the profane."[101]

With reference to the norm regarding collaboration, Thomas Gieryn points out that Merton postulated the impetus for "competitive cooperation" in scientific culture, which, notwithstanding the imperative for originality and quest for priority, he perceived to be transgenerational. Thus, according to Merton, the process of discovery is "essentially cooperative [and] results from the realization that scientific advance involves the collaboration of past and present generations."[102] Accordingly, Merton would recur to the celebrated observation by Sir Isaac Newton that he had inevitably "seen farther than others" because he was "standing on the shoulders of giants."[103] But although knowledge production may be both competitive and cooperative, as Gieryn elaborates, disinterestedness demands that "provisional knowledge claims be evaluated by a scientist's expert and authorized competitors."[104]

It would be superfluous in the present context to attempt to represent the full scope of structural transformation in American higher education associated with the Fourth Wave. Such an account would approach the Fourth Wave as situated within and constituted by its epistemological, administrative, and sociocultural dimensions and interrelations. No account of the Fourth Wave, of course, would be complete without some attempt to suggest the extent to which its modes of knowledge production have defined not only the domains of contemporary academic culture but, more broadly, the norms and values and institutions of contemporary society. We attempt to suggest the extent to which the Fourth Wave took up the mantle of the German research university to claim what Chad Wellmon termed its uncontested "epistemic authority" and prerogative to legitimate knowledge, especially as it could be deemed sufficiently "scientific." Knowledge production itself would become institutionally dependent, especially insofar as knowledge would be organized by disciplines,[105] beginning with the implementation of the conventional tripartite organization of humanities, social sciences, and natural and physical sciences. This process coevolved with the organization of faculty into academic departments defined by disciplines, which then corresponded to undergraduate majors and graduate fields of study. Because of their "extraordinary ability to organize individual careers, faculty hiring, and undergraduate education," sociologist Andrew Abbott observes, disciplinary departments appear to be the "essential and irreplaceable building blocks" of American academia.[106] A fuller account than is possible here would include, for example, some consideration of their influence on the formation of national scholarly associations, such as the American Historical Association (1884), American Economic Association (1885), American Psychological Association (1892), American Political Science Association (1903), American Sociological Association (1905), and the Social Science Research Council (1923), each of which publishes various scholarly journals. The organizations and journals are part and parcel of an ethos that Thelin describes as a "new conception of academic professionalism essential to the creation of a university professoriate," which included the codification of academic rank and formalization of the processes associated with promotion and tenure.[107] Such an account would approach the Fourth Wave as a progenitor of professional schools in such fields as business, law, and medicine. The formation of university affiliated postbaccalaureate professional schools established a pattern that in some sense defined professional education. As Abbott points out, "While in fact professional education by no means required university affiliation . . . profession after profession turned to the university for help in seizing control of its own educational apparatus." But all of this is just to scratch the surface of what Abbott terms the "slow structural metamorphosis that leads to the modern university." Moreover, "University structure is then a slowly changing fact of competitive life that is eventually transformed, in part by that very competition."[108]

Among the most significant structural transformations that defined American higher education beginning in the late nineteenth century was the colocation of teaching and organized research in the set of Fourth Wave universities. As Calhoun elaborates, "Research was redefined in many fields from a part-time activity of individual faculty employed largely as teachers into a large-scale, high-cost, externally funded under-taking often requiring complex organizational structures."[109] Espe-cially in the postwar decades, the prominence of research in this set of institutions was consolidated by a federal science policy that brought massive investment to research deemed to be in the national interest. We take this up in chapter 4, but for now simply remark that despite the fa-miliar tension in contemporary academic culture between teaching and research, a significant portion of the investment in the research and development efforts of the set of major research universities yields com-plementary outcomes in the enhanced education of both undergradu-ates and graduate students. As former University of California provost C. Judson King observes, "Lest we conclude that research standing and educational effectiveness are two entirely different things not much re-lated, it is important to recognize the essential feature of research uni-versities, which is that research bears heavily on education, especially the education of researchers and other creative people."[110]

Moreover, apart from the portion of benefits of university-based re-search that are privatized through intellectual property rights like pat-ents, McMahon explains, the "benefits from most research performed at universities are social benefits since there is distribution of the results required through publication and also since master's and PhD graduates spread the methods and results of basic and applied research to others throughout the society." The social aspect of the benefits derive in part from the ubiquity of the products of research from across all fields so pervasive as to escape our notice: "Very few ideas and results from re-search in the social sciences, humanities, mathematics, business, agri-cultural economics, or other fields result in objects that can be patented and manufactured, although they can sometimes have sweeping effects on the economy, the rule of law, or other aspects of the quality of life."[111]

In the context of undergraduate education this approach has been termed "research-based" or "inquiry-based" learning or, more commonly, simply "research learning." Chief among the recommendations of the Boyer Commission on Educating Undergraduates in Research Universities, convened by the Carnegie Foundation for the Advancement of Teaching, is that research-based learning become the standard. The report attributes to John Dewey the insight that learning is optimally based on "discovery guided by mentoring rather than the transmission of information," an arrangement moreover that encourages reciprocity between scholar-teachers and students. However, and consistent with our contention that the design constraints of Fourth Wave institutions demand remediation, "This concept of integrated education requires restructuring both the pedagogical and integrative aspects of the research university experience." With reference to the imperative for new approaches to undergraduate education, the report, which was published in 1998, concluded that "for the most part fundamental change has been shunned; universities have opted for cosmetic surgery, taking a nip here and a tuck there, when radical reconstruction is called for."[112]

Engagement in research learning—the sort of competitive world-class education characteristic of research-grade institutions that we term research-pedagogic—offers opportunities not always available to students enrolled in other institutional types. The unique attributes of undergraduate education in a highly productive research-pedagogic academic milieu are delineated in a report from the Committee on Institutional Cooperation, a consortium that links twelve major research universities in the Midwest. Advantages and added value include student exposure to cutting-edge research and incorporation of the latest research and breaking developments into course curricula; increased opportunities for student engagement in research conducted by leading experts in respective fields; access to state-of-the-art laboratories and libraries; increased network of connections with experts in respective fields as well as exposure to institutional engagement with industry leaders; co-curricular and experiential learning opportunities; internationalized peer and faculty populations and curricula; and the employability of graduates of top-ranked major research universities.[113] As the late

Charles M. Vest, then president of MIT, observed in a 1994 letter to parents, the distinctive character of a major research university encourages undergraduates to participate in research guided by scientists and scholars working at the frontiers of knowledge: "Our society will ask much more of these students—and they will ask more of themselves—than just to know what others have accomplished. If they are going to help us expand our knowledge and solve our problems, they are going to have to know how to research, to analyze, to synthesize, and to communicate. They must learn how to gather data, to develop hypotheses, to test and refine them, or throw them out when necessary and start over."[114] Of course, research learning is certainly characteristic of many liberal arts colleges as well. William Durden, president emeritus of Dickinson College—a quintessential First Wave college founded in 1773—points out in this context that by one estimate liberal arts colleges produce twice as many students who eventually complete doctorates in the natural sciences as other categories of institutions.[115]

But, despite the success of the model and the contributions of contemporary academic culture to the quality of life and standard of living for billions, the major research universities of the Fourth Wave tend to perpetuate the academic infrastructure of the mid-twentieth century, with some institutions expanding only nominally despite surging enrollment demand and projections of shortfalls of highly educated participants in the workforce. Despite their pivotal role during the initialization of the knowledge economy, most have become increasingly exclusive and limit admissions to a small fraction of academically qualified applicants. The determinants of scale and accessibility, moreover, are not exclusively or even primarily the outcomes of fiscal constraint, however much public disinvestment spikes the costs of tuition and exacerbates the incommensurabilities of supply and demand.

## Knowledge Production as Socially Useful as It Is Scientifically Meritorious

The Fifth Wave must be unified by the pursuit of knowledge that is as socially useful as it is scientifically meritorious. Beginning with the modern research university that emerged during the first decade of the nineteenth century in Berlin, academic culture claimed the prerogative to legitimate knowledge. The research university institutionalized science and conferred epistemic authority on knowledge deemed sufficiently "scientific." Inasmuch as the scientific culture of the modern era has shaped the research university, knowledge production itself has become institutionally dependent.[116] But whereas Fourth Wave research universities have prioritized the pursuit of the unknown and the isolation and analysis of increasingly specialized knowledge, Fifth Wave institutions will seek to advance adaptive knowledge creation and recalibrate their orientation to promote broad societal advancement. Much research may be socially valuable even if pursued primarily for the purpose of expanding knowledge, but the complexity of the challenges that confront global society demands that research be increasingly organized to advance desired social outcomes.

From an epistemological perspective, Fourth Wave research universities have institutionalized scientific culture and prioritized its reductionist approaches. Knowledge production remains largely organized and legitimated disciplinarily. But recognition of the limitations of our collective ability to acquire, integrate, and apply knowledge is rarely explicit in Fourth Wave academic culture. Recognition of human limitation would ideally inform Fifth Wave knowledge production as it emerges and serve as an incentive for further inquiry and action directed toward the realization of what Cole terms a "more perfect American research university." Among the values of contemporary academic culture that Cole enumerates, "organized skepticism . . . of almost anything proposed as fact or dogma" and the application of "appropriately rigorous methodological criteria to claims of discovery or truth" must remain deployed in the assessment of our knowledge enterprises with deliberate, reflexive, and normative intent.[117] The Fifth Wave must thus concede its limitations in the face of uncertainty and complexity as well as confront the implication of academic culture in the broader societal failure to ensure the equitable distribution of the benefits of academic research.

In his seminal account of what he terms the "republic of science," Michael Polanyi represents the values of pure science governed by an "invisible hand" guiding scientific culture toward discovery that would inevitably benefit society.[118] With reference to this presumption, Roger Pielke paraphrases the assessment of the physicist Alvin Weinberg regarding the "explicitly normative axiological attitudes—statements of value—that scientists hold about their profession" in the following terms: "Pure is better than applied; general is better than particular; search is better than codification; paradigm breaking is better than spectroscopy."[119] As one team of scholars addressing the often overlooked nuances of the dilemma put it: "A combination of social values, political contexts, technological innovation and diffusion, and the obduracy of infrastructure and economic and institutional structures often impede effective social, political, and technological action."[120] Indeed, in a *locus classicus* discussion of the formulation of science and technology policy, Daniel Sarewitz examines what he terms the myths perpetuated by scientific culture, which in a more general context serves equally to characterize the presumptions that guide Fourth Wave academic culture:

> The myth of infinite benefit ("More science and more technology will lead to more public good"); the myth of unfettered research ("Any scientifically reasonable line of research into fundamental natural processes is as likely to yield societal benefit as any other"); the myth of accountability ("Peer review, reproducibility of results, and other controls on the quality of scientific research embody the principal ethical responsibilities of the research system"); the myth of authoritativeness ("Scientific information provides an objective basis for resolving political disputes"); the myth of the endless frontier ("New knowledge generated at the frontiers of science is autonomous from its moral and practical consequences in society").[121]

Implicit in any conception of the Fifth Wave then is the assumption—framed in terms consonant with the tenets of American pragmatism—that knowledge should be useful and thus lead to practical action.[122] Undergirding this assumption is the corollary that knowledge is a product of negotiation and consensus, a collaborative process that Habermas terms "communicative rationality."[123] Pragmatism, with its insistence on the indivisibility of thought and action and emphasis on the practical application of knowledge within the context of social practice, emerged contemporaneously with the consolidation of the model for the American research university in the final quarter of the nineteenth century. Because the pragmatist conviction that knowledge should lead to action competes with the Fourth Wave valorization of increasingly specialized knowledge, the objective of real-world impact should ideally become an explicit mandate, even if belatedly.

The Fifth Wave thus seeks to advance the impact of knowledge on human affairs, and with this commitment comes a unique set of complex challenges and responsibilities. New knowledge is essential but not necessarily sufficient to motivate let alone guide researchers and policy-makers to seek both to optimize and operationalize its social impacts. This is not to suggest that Fourth Wave academic culture has in some sense been deliberately reluctant to guide research toward the achievement of desired outcomes. Scientists and technologists have written entire books about the practical application of their discoveries and inventions while others have addressed ethical issues surrounding their potential misuse. But in its accustomed effort to produce novel and abstract knowledge, contemporary academic culture sometimes overlooks its potential to give direction and purpose to humanist and social scientific insight, scientific discovery, and technological application to advance desired outcomes or to create useful products, processes, and ideas. In this context the philosopher Robert Frodeman laments the limitations of the "epistemological regime we have been living within, that of infinite, largely laissez-faire knowledge production." As evidence he cites research that estimates that from among the millions of peer-reviewed journal articles published a decade ago, fewer than half were cited during the first five years following their publication. According to another estimate, 48 percent of all articles ever published have never been cited.[124]

Accordingly, the sociotechnically integrated institutional platforms of the Fifth Wave are designed both to permit and enable researchers to seek solutions and transformation through a use-inspired agenda that addresses complex and intractable problems, which are inevitably fraught with uncertainty and contested values.[125] In an effort to reveal the limitations of the standard binary opposition between basic and applied research, the policy scholar Donald Stokes constructed a table to represent types of research ("Quadrant Model of Scientific Research"), which may variously be inspired by the quest for fundamental understanding or considerations of use. In this conceptualization, Bohr's quadrant—so-called, he explains, in honor of the quest for a model of atomic structure by Niels Bohr—represents basic research unfettered by concern with application. The quadrant named for the quintessential system builder, Thomas Edison, represents applied research. Pasteur's quadrant, however, combines the approaches of Bohr and Edison and stands for "basic research that seeks to extend the frontiers of understanding but is also inspired by considerations of use." The designation memorializes the approach to research pioneered by Louis Pasteur, the eminent chemist and microbiologist, whose late career was devoted to the development of vaccines that have protected millions from disease: "Pasteur's drive toward understanding and use illustrates this combination of goals."[126] By building on the accomplishments of the Fourth Wave, the Fifth Wave seeks to ameliorate problems by invoking the spirit of Pasteur's quadrant.

The research enterprises of the Fifth Wave thus encourage integrative research that transcends the spurious dichotomy between the categories of fundamental and applied posited in the standard linear model of innovation. Venkatesh Narayanamurti and Toluwalogo Odumosu explain that the linear model "represents the belief that the technological products of modernity are driven by a process that begins with basic (sometimes referred to as fundamental) research, which is then taken up in further research activities that aim to solve specific problems, the outcomes of which may lead to the development of products and services that may prove to be marketable."[127] Integrative research moreover advances know-how, which "denotes the knowledge, some articulated and some tacit, that guides the actions of skilled agents who aim to achieve a particular practical objective," as Sarewitz and Richard R. Nelson explain. "That is, the state of know-how defines best practice in an arena of human activity."[128] The Fifth Wave accordingly seeks to calibrate institutional platforms to advance and sustain know-how.

The Fifth Wave in a sense institutionalizes the emerging paradigm of knowledge production that science policy scholar Michael Gibbons and colleagues characterize as "Mode 2," referring to the proposition that an ongoing transition in the cognitive orientation and social practices of contemporary academic culture has increasingly superseded the scientistic and disciplinary norms that were institutionalized with the formation of the modern research university in the wake of the Scientific Revolution and Enlightenment. Whereas Mode 1 knowledge production is said to be correlated with the disciplinary framework, scientific dominance, and theoretical hegemony of the academy, Mode 2 knowledge production is largely transdisciplinary and undertaken in a context of application and broad social accountability.[129] Mode 2 moreover corresponds to integrative problem-driven collaborative research that transcends the conventional dichotomy between basic and applied research posited in the standard linear model of innovation.[130] As we assess in chapter 5, it is thus possible to correlate Mode 1 knowledge production with the Fourth Wave, which consolidated its model in the wake of the scientific enterprise of nineteenth-century German academic culture, and Mode 2 with the Fifth Wave. Indeed, we contend that Fifth Wave research universities are the key nodes in the network of heterogeneous institutional actors that have operationalized and continue to sustain Mode 2 knowledge production. In this sense, Mode 2 knowledge production represents the culmination of processes that have been gathering momentum in Fourth Wave research universities throughout their ascendency. Through their operationalization of Mode 2 knowledge production, Fifth Wave institutions will become better equipped to transcend the design constraints of the Fourth Wave as well as mount responses to the intractable challenges that confront humanity.

A further glimpse of the epistemological limitations of the scientific culture of the contemporary academy comes with the acknowledgment of uncertainty and recognition of contingency. The literary scholar M. H. Abrams captures this dilemma with his observation that, in circumstances where "valid knowledge and understanding are essential but certainty is impossible," because the "rules are uncodified and elusive and there is room for the play of irreducible temperamental differences," we must consult the subtler calculus of the humanities, which, he reminds us, were "designed for use in the human predicament."[131] At the very least we must recognize that the humanities may serve as a guide when there are "questions which can be asked of science and yet which cannot be answered by science," referring to what Weinberg in a seminal 1972 essay termed the domain of "trans-science."[132]

The Fifth Wave must accommodate the socially robust knowledge that is a product of its increasing contextualization among academic institutions, business and industry, government agencies and laboratories, and organizations in civil society, as well as currents from the broader cultural Zeitgeist—the boundaries of which are becoming increasingly "fuzzy." As Helga Nowotny, Peter Scott, and Michael Gibbons point out: "The increasing emphasis on the contribution of science to wealth creation and social improvement, the growing deference to so-called user perspectives, the great weight now attached to ethical and environmental considerations, are all examples of the intensification of what we have called contextualization."[133] The Fifth Wave must accommodate an academic culture that reaffirms the pragmatist tenet that truth is a matter of social consensus. As philosopher Richard Rorty reminds us, the recognition that our "vocabularies" may be contingent does not prevent us from imagining and constructing a better world. Indeed, in the "literary culture" he envisions, the "intellectuals will have given up the idea that there is a standard against which the products of the human imagination can be measured other than their social utility, as this utility is judged by a maximally free, leisured, and tolerant global community."[134]

The preponderant commitment to discovery and innovation that distinguishes the research university from other institutional types must be reconciled with the imperatives of social responsibility and societal engagement. The assumption that the intellectual objectives of the Fourth Wave, especially in terms of scientific research and technological innovation, are automatically and inevitably aligned with our most important goals as a society is erroneous. Instead the intent to create knowledge that is socially useful as well as scientifically meritorious will require that academic culture assume significantly greater responsibility for the role of knowledge in society. If the Fifth Wave is to function as a framework for responsible innovation and sustainable development, academic culture must embrace the imperative of responsibility described by philosopher Hans Jonas. With reference to what he terms our "Promethean technological attainments," Jonas observes: "The lengthened reach of our deeds moves responsibility, with no less than man's fate for its object, into the center of the ethical stage." Moreover, "Its axiom is that responsibility is a correlate of power and must be commensurate with the latter's scope and that of its exercise."[135] Equivocal outcomes are in some instances indicators of fallibility in academic governance or science and technology policy, but in a broader sense they merely illumine the contours of inevitable human limitation. There is no recourse but to attempt to negotiate our limitations, however, and the quest to advance institutional evolution in the American research university that Cole envisions represents one important aspect of that impulse. This is surely the basis for envisioning the Fifth Wave.

## Transcending the Conflict between Accessibility and Excellence

The arguments set forth in our previous book regarding the imperative for broad accessibility to research-grade higher education achieve heightened relevance in the conceptualization of a league of institutions that collectively have the potential to exert substantive impact on admissions practices that typically favor students from families in the top quintile or even decile of income distribution in our nation. For those alarmed over the increasing inequality in our society and the threat such inequity poses to our social cohesion and collective prosperity, it should be a matter of urgent concern that, among families in the top quartile of household incomes, 82 percent of children will attend college compared with only 45 percent from families in the bottom quartile. Students from families in the top income quartile are five times more likely to graduate from college with a bachelor's degree by the age of twenty-four than those from the lowest income quartile—58 percent as opposed to 11 percent. For the second-to-bottom quartile, the rate is 20 percent. A bachelor's degree is a key determinant of social mobility and economic potential, but the degree attainment rate for half of our population does not exceed 16 percent. Although the rate for the various income quartiles fluctuates, it remains highly unequal. The disparity between the lowest and highest income quartiles was even starker just a few years ago. In 2013 students from families in the top income quartile were eight times more likely to graduate from college with a bachelor's degree than their peers from the bottom quartile—77 percent as opposed to 9 percent.[136]

In her useful primer to some of the dilemmas that confront American higher education, Goldie Blumenstyk puts the correlation between affluence and academic success in the following terms: "Between 1970 and 2012 . . . the proportion of low-income twenty-four-year-olds (family income of $34,160 and below) with bachelor's degrees went from just 6 percent to slightly over 8 percent. Meanwhile, the proportion of upper income twenty-four-year-olds (family income of $108,650 and up) with a bachelor's degree increased from 40 percent to 73 percent." Moreover, attainment of bachelor's degrees among twenty-four-year-olds from the bottom half of income distribution actually dropped by 5 percentage points between 1980 and 2011.[137] From figures such as these one can only conclude that socioeconomic status at birth still determines far too many learning outcomes and family income remains the greatest predictor of whether or not an individual will obtain a college degree. The college completion gap threatens the potential for social mobility that is the basis of our social fabric. It relegates the children of lower-income Americans to unskilled, low-paying jobs—the very kind of work that is most vulnerable to automation and disruption—and leaves the American dream out of reach for millions.

The correlation between affluence and admissions—what has been termed the "reproduction of privilege" in an increasingly "hereditary meritocracy"[138]—becomes especially conspicuous in any account of the family income of students enrolled in our nation's leading private research universities. More students from what has been termed the set of "Ivy-Plus colleges"—the eight schools of the Ivy League and the University of Chicago, Stanford, MIT, and Duke—come from families from the top 1 percent of income distribution than all their peers from the entire bottom half, 14.5 percent and 13.5 percent, respectively. A student born to that level of affluence is seventy-seven times more likely to attend one of these schools than his or her counterpart from the bottom quintile. Raj Chetty and his colleagues at the Economic Mobility Project moreover dispel the perception that middle-class students are underrepresented at highly selective institutions as a consequence of recruitment efforts that favor the socioeconomically disadvantaged: "Students from the lowest-income families have the smallest enrollment shares at the most selective private colleges, both in absolute numbers and relative to comparably ranked public schools. Only 3.8 percent of students come from the bottom 20 percent of the income distribution at Ivy-Plus colleges."[139] Thirty-eight colleges—among them Brown, Dartmouth, Penn, Princeton, and Yale—had more students from families in the top 1 percent of income distribution than from the bottom 60 percent.[140] The average family income among Harvard students, for example, is roughly $450,000, which positions this group among the top 2 percent nationally. Piketty finds that family income has become an "almost perfect predictor of university access." He elaborates: "Research has shown that the proportion of college degrees earned by children whose parents belong to the bottom two quartiles of the income hierarchy stagnated at 10–20 percent in 1970–2010, while it rose from 40 to 80 percent for children with parents in the top quartile."[141]

While the prosperity of the Ivy League student body would surprise no one, the socioeconomic profile of students admitted to leading public research universities—the so-called flagships or Public Ivies—departs only somewhat from the topmost stratum. At the University of Michigan, for example, David Leonhardt reports that during one recent academic year more entering freshmen were products of families with incomes exceeding $200,000 than all of their peers originating from families in the bottom half of income distribution.[142] According to one recent estimate, in our nation's 193 most selective institutions, students from the top economic quartile outnumber their socioeconomically disadvantaged peers by fourteen to one.[143] By another estimate, three-fourths of students who attend institutions the College Board deems highly selective are products of families from the top income quartile, with only 3 percent from the bottom quartile.[144] "When compared with children in families earning less than $50,000 per year in 2002 (the bottom 54 percent of families), children in families with income above $100,000 (i.e., the top 13 percent) are 50 percent more likely to attend a postsecondary institution of some type—a 90 percent attendance rate for the latter as compared to 60 percent for the former," reports demographer Nathan Grawe. Children from affluent families enjoy a 43-point advantage over low-income peers (73 percent versus 30 percent, respectively), Grawe elaborates. At more highly selective institutions, "children from high-income families are more than six times as likely to attend an institution ranked among the top fifth colleges or universities (13 percent as compared to 2 percent)."[145]

Public disinvestment in higher education—often concentrated in places most in need of precisely the opposite—is an important factor stemming the momentum of increased accessibility to our nation's colleges and universities. Over the past decade, average published tuition and fees at public four-year colleges and universities has increased by 35 percent in 2018 dollars.[146] Between 1980 and 2015 tuition and fees at public universities increased by more than four times the rate of inflation.[147] Average net price of attendance as a percentage of average family income for students from the lowest income quartile in 2012 was 84 percent as opposed to 15 percent for students from the highest quartile.[148] As a result, many of the students who would most benefit from this most obvious avenue of upward mobility—those whom we broadly categorize as socioeconomically disadvantaged or historically underrepresented—have few prospects for admission to a research-grade university. The decline comes at a time when more and more Americans of all ages, socioeconomic backgrounds, levels of academic preparation, and types of intelligence and creativity are seeking enrollment, overwhelming a set of institutions built to accommodate the needs of our country prior to World War II, when the population was fewer than half its present number, and only slightly more than 1 percent of Americans enrolled in college. Indeed, enrollment capacity, accessibility, and equity have been identified as the "critical triumvirate" of overarching concerns in higher education worldwide, along with quality assurance, accountability, and assessment.[149] While restoration of public support is essential, institutions themselves must rethink their strategic objectives and reconceptualize their designs, especially in terms of their potential to expand enrollment capacity to provide broad accessibility commensurate with the scale of demand and the socioeconomic and intellectual diversity of our society.

Admissions practices that perpetuate the intergenerational reproduction of privilege dovetail with institutional policies that maintain the status quo in enrollment levels. But the global dominance of a relative handful of elite institutions is insufficient to ensure our continued prosperity and competitiveness, especially if we stop to consider the disproportionately few students fortunate enough to be admitted to these top schools. This dilemma that defines the Fourth Wave has been aptly framed as a contest between "equity and excellence in American higher education" by economist and former Princeton president William Bowen and colleagues Martin Kurzweil and Eugene Tobin. In their acclaimed 2006 book, they describe the "simmering debate over whether it is better to educate a small number of people to a very high standard or to extend educational opportunities much more broadly—even if this means accepting a somewhat lower standard of performance and, in general, spreading resources more thinly." Equity and excellence are complementary, the authors observe, because talent is distributed throughout the socioeconomic spectrum, national competitiveness depends on extending opportunities to sufficient numbers from all demographic strata, diversity enhances the quality of the educational experience, and the success of our democracy depends on an educated citizenry. "In its most shallow construction, this linkage [between equity and excellence] takes the form of a direct, zero-sum tradeoff between the two ideals." The authors recognize that to move beyond this justification for the exclusionary business model, "society at large can build the educational scale that it requires only if its institutions of higher education tap every pool of talent."[150]

As Newfield aptly frames the dilemma: "The entrenched practices, the deep culture, the lived ideology, the life-world of American higher education all point toward defining excellence through selectivity, and would seek to improve any university regardless of mission by tightening admissions standards." The apparent conflict between accessibility and excellence is a product of the systemic inequality of American higher education, Newfield elaborates, and he is blunt in his assessment of the prospects for students relegated to less selective institutions, which, despite the motivation of students and commitment of faculty, staff, and administrators, are "unable to deliver solid academic outcomes."[151] More selective institutions produce better educational outcomes—selectivity in the conventional model is an index of quality. "More selective universities, by definition, enroll students with stronger entering credentials who are more likely to graduate regardless of where they go to college," Bowen points out in a subsequent study coauthored with colleagues Matthew Chingos and Michael McPherson.[152] Newfield paraphrases the major thrust of their assessment: "The most important factor affecting graduation rates is the university's selectivity: the greater the selectivity, the higher the graduation rate." For institutions entrenched in the conventional model, the motivations behind increasingly rigorous admissions standards are obvious: "The promise is that the outcome of increased selectivity will be both more money and better students who are more likely to succeed and who will produce better work while allowing their professors to do better research and their institution to in turn attract better incoming students and better—wealthier—donors."[153] Graduation from a highly selective institution moreover yields a substantial premium in earnings and professional prospects, especially for socioeconomically disadvantaged students.[154] Despite the narrative of crisis and dysfunction that now attaches to discussions of higher education, graduation from a top liberal arts college or major research university remains for most individuals the most likely scenario to advance socioeconomic mobility. Mettler underscores the premium of enrollment in the highly selective institutions of the Fourth Wave: "Degrees from elite institutions generally yield the most impressive returns for their graduates: their earnings are 45 percent higher than those who receive college degrees elsewhere, and they produce a disproportionate share of the nation's top corporate and government leaders."[155]

Because the New American University model operationalized at appropriate scale in the Fifth Wave brooks no compromise in the quality of knowledge production and insists that equity is attained only when all academically qualified students are offered an opportunity for access to a research-grade education regardless of socioeconomic background, the Fifth Wave transcends the constraints of this self-aggrandizing but spurious zero-sum trade-off. And whereas Bowen and his colleagues focus on the socioeconomically disadvantaged and historically underrepresented, the Fifth Wave model welcomes students from all demographic strata capable of accomplishment in a research-grade environment, including the gifted and creative students who do not necessarily conform to a conventional academic profile. Fifth Wave institutions will moreover recalibrate their orientation from predominant faculty-centrism to student-centrism. Because socioeconomic status need no longer serve to predict outcomes in educational attainment, the objective of the new model is to overcome social, cultural, and financial constraints for individual students as well as to advance research learning to promote broad societal advancement.

Recruitment efforts focused on academically gifted students from socioeconomically disadvantaged and historically underrepresented backgrounds shortchange capable students who lack the profiles targeted by recruiters. These measures sometimes merely produce the appearance of diversity because it is always possible to skim from an arbitrarily defined upper echelon without drawing more deeply from the pools of academic talent found throughout our society. As economist Robert Gordon observes, "Presidents of Ivy League colleges and other elite schools point to the lavish subsidies they provide as tuition discounts for low- and middle-income students, but this leaves behind the vast majority of American college students who are not lucky or smart enough to attend these elite institutions."[156] But intelligence is distributed throughout the population, and for millions of individuals it manifests through skills, abilities, and experience that elude current admissions protocols. Admissions policies that merely skim from the conventionally defined top 5 or 10 percent shortchange countless gifted and creative individuals. As we contended at the outset of this chapter, at issue is not the education of students graduating from the top 5 or 10 percent of their high school classes, which represents business as usual at gold standard institutions, but rather the imperative to educate the top quarter or third of respective age cohorts to internationally competitive levels of achievement and through universal learning frameworks to provide opportunities for lifelong learning to more than half the population of the United States.

We reiterate that the exclusion of academically qualified students is the product of limitations in the infrastructure of American higher education. In our previous book we estimated that aggregate undergraduate enrollment in the Ivy League schools, together with the fifty top liberal arts colleges, accounted for less than 1 percent of what in 2015 represented the total U.S. undergraduate population of 18.2 million students. Among the sixty member institutions that constitute the prestigious Association of American Universities (AAU), undergraduate enrollment then represented approximately 6 percent of college students in the United States. The combined undergraduate enrollment of what were then the 108 research-extensive universities, which the Carnegie Foundation for the Advancement of Teaching designates as R1 institutions and includes all sixty AAU schools, numbered little more than two million, or roughly 11 percent of American students. The numbers have changed slightly, as we assess more fully in chapter 3, but as we then framed the dilemma, this meant that in a nation with roughly 18.2 million undergraduates enrolled in postsecondary education—including 45 percent attending community colleges and 10 percent then enrolled in for-profit sector institutions—the combined undergraduate enrollment of all research-extensive universities, which includes all sixty AAU schools, numbered little more 11 percent of all American students enrolled in two- and four-year degree-granting institutions.[157] If to the set of research-extensive, or R1, institutions we factor in the second tier of research universities, which Carnegie alternately characterizes as research-intensive or R2 institutions, aggregate undergraduate enrollment climbs to 3.7 million, or roughly 22.1 percent of overall undergraduate enrollment.[158] Enrollments have ticked down marginally five years hence, and more recent estimates may somewhat temper the dire scenario, but the numbers have not changed all that substantially. As we assess in the following section, enrollment growth in less selective second-tier or even nonselective institutions such as community colleges and explicitly vocational schools continues to far outpace enrollments in research-grade institutions.

The intent to enroll in college is nearly universal among the roughly 3.5 million American high school seniors who graduate each spring, observes Oren Cass, a senior fellow at the Manhattan Institute for Policy Research. But the trajectories of recent cohorts of students diverge starkly according to a predictable pattern. Cass offers the following rough estimates: One-fifth will fail to receive a high school diploma; one-fifth will pursue no further formal schooling; one-fifth will enroll in college but fail to graduate; one-fifth will complete some level of college but subsequently enter the workforce in a position that does not require a degree. "Despite decades of reform in teacher training, student testing, and standards, as well as school choice and hundreds of billions of dollars in new annual education spending, only a final fifth will successfully navigate the path—high school to college to career—that is our education system's ideal."[159] As Brooks remarks of this assessment, "We build a broken system and then ask people to try to fit into the system instead of tailoring a system around people's actual needs."[160]

Although roughly one-third of Americans hold a four-year degree, outcomes for graduates are often subpar and vary drastically according to institutional types. Completion of a bachelor's degree—graduation as opposed to enrollment and attendance—may demonstrably be the "single most important indicator of educational attainment," as Bowen, Chingos, and McPherson point out,[161] yet it would be a fallacy to infer from such assessments that all bachelor's degrees may be taken to be equivalent. Nearly half of all students who begin college never graduate, according to U.S. Department of Education figures from 2015.[162] A more recent estimate places that number at more than one-third of college students, many of whom acquire significant student loan debt in the process. More than one in five full-time freshmen nationwide fail to return for their sophomore year.[163] The prospects are even more alarming for students enrolled in community colleges, where two-year graduation rates do not exceed 13 percent.[164] For students who begin their undergraduate trajectories at community colleges, an unexpected penalty sometimes attaches. Economists report a reduction of 32 percentage points in the likelihood of graduation with a bachelor's degree in six years.[165] Despite generally weaker entering academic credentials that correlate to socioeconomic disadvantage, however, Bowen, Chingos, and McPherson cite data that show that community college students who graduate and successfully transfer to four-year institutions complete four-year degrees at comparable or even superior rates: "Compared to freshmen with similar high school GPAs and SAT/ACT scores, transfer students are much more likely to graduate." At selective state universities, the differential can be as much as seven to ten percentage points.[166]

Moreover, since 2000 the federal government has spent more than $300 billion on the Pell Grant program, which has been described as the "nation's single most expensive education program . . . with no way of knowing how many of the recipients ever actually earned degrees."[167] According to the U.S. Department of Education, the program, which awards grants based on family earnings to help low-income students obtain access to higher education, cost taxpayers $26.6 billion in academic year 2016–2017, down from a high of $39.4 billion during 2010–2011. Recipients during these academic years numbered 7.1 million and 9.4 million, respectively.[168] Taxpayers may have spent something like $500 billion on the program since it was initiated in 1972. Yet more than half of Pell Grant recipients never obtain a degree of any type from either a community college or public university.[169]

For the majority of Americans, the prospects for academic success are uneven at best. Among these are our fellow citizens most likely to be socially and economically excluded from the direct and indirect benefits of higher education. Because our nation's leading universities deem it appropriate to maintain modest levels of enrollment, which is to say that these institutions increasingly define their excellence through admissions practices based on the exclusion of the majority of academically qualified applicants, other research-grade academic platforms must emerge that offer accessibility to greater numbers of students. We reiterate that the imperative for the Fifth Wave thus stems from the potential of its academic platforms to combine knowledge production and innovation with research-grade education accessible to the broadest possible demographic representative of the socioeconomic and intellectual diversity of our nation. We underscore yet again that mere access to standardized forms of instruction decoupled from discovery and knowledge production will not deliver desired societal outcomes.

## The Tension between Accessibility and Academic Excellence

The proposition that accessibility and academic excellence need not be mutually exclusive is implicit in the conception of the New American University and the Fifth Wave. However, if one accepts the explicit dimensions of accessibility and excellence, their juxtaposition evokes tensions inherent in contemporary academic culture that Craig Calhoun perceives to be both ideological and unlikely to be resolved. His explication of the relationship between accessibility and excellence reveals tacit dimensions of both concepts that are essential and fundamental to our understanding of the imperative for the Fifth Wave. Whether or not one subscribes to the notion that the quest for excellence inherently and inevitably reduces accessibility to higher education for large numbers of underrepresented students, Calhoun finds that the pursuit of excellence as it is commonly understood by academic culture has compelled institutions to "invest in a competition that has become an end in itself." As a consequence, he observes, "Universities are becoming much more unequal at the same time that higher education and research are being organized, funded, and marketed in more integrated ways and on larger scales— nationally, regionally, and globally."[170] Fifth Wave universities oppose narrow consequences that accrue primarily to students of affluent parents. Instead, the Fifth Wave will provide access to academic excellence to students from the broadest possible demographic through academic enterprise that is funded and marketed in a manner that is scalable.

As the common term used by academic culture to convey "nonreferentially specific claims of quality or merit," Calhoun observes, *excellence* is fraught with connotations that reflect societal values in transition. In this context he cites the explication of excellence proposed by Bill

Readings, a Canadian literary scholar and astute critic of academic culture. According to Readings, excellence was formerly an estimation of merit bestowed by what he termed the "university of culture," referring to an institution primarily concerned with the collective and committed to public value. However, legitimation of merit has more recently been conferred by the "university of excellence," which, Readings contends, has largely superseded the university of culture and reflects private values consistent with the neoliberal global order. Calhoun finds that the rhetoric of excellence had been transformed by "evacuating much specific meaning (and especially Aristotelian heritage) from the notion of excellence, treating it as a term of commensuration like price rather than the quality of doing well in very different and largely incommensurable dimensions of life." The formerly robust rhetoric of excellence has degenerated into the mindless "pursuit of recognition and especially the positional good of being seen to be better than others."[171] Fifth Wave universities seek to resurrect the useful public values of accessibility and excellence and apply them to higher education.

Calhoun maintains that excellence and accessibility are difficult to integrate because conceptions of excellence have degenerated into facile and irrelevant hierarchical rankings that do not accurately reflect any aspect of academic quality. The distortion is especially pernicious because rankings related to excellence are based on excluding worthy but disadvantaged applicants, not actual academic performance. The resulting hierarchies heralded in the media are both taller and narrower than they need to be because they exaggerate the excellence of a few elite institutions that educate a relatively small number of generally affluent students. Under the current regime, accessibility is constructed to mean opening up the system to allegedly unqualified students and excellence is framed in ways that are incommensurable with admitting qualified but disadvantaged students, all of whom would benefit equally from an academic milieu fueled by world-class research. In contrast, the Fifth Wave league of national service universities reconstructs the alleged incommensurability by integrating research excellence with broad accessibility in ways that are consistent with the democratic ideals and egalitarian values of our society.[172]

Jason Owen-Smith pinpoints an inflection point in the transition from the "university of culture" to the "university of excellence" in outcomes advocated by the Truman Commission on Higher Education, which in 1947 issued a report that defined national goals for higher education. Among the overarching goals for higher education specified by the commission was the "fuller realization of democracy in every phase of living." The report enjoined the federal government to partner with states to support universities in providing "the means by which every citizen, youth, and adult is enabled and encouraged to carry his education, formal and informal, as far as his native capacities permit." However, Owen-Smith observes: "This focus on education for the purpose of supporting a distinctive national culture eventually gave way to languages of individual excellence, identity, and efficiency."[173]

With reference to accessibility, Calhoun found the term to be an "ideological shorthand for the transformations demanded of older forms of elite and often sequestered universities as they became central institutions in modern and increasingly democratic societies." But to the extent that institutions accommodate enrollment demand, increased accessibility could impact the credentialing functions of universities: "Expanded access may imply more open and meritocratic distribution of existing credentials, but of course it actually produces an inflation in credentials and a new emphasis on prestige differentiations among apparently identical credentials."[174]

Indeed, an appreciation of the tensions between excellence and accessibility that Calhoun identifies is essential to a thorough assessment of the extent to which the contemporary university serves the public interest and the potential of the Fifth Wave to leverage this publicness. In this context Calhoun quotes sociologist Gerard Delanty, who terms the university the "paradigmatic institution of the public sphere and of modernity more generally." But to understand the public dimensions of research universities more fully, Calhoun elaborates, it is essential to evaluate four senses of "public": "(1) where does the money come from? (2) who governs? (3) who benefits? and (4) how is knowledge produced and circulated?"[175] Alongside these questions, David Guston suggests that from an historical perspective it may well be worth considering who contributed and who sacrificed to build our colleges and universities.[176] Whether universities are part of the public sphere as defined by Habermas or Delanty or, instead constitute a multitude of publics that contribute to the conversation, we believe along with Calhoun that universities contribute substantial public value and that much of the value of public universities has been privatized. We propose that the Fifth Wave constitutes a structural transformation that will reinvigorate the public value of higher education.

Labaree points to stratification among institutional types of universities as the de facto mechanism to diffuse the tension between accessibility and excellence, which is to say, as he puts it, the "tension between social accessibility and social exclusivity, between admitting everyone and limiting access to the elite." He perceives this tension as inherent in liberal democracy, with its "willingness to constrain liberty in order to maximize social equality, and liberal markets, with their willingness to tolerate inequality in order to maximize liberty." Stratification accommodates both tendencies: "We can make universities both accessible and elite by creating a pyramid of institutions in which access is inclusive at the bottom and exclusive at the top." A system that "simultaneously extends opportunity and protects privilege," he contends, results in a "structure in which universities are formally equal but functionally quite different, where those institutions that are most accessible provide the least social benefit, and those that are the least accessible open the most doors."[177]

But the Fifth Wave dynamically manages accessibility and academic excellence without stratification across universities, which tends to funnel many academically qualified but socioeconomically disadvantaged students downward in the hierarchy of institutional types. As we elaborate in chapter 2, as the foundational prototype for the New American University and Fifth Wave models, Arizona State University represents an organizational framework that combines academic excellence with broad accessibility, which may be likened to coupling within a single institution the world-class research excellence of the University of California system with the accessibility offered by the Cal State system.

## The Alignment of Hierarchical Differentiation and Stratification

Roughly three-fourths of high school graduates now enroll in some form of college, including community colleges and for-profit sector institutions—a fourfold increase since mid-century. The overall college enrollment rate among young adults, defined as the percentage of eighteen- to-twenty-four-year-olds enrolled as undergraduates or graduate students, increased from 35 percent in 2000 to 42 percent in 2016. Nearly 70 percent of 2016 high school graduates enrolled in college in fall of that year. According to the Bureau of Labor Statistics, "Of the 3.1 million people ages 16 to 24 who graduated from high school [in] 2016, about 2.2 million, or 69.7 percent, were enrolled in college in October 2016," a figure little changed from the previous year. The corresponding figure for 1995 was 61 percent. Although the discrepancy in enrollment rates between students from socioeconomically disadvantaged and upper-income families has progressively narrowed, 83 percent of students from high-income families enrolled in college in 2016, whereas the rate for middle-income students was 64 percent and for low-income students 67 percent.[178]

College participation rates may be on the uptick, but the expansion of accessibility in research-grade higher education is a vastly different proposition than what is conventionally espoused in perennial efforts to boost college enrollments and graduation numbers among disadvantaged and underrepresented student populations. Growth and expansion in higher education characteristically follows a pattern of development from the elite to mass to universal phases, according to sociologist Martin Trow, whose analysis corroborates the disproportionate impact of growth on research-grade institutions. Growth manifests in terms of changes in the rates of growth of systems or institutions; in the absolute size of systems or institutions; and in the rates of participation of respective cohorts through three phases of access: elite, mass, and universal. The phases differ both quantitatively and qualitatively.[179] Access in the elite phase is highly limited and perceived as a "privilege, either of birth or talent or both." Trow characterizes the elite phase as concerned "primarily with shaping the mind and character of the ruling class, as it prepares students for elite roles in government and the learned professions."[180] Mass higher education represents participation of respective age cohorts exceeding 15 percent; the universal phase participation exceeding 50 percent. Access in the mass phase is perceived as a "right for those who have certain formal qualifications," and in the universal phase, an obligation for children from the middle and upper middle classes. In the mass phase, priorities shift toward the "transmission of skills for specific technical roles" for a broader elite ("the leading strata of all the technical and economic organizations of the society"). Universal access potentially implicates the entire population, and the "primary concern is to maximize the adaptability of that population to a society whose chief characteristic is rapid social and technological change."[181] As policy scholar Simon Marginson summarizes, "Access to higher education shifted from being a privilege in the elite phase to a right in the mass phase and then to an 'obligation' in the universal phase, when higher qualifications become mandatory for full and effective social engagement."[182]

During the three decades following World War II—the period of expansion for colleges and universities that has been termed the "Golden Age" of American higher education—growth in undergraduate enrollments, including community colleges, increased fivefold, and graduate school enrollment increased nearly 900 percent, bolstered by returning veterans, women, and historically excluded minorities.[183] The expansion was a function of the demographic patterns that produced the baby boom, the economic growth rate of the thriving postwar economy, and the Cold War, which institutionalized wartime federal investment in university-based research and development associated with national defense, economic prosperity, and public health.[184] But that expansion has increasingly been accompanied by the hierarchical differentiation of sectors, which has been termed "vertical institutional segmentation or stratification." As Brendan Cantwell and Simon Marginson explain: "Vertical stratification includes: (1) differential value from participation; (2) segmentation of the student body on a hierarchical basis; and (3) institutional hierarchy."[185] As the epigraph for their chapter on vertical stratification, Cantwell and Marginson aptly cite the sociologist Fred Hirsch on what he termed "positional competition," by which he meant "competition that is fundamentally for a higher place within some explicit or implicit hierarchy and that thereby yields gains for some only by dint of losses for others. Positional competition, in the language of game theory, is a zero-sum game: what winners win, losers lose."[186]

Although enrollment growth in less selective second-tier or even nonselective institutions such as community colleges and explicitly vocational schools far outpaces increased enrollment in research-grade institutions, some major research universities have undeniably attempted to accommodate increased enrollment through the development of satellite campuses, which invariably base admissions decisions on less stringent standards. Such hierarchical differentiation may be perceived to be diversion, which, in effect, funnels students from socioeconomically disadvantaged and historically underrepresented backgrounds into positions of lower status.[187] Chetty and colleagues corroborate that growth in college attendance among low-income students for the period between 2000 and 2011 was primarily limited to for-profit institutions and two-year colleges. "Even at the Ivy-Plus colleges, which enacted substantial tuition reductions and other outreach policies during this period, the fraction of students from the bottom quintile of the parent income distribution increased by only 0.65 pp." Moreover, "The fraction of students from the bottom 60 percent of the income distribution exhibits very similar time trends, with an increase of 0.8 percentage points at Ivy-Plus colleges and a decline of 3.1 percentage points at other elite schools."[188]

"The key question about educational expansion is whether it reduces inequality by providing more opportunities for persons from disadvantaged strata, or magnifies inequality by expanding opportunities disproportionately for those who are already privileged," Richard Arum Adam Gamoran, and Yossi Shavit contend.[189] Another assessment found that "inequality between any two social strata in the odds of attaining a given level of education persists until the advantaged class reaches the point of saturation."[190] As Marginson explains, "High and growing participation in higher education does not necessarily trigger upward social mobility on a broad scale when social stratification is aligned to vertical institutional segmentation." In this context he quotes Trow: "The establishment of different sectors, reflecting the status hierarchies in the larger society, is a more effective way of using higher education to buttress rather than undermine class structure."[191] As Mettler cautions: "All told, higher education today is becoming a caste system in which students from different socioeconomic backgrounds occupy distinct strata, and their experiences within those tiers end up making them increasingly unequal."[192]

Awareness of the pernicious ramifications of stratification in higher education was evident decades before the concept entered the discourse of socioeconomic opportunity. In his foreword to the 1947 report of the Commission on Higher Education, President Harry Truman warned of its consequences: "If the ladder of educational opportunity rises high at the doors of some youths and scarcely rises at the doors of others, while at the same time formal education is made a prerequisite to occupational and social advance, then education may become the means, not of eliminating race and class distinctions, but of deepening and solidifying them."[193] The Fifth Wave seeks to redress the inequities associated with the hierarchical differentiation of sectors, or vertical institutional segmentation. And although the imperative for the formation of the Fifth Wave is not exclusively an argument about whether the admissions policies and enrollment capacities of research-grade institutions are commensurate with demand or appropriate in scale to the needs of the nation, projected shortfalls in the numbers of highly educated college graduates threaten our nation's prosperity and economic competitiveness.[194] Because the admissions policies of our leading institutions cull all but a fraction of academically qualified applicants, and the demographic trends shaping our nation militate against the success of students from the middle classes and especially those from socioeconomically disadvantaged and historically underrepresented backgrounds, if our society is to continue to prosper, the Fourth Wave must be augmented by a league of institutions that draw from the broader talent pool of socioeconomic and intellectual diversity and integrate the production and distribution of knowledge at socially meaningful scale.

## Toward the Emergence of the Fifth Wave

To underscore one of the major arguments of these chapters, inasmuch as access to knowledge underpins the societal objectives of a pluralistic democracy, scalability and thus accessibility must be at the core of evolving institutional models. To reiterate a corollary point: As de facto national policy, excluding the majority of academically qualified students from the excellence of a research-grade university education is both counterproductive and ethically unacceptable. The imperative for broad accessibility to research-grade academic platforms is far more urgent than policymakers realize, even those on the national stage charged with advancing higher education policy. Our national discussion on higher education must not be limited merely to arbitrary goals for the production of more college graduates. We reiterate the point yet again: Mere access to standardized forms of instruction decoupled from knowledge production and discovery will not deliver desired societal outcomes. Inasmuch as education is a public good, the meritocratic pretense used to justify current admissions protocols must be regarded a defensive posture and abdication of the social compact implicit in American public higher education. College is not for everyone, but if our nation is to remain competitive in the global knowledge economy, our society must begin in earnest to build a higher education infrastructure proportionate to the task of educating to competitive levels of achievement not only the conventionally measured top 5 or 10 percent but at a minimum a quarter or third of respective cohorts of academically qualified students representative of the socioeconomic and intellectual diversity of our society, and through universal learning frameworks to provide opportunities for lifelong learning to more than half the population of the United States. A universal learning framework serves any learner from any socioeconomic background at any stage of work and learning through educational, training, and skills-building opportunities.

To underscore the principal interrelated corollary argument, the nation must advance discovery, creativity, and innovation to ensure the well-being and prosperity of individuals and economic growth and competitiveness for the collective. Toward this end the Fifth Wave will ultimately encompass a network of public and private research universities and liberal arts colleges linked with business and industry, government agencies and laboratories, and organizations in civil society—a plurality of differentiated institutional actors from throughout the national innovation system aligned through academic enterprise, transdisciplinary collaboration, and public purpose. In the near term, the nation needs a new model for the subset of large-scale public research universities that will constitute the vanguard of the Fifth Wave—a model for a complementary subset of institutions that combines accessibility with world-class knowledge production and societal impact that would leverage the complementarities and synergies between discovery and accessibility.

Fifth Wave universities thus advance processes that have been gathering momentum in Fourth Wave research universities throughout their ascendency, beginning with the integration of teaching and research that has been a central tenet of the Fourth Wave since its inception. But building on the accomplishments of the Fourth Wave in this context, Fifth Wave universities will deliberately aspire to transcend the spurious dichotomy between teaching and research through the integration of cutting-edge technological innovation with institutional cultures dedicated to the advancement of learning outcomes. In research-grade institutions, academic quality in undergraduate and graduate education correlates directly with the breadth of the research enterprise, driven in a research-intensive milieu by the interaction of students with scientists and scholars working at the frontiers of discovery. The objective of the new model is to produce not only knowledge and innovation but also students who are adaptive master learners empowered to integrate a broad array of interrelated disciplines and negotiate over their lifetimes the changing workforce demands and shifts in the knowledge economy driven by perpetual innovation.[195]

The prospect of becoming a member institution in the league of Fifth Wave universities will have little resonance for many colleges and universities. Most First Wave schools—leading liberal arts colleges such as Bowdoin, Williams, Amherst, Grinnell, or Colorado College, for example—will elect to continue to evolve within their present institutional category (wave type) because of their unique missions and purposes. The models associated with successive waves will not supplant preceding waves, and each will operate in parallel with the others, although some institutions in each wave may elect to interrelate with others through collaboration. To reiterate the point, whereas innovation and evolution from relatively simple to increasingly complex institutional forms is the mechanism that impels transition from one wave to the next—from the First Wave to the Fourth Wave, as in the case of the transformation of Harvard College into Harvard University during the nineteenth century—innovation and evolution are ongoing processes within each of the waves. Not all innovation and evolution signals inevitable transition between waves. Nevertheless, new Fifth Wave institutions will likely continue to emerge from preceding waves, as in the case of Arizona State University, which was founded in 1885 as a normal school, or territorial teachers' college, and thus a late-stage entrant to the Second Wave, and subsequently morphed, after 1960, first into a large regional public university, and then, following 1990, a late-entrant Fourth Wave research university now on the cusp of the emerging Fifth Wave. We reiterate our contention that whereas ASU could be regarded the institutional progenitor of the Fifth Wave, potential institutional peers in transition to the Fifth Wave would arguably include Purdue University, Pennsylvania State University, and the University System of Maryland.

The Fifth Wave will address many of the core educational challenges faced by American higher education in the twenty-first century by adding new organizational types to augment the existing types. In recent years, the federal government and various state governments have announced initiatives outlining measures to achieve for our nation a return to the highest rates of educational attainment in the world. However, our current models operate under serious limits to growth. Increasing the postsecondary degree attainment rate requires systematic improvements throughout the entire education pipeline—including high school graduation rates, college-going rates, and two- and four-year college graduation rates. Within this context, attaining a 50 percent postsecondary degree attainment rate among graduating high school seniors would require roughly doubling the number of students progressing through the system. But there is more to the challenge than increasing the scale of the existing system.

Without innovation and reforms, including new institutional models, increasing the number of high school students graduating and attending college would likely only decrease the graduation rates of colleges. Fifth Wave universities will address this issue by assuming responsibility for the success of each student and dramatically reconfiguring the delivery of content through adaptive learning and other technology-enabled strategies. We reiterate that it is conceivable that many Fifth Wave universities will likely scale up to include twice as many students as are currently enrolled, producing three to five times as many graduates, and serving more than ten times the number of engaged learners. The nation would need perhaps thirty to forty such large-scale public research universities to commit to these sorts of scale objectives in order to make meaningful gains on our national higher education attainment goals. Achieving these outcomes requires broad-based commitments to both accessibility and academic excellence as well as public service and necessarily requires sociological and technological interventions. Specification of these outcome-oriented objectives serves to highlight the process whereby universities, should they choose to do so, might transition toward the Fifth Wave.

Clark Kerr, then University of California president, coined the term "multiversity" more than half a century ago to characterize an institution he deemed "central to the conduct of an entire society." As a "whole series of communities and activities held together by a common name, a common governing board, and related purposes," which, he noted, include a "series of individual faculty entrepreneurs held together by a common grievance over parking,"[196] the contemporary university has become so complex an organizational structure and "bundled together" so many disparate functions that Craig Calhoun suggests replacing the term multiversity with *megaversity*.[197] This coinage perhaps effectively conveys the structural complexities inherent in the Fifth Wave model, which, as Christopher Newfield pointed out with reference to the New American University model, "functions through synthesis and integration rather than unbundling." Newfield aptly characterizes the administration of such an institution as the "complex orchestration of multiple goals that better serves our dauntingly complicated societies than corporate-style command-and-control." The essential point is that such administration is "not just bureaucratic bloat but a multifaceted instrument of social development."[198]

Calls for purported greater efficiencies and cost controls to be realized through the "unbundling" of higher education[199] stand in stark contrast to the objective of a comprehensive liberal education that is the hallmark of research-grade universities. Clayton Christensen laments that because research universities are saddled with the "multiple value propositions" of "knowledge creation (research), knowledge proliferation and learning (teaching), and preparation for life and careers," they are "conflations of the three generic types of business models—solution shops, value-adding process businesses, and facilitated user networks." The average state university is thus likened to a merger of "consulting firm McKinsey with Whirlpool's manufacturing operations and Northwestern Mutual Life Insurance Company"—which is to say, "three fundamentally different and incompatible business models all housed within the same organization."[200] In *The Innovative University*, Christensen and Henry Eyring pursue an economic argument by comparing the ability of Harvard and BYU-Idaho to graduate undergraduates with bachelor's degrees and discount the value of academic research in achieving that goal. Although their analysis has important economic implications, research excellence at both the undergraduate and graduate levels is fundamental to the research-pedagogic learning environments of the Fifth Wave.[201] Newfield characterizes the assumptions behind the impetus that proponents of unbundling advocate in the following terms: "Universities are degree factories and to cut costs their governments could split the credentialing function from research and isolate training programs from comprehensive four-year degrees. Students would pay for exactly the workforce knowledge they need and not a dollar more for something extra." There is just one hitch: "The downside is that this would destroy the comprehensive cognitive development that an integrated curriculum is designed to produce."[202] As he put this matter elsewhere, "The idea seems to be to convert college to a large volume of certificate programs and put most teaching online."[203] While the trend toward cafeteria-style approaches to certification may serve for some as an alternative to enrollment in traditional degree programs, coursework undertaken with the objective of professional certification is ideally complementary to a balanced and integrated liberal arts curriculum that is both foundational intellectually as well as a prerequisite to competitiveness in the global knowledge economy.

Although the demand for advanced teaching and research, and for the production of new ideas, products, and processes that are its outputs, is at fever pitch and far exceeds the current supply, public sector investment in higher education is unlikely to be restored to prerecession levels. In response to constraints on state resources, colleges and universities will need to innovate, beginning with diversification of sources of revenue and the implementation of creative strategies to improve cost-effectiveness, including leveraging new interactive learning technologies. Put simply, while state leaders with strategic vision will invest in higher education, public universities can no longer afford to expect that the state will be a reliable benefactor. Appropriate historical models from which to derive a course of action in the present context do not exist. Entrenched assumptions and rigid social constructs hinder adaptability, while inherent design limitations hamper organizational change in response to real-time demand. Risk-taking in the academic sector is thus essential if our society is to thrive. Moreover, how do we assess the scale of unmet demand? Or that there would not be even more demand but that countless students have abandoned their aspirations and effectively dropped out of the pool of potential applicants, much in the same way that millions have chosen no longer to participate in the labor force?

Accounts of disruption, dysfunction, and rancor in American higher education abound.[204] But universities have evolved to address societal challenges over the past millennium, and the differentiated new models of the Fifth Wave offer new possibilities to rethink our approaches to the complex challenges that confront global society. What if curricula sought to establish competency among students in a collective knowledge base prior to subsequent differentiation and individuation? What if the socio-economic status of incoming students no longer predicted outcomes in educational attainment? What if all students achieved quantitative and scientific literacy as well as critical acumen in the social sciences and the humanities? What if two or three majors became the norm for under-graduates, and through reduced costs colleges and universities pro-duced three times the output? If new approaches to teaching and learn-ing can accomplish some or all of these outcomes, Fifth Wave institutions will take a significant step toward societal transformation at scale.

Scale and accessibility on the one hand and quickening the pace of innovation on the other are by no means the sole challenges confront-ing the major research universities that constitute the Fourth Wave, nor are they the exclusive dimensions to the New American University model operationalized in Arizona that serves as the prototype for the emerg-ing Fifth Wave. But to reiterate a crucial point, if leading Fourth Wave universities deem it appropriate to maintain fixed levels of enroll-ment while excluding the majority of academically qualified applicants, alternative research-grade academic platforms must emerge that offer broader accessibility to academic excellence. The imperative to educate to competitive levels of achievement not only the conventionally mea-sured top 5 or 10 percent but also the most capable quarter or third of respective age cohorts of academically qualified students representative of the socioeconomic and intellectual diversity of our society requires investment in a higher education infrastructure proportional to the task. Such an infrastructure would simultaneously drive discovery, creativity, and innovation. If our nation is to prosper in the twenty-first century, then, a subset of public universities operating independently and in co-ordination through networks must take up the challenge to evolve in scope and at social scale to promote both academic excellence and broad accessibility. The demands of both equity and prosperity argue that society needs to expand its capacity to produce millions of additional graduates during the next several decades capable of both catalyzing and benefiting from an economy increasingly based on the generation and application of useful knowledge. In this sense, the universities of the Fifth Wave could thus be said to collectively constitute the national university envisioned by the founders of our nation—a set of institutions committed to service to the nation that might appropriately be characterized as a league of national service universities.

## Notes

1. Jonathan R. Cole, *The Great American University: Its Rise to Preeminence, Its Indispensable National Role, and Why It Must Be Protected* (New York: Public Affairs, 2009), 13.

2. American Academy of Arts and Sciences, *Public Research Universities: Recommitting to Lincoln's Vision: An Educational Compact for the Twenty-First Century* (Cambridge, MA: American Academy of Arts and Sciences, 2016).

3. Nathan Rosenberg, "America's Entrepreneurial Universities," in *The Emergence of Entrepreneurship Policy: Governance, Start-Ups, and Growth in the U.S. Knowledge Economy*, ed. David M. Hart (Cambridge: Cambridge University Press, 2003), 113–137. See also Walter W. Powell and Kaisa Snellman, "The Knowledge Economy," *Annual Review of Sociology* 30 (2004): 199–220; Nathan Rosenberg and Richard R. Nelson, "American Universities and Technical Advance in Industry," *Research Policy* 23, no. 3 (1994): 323–348; and Richard C. Atkinson and William A. Blanpied, "Research Universities: Core of the U.S. Science and Technology System," *Technology in Society* 30 (2008): 30–38.

4. See especially Cole, *Great American University,* ch. 4; Jason Owen-Smith, *Research Universities and the Public Good: Discovery for an Uncertain Future* (Stanford: Stanford University Press, 2018); Roger L. Geiger, *Research and Relevant Knowledge: American Research Universities since World War II* (Oxford: Oxford University Press, 1993).

5. Michael M. Crow and William B. Dabars, *Designing the New American University* (Baltimore: Johns Hopkins University Press, 2015).

6. David H. Guston et al., "Responsible Innovation: Motivations for a New Journal," *Journal of Responsible Innovation* 1, no. 1 (2014): 1–8.

7. For a comprehensive yet nuanced single volume compendium, see Roger L. Geiger, *The History of American Higher Education: Learning and Culture from the Founding to World War II* (Princeton, NJ: Princeton University Press, 2015).

8. A concept borrowed from the nomenclature of developmental biology, *morphology* refers to "shape, form, external structure or arrangement, especially as an object

of study or classification," and more generally to the "history of variation in form." *Oxford English Dictionary (OED)*, 3rd ed. (Oxford: Oxford University Press, 2012), online version accessed May 2018, s.v. "morphology." Pierre Bourdieu utilized the concept in an academic context. See his *Homo Academicus*, trans. Peter Collier (Stanford: Stanford University Press, 1988).

9. Roger L. Geiger, "The Ten Generations of American Higher Education," in *American Higher Education in the Twenty-First Century: Social, Political, and Economic Challenges*, 4th ed., ed. Michael N. Bastedo, Philip G. Altbach, and Patricia J. Gumport (Baltimore: Johns Hopkins University Press, 2016), 3.

10. Hans Henrik Bruun, *Science, Values, and Politics in Max Weber's Methodology* (London: Routledge, 2016), 208–209.

11. Caroline Winterer, *The Culture of Classicism: Ancient Greece and Rome in American Intellectual Life, 1780–1910* (Baltimore: Johns Hopkins University Press, 2002).

12. Steven Koblik, foreword to *Distinctively American: The Residential Liberal Arts Colleges*, ed. Koblik and Stephen R. Graubard (New Brunswick, NJ: Transaction, 2000), xv.

13. Rosenberg and Nelson, "American Universities and Technical Advance in Industry."

14. Roger L. Geiger, *To Advance Knowledge: The Growth of American Research Universities, 1900–1940* (Oxford: Oxford University Press, 1986), 2–3.

15. Geiger, *To Advance Knowledge*, 2–3.

16. Paul J. DiMaggio and Walter W. Powell, "The Iron Cage Revisited: Institutional Isomorphism and Collective Rationality in Organizational Fields," *American Sociological Review* 48, no. 2 (1983): 147–149.

17. Laurence R. Veysey, *The Emergence of the American University* (Chicago: University of Chicago Press, 1965), 339–340.

18. Crow and Dabars, *Designing the New American University*, 29, 306.

19. George Thomas, *The Founders and the Idea of a National University: Constituting the American Mind* (Cambridge: Cambridge University Press, 2015). See also Albert Castel, "The Founding Fathers and the Vision of a National University," *History of Education Quarterly* 4, no. 4 (December 1964): 280–302.

20. Martin Trow, "In Praise of Weakness: Chartering, the University of the United States, and Dartmouth College," *Higher Education Policy* 16 (2003): 17–21; Hugh Davis Graham and Nancy Diamond, *The Rise of American Research Universities: Elites and Challengers in the Postwar Era* (Baltimore: Johns Hopkins University Press, 1997), 12–14.

21. Rosenberg, "America's Entrepreneurial Universities," 114.

22. David F. Labaree, *A Perfect Mess: The Unlikely Ascendency of American Higher Education* (Chicago: University of Chicago Press, 2017).

23. Mitchell L. Stevens and Benjamin Gebre-Medhin, "Association, Service, Market: Higher Education in American Political Development," *Annual Review of Sociology* 42 (2016): 127–128.

24. Stephen M. Gavazzi and E. Gordon Gee, *Land-Grant Universities for the Future: Higher Education for the Public Good* (Baltimore: Johns Hopkins University Press, 2018).

25. John R. Thelin, *A History of American Higher Education*, 3rd ed. (Baltimore: Johns Hopkins University Press, 2019), 45–46.

26. Frank H. T. Rhodes, *The Creation of the Future: The Role of the American University* (Ithaca, NY: Cornell University Press, 2001), 2. Inasmuch as it is common to trace the lineage of institutional antecedents of American colleges and universities to the earliest universities of the European Middle Ages, Rhodes begins his list with the University of Bologna, which by some accounts was founded in 1088: "Bologna, like other older universities, was—to use modern jargon—a virtual learning community long before it was formally recognized as an institution." The canonical account of the earliest European universities remains Hastings Rashdall, *The Universities of Europe in the Middle Ages* (Oxford: Oxford University Press, 1895).

27. Michael M. Crow and Derrick M. Anderson, "National Service Universities: Fulfilling the Promise of Excellence at Scale in American Higher Education," working paper (Tempe: Office of the President, Arizona State University, 2019). The discussion of the Fifth Wave as a league of national service universities in this section derives from this document without further explicit citation.

28. Jeff Selingo et al., "The Next Generation University" (Washington, DC: New America, 2013).

29. Michael M. Crow et al., "Universal Learning as a New Aspiration for Higher Education," working paper (Tempe: Office of the President, Arizona State University, 2019). The discussion of the Fifth Wave as a platform for universal learning in this section derives from this document without further explicit citation.

30. Peter McPherson et al., "Competitiveness of Public Research Universities and Consequences for the Country: Recommendations for Change," NASULGC Discussion Paper (Washington, DC: Association of Public and Land-Grant Universities, 2009).

31. *Oxford English Dictionary (OED)*, 3rd ed. (Oxford: Oxford University Press, 2012), online version accessed May 2018, s.v. "heuristic."

32. John F. Padgett and Walter W. Powell, *The Emergence of Organizations and Markets* (Princeton, NJ: Princeton University Press, 2012), 1.

33. *Teleonomy* is the "property of living systems of being organized in such a way that structures and processes tend towards the attainment of particular ends or outcomes." Evolutionary biologists introduced the term to "avoid the imputation of purpose as an explanation of biological adaptation," as in the concept of teleology. *OED*, accessed December 2016, s.v. "teleonomy."

34. Jürgen Habermas, *The Structural Transformation of the Public Sphere: An Inquiry into a Category of Bourgeois Society*, trans. Thomas Burger (Cambridge, MA: MIT Press, 1991 [1962]).

35. Craig Calhoun, "The University and the Public Good," *Thesis Eleven* 84 (February 2006): 15–16.

36. In his essay "Objectivity in Social Science and Social Policy" (1904), Weber defined the ideal type as a "mental image (*Gedankenbild*) [that] brings together certain relationships and events of historical life to form an internally consistent cosmos of conceptual interrelations." It is thus a construct that accentuates and synthesizes various

viewpoints into a comprehensible mental image. In *The Methodology of the Social Sciences*, trans. Edward A. Shils and Henry A. Finch (London: Routledge, 2011), 90–91, quoted in Bruun, *Science, Values, and Politics in Max Weber's Methodology*, 208–209. Bruun offers the further clarification: "In Weber's view, a mental or intellectual abstraction, a concept, is, of course, always unreal in the sense that it cannot reproduce reality; but the unreality referred to here is so to speak, of the second degree, in that the concept has no actual correlate in empirical reality: it is a construct" (209n12).

37. Martin Trow, "Problems in the Transition from Elite to Mass Higher Education" (Berkeley: Carnegie Commission on Higher Education, 1973), 18.

38. Michael D. Cohen, James G. March, and Johan P. Olsen, "A Garbage Can Model of Organizational Choice," *Administrative Science Quarterly* 17, no. 1 (1972): 1.

39. Peter J. Caws, "Design for a University," *Daedalus* 99, no. 1 (Winter 1970): 88.

40. Neil J. Smelser, *Dynamics of the Contemporary University: Growth, Accretion, and Conflict* (Berkeley: University of California Press, 2013), 12–14.

41. Bruun, *Science, Values, and Politics*, 208–209.

42. Jonathan Cole, personal correspondence, February 9, 2019; Thomas S. Kuhn, *The Structure of Scientific Revolutions*, 50th anniv. ed. (1962; Chicago: University of Chicago Press, 2012), x–xi.

43. Ian Hacking, "Introductory Essay," in Kuhn, *Structure of Scientific Revolutions*, xi.

44. Kuhn, *Structure of Scientific Revolutions*, 35.

45. Hacking, "Introductory Essay," xvi.

46. Kuhn, *Structure of Scientific Revolutions*, 112.

47. Robert Donmoyer, "Take My Paradigm ... Please! The Legacy of Kuhn's Construct in Educational Research," *International Journal of Qualitative Studies in Education* 19, no. 1 (2006): 21.

48. Imre Lakatos, *The Methodology of Scientific Research Programmes: Philosophical Papers*, vol. 1 (Cambridge: Cambridge University Press, 1978).

49. Peter Godfrey-Smith, *Theory and Reality: An Introduction to the Philosophy of Science* (Chicago: University of Chicago Press, 2003), 102.

50. Suzanne Mettler, *Degrees of Inequality: How the Politics of Higher Education Sabotaged the American Dream* (New York: Basic Books, 2014).

51. Michael Mitchell et al., "Unkept Promises: State Cuts to Higher Education Threaten Access and Equity" (Washington, DC: Center on Budget and Policy Priorities, 2018).

52. National Center for Statistics, *The Condition of Education 2015* (Washington, DC: U.S. Department of Education, 2015).

53. Josipa Roksa et al., "United States: Changes in Higher Education and Stratification," in *Stratification in Higher Education: A Comparative Study*, ed. Yossi Shavit, Richard Arum, and Adam Gamoran (Stanford: Stanford University Press, 2007), 165–167; Raj Chetty et al., "Mobility Report Cards: The Role of Colleges in Intergenerational Mobility," NBER Working Paper no. 23618 (Cambridge, MA: National Bureau of Economic Research, December 2017), 35.

54. Roger L. Geiger, *Knowledge and Money: Research Universities and the Paradox of the Marketplace* (Stanford: Stanford University Press, 2004), 19–20.

55. Jonathan Cole, personal correspondence, February 9, 2019.

56. J. Douglas Toma, "Institutional Strategy: Positioning for Prestige," in *The Organization of Higher Education: Managing Colleges for a New Era*, ed. Michael N. Bastedo (Baltimore: Johns Hopkins University Press, 2012), 118–159.

57. Robert Samuels, *Why Public Higher Education Should Be Free: How to Decrease Cost and Increase Quality at American Universities* (New Brunswick, NJ: Rutgers University Press, 2013), 4–5, quoted in Christopher Newfield, *The Great Mistake: How We Wrecked Public Universities and How We Can Fix Them* (Baltimore: Johns Hopkins University Press, 2016), 297.

58. Joseph A. Soares, *The Power of Privilege: Yale and America's Elite Colleges* (Stanford: Stanford University Press, 2007), 1.

59. Jerome Karabel, *The Chosen: The Hidden History of Admission and Exclusion at Harvard, Yale, and Princeton* (Boston: Houghton Mifflin, 2005), 555. For additional perspective on admissions, see Daniel Golden, *The Price of Admission: How America's Ruling Class Buys Its Way into Elite Colleges—and Who Gets Left Outside the Gates* (New York: Random House, 2006).

60. Christopher Newfield, *Unmaking the Public University: The Forty-Year Assault on the Middle Class* (Cambridge, MA: Harvard University Press, 2008), 97.

61. Karabel, *The Chosen*, 550.

62. Christopher Lasch, *The Revolt of the Elites and the Betrayal of Democracy* (New York: W. W. Norton and Company, 1995), 64, quoted in Newfield, *Unmaking the Public University*, 99.

63. American Academy of Arts and Sciences, *Public Research Universities*, 30.

64. Claudia Goldin and Lawrence F. Katz, *The Race between Education and Technology* (Cambridge, MA: Belknap Press of Harvard University Press, 2008), 11–43, 44–46.

65. John Aubrey Douglass, *The Conditions for Admission: Access, Equity, and the Social Contract of Public Universities* (Stanford: Stanford University Press, 2007), 7–8.

66. Newfield, *Great Mistake*, 46–47.

67. Michael Mitchell and Michael Leachman, "Years of Cuts Threaten to Put College Out of Reach for More Students" (Washington, DC: Center on Budget and Policy Priorities, 2015).

68. Goldin and Katz, *Race between Education and Technology*, 44–46, 303.

69. Emmanuel Saez and Gabriel Zucman, "Wealth Inequality in the United States since 1913: Evidence from Capitalized Income Tax Data," *Quarterly Journal of Economics* 131, no. 2 (May 2016): 519–578; Gabriel Zucman, "Global Wealth Inequality," Working Paper 25462 (Cambridge, MA: National Bureau of Economic Research, January 2019).

70. Thomas Piketty, *Capital in the Twenty-First Century*, trans. Arthur Goldhammer (Cambridge, MA: Belknap Press of Harvard University Press, 2014), 71.

71. Paul A. Samuelson, "The Pure Theory of Public Expenditures," *Review of Economics and Statistics* 36, no. 4 (1954): 387–389. See also Joseph E. Stiglitz, "Knowledge

as a Global Public Good," in *Global Public Goods: International Cooperation in the Twenty-First Century*, ed. Inge Kaul, Isabelle Grunberg, and Marc Stern (Oxford: Oxford University Press, 1999), 308.

72. Joel Mokyr, *The Gifts of Athena: Historical Origins of the Knowledge Economy* (Princeton, NJ: Princeton University Press, 2002).

73. Rhodes, *The Creation of the Future*, xi.

74. Alan Wilson, *Knowledge Power: Interdisciplinary Education for a Complex World* (London: Routledge, 2010), ix, 1.

75. Theodore W. Schultz, "Investment in Human Capital," *American Economic Review* 51, no. 1 (March 1961): 1–17. For analysis of the correlation between investment in education and training and economic growth, see Gary S. Becker, *Human Capital: A Theoretical and Empirical Analysis, With Special Reference to Education*, 3rd ed. (Chicago: University of Chicago Press, 1993). The point that knowledge is the source of cultural capital and thus interrelated with social capital is associated with sociologist Pierre Bourdieu. See, for example, Bourdieu, "The Forms of Capital," in *Handbook for Theory and Research in the Sociology of Education*, ed. John G. Richardson (Westport, CT: Greenwood Press, 1986), 241–258. And although the aphorism that knowledge is power has been a rhetorical commonplace for millennia, Michel Foucault is oft cited for his illumination of the contours of the correlation between knowledge and power from an ideological perspective. See, for example, Foucault, *Power/Knowledge: Selected Interviews and Other Writings, 1972–1977* (New York: Pantheon, 1980).

76. Walter W. McMahon, *Higher Learning, Greater Good: The Private and Social Benefits of Higher Education* (Baltimore: Johns Hopkins University Press, 2009).

77. Thomas G. Mortenson et al., "Why College? Private Correlates of Educational Attainment," *Postsecondary Education Opportunity: The Mortenson Research Seminar on Public Policy Analysis of Opportunity for Postsecondary Education* 81 (March 1999).

78. U.S. Department of Treasury with the U.S. Department of Education, "The Economics of Higher Education" (Washington, DC, U.S. Department of Treasury, December 2012), 15; 16, figure 6. Whereas for those without college degrees from families in the bottom quintile of income distribution the prospects of remaining in the two bottom quintiles are estimated to be roughly 70 percent, those who graduate are equally likely to end up in any of the upper income quintiles.

79. McMahon, *Higher Learning, Greater Good*, 181–255.

80. Enrico Moretti, "Estimating the Social Return to Higher Education: Evidence from Longitudinal and Repeated Cross-Sectional Data," *Journal of Econometrics* 121 (2004): 175–212.

81. David Brooks, "The Education Gap," *New York Times* (September 25, 2005).

82. Mettler, *Degrees of Inequality*, 190.

83. Anthony P. Carnevale and Stephen J. Rose, "The Undereducated American" (Washington, DC: Georgetown University Center on Education and the Workforce, June 2011), 1, 8, 10.

84. Mettler, *Degrees of Inequality*, 190–191.

85. Brooks, "Education Gap."

86. For discussions of national systems of innovation, see, for example, David C. Mowery and Nathan Rosenberg, "The U.S. National Innovation System," in *National Innovation Systems: A Comparative Analysis*, ed. Richard R. Nelson (Oxford: Oxford University Press, 1993), 29–75; Jorge Niosi et al., "National Systems of Innovation: In Search of a Workable Concept," *Technology in Society* 15 (1993): 207–227; Christopher Tucker and Bhaven Sampat, "Laboratory-Based Innovation in the American National Innovation System," in *Limited by Design: R&D Laboratories in the U.S. National Innovation System*, ed. Michael M. Crow and Barry Bozeman (New York: Columbia University Press, 1998), 41–72.

87. Mariana Mazzucato, *The Entrepreneurial State: Debunking Public vs. Private Sector Myths* (New York: Public Affairs, 2013). Regarding the role of the State, Mazzucato elaborates: "Support for innovation can take the form of investments made in R&D, infrastructure, labour skills, and direct and indirect support for specific technologies and companies" (37).

88. Graham and Diamond, *Rise of American Research Universities*.

89. According to figures calculated from the Integrated Postsecondary Education Data System (IPEDS), Jason Owen-Smith reports: "The U.S. Department of Education identified 5,071 degree-granting higher-education institutions that awarded federal financial aid in 2015." *Research Universities and the Public Good*, 2. But, according to the Pell Institute for the Study of Opportunity in Higher Education, "In 2015–16, there were 4,583 two-year and four-year undergraduate degree-granting institutions in the United States; 34 percent were two-year institutions and 66 percent were four-year." Margaret Cahalan et al., *Indicators of Higher Education Equity in the United States: 2018 Historical Trend Report* (Washington, DC: Pell Institute for the Study of Opportunity in Higher Education, 2018), 10.

90. Owen-Smith, *Research Universities and the Public Good*, 2.

91. Institute of Higher Education, Shanghai Jiao Tong University, Academic Ranking of World Universities (ARWU), http://www.shanghairanking.com/ARWU-Methodology-2019.html. *The Economist* called ARWU "the most widely used annual ranking of the world's research universities," and the *Chronicle of Higher Education* termed it "the most influential international ranking." Their methodology evaluates the scientific and scholarly contributions of alumni (10 percent); scientific and scholarly contributions of faculty (20 percent); citations of researchers in twenty-one broad subject categories (20 percent); research output, measured by the number of articles published in leading journals such as *Nature* and *Science* (20 percent); research output, measured by articles in *Science Citation Index Expanded* and *Social Science Citation Index* (20 percent); assessing academic performance with respect to the size of an institution (10 percent). *Times Higher Education World University Rankings*, https://www.timeshighereducation.com.

92. Cole, *Great American University*, 299–300.

93. Kevin Carey, "Americans Think We Have the World's Best Colleges," *New York Times* (June 28, 2014). Carey explicates the distinction as follows: "America's perceived international dominance of higher education . . . rests largely on global rankings of top

universities. . . . When President Obama has said, 'We have the best universities,' he has not meant: 'Our universities are, on average, the best'—even though that is what many people hear. He means, 'Of the best universities, most are ours.'"

94. Philip G. Altbach, *Global Perspectives on Higher Education* (Baltimore: Johns Hopkins University Press, 2016), 86–87.

95. Charles T. Clotfelter, *Unequal Colleges in the Age of Disparity* (Cambridge, MA: Harvard University Press, 2017), 15.

96. Christopher Newfield, "The End of the American Funding Model: What Comes Next?" *American Literature* 82, no. 3 (September 2010): 611–635.

97. Cole, *Great American University*, 5.

98. Craig Calhoun, "The Public Mission of the Research University," in *Knowledge Matters: The Public Mission of the Research University*, ed. Diana Rhoten and Craig Calhoun (New York: Columbia University Press, 2011), 2–3.

99. Simon Marginson, "Public/Private in Higher Education: A Synthesis of Economic and Political Approaches," *Studies in Higher Education* 43, no. 2 (2018): 322–337. Marginson cites Samuelson, "The Pure Theory of Public Expenditure," 387–389 and John Dewey, *The Public and Its Problems* (New York: Henry Holt and Company, 1927).

100. Cole, *Great American University*, 61–70.

101. Robert K. Merton, "The Normative Structure of Science" (1942), in Robert K. Merton, *The Sociology of Science: Theoretical and Empirical Investigations*, ed. Norman W. Storer (Chicago: University of Chicago Press, 1973), 267–268. The essay was originally published as "Science and Technology in a Democratic Order," *Journal of Legal and Political Sociology* 1 (1942): 115–126.

102. Robert K. Merton, *On Social Structure and Science* (Chicago: University of Chicago Press, 1996 [1942]): 272–273, quoted in Thomas F. Gieryn, "Paradigm for the Sociology of Science," in Robert K. Merton, *Sociology of Science and Sociology as Science*, ed. Craig Calhoun (New York: Columbia University Press, 2010), 124–125. Some scholars have proposed that originality be designated one of five CUDOS norms. See Bruce Macfarlane and Ming Cheng, "Communism, Universalism, and Disinterestedness: Reexamining Contemporary Support among Academics for Merton's Scientific Norms," *Journal of Academic Ethics* 6 (2008): 67–78.

103. Sir Isaac Newton to Robert Hooke (February 5, 1676): "If I have seen farther than others, it is because I was standing on the shoulders of giants." Quoted in Robert K. Merton, *On the Shoulders of Giants: A Shandean Postscript* (Chicago: University of Chicago Press, 1993). For a genealogy of the theme, see Matei Calinescu, *Five Faces of Modernity: Modernism, Avant-Garde, Decadence, Kitsch, Postmodernism* (Durham, NC: Duke University Press, 1987), 15–17.

104. Gieryn, "Paradigm for the Sociology of Science."

105. Chad Wellmon, *Organizing Enlightenment: Information Overload and the Invention of the Modern Research University* (Baltimore: Johns Hopkins University Press, 2015), 3–4, 13, 22.

106. Andrew Abbott, *Chaos of Disciplines* (Chicago: University of Chicago Press, 2001), 126–128.

107. Thelin, *History of American Higher Education*, 127–128.

108. Andrew Abbott, *The System of Professions: An Essay on the Division of Expert Labor* (Chicago: University of Chicago Press, 1988), 205–208, 321–322.

109. Calhoun, "The University and the Public Good," 17–19.

110. C. Judson King, *The University of California: Creating, Nurturing, and Maintaining Academic Quality in a Public Research University Setting* (Berkeley: Center for Studies in Higher Education, University of California, 2018), 755n3.

111. McMahon, *Higher Learning, Greater Good*, 256–257.

112. Boyer Commission on Educating Undergraduates in the Research University, "Reinventing Undergraduate Education: A Blueprint for America's Research Universities" (Stony Brook: State University of New York, 1998), 6, 14–16.

113. Committee on Institutional Cooperation, "Values Added: Undergraduate Education at the Universities of the CIC" (2015), https://www.btaa.org/about/reports. The academic consortium, which was initiated by the University of Chicago in 1958, became the Big Ten Academic Alliance in 2016.

114. Charles M. Vest, "The Object of Research, the Object of Education," excerpt from a letter to the parents of MIT undergraduates, 1994.

115. William G. Durden, review of *Designing the New American University*, by Michael M. Crow and William B. Dabars, *Journal of College and University Law* 42, no. 2 (2016): 556.

116. Wellmon, *Organizing Enlightenment*, 3–4, 13, 22.

117. Jonathan R. Cole, *Toward a More Perfect University* (New York: Public Affairs, 2016), 16, 218.

118. Michael Polanyi, "The Republic of Science," *Minerva* 1, no. 1 (1962): 54–73. For perspective on this seminal essay, see John Ziman, "Commentary," in the special issue on Polanyi's article, *Minerva* 38 (2000): 21–25.

119. Alvin Weinberg, "The Axiology of Science," *American Scientist* 58, no. 6 (November–December 1970): 612–617, cited in Roger A. Pielke, *The Honest Broker: Making Sense of Science in Policy and Politics* (Cambridge: Cambridge University Press, 2007).

120. Thaddeus R. Miller et al., "The Future of Sustainability Science: A Solutions-Oriented Research Agenda," *Sustainability Science* 9 (2014): 239–246.

121. Daniel Sarewitz, *Frontiers of Illusion: Science, Technology, and the Politics of Progress* (Philadelphia: Temple University Press, 1996), 10–11.

122. Richard J. Bernstein, *The Pragmatic Turn* (Cambridge: Polity, 2010).

123. Jürgen Habermas, *The Theory of Communicative Action*, vol. 2, *Reason and the Rationalization of Society*, trans. Thomas McCarthy (Cambridge, MA: MIT Press, 1987).

124. Robert Frodeman, *Sustainable Knowledge: A Theory of Interdisciplinarity* (Basingstoke: Palgrave Macmillan, 2014), 62, 76, 82n5. Frodeman cites Arif E. Jinha, "Article 50 Million: An Estimate of the Number of Scholarly Articles in Existence," *Learned Publishing* 23: 258–263; Mark Bauerlein, et al., "We Must Stop the Avalanche of Low-Quality Research," *Chronicle of Higher Education*, June 13, 2010.

125. Miller et al., "Future of Sustainability Science," 239–240.

126. Donald E. Stokes, *Pasteur's Quadrant: Basic Science and Technological Innovation* (Washington, DC: Brookings Institution Press, 1997), 72–75.

127. Venkatesh Narayanamurti and Toluwalogo Odumosu, *Cycles of Invention and Discovery: Rethinking the Endless Frontier* (Cambridge, MA: Harvard University Press, 2016), 21.

128. Daniel Sarewitz and Richard R. Nelson, "Progress in Know-How: Its Origins and Limits," *Innovations: Technology, Governance, and Globalization* 3, no. 1 (Winter 2008): 101–117. For an epistemological account of know-how, see Jason Stanley, *Know How* (Oxford: Oxford University Press, 2011).

129. Michael Gibbons et al., *The New Production of Knowledge: The Dynamics of Science and Research in Contemporary Societies* (London: Sage, 1994); Helga Nowotny, Peter Scott, and Michael Gibbons, "Mode 2 Revisited: The New Production of Knowledge," *Minerva* 41 (2003): 179–194.

130. Ben Shneiderman, *The New ABCs of Research: Achieving Breakthrough Collaborations* (Oxford: Oxford University Press, 2016).

131. M. H. Abrams, "What's the Use of Theorizing About the Arts?" in *In Search of Literary Theory*, ed. Morton W. Bloomfield (Ithaca, NY: Cornell University Press, 1972), 52–54, quoted in Daniel Mark Fogel, "Challenges to Equilibrium: The Place of the Arts and Humanities in Public Research Universities," in *Precipice or Crossroads: Where America's Great Public Universities Stand and Where They Are Going Midway Through Their Second Century*, ed. Daniel Mark Fogel (Albany: State University of New York Press, 2012), 253–254.

132. Alvin M. Weinberg, "Science and Trans-Science," *Minerva* 10, no. 2 (April 1972): 209–222, quoted in Daniel Sarewitz, "Animals and Beggars: Imaginative Numbers in the Real World," in *Science, Philosophy, and Sustainability: The End of the Cartesian Dream*, ed. Ângela Guimarães Pereira and Silvio Funtowicz (London: Routledge, 2015): 135–146.

133. Helga Nowotny, Peter Scott, and Michael Gibbons, *Rethinking Science: Knowledge and the Public in an Age of Uncertainty* (Cambridge: Polity Press, 2001).

134. Richard Rorty, "Philosophy as a Transitional Genre," in *Pragmatism, Critique, Judgment: Essays for Richard J. Bernstein*, ed. Seyla Benhabib and Nancy Fraser (Cambridge, MA: MIT Press, 2004), 27.

135. Hans Jonas, *The Imperative of Responsibility: In Search of an Ethics for the Technological Age* (Chicago: University of Chicago Press, 1984), x.

136. Cahalan et al., *Indicators of Higher Education Equity,* Equity Indicator 5a, 96–99. Figures are for 2016, the most recent available. The 2013 figures are found in Margaret Cahalan and Laura Perna, *Indicators of Higher Education Equity in the United States: 45-Year Trend Report* (Washington, DC: Pell Institute for the Study of Opportunity in Higher Education, 2015), 30.

137. Goldie Blumenstyk, *American Higher Education in Crisis? What Everyone Needs to Know* (Oxford: Oxford University Press, 2015), 21–24. Blumenstyk cites data from Thomas G. Mortenson, "Unequal Family Income and Unequal Educational Opportunity, 1970–2012," *Postsecondary Education Opportunity* (Washington, DC: Pell

Institute for the Study of Opportunity in Higher Education, October 2013); Mortenson, "Family Income and Unequal Educational Opportunity," *Postsecondary Education Opportunity* (November 2012).

138. Thomas B. Edsall, "The Reproduction of Privilege," *New York Times* (March 12, 2012); Stephen J. McNamee and Robert K. Miller, *The Meritocracy Myth*, 2nd ed. (Lanham, MD: Rowman and Littlefield, 2009).

139. Chetty et al., "Mobility Report Cards: The Role of Colleges in Intergenerational Mobility," 2.

140. Gregor Aisch et al., "Some Colleges Have More Students from the Top 1 Percent than the Bottom 60," *New York Times* (January 18, 2017). As their source the authors cite the report from Chetty et al.

141. Piketty, *Capital in the Twenty-First Century*, 485.

142. David Leonhardt, "Top Colleges Largely for the Elite," *New York Times* (May 25, 2011).

143. Peter Dreier and Richard D. Kahlenberg, "Making Top Colleges Less Aristocratic and More Meritocratic," *New York Times* (September 12, 2014).

144. Edsall, "Reproduction of Privilege."

145. Nathan D. Grawe, *Demographics and the Demand for Higher Education* (Baltimore: Johns Hopkins University Press, 2018), 24.

146. College Board, "Trends in College Pricing 2018," 18, figure 8.

147. Steven Brint, *Two Cheers for Higher Education: Why American Universities Are Stronger Than Ever—and How to Meet the Challenges They Face* (Princeton, NJ: Princeton University Press, 2018).

148. Cahalan et al., *Indicators of Higher Education Equity in the United States: 2018 Historical Trend Report*, Equity Indicator 4b(ii), 85.

149. John H. Hawkins and W. James Jacob, introduction to *The New Flagship University: Changing the Paradigm from Global Ranking to National Relevancy*, ed. John Aubrey Douglass (London: Palgrave Macmillan, 2016), xi.

150. William G. Bowen, Martin A. Kurzweil, and Eugene M. Tobin, *Equity and Excellence in American Higher Education* (Charlottesville: University of Virginia Press, 2006), 1–4.

151. Newfield, "End of the American Funding Model," 620–21.

152. William G. Bowen, Matthew M. Chingos, and Michael S. McPherson, *Crossing the Finish Line: Completing College at America's Public Universities* (Princeton, NJ: Princeton University Press, 2009), 192.

153. Newfield, "End of the American Funding Model," 613, 617, 619–621.

154. Richard D. Kahlenberg, *Rewarding Strivers: Helping Low-Income Students Succeed in College* (New York: Century Foundation, 2010).

155. Mettler, *Degrees of Inequality*, 31.

156. Robert J. Gordon, "The Demise of U.S. Economic Growth: Restatement, Rebuttal, and Reflections," NBER Working Paper 19895 (Cambridge, MA: National Bureau of Economic Research, February 2014), 10.

157. Crow and Dabars, *Designing the New American University*, 30–32. Academic year 2012–2013 data was the most recent available from IPEDS in 2015 (Integrated Postsecondary Education Data System).

158. Scott A. Ginder, Janice E. Kelly-Reid, and Farrah B. Mann, *Enrollment and Employees in Postsecondary Institutions, Fall 2017; and Financial Statistics and Academic Libraries, Fiscal Year 2017: First Look (Provisional Data)* (Washington, DC: National Center for Education Statistics, 2019), table 1, 6–7. Our tally of fall 2017 enrollments at the 115 Carnegie R1—formerly RU/VH—institutions showed 2,465,602 undergraduates, which represents 14.4 percent of total Title IV undergraduate enrollment. Adding R2 institutions, undergraduate enrollment climbs to 3,791,658, or 22.1 percent of total Title IV undergraduate enrollment.

159. Oren Cass, *The Once and Future Worker: A Vision for the Renewal of Work in America* (New York: Encounter, 2018). Cass derives his estimates in part from the Digest of Education Statistics, tables 219.10, 302.10, and 326.40.

160. David Brooks, "What the Working Class Is Still Trying to Tell Us," *New York Times* (November 8, 2018).

161. Bowen, Chingos, and McPherson, *Crossing the Finish Line*, 2.

162. U.S. Department of Education, "Fact Sheet: Focusing Higher Education on Student Success" (Washington, DC: U.S. Department of Education, July 27, 2015; Doug Shapiro et al., "Completing College: A National View of Student Attainment Rates, Fall 2009 Cohort" (Herndon, VA: National Student Clearinghouse Research Center, 2015).

163. Jon Marcus, "More High School Grads Than Ever Are Going to College, but One in Five Will Quit," *Hechinger Report* (July 5, 2018), https://hechingerreport.org/more-high-school-grads-than-ever-are-going-to-college-but-1-in-5-will-quit/.

164. Robert J. Gordon, *The Rise and Fall of American Growth: The U.S. Standard of Living Since the Civil War* (Princeton, NJ: Princeton University Press, 2016), 627. Gordon notes that the percentage for the four-year graduation rate among community college students rises to 28 percent. See also Gordon, "The Great Stagnation of American Education," *New York Times* (September 7, 2013).

165. Gary C. Fethke and Andrew J. Policano, *Public No More: A New Path to Excellence for America's Public Universities* (Stanford: Stanford University Press, 2012), 15. Fethke and Policano cite John Bound and Sarah Turner, "Collegiate Attainment: Understanding Degree Completion," NBER Report 2010, no. 4 (Cambridge, MA: National Bureau of Economic Research, 2010).

166. Bowen, Chingos, and McPherson, *Crossing the Finish Line*, 230.

167. Sarah Butrymowicz, "Billions in Pell Dollars Go to Students Who Never Graduate," *Hechinger Report* (August 17, 2015).

168. U.S. Department of Education, "Federal Pell Grant Program End-of-Year Report, 1981–82 through 2015–16" (Washington, DC: U.S. Department of Education, 2018), fig. 15b: "Total Pell Expenditures and Number of Recipients, 1976–77 to 2016 17."

169. Education Trust, "The Pell Partnership: Ensuring Shared Responsibility for Low-Income Student Success" (Washington, DC: Education Trust, 2015).

170. Calhoun, "The University and the Public Good," 8–9.

171. Calhoun, "The University and the Public Good," 8–9, 38n12; Calhoun cites Bill Readings, *The University in Ruins* (Cambridge, MA: Harvard University Press, 1996), xx.

172. Calhoun, personal correspondence, September 19, 2019.

173. President's Commission on Higher Education, *Higher Education for American Democracy* (Washington, DC: U.S. Government Printing Office, 1947), 1:v, cited in Owen-Smith, *Research Universities and the Public Good*, 38.

174. Calhoun, "The University and the Public Good," 9, cites Randall Collins, "Credential Inflation and the Future of Universities," in *The Future of the City of Intellect,* ed. Steven Brint (Stanford: Stanford University Press, 2002).

175. Gerard Delanty, "The Sociology of the University and Higher Education: The Consequences of Globalization," in *The Sage Handbook of Sociology,* ed. Craig Calhoun, Chris Rojek, and Bryan Turner (London: Sage, 2005), 530, cited in Calhoun, "The University and the Public Good," 10.

176. David Guston, personal correspondence, May 1, 2019.

177. Labaree, *A Perfect Mess.*

178. Among high school graduates in 2016, the college enrollment rate was 71.9 percent for women and 67.4 percent for men. Asian graduates enrolled at a rate of 92.4 percent, followed by Hispanics (72 percent), Whites (69.7 percent), and Blacks (58.2 percent). Bureau of Labor Statistics, U.S. Department of Labor, *The Economics Daily* (October 2016).

179. Trow, "Problems in the Transition," 2, 6–7.

180. Martin Trow, "Reflections on the Transition from Mass to Universal Higher Education," *Daedalus* 99, no. 1 (1970): 2.

181. Trow, "Problems in the Transition," 7–8. In the universal phase, as Trow puts it: "Failure to go on to higher education from secondary school is increasingly a mark of some defect of mind or character that has to be explained or justified or apologized for" (7).

182. Simon Marginson, *The Dream Is Over: The Crisis of Clark Kerr's California Idea of Higher Education* (Oakland: University of California Press, 2016), 28–29.

183. Geiger, "The Ten Generations of American Higher Education," 24–25.

184. Louis Menand, *The Marketplace of Ideas: Reform and Resistance in the American University* (New York: W. W. Norton and Company, 2010), 64–73.

185. Brendan Cantwell and Simon Marginson, "Vertical Stratification," in *High Participation Systems of Higher Education,* ed. Brendan Cantwell, Simon Marginson, and Anna Smolentseva (Oxford: Oxford University Press, 2018), 125.

186. Fred Hirsch, *Social Limits to Growth* (Cambridge, MA: Harvard University Press, 1976), 52, quoted in Cantwell and Marginson, "Vertical Stratification," 125.

187. Roksa et al., "United States: Changes in Higher Education and Stratification," 165–167. With reference to expansion as differentiation and diversion, the authors cite Steven G. Brint and Jerome Karabel, *The Diverted Dream: Community Colleges and the Promise of Educational Opportunity in America, 1900–1985* (Oxford: Oxford University Press, 1989).

188. Chetty et al., "Mobility Report Cards," 35.

189. Richard Arum, Adam Gamoran, and Yossi Shavit, "More Inclusion Than Diversion: Expansion, Differentiation, and Market Structure in Higher Education," in *Stratification in Higher Education: A Comparative Study*, ed. Yossi Shavit, Richard Arum, and Adam Gamoran (Stanford: Stanford University Press, 2007), 1.

190. Adrian E. Raftery and Michael Hout, "Maximally Maintained Inequality: Expansion, Reform, and Opportunity in Irish Education, 1921–75," *Sociology of Education* 66 (1993): 41–62, cited in Arum, Gamoran, and Shavit, "More Inclusion Than Diversion," 3–4.

191. Marginson, *The Dream Is Over*, 34; Trow, "Problems in the Transition," 25.

192. Mettler, *Degrees of Inequality*, 4–5.

193. Harry S. Truman, "Statement by the President Making Public a Report of the Commission on Higher Education," December 15, 1947, quoted in Cahalan et al., *Indicators of Higher Education Equity*, 6.

194. Anthony P. Carnevale, Nicole Smith, and Jeff Strohl, "Recovery: Job Growth and Education Requirements through 2020" (Washington, DC: Georgetown University Center for Education and the Workforce, June 2013).

195. Don E. Kash, *Perpetual Innovation: The New World of Competition* (New York: Basic Books, 1989).

196. Clark Kerr, *The Uses of the University*, 5th ed. (1963; Cambridge, MA: Harvard University Press, 2001), 1, 15.

197. Calhoun, "The University and the Public Good," 17.

198. Christopher Newfield, "What Is New about the New American University?" *Los Angeles Review of Books* (April 5, 2015).

199. See, for example, Ryan Craig, *College Disrupted: The Great Unbundling of Higher Education* (New York: Palgrave Macmillan, 2014); Anya Kamenetz, *DIY U: Edupunks, Edupreneurs, and the Coming Transformation of Higher Education* (White River Junction, VT: Chelsea Green, 2010); and Jeffrey J. Selingo, *College Unbound: The Future of Higher Education and What It Means for Students* (New York: Houghton Mifflin Harcourt, 2013).

200. Clayton M. Christensen et al., "Disrupting College: How Disruptive Innovation Can Deliver Quality and Affordability to Postsecondary Education" (Washington, DC: Center for American Progress, February 2011), 3.

201. Clayton M. Christensen and Henry J. Eyring, *The Innovative University: Changing the DNA of Higher Education from the Inside Out* (San Francisco: Jossey-Bass, 2011).

202. Newfield, "What Is New about the New American University?"

203. Newfield, *Great Mistake*, 15.

204. See, for example, Bryan Caplan, *The Case against Education: Why the Education System Is a Waste of Time and Money* (Princeton, NJ: Princeton University Press, 2018); and Kevin Carey, *The End of College: Creating the Future of Learning and the University of Everywhere* (New York: Riverhead Books, 2015).

# TWO

# A Prototype for a Fifth Wave University

Although the emerging Fifth Wave comprises varied and differentiated institutional actors spanning academia, business and industry, government, and civil society, the envisioned formation of a league of Fifth Wave colleges and universities builds most proximately on the foundations of the New American University model operationalized at Arizona State University. This new model complements the existing model for large-scale public research universities and represents an inflection point in the transition from the late stages of the Fourth Wave to the emergence of the Fifth Wave. The model combines accessibility to an academic milieu characterized by discovery and a pedagogical foundation of knowledge production, inclusiveness to a broad demographic representative of the socioeconomic diversity of the region and nation, and, through its breadth of functionality, maximization of societal impact. The foundational prototype of the New American University model has been operationalized at Arizona State University since 2002 through a comprehensive reconceptualization that has produced an institution with sufficient scope and scale to offer broad accessibility to an academic platform of world-class knowledge production focused on societal outcomes.

The scope and scale of transformation undertaken by Arizona State University—one of the nation's youngest and largest major public research universities governed by a single administration—is arguably unprecedented in American higher education. The demonstrable success of the reconceptualization across varied and interrelated indicators substantiates the proposition that world-class knowledge production, broad accessibility, and social impact are not mutually exclusive.

The trajectory of soaring enrollment growth that may be attributed to the new model continues to be accompanied by significant increases in freshman persistence, degree production, learning outcomes, minority enrollment, academic success, and all measures of quality of graduates. ASU has succeeded in advancing both the academic rigor and diversity of its student body, which increasingly includes more and more students from socioeconomically disadvantaged and underrepresented backgrounds, including a significant cohort of first-generation college applicants. Corollary achievements include robust growth in research infrastructure and sponsored expenditures, which since 2004 have made the ASU research enterprise the fastest growing in the nation; unparalleled academic accomplishment for scholars and students alike; and the formation of transdisciplinary colleges, schools, institutes, and research centers reconfigured according to broad societal challenges rather than historically entrenched disciplines.

Before we evaluate institutional statistics in greater detail and elaborate regarding their significance subsequently in this chapter, we begin with an initial overview of some of the outcomes of the reconceptualization of ASU between 2002 and 2019. During this timeframe, overall enrollment has increased by 116 percent—from 55,491 undergraduate, graduate, and professional students in fall semester 2002 to 119,979 in fall 2019. Of this number, 44,253 are enrolled through ASU Online. Undergraduate enrollment has increased by 126 percent—from 42,877 in fall semester 2002 to 96,727 in fall 2019, including 33,410 enrolled through ASU Online. The fall 2019 freshman class numbered 15,606, which represents a 128.8 percent increase over the fall 2002 class. Degree production has increased even more sharply—more than 133 percent. ASU awarded 27,485 degrees in academic year 2018–2019, including 8,145 graduate and professional degrees, up from 11,803 during academic year 2002–2003. The university has conferred more than 139,500 degrees during the past six academic years. ASU demonstrates that academic excellence is a correlate of diversity. Minority enrollment has soared 310 percent, from 11,487 to 47,104 in fall 2019, constituting 39.3 percent of total enrollment and 46.1 percent of the freshman class. While the absolute number of white freshmen increased, the proportion was less than 50 percent of the class for the first time in ASU history in fall 2017 (49.4 percent that semester and 46.8 percent in fall 2019). During academic year 2018, 35 percent of undergraduates were first-generation college students. Since 2002 the number of first-generation students has more than tripled, from 7,560 in 2002 to 23,583 in 2018. More than 22.2 percent of the freshman class come from families that meet federal poverty guidelines. In an increasingly diverse student body, freshman persistence for the fall 2017 cohort was 85.5 percent, 11.5 percent higher than the fall 2002 cohort. The four-year graduation rate has increased to 51.0 percent, but for students with 4.0-range grade point averages (> 3.67), the rate is 70.3 percent.[1] Academic excellence is moreover a correlate of diversity. ASU ranks among the top ten public universities in its enrollment of National Merit Scholars, surpassing Stanford, MIT, Duke, Brown, UCLA, and Berkeley, and among the top three producers of Fulbright Scholars, tied with Princeton and Rutgers and coming in behind only Harvard and the University of Michigan.

Most of the benefits from university-based research are social and contribute to the economic productivity and well-being of society.[2] As a consequence of continued progress in the ambitious expansion of the research enterprise initiated at ASU in 2002, research-related expenditures over the period FY 2002 to FY 2018 have grown by more than a factor of five—without significant growth in the size of the faculty—reaching a record of $618 million in FY 2018, up from $123 million in FY 2002. According to the most recent data published by the National Science Foundation,[3] ASU is among the fastest-growing university research enterprises in the nation. ASU's total research expenditures have grown by 143 percent over the past decade, more than tripling the national growth rate in total university research expenditures of 46 percent. Federally funded research expenditures at ASU have grown by 92 percent, more than tripling national growth in federally funded university research expenditures of 29 percent. According to the National Science Foundation, ASU ranks eighth of 747 universities without medical schools in terms of total research expenditures—ahead of Caltech, Princeton, and Carnegie Mellon. Growth in research expenditures across all disciplines and investment from an increasing number of funding agencies indicates that ASU's research enterprise is on track to reach $815 million in annual research expenditures by 2025.

Recapitulation and reevaluation of the case study from our previous book in the present chapter is intended to serve as proof of concept and as a point of departure for further empirical analysis of the emergent Fifth Wave.[4] The following thus offers not only an opportunity to revisit the institutional objectives that motivated the so-termed design process undertaken in 2003 but outlines the challenges and suggests strategies applicable in other proto–Fifth Wave contexts. The design process has been characterized as an institutional experiment conducted at scale and in real time; the proposition that it be regarded as a case study in American higher education derives in part from its scale and scope as well as the rigor of its implementation across interrelated and mutually interdependent dimensions, as well as its reflexive implementation. We refer to this chapter as a case study loosely but concede that our efforts lack the rigor of a full-blown case study that satisfies the requirements of the qualitative method properly executed. In his widely cited book, Robert Yin distinguishes between case study research as the "*mode* of inquiry," case studies as the "*method* of inquiry, or *research method* used in doing case study research," and case(s) as the "*unit* of inquiry of a case study."[5] In contrast to the precise analytical knife that Yin wields, our case study focuses on ASU as a particular case, or unit of inquiry, to further our explication of and argument in favor of the New American University and Fifth Wave models.

Nevertheless, it may be useful to consider the two-part definition of the case study method as defined by Yin. First, he maintains that the method addresses real-world cases empirically—ASU, for instance—in which boundaries between the case under consideration and its environment or context may not be well defined. In addition, the case study method is appropriate for phenomena that are plagued by a large number of variables that exceed data available to address them, that may benefit from theoretical propositions to guide research efforts, and that rely on evidence from many sources that converge into generalizable findings—all of which apply to our admittedly biased argument.[6] In the end, this chapter may more accurately be described as rhetoric supported by statistics that does not consider rival plausible hypotheses or explanations. Our argument may be more consistent with the characterization of an analytical framework put forth by John Padgett and Walter Powell: an inductive history coupled with a deductive model. "Inductive histories and deductive models are viewed as complementary (not competitive) research strategies, both being dedicated to the discovery of social processes of organizational genesis and emergence."[7] The inductive history builds on empirical, real-world evidence, and the deductive model is the New American University and Fifth Wave construct that we describe throughout these chapters.

Although we employ quantitative evidence and associated statistics to bolster our argument that ASU represents a prototype for the Fifth Wave university model, our argument relies primarily on qualitative evidence because ASU is a complex institution embedded in local, state, national, international, and even interstellar environments. In contrast to quantitative methods like surveys or tests in which researchers seek to be blind to the effects of the instruments on the subjects under investigation, the academic community is intimately involved in the design and operation of an enterprise that must be assessed through qualitative interactions with many individuals, groups, communities, and cultures on an ongoing basis.[8] In the final analysis, we propose that calling our chapter a case study may be acceptable in a colloquial if not a technical sense.

## The Imperative for the Reconceptualization

The operationalization of the New American University model represents a reconceptualization of the American research university as a complex and adaptive comprehensive knowledge enterprise committed to discovery, creativity, and innovation, an institution accessible to the broadest possible demographic, both socioeconomically and intellectually. We take up assessment of the conceptual underpinnings of this formulation in chapter 5. Reconceptualization refers to institutional design, which proceeds through a design process that we consider more fully subsequently in this chapter. In this case the design process represents an effort by the academic community to build an institution committed to public value and the public interest, as well as to accelerate a process of institutional evolution that might otherwise have proceeded at best only incrementally, or possibly only in the face of crisis. Motivated initially by the imperative for an institutional response to the lagging educational attainment, lackluster economic output, and unprecedented shift in the regional demographic profile from the sole comprehensive research university in a metropolitan region projected to double in population by midcentury, the reconceptualization sought to reevaluate and, as appropriate, redesign all aspects of the curriculum, organization, and operations of the institution. "There is no argument: demographic change is reshaping the population of the United States in ways that raise challenges for higher education," writes demographer Nathan Grawe. "Through immigration, interstate migration, and fertility differences across demographic groups, the country's population is tilting toward the Southwest in general and the Hispanic Southwest in particular." Of particular relevance to the imperative for the reconceptualization of ASU, Grawe observes: "From the perspective of the higher education sector, these changes adversely shift the population away from traditionally strong markets toward those with lower rates of educational acquisition."[9]

Educational attainment remains the most obvious contributor to the development of human capital and knowledge capital, and its impact on individual prosperity is well documented. There is still no better investment than a four-year degree: with annual returns greater than 15 percent by some estimates, college education offers twice the return on investment of stocks, and at least three times the return for corporate bonds, gold, treasury bills, and housing.[10] There is moreover no better safeguard against poverty than the attainment of a bachelor's degree. The unemployment rate of those with only a high school diploma is nearly twice that of those who have obtained a bachelor's degree. There is a clear relationship between growth in degree attainment and growth in per capita GDP across the country. The states with higher growth in college degree attainment have generally had higher increases in per capita GDP as well (figure 2). Arizona's degree attainment rates were among the lowest in the nation from 2000 to 2010, and its GDP per capita actually declined during this period (figure 3). The links between human capital, industrial clusters, economic growth, and the prosperity of individual citizens are clear: when a state does not develop its human capital infrastructure, it cannot attract high-value industries, because people do not acquire the credentials and skills necessary to obtain higher-paying jobs, and are therefore forced to take jobs in industries that offer lower wages. High-value industries are inherently human-capital intensive. Since 2005 output growth in Arizona has been nearly flat in professional, scientific, and technical services as well as in manufacturing. Although output in the information sector has grown, its

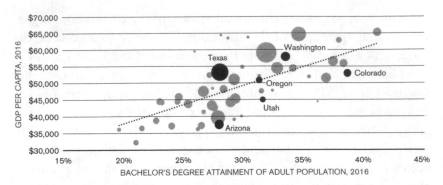

FIGURE 2. Per capita GDP correlates with educational attainment: bachelor's degree attainment and real per capita GDP by state (2016). Source: U.S. Census Bureau, American Community Survey, and U.S. Bureau of Economic Analysis

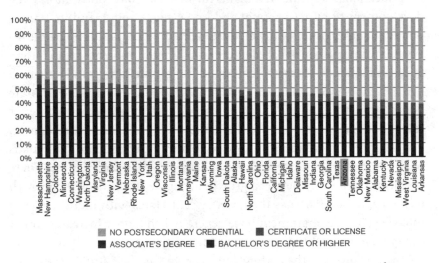

FIGURE 3. Arizona's educational attainment is lower than most states: working-age population by educational attainment by state (2016–2017). Source: Arizona Board of Regents analysis data from American Community Survey and Current Population Survey, http://us-attainment.azregents.edu

contribution to state GDP is still 40.4 percent less than the national average. Because taxes and the cost of doing business are already low in Arizona, low-output growth in these sectors suggests the impact of low availability of skilled professionals. The industries that are best able to make use of less-skilled workers deliver less total economic value to the state because the goods and services they provide are less valuable to trade with other states and countries.[11]

How does Arizona fare at producing human capital, and what does this mean for the prosperity of individuals and families in the state? It turns out that in Arizona, only nine out of one hundred students in the ninth grade will complete a bachelor's degree in six years. In Arizona, for every one hundred children in the ninth grade, sixty-four will graduate from high school four years later, eighteen will enter a four-year program of higher education within one year, but only nine will complete their bachelor's degree within six years. These figures belie a perfect storm of social and economic challenges that is making landfall in Arizona. For decades, Arizona's economic development strategy, which seeks to create a low-cost, tax-friendly business environment but does not aim to produce human capital has predictably attracted and grown lower-value industries. While it is undeniable that these industries create jobs, it is also true that the specific jobs these industries create are among the most likely to be replaced by new technologies as our economy becomes more efficient. The creation of jobs and demands for labor in fields that are certain to be disrupted places Arizona's families in economically and socially vulnerable positions. This approach also limits the state's capacity to adapt to new opportunities and respond to new challenges. Arizona's economy suffered more than others and took longer to recover. While we can never fully understand every aspect of regional economic growth, we can commit to supporting the forces that empower every proven pathway: human capital and knowledge capital. We call attention to the shortcomings of Arizona's economic development strategies to suggest a better alternative for the state. With this background, the mandate for Arizona State University becomes clear: ASU is to efficiently and effectively generate for Arizona the people, ideas, and technologies that will enable long-term, adaptive, knowledge-intensive growth. Academic enterprise is the obvious operational model that will bring about this massive transformation.[12]

The data on Arizona's response to the Great Recession support this general hypothesis. Public investment for higher education remains well below levels prior to the Great Recession in nearly every state. The Center on Budget and Policy Priorities found that, in the academic year ending in 2017, state investment in higher education was nearly $9 billion below 2008 levels when adjusted for inflation. Even as state revenues have been restored, all but five states were spending less per student than prior to academic year 2008. Average state spending remained 16 percent below prerecession levels. Appropriations per student declined more than 30 percent over this decade in eight states, including Arizona, which cut student funding by 53.8 percent.[13] In fact, Arizona has led the nation in its funding cuts in support for higher education since the recession. State disinvestment in ASU has represented the largest reduction both in absolute dollars and as a percentage of general funds from legislative appropriations for any public university in the nation and, by our estimates, in the history of American higher education (figure 4). In fact, per capita spending on higher education in Arizona has declined by 75 percent since 1979 (figure 5). The reduction in support coincides with the aforementioned period of record enrollment growth, which between fall semester 2002 and fall 2019 accounted for a roughly 116 percent increase and, within this same timeframe, a 310 percent increase in minority enrollment and a 133 percent increase in annual degree production.

Rather than extrapolate from existing academic structures and operations, the design process for ASU sought to articulate a unique and self-determined institutional profile, which is especially critical for public universities if institutional identity is not to be generic or imposed by

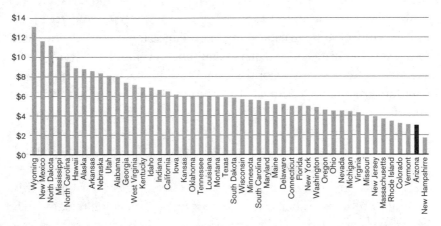

FIGURE 4. Arizona lags in state postsecondary investment: higher education spending per $1,000 in personal income (FY 2016). Source: Center for the Study of Education Policy, Illinois State University

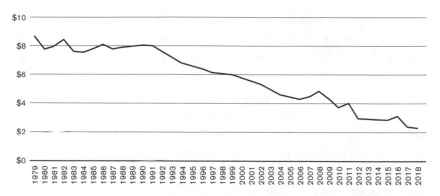

FIGURE 5. Arizona higher education spending per capita has declined by 75 percent since 1979: spending per $1,000 in personal income (1979–2018). Source: ASU analysis of data from U.S. Department of Commerce, U.S. Bureau of Economic Analysis, and State of Arizona Joint Legislative Budget Committee

legislative fiat. Self-determination is the crux of the distinction between the bureaucratic mind-set of an agency and the boundary-spanning dynamism of an academic enterprise. Absent self-determination, the forces of isomorphic replication would likely lead to reversion to the norm—the Generic Public University. Isomorphism encourages bureaucratization, which, as Anthony Downs points out, promotes routine, standardization, and inertia, as well as conformity to rules,[14] all of which are inimical to the purposes of what should be an autonomous enterprise. Bureaucratization is nowhere more evident than in generic public universities that conform to the obsolete service model that values universities principally for the basic task of undergraduate education. The new model establishes the conditions for substantive and rapid rather than incremental and cumulative evolution. Because the model disrupts inertia and stasis, its implementation offers the potential to unleash the revolutionary change characteristic of punctuated equilibrium.[15]

Any model for a Fifth Wave university would necessarily be defined by its alignment with public values as well as service to the public interest.[16] Accordingly, to restore the social compact implicit in American public higher education, ASU sought to revive the intentions and aspirations of the historical public university model, which, building on the ideals of the Morrill Act of 1862 that produced the system of land-grant universities, sought to provide broad accessibility as well as engagement with society. The new institutional model expands enrollment capacity, promotes diversity, and offers accessibility to world-class research and scholarship to a diverse and heterogeneous student body representative of the demographic profile of the state, which includes a significant proportion of students from socioeconomically diverse and underrepresented backgrounds, as well as a preponderant share of first-generation college applicants. At the same time, the model facilitates knowledge production and innovation, advancing the objective of transforming ASU into a leading global center for interdisciplinary research, discovery, and development by 2025.

The model facilitates accessibility to students from all demographic strata capable of accomplishment in a research-grade milieu, including gifted and creative students who do not conform to a standard academic profile.[17] Nearly all leading colleges and universities offer opportunities to students of exceptional academic ability from underrepresented and socioeconomically disadvantaged backgrounds. In this manner a measure of diversity can be achieved without actually drawing more deeply from the broader talent pool of socioeconomically and ethnically diverse populations. But intelligence is distributed throughout the population, and for many it manifests through skills, abilities, and experiences that current admissions protocols disregard. Admissions policies that merely skim from the conventionally defined top shortchange countless gifted and creative individuals.

Multiple strategies have guided ASU's efforts to provide a world-class educational experience and to excel in its research portfolio. These include the application of technology in educational design and delivery, innovation in advising and course scheduling to speed time to degree, and aggressive improvements in retention and graduation rates to drive down the resources needed per degree produced. Complementary strategies include maintaining a single unified administrative hierarchy that spans four campuses that constitute the largest American university governed by a single administration; use of collaborative investment to build physical infrastructure; continuous improvement in the ability to operate effectively at scale, in recognition that quantity need not preclude quality; monetization of assets often ignored by colleges and universities, including intellectual capital; and, perhaps most uniquely, recognizing the value of thinking differently, resulting in the opportunity to be a "first mover" in boundary-spanning collaborations with business and industry and government.

Cost effectiveness has been a correlate key metric for ASU even as the university has increased its student population to among the largest in the nation. As we delineate in this chapter, through strategic organizational streamlining designed to cut costs while preserving the quality of the academic core, ASU has become one of the nation's most efficient producers of both college graduates and cutting-edge research, which contributes hundreds of millions of dollars annually to the Arizona economy. ASU's cost per degree is nearly 20 percent below the national median (figure 6).[18] Further, through a combination of fiscal discipline and strategic use of partnerships to control costs, ASU has consistently operated with about half the staff per student as its peers. ASU has 12.42 employees per 100 students, whereas the median among the fifteen research universities designated as aspirational peers is 25.18.[19] Whether the indicator is total spending per degree produced or the output of its research enterprise, the advancement of the university is demonstrable when measured against all other public research universities. Cost discipline, application of technology, and economies of scale are projected to maintain current cost levels.

In an effort to develop strategies to advance what the New America Foundation termed "The Next Generation University," we reiterate the four key conclusions of the authors: "An intentional student-focused

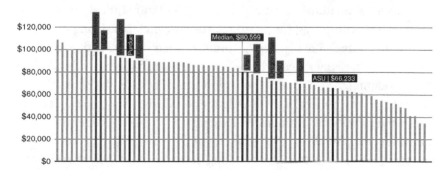

FIGURE 6. ASU uses 17 percent fewer resources per degree awarded than the national median: tuition and state appropriations per degree awarded at R1 public research universities (FY 2017). Source: IPEDS

vision matters; bigger can be good; it is possible to enroll and educate large numbers of unevenly prepared students well without diminishing quality; and it is possible for institutions of higher education to innovate fast and at scale."[20] The New American University and Fifth Wave approaches are consistent with the tenets of the New America report and contrary to the norm in public higher education. As Christopher Newfield points out, "Public universities have always spent less per student than their private counterparts through factory-style efficiencies such as large lectures, mechanized grading, minimal personal contact between students and faculty, and, for four decades, increasing use of contingent instructors." He cites the heedless implementation of MOOCs as emblematic in this context and underscores that such efforts to enforce efficiencies may be counterproductive: "Saving money on higher education makes it less suited to a knowledge economy by forcing its standardization."[21] By contrast, standardization is anathema to the New American University model, and preservation of the academic core outweighs efforts to maximize efficiencies.

## Accessibility to Academic Excellence for a Broad Demographic

Given the overwhelming evidence regarding the returns to individuals and to society of a college degree, we characterize the creation of human capital in terms of empowering individuals. We measure the production of empowered individuals through our performance on various metrics related to students. Among the most important are growth in total enrollment, which shows the growth of our student body across all four ASU campuses; freshman retention, which is a strong indicator of whether a student will go on to complete their degree; and graduation rates and degrees awarded, which show our overall success in producing human capital. ASU is one of the largest universities in the United States in terms of enrollment. This is a deliberate design choice that reflects the university's commitment to its charter. We are frequently asked questions like, When is ASU going to stop growing? This is the wrong question. When we consider the long-term implications of Arizona's lack of human capital development, and especially how few high school freshmen end up graduating from college, perhaps we should be asking, How can we grow faster? How can we do more to solve these problems?

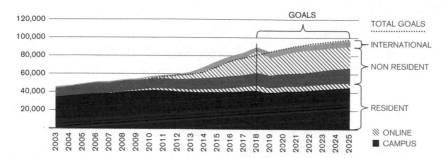

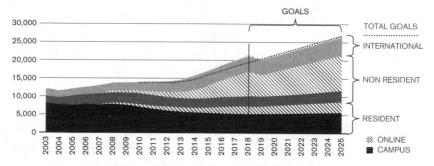

FIGURE 7. Between fall semester 2002 and 2019, ASU undergraduate enrollment has increased by 126 percent—from 42,877 to 96,727, including 33,410 enrolled through ASU Online. Undergraduate enrollment is up 43 percent in five years: actual figures and metric goals (2003–2025). (Chart reflects data available AY 2017–2018.) Source: ASU Office of Institutional Analysis

FIGURE 8. Between fall semester 2002 and 2019, ASU graduate and professional student enrollment has increased by 84 percent—from 12,614 to 23,252, including 10,843 enrolled through ASU Online. Graduate enrollment is up 47 percent in five years: actual figures and metric goals (2003–2025). Source: ASU Office of Institutional Analysis

ASU's response to these challenges is to embrace the audacious goal of achieving enrollment in excess of 120,000 students by 2025. With well over 100,000 students currently enrolled, we are on track to meet this goal (figures 7 and 8).[22]

The New American University model calls for accessibility at scale, inclusivity rather than exclusivity, and an emphasis on outcomes rather than inputs. At the beginning of the chapter we reported some key numbers, including a 116 percent increase in enrollment growth in undergraduate, graduate, and professional students—from 55,491 in fall semester 2002 to 119,979 in fall 2019. Of this number, 44,253 are enrolled through ASU Online, which augments the full-immersion campuses that ASU operates, as assessed in the discussion of teaching and learning realms that follows. To appreciate the pace of enrollment growth in a single year, total enrollment in fall semester 2018 had been 111,291, and of that number, 37,384 had been enrolled through ASU Online. We reiterate that undergraduate enrollment has increased by 126 percent—from 42,877 in fall semester 2002 to 96,727 in fall 2019, including 33,410 enrolled through ASU Online. During this timeframe, graduate enrollment has increased by 84 percent—from 12,614 graduate and professional students in fall semester 2002 to 23,252 in fall 2019, including 10,843 enrolled through ASU Online. The fall 2019 freshman class numbers 15,606, up from 13,975 in fall 2018, with a mean high school grade point average of 3.45 and median SAT score of 1210. The median SAT score of the fall 2017 freshman class had been 1200, but with scores adjusted for the redesigned test in March 2016, 1180 for the 2018 freshman class. The size of the fall 2019 freshman class represents a 128.8 percent increase over the fall 2002 class. Of those who reported class rank in fall 2018, 27.5 percent graduated in the top 10 percent of their classes. A cohort with these academic qualifications comprises nearly one thousand more freshmen from the top decile than the total number of students in the current freshman class of Harvard University.[23]

The four-year graduation rate has increased to 51.0 percent, but for students with 4.0-range grade point averages (> 3.67), the rate is 70.3 percent, as we pointed out. From 2003 to 2012, ASU's four-year graduation rate nearly doubled, five-year graduation rate increased by nearly 15 percent, and six-year graduation rate grew by more than 20 percent. The six-year graduation rate for the freshman cohort entering in 2012 was 67.7 percent, up 37.6 percent from the 49.2 percent rate for the cohort that entered in fall 1995. The six-year graduation rate for the freshman cohort entering in 2011 had been 63.1 percent, up 28.3 percent from the rate for the cohort that entered in fall 1995 (figure 9). The most recent overall six-year graduation rate available for four-year public institutions is 58.9 percent, for the 2010 cohort. In an increasingly diverse student body, freshman persistence for the fall 2017 cohort at ASU was 85.5 percent, 11.5 percent higher than the fall 2002 cohort (figure 10).

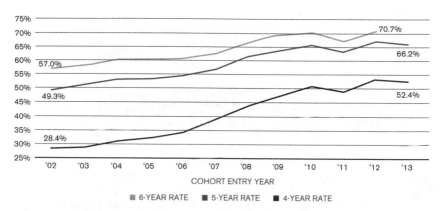

FIGURE 9. ASU four-year graduation rate is up 85 percent since 2002: resident freshman graduation rate by entry-year cohort (2002–2013). Source: ASU Office of Institutional Analysis

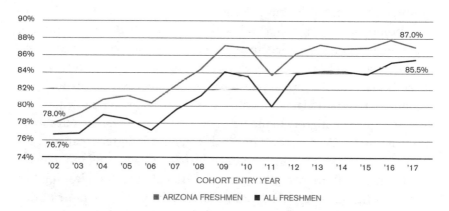

FIGURE 10. First-year freshman retention is nearing 90 percent goal: first-year freshman retention rates (2002–2017). Source: ASU Office of Institutional Analysis

Higher graduation rates have translated into more degrees awarded. Here again, the growth rate of ASU degrees awarded exceeds that of leading peer institutions and has accelerated dramatically during the past five years as a result of our expansion of online digital immersion programs. Degree production has increased more than 133 percent, from 11,803 during academic year 2002–2003 to 27,485 in academic year 2018–2019, which included 8,145 graduate and professional degrees. The university has conferred more than 139,500 degrees during the past six

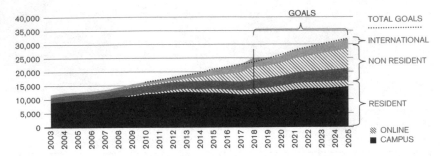

FIGURE 11. Degree production has increased more than 133 percent, from 11,803 during academic year 2002–2003 to 27,485 in academic year 2018–2019, which included 8,145 graduate and professional degrees. (Chart reflects data available AY 2017–2018.) Source: ASU Office of Institutional Analysis

academic years (figure 11). Beyond increasing the number of degrees awarded each year, ASU has placed special emphasis on increasing degree production in high-demand fields. ASU has made great strides in increasing degrees awarded in science, technology, engineering, and mathematics (STEM) fields, as well as in education and the health professions. These fields are key focus areas for improving Arizona's national and international competitiveness. ASU plans to double production of degrees in high-demand fields by 2025. Increasing the number of graduates in STEM fields will improve Arizona's long-term capacity for the growth of high-tech, high-value industries. Graduating more qualified teachers will improve Arizona's educational outcomes, leading to a better pipeline of college-ready students. And, by preparing more nurses and healthcare professionals, ASU is helping to ensure that Arizona's healthcare system can meet the needs of a growing population.

To reiterate a point underscored in the initial case study, an appreciation for the significance of continued improvement in the graduation rates cited requires more nuanced explication. The graduation rates for the most recent four-year and six-year cohorts—2014 and 2012, respectively—vary significantly depending on the entering high school grade point averages of students. As is evident from the following figures, the differences in graduation achievement between students with GPAs of 4.0 (A students) and 3.0 (B students) diminishes over time, as we move from four to six years postentry to the university. Four-year graduation rates for B/B+ students are 48.7 percent, 68.2 percent for A- students, and

77.2 percent for students with GPAs of 4.0. The latter figure for the prior cohort had been 78.9 percent. Six-year graduation rates for B/B+ students are 64.1 percent, 81.7 percent for A- students, and 87.1 percent for A students. The latter figure for the prior cohort had been 85.2 percent. A higher percentage of A students (41 percent) entered the university having completed college credits than B/B+ students (26 percent), which enables them to complete their degrees more quickly.

Since it is broadly understood in the conventional model that the academic preparation of students is highly predictive of persistence and graduation, these distinctions are important to note, particularly for institutions that admit students with more varied levels of academic preparation. Observing only the overall average for universities that welcome diverse cohorts masks the accomplishments of such institutions in improving the success of all students, particularly if they are compared to schools that admit only students from the uppermost A-level GPA range.[24] Moreover, ASU figures for four- and six-year graduation rates compare favorably with those of the highly selective University of California system, which recently reported figures of 63 percent and 83 percent, respectively. The UC figures are said to reflect the "high academic caliber of entering students."[25] ASU now boasts graduation rates that exceed those of peer universities such as Ohio State University and the University of Texas at Austin.

Minority enrollment from fall 2002 through fall 2019 soared 310 percent, from 11,487 to 47,104, the latter constituting 39.3 percent of total enrollment. While the first-time full-time freshman class has increased in size by 129 percent since 2002, enrollment of students of color has significantly outpaced this growth. Students from historically underrepresented racial and ethnic backgrounds made up 46.1 percent of the fall 2019 first-time freshman class, which represents a 373 percent increase in minority enrollment in the entering freshman class since 2002. Overall, total minority undergraduate enrollment has increased 324 percent during this period. The number of African American students grew 262.2 percent, from 1,768 to 6,404; the number of Asian students grew from 2,535 to 7,434, a 193.3 percent increase; and the number of Hispanic students grew from 6,018 to 26,350, marking a 338 percent increase. While the absolute number of white freshmen increased, the proportion was less than 50 percent of the class for the first time in ASU

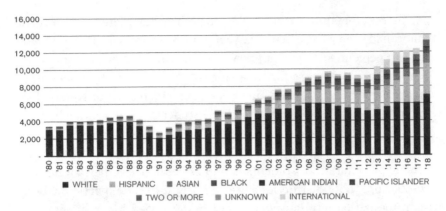

FIGURE 12. Students from historically underrepresented racial and ethnic backgrounds made up 46.1 percent of the fall 2019 first-time freshman class, which represents a 373 percent increase in minority enrollment among freshmen since 2002. First-time freshman enrollment by race (fall 1980–fall 2018). Source: ASU Office of Institutional Analysis

history in fall 2017—49.4 percent that semester and 46.8 percent in fall 2019 (figure 12).

Needless to say, academic talent among high school graduates is not limited to students from privileged backgrounds. Because ASU is committed to the principle that academic excellence is a correlate of diversity, the university seeks to accelerate efforts to ensure that qualified Arizona undergraduates from diverse and previously underrepresented socioeconomic backgrounds are eligible for access to a research-grade academic milieu. For example, during academic year 2018, 35 percent of undergraduates were first-generation college students. Access and outreach efforts combined with financial aid policies and student success programs have resulted in a doubling of the numbers of first-generation students in the last decade. Since 2002 the number of first-generation students has more than tripled, from 7,560 in 2002 to 23,583 in 2018 (figure 13).

Since FY 2002 ASU has made significant headway in delivering on its promise that no qualified Arizona student will ever be denied access to a baccalaureate degree for lack of financial means. During this period the university has transitioned from a low-tuition but low-access model to charging moderate tuition, which permits the university to increase ac-

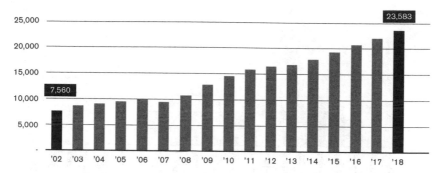

FIGURE 13. Number of ASU first-generation students has more than tripled (2002–2018). Source: ASU Office of Institutional Analysis

cess by setting aside a portion of tuition revenues for need-based financial aid. As a result, the number of first-time, full-time Arizona freshmen whose families meet federal poverty guidelines increased from 300 in FY 2002, which represented 6.9 percent of the freshman class, to 1,514 in FY 2018, which according to preliminary figures represents 22.2 percent of the freshman class. Enrollment of freshmen coming from families with incomes below $20,000 per year increased from 219 in fall 2002 to 1,036 (resident dependent first-time freshmen) in fall 2017, an increase of 373 percent (figure 14). The keystone initiative in this context is the President Barack Obama Scholars Program, which, since May 2009, has ensured that in-state freshmen from families with moderate annual incomes are able to earn baccalaureate degrees with little or no debt. The Obama Scholars program continues to serve students from families with the greatest financial need who are eligible for financial aid that covers the direct cost of college attendance.

In FY 2018 ASU awarded a record $1.58 billion in all forms of financial aid to 101,400 students. Of that total, $760 million was awarded in the form of scholarships and grants to 80,443 students. Total financial aid for undergraduate students grew from $195 million in FY 2002 to more than $1.2 billion in FY 2018, an increase of 516 percent. The number of undergraduate students receiving financial aid grew from 25,594 in FY 2002 to 83,297 in FY 2018, a 225 percent increase. The number of Pell Grant recipients has increased from 10,344 during the 2002–2003 academic year to 35,595 in 2017–2018. These awards provide need-based

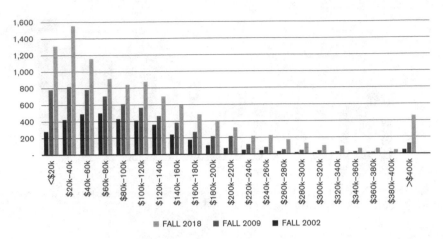

FIGURE 14. ASU is far more accessible to low-income students: freshman enrollment by income (2002, 2009, 2018). All incomes adjusted to 2018 dollars.

grants to low-income undergraduate and certain postbaccalaureate students to promote access to postsecondary education. First-time freshman Pell Grant recipients increased 289 percent from FY 2003 to FY 2018, from 1,209 to 4,706 students. In FY 2018, 62 percent of undergraduate students received financial aid. The average student financial aid package for full-time Arizona resident undergraduate students with need was $14,227. ASU baccalaureate degree recipients who were Arizona residents had an average loan debt of $22,579 in FY 2018. According to the College Board, average indebtedness of ASU undergraduates remains well below the national average for public universities, which for the academic year 2015–2016 was estimated to be $30,100. ASU's success in offering access to resident undergraduates regardless of their financial means remains one of the most significant achievements in the history of the institution.

For five consecutive years ASU has topped the list of most innovative schools in the nation, according to the *U.S. News & World Report* ranking, recognizing the university's groundbreaking initiatives, partnerships, programs, and research. The widely touted set of annual rankings compares more than 1,500 institutions on a variety of metrics and the assessments of peers, including college and university presidents, provosts, and admissions deans, who nominate up to ten institutions that are making the most innovative improvements to curriculum, faculty, students, campus life, technology, or facilities. Following ASU, the second- and third-most innovative universities were Stanford and MIT. The innovation ranking is due at least in part to the more than 80 percent improvement in ASU's graduation rate in the past fifteen years, the fact that ASU is the fastest-growing research university in the nation, and the emphasis on inclusion and student success that has led to more than 50 percent of the school's in-state freshman coming from minority backgrounds. In addition, the magazine designated ASU as an "A+ School for B Students," a list of universities that are not ranked. Schools on the list had to admit a meaningful proportion of applicants whose test scores and class standing put them in non-A territory but whose freshmen retention rate was at least 75 percent.

Measures such as increases in degree production, socioeconomic diversity, minority enrollment, and freshman persistence; improvements in academic achievement and faculty accomplishment and diversity; and the expansion of the research enterprise must be evaluated within the context of their accomplishment by a university committed to offering admission to all academically qualified Arizona residents regardless of financial means, and that strives to maintain a student body representative of the spectrum of socioeconomic diversity of American society. Improvement of graduation rates or freshman persistence could readily be achieved by limiting admissions to ever-more handpicked classes. The entering freshman class currently numbers 13,975 students and correlates with the socioeconomic and ethnic diversity of the region. Despite such expanded accessibility, ASU nevertheless remains above the national average in freshman retention and graduation rates among four-year public universities, at 85.5 percent and 67.7 percent, respectively. Moreover, the academic qualifications of a significant cohort of each entering freshmen class match those of students admitted to the Ivy League and the nation's top liberal arts colleges. ASU has accomplished these objectives by offering admission to a broad demographic spectrum of academically qualified students of varied and diverse backgrounds to whom admission to a world-class research university would otherwise be denied. And it has done so during a period of both robust enrollment growth and historic disinvestment in public higher education. The attainment of these objectives is an outcome of an institutional culture committed to academic enterprise and improved cost effectiveness through productivity gains and constant innovation. These goals are moreover representative of the intent of the nation's youngest major research university to redefine its terms of engagement rather than entering into head-to-head competition with institutions that have matured over the course of centuries.

## A Commitment to National Goals and Global Well-Being

A determination to advance the frontiers of knowledge corresponds to the maturation of the research enterprise of an institution and aligns with the Fifth Wave commitment to advance national goals and the well-being of global society. The advancement of the research enterprise at ASU must be appreciated in the context of an institution that did not achieve university status until 1958 and designation as a research-extensive ("Research I") university from the Carnegie Foundation for the Advancement of Teaching until 1994,[26] conferring on it recognition as one of only eighty-eight institutions then so classified. Even more significantly, it was one of a mere handful of major research universities without both an agricultural and medical school to be thus designated. In its research orientation, ASU has become increasingly determined to focus on societal outcomes and public well-being, advancing innovation on all fronts and mounting responses commensurate with the scale and complexity of the challenges that confront the global community. The most prominent research initiatives are in alignment with critical national goals in such strategic areas as earth and space exploration, sustainability and renewable energy, advanced materials, flexible electronics, healthcare, national security, urban systems design, and STEM education.

As a consequence of continued progress in the ambitious expansion of the research enterprise initiated in 2002, research-related expenditures over the period FY 2002 to FY 2018 have grown by more than a factor of five—without significant growth in the size of the faculty—reaching a record of $618 million in FY 2018, up from $123 million in FY 2002 (figure 15). This figure represents a 13 percent increase in expenditures over FY 2017 ($545 million) and is the largest absolute dollar and percentage increase in research expenditures over the past decade.

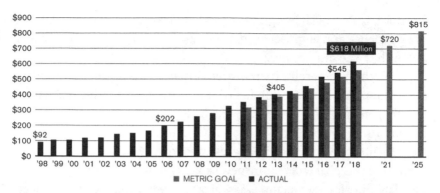

FIGURE 15. Arizona State University actual and projected research expenditures, 1998–2025. Source: National Science Foundation, Higher Education Research and Development (HERD) Surveys; ASU Knowledge Enterprise

According to the most recent data published by the National Science Foundation,[27] ASU has continued to be one of the fastest-growing university research enterprises over the last decade (2007–2017) among all institutions with annual research expenditures exceeding $100 million annually. ASU's research growth was outpaced only by Indiana University, which assumed control of the medical school formerly reported as part of Indiana University–Purdue University Indianapolis, and New York University, which consolidated its previously separately reported Polytechnic Institute. ASU's total research expenditures have grown by 143 percent over the last decade, more than tripling the national growth rate in total university research expenditures of 46 percent. ASU's federally funded research expenditures have grown by 92 percent, more than tripling the national growth in federally funded university research expenditures of 29 percent. According to the National Science Foundation, ASU ranks eighth of 747 universities without medical schools in terms of total research expenditures—ahead of Caltech, Princeton, and Carnegie Mellon.[28] Among all 903 institutions participating in the survey, ASU ranked forty-fourth. In terms of non–medical school expenditures, ASU ranked twenty-first of 903 institutions. In terms of NSF-funded expenditures, ASU ranked twenty second—ahead of Harvard, University of Chicago, University of Pennsylvania, Princeton, Duke, and Johns Hopkins—and eighth in NASA-funded expenditures—ahead of

Stanford, Columbia, Georgia Tech, and UCLA. ASU ranked thirteenth in nonscience and engineering disciplines, fourth in the social sciences, and fifth in the humanities.[29]

Growth in research expenditures across all disciplines and investment from an increasing number of funding agencies indicates that the research enterprise is on track to reach $815 million in annual research expenditures by 2025, consistent with the intent to establish ASU as a global center for interdisciplinary research, discovery, and development. Achieving this goal will require new capacity building investment in faculty, laboratories, and facilities as well as the ambitious pursuit of large-scale federal projects, partnership building, and growth into new funding areas including international development. Perspective regarding the projected attainment of $815 million in research expenditures comes from consideration of current figures. During FY 2017, only two institutions without medical schools reported total research expenditures exceeding $815 million: Massachusetts Institute of Technology ($952 million) and the University of Texas M. D. Anderson Cancer Center ($888 million). Only twenty-one other institutions with medical schools reported $815 million in research expenditures.[30]

The expansion and intensification of the research enterprise without significant growth in the size of the faculty—ASU's student-to-faculty ratio of 21:1 has remained consistent since 2002—attests not only to faculty accomplishments but also their creativity and productivity. The faculty presently includes five Nobel laureates, five MacArthur fellows, seven Pulitzer Prize recipients, thirty-five Guggenheim fellows, 196 Fulbright American Scholars, and more members of the National Academies than have served on the faculty during the entire history of the institution, including ten members of the National Academy of Engineering, twenty-three members of the National Academy of Sciences, and three members of the National Academy of Medicine, as well as twenty-two fellows of the American Academy of Arts and Sciences and seventy-seven fellows of the National Endowment for the Humanities. Excellence in this context as well is a correlate of increasing diversity: between fall 2002 and 2018, minority tenured and tenure-track faculty as a percentage of the total for this category increased from 18.5 percent to 28.9 percent, a 56.2 percent increase. In this timeframe total tenured and tenure-track faculty grew from 1,671 to 1,994, a 19.3 percent increase, while minority tenured and tenure-track faculty grew from 309 to 576, an 86.4 percent increase.

The momentum of interdisciplinary collaboration at ASU may in part be attested by the growth in the number of active sponsored projects involving investigators from different academic units, which rose by 182 percent between FY 2003 and FY 2018, outpacing projects involving researchers in single units, which increased by only 27 percent. In FY 2003, 20 percent of active projects involved more than one unit. In FY 2018, this number increased to 35 percent. The total value of active sponsored projects from single units during this timeframe increased 106 percent, while the value of projects involving more than one unit increased 367 percent.

ASU maintains one of the most productive technology transfer operations as well when compared with the performance metrics of peer research institutions. As of 2018, ASU has advanced into the top ten of all universities worldwide for U.S. patents issued to researchers and third among U.S. universities without a medical school, behind MIT and Caltech. ASU tied with the University of Michigan to rank tenth overall in a roster that also includes the University of California, Stanford, Harvard, and Johns Hopkins.[31] Management of patents for campus-based discoveries is provided by Skysong Innovations—formerly known as Arizona Technology Enterprises (AzTE)—which was formed in 2003 as the exclusive intellectual property management and technology transfer operation for the university. Skysong Innovations works with faculty, investors, and industry partners to speed the flow of innovation from the laboratory to the marketplace. Its focus on organizational scaling and operational efficiencies dramatically increases the flow of technology from ASU labs into commercial application. Skysong Innovations operates at a high rate of deal flow as measured by cross-university output statistics, but its mastery of process leverages its impact. An institutional culture of entrepreneurship facilitates a proactive data-driven approach to identifying potential licensees, development partners, and investors, resulting in greater external interest in partnership, licensing, and acquisition.

ASU consistently ranks among the top-performing U.S. universities in terms of intellectual property inputs (inventions disclosed by ASU researchers) and outputs (licensing deals and startups) relative to the size of the university's research enterprise, according to annual surveys by the Association of University Technology Managers (AUTM). The Milken Institute ranks ASU twenty-first for best universities for tech transfer and commercialization—sixth among institutions without a medical school. The ranking underscores that universities are among the nation's most powerful engines for domestic economic growth. To date, more than 120 companies have been launched based on ASU innovations. The economic impact of these companies is considerable, having now raised more than $700 million in venture capital and other funding. The Seidman Research Institute studied thirty-six ASU-linked companies in the Skysong Innovations portfolio—all founded during the previous decade—and estimated their collective contribution to the state's economy for 2016 and 2017 included approximately 2,600 job-years; $250 million contributed to Gross State Product; $170 million in additional wages; and $22 million in additional state and local tax revenue. Beyond Arizona, Skysong Innovations maintains a continued physical presence at the ASU California Center in Santa Monica, which fosters connections between the Arizona and California innovation ecosystems.

ASU's unprecedented success in growing research expenditures and driving socially impactful research is the result of more than fifteen years of ongoing organizational redesign. Now that the university has realized an institutional shift toward innovation at all levels and made transdisciplinary collaboration the norm, ASU is moving on to the next phase in organizational development for innovation: the creation of external affiliated organizations that allow the academic community to push the frontiers of knowledge and discovery far beyond the capabilities of a traditional public university. ASU Research Enterprise (ASURE) is an ASU-affiliated not-for-profit corporation created to build capacity for security and defense-relevant research that serves national interests. ASURE acts as an intermediary between national defense agencies and ASU scientists, allowing the university to transcend organizational and cultural boundaries to research collaboration. The U.S. Department of Defense and agencies in the intelligence community issue billions of dollars of contracts for research and development each year, but university research scientists often lack the support needed to interface with agencies, meet security requirements, and understand federal technology acquisition systems. ASURE employs experienced professionals with military, defense, and technology backgrounds to provide the technical expertise, operational capabilities, and domain knowledge to close this gap. The ASURE team assembles expert faculty teams to tackle national security projects across multiple domains such as computer networking, supply-chain management, data mining, unmanned vehicle control, human-machine decision making, water purification, and health care. ASURE's status as an affiliated but self-governed organization allows for streamlined security clearance acquisition, simplified compliance, and greater overall agility in project execution. By handling the bureaucratic requirements associated with executing projects under defense and intelligence acquisitions, ASURE brings the full depth and breadth of faculty expertise to the fore.[32]

The ASU Research Collaboratory is another important new venture that builds ASU's capacity for innovation in research and services delivery. The Research Collaboratory serves as an incubator for high-impact initiatives of university faculty and students, providing the legal, financial reporting, and governance support to shepherd ideas into the market. The first major initiative of the Research Collaboratory, the National Biomarker Development Alliance, advances global standards for the development of biomarkers and guides their trajectory into widespread clinical application. The Research Collaboratory allows ASU to provide indirect support in endeavors of tremendous complexity that require a high degree of agility and independence to succeed. The initiative positions the university at the forefront of the personalized medicine revolution, for example. As a privately administered 501(c)3 organization, the Research Collaboratory is also able to manage the finances of some university international projects, widening ASU's global reach. For example, the Research Collaboratory allows ASU to maintain a repository of historical artifacts and artwork in Mexico for the university's Teotihuacan Research Laboratory.[33]

Among authoritative assessments of comparative institutional rankings, the Academic Ranking of World Universities (ARWU), compiled by the Institute of Higher Education, Shanghai Jiao Tong University, is generally regarded as credible proxy for achievement in discovery and innovation. ARWU ranked ASU ninety-third among the top one hundred universities in the world in 2015, which corresponds to forty-seventh among all universities in the United States. Although ASU currently appears in the cluster of institutions ranked between 100 and 150, the university did not even rank among the top 200 institutions in 2002 and first achieved top 100 status only in 2006. The assessment compares 1,200 institutions worldwide and is considered among the most rigorous such evaluations.[34] ASU ranks in the top 1 percent of the world's most prestigious universities, according to one 2018 assessment. The *Times Higher Education World University Rankings* placed ASU 126th in the world, using measures of excellence in teaching, research, knowledge transfer, and international outlook. ASU ranked 35th worldwide in the *THE* 2019 *University Impact Rankings*, which assess universities against the United Nations' Sustainable Development Goals.[35]

## The Terms of the Reconceptualization

Arizona State University is committed to offering admission to all academically qualified Arizona residents regardless of financial need.[36] To promote accessibility to a student body representative of the socioeconomic and intellectual diversity of the region, admissions policies similar to those of the University of California in the mid-twentieth century were implemented.[37] Consistent with the tenet that the Fifth Wave comprises a subset of major public research universities that have reinvigorated the public dimension of their mission and purpose and undertaken deliberate expansion of scope and scale to offer broad accessibility to academically qualified student populations representative of the socioeconomic and intellectual diversity of the nation, ASU articulated a charter statement in 2014 that expresses the intent of the academic community to maximize the public value of the institution: *Arizona State University is a comprehensive public research university, measured not by whom it excludes, but by whom it includes and how they succeed; advancing research and discovery of public value; and assuming fundamental responsibility for the economic, social, cultural, and overall health of the communities it serves.*[38]

The charter statement reaffirms the longstanding social compact implicit in the institutional type of the public university and represents as well a deliberate affirmation of institutional autonomy and self-determination. The charter represents the culmination of a series of documents, beginning with the 2004 foundational white paper that first announced the reconceptualization and delineated its objectives and the parameters of its operationalization through what would be termed the design process. Among the associated challenges that motivated the establishment of a new institutional platform apart from subpar performance in economic output and the unprecedented shift in the regional demographic profile cited in the report were lagging educational attainment in an underperforming prekindergarten through grade 12 educational system; limited public and private support for the university, including declining state government investment when measured on a per-student basis; and the need for the advancement of knowledge-based economic development in an economy insufficiently diversified to accommodate population expansion. A recent estimate of the college participation rate for students from low-income families in Arizona attests to the continued imperative for the new model. Whereas the national median is 34 percent and some northeastern states achieve rates as high as 56 percent, at 27 percent, Arizona ranks among the lowest dozen states.[39]

The objective was initially formulated as the intent to build a comprehensive metropolitan research university that would become an "unparalleled combination of academic excellence and commitment to its social, economic, cultural, and environmental setting." The self-appointed mandate to advance the well-being of the communities served by the university thus called for an institution that "measures its academic quality by the education that its graduates have received rather than the academic credentials of its incoming freshman class; one at which researchers, while pursuing their scholarly interests, also consider the public good; one that does not just engage in community service, but rather takes on major responsibility for the economic, social, and cultural vitality of its community."[40]

The foundational white paper introduced the set of eight interrelated and mutually interdependent design aspirations, which represent ideals for institutional culture as well as strategic approaches to the accomplishment of goals and objectives. To be understood as general guidelines intended to inspire creativity, spark innovation, and foster institutional individuation, these call for the academic community to (1) respond to its cultural, socioeconomic, and physical setting; (2) become a force for societal transformation; (3) pursue a culture of academic enterprise and knowledge entrepreneurship; (4) conduct use-inspired research; (5) focus on the individual in a milieu of intellectual and cultural diversity; (6) transcend disciplinary limitations in pursuit of intellectual fusion (transdisciplinarity); (7) embed the university socially, thereby advancing social enterprise development through direct engagement; and (8) advance global engagement. A number of variant formulations of the design aspirations have appeared, including the following more succinct delineation:

1. Leverage Our Place: ASU embraces its cultural, socioeconomic, and physical setting.
2. Transform Society: ASU catalyzes social change by being connected to social needs.
3. Value Entrepreneurship: ASU uses its knowledge and encourages innovation.
4. Conduct Use-Inspired Research: ASU research has purpose and impact.
5. Enable Student Success: ASU is committed to the success of each unique student.
6. Fuse Intellectual Disciplines: ASU creates knowledge by transcending academic disciplines.
7. Be Socially Embedded: ASU connects with communities through mutually beneficial partnerships.
8. Engage Globally: ASU engages with people and issues locally, nationally, and internationally.

The revised mission and goals ("Toward 2025 and Beyond") reflect the outcome of achievements between 2002 and 2017. The objectives specified correspond to the outputs of the most highly selective public universities and must be evaluated within the context of their accomplishment by a large public university committed to drawing from the broader talent pool of socioeconomic diversity. Their attainment assumes an institutional culture committed to academic enterprise and improved cost effectiveness through productivity gains and constant innovation:

*Demonstrate leadership in academic excellence and accessibility*
Maintain the fundamental principle of accessibility to all students
    qualified to study at a research university;

Maintain university accessibility to match Arizona's socioeconomic
    diversity with undifferentiated outcomes for success;
Improve freshmen persistence to greater than 90 percent;
Enhance university graduation rate to 80 percent and more than
    32,000 graduates;
Enhance quality while reducing the cost of a degree;
Enroll 100,000 online and distance-education degree-seeking students;
Enhance measured student development and individual student
    learning to national leadership levels;
Enhance linkages to the university at all levels for all learners.

*Establish national standing in academic quality and impact of colleges
and schools in every field*
Attain national standing in academic quality for each college and
    school (top 5 percent);
Attain national standing in the learning value added to our graduates
    in each college and school;
Become the leading university academically, in terms of faculty,
    discovery, research, and creativity, in at least one department or
    school within each school/college.

*Establish ASU as a leading global center for interdisciplinary research,
discovery, and development by 2025*
Become the leading American center for discovery and scholarship in
    the integrated social sciences and comprehensive arts and sciences;
Enhance research competitiveness to more than $815 million in
    annual research expenditures;
Transform regional economic competitiveness through research and
    discovery and value-added programs;
Become a leading American center for innovation and entrepreneur-
    ship at all levels.

*Enhance our local impact and social embeddedness*
Strengthen Arizona's interactive network of teaching, learning, and
    discovery resources that reflects the scope of ASU's comprehensive
    knowledge enterprise;
Co-develop solutions to the critical social, technical, cultural, and
    environmental issues facing twenty-first-century Arizona;

Meet the needs of twenty-first-century learners by empowering
families in the education of their children, increasing student
success through personalized learning pathways, and promoting a
college-going culture in Arizona's K–12 schools;
Establish, with Mayo Clinic, innovative health solutions pathways
capable of educating 200 million people about health care; engaging 20 million people in online health care delivery; and enhancing
treatment for 2 million patients.

### From Bureaucratic Agency to Academic Enterprise

To achieve the ambitious objectives of the New American University
model, ASU adopted academic enterprise as its operational model. Characterized by a commitment to responsivity, maximization of clear goals,
and adaptiveness, the academic enterprise model emerging from ASU
represents a new approach to advancing knowledge production and innovation and the multidimensional social, cultural, and economic
mission of a publicly purposed major research university. In the following we articulate the rationale for ASU's transformation into an academic
enterprise and the opportunities that come from rethinking the foundational bureaucratic and public agency assumptions upon which higher
education in the United States has to this point emerged.[41]

To the extent that a public university succeeds in reconstituting itself
as an academic enterprise, it rejects the constraints associated with the
designation of government agency. The language of government and bureaucracy is frequently invoked in discussions of public colleges and
universities. Sometimes this discourse is associated with praise for institutional commitment to public service and stability. At other times,
critics of public higher education level the accusation of bureaucracy to
suggest inherent inefficiencies and excessive costs. Bureaucracy, however,
is an essential feature of all modern societies and is integral to many
important organizations—whether publicly funded and mission driven,
as in the case of state-assisted universities, or privately owned, as in the
case of businesses that are designed to maximize profit. Max Weber, the
German political economist and sociologist whose ideas have shaped our
understanding of capitalism and governance, noted that bureaucratic
organization is ubiquitous across many types of organizations—"fully
developed in political and ecclesiastical communities only in the mod-

ern state, and in the private economy only in the most advanced institutions of capitalism." Moreover, "It does not matter for the character of
bureaucracy whether its authority is called 'private' or 'public.'"[42] Similarly, the economist Joseph Schumpeter observed, "Bureaucracy is not an
obstacle to democracy but an inevitable complement to it."[43] Policy
scholar Anthony Downs observes, "It is ironic that bureaucracy is still
primarily a term of scorn, even though bureaus are among the most
important institutions in every nation in the world. . . . They make critical decisions which shape the economic, political, social, and even moral
lives of everyone on earth."[44]

Although bureaucratic organizational models like government agencies perform critical functions that facilitate the operations of society,
constraints associated with large impersonal public agencies whose re-
mit is to perform standardized and repetitive tasks efficiently is not normally conducive to discovery, creativity, and innovation. The *Oxford
English Dictionary* defines *bureaucracy* as "administration by a hierarchy of professional administrators following clearly defined procedures
in a routine and organized manner," and in the pejorative sense as a system that is "characterized by such features as an excessive concern with
formal processes and a tendency for administrative power to increase
and become more centralized, and hence by inefficiency and imperson-
ality, officialism, [and] red tape."[45] Indeed, Downs identifies routine,
standardization, and inertia as among the chief attributes of bureaucracies. He observes that bureaus often "struggle for autonomy." As he
elaborates, "No bureau can survive unless it is able to demonstrate that
its services are worthwhile to some group with influence over sufficient
resources to keep it alive. . . . If it is a government bureau, it must impress
those politicians who control the budget that its functions generate political support or meet vital social needs." Because generic public universities perpetuate the obsolete service model that accords value to universities principally for their role in undergraduate education, one may
extrapolate in this context from Downs's assessment: "Once the users of
the bureau's services have become convinced of their gains from it, and
have developed routinized relations with it, the bureau can rely upon a
certain amount of inertia to keep on generating the external support it
needs." Moreover, "As bureaus grow older, they tend to develop more formalized rule systems . . . [which] tend to divert the attention of officials

from achieving the social functions of the bureau to conforming to its rules—the 'goal displacement' described by sociologists," Downs explains. Entrenched protocols "increase the bureau's structural complexity, which in turn strengthens its inertia because of greater sunken costs in current procedures. The resulting resistance to change further reduces the bureau's ability to adjust to new circumstances."[46] As James Q. Wilson observes of agencies, the quantity of outputs does not necessarily correspond to the quality of outcomes: "How, if at all, the world changes because of the outputs."[47]

In contrast to the rigidities and entrenchment associated with agencies, enterprises are defined by their initiative, autonomy, and self-determination. To the extent that universities function as agencies rather than enterprises, they may fail to realize their full potential. Although one generally associates the term *enterprise* with business or commerce, the attribute of enterprise is not restricted to any particular sector. The *Oxford English Dictionary* defines *enterprise* as a "bold, arduous, or momentous undertaking," and the "disposition or readiness to engage in undertakings of difficulty, risk, or danger." To be described as an enterprise, an organization simply requires an entrepreneurial spirit. As an academic enterprise, ASU embodies the spirit of creative risk taking through which knowledge is brought to scale to exert impact on societal development and economic competitiveness. An entrepreneurial approach to knowledge production encourages experimentation as well as deliberation and risk taking in all fields and sets the pattern for vanguard scientific discovery, technological innovation, humanistic insight, social scientific rigor, and creative expression. The emerging enterprise model embraces the pragmatist unification of thought and action and demands the reorganization of institutions to achieve more optimal societal outcomes. The model transcends the spurious dichotomy between public value and market value and recognizes the imperative to succeed in terms of both. Awareness of the multidimensional nature of success according to both social and economic criteria allows academic communities to contextualize the challenge for new models of higher education: designing institutions that are successful according to the standards of both the market and society. New institutions will be expected to advance the social and scientific outcomes of a traditional agency-oriented university design coupled with the innovative and adaptive commitments of emerging enterprise models. The model moreover affirms the unrivalled status of the university as a chief player in a highly competitive arena that produces knowledge capital—not only goods and services but also human capital, referring to the measure of the value of the stock of knowledge, skills, and creativity that may be acquired through investment in education and training. Through investment in human capital, the economist Theodore W. Schultz observed, "the quality of human effort can be greatly improved and its productivity enhanced."[48]

Among the best and the worst of what economist and policy scholar Charles Clotfelter terms the "vast and variegated" subset of four-year institutions in American higher education: "some 1,600 colleges and universities offering baccalaureate degrees [of which] roughly 40 percent are creatures of government—mostly state governments—and the rest beholden only to their boards of trustees," he identifies the grip of isomorphic replication. "Ironically, this diversity coexists with what appears to be a persistent urge to standardize." As we contend throughout these chapters, only generic public universities willingly blinkered by the bureaucratic constraints of the agency model should be content to be designated merely "creatures of government." And to revisit yet again two essential corollary points, not all colleges and universities are alike and not all degrees carry equal value. In the passage that follows, Clotfelter captures perfectly the conventional wisdom that all colleges and universities offer pretty much the same product:

> These unequal colleges share more than a few common outward features, such as degree names, grading conventions, departmental organization, and occupational titles. Within this industry we behold a collection of "firms" all of which purport to sell (to customers able to perform certain tasks) one of several seemingly standardized commodities—degrees—each beginning with the words "bachelor of." So standardized are these degrees that, for many employers and universities and for virtually all statistical purposes, a degree from any college whose quality has been certified by one of the country's regional accrediting agencies will be treated as representing a common level of educational achievement. To be a college graduate means simply having a bachelor's degree from any accredited college or university.[49]

Inasmuch as the Fifth Wave represents the effort to differentiate and evolve new organizational frameworks to spur knowledge production and innovation, the standardization associated with generic public universities is anathema to the orientation of the enterprise model.

Academic enterprise is not to be taken to refer to what is termed the "corporate university." Although what the economist Henry Etzkowitz called the "triple helix" of university-industry-government innovation is essential to the national innovation system,[50] critics allege that collaboration between the academy and business and industry commoditizes knowledge and compromises disinterested inquiry.[51] Yet such engagement across sectors is essential if universities are to leverage their knowledge production to catalyze innovation that benefits the public good. Nor does it imply a business model guided solely by financial considerations. Academic enterprise is not just about the money but, needless to say, money is necessarily a dimension of academic enterprise. As John Lombardi, former president of the Louisiana State University system puts it, "While most university conversations focus on issues of academic substance—program content, research results, and curriculum issues, for example—almost every conversation carries a subtext about money." As Lombardi quips, "Universities use special words to describe money questions. They talk about 'resources' or 'program support' when what they actually mean is 'money.'"[52]

Strategic management perspectives of academia are common enough, as in the assessment of the "conglomerate challenge" that is said to confront the contemporary research university in the estimation of Bernard Ferrari, dean of the Johns Hopkins Carey Business School, and strategic management theorist Phillip Phan. Ferrari and Phan characterize the business model of this set of institutions as a "diversified conglomerate of independent strategic business units (SBUs)," referring to academic units such as divisions and colleges and schools. Academic conglomerates allocate resources to individual units but must contend with such issues as the "carrying of economically inefficient academic units (defined as those chronically unable to earn their cost of capital in tuition, endowment, or research funding); the non-fungibility of specialized real estate assets and scientific equipment; and the immovability of the tenured faculty." But whereas conglomerates are free to restructure and sell off or spin out unprofitable and underutilized assets, the authors argue, universities remain shackled by the norms and rigidities of academic culture. To longstanding impediments are now added such new dynamics as skyrocketing tuition costs, demographic reconfigurations, diminished research funding, the advent of ubiquitous online learning, and skepticism regarding the value of higher education. Ferrari and Phan recommend that trustees from the corporate sector encourage academic leaders and fellow board members to "start thinking of the university not as a collection of individual SBUs but as a portfolio of revenue-producing or cost-incurring assets, each with different risk profiles and possibilities for navigating disruptive change." Dispassionate and sober stocktaking among administrators and trustees would address such questions as the following:

> What mix of academic programs is best able to generate sustainable growth, stable cash flows (in portfolio parlance, businesses with countercyclical demand patterns), and brand equity? What programs are truly critical, and which are "nice to have"? What current academic programs and areas of research do not contribute to sustainability, stability, and reputation of the whole? What new innovations (academic programs and emerging domains of research) deserve further investment to create new sources of revenue and new opportunities for mission and brand building?[53]

Consistent with the trajectory from bureaucratic agency to academic enterprise envisioned for the Fifth Wave, higher education policy scholar Burton Clark identifies five key aspects essential to the transformation: (1) a more robust managerial approach; (2) the formation of entities to mediate between academic units and corporate and industry partners, which he terms "developmental peripheries"; (3) a diversified funding base; (4) what he terms a "stimulated academic heartland;" and (5) an entrepreneurial culture. Clark thus frames the limitations of the agency model: research universities can "passively fall in line and undergo parallel financial increases and decreases—as goes the government, so they go—with the governmental stimulus determining university response." The alternative is to actively pursue a diversified funding base and develop additional revenue streams. While ambition encourages this option, he points out, the competitive ecosystem of research-grade institutions essentially necessitates the transition to entrepreneurship. His assessment of what he calls the "entrepreneurial response" merits extended quotation:

> The entrepreneurial response offers a formula for institutional development that puts autonomy on a self-defined basis: diversify income to increase financial resources, provide discretionary money, *and* reduce governmental dependency; develop new units outside traditional departments to introduce new environmental relationships and new modes of thought and training; convince heartland departments that they too can look out for themselves, raise money, actively choose among sustainable specialities, and otherwise take on an entrepreneurial outlook; evolve a set of overarching beliefs that guide and rationalize the structural changes that provide a stronger response capability; and build a central steering capacity to make large choices that help focus the institution. The entrepreneurial response in all its fullness gives universities better means for redefining their reach— to include more useful knowledge, to move more flexibly over time from one programme emphasis to another, and finally to build an organizational identity and focus.[54]

To appreciate the potential of new and more entrepreneurial models in higher education, we must first revisit the institutional logics that define the missions and drive the operations of present-day universities. Narrowly defined notions of discovery and pedagogy that date back to the guild culture of thirteenth-century Europe inform the governance of academic institutions to this day. In what we might term the "traditional" academic model, university faculty act as stewards of the accumulated knowledge of civilization, sometimes perceiving themselves as guardians against the pressures of both the market and social change. Many of America's most venerated (and usually private) institutions remain organizationally most akin to the hybrid of British and German academic models whose designs they emulate, following a long heritage of valuing tradition at the expense of socially responsive innovation. This tendency bears heavily on university leadership, often resulting in reluctance to respond to social needs and a myopic focus on the walled garden of the academy. As a result, these universities fail to respond to growing demand for educational accessibility, admitting relatively fewer students than public universities and giving faculty free rein to determine research priorities rather than systematically pursuing public value-oriented discovery.[55]

In terms of social benefit, public universities are often remarkably successful, offering pathways to skills and credentials that help individuals realize greater prosperity and socioeconomic mobility and producing research that drives economic growth. Most public research universities were initially designed around the traditional academic model, but because they were created to be more accessible and oriented toward serving the public, they had to adopt a new model to succeed. Public universities therefore usually operate under the model of academic bureaucracy, marked by complex administrative structures that allow them to serve larger numbers of students and comply with the directives and goals of the states that fund them. Although academic bureaucracies do successfully graduate many more students than their smaller, more traditional counterparts, they are prone to organizational inertia and what is termed by organizational theorists a "conserver mentality." Aware that state legislatures control their budgets, they seek to use resources as efficiently as possible, often at the expense of innovation and quality outcomes in teaching, learning, and research. Universities that operate as academic bureaucracies often fail to realize their full potential, being slow to change, cost ineffective, and unresponsive to the needs of nontraditional students. Like the institutions of the traditional academic model, academic bureaucracies are risk-averse, but for entirely different reasons. The bureaucratic logic that animates academic bureaucracies diminishes the agency of faculty, causes administrators to obsess over reporting metrics rather than results, and constrains the vision of leadership to near term outcomes rooted in institutional survival rather than growth and progress.[56]

For-profit universities occupy a special niche in American higher education, following a market model that values neither the pursuit of knowledge for enlightenment and discovery nor service to the public. For-profit institutions seek only to maximize profit for their shareholders—sometimes at the expense of academic quality—and although their ability to survive confirms that they create market value, they are inherently incapable of advancing public value. Because neither universities operating under the traditional academic model nor

for-profit universities driven by the market model are designed to respond to social and economic needs, public research universities remain
the best vehicle for advancing public value. To do so most effectively,
they must overcome the shortcomings of academic bureaucracy by embracing academic enterprise. This emergent organizational logic is
based on the premise that the purpose of public universities should be
social transformation—that is, to create positive social, economic, and
environmental outcomes not only for stakeholders but also for all of society. Rather than narrowly focusing on the needs of academic communities, or even communities and states, academic enterprise universities
recognize their ability to exert national and even global impact through
their knowledge production and innovation. The culture of academic
enterprise is remarkably different from other models. Faculty contribute
to university management and work alongside administrators and managers, all of whom collectively take responsibility for maximizing the
value the institution provides rather than merely conserving resources.
As knowledge entrepreneurs, faculty members are empowered to take
meaningful risks to improve teaching and learning, forge meaningful
collaborations, and make impactful discoveries.[57]

Entrepreneurial leadership is the differentiator in determining
whether a university will function as an academic bureaucracy or as an
academic enterprise that takes meaningful and innovative risks to enhance its value for stakeholders. Schumpeter argued that, in capitalist
systems, the role of entrepreneurs is to fundamentally reform the patterns of production by leveraging technology to produce new commodities, produce old commodities in new ways, capitalize upon new sources
of supply, and open new markets for products, or even to reorganize
entire industries.[58] Academic enterprise leverages technology, as Schumpeter describes, and draws upon previously untapped knowledge, talent,
and resources from outside and within the organization to achieve
breakthroughs in educational quality and research impact. Academic
entrepreneurship that leads to radical change depends upon leadership
that is not only committed to creative risk-taking but also to new values
that redefine the purposes of colleges and universities in society. Entrepreneurial leadership in higher education thus entails a parting of ways
with the assumptions, traditions, and inertia that have hampered the
evolution of the academy from the medieval period through the present,

and an embrace of forward-looking future-oriented thought and action that demand the reorganization of institutions to achieve better outcomes for society.[59]

Organizational variation in higher education is narrowly construed and underappreciated, and current classification systems stifle the potential for institutional diversity. One cluster analysis of 1,525 four-year public and private colleges and universities found at least twelve organizational types.[60] A more nuanced classification system that acknowledges the imperative for institutional diversity would enrich the present discussion, which, we concede, at times tendentiously reduces the scope of analysis in an attempt to conceptualize the Fifth Wave in terms of the Fourth Wave. An alternative classification regime might more precisely identify the nature of variation in American higher education. Generic information-transfer organizations such as the University of Phoenix, for example, are designed primarily to efficiently transfer existing codified knowledge. Research-grade institutions prioritize knowledge production, including its discovery, analysis, synthesis, and dissemination, but vary according to their accessibility, admissions practices, levels of enrollment, research intensity, and a host of other variables. Suffice it to say for the present that Fifth Wave universities build on the core of knowledge with various forms of enterprise, including academic enterprise, which among its multiplicity of functions operates and evolves immersive teaching and learning systems; knowledge enterprise, which supports and advances discovery, innovation, and translation throughout the university and its nexus of interrelations with business and industry, government agencies and laboratories, and organizations in civil society; learning enterprise, which creates and operates new pedagogical tools for massive-scale digital immersion and lifelong learning opportunities; and partnership enterprise, which develops and leverages external partners to help the university achieve its broad mission of societal transformation.[61]

Academic enterprise is an operational logic that attempts to recharacterize both the college or university and its governance in terms of its potential to advance new opportunities to achieve critical social outcomes. Governance and the pursuit of public value vary according to whether an institution embraces the logic of the academy model; the bureaucratic, or agency, model; the market model characteristic of the for-profit sector; or the enterprise model that is the basis of the New American University and the Fifth Wave. Whereas the animating purpose of institutions guided by the academy model is the enlightenment of individual students, it is organizational preservation for agencies, profit maximization for owners and shareholders among for-profits, but social transformation in the enterprise model. Immersive instruction is the path to public value in the academy model, achievement of state-specified goals in the agency model, efficiency and cost reduction among for-profits, but connecting instruction to knowledge generation at a scale that impacts society in the enterprise model. Faculty members are assumed to be self-governing professionals in the academy model, bureaucrats responding to rules in the agency model, commodity labor but not entrepreneurial in the market model, but knowledge entrepreneurs in the enterprise model. Administration, or management, is drawn from and blended with the faculty in the academy model but remains distinct from faculty in the agency model, where administrators often follow patterns established in traditional public management. Although professional management functions entrepreneurially in the market model, managers remain distinct from faculty. In the enterprise model, administrators act entrepreneurially but are drawn from and blend with the faculty.

Whereas in the academy model accountability mechanisms among the faculty are prescribed by professional guidelines, in the state control model accountability derives from such mechanisms as audits, public reporting, and standardized testing, the latter of which, along with consumer choice, also governs the for-profit sector. Accountability in the enterprise model, however, is achieved through demonstrated economic and social progress. Tuition and endowment income, and for public colleges and universities, enrollment funding from state governments, constitute in varying proportions the primary funding mechanisms in both the academy and agency models. Apart from tuition and fees, for-profit institutions often rely on vouchers and performance-based funding from the state. But as we have delineated in this discussion, academic enterprise thrives from diverse sources of revenue that vary according to the tilt of entrepreneurial initiative. Finally, the organizational scale of impact in the academy model is the individual, or cohorts of individuals, and for the agency model the state or community. The scale of impact remains indeterminate in the market model because for-profits will seek to attain any scale from which profit can be derived. The organizational scale of impact in the enterprise model, however, is societal, with the intent to attain national and global reach.[62]

Disavowal of the agency model should not be taken to suggest that government has no role in the enterprise model. Although the challenge of defining the proper role of government in the provision of education remains unresolved to the present day,[63] public research universities shifting from the agency model to an enterprise model need to maximize all available resources and thus require supportive policies from state and federal government. As delineated in the report of the Lincoln Project of the American Academy of Arts and Sciences, "Any solution will require an infusion of strategies, ideas, partnerships, and revenue streams—a new compact among the federal government, state governments, corporations, foundations, philanthropists, students, and, of course, universities themselves."[64] The National Research Council has similarly recommended strategic actions to consolidate the competitive stance of both public and private research universities. Among those most relevant to the advancement of a league of Fifth Wave universities are federal policies that support both university-performed research and development consistent with national innovation strategies and funding for graduate education, and state policies that provide autonomy to public research universities and restore state appropriations to levels sufficient for institutions to attain world-class competitiveness. The report similarly calls for business and industry to facilitate knowledge transfer in support of national goals.[65]

The Strategic Enterprise Plan, adopted in 2009, sought to articulate the rationale for ASU's transformation into an academic enterprise. Its tenets build on the foundational 2004 white paper and seek to advance the longstanding imperative for an institutional response to the lagging economic output and unprecedented shift in the regional demographic profile. Because ASU has assumed responsibility to fulfill the requirements of the Arizona Constitution to provide public education, its commitment to educate all academically qualified citizens of Arizona, conduct world-leading research in the interests of the nation, and advance public well-being can no longer be contingent on arbitrarily determined levels of support from the state legislature.[66] Implicit in the charter statement is the affirmation that ASU will find the means to meet its obligations to fulfill its charter regardless of the extent to which it benefits from appropriate and equitable public investment. Because the charter thus presumes that ASU will seek appropriate and fair public investment in the costs of education for Arizona resident students, it is incumbent on the institution to reconstitute itself as an academic enterprise rather than a mere agency of state government. To the extent that ASU succeeds in advancing this different institutional logic, its transformation into an academic enterprise challenges the foundational assumptions of the compact between state governments and their public universities as well as the patterns and processes that guide bureaucratic public organizations.

The Strategic Enterprise Plan was created to realize the aspirations of the charter of the university. Unlike the strategic plans of traditional colleges and universities, ASU's operational model reflects its unique identity as an academic enterprise that takes reasonable risks to achieve meaningful outcomes. Performance data show that as an academic enterprise ASU is achieving the transformative outcomes it seeks in two key human capital and knowledge capital areas: the empowerment of individuals and cutting-edge knowledge production and innovation. An internationally competitive higher education enterprise is crucial if Arizona and its citizens are to prosper financially and socially. Supporting academic enterprise requires not only the continuation of traditional educational activities at accelerated rates but also the development of new enterprise programs that fill resource gaps. The Strategic Enterprise Plan will continue to advance the transformation of the university from an underperforming public agency model to a public enterprise model, enabling its capability to improve its performance and meet its metric targets.

ASU's new enterprise programs drive the university's continued growth and impact and enable the success of the Strategic Enterprise Plan. Closing resource gaps in order to drive the university to its 2025 goals requires entirely new enterprise programs. These programs are creative investments in new endeavors that will raise revenue to build the capacity of the university to fulfill the mandates of its charter. ASU's reorganization as a New American University reflects its new capacities as an academic enterprise to create greater value for the public it serves. Through new ways of thinking, ASU is putting existing capabilities to work and redefining the boundaries of what universities can do without losing sight of principles consistent with its charter. Rather than detract from the mission of the university, these ventures draw upon and bolster capacities while creating new revenue that will be reinvested in the production of human capital and knowledge capital to drive the economic, social, and cultural vitality of Arizona and the nation. New enterprise focus areas include innovation in educational delivery; leveraging technology and organizational change for student success; organizing for research innovation; technology commercialization and entrepreneurship; international development; and reinventing university philanthropy.

## From Agency in 1985 to Enterprise in 2025

The New American University model implicitly rejects the premise that broad accessibility and academic excellence are antithetical. But this claim is no longer merely rhetorical or conjectural. ASU's rapid improvement across all indicators of institutional performance, ascent in national and international stature, and track record of garnered accomplishments during the first fifteen years of its reconceptualization as an academic enterprise and more inclusive public research university provide indisputable empirical evidence of the success of the model. But its transformation from an institution dominated by what might be termed an underperforming public agency model to the public enterprise of a new era can best be appreciated by comparison of some key indicators of institutional performance at four points beginning in 1985. ASU did not attain university status until 1958 and conducted no significant funded research prior to 1980—roughly one hundred years later than most other major research universities. Because the Carnegie Foundation did not grant ASU research-extensive ("Research I") status until 1994, conferring on it recognition as one of a handful of institutions without both an agricultural and medical school to be thus designated, ASU may legitimately claim to be one of the nation's youngest major research universities.

As an underperforming public agency in FY 1985, ASU depended on high levels of investment from the state government: $8,755 in base state investment per full-time equivalent (FTE) student expressed in 2017 dollars. The operating budget amounted to $238 million. With a four-year graduation rate of 13.8 percent, student outcomes were clearly inadequate.

Tuition was low and as a consequence so too was available financial aid: resident undergraduate tuition and fees were $2,577 per year and less than 2 percent of undergraduates received Pell Grants. Freshman diversity was strikingly low: 84.9 percent of the student population reported as white, and only 9.9 percent reported as underrepresented minorities. Moreover, the contribution of the institution to knowledge generation was nominal: annual research expenditures amounted to a mere $28 million.

By 2002 ASU could have been characterized as a minimally performing public agency. At $9,230 per FTE student, base state investment remained high when compared with institutional peers among public research universities. The operating budget had increased to $750 million. A four-year graduation rate of 28.4 percent meant that student outcomes had marginally improved. Resident undergraduate tuition and fees had increased to $3,527 per year and 22 percent of undergraduates received Pell Grants. Thus, one might term these levels of tuition and fees and aid middling. Freshman diversity could be characterized as middling as well: 71.2 percent of the student population reported as white and 17.2 percent reported as underrepresented minorities. At this point the institution made a correspondingly middling contribution to knowledge production: annual research expenditures had climbed to a mere $123 million.

By 2018 ASU can finally be characterized as an established public academic enterprise. Although the operating budget of the university has increased to $3.1 billion, state investment per FTE student has dipped from $9,230 in 2002 to $3,141 in 2017 dollars. Moreover, state appropriations per degree awarded have plummeted from $39,830 in 2017 dollars to $12,905 in FY 2017. As delineated in this chapter, student outcomes, including retention and graduation rates for all students—but in particular, Arizona residents—are at their highest levels ever. During the past academic year, ASU welcomed the largest freshman class of Arizona residents in the history of the university or any Arizona university. Roughly half of Arizona undergraduate resident students arrived from families earning below the state's median income. Approximately 84 percent of Arizona undergraduate resident students, spanning every income level, received need- or merit-based gift aid, with an average gift award of approximately $8,300. Arizona ranks fourth in the nation for students graduating with the lowest amount of debt. Forty percent of resident students graduate debt-free. ASU has become far more accessible and attractive to students from families with lower and modest incomes during a period of tuition increases. This has been achieved at the same time that ASU has become a school of choice for students for whom affordability is not an issue.

These data represent years of intense focus on enhancing the performance of the university, including cost control, which has positioned ASU among the most efficient producers of higher education in the nation. ASU has reduced the cost to the state to produce a degree by approximately 75 percent. Moreover, ASU has increased the number of degrees awarded by approximately 300 percent during the past twelve years and the number of high-need degrees by even more. ASU has lowered the needed resources per student from the state by more than 50 percent, but, even at this new level, state investment remains insufficient. Despite the state's continued lack of sufficient investment in Arizona students during a period of unprecedented enrollment growth, the strong financial position of the university may be attributed to the continued focus of the university on both excellence and efficiency.

Within the context of the Strategic Enterprise Plan, ASU proposes a new model for public university finance in Arizona, which includes the following: (1) the university will cover all the operating and capital costs of the university from nonstate sources; (2) the state will support 50 percent of the cost of instruction for Arizona resident students—more than 50,000 at present—at the new audited low cost basis of $16,000 per year; (3) the state will allow the university to operate as a public enterprise and in that mode use market forces, advanced management practices, and the most advanced technological foundation conceivable to advance the university; and (4) the state will occasionally—every decade or so—support the development of state-of-the-art research infrastructure.

Strong economies are inextricably linked with an educated workforce and thriving colleges and universities. ASU drives the economy forward by creating new knowledge and supporting existing business, social, and public service enterprises, as well as attracting new companies and other interests to Arizona. But because ASU is an academic enterprise, the commitment of the university to discovery, creativity, and innovation, and to the students of Arizona, is not contingent upon state support. As a consequence of organizational design changes, technological innovations, and an entrepreneurial spirit that permeates the entire institution, it costs substantially less to educate a student in 2018 than in 2008. Costs are 21 percent below the average of all four-year public research universities nationwide. These figures assume even more significance when one considers that ASU ranks among the top 16 percent worldwide for graduate employability, ranking ahead of such institutions as Penn State, Georgetown, and Michigan State, according to *QS World University Rankings.*

Meanwhile, the value of an ASU degree continues to rise. More than seven thousand companies scout ASU student talent every year, and blue-chip companies, including Apple, Ford Motor Company, Mayo Clinic, and Honeywell have designated ASU a premier university for recruiting. Nine out of ten ASU graduates have received a job offer or are in graduate school within three months of graduation. These outcomes and those delineated in this case study did not happen overnight or as a result of political pressure but are a result of the high demand for world-class university graduates and the unwavering commitment of the university to providing the highest quality education at the lowest price possible. The institution has retained its medium price point in terms of resident undergraduate tuition and fees, which in 2018 were $10,792, but has shifted to significantly higher levels of financial aid, with 36.1 percent of undergraduates receiving Pell Grants.

As a large-scale, sociotechnically integrated, research-extensive institution that through scale, scope, and differentiation has achieved the potential to dramatically impact Arizona, by 2025 ASU will be producing 60 percent of the high-demand degrees in Arizona, conducting 50 percent of the research for all the public universities in the state, awarding 55 percent of all degrees, and managing 55 percent of all student enrollment. As subsequently assessed, ASU has already become one of the top ten institutions in the nation for research expenditures among institutions without a medical school. Metric targets for the public enterprise model in 2025 project total enrollment of 125,000 students, including both immersion and online. Total degrees conferred will number 32,000, with 15,000 in STEM, education, and health professions. Research expenditures are projected to soar to $815 million. Net tuition—after grants, gift aid, and tuition benefits but no loans—will remain roughly $2,200 per year (figures 16 and 17).

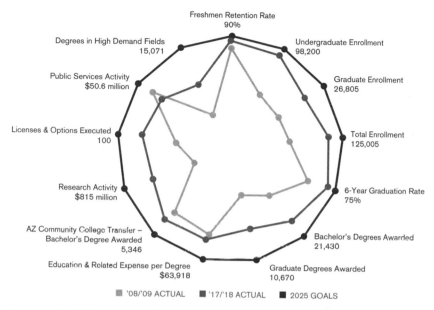

FIGURE 16. ASU has made substantial progress on its metric goals since 2008–2009. Analysis: Kyle Whitman

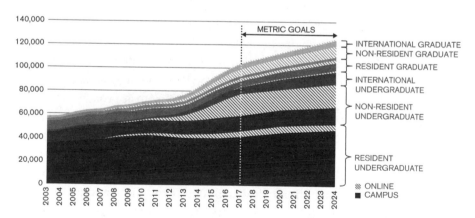

FIGURE 17. History of enrollment changes by type of student and targets for enrollment through 2025

Universities facilitated the birth of alternative learning platforms such as massive open online courses (MOOCs) by developing and validating their instructional methods and supplying their content. New learning models in online education, including degree-granting online platforms bear little resemblance to preceding efforts in this context. For example, ASU's EdPlus is an enterprise design unit that advances the design and scalable delivery of digital education and incorporates adaptive learning methodologies to personalize the online experience for more than 47,000 students. Adaptive learning and artificial intelligence technologies developed by EdPlus have turned online learning into a fully personalized experience that tracks the pace of individual students. These tools can facilitate teaching and learning across the entire network of national service universities. These and other new online education methodologies are supported by research-based advances in the theory and practice of teaching, driven by innovative colleges of education such as the ASU Mary Lou Fulton Teachers College, which integrates these findings into new technologies and approaches that are tested in the field through partnerships with school systems.[67]

## A New Framework for a Fifth Wave University

At the heart of the deliberate effort to reconceptualize a late-stage Fourth Wave research university first as a New American University and then more recently as a prototype knowledge enterprise spearheading the emergence of the Fifth Wave is the collaborative "design process" first assessed in our previous book. Given the central role of the design process in the transformation of the institution, we offer the following synopsis of the process as well as assess the theoretical aspects of institutional design in chapter 6. An inclusive, bottom-up approach enabled by top-down and center-out empowerment of relatively autonomous faculty committees, or design teams, restructured the academic framework of the entire institution. Organizational theorists thus envision optimal institutional change driven not by an administrative elite but rather by "passionate individuals distributed throughout and even outside the institution, supported by institutional leaders who . . . realize that this wave of change cannot be imposed from the top down."[68]

Application of an iterative "design-build" method—a concept borrowed from the architectural profession and construction industry—remains among the most effective of possible approaches to restructuring academic and administrative frameworks. Design-build refers to the integration of conception and execution by a single team. The process may be likened to a sequence of *charettes*, which the *Oxford English Dic-*

*tionary* defines as a "period of intense (group) work, typically undertaken in order to meet a deadline. Also: a collaborative workshop focusing on a particular problem or project." In some cases the relative autonomy of design teams assumed the tenor of a "skunkworks," an industry term that in broad usage specifies an informal and autonomous group often working in isolation. Retrenchment to the proverbial drawing board permitted teams to assume a "blank slate" standpoint that encourages thought experiments. The architectonic metaphors enlisted in this context suggest the imperative for structural change as well as continuous adaptation and recalibration through repeated course corrections.[69]

The overarching objective of the reconfiguration of academic organization was to advance teaching and research through the development of a federation of unique and differentiated transdisciplinary departments, research centers, institutes, schools, and colleges—organizational constructs henceforth generally referred to as "colleges and schools," with colleges representing a particular amalgamation of schools. These new academic entities ("new schools") have been conceptualized to advance research-pedagogical learning and research and development that possess the interdisciplinary breadth to address the large-scale grand challenges that confront global humanity. The restructuring of academic organization also represents the operationalization of an institutional context for interdisciplinarity that promotes collaborative engagement and must be appreciated within the broader context of the comprehensive reconceptualization of all aspects of the entire institution. Following reconceptualization, some core disciplines remain departmentally based, while faculty associated with other disciplines have become resident in a growing number of explicitly interdisciplinary academic units. The accommodation of interdisciplinarity generally aligns with the intent to facilitate teaching and research or, more narrowly, to address a specific research challenge. Although administrative efficiency is sometimes cited as an objective, the identification of a research problem or theme, whether strategic, tactical, or methodological, has generally motivated the establishment or reorganization of a particular academic unit. A glimpse at some of the new schools and initiatives suggests their alignment with the design aspirations of the New American University model and ambitions of the Fifth Wave.

The university was reconceptualized as a single and unified academic and administrative infrastructure distributed across four campuses without campus-level governance. In this decentralized model, deans and directors of colleges and schools assume responsibility for academic leadership. Because the implicit hierarchization of what are inevitably termed satellite campuses of large public universities is counterproductive to student success, an explicit non-hierarchical relationship obtains between the four campuses. Because the "school-centric" model devolves intellectual and entrepreneurial responsibility to the level of the college and school, academic units are empowered to exercise a measure of autonomy and compete for renown and resources not intramurally but to the extent of market limits with peer entities globally. Although the design process sought to extrapolate from the existing academic structure and operations rather than recur to historical models, the federation of semi-autonomous constituent academic units loosely corresponds to the prototype of the University of London, which was formed in 1836 primarily for administrative purposes to join University College London with King's College London, established respectively in 1826 and 1829. Nineteen autonomous and self-governing institutions presently constitute the University of London federation, which apart from the two founding universities includes such heterogeneous and differentiated world-class institutions as the London School of Economics and Political Science, London Business School, London School of Hygiene and Tropical Medicine, and SOAS, formerly the School of Oriental and African Studies.[70]

The reorganization of the life sciences faculties that coincided with the initiation of the reconceptualization appears in retrospect to adumbrate the extent of the impending interdisciplinary reconfiguration. In July 2003, the biology, microbiology, and plant biology departments and the program in molecular and cellular biology merged to form the new ASU School of Life Sciences (SOLS). Within a framework of seven faculty groups, more than one hundred life scientists, engineers, philosophers, social scientists, and ethicists now self-organize around key societal and environmental challenges. An allied bioscience endeavor formed a decade ago, the Biodesign Institute is a major transdisciplinary research center addressing critical global challenges in health care, sustainability, and national security by developing solutions inspired from natural systems and translating those into commercially viable products and clinical practices. By advancing biologically inspired design and fostering the convergence of the broad scientific fields of biology, nanotechnology, informatics, and engineering under one roof, the institute advances understanding in human health and the environment through research in such areas as personalized diagnostics and treatment, infectious diseases and pandemics, national security threats, ubiquitous sensing, optimized human performance, environmental sustainability, and renewable sources of energy. As one of a small cadre of institutions that have embraced a mandate for fundamental transformation, ASU recognizes the imperative to scale to support vanguard research on problems that will be solved only through large-scale collaborative inter- and transdisciplinary efforts. The intent to pioneer vanguard research and development capabilities represents a significant departure from the traditional model of individual-investigator initiatives and requires Biodesign researchers to predict the trajectory of advances in the biosciences and establish large-scale collaborative and convergent programs.

Among the fifteen constituent research centers of the Biodesign Institute are the Center for Innovations in Medicine, dedicated to the improvement of medical diagnostics and the treatment and prevention of disease; ASU-Banner Neurodegenerative Disease Research Center, a research alliance to advance the treatment of Alzheimer's, Parkinson's, and other neurodegenerative diseases; the Virginia G. Piper Center for Personalized Diagnostics, where research teams seek to identify and test new biomarkers associated with biological subtypes of diseases like cancer to improve treatment outcomes and survivability; and the Center for Mechanisms of Evolution, which focuses on mechanisms of organismal adaptation across all the genetic, cellular, and phenotypic levels and the role of random genetic drift and recombination across populations. Biodesign teams moreover collaborate with researchers from Mayo Clinic Arizona. In collaboration with Mayo Clinic, ASU has established joint degree programs in law, business, and nursing; collaboration in bioengineering and bioinformatics research; and innovative health solutions pathways with the potential to educate 200 million people about healthcare, engage 20 million people in online health-care delivery, and enhance treatment for 2 million patients. Students who attend Mayo Medical School will have the opportunity to participate in a number of dual-degree programs, including ASU's Master's of Healthcare Delivery. A joint team science program is advancing high-impact projects with near-term clinical translation potential in biomedical engineering, sensing, and functional restoration.

In a sense, each of the Biodesign Institute research centers represents a discrete albeit interrelated team, or set of teams, which frequently include researchers from academic units throughout the university as well as industry and government partners. Team collaboration is behind the success of a new effort in synthetic biology to demonstrate how the biological information contained within ribonucleic acid (RNA) can be adapted to create logic circuits capable of performing computations; development of a diagnostic platform called ImmunoSignature, which with a single drop of blood can detect diseases that involve an immune response, including cancer, autoimmune, infectious, metabolic, and neurologic diseases; and a project to enable large-scale cultivation of microalgae—species of microscopic single-cell organisms that can be used to produce renewable biofuels that recycle carbon dioxide from the atmosphere. The Atmospheric Carbon Dioxide Capture and Membrane Delivery project, undertaken to assist the U.S. Department of Energy (DOE) in its efforts to promote the advancement of clean and renewable energy, brings together teams of researchers from the Swette Center for Environmental Biotechnology, Center for Negative Carbon Emissions, and Center for Applied Structural Discovery (CASD)—constituent research centers of the Biodesign Institute—with physicists and civil, environmental, and sustainability engineers from the School of Sustainable Engineering and the Built Environment.[71]

Among the new transdisciplinary schools conceptualized and operationalized during the past decade are the School of Earth and Space Exploration (SESE); School of Human Evolution and Social Change (SHESC); School of Politics and Global Studies; School of Social Transformation; and School of Historical, Philosophical, and Religious Studies (SHPRS). SESE epitomizes efforts to institutionalize interdisciplinary collaboration. Established through an amalgamation of the former Department of Geological Sciences and the astronomy, astrophysics, and cosmology faculties of the former Department of Physics and Astronomy—thereafter the Department of Physics—SESE includes theoretical physicists, systems biologists, biogeochemists, and engineers who advance the development and deployment of critical scientific instrumentation. Transdisciplinary fluidity facilitates collaboration among more than sixty faculty members and one hundred research scientists, engineers, and postdoctoral scholars. Subfields within astrophysics and cosmology, for example, include computational astrophysics; physics of the early universe; and the formation of galaxies, stars, and planetary systems. The broad theme of exploration represents a transdisciplinary conceptualization of the quest to discover the origins of the universe and expand our understanding of space, matter, and time.

The set of new schools complements existing academic units reconceptualized along interdisciplinary lines. The Ira A. Fulton Schools of Engineering, for example, have evolved from a single conventional college of engineering and applied sciences to comprise five distinct research-intensive transdisciplinary schools: the School of Biological and Health Systems Engineering; School of Computing, Informatics, and Decision Systems Engineering; School of Electrical, Computer, and Energy Engineering; School for Engineering of Matter, Transport, and Energy; and School for Sustainable Engineering and the Built Environment. A sixth school, the Polytechnic School, focuses on use-inspired translational research and offers students interested in direct entry into the workforce an experiential learning environment. Within these six schools, more than two dozen research centers advance interdisciplinary collaboration, including the Security and Defense Systems Initiative, which addresses national and global security and defense challenges through an integrative systems approach; Flexible Display Center, a cooperative agreement with the U.S. Army to advance the emerging flexible electronics industry; and LightWorks, an endeavor in renewable energy fields, including artificial photosynthesis, biofuels, and next-generation photovoltaics. Prominent transdisciplinary initiatives in the humanities and social sciences include the Institute for Humanities Research; Center for the Study of Religion and Conflict, which promotes research on the dynamics of religion in contemporary society with the objective of seeking solutions and informing policy; Complex Adaptive Systems Initiative (CASI), a collaborative effort to address global challenges in health, sustainability, and national security; and the Consortium for Science, Policy, and Outcomes (CSPO). CSPO is dedicated to interdisciplinary examination of the societal and cultural context within which science is conducted and seeks to enhance the contributions of science and technology to an improved quality of life, with particular attention to distributional impacts—questions of who is likely to benefit from public investments in knowledge production and innovation. A new Washington, DC, Center serves as a platform for engagement with national and global affairs, increasing the visibility of the university as well as its capacity for impact. Just three blocks from the White House, this renovated historic eight-floor structure facilitates the activities of eighteen academic units, providing space for visiting scholars and student interns, and even housing a news studio for broadcast journalism students from ASU's Walter Cronkite School of Journalism and Mass Communication.

With more than six thousand artists, designers, and scholars collaborating across five schools and a major university art museum, the Herberger Institute for Design and the Arts comprises the School of Art; School of Film, Dance, and Theater; Design School, which offers degrees in architecture, environmental design, industrial design, interior design, landscape architecture, urban design, and visual communication; School of Music; and the School of Arts, Media, and Engineering (AME), which conducts research on experiential media that integrate computation and digital media with the physical human experience. Established as a joint initiative between the Herberger Institute and the Ira A. Fulton Schools of Engineering, AME transcends the constraints of existing technologies to solve real-world problems in an increasingly digital world. The school will play a key role in the new Creative Futures immersive media studio, which trains students in the transdisciplinary digital expertise essential to augmented reality, virtual reality, and immersive and interactive media spaces. Innovation Space pairs business, engineering, design, and sustainability students with clients to prepare leaders with the mind-set, skill sets, and practice needed to design and develop successful ventures and products in any industry or sector. Students acquire both the expert skills and core competencies needed to think across complex systems to create products, services, and business models that provide value to all stakeholders in a world of growing uncertainty and ambiguity.

The National Accelerator for Cultural Innovation works with field partners to advance the roles of artists and designers in facilitating social change and reimagining the public good. Recognizing that gradu-

ates will not necessarily find themselves on the concert stage or in traditional art and design spaces, Dean Steven J. Tepper devised the
initiative to elevate the role of artists and designers as key contributors
to societal well-being. Under the auspices of the Accelerator and funded
in part by a grant from the National Endowment for the Arts, ASU established the Practices for Change fellowship, which is rooted in the belief that creative practices have the potential to scale up new ways of
integrating art and design as powerful tools for social change. A new online digital photography program exemplifies the commitment of the
Herberger Institute to scaling studio-based design to make the arts accessible to nontraditional students.

In May 2018 the Los Angeles County Museum of Art (LACMA) and
Herberger Institute announced an unprecedented partnership designed
to increase curatorial and leadership diversity in the museum field. The
fellowship for curators from diverse backgrounds combines rigorous academic instruction with on-the-job experience at LACMA or the ASU
Art Museum. An unconventional partnership with renowned artist
James Turrell exemplifies the sort of collaboration that is a hallmark of
the New American University model. Turrell has transformed Roden
Crater, an extinct volcano on the edge of the Painted Desert in northern
Arizona, into a large-scale installation fusing art, engineering, astronomy, and architecture that plays with viewers' perceptions of light and
space. The partnership has permitted ASU to leverage the project for
educational purposes and aid in its completion so that it can be opened
to the public. In 2018–2019, ASU students from five field lab classes vis-
ited and studied the project in such contexts as sacred architecture and
indigenous astronomy, learned about color from a theoretical astrophys-
icist, and participated in a workshop on the sense of taste. Students described their visits as inspirational and transformative, a testament to the
power of art to transform knowledge and the human experience.

Design is a critical dimension of the University City Exchange (UCX),
a university-wide initiative directed by designer and architect Wellington ("Duke") Reiter that exemplifies ASU's commitment to "leveraging
place," the first of the eight design principles of the New American University. Finding common cause with our immediate surroundings and
municipalities is a prominent feature of our agenda as the fortunes of the
university and the city of which it is a part are inextricably linked. With

this in mind, the essential function of UCX is to ensure a consistent, nimble, and innovative address for this mutually beneficial pairing. Locally, UCX is especially attentive to the still-forming urban experiment in the heart of the Sonoran Desert that is Phoenix—one of the fastest-growing metropolitan regions in the United States. Accordingly, as the premier educational and research entity in the region, ASU has assumed a "fundamental responsibility for the economic, social, cultural, and overall health of the communities it serves," as stated in the ASU Charter.

Probably the most overt demonstration of conjoining the interests of the university and the city is the ASU Phoenix Downtown campus. In the early 2000s, the urban core of the nation's sixth-largest city lacked the vitality one would expect, and the installation of several large sports facilities had not altered that equation. The idea of creating an academic and research enterprise in close proximity to business, government, hospitals, media, nonprofits, and entrepreneurs seemed a win on many fronts. The citizens agreed, and in 2006 passed a bond election, 2:1, to make this vision possible. Today, the stated goal of fifteen thousand students living and learning in the city is a fulfillment of the "leveraging place" imperative, and the unique cluster of colleges and schools on the downtown campus exemplifies the public mission of the university. An urban educational environment combines the syncopation of everyday life with the regimented demands of the college curriculum and academic calendar. The offerings of the ASU Downtown Phoenix campus were chosen expressly because students would be in the company of working journalists, health-care professionals, public officials, and experts and practitioners of all backgrounds. Unquestionably, both Phoenix and ASU are enriched as a result, as are the students who are enhancing and benefiting from each. The collaboration has become a national model. The University of Central Florida, for example, worked with ASU representatives to re-create a similar university-city partnership for a new purpose-built facility in downtown Orlando.

But UCX and ASU are about more than buildings, campuses, and real estate. We have moved well beyond the frequently invoked "town-gown" frictions in many other locales. Instead, our attention is directed toward a dynamic public realm, the highest design standards, integral economic development, sustainability in all of its manifestations, and the building of an inclusive and equitable city. The overarching goal is to optimize the deep intellectual and research assets of the university and apply them to significant questions associated with the world we are building. Demonstrations of the geographic and programmatic expansiveness of the UCX "leveraging place" mandate include a number of long-term projects, beginning with Rio Reimagined. At the request of the late senator John McCain, the university is leading the rejuvenation of more than fifty miles of the Salt River so that it will become an engine for economic development, community advancement, and water responsibility. With the world's fifth-largest economy immediately to our west and tens of thousands of students coming to ASU from Southern California, ASU is establishing a high-impact presence in Los Angeles via the renovation of the historic Herald Examiner Building. And in keeping with the New American University orientation and contextualization, an initiative termed Ten Across (10X) illustrates how the 2,400-mile U.S. Interstate 10 corridor provides a compelling window on the future of the country.

### "The Future Is for Everyone"

As platforms for knowledge production, economic growth, and societal transformation, our nation's research universities must seek to ensure that scientific discovery and technological innovation lead to equitable societal benefit and contribute to global prosperity and well-being. Accordingly, the Consortium for Science, Policy and Outcomes (CSPO) has for the past two decades served as an intellectual network committed to enhancing the contributions of science and technology to society's pursuit of equality, justice, freedom, prosperity, and overall quality of life. CSPO has emerged as a globally preeminent science and technology policy think tank; productive contributor to urgent public discussions about science, innovation, and society; and source of solutions with broad societal impact as well as significant agent of change within the university itself. For the fifth consecutive year, CSPO has been named one of the top ten think tanks for science and technology policy by the Think Tanks and Civil Societies Program of the Lauder Institute of the University of Pennsylvania.[72] With the more recent creation of the university-wide Institute for the Future of Innovation in Society (IF/IS) and School for the Future of Innovation in Society (SFIS), launched in

2015, CSPO is now positioned to pursue a more comprehensive and strategic set of ambitions aimed at enhancing societal capacity for understanding and managing sociotechnical change. The formation of the institute and school constitute a major amplification of institutional capacities, while building directly on and from current activities. These efforts place the role of human agency and responsibility at the forefront of considerations of innovation and seek to transform ASU into a test bed and driving force for defining and promoting the responsible role of knowledge-based innovation in addressing the grand challenges of the twenty-first century.[73]

Initially conceived in 1997 as the Center for Science, Policy, and Outcomes, CSPO—a project of Columbia University—was located in Washington, DC, and augmented by strategic alliances with other institutions and foundations. The center connected science policy scholarship with policy discourse aimed at enhancing the contributions of science and technology to an improved quality of life, with particular attention to distributional impacts—questions of who is likely to benefit from public investments in knowledge production and innovation. The center was reconstituted as the consortium at ASU in July 2004 and retains an orientation toward scholarship associated with key concepts operative during the formative period of conceptualization. These include that desired outcomes can drive science, that the societal value of new knowledge is determined by how it is used and by whom, and that the definition of the problem helps determine the relevance of the research.[74] Since 2008, the reconstituted CSPO has operated a center in Washington, DC (CSPO-DC), that serves as a nucleus for a diverse array of collaborations and partnerships with government agencies and NGOs.

With the formation of the School for the Future of Innovation in Society, the school assumed the status of overarching institutional structure. SFIS exercises formidable strategic capacities in three broad areas: governance of emerging technologies, science policy and social outcomes, and science-society engagement. Its influential scholarship, academic networks, and policy and public outreach programs contribute to a model of institutional innovation that catalyzes an evolving international agenda for responsible innovation. This work includes the fundamental theoretical contribution of anticipatory governance, implementation of research and engagement methods of real-time technology assessment, and prototyping of both across major science and engineering initiatives. An important related research thrust advances sociotechnical integration, which brings social scientists and natural scientists into collaboration with engineers in the laboratory and experts and practitioners in industry. CSPO and SFIS scholarship on technological governance embodies a comprehensive agenda for public engagement and outreach. Both CSPO and SFIS have developed innovative deliberative and learning environments for scientists and engineers and have spurred a prodigious publication output that includes two book series, notably *The Rightful Place of Science*, and various journals, including the *Journal of Responsible Innovation* and, in partnership with the National Academies, *Issues in Science and Technology*.

An array of independent but related projects are coalescing as cornerstones for strategic development and as a foundation for research and training, with such themes as energy and society, sociotechnical futures, and the intersection of development, sustainability, and innovation. Initiatives in this latter context, for example, may include participatory technology development, community-based adaptation, and the resilience of farmers in South Asia; the emergence and evolution of innovation systems in Africa; the role of social media in democracy movements; higher education as a focus of national development; and the importance of multiple knowledge systems in solution-based approaches to sustainable development. Global engagement is represented by research projects in Ecuador, India, Kenya, Morocco, Nepal, Pakistan, Turkey, and Uganda, some of which has been conducted collaboratively with the School of Sustainability. Moreover, collaboration with universities abroad and international organizations, including the World Bank, United Nations Development Program, International Center for Integrated Mountain Development, and an array of nongovernmental organizations (NGOs) provides expanded platforms for scholarly engagement. CSPO-DC has led efforts to build a community of practice around innovative R&D program management that has resulted in strong ties to programs in several federal agencies, including NOAA, NASA, GAO, and NSF, as well as OMB and OSTP, where SFIS and agency personnel regularly interact to strengthen the social outcomes of federal R&D activities.

SFIS coordinates dynamic collaborative initiatives with colleges, schools, institutes, and research centers throughout the university, some of which are critical centripetal forces within the university as a whole. "The future is for everyone" is the tagline of the school, and because questions regarding the outcomes of science and technology are inherently forward looking, SFIS strategically confronts this orientation by building capacity for future-oriented scholarship that also involves a strong participatory and deliberative dimension. Exploring issues such as energy, geoengineering, human enhancement, personalized medicine, and the future of the city, research engages scientists developing emerging technologies, stakeholders deliberating the societal consequences of nanotechnology, and policy and industrial audiences exploring the implications of responsible innovation. Incubated within the Center for Nanotechnology and Society (CNS-ASU), a semiautonomous research center within CSPO, this thrust involves a widening network of collaborations, including the Biodesign Institute on medical diagnostics, LightWorks on solar to fuels, and the School of Sustainability and City of Phoenix Planning Department on sustainable urban futures.

SFIS is centrally involved in various partnerships aimed at bringing complex science-society issues more compellingly into the public sphere. Emerge is an annual festival that brings scientists, engineers, artists, and designers together with the academic community and local public to reinvent the future. Future Tense, a partnership among ASU, New America Foundation, and *Slate* magazine, hosts a variety of DC-based activities aimed at catalyzing broader awareness of complex challenges of science, technology, policy, and society. The Frankenstein Bicentennial Project, a global celebration of the bicentennial of the publication of the novel *Frankenstein; or The Modern Prometheus*, by Mary Shelley, in 1818, was led by SFIS and the Center for Science and the Imagination. In a new annotated edition of the novel, SFIS founding director David Guston and colleagues observe that the novel enduringly "influences the way we confront emerging science and technology, conceptualize the process of scientific research, imagine the motivations and ethical struggles of scientists, and weigh the benefits of scientific research against its anticipated and unforeseen pitfalls."[75]

While it is entirely possible to argue that the speed and transformative nature of technological innovation is in the eye of the beholder—

always fastest and most disruptive to the present-day observer—it is hard to ignore indicators that global society is at an inflection point in what we can achieve through emerging science and technology, and the profound implications of how these play out within an increasingly interconnected and dynamic society. Some of these indicators lie in technological advances themselves: our increasing mastery of biological code; the emergence of powerful new computer technologies, including artificial intelligence; and our growing ability to design and construct the very materials our lives depend on. Our ability to not only code in biological bases, computer bits, and atoms, but to cross-code between these, is releasing us from the constraints imposed by the natural world, and is opening the way to technologies that would have been impossible just a few short years ago. Yet these purely technological advances are being modulated and amplified by equally powerful changes in the social, economic, legal, and political ecosystems within which they exist. The interplay between growing connectivity, shifting social norms and expectations, and new technologies, is leading to feedback loops that are making the future increasingly hard to predict. Except that we know that it will be radically different from the present we live in. This maelstrom of change is captured in the discourse surrounding technological convergence and the so-termed Fourth Industrial Revolution, the new ethics of transformative technologies, and what socially responsible innovation means in a changing world. And at the heart of these conversations there are two dominant narratives: (1) the need for thinking and understanding around innovation-driven change that transcends traditional disciplines and concepts and (2) the need to equip people to survive and thrive in a future where there is no guarantee that the knowledge and skills of yesterday will be the those needed tomorrow. This is the space that SFIS sets out to occupy. By enabling experts to combine knowledge and insights in innovative ways, the school is mapping out the emerging landscape around new technologies in an evolving society. But more than this, it is helping reveal new pathways through this landscape. And through its research and educational programs and engagement with innovators, policymakers, and members of the public, it is working toward the knowledge, understanding, tools, and skills that will be essential for ensuring that society thrives through the transitions that confront us.[76]

SFIS offers undergraduate and graduate degree programs, including the PhD program in Human and Social Dimensions of Science and Technology (HSD), which fuses knowledge and insights from the humanities, social and natural sciences, and fields of engineering to rethink human agency in science and technology to confront the fundamental governance challenges of our time in such sectors as energy, health care, information, development, sustainability, and biotechnology. The Master of Science and Technology Policy (MSTP) helps students build a professional foundation for working in the public and private sectors at the interface of science, technology, policy, and society. The program has placed interns and graduates in the U.S. Government Accountability Office (GAO), White House Office of Science and Technology Policy (OSTP), International Food Policy Research Institute, NASA, and various scientific professional societies, nonprofit agencies, and technology companies. The Master of Science in Global Technology and Development (GTD) is a professional program for practitioners in the field of development that empowers students with the capacity to understand and analyze the intersections of technological and human development across comparative social, political, and economic contexts, to use that knowledge to assess the impacts and implications of development for society, and to influence appropriate policies and programs for the future. A new PhD program in Innovation and Global Development complements GTD and provides an opportunity for students to pursue research on the global interplay among innovation and political, social, and economic development in a low-residency fashion.

Looking ahead, SFIS has proposed a new master of science in public interest technology, meant to advance the training of professional students who can blend technical and social expertise to create policies and technologies that advance the public good. A growing population of CSPO and SFIS alums are working in settings where they are putting their academic training into real world practice, in organizations including the American Association for the Advancement of Science (AAAS), Argonne National Laboratory, Booz Allen Hamilton, Brookings Institution, California Ocean Sciences Trust, Federal Aviation Administration, Mercatus Center at George Mason University, NASA, United Nations, U.S. Army, U.S. Department of Agriculture, GAO, and Peace Corps.

The underlying philosophy within SFIS of constructive co-creation of ideas and insights between very different areas of expertise is a powerful catalyst for new thinking on risk. This is where concepts such as risk as a threat to value and approaching complex challenges as a multidimensional "risk landscape" between the present and the future draw on the creativity and innovation that comes from partnerships that transcend conventional boundaries. Risk innovation is a framework for thinking about emerging risks that is championed by the ASU Risk Innovation Lab. Andrew Maynard, professor and director of the program, explains that risk innovation grapples with the growing divide between novel ways in which innovation can lead to harm and the inadequacies of conventional approaches to risk. At its core, this framework recognizes that risks emerging from innovation—especially technological innovation—demand parallel innovation in how to understand them and respond to them. This is clear where science and technology are leading to step-changes in capabilities, such as gene editing, self-driving cars, advanced applications of artificial intelligence, and the development of esoteric new materials. In these and similar cases, existing risk paradigms are often inadequate to the task of identifying potential harm arising from new technological capabilities and of informing appropriate courses of action. Yet as the coupling between technology innovation, the environment, and society, becomes increasingly tight, further categories of risk are emerging that transcend conventional thinking. These include the potential impacts of technologies on social justice, privacy, and personal and national security. But they also involve how a shifting sociotechnological landscape potentially threatens values such as dignity, self-worth, deeply held beliefs, and sense of community. Here, a radical rethink of what risk means and how to use this to not only survive but thrive in the future is critical. Through such areas of programmatic focus as the Risk Innovation Lab, the school's students become part of a larger community of thinkers, knowledge-generators, and practitioners who are both equipped for and committed to ensuring that, whatever the future brings, society will have the insights, skills, and tools to ensure that it is beneficial for as many people as possible.[77]

Keeping Our Planet Habitable

Acknowledging the certainty of major environmental and societal crises in the decades ahead, ASU has announced the formation of the Global Futures Laboratory, which seeks to position the university as a global hub of international alliances and networks of scientists and scholars collaborating to address the most critical issues related to human society and the future of our planet, including the transition of the societal, natural, and biogeochemical systems of planet Earth. Specific focal areas explore new energy systems, food security and land degradation, environmental and public health, depletion of natural resources, water scarcity, decision-making and behavior, and the imperative for new economies. The natural and socioeconomic systems of our planet are on nonsustainable paths, and some subsystems are close to or have exceeded critical thresholds. Global Futures represents the commitment of the university to advancing knowledge production and innovation that seek to secure a habitable planet and future in which prosperity and well-being are broadly attainable. Harnessing the capacities of academia for discovery and innovation, Global Futures will develop options for the purposeful design of our future and proactive planetary management to achieve sustained habitability and improved well-being for all humankind. Global Futures seeks to assert and advance the role of academia in the debate about and decision making for the future of our planet and global society. Academia will play a key role in shaping this debate by informing it with the best knowledge available and by anticipating— through effective exchange with a broad stakeholder community— which critical interventions will steer us toward a sustainable and globally connected future. The initiative leverages ASU's proven ability to work seamlessly across disciplines to address complex global challenges and is rooted in the conviction that ASU possesses the intellectual and creative capacity to connect thinkers and makers, forge partnerships within and beyond academia, and explore the right questions and develop the most fruitful responses. The willingness of society to change and recognize planetary boundaries, however, will be key to success in embarking on a trajectory toward a sustainable future.[78]

Academic culture has responded slowly to human impact on the dynamic and interactive system of complex biogeochemical cycles that constitutes the Earth system, which since the advent of industrialization has fallen increasingly under the influence of humankind. Academia contributed to enabling the Industrial Revolution by providing scientific knowledge to the epistemic base of technological innovation but was not equipped to guide society vis-à-vis the rapid changes triggered by this accelerated phase of development. Nor has it more recently proactively led the processes of rapid technological and societal change. Humankind is pushing hard against planetary boundaries and using more resources than the planet has to offer. The Earth system is out of equilibrium and has reached a state of imbalance that threatens the habitability of the planet. As a consequence, humankind has left the domain of a safe operating space, and academia must assume a mandate to chart a pathway toward a sustainable future for our planet. Global society, through its knowledge enterprises and decision-making entities, must embark on a trajectory that reestablishes a balance that will allow further prospering of global society in the so-called Anthropocene era.[79]

Global Futures will serve as a matrix for transdisciplinary holistic knowledge production and cutting-edge technological innovation and facilitate the engagement of scientists and scholars with a global network encompassing business and industry, government laboratories agencies, and organizations in civil society. Successful implementation assumes breaking new intellectual ground in understanding, quantifying, and projecting/predicting complex systems, as well as modifying (engineering) them while minimizing negative effects to the extent they can be recognized or anticipated. Research, for example, might seek to provide basic understanding of the factors determining the capacity and limits of the planet for further development vis-à-vis physical and biogeochemical systems, socioeconomic and sociocultural dynamics, political institutions, and societal choices. This research would also include design solutions to problems caused by anthropogenic pressure on the environment, vis-à-vis degradation of life supporting systems and depletion of natural resources, and analysis of the economic feasibility of implementations on local, regional, and global scales. The attainment of a sustainable future critically depends on expanding the role of academia in bridging the spaces between idea generation, design of solutions, translation, and application and implementation. Utilizing the full breadth and depth of the innovative capacity of academia, Global Futures will conduct Planetary Management Symposia that convene leading international experts around timely topics related to the future of the planet. Examples of topics are climate engineering, new global commons, stability of societal structures, environmental decision-making and value systems, global connectivity, and emerging hotspots approaching critical thresholds. The laboratory will advance the formation of networks and leagues to connect scientists and scholars to create a platform for wide-ranging exchange about global futures across all knowledge domains. An initiative termed Earth Observation, for example, would monitor human behavior and function to provide inputs for real-time visualization of the state of the planet and contribute to the capacity of academic research to impact long-term decision making.

Because stakeholders are frequently key facilitators of knowledge transfer and essential in defining the directions of research, engagement with a broadly defined group will be essential, especially to expand the discourse beyond the traditional confines of academia. A stakeholder dialogue platform has the potential to advance academia's engagement in problems of immediate concern to society and engage stakeholders in academic research and education from project design to synthesis of results and recommendations for implementation of solutions from local to global scales. A more operationally oriented approach combines the imperative to address such challenges as the accelerating climate crisis, the global water challenge, ecosystem degradation, and the effects of pollution on public health with emerging opportunities and new insights from the natural and social sciences as well as the humanities to create new platforms to advance synergies. Despite lingering resistance from traditional disciplines to new transdisciplinary training of new generations of students, Global Futures will educate problem solvers and innovators to build the capacity of a diverse and inclusive workforce.

More than a decade ago, ASU declared its intent to become the world leader in sustainability research and education, taking the first steps in 2004 with the launch of the Global Institute of Sustainability and, two years later, with the charter of the School of Sustainability, the first in academia. Scientists, scholars, policymakers, and experts in sustainability from ASU and around the world gathered in Temozón, Mexico, that year to consider how a large public research university could best commit itself to sustainability as a core value in its teaching, research, and public engagement. The discourse from that gathering led to the establishment of the Julie Ann Wrigley Global Institute of Sustainability, envisioned to function as the hub for all of ASU's global sustainability efforts. With the establishment of the Julie Ann Wrigley Global Institute of Sustainability (GIOS) in 2004 and the charter of the School of Sustainability in 2006, ASU assumed a mandate to advance transdisciplinary teaching and research on social, economic, and environmental sustainability. GIOS facilitates solutions-focused transdisciplinary research that is often not rewarded in traditional academia and brings into collaboration scholars, scientists, and engineers with citizen stakeholders, government policy makers, and industry leaders to share knowledge and expertise and develop solutions to the challenges of sustainability. With research in areas as diverse as air quality, arts, humanities, economics, food systems, marine ecology, mathematics, materials design, medicine, nanotechnology, policy and governance, renewable energy, risk assessment, transportation, urban ecology, and urban infrastructure, the faculty members affiliated with GIOS are addressing some of the most critical challenges of our time as well as training future generations of scholars, scientists, and practitioners.

Among many collaborative, stakeholder-engaged, and solutions-focused initiatives in GIOS that represent the university's commitment to use-inspired, socially embedded, transdisciplinary teaching and research is the Decision Center for a Desert City (DCDC), which seeks to understand the impacts of regional climate and land-use changes on urban water systems. The center works in the context of sustainability transitions in the Colorado River Basin and uses simulation modeling and visual analytics to integrate knowledge and the biophysical and socioeconomic determinants of water-systems policymaking. We assess DCDC as a boundary organization in chapter 5. An initiative in urban ecology has led its founding investigators to develop the Urban Resilience to Extremes Sustainability Research Network (UREx SRN). Working with a growing number of cities in the western hemisphere, researchers are conceptualizing and deploying strategies for the development of resilient infrastructure, many of which are ecologically based and designed to improve the quality of life from day to day and mitigate effects of extreme weather events.

Since 2012, ASU's Rob and Melani Walton Sustainability Solutions Initiatives have engaged organizations and more than half a million individuals in their quest to solve global sustainability problems. A sustainability consultancy, the initiative was established to work with external clients and partners around the world. A Knowledge Exchange for Resilience builds on the success of the university in building mutually beneficial partnerships with the goal of making Maricopa County a model for university-community collaboration to foster positive change and improve resilience in economic and environmental stresses.

The School of Sustainability is the first school in the United States to offer graduate and undergraduate degrees specifically in sustainability. The school is educating a new generation of leaders through collaborative, transdisciplinary, and solution-oriented training that addresses social, economic, and environmental challenges. The school prepares students to view complex problems and solutions systemically, work collaboratively with people of differing perspectives, and create strategic solutions for a desirable and more sustainable future. Teaching and research seek adaptive solutions to such issues as rapid urbanization, water shortages, food insecurity, loss of biodiversity, energy affordability, and the development of sustainable energy, materials, and technologies. To engender an institutional culture of sustainability, ASU offers sustainability-themed courses in fields as diverse as anthropology, architecture, biology, economics, engineering, industrial design, law, philosophy, nonprofit leadership, tourism, and urban planning. Along with such guiding principles of modern societies as human rights, sustainability is an epochal question that must be addressed by the citizens of a planet with a population that already exceeds seven billion and is projected to approach ten billion. Entrenchment in disciplinary silos undermines the capacity of our institutions to advance research that can provide us with the means to balance wealth generation with continuously enhanced environmental quality and social well-being. Interdisciplinary research and teaching associated with sustainability is representative of the ASU effort to design a new model for the American research university. Today, the School of Sustainability boasts over 1,400 alumni, and ASU has served as the model for many of the hundreds of sustainability degree programs around the country.

An exhaustive survey of the hundreds of transdisciplinary centers and institutes embedded within the framework of colleges, schools, and departments that constitute the overarching academic organization of ASU would be inconceivable within the scope of a single volume. Those profiled in this chapter are intended merely to suggest the intent of the research enterprise to address the complex problems and seemingly intractable challenges that confront society in hopes of finding solutions and working toward positive change locally, nationally, internationally, and beyond, and to underscore its interrelation with the research-pedagogic curriculum.[80] Through the design process that operationalized the New American University model, the academic community has sought to rethink the institution from the ground up and, by establishing new criteria to measure success, has chosen to redefine the terms of competition with institutions that have matured over the course of centuries. The experiment has succeeded in demonstrating that an institution can compete with the world's leading universities academically, yet remain broadly inclusive even while advancing a vanguard research enterprise dedicated to the public interest.

## Toward Frameworks for Universal Learning

Arizona State University has adopted universal learning as an aspirational initiative and is designing products, processes, and capacities accordingly. Through education, training, and skill-building opportunities, ASU is evolving a model capable of being of service at scale to an ever-broadening spectrum of learners. ASU has embraced the challenge of expanding educational access to disadvantaged learners throughout the United States and around the world without compromising quality, while maintaining its commitment to research and discovery that advances public value.[81] ASU has identified three design principles that guide its pursuit of universal learning: radical access, entrepreneurial partnerships, and perpetual innovation and discovery. The concept of radical access addresses the exclusionary practices of America's colleges and universities. ASU does not ask whether a learner is ready for us but whether we are ready to serve their needs in the learning environment best suited for them—whether a college degree pathway or customized learning pathway. ASU is overcoming geographic access barriers through the work of EdPlus, which designs and implements cutting-edge online learning solutions to reach learners in all corners of the nation and world. Likewise, ASU is taking on cost barriers through innovation in financial aid that allows the university to serve an unprecedented number of Pell recipients and promises the lowest possible tuition given each student's individual circumstances.[82]

As a university that engages globally, ASU seeks to overcome barriers to educational access at global scale. Through Open Scale Courseware, ASU offers free courses and transferable credits to students in nearly every country in the world. Through Global Launch, the largest intensive English program in the United States, ASU provides English instruction to the largest international student population of any university in the nation. ASU's mission extends to learners in the most challenging economic and geopolitical circumstances in the world. With support from the U.S. Agency for International Development (USAID), ASU is helping universities in Malawi to build their capacity for online and distance learning and to serve young women and vulnerable students. In Vietnam, ASU has partnered with USAID, Intel, and a growing private-sector consortium to improve the quality of university engineering programs to support technology-led economic growth. Consistent with the objectives of universal-learning frameworks, ASU has developed Education for Humanity, an initiative to facilitate the education of the more than 44,000 people that the United Nations Refugee Agency (UNHCR) estimates are forced to flee from their accustomed lives each day as a consequence of conflict, persecution, or generalized violence. According to the agency, among the unprecedented 68.5 million individuals who have been displaced worldwide, 25.4 million are refugees, over half of whom are under the age of eighteen. More than 85 percent of refugees flee to developing countries, where most are unable to continue their educations. Most education programs for refugees, however, focus on primary schooling. Education for Humanity by contrast seeks to meet the needs of the tens of thousands of young adults who would otherwise be enrolled in college by offering rapidly deployable online courses to refugees in Lebanon, Jordan, Iraq, Uganda, and Rwanda, with the program expected soon to expand to Ethiopia and Kenya.

Advancing universal learning as a broad social aspiration necessitates diverse, far-reaching partnerships with other universities and the private sector. Accordingly, ASU is building partner networks with other institutions capable of advancing universal learning. Through the University Innovation Alliance, a consortium of large-scale public research universities that we subsequently assess in this chapter, ASU is enabling the sharing of data and solutions to support better educational outcomes and expanded educational access. The PLuS Alliance is an educational cluster including ASU, King's College London, and University of New South Wales that is advancing cross-border research and education to take on challenges that extend beyond borders in areas such as health, sustainability, innovation, and social justice. ASU's commitment to universal learning informs its partnerships with the private sector. Through its collaboration with Chemonics, the largest implementer of USAID projects globally, ASU is training the global workforce of Chemonics—many of whom reside in developing countries and are otherwise unable to access educational opportunities to support their critical work in international development. Through the Starbucks College Achievement Plan, ASU offers fully online degrees to Starbucks partners (baristas) around the world at no cost. ASU is also providing skills training and degrees to employees of Adidas and Uber, promoting a new model for public-private collaboration that creates learning opportunities for individuals in the workforce, and working with large businesses to enable large employee cohorts to gain new skills and pathways.

Knowledge-based organizations subject to market forces can rarely justify the costs of sustained commitment to innovation, and those in the public sector rarely gather the political support to tackle new initiatives. With their missions to advance and disseminate knowledge, however, research universities are different. While most knowledge organizations view knowledge as instrumentally valuable, universities see knowledge as intrinsically valuable. When knowledge is merely instrumentally valuable, its role in driving innovation can be mediated by demand. When knowledge is intrinsically valuable, there are no demand limitations. For research universities, innovation for the benefit of knowledge production and knowledge production for the benefit of innovation can advance perpetually. This unceasing commitment to discovery and innovation and integrating new knowledge into operations and educational experiences is an important foundation for universal learning. Accordingly, it is essential that research universities operate at the core of any universal-learning system.

Two major factors presently make universal learning a realistic prospect. As a result of increasing prosperity, education is more accessible than at any previous time in human history, and more learners enter adulthood equipped with the skills they need to learn at higher levels. The maturity of education systems in developed countries, combined with responsive, proactive international development programs, is assisting the growth of educational systems in the developing world to drive increased standards of living and technology-led growth. The advent of low-cost and effective technologies allow high-quality teaching and learning at scale. Over the last decade, MOOCs established proof of concept for how to leverage technology to overcome geographic and cost barriers to access. Most recently, artificial intelligence and adaptive and assisted-learning technologies have been used to decrease faculty-to-student ratios while increasing learning outcomes, providing learners with highly personalized educational experiences tailored to their life circumstances and level of intellectual development. These technologies offer the potential for testing new instructional modalities that only ratchet up in effectiveness for any given student and across cohorts of students. Collectively, these technologies allow us to provide a complete educational experience to learners in fully online and mixed teaching modes at lower cost without compromising quality. Importantly, all of these technologies are in their infancy, representing a fraction of the value they will be able to provide as they mature. College may not be for everyone, but for the many who regard degree completion as essential to the fulfillment of their potential, the configuration of higher education in the United States is poorly designed, as assessed in chapter 1. As a consequence, thirty-six million individuals between the ages of twenty-five and sixty-five started college but did not complete an associate's or bachelor's degree. To advance a universal-learning framework, ASU will optimize degree completion via a pipeline approach directed toward that end. A universal-learning framework will broaden the end goal to include other forms of postsecondary learning and therefore require changing institutional culture to embrace non-pipeline lifelong learning approaches. Such a framework would be particularly important for the university to respond to the needs of a workforce destabilized by increasing automation and the rise of the gig economy, which necessitates more frequent upskilling and reskilling.

Connecting the workforce to lifelong learning opportunities will require the design of large-scale partnerships between universities and workplaces that understand that access to education is a social imperative to national success. Colleges and universities do not easily fit together with potential corporate partners and require boundary-spanning organizations to bridge the gaps. To develop new pathways for learners, we must accelerate our understanding of corporate social impact and develop new conceptualizations of the return on investment of employee education. Designing partnerships for social impact and transformation will require the evolution of cultural norms and expectations. Within academe, these would include increased clock speed in designing and launching courses, active recognition of the emerging human potential revolution, and the adoption of entrepreneurial methods and mindsets. For employers these would include the decommodification of labor, creation of a culture of reward around education and learning, and the recognition that employee upskilling improves enterprise competitiveness. State and local governments would strive to correlate support of advanced education and training with long-term regional and global labor market trends. A sea change in public perception in this context would begin with the recognition that learning within formal organizations does not inevitably end at some arbitrarily predetermined age.

## Innovation in Educational Delivery

ASU is pursuing innovation in educational delivery across four realms of teaching and learning, each of which bears the hallmarks of technological enhancement and broad educational access. As a large-scale sociotechnologically enhanced research-pedagogic institution, ASU is leading the development of differentiated, technology-based teaching and learning realms that operate across varied learning environments. Through robust collaboration with educational technology partners, utilizing more than 150 third-party tools and services to expand and improve the increasingly personalized online learning experience, ASU has been able to achieve significant positive outcome differentiators. Instructional designers work with faculty members to reconceptualize course content for online students, with an emphasis on engagement and interaction. Innovations in teaching and learning can be leveraged across the four realms to improve outcomes and reduce costs. Customized technology platforms include personalized learning at scale, ubiquitous content-delivery mechanisms, and artificial-intelligence-based advising.

Teaching and Learning Realm 1 encompasses the totality of the genetic inputs of the academic tradition, which traces its lineage to the Greek academies and spans more than two millennia, enhanced by technology to facilitate mixed-mode/hybrid online learning and boost retention and graduation rates. Realm 1 serves students pursuing degrees on four so-termed full-immersion campuses, beginning with the historic campus in Tempe, and three newer campuses—the Polytechnic, Glendale, and downtown Phoenix—which serve as platforms for the teaching, research, and innovation essential to advancing social and economic development. Full-immersion on-campus technology-enhanced learning engages 3,400 faculty members, nearly 17,000 support staff, and more than 73,000 students. Regional centers in Yuma, Safford, Payson, and Lake Havasu extend ASU's reach into growing communities that are presently served only by community colleges or university branch campuses, allowing ASU to increase enrollments.

Realm 1 is characterized by quantitative, scientific, and technological literacy among all students, many of whom pursue two or even three academic majors. Broad admissions standards, fluid interface with community colleges, and lower costs permit operations scalable to three times the historic norm. Realm 1 is moreover predicated on the supposition that the socioeconomic status of incoming students does not predict outcomes. To maximize accessibility, as previously noted, ASU maintains the historical admissions standards of leading American research universities during the 1950s, such as the University of California at Berkeley, UCLA, and the University of Michigan. New enterprise programs associated with Realm 1 include Global Launch, which is a significant expansion of ASU's successful intensive English program for international learners. ASU Preparatory Academies (ASU Prep) are two charter schools located in downtown Phoenix and East Mesa that utilize cutting-edge pedagogical methods to improve outcomes for underserved students and maximize college preparedness. Of the two thousand K–12 students enrolled at ASU Prep, 76 percent come from low-income households. The two schools have seen a 330 percent increase in enrollment over three years and maintain waiting lists numbering over one thousand students. Me3 is a mobile app that helps high school students determine potential college majors and identify courses needed for college acceptance. Through ASU Prep and Me3, ASU is expanding the college pipeline while making a significant impact on the educational preparedness of Arizona high school students.

Institutions from the first four waves have mastered traditional classroom instruction, but most have undertaken only incremental measures to realize the potential of new and ubiquitous information technologies. From pedagogical innovation to academic advising to data analytics and institutional modeling, new technology platforms promise to enhance teaching and learning and improve outcomes, particularly among students from diverse socioeconomic and cultural backgrounds. Through a combination of traditional classroom instruction with online technologies that deliver interactive content, monitor individual progress, and accommodate multiple learning styles, universities now have the potential to offer education customized to individual students while lowering costs. Conflation of online learning with MOOCs led to initial skepticism about learning technologies: "The rise of online instruction through the MOOC wave of 2011–2013 was the most ambitious attempt to extend existing cost reductions without hurting instruction, but it failed," Christopher Newfield contends. "Today's students need more personalized instruction, not less, and yet public universities are decreasingly able to offer this."[83] The personalized approach to learning technologies operationalized by ASU suggests that concerns regarding enforced standardization are unwarranted.

Teaching and Learning Realm 2 refers to fully online digital immersion programming. Realm 2 provides the university the capability to increase degree attainment by reaching potential students otherwise unable to attend. Realm 2 is operationalized through EdPlus, ASU's signature platform for advancing online learning. EdPlus advances research, instruction, educational design, and partnerships to extend the reach of the university using digital technologies, which permit the conceptualization, design, implementation, and evaluation of online curricula that reach tens of thousands of students domestically and internationally. ASU Online, a part of EdPlus, is our platform for full digital immersion that allows students to obtain a degree without ever setting foot on campus. ASU Online meets the needs of the largest and fastest-growing segment of the student population: nontraditional learners. Less than one in five students currently enrolled in U.S. postsecondary institutions started on a four-year campus following graduation from high school. Our commitment to online learning recognizes and works to accommodate the diverse and sometimes challenging life circumstances that confront nontraditional learners. Lifelong personalized learning through digital immersion offers a majority of the population the potential to achieve college completion. The objective is to increase online enrollment from within Arizona and across the nation from 20,000 to 100,000 by 2025.

ASU has leveraged the strength of its online infrastructure to pursue two significant partnerships that will have a significant impact on enrollments. The Starbucks College Achievement Plan (SCAP), a first-of-its-kind partnership between ASU and Starbucks launched in June 2014, creates an opportunity for all eligible Starbucks associates in the United States to earn bachelor's degrees. The corporation provides full tuition reimbursement toward online baccalaureate completion for qualified associates who enroll in one of more than fifty online degree programs. Spring semester 2018 enrollment was at 113 percent of goal, with more than 7,000 total enrollees. As of that semester, 51 percent of Starbucks stores in the United States have at least one partner enrolled, which is up from 39 percent the prior year. Overall, nearly 1,800 SCAP graduates had degrees conferred by 2018, bringing the partnership closer to its aspirational goal of graduating 25,000 scholars by 2025. The program is an example of the potential of academic enterprise to promote economic and social development. The PLuS (Phoenix-London-Sydney) Alliance, a partnership with King's College London and the University of New South Wales, in Sydney, Australia, represents an expansion of ASU Online into international markets to offer a mix of certificate and degree programs to underserved populations. Innovations required to implement Realm 2 include technology to support human relationships and build organizational affinity, integrated human-tutor interfaces, real-time and development-based assessment, and quantitative and scientific literacy for all participants.

Teaching and Learning Realm 3 operates through digital immersion-based programming delivered at massive scale. Realm 3 includes boundary-spanning initiatives with demonstrated capacities to reach millions of nontraditional learners and offers potential students with limited resources opportunities to explore courses, obtain a certificate, or pursue enrollment in degree programs. In collaboration with edX, the nonprofit provider of online education affiliated with MIT, ASU offers the Global Freshman Academy, which allows students to earn freshman credit after completing digital immersion courses hosted by edX and designed and taught by ASU faculty in an enhanced MOOC format. The program, launched in 2015, is the first ever to provide students with the option of university credit for the completion of MOOC courses. Initial enrollment in the first three courses exceeded 50,000 students from 192 countries, with more than 30 percent demonstrating interest in receiving credit. During the next few years, ASU plans to scale the program to offer more courses to more students and find new ways of converting them into full-time, degree-seeking students. Another new enterprise program in Realm 3 is ASU Prep Digital, a fully online high school that offers high-level coursework to Arizona students who are unable to physically attend high school. The curriculum of ASU Prep Digital is designed by the teachers at ASU Prep and delivered fully online along with access to counseling and coaching. Innovations required to implement Realm 3 include technologies that derive value from scale, content and delivery mechanisms appropriate to all life stages, multi-organizational pathway mapping, and quantitative and scientific literacy for all participants.

Teaching and Learning Realm 4 refers to a new form of totally personalized technology-enhanced learning being pioneered at ASU termed "education through exploration." The intent is for students to establish competency in a collective knowledge base and then pursue differentiation and individuation. Whereas traditional pedagogy emphasizes mastery of existing knowledge, the Center for Education Through Exploration (ETX) is developing approaches to learning through participatory individualized exploration of the unknown. ETX designs, develops, and deploys interactive, transdisciplinary, exploration-based digital platforms and teaching networks intended to extend personalized learning to millions of underserved students globally. Through short interactive lessons, ETX facilitates engagement with potential students for the other three realms. The effort represents a moon shot that has the potential to expand the frontiers of higher education. Innovations required to implement Realm 4 include virtual augmented reality, direct human cognition linkages, intelligent tutoring through verbal query, new group-learning tools, and quantitative and scientific literacy for participants.

Teaching and Learning Realm 5 represents infinitely scalable learning and aspires to the seamless integration of individualized learning across all life stages. Innovations required to implement Realm 5 include lifelong intelligent tutoring and quantitative and scientific literacy for all participants.

## Leveraging Technology for Student Success

American colleges and universities have long relied on the admissions process as a way of preselecting students who are most likely to succeed, and excluding those who may meet admissions standards but are less likely by various indicators to graduate. This approach fares well enough for freshmen who begin college with the requisite study skills, social support, financial stability, and grit to propel themselves through the college experience, but decreases educational access for those who face challenging life circumstances or have less understanding of how to navigate the academic world. These obstacles are especially common among students from disadvantaged backgrounds, whether they are the first in their family to attend college, are foster children or were orphaned, or are economically challenged, perhaps even to the point of needing to provide for their siblings or extended family while they matriculate as undergraduates. ASU's charter addresses these students specifically. By measuring the success of the university not by those whom we exclude but those we include and how they succeed, ASU assumes responsibility for creating educational opportunities for all qualified students. Recall that in Arizona, only nine out of one hundred high school students will go on to obtain a college degree, exacerbating the state's shortfall in human capital and limiting the lifelong economic and social potential of its youth. The solution to this problem is not to weed out "risky" students in the admissions process, but rather to ensure that these very students thrive at ASU and go on to graduate despite their disadvantages. As a university that acts entrepreneurially, ASU is leveraging technology and undertaking organizational innovations to make college affordable to all students, meet their needs through better student support and enhanced advising capabilities, and provide an educational experience that dynamically adapts to the needs of individual students. As evidenced by ASU's year-over-year growth in freshman retention and graduation rates, especially among disadvantaged students, it is clear that our approach is succeeding.[84]

ASU has instituted major reforms to its admissions process that have allowed it to grow at scale. The university admits any student who meets the requirements set forth by the Arizona Board of Regents and does not arbitrarily cap the number of students it admits to a given program or in a given year. From 2007 onward, the university has used a rapid admissions process that decreases decision time from two weeks to twenty-four hours, and streamlines acceptance of a student's transfer credits. Upon being admitted, students are provided specialized support in acquiring financial aid. ASU has made the express pledge to all incoming Arizona freshmen—the ASU Promise—that it will help them find an appropriate mix of loans, scholarships, and other forms of support so that they can afford to attend the university regardless of their financial situation. A differential approach to distribution of financial aid has benefited low-income students while keeping tuition affordable for other students, allowing ASU to increase the number of Pell recipients enrolled from just over 10,000 in 2002 to nearly 36,000 in 2017. During the same time frame, ASU increased institutional aid to students from $138 million to $288 million, sponsoring an average of 67 percent of tuition for in-state full-time enrolled freshmen. These dramatic policy changes have set ASU apart from nearly every university in the United States and account for the success of the university in growing its student population to the largest in the nation.

ASU has also developed a suite of resources targeted at freshmen to put them on track for long-term success. With the understanding that many students will start college without a clear understanding of what may be required of them, ASU implemented ASU 101 and ASU 111, two semester-long courses that help students to understand the resources that the university offers; enhance their learning and study skills; and introduce them to opportunities for engagement—a strong predictor of persistence and graduation. Freshmen are also offered one-on-one peer mentoring through the First Year Success program, in which exemplary juniors and seniors help new students to understand their strengths and weaknesses and develop an individualized plan for making the most of their college experience. ASU has also designed and tested the LEAD (Learn Explore Advance Design) program, a seminar-style class for freshmen identified as at-risk based on high school GPA and SAT scores. The LEAD program uses small-group interaction and discussion to equip students with skills in critical reasoning, reading, communication, emotional intelligence, teamwork, and personal time management. LEAD has been demonstrated to increase the first semester GPA of at-risk students from 2.4 to 3.3 and is being scaled to reach more students in the years ahead.

In 2008 ASU built and implemented the eAdvisor suite, a dashboard for students and their advisors that integrates financial aid, academic progress, and personalized campus housing information to provide customized, holistic support to every student. The eAdvisor suite has since become a nationally recognized tool par excellence and is one of the major factors in driving ASU's increase in retention and graduation rates. The eAdvisor suite guides students toward selecting a major that suits their aptitude and interests and gives them a complete road map toward degree completion. Students meet with their advisor in person during their first semester and as necessary based upon data that the program collects about student performance. As students progress through their degree programs, eAdvisor keeps them informed on which courses to take next, ensuring that high-demand or limited courses are always available for those who need to take them to continue. If a student falls off track, such as by failing a required course or neglecting to enroll in necessary courses according to the timeline of their major, eAdvisor automatically contacts the student and their advisor so they can meet and resolve the issue. The eAdvisor suite provides students with greater awareness and accountability for pursuing their major to completion, and empowers advisors with robust data about every student they serve to increase the quality of interactions with students, while reducing the number of meetings required between students and advisors to address predictable and avoidable problems. It also allows departments to match supply and demand for courses by anticipating the number of students within each major that will need to take required courses. Additionally, eAdvisor has been made available to the Maricopa County Community Colleges to facilitate a smoother transition for incoming transfer students.

One important facet of ASU's shift into digital learning is the design and testing of adaptive-active hybrid courses, a new approach to educational delivery that represents a fundamental departure from traditional instruction modules. The adaptive courseware approach engages students with online content prior to class, allowing them to learn at different speeds based upon their performance as evaluated by courseware algorithms. In class, students respond to material in active learning sessions. ASU initially implemented this approach in freshman math, chemistry, and biology courses—the courses in which passage is most associated with higher retention rates. Adaptive courseware increased success rates in math from 66 percent in 2009 to 85 percent in 2015 and has been shown to increase pre- to post-test scores in chemistry and biology by significant margins. Twenty thousand students already engage with the adaptive courseware each year, and the university is working to expand adaptive courseware to up to seventy-five undergraduate courses, which will reach 75 percent of undergraduate students.

The university has also made significant changes to the way that academic departments guide students toward graduation. Through policy changes that effect greater accountability for departments to increase student retention and degree acquisition, ASU has made it easier for students to focus on their studies rather than navigating academic bureaucracy. We have incentivized college deans to improve retention rates in the departments they oversee and set specific goals and metrics to drive student progress toward graduation. Since 2007 students have been required to declare majors after forty-five credit hours rather than eighty, which pushes students to departments where they can be supported along clear pathways toward degrees. With the help of eAdvisor, departments have improved advising practices to maximize positive outcomes for students and are now technologically equipped to anticipate and respond to course demand. These policy changes have been accompanied by a cultural shift toward a proactive orientation. Even in programs known for their intensity and rigor, the most challenging courses have been redesigned to be more adaptive and dynamic, so that students improve and proceed rather than being "weeded out."

## Global Engagement and International Development

Commitment to global engagement is among the core design aspirations that have guided institutional innovation. By established metrics, ASU has become an undisputed leader in the internationalization of higher education. ASU welcomes students from 136 countries around the world and endeavors to be of service to individuals from all nations. For the third consecutive year, ASU is among the leading host institutions in the United States for international students. With more than 13,000 international students enrolled in 2017, the university is home to the largest international student population in the nation among public universities. According to the Institute of International Education (IIE), the profile of the international student population at ASU corresponds to the IIE compilation of leading places of origin for international students in the United States: China, followed by India, Saudi Arabia, and South Korea. ASU sends over two thousand students to study abroad each year, and maintains international partnerships with universities on six continents.

As a public and social value enterprise, ASU endeavors to solve challenges of global scale, enhance the quality of life for people around the world, and promote global stability that benefits national security interests. These projects fall under the broad umbrella of international development, and are funded by the federal government through agencies such as USAID, the U.S. Department of State, Millennium Challenge Corporation, and international organizations such as the World Bank and United Nations World Food Programme. The international development industry consists of more than two hundred highly specialized for-profit firms and NGOs that compete for federal and private funds to implement projects around the world. The extremely competitive and nearly impenetrable culture of the industry means that few universities bid on international development projects, and those that do often focus on single areas of expertise, such as Johns Hopkins University in medicine and Michigan State University in agriculture. And because of their often well-deserved reputation as cumbersome bureaucracies, universities are frequently dismissed as viable partners by international development firms and agencies. But as a university that conducts itself as an academic enterprise, ASU has demonstrated its capacities to leverage opportunities where others would perceive insurmountable challenges. Over the past five years, ASU has strategically built relationships with international development agencies and many of the top firms in the industry, garnering a reputation as a capable and agile implementer for large-scale projects. To carry out this work, the university established ASU International Development (ASU ID), a specialized office that retains top industry experts in the international development funding landscape. With personnel in both Arizona and Washington, DC, ASU ID allows the university to bridge the cultural and knowledge gap between the spheres of academe and international development.[85]

ASU is a national leader in growing research expenditures from traditional funding sources, including federal agencies such as the National Institutes of Health and National Science Foundation, as well as private industries and philanthropic foundations. The university research supported by these public and private investments is often relevant to global development, and ASU is one of the few institutions in the nation to systematically leverage its research capabilities to pursue international development funding to solve global development challenges. ASU ID specializes in seven focus areas that reflect the university's geography, design aspirations, and unique research portfolio: (1) data and decision-making, (2) economic growth, (3) education, (4) global health, (5) rule of law (citizen security), (6) sustainability, and (7) women and gender. ASU ID systematically surveys the funding environment for opportunities to apply the university's expertise across these areas, identifies prospective partner organizations, and assembles expert interdisciplinary teams with country-specific knowledge to tackle projects.

As a new enterprise strategy, ASU's work in international development is not only a success from the perspective of increasing research expenditures but especially in terms of its impact on the developing world. ASU ID translates the university's research into innovative solutions that are deployed in-situ across the developing world, bridging the gap between theory and application to exert meaningful impact. Through the Women and Entrepreneurship in the Americas program, which is supported by USAID, Inter-American Development Bank, and

Goldman Sachs, experts at ASU's Thunderbird School of Global Management provide training and mentorship to female entrepreneurs to promote community development and economic prosperity. In the recently concluded India Support for Teacher Education Program (In-STEP), funded by USAID, faculty researchers and practitioners at ASU's Mary Lou Fulton Teachers College trained more than one hundred Indian educators in cutting-edge teaching methodologies, information technology, and accountability and reform measures. And in El Salvador, a country where citizens and communities face some of the highest rates of violent crime in the world, ASU is enhancing the capacities of civil society and the private sector to address gang violence and broker peace between criminal organizations. Around the world, ASU's work is empowering women, driving economic growth, building local educational capacity, improving health-care outcomes, promoting sustainable development, creating freer and safer societies, and enhancing the abilities of governments and communities to make accurate, data-driven policy choices.

Because stability and prosperity in Pakistan is critical to U.S. and global security interests, for example, ASU sought and successfully secured $18 million in USAID funds in 2016 to lead the U.S.-Pakistan Centers for Advanced Studies in Energy (USPCAS-E), a partnership between ASU and two leading universities in Pakistan focused on applied research in the energy sector. The partnership leverages ASU's expertise in university design, applied research, and energy to help Pakistan realize its potential for economic growth. USPCAS-E seeks to generate cost-effective and sustainable solutions for Pakistan's energy challenges and empower the next generation of energy experts, especially women and youths from disadvantaged backgrounds. USPCAS-E is a model for how ASU is expanding its global footprint in meaningful ways, realizing its potential as an idea generator with the influence and potential to change lives throughout the developing world.

The Vocational Training and Education for Clean Energy (VOCTEC) program, a partnership between ASU, USAID, and the International Renewable Energy Agency, mobilizes ASU's leadership and expertise to promote sustainable, renewable energy infrastructure and investment in developing countries. Through VOCTEC, ASU provides local technicians with the knowledge, training, and capacity to install, operate, and maintain solar photovoltaic, micro-hydro, wind energy, and micro/ mini-grid power systems. VOCTEC builds human capacity for clean energy systems, developing lab and training infrastructure, preparing clean energy workers for certification for international standards, and establishing the foundation to pass this knowledge on to future generations. To date, VOCTEC has trained hundreds of technical professionals, leaders, educators, and entrepreneurs, including women, in twenty countries, including Vietnam, Guyana, Liberia, India, Sierra Leone, Kenya, Nepal, and numerous Pacific Island nations.

The Higher Engineering Education Alliance Program (HEEAP) is an ASU-led public-private partnership to build Vietnam's high-tech manufacturing industry and workforce. HEEAP targets Vietnamese higher education, scaling ASU's entrepreneurial model of the university as a use-inspired research and economic development engine, to build their capacity to produce highly skilled workers to meet the needs of industry. Starting in 2011 as a partnership between ASU's Ira A. Fulton Schools of Engineering, USAID, and Intel, HEEAP has grown into a $25-million program that includes Vietnam's top technical universities and vocational schools, additional U.S. university partners, and a growing coalition of industry partners. Through the Vocational and University Leadership and Innovation Institute (VULII), a three-year HEEAP project funded by USAID, ASU is fostering systemic change in higher education to build research and training capacity and promote academic leadership within the Vietnamese educational system. USAID also awarded ASU with an additional $10.8 million in 2015 to support Building University-Industry Learning and Development Through Innovation and Technology (BUILD-IT), a follow-up initiative to align STEM instruction in Vietnamese institutions to the needs and capabilities of industry partners. HEEAP's instructional approach produces technically competent, work-ready graduates who have in-demand skills and knowledge. To date, HEEAP has trained 3,500 participants in U.S.-based and in-country workshops.

## An Alliance to Advance Accessibility

Consistent with the tenets of the Fifth Wave, accessibility to research-grade academic platforms and institutional innovation is similarly the context for the formation of the University Innovation Alliance (UIA), a coalition of eleven major public research universities established in September 2014 that endeavors to promote educational attainment, and especially to advance rates of graduation among historically underrepresented and socioeconomically disadvantaged students. Apart from ASU, member institutions that constitute the alliance are Georgia State University; Iowa State University; Michigan State University; Ohio State University; Oregon State University; Purdue University; University of California, Riverside; University of Central Florida; University of Kansas; and University of Texas, Austin. In the ferociously competitive arena of research-grade higher education, the universities that constitute the alliance are committed to collaboration to reshape the future of American higher education. As the UIA prospectus framed its intent: "Our collective vision is that by piloting new student success interventions, sharing insights about their relative costs and effectiveness, and scaling those interventions that are successful, we will significantly increase the number of low-income Americans and first-generation college students graduating with high-quality college degrees—and that, over time, our collaborative work will catalyze systemic changes in the entire higher education sector."[86]

In response to the critical imperative for our nation's colleges and universities to provide advanced levels of education to a broader spectrum of students, the UIA launched with a public goal to award collectively an additional 68,000 undergraduate degrees above baseline within ten years, with at least half of these awarded to students from socioeconomically disadvantaged backgrounds. As of 2018 this community of practice is on track to surpass this goal by more than 50,000 degrees. More significantly, alliance member institutions have succeeded in increasing the number of degrees awarded annually to students from low-income families by 29.6 percent over five years, which represents nearly 6,000 additional degrees awarded per year. The share of degrees awarded to students from low-income families has risen from 28.2 percent to 31.5 percent from 2012–2013 to 2017–2018. The UIA has garnered substantial interest from policymakers and sparked a national conversation about the imperative for improvement in educational outcomes and collaboration as a means of accelerating innovation. In April 2018 the alliance hosted the first National Summit on Student Success Innovation and Campus Transformation, which convened more than three hundred representatives of over seventy institutions and thirty organizations to engage in methods of collaboration honed by the UIA in its first three years. Through challenge grants funded by ECMC Foundation, the summit also spawned three new collaboratives composed of ten colleges and universities advancing aims similar to those of the UIA.

A summary of collective outcomes among alliance member institutions shows significant progress on key indicators.[87] Between 2012–2013 and 2017–2018, the total number of undergraduates awarded degrees at UIA institutions increased by 16.1 percent, from 79,073 to 91,823. The number of low-income students graduating increased by 29.6 percent. Across the UIA, low-income students in 2017–2018 represented 31.5 percent of total degree awards, compared to 28.2 percent in 2012–2013—a gain of 3.3 percentage points. Other measures of progress over those four years include:

- Overall freshmen first-year retention at UIA schools increased from 88.4 percent to 89.4 percent. The gap between overall and lower-income freshmen narrowed slightly, from 3.8 percent in 2012–2013 to 3.5 percent in 2017–2018.
- The thirty-hour freshmen progression metric (freshmen with thirty credits when entering their second fall) increased from 71.1 percent to 76.3 percent.
- The sixty-hour freshmen progression metric (freshmen with sixty credits when entering their third fall) increased from 62.2 percent to 69.1 percent.
- The ninety-hour freshmen progression metric (freshmen with ninety credits by their fourth fall) increased from 59.5 percent to 65.7 percent.
- Retention rates for transfer students with fewer than sixty credits improved from 81.6 percent to 83 percent for all students, and from 77.4 percent to 77.8 percent for low-income students.
- For transfer students with more than sixty credits, the retention rate improved slightly from 84.3 percent in 2012–2013 to 85.6 percent in 2017–2018. The low-income figure, however, remained at 84.7 percent from 2012–2013 to 2017–2018.

In the effort to scale innovations and maximize collaboration across the network, UIA member institutions have undertaken a number of joint projects. These include the implementation of predictive analytics systems on all alliance campuses; using predictive analytics to implement a proactive advising initiative supported by a U.S. Department of Education First in the World grant; a completion grant initiative to provide targeted financial interventions to students whose unmet financial need poses a barrier to their registration and graduation; and a project to modernize transitions from college to career by mobilizing interdisciplinary teams of campus professionals in tandem with cross-sector business and organizational leaders. Alliance institutions also exchange knowledge about techniques such as process mapping, organic scaling, and program replication.

The formation of the alliance recognizes that both personal income and collective prosperity are correlated with educational attainment and comes at a time when the United States must confront a critical shortfall in college-educated workers. At the time of the UIA's founding in 2014, the rate of poverty for Americans twenty-five years and older with no college degree (13.1 percent) was three times higher than the rate for those with at least a bachelor's degree (4.1 percent).[88] In 2017, data show a slight narrowing of this gap (12.7 percent for those with only a high school degree, compared with 4.8 for those with a bachelor's degree or higher), but individuals with at least a bachelor's degree continued to show the lowest poverty rates.[89] American workers with a college degree earn an estimated 80 percent more than those without a degree. Researchers argue that producing twenty million additional college-educated workers over the next fifteen years can reduce American income inequality; however, on its current course, the country is poised to add just eight million.[90] The consequences of lack of educational attainment are borne disproportionately by members of minority groups, which represent the fastest-growing segment of the population.[91]

The correlation between family income and academic success is well documented. The demographic trends shaping our nation militate against the success of students from socioeconomically disadvantaged and historically underrepresented backgrounds, whose prospects for advanced educational attainment and economic prosperity remain bleak. Alliance member institutions enroll a diverse ethnic and socioeconomic cross-section of students, including a higher percentage of transfer students, undergraduate recipients of Pell grants, and students age twenty-five and older than nonmember very high research universities.[92] Enrollment patterns among UIA institutions position the alliance to address the shortfall in college-educated citizens that threatens our nation's prosperity and economic competitiveness.[93]

American higher education valorizes competition at all levels, but cooperation and collaboration as well as competition among institutions will be required if we are to move beyond current patterns that exclude a majority of academically qualified students. The commitment to cooperation and collaboration of alliance member institutions is predicated on the recognition that the metrics of competitive evaluation encourage exclusion rather than accessibility. Collective impact has been defined as the "commitment of a group of important actors from different sectors to a common agenda for solving a specific social problem." As innovation theorists John Kania and Mark Kramer observe, "Large-scale social change requires broad cross-sector coordination, yet the social sector remains focused on the isolated intervention of individual organizations." Similarly, the diffusion of innovation is facilitated through networks.[94] Disruptive innovation remains a buzzword, but the application of the concept is generally restricted to online education while the real innovation heralded by the formation of the alliance is cooperation and collaboration.

The University Innovation Alliance is wholly unlike existing organizations committed to the advancement of colleges and universities. As the UIA report observes: "This is the first time a group of large public research universities has self-organized across state and conference lines specifically to test and scale solutions to problems of access and graduation in higher education." The primary objective cited is the improvement of student outcomes through the formation of an "innovation cluster that develops and tests new initiatives, shares data, and scales best practices across the alliance and beyond." Moreover, these innovations are expected to be scalable and adaptable by other institutions. Scale is key in this undertaking. Collectively these institutions represent 20 percent of the student population at our nation's very high research universities, as designated by Carnegie.[95] As the vision and prospectus statement reports regarding member institutions: "Together we draw from every region in the country and span the spectrum of public research universities, from emergent institutions to land-grant universities and state flagships."[96]

## Purdue University as a Fifth Wave University

Alliance member institutions comprise differentiated institutional models and in the idiom of the Fifth Wave, could be said to function as national service universities. For example, Purdue University is Indiana's public land-grant research university and thus representative of a Third Wave university that transitioned to the Fourth Wave. Purdue has buttressed its public service mission and commitment to access through its innovative acquisition in 2017 of Kaplan University, a former for-profit, primarily online university. By increasing its student population by thirty thousand through this technology-enabled strategy and the formation of Purdue University Global, Purdue consolidates its position as one of the leading national land-grant university member institutions heralding the Fifth Wave.[97]

Institutional rivalries among the country's seven hundred public universities hamper the collective ability of higher education to produce the graduates needed to improve America's global competitiveness.[98] Because the United States will need sixteen million more graduates by 2025 than the current system of higher education can produce under conditions that now prevail, the institutions of the Fifth Wave must find ways to collaborate on a differentiated basis to fulfill their collective mission to produce graduates and research needed to respond to looming economic, social, and environmental challenges.

The market for online education is developing rapidly. According to the National Center for Education Statistics, about one-third of undergraduates, or 5.2 million students, received some part of their education online in 2016, while 13 percent of undergraduates, or 2.2 million, took distance-education classes exclusively. Of those 2.2 million students, 774,000 were enrolled at colleges and universities in states where they do not reside, while 1.3 million were registered at institutions in their home states.[99] After many false starts by some of the most prestigious universities in the world,[100] information and communication technologies now allow Fifth Wave universities to offer personalized interactive online education that is comparable to that delivered on traditional immersion campuses. The advent of online delivery of education allows the most stellar scholars, programs, and schools to reach qualified students literally anywhere in the world, which in turn will facilitate the knowledge production and innovation needed to advance the interests of humanity.

The eleven member institutions of the alliance have banded together in a league not only to dramatically increase the number of master learners needed to meet the challenges of our era but also to simultaneously promote diversity, lower costs, and improve the efficiency of the resources directed toward higher education, as well as to promote collaboration at a scale commensurate with the challenges. Collaboration among Fifth Wave institutions leagued together beneath the banner of the alliance represents a systemic but diversified adaptation to a changing educational environment. Through its acquisition of Kaplan and formation of Purdue Global, Purdue University is filling an important niche in a changing environment—the education of the thirty-five million citizens who began but have not finished their college degrees.[101]

Although Purdue will continue to offer top-tier research-grade immersion at its historic flagship campus in West Lafayette, Indiana, the acquisition of Kaplan demonstrates that Fourth Wave universities can transcend the status quo to deliver flexible educational opportunities at a scale requisite to societal need. For those concerned that the online venture will drain the resources of an established and respected institution, Purdue Global is financially sequestered from the rest of the Purdue system and will rely only on tuition and fund-raising to meet its obligations. No appropriations from the state of Indiana will be used to support the new venture. Kaplan University operated fifteen brick-and-mortar facilities across the United States, including one in Indianapolis that may expand across the state of Indiana. Consistent with a Fifth Wave university embedded in local environments, students who reside in Indiana are eligible for discounted tuition at Purdue Global.[102]

In recent years, online for-profit colleges have come under fire for encouraging students to assume debt that they could not pay back from earnings available from the jobs that they were qualified for when they graduated. To protect future students from unfair trade practices, the Obama Administration imposed regulatory sanctions, which disrupted the for-profit college market. The advent of Purdue Global is an example of the restructuring that resulted after the disruption.[103] Despite the upheaval in the for-profit college market, Fifth Wave universities understand that they must reach out to and meet students whether at home

or on campus. Online higher education fills an important niche by offering learning opportunities to those who may not be able to take advantage of a traditional college education on brick-and-mortar campuses, including students with disabilities and those engaged in military
service.[104]

Purdue Global advances the efforts of Fifth Wave universities to pursue innovative ways to reach out to qualified adult learners. Ted Mitchell, president of the American Council on Education, has deemed the
acquisition an effort by Purdue to "extend its unquestioned tradition of
educational excellence and its land grant mission by leveraging the tools,
technologies, and practices that Kaplan has developed to reach more and
different students." Among these he envisions the twenty-two-year-old
returning veteran, the thirty-year-old single mom, the first-generation
college goer, the fifty-year-old displaced worker, and the underprepared
low-income high school graduate.[105] Reaching out to fellow citizens from
socioeconomically disadvantaged and historically underrepresented
groups as well as the broad spectrum of lifelong learners with differing
indicators of intelligence and creativity promotes the diversity needed to
expand the pool of applicants required to meet the needs of a twenty-
first-century society.

## Toward a League of Differentiated Models

In chapter 1 we proposed that as the vanguard of a potential cohort
of peer institutions positioned to negotiate the demands of broad accessibility and academic excellence, ASU be regarded as the institutional
progenitor of the Fifth Wave, which is to say, a league of national service
universities. And that inasmuch as attributes of the Fifth Wave include
a commitment to scale both on campus and online, a refusal to exclude
academically qualified students on the basis of arbitrary admissions
standards, and evidence of a world-class research profile, potential institutional peers in transition to the Fifth Wave could include Purdue
University, Pennsylvania State University, and the University System of
Maryland.

Most leagues of universities are dedicated exclusively to the advancement of academic excellence rather than broad accessibility. Notable examples are the Association of American Universities (AAU), the Russell Group in Great Britain, and the League of European Research

Universities. But of course a league could dedicate member institutions to the advancement of collective action. Elinor Ostrom, Nobel laureate in economics recognized for her analysis of economic governance, sought to understand collaboration in this context and frames this objective in terms of governing the commons. This assumes the conception of knowledge as a commons, which is to say, a shared resource.[106] But, unlike the tragedy of the commons assessed by Garrett Hardin, wherein shared resources are inevitably degraded as stakeholders each seek to maximize personal gain—he provides the example of herdsmen whose increasing numbers of cattle will eventually overgraze an open pasture[107]—knowledge is never diminished with its use. But any framework for analyzing the knowledge commons, as Ostrom and Charlotte Hess explain, must "factor in the economic, legal, technological, political, social, and psychological components—each complex in its own right—that make up this global commons."[108]

The proposition that the Fifth Wave could be said to constitute a league of national service universities is moreover consistent with the recommendation by Jonathan Cole that the formation of what he terms academic leagues could advance research and teaching. Because such leagues represent collaboration among scientists and scholars affiliated with arrays of leading universities, both nationally and internationally, the approach comports with the objectives of the Fifth Wave. Such de facto alliances—rather than formal mergers—would coordinate top complementary programs, especially from different fields. Cole offers the hypothetical example of the Earth Institute at Columbia University leading an interdisciplinary consortium of fifteen to twenty universities worldwide to advance sustainability. And whereas most such collaboration is spurred by objectives of research, Cole recommends the development of what he terms quasi-mergers for teaching as well as joint degree programs. Although such programs may be cost effective, however, he cautions that requisite new structural relationships could threaten perceptions of institutional autonomy.[109] Consistent with the recommendation regarding the formation of academic leagues to advance research and teaching, the PLuS Alliance—the acronym derived from Phoenix, London, and Sydney, the locales of Arizona State University, King's College London, and the University of New South Wales—represents the collaboration of three leading research universities situated on three continents allied to tackle global challenges associated with health care, social justice, sustainability, and technology and innovation that lie beyond the capacity of any single institution, public or private, to address.

Our analysis of organizational evolution in American higher education and the evolutionary scheme of the five waves is not intended as overtly teleological, nor is it constructed to justify any particular model. The New American University, or emergent Fifth Wave, model is only one among many possible variants. Thus, in our first book we suggested that the predication of a New American University model comes with the caveat that institutions seeking reconceptualization must not succumb to a new form of isomorphism in attempting to embrace the foundational prototype. Similarly, we assessed that it may be counterproductive to profess the prescription of a set of design strategies applicable in all contexts because no such algorithm or protocol exists. While we recognize that the model might encourage emulation of the prototype, we recommend in other institutional contexts the sustained deployment of design strategies uniquely correlated to address the objectives of respective institutions. While the reflexive instantiation of the model incontrovertibly demands that it be treated as a case study, the intent remains to advocate for institutional differentiation and self-determination.

The Fifth Wave builds on structural transformations initiated by earlier waves, particularly the Fourth Wave, especially by assessing, analyzing, and integrating the tension between research excellence and broad accessibility identified by Craig Calhoun, which we assessed in chapter 1.[110] ASU has endeavored to redesign itself to produce students equipped to respond to the festering social, economic, and environmental challenges facing humanity. Such innovations as the improved online learning adopted by ASU, Purdue Global University, the University of Central Florida, and other schools we have identified as potential members of the league of national service universities, will leverage the structural transformations of preceding waves. As circumstances change, universities that anticipate future waves will in turn pragmatically assess, analyze, and address challenges as they arise. Although each university is embedded in a unique complex local ecosystem, groups of universities at the regional, national, and international levels may encounter similar challenges and devise coordinated responses through new or existing groups or leagues. Our nation's universities must break out of stultifying isomorphism and filiopiety to meet emerging challenges in real time and evolve appropriate responses at socially meaningful scale.

## Notes

1. Although newly released institutional statistics for fall 2019 are reported as available, some figures cited represent data from prior academic years, which are the most recent available. All charts in chapter 2 reflect enrollment numbers through fall 2018. Unless otherwise indicated, all data pertaining to ASU throughout these chapters are provided by the Arizona State University Office of Institutional Analysis, https://uoia .asu.edu.

2. Walter W. McMahon, *Higher Learning, Greater Good: The Private and Social Benefits of Higher Education* (Baltimore: Johns Hopkins University Press, 2009).

3. National Science Foundation (NSF), Higher Education Research and Development (HERD) Survey (2017), https://www.nsf.gov/statistics/srvyherd/#sd&tabs-1.

4. Michael M. Crow and William B. Dabars, *Designing the New American University* (Baltimore: Johns Hopkins University Press, 2015), 7–8, 60–64, 240–303.

5. Robert K. Yin, *Case Study Research and Applications: Design and Methods* (Los Angeles: Sage, 2018), xx.

6. Yin, *Case Study Research and Applications*, 22.

7. John F. Padgett and Walter W. Powell, *The Emergence of Organizations and Markets* (Princeton, NJ: Princeton University Press, 2012), 2.

8. Dawson R. Hancock and Bob Algozzine, *Doing Case Study Research: A Practical Guide for Beginning Researchers* (New York: Teachers College Press, 2011), 8–12.

9. Nathan D. Grawe, *Demographics and the Demand for Higher Education* (Baltimore: Johns Hopkins University Press, 2018).

10. Michael Greenstone and Adam Looney, "Where is the Best Place to Invest $102,000—In Stocks, Bonds, or a College Degree?" (June 25, 2011), www.brookings.edu /research/where-is-the-best-place-to-invest-102000-in-stocks-bonds-or-a-college -degree.

11. Michael M. Crow and Derrick M. Anderson, "From Agency to Enterprise: Arizona State University and a New Institutional Paradigm for American Higher Education," working paper (Tempe: Office of the President, Arizona State University, 2018), 20–23.

12. Crow and Anderson, "From Agency to Enterprise," 24.

13. Michael Mitchell, Michael Leachman, and Kathleen Masterson, "A Lost Decade in Higher Education Funding: State Cuts Have Driven Up Tuition and Reduced Quality" (Washington, DC: Center on Budget and Policy Priorities, August 2017), 1–4. For historical perspective on the extent of public disinvestment in higher education, see Donald E. Heller, "State Support of Higher Education: Past, Present, and Future," in

*Privatization and Public Universities,* ed. Douglas M. Priest and Edward P. St. John (Bloomington: Indiana University Press, 2006), 11–37.

14. Anthony Downs, *Inside Bureaucracy* (Boston: Little, Brown, 1967).

15. For relevant discussions of the theory of punctuated equilibrium applied to organizational change, see Elaine Romanelli and Michael L. Tushman, "Organizational Transformation as Punctuated Equilibrium," *Academy of Management Journal* 37, no. 5 (1994): 1141–1166; C. J. G. Gersick, "Revolutionary Change Theories: A Multilevel Exploration of the Punctuated Equilibrium Paradigm," *Academy of Management Review* 16, no. 1: 10–36; Karl E. Weick and Robert E. Quinn, "Organizational Change and Development," *Annual Review of Psychology* 50 (1999): 361–386.

16. Torben Beck Jørgensen and Barry Bozeman, "Public Values: An Inventory," *Administration and Society* 39, no. 3 (May 2007): 354–381.

17. Howard Gardner, *Frames of Mind: The Theory of Multiple Intelligences* (New York: Basic Books, 1983); *Multiple Intelligences: New Horizons* (New York: Basic Books, 1993).

18. During FY 2015–2016 and generally reported as AY 2016, the calculation reported as median cost per degree among public research universities was $81,109. The set refers to the seventy-six public universities then designated as research-extensive. Whereas the figure for ASU is $65,447, cost per degree at the University of Washington, for example, is $92,395. According to Richard H. Stanley, senior vice president and university planner, the figures are proxies derived by dividing the total reported state appropriation and tuition and fees after discounts and allowances by the number of degrees awarded. Revenue sources used are for education and exclude research awards, auxiliary revenues, and restricted sources. Because the high cost of teaching medicine can skew comparisons, a more relevant comparison is to the set of thirty-seven research-extensive institutions without medical schools. The median for that subset is $72,547, and because they do not have medical schools, one might cite Purdue ($92,972) or Texas A&M ($83,847).

19. U.S. Department of Education, IPEDS (Integrated Postsecondary Education Data System) dataset (FY 2016), https://nces.ed.gov/ipeds/use-the-data. Employees are counted as full-time equivalent (FTE) and include all faculty and staff excluding those that work at medical schools and student employees. Contracted workers are not included in FTE counts.

20. Jeff Selingo et al., "The Next Generation University" (Washington, DC: New America, 2013).

21. Christopher Newfield, *The Great Mistake: How We Wrecked Public Universities and How We Can Fix Them* (Baltimore: Johns Hopkins University Press, 2016).

22. Crow and Anderson, "From Agency to Enterprise," 26.

23. Roughly 68 percent of freshmen in this cohort reported class rank. Of these, 2,634 graduated in the top 10 percent of their class—more students than constitute Harvard's entire freshman class of 2022, which numbers 1,661. See https://features.the crimson.com/2018/freshman-survey/makeup-narrative/.

24. The U.S. Department of Education IPEDS dataset reveals that only 12.8 percent of all colleges and universities that reported five-year graduation rates experienced rates greater than 75 percent in 2013. These highly selective institutions enrolled 401,141 Pell-eligible students in 2013–2014, or no more than 10 percent of all Pell-eligible students in the United States.

25. "Undergraduate Student Success," chapter 4 in Accountability Report 2014, University of California, quoted in C. Judson King, *The University of California: Creating, Nurturing, and Maintaining Academic Quality in a Public Research University Setting* (Berkeley: Center for Studies in Higher Education, University of California, 2018), 152.

26. Boyer Commission on Educating Undergraduates in the Research University, "Reinventing Undergraduate Education: A Blueprint for America's Research Universities" (Stony Brook: State University of New York, 1998), 2.

27. NSF, HERD Survey (2017). The HERD survey is generally held to be the preeminent standard for measuring university research and development activities.

28. In terms of total research expenditures for institutions without a medical school, the top ten leading schools are 1. Massachusetts Institute of Technology; 2. University of Texas M. D. Anderson Cancer Center; 3. Georgia Institute of Technology; 4. University of California, Berkeley; 5. University of Illinois at Urbana-Champaign; 6. Purdue University, West Lafayette; 7. University of Maryland, College Park; 8. Arizona State University; 9. Virginia Polytechnic Institute and State University; 10. North Carolina State University. NSF, HERD Survey (2017).

29. NSF, HERD Survey (2017).

30. NSF, HERD Survey (2017). In descending order, these are Johns Hopkins University; University of Michigan; University of California, San Francisco; University of Pennsylvania; University of Washington; University of Wisconsin; University of California, San Diego; Duke University; Harvard University; Stanford University; Duke University; University of North Carolina, Chapel Hill; University of California, Los Angeles; Cornell University; Yale University; University of Pittsburgh; University of Minnesota; New York University; Texas A&M University; University of Pittsburgh; Yale University; Columbia University; Ohio State University; and Pennsylvania State University.

31. National Academy of Inventors and Intellectual Property Owners Assocation, "Top 100 Worldwide Universities Granted U.S. Utility Patents in 2018," which is based on data from the U.S. Patent and Trademark Office (PTO).

32. Crow and Anderson, "From Agency to Enterprise," 56.

33. Crow and Anderson, "From Agency to Enterprise," 57.

34. Institute of Higher Education, Shanghai Jiao Tong University, Academic Ranking of World Universities (ARWU), http://www.shanghairanking.com/ARWU -Methodology-2019.html. For an explication of the methodology, see 90n91.

35. *Times Higher Education World University Rankings* and *University Impact Rankings*, https://www.timeshighereducation.com/world-university-rankings.

36. Requirements for assured admission for Arizona residents conform to Arizona Board of Regents (ABOR) policy 2-121, which specifies criteria for general aptitude and competence. General aptitude requires graduation from a regionally accredited high school in the upper quartile of the graduating class. Competence is evaluated through the completion of appropriate course work with a 3.0 grade point average in the following areas: English (four years), math (four years), laboratory science (three years), social science (two years), foreign language (two years), and fine arts (one year). In some cases, admission may be granted despite deficiencies, except in both math and laboratory science. However, consistent with ABOR policy, the university may exercise discretion in admissions for applicants who do not meet these requirements. Admissions criteria vary for transfer students, nonresidents, and international students. ABOR academic policy 2-121B creates two additional categories of admission: delegated and special. Delegated admission may be used for students earning at least a 2.5 GPA who demonstrate completion of a minimum of fourteen of the sixteen core competencies, while special admission allows universities to admit students not meeting either assured or delegated requirements up to a maximum of 10 percent of incoming classes. See https://students.asu.edu/freshman/requirements.

37. John Aubrey Douglass, *The Conditions for Admission: Access, Equity, and the Social Contract of Public Universities* (Stanford: Stanford University Press, 2007), 42, 80, 112. The 1960 Master Plan for Higher Education in California specified that the top 12.5 percent of California public high school graduates would be eligible for admission to the University of California, a reduction from the historical figure of roughly 15 percent. Douglass explains that the trajectory toward increasingly selective admissions arrived with the establishment in 1979 of the eligibility index—a sliding scale of grade point average in required courses combined with SAT scores—coupled with the slowing of enrollment growth. In the late 1950s, the subject area requirement for resident freshman applicants from accredited high schools specified a B average in the last three years in a pattern of ten high school academic subjects: "one year in American history and civics, three in English, one in algebra, one in geometry, one in laboratory science, two in foreign language, and one additional in either mathematics, foreign language, or laboratory science." Approximately 10 percent of students were eligible for admission by "exception" or through other means (42). See chapter 5 in this volume for a discussion of the implications of the Master Plan in terms of the historical context of the Fourth Wave.

38. https://newamericanuniversity.asu.edu/about/asu-charter-mission-and-goals.

39. Tom Mortenson, "College Participation Rates for Students from Low-Income Families by State and Sector, 1998 to 2016," *Postsecondary Education Opportunity* 290 (2017), cited in Margaret Cahalan et al., *Indicators of Higher Education Equity in the United States: 2018 Historical Trend Report* (Washington, DC: Pell Institute for the Study of Opportunity in Higher Education, 2018): 48, figure 1i(i).

40. "One University in Many Places: Transitional Design to Twenty-First-Century Excellence" (Tempe: Arizona State University, 2004). Throughout this chapter, exposition of the argument and rationale behind the design process extrapolates from this

and other institutional white papers, which in some instances are not cited, and, most importantly, from our previous book.

41. Crow and Anderson, "From Agency to Enterprise," 1.

42. Max Weber, "Characteristics of Modern Bureaucracy" (1925), in *Economy and Society*, 2 vols., translated and edited by Guenther Roth and Claus Wittich (Berkeley: University of California Press, 2013), vol. 2, 183.

43. Joseph A. Schumpeter, *Capitalism, Socialism, and Democracy* (London: Routledge, 1994), 206.

44. Downs, *Inside Bureaucracy*, 1.

45. *Oxford English Dictionary (OED)*, 3rd ed. (Oxford: Oxford University Press, 2012), online version accessed May 2018, s.v. "bureaucracy."

46. Downs, *Inside Bureaucracy*, 8, 18–19.

47. James Q. Wilson, *Bureaucracy: What Government Agencies Do and Why They Do It* (New York: Basic Books, 1989), 158.

48. Theodore W. Schultz, "Investment in Human Capital," *American Economic Review* 51, no. 1 (March 1961): 1–17. For analysis of the correlation between investment in education and training and economic growth, see Gary S. Becker, *Human Capital: A Theoretical and Empirical Analysis, With Special Reference to Education*, 3rd ed. (Chicago: University of Chicago Press, 1993).

49. Charles T. Clotfelter, *Unequal Colleges in the Age of Disparity* (Cambridge, MA: Harvard University Press, 2017), 17.

50. Henry Etzkowitz, *The Triple Helix: University-Industry-Government Innovation in Action* (New York: Routledge, 2008).

51. For an indictment of what is perceived to be the peril of corporatist influence in academia, see Eyal Press and Jennifer Washburn, "The Kept University," *Atlantic Monthly* 285, no. 3 (March 2000): 39–54. More balanced discussion is to be found in David H. Guston, "Responsible Innovation in the Commercialized University," in *Buying in or Selling Out: The Commercialization of the American Research University*, ed. Donald G. Stein (New Brunswick, NJ: Rutgers University Press, 2004), 161–174; Sheila Slaughter and Larry L. Leslie, *Academic Capitalism: Politics, Policies, and the Entrepreneurial University* (Baltimore: Johns Hopkins University Press, 1997); and Sheila Slaughter and Gary Rhoades, *Academic Capitalism and the New Economy: Markets, State, and Higher Education* (Baltimore: Johns Hopkins University Press, 2004).

52. John V. Lombardi, *How Universities Work* (Baltimore: Johns Hopkins University Press, 2013), 69.

53. Bernard T. Ferrari and Phillip H. Phan, "Universities and the Conglomerate Challenge," *McKinsey Quarterly* (September 2018).

54. Burton R. Clark, "The Entrepreneurial University: Demand and Response," *Tertiary Education and Management* 4, no. 1 (1998): 5–16. See also Burton R. Clark, *Creating Entrepreneurial Universities: Organizational Pathways of Transformation* (Oxford: Elsevier, 1998).

55. Crow and Anderson, "From Agency to Enterprise," 6.

56. Crow and Anderson, "From Agency to Enterprise," 6–7.

57. Crow and Anderson, "From Agency to Enterprise," 7.

58. Joseph A. Schumpeter, *The Theory of Economic Development* (Cambridge, MA: Harvard University Press, 1934). Schumpeter ascribes the innovation intrinsic to "creative destruction" to entrepreneurs: "The function of entrepreneurs is to reform or revolutionize the pattern of production by exploiting invention or, more generally, an untried technological possibility for producing new commodities or producing an old one in a new way" (8).

59. Crow and Anderson, "From Agency to Enterprise," 10.

60. Kyle Whitman, "Organizational Systematics in the Public Sector: The Case of American Higher Education," dissertation prospectus, Arizona State University (2019).

61. Michael M. Crow, "Designing Partnerships for Social Impact and Transformation," presentation at ASU-GSV Summit, San Diego, California (April 9, 2019).

62. Michael M. Crow, Kyle Whitman, and Derrick M. Anderson, "Rethinking Academic Entrepreneurship: University Governance and the Emergence of the Academic Enterprise," *Public Administration Review* (in press), https://onlinelibrary.wiley.com/doi/abs/10.1111/puar.13069.

63. Amy Gutmann, *Democratic Education* (Princeton, NJ: Princeton University Press, 1987). See also Mariana Mazzucato, *The Entrepreneurial State: Debunking Public vs. Private Sector Myths* (New York: Public Affairs, 2013).

64. American Academy of Arts and Sciences, *Public Research Universities: Recommitting to Lincoln's Vision: An Educational Compact for the Twenty-First Century* (Washington, DC: American Academy of Arts and Sciences, 2016), 13.

65. National Research Council, *Research Universities and the Future of America: Ten Breakthrough Actions Vital to Our Nation's Prosperity and Security* (Washington, DC: National Academies Press, 2012), 7, 9, 11.

66. The Constitution of the State of Arizona (Article 11, section 10) specifies "the legislature shall make such appropriations, to be met by taxation, as shall insure the proper maintenance of all state educational institutions and shall make such special appropriations as shall provide for their development and improvement."

67. Michael M. Crow and Derrick M. Anderson, "National Service Universities: Fulfilling the Promise of Excellence at Scale in American Higher Education," working paper (Tempe: Office of the President, Arizona State University, 2019).

68. John Hagel, John Seely Brown, and Lang Davison, *The Power of Pull: How Small Moves, Smartly Made, Can Set Big Things in Motion* (New York: Basic Books, 2010), 7, 11, 73.

69. Crow and Dabars, *Designing the New American University*, 247. *Oxford English Dictionary (OED)*, 3rd ed. (Oxford: Oxford University Press, 2012), online version accessed May 2018, s.v. "charette" and "skunkworks." The dictionary informs us that the latter term derives from the name of an outdoor still in the comic strip *L'il Abner*, where moonshine was produced from "old shoes and dead skunk."

70. For an overview of the federated system, see Negley Harte, *The University of London, 1836–1986* (London: Athlone Press, 1986). For a historical overview of academic federation, see Sheldon Rothblatt, "Historical and Comparative Remarks on the Fed-

eral Principle in Higher Education," *History of Education* 16, no. 3 (1987): 151–180. For a sense of the challenges associated with continued federation, see Malcolm Grant, "The Future of the University of London: A Discussion Paper from the Provost of University College London" (March 2005).

71. Joseph Caspermeyer, R. Harth, and J. Kullman, personal correspondence and news releases, Biodesign Institute, Arizona State University, 2015–2017.

72. "Think Tanks and Civil Societies Program (TTCSP)," Lauder Institute, University of Pennsylvania, https://www.gotothinktank.com.

73. David Guston, Lori Hidinger, and Daniel Sarewitz, "IF/IS: The Institute for the Future of Innovation in Society" (2018). The discussion of CSPO, IF/IS, and SFIS in this chapter is adapted from this unpublished SFIS working paper and related documents without further explicit citation.

74. Further insight into the formative period of CSPO is to be found in the collection of essays that explore issues and themes discussed at a major conference held at Columbia University in 2002. "Living with the Genie: Governing the Scientific and Technological Transformation of Society in the Twenty-First Century" convened leading thinkers from diverse fields to help legitimate the urgency of serious discourse about science, technology, and society. See Alan Lightman, Daniel Sarewitz, and Christina Desser, eds., *Living with the Genie: Essays on Technology and the Quest for Human Mastery* (Washington DC: Island Press, 2003).

75. Mary Shelley, *Frankenstein: Annotated for Scientists, Engineers, and Creators of All Kinds*, ed. David H. Guston, Ed Finn, and Jason Scott Robert (Cambridge, MA: MIT Press, 2017), i.

76. Andrew Maynard, personal correspondence, June 27, 2019.

77. Andrew Maynard, personal correspondence, June 27, 2019.

78. Peter Schlosser, "Global Futures Initiative: Outline of Concept and Draft of Charter," December 14, 2017. The discussion of the Global Futures Laboratory in this chapter is adapted from this document and various presentations without further explicit citation. Schlosser is vice president and vice provost of Global Futures and University Global Futures professor.

79. Will Steffen, Paul J. Crutzen, and John R. McNeill, "The Anthropocene: Are Humans Now Overwhelming the Great Forces of Nature?" *Ambio* 36, no. 8 (December 2007): 614–621.

80. https://www.asu.edu/about/centers-and-institutes#university-provost.

81. See "ASU Charter," https://president.asu.edu/asu-mission-goals.

82. Michael M. Crow, Derrick M. Anderson, Jacqueline Smith, and Luke Tate, "Universal Learning as a New Aspiration for Higher Education," working paper (Tempe: Office of the President, Arizona State University, 2019). The introductory discussion of universal learning in this chapter derives from this document without further explicit citation.

83. Newfield, *Great Mistake*, 20.

84. Crow and Anderson, "From Agency to Enterprise," 50. The subsequent paragraphs in this section derive from pages 50–55 of this working paper.

85. Crow and Anderson, "From Agency to Enterprise," 60–61. The subsequent paragraphs in this section derive from pages 60–65 of this working paper.

86. "The University Innovation Alliance to Enhance Access and Success at Public Research Universities: Vision and Prospectus" (2014), 4. Development of this working paper was supported by funding from the Lumina Foundation and the Bill and Melinda Gates Foundation. Michael Crow chairs the alliance with Mark Becker, president, Georgia State University, serving as co-chair.

87. Bridget Burns, "University Innovation Alliance Background and Proof Points of Success," working paper (2018).

88. U.S. Census Bureau, 2008–2012 American Community Survey, cited in "University Innovation Alliance: Vision and Prospectus," 3.

89. Kayla Fontenot, Jessica Semega, and Melissa Kollar, *Income and Poverty in the United States: 2017,* Current Population Reports, P60-263 (Washington, DC: U.S. Census Bureau, 2018).

90. Anthony Carnevale and Stephen Rose, "The Economy Goes to College: The Hidden Promise of Higher Education in the Post-Industrial Service Economy" (Washington, DC: Georgetown University Center for Education and the Workforce, 2015).

91. U.S. Census Bureau, 2008–2012 American Community Survey, cited in "University Innovation Alliance: Vision and Prospectus," 3–4.

92. "University Innovation Alliance: Vision and Prospectus," 5.

93. Anthony Carnevale, Nicole Smith, and Jeff Strohl, "Recovery: Job Growth and Education Requirement through 2020" (Washington, DC: Georgetown University Center for Education and the Workforce, 2014); Carnevale, Smith, and Strohl, "Help Wanted: Projections of Jobs and Education Requirements Through 2018" (Washington, DC: Georgetown University Center for Education and the Workforce, June 2010).

94. "University Innovation Alliance: Vision and Prospectus," 6. See John Kania and Mark Kramer, "Collective Impact," *Stanford Social Innovation Review* (Winter 2011): 36–41, and E. M. Rogers, *The Diffusion of Innovations* (New York: Free Press, 2003), both cited in the prospectus.

95. Integrated Postsecondary Education Data System (IPEDS), cited in "University Innovation Alliance: Vision and Prospectus," 5.

96. "University Innovation Alliance: Vision and Prospectus," 4.

97. Tunku Varadarajan, "College Bloat Meets 'The Blade,'" *Wall Street Journal* (December 14, 2018).

98. "University Innovation Alliance Vision," University Innovation Alliance, accessed on September 21, 2018, https://www.youtube.com/watch?v=KioAdLTEwbs.

99. Joel McFarland, et al., *The Condition of Education 2018* (NCES 2018-144) (Washington, DC: U.S. Department of Education, National Center for Education Statistics, 2018), 163.

100. Taylor Walsh, *Unlocking the Gates: How and Why Leading Universities Are Opening Up Access to Their Courses* (Princeton, NJ: Princeton University Press, 2010).

101. "U.S. Department of Education Acts on Purdue NewU Plan to Acquire Kaplan, Operate as Indiana's Newest Public Institution," *Purdue University News,* accessed on

September 19, 2017, https://www.purdue.edu/newsroom/releases/2017/Q3/u.s.-department
-of-education-acts-on-purdue-newu-plan-to-acquire-kaplan,-operate-as-indianas
-newest-public-institution.html.

102. Andy Thomason, "Purdue U. Buys Mega For-Profit Kaplan U., Plans to Turn
It into a Public University," *Chronicle of Higher Education*, April 27, 2017, https://www
-chronicle-com.ezproxy1.lib.asu.edu/blogs/ticker/purdue-u-is-expected-to-buy-mega
-for-profit-kaplan-u-turn-it-into-a-public-university/118020.

103. Dan Bauman and Goldie Blumenstyk, "A Sector in Flux: How For-Profit Higher
Ed Has Shifted," *Chronicle of Higher Education*, March 13, 2018, https://www-chronicle
-com.ezproxy1.lib.asu.edu/article/A-Sector-in-Flux-How/242813.

104. Goldie Blumenstyk, "Online Learning Is Misunderstood: Here's How," *Chronicle of Higher Education*, August 22, 2018, https://www.chronicle.com/article/Online
-Learning-Is/244173.

105. Ted Mitchell, letter to Barbara Gellman-Danley, January 25, 2018, https://www
.purdue.edu/president/email/2018/NewU-quotes.pdf.

106. Elinor Ostrom, *Governing the Commons: The Evolution of Institutions for Collective Action* (Cambridge: Cambridge University Press, 1990).

107. Garrett Hardin, "The Tragedy of the Commons," *Science* 162, no. 3859 (December 13, 1968): 1243–1248.

108. Elinor Ostrom and Charlotte Hess, "A Framework for Analyzing the Knowledge Commons," in *Understanding Knowledge as a Commons: From Theory to Practice*,
ed. Charlotte Hess and Elinor Ostrom (Cambridge, MA: MIT Press, 2007), 41.

109. Jonathan R. Cole, *Toward a More Perfect University* (New York: Public Affairs,
2016), 171–183.

110. Craig Calhoun, "The University and the Public Good," *Thesis Eleven* 84 (February 2006): 7–43.

# THREE

# Boutique Production Strategies and Appropriate Scale

In its intent to balance the imperative to accommodate enrollment growth with the effort to advance world-class knowledge production, the California Master Plan for Higher Education could to some extent be said to anticipate the emergence of the New American University and Fifth Wave models. The 1960 Master Plan codified the tripartite hierarchical differentiation of the three sectors of public higher education in that state, beginning with the University of California system, which emerged with the Third Wave and transitioned to the Fourth Wave; the state colleges that would subsequently constitute the California State University system, which originated with the teachers' colleges of the Second Wave; and the community colleges, which would come to form a third system that exemplifies the broad accessibility of the Second Wave. With its provisions for the coordination of differentiated sectors, permitting broad accessibility both in the community colleges and Cal State campuses while advancing research-grade knowledge production in the University of California, the plan has been characterized as an "internationally acclaimed blueprint for the transition to mass higher education."[1] Jonathan Cole pinpoints the upshot: "In short, [Kerr] wanted to build a state system that was designed for both access and excellence."[2] The lineage of the fundamental tenets of the New American University model is plainly evident, and to reiterate an essential point, the effort by Arizona State University to combine broad accessibility with world-class knowledge production arguably integrates in a single academic platform the research-grade infrastructure of the University of California system with the accessibility offered by the Cal State system. And although the Master Plan represents a historically successful prototype conceived with the intent to promote accessibility to research-grade academic platforms, the top-tier UC campuses, especially Berkeley and UCLA, instead increasingly rival their institutional peers among the Ivy League and Fourth Wave counterparts in restricting access to the majority of academically qualified applicants.

A closer look at the terms of the Master Plan reveals the extent to which its provisions were motivated by the twin imperatives of accessibility and knowledge production. In brief, the University of California was to retain its nearly exclusive responsibility for research and prerogative to confer doctoral degrees as well as assume the mandate to educate the top 12.5 percent of California public high school graduates. As former UC provost C. Judson King points out, "UC de facto became the designated research arm of the state." The state colleges that would subsequently form the California State University system would educate the top third of high school graduates as well as confer a range of master's degrees. The balance of students (all students "capable of benefitting from instruction") would be eligible for enrollment in community colleges, which were authorized to grant associate's degrees, offer remedial instruction, and focus on workforce preparation. The provision for students who succeeded in the community colleges or Cal State system to transfer to the UC system would be an important component of the arrangement. To facilitate the transfer process, the Master Plan specifies that UC maintain a 60 to 40 ratio between upper and lower division enrollments. Although rates of transfer have substantially declined, from up to 35 percent in the 1980s to as low as 15 percent for the cohort entering in 2003, King points out that up to 28 percent of bachelor's degree recipients in the UC system transferred from community colleges. No less critical to the Master Plan was the intent to ensure that no student would be denied admission for lack of financial resources.[3]

"Although the Master Plan gives the impression of being a grand design put together starting afresh," writes King, "it was in fact the result of complex negotiations in a contentious and politicized environment."[4] Motivated in part by a projected fourfold increase in overall enrollment demand in the state by 1975, University of California administrators in the late 1950s sought to negotiate the terms of an expansion of statewide enrollment capacity. But Clark Kerr, then only recently inaugurated as president, also intended to consolidate the position of the university as the preeminent research institution in California. As John Aubrey Douglass points out, "For California's land-grant university, the advantages of the tripartite system were tremendous. The university maintained its central and elevated role in graduate education and research, and the university was given license to continue its relatively high admissions standards—indeed, to raise them."[5] Because the Cal State system absorbed a majority of the student population seeking bachelor's degrees, the UC research enterprise did not need to fear inevitable "dilution," as King puts it, by the greater effort that would have had to be expended on undergraduate education.[6]

Under the terms of the eventual agreement, as Douglass explains, UC and Cal State would both recalibrate their existing social contracts and benefit by raising admissions standards. At one stroke, reducing access would produce more selective student populations. "The main motivation was financial," Douglass explains:

> To reduce costs, the University of California and the state colleges (what would become CSU) agreed to reduce their eligibility pools of high school graduates. The University of California would raise its admission standards with the purpose of lowering its pool of eligible freshmen from approximately its historical figure of the top 15 percent to the top 12.5 percent of public high school graduates. California State University raised its admissions standards and lowered its eligibility pool from approximately the top 50 percent to the top 33.3 percent of California's secondary school graduates. In turn, these revised targets would shift in the near term approximately 50,000 students to the junior colleges (what would be renamed the California Community Colleges) with lower operating costs and funding primarily from local property taxes.[7]

Despite explosive population growth in California over the past half-century, the eligibility criteria specified in 1960 remain fixed. Because of the increasing selectivity of the UC and Cal State systems, California has relied more heavily on its community colleges to provide initial lower-division enrollment than any other state. As a consequence, California reports the highest proportion of enrollment in community colleges in the nation, a figure that peaked at 74 percent in 2006–2007. The broader implications are considerable. King reports: "While California stands second among the fifty states in higher education enrollment per one thousand in the eighteen-to-twenty-nine range, it stands dead last among the states in the proportion of students (only 26 percent) enrolled in four-year institutions." Despite projected shortfalls of highly educated workers, California ranks forty-third among the fifty states in baccalaureate recipients in this cohort: 23.8 per thousand.[8] Needless to add, the broad accessibility to research-grade academic platforms offered by the Fifth Wave suggests a solution to the suboptimal societal outcomes of the conventional segmentation of sectors in higher education, here exemplified in California.

Simon Marginson terms the Master Plan the "best known of all blueprints for system organization, one that helped to shape higher education across the country and across the world." And indeed, the tenets of the Master Plan would resonate worldwide. As Marginson points out, "Something of the same optimism and faith in common and constructed solutions was evident in Europe and Britain—for example, in the 1963 Robbins Report, which called for a major expansion in British higher education."[9] We consider the Robbins Report in chapter 7 as well as other attempts to reconcile the demands of enrollment growth with the imperative for knowledge production internationally.

## A Glimpse at the Assessment of Appropriate Scale

The claim that Arizona State University represents the attempt to realize an organizational framework that combines academic excellence with broad accessibility, which, as we propose throughout these chapters, may be likened to coupling within a single institution the world-class research excellence of the University of California system with the accessibility offered by the Cal State system, deserves closer scrutiny. With 481,000 students on twenty-three campuses, the California State University system is among the largest in the nation. Relative to the conventional college-age population in the state of Arizona, ASU as a single institution is nearly as large as the entire Cal State system, while its relative enrollment of socioeconomically disadvantaged students dwarfs the enrollment rate of comparable students at any single UC campus.

The proposition that the Fifth Wave will initially comprise a subset of large-scale public research universities that have undertaken deliberate expansion of scale sufficient to offer broad accessibility to learning environments of world-class knowledge production neglects to define and consider the implications of one of its integral concepts. What constitutes appropriate or optimal scale for this set of institutions? Is this simply to posit that colleges and universities attain some sort of homeostatic equilibrium and optimal function when their capacity becomes proportionate to enrollment demand and population growth? Is it simplistic or tautological to argue that the scale of the set of major research universities should be sufficient to fulfill their various missions? And to what extent are these institutions even scalable?

Scale is generally conceptualized in terms of enrollment numbers and is inextricably linked with the concept of access, but the concept of scale is both far more complicated and complex. Of course, one might speak of the scale of the impact of an institution in terms of its research enterprise, for example, in which case a small institution like Caltech has outsized impact. Or one could evaluate the scale of the impact of an institution in terms of its public engagement or societal advancement. Scale is a multidimensional assessment that must not only consider size but also representation—is a university large enough for the population it is tasked with serving? Two institutions of the same size in terms of enrollment can exert drastically different levels of impact depending on their missions and objectives and the demographics of their respective student populations. Scale, then, must be an assessment of how much value a university can contribute to society.

Inasmuch as we benchmark the University of California as an exemplar of world-class research excellence, we take the liberty of gauging its performance in another context. In 2017, 1,233,775 Californians and 252,586 Arizonans between the ages of eighteen and twenty-four earned less than 175 percent of the Federal Poverty Level in 2017, according to the American Community Survey. These socioeconomically disadvantaged residents made up 35 percent and 40.5 percent of the total population in this age bracket in California and Arizona, respectively. The enrollment of undergraduate Pell-eligible students in the University of California system in 2017 was equal to 6.7 percent of the lower-income college age population in the state, compared to 11.9 percent at Arizona State University. From 2007 to 2017, UC's performance on this measure increased by 2.5 percentage points, but ASU increased by 7 percentage points.

The enrollment of Pell students at ASU relative to the socioeconomically disadvantaged college-age population in Arizona dwarfs the enrollment rate of similar students at any single UC campus. Of the UC campuses, Irvine had the highest enrollment intensity of lower-income students at only 1 percent of the total eighteen-to-twenty-four-year-old lower-income population in the state. Consider that, in order for UCLA to match the performance of ASU on this measure, it would have had to enroll 146,820 Pell students in 2017, which would have been 115,818 more than actual enrollment. While these hypothetical students could be freshmen or transfers, consider that 64 percent of admitted freshman to UCLA in fall 2018 had a weighted high school GPA of 4.2 or above. (In 2012 that figure had been 92.6 percent. The drastic reduction may be attributed to a systemwide change in policy regarding the calculation of GPAs.) Given that the population of lower-income students in California is so large and the enrollment capacity of the UC campuses so limited, UC can in effect cherry-pick the highest-performing lower-income students. UC's low-access model is what drives UC's high graduation rates. In other words, the high graduation rates are not evidence that the University of California has discovered a new model for higher education that enables upward economic mobility. The graduation rates are instead in part an outcome of the systematic selection of only high-achieving lower-income students. To the extent that these students are upwardly mobile, then, it could be argued that antecedent traits and experiences— the sort of profiles that predict selection for admission—rather than primarily their experience while enrolled, fundamentally contributed to their success.

ASU has undertaken efforts to develop a graduation-rate reporting framework that provides more detailed and meaningful data than the current cohort-based reporting system and found that the graduation rate for ASU freshmen who entered in fall 2013 with a high school GPA of 3.67 or higher was 70.7 percent. Students in this cohort who received a Pell Grant graduated at a rate of 66.8 percent. While direct comparisons between ASU and UC at this level of detail are not possible given data availability, consider that the average unweighted GPA for the incoming class of 2013 at UC San Diego was 3.77, but their four-year graduation rate was just 65.1 percent in 2013.[10]

If the objective of the reconceptualization described in the previous chapter had been incremental improvement of an historical model, ASU could readily have followed the path from Point A, representing its status prior to the design process, to Point B, with B representing a conventional Fourth Wave research university. The framework for such a generic public university would include the perpetuation of disciplinary silos, establishment of a medical school, culling of the student body through the selection of handpicked freshmen classes leading to the elimination of the bottom quarter of the undergraduate student body based on the criterion of prior academic preparation, and a reduction in the number of students admitted with Pell Grants. The conventional approach would have sought to transform ASU into another very large "flagship" public research university such as UCLA or the University of Washington. The Fourth Wave model has been immensely successful, but the limitations of the present model in the context of the changing demographics of metropolitan Phoenix motivated the academic community to aspire to move beyond Point B—the Fourth Wave research university—to Point C, which represents the operationalization of an academic platform characterized by differentiated transdisciplinary academic units and new approaches to teaching, learning, and research at scale, with scale correlated with enrollment demand, socioeconomic diversity, and the intent to realize societal impact. The Fifth Wave thus embraces scale and scope as assets, and leverages technology to realize an expansive social footprint while simultaneously increasing performance and quality.

## The Scale of Elite Higher Education

"In every advanced society the problems of higher education are problems associated with growth," sociologist Martin Trow proposed more than four decades ago in a report that codified conventional notions of elite, mass, and universal higher education.[11] "One thing is certain: mass higher education is a permanent condition of higher education throughout the world," Philip Altbach corroborates with reference to the transition from elite to mass higher education in a comparative context.[12] "If there is a single factor most basic to the structural transformation of higher education and research it is simply growth in scale," observes Craig Calhoun.[13] And indeed it is growth in scale and complexity and the attendant structural transformation of institutional types that provokes the emergence of successive waves in our typology. But in the United States, the "very idea of expansion is anathema to the elite," as David Kirp reminds us. "Instead these schools set ever-higher standards for admission. The most selective reject seven out of eight applicants, almost all of whom are qualified."[14] The determination to moderate enrollments, of course, is not the consequence of some nefarious intent to curtail intergenerational socioeconomic mobility but generally correlates with fiscal constraints. "To extend enrollments beyond an optimal point requires extraordinary expense for additional space or personnel—a jump in marginal costs," as Roger Geiger points out. "One cannot generalize across hundreds of institutions, each of which carefully evaluates when, where, how, and which additional students might be accommodated, but the calculus on balance has not favored expansion."[15]

Boutique production strategies predominate in elite higher education. The term refers to the sort of small-scale craft production characteristic of the manufacturing operations of the pre-industrial era. Of course, production strategies of this scale are precisely what characterize the artisanal approaches of the upper tiers of academic practice, which the economist William Baumol likened to handicraft industries. Baumol and his colleague William Bowen focused on the performing arts to examine the implications of lack of productivity gains in labor-intensive "industries" such as higher education.[16] Faculties within respective disciplinary fields are essentially guilds, betraying the medieval origins of the modern research university, and disciplinary acculturation accordingly is essentially an apprenticeship, which is "not merely the preferred method of 'manual' trades but also of the higher reaches of academic disciplines."[17] Boutique manufacturing production comports with the artisanal practices characteristic of research in the top tiers of academe because all aspects of the process can be minutely calibrated and individualized.[18] Artisanal modes may remain essential to discovery, creativity, and innovation—there is no efficient way to discover the origins of the universe—but at issue are the productivity gains permitted only through sociotechnical integration.

But whereas enrollment growth is invariably associated with less-selective second-tier institutions explicitly committed to accessibility, the Fifth Wave has the potential to integrate world-class knowledge production and innovation with broad accessibility and thus conjoin in a single institutional platform the missions and objectives of the set of leading major research universities and liberal arts colleges—the sector in academic culture associated with elite higher education—with the egalitarian objectives inaugurated by the second and third waves. The Fifth Wave thus accommodates and may even be said to guide or structure the transition from the elite to mass to universal phases and in so doing establish the conditions for mass access to the sort of comprehensive liberal arts education and research-pedagogic academic milieu historically characteristic of the elite phase of higher education. Indeed, the Fifth Wave aspires to serve as a framework for universal learning.

Although our nation's leading research universities, both public and private, consistently dominate global rankings, U.S. success in establishing world-class excellence in a relative handful of elite institutions does little to ensure the broad distribution of the benefits of educational attainment, nor does it secure conditions conducive to the innovation that contributes to our continued national competitiveness, especially if we stop to consider the disproportionately scant number of students deemed sufficiently meritorious to be admitted to these top schools. When historian Anthony Grafton referred to the "little group of traditional liberal arts colleges, all of whose students could fit in the football stadium of a single Big Ten school," his characterization of the incommensurability of the mismatch between supply and demand in elite higher education was no mere hyperbole.[19] He may have had in mind the assessment of the dilemma by Michael McPherson and Morton Schapiro, who observed that "all of the nation's liberal arts college students would almost certainly fit easily inside a Big Ten football stadium: fewer than 100,000 students."[20]

And indeed, in our previous book we cited data that showed that the top fifty liberal arts colleges collectively enrolled 95,496 undergraduates, excluding the three service academies, a number that would not quite fill the 110,000 seats in Michigan Stadium in Ann Arbor. Revised figures indicate that enrollment in this set of schools has now declined to 94,324. If we were to include West Point, Annapolis, and the Air Force Academy in the calculation, which rank among the top fifty liberal arts colleges in the *U.S. News & World Report* assessment that serves as our guide in this context, this figure would increase to 107,586 or, excluding the military academies but including the next three colleges in the rankings, 100,373.[21]

Regardless of which numbers one cites, seats for nearly all of these students would still be available in Michigan Stadium.

In our previous tally we then calculated that aggregate undergraduate enrollment in the Ivy League schools, together with the fifty top liberal arts colleges, accounted for less than 1 percent of the total U.S. undergraduate population of 18.2 million. The eight traditional Ivies enrolled 65,677 undergraduates during academic year 2013–2014, a figure that has increased nominally to 67,296 in fall 2017. As a consequence, even more students would have to be turned away from Yale Bowl, which still only accommodates 61,446. But although the total number of undergraduates in the nation declined to 17.1 million in 2017, all the undergraduates in the Ivies together with their peers in the fifty top liberal arts colleges still accounted for less than 1 percent of the total U.S. undergraduate population.[22]

But perhaps this assessment unfairly circumscribes the extent of the elite student body. If we take institutional membership in the prestigious Association of American Universities (AAU), which comprises sixty leading research universities in the United States, both public and private, as proxy for elite higher education, the number of seats available for undergraduates in highly selective institutions climbed from 1.1 million in AY 2013–2014 to 1.2 million in AY 2017–2018. In 2012 AAU reported that its public member institutions enrolled 918,221, while AAU private schools enrolled 211,500. We estimate in 2019 that the public AAU schools enroll 1,008,779 and the privates 222,173. As a consequence, if we consider only the thirty-four public AAU member institutions, their share of overall enrollment in the nation climbed from 5 percent to 5.89 percent, while enrollment in the twenty-six private member institutions ticked up from 1.14 percent to 1.3 percent. And total undergraduate enrollment at AAU schools increased from approximately 6 percent to 7.18 percent of American undergraduates.[23]

But we might frame the scale of the dilemma yet another way. In our previous book we reported that in a nation with roughly 18.2 million undergraduates enrolled in postsecondary education—including 45 percent attending community colleges and 10 percent enrolled in for-profit sector institutions—the combined undergraduate enrollments of the 108 research-extensive universities, which include all sixty AAU schools and thus the Ivies as well, numbered little more than 2 million, or roughly 11 percent of the undergraduate population.[24] We estimate in 2019 that in a nation with 17.1 million undergraduates enrolled in post-secondary institutions—including 41 percent enrolled in community colleges and 6 percent enrolled in for-profits—the combined undergraduate enrollment of the 115 research-extensive universities, including the sixty AAU schools and thus the Ivies—numbers 2.4 million, or roughly 14.4 percent of American college students. If we factor in the second tier of research universities, which the Carnegie scheme previously termed merely research-intensive and now designates as R2 institutions, undergraduate enrollment climbs to 3.7 million, or roughly 22.1 percent of overall undergraduate enrollment.[25]

At this point it is appropriate to reiterate the proposition that what is at issue is not the education of students who graduate in the top 5 or 10 percent of their high school classes, which represents business as usual at our leading universities, but rather the imperative addressed by the Fifth Wave to educate to internationally competitive levels of achievement the top quarter or third of respective age cohorts in traditional brackets, that is, eighteen-to-twenty-four-year-olds, and through universal-learning frameworks to provide opportunities for lifelong learning to more than half the population of the United States.

It is worth noting that the observed decrease in total undergraduate enrollments since the analysis of our previous book should be viewed within the broader context in which college enrollment is, to a certain extent, a function of economic prosperity. Between 2006 and 2010, the relatively brief period encompassing the global financial crisis, overall enrollment at degree-granting postsecondary institutions rose 18 percent. In the subsequent six years, enrollment decreased by 6 percent, with total enrollment at all Title IV degree-granting institutions decreasing by 1.7 percent and 1.0 percent in 2016 and 2017, respectively.[26] Rising unemployment and decreasing job prospects drove more students to seek a college education. But as the economy recovered, unemployment decreased, workforce numbers rebounded, and college enrollment figures declined as a consequence. For-profit institutions, in particular, have seen precipitous decreases in enrollment—13.7, 14.5, and 7.1 percent in 2015, 2016, and 2017, respectively. In that timeframe, enrollment at four-year degree-granting for-profit institutions alone dropped by 141,805—a

12.5 percent decrease.[27] A large share of these enrollment declines are attributable to the highly publicized closures of Corinthian Colleges and ITT Technical Institute, which, when combined, accounted for approximately 73,000 students at the time of their dissolution.

Christopher Newfield offers some alternative numbers that further illustrate the gap between the supply and demand for research-grade higher education. He estimates that 0.7 percent of students will attend an Ivy League or Ivy-comparable private research university and 2.4 percent will attend an elite liberal arts college. He cites the observation that "the 225 private liberal arts colleges described in *America's Best Colleges* enroll 349,000 students, which is the same number of students that attend just three large urban community college systems (Miami-Dade College, Northern Virginia Community College, and the Houston Community College System)." Regardless of which figures one considers, the allocation of opportunity that these and other readily available statistics betoken heralds what Newfield terms the "devolutionary cycle" that undermines the benefits that society should expect from its support of public research universities and threatens the "democratization of intelligence" and "collective enlightenment" to which our society might otherwise aspire.[28]

Scale is a correlate of accessibility, but a recent assessment underscores the significance of scale as a correlate of research performance among major research universities. Competitive success in research performance is moreover assessed as a correlate of overall academic quality for research institutions. Taking federal science and engineering expenditures as a leading indicator of success, the authors of the study—William B. Rouse, John V. Lombardi, and Diane D. Craig—identified 160 single campus institutions, both public and private, that each reported over $40 million in this category of expenditures in 2014. This subset represents 7 percent of the 2,285 four-year nonprofit institutions of higher education and 19 percent of all institutions that receive federal research funding. The subset, however, reports 92 percent of all federal research expenditures. This "concentration of research performance" among the most highly competitive major research universities builds atop robust institutional financial foundations. "Endowment assets serve as a proxy for institutional wealth," the authors observe, and report that this subset of institutions raises 75 percent of all endowment assets. "Scale is important in research university success," Rouse and colleagues conclude. "Larger scale spreads the costs of research over more projects, faculty, and research programs. Many research institutions have significant undergraduate student bodies whose numbers, through tuition, fees, state support, and alumni commitment, drive resources and support the teaching and other work associated with instruction." Where this set of institutions arguably falls short is in their accessibility. These 160 institutions enroll roughly 3.5 million students, which in 2014 represented only 18 percent of the 20.2 million students enrolled at all levels in American higher education.[29]

Although Fourth Wave public research universities represent the attainment of remarkable public value because of their unparalleled contributions to society, in a sense they could be said to have hit scale limits. They have proven resistant to scaling in response to the demand for their services, responding to rapid changes in technology and demographics, and addressing problems in the financing of higher education, which manifest in high costs and increasing tuition. To some extent the first attempts to shift toward societal-scale impact levels in higher education were led by for-profit institutions sensing a market opportunity that public universities were not able to accommodate or chose to disregard. In most cases, these efforts have proven to be unsuccessful. The purpose of for-profit universities is to increase shareholder value, an end that is often in conflict with the creation of public value, which has been characterized as "the prerogatives, normative standards, social supports, rights and procedural guarantees that a given society aspires to provide to all citizens."[30] Many goods that are successful in the market fail to produce public value, of course. For-profit universities may sometimes respond to particular market segments, but in terms of returns for society—increased student indebtedness, decreased graduation rates, and poor outcomes for veterans and low-income and minority students— have been public value failures.[31] Emerging Fifth Wave institutions should be designed to offer a remedy to these various limitations by becoming more adaptive and responsive to the full set of stakeholder demands. They also offer a remedy to the public value failures of the unsuccessful profit-driven models by leveraging technology to enhance quality and responsivity rather than to maximize profit margins.

At issue is the scale of enrollment capacity in research-grade American higher education. Assessments of scale in higher education generally focus on aggregate enrollment demand. As educational theorist Mitchell Stevens points out, "It has been methodologically convenient to model U.S. higher education as the sum of individual students making individual choices about where, when, and under what statistically described conditions they attend college." But the focus on enrollment demand by social scientists—what he terms "linear models of students moving through college"—minimizes the imperative to focus on the enrollment capacities of individual institutions, including the aggregate supply of places in research-grade institutions. As Stevens elaborates: "Economists describe the problem succinctly: social scientists focus primarily on the demand side and are weak on the supply side of higher education."[32] But as Geiger points out, despite significant fluctuations in the number of high school graduates over the final quarter of the twentieth century, freshman enrollments remained remarkably consistent: "This fact strongly suggests that freshman enrollments at these institutions are in the aggregate largely determined by the supply of places."[33] And among the implications of such boutique production strategies are enrollment capacities that have failed to scale with demand. The mismatch leads to stagnation in the supply of college graduates, educated citizens, and members of the workforce—in short, the human capital essential to the competitiveness, prosperity, and well-being of our society.

Moreover, the present level of accessibility to research-grade institutions will not keep pace with workforce projections that predict a significant shortfall of educated workers and disregards estimates that population growth will likely exceed 100 million by midcentury. In the postrecession economy, workforce experts reaffirm the well-established correlation between educational attainment and employment outcomes, and especially the premium in wages, as well as the projected large-scale shortfalls of educated workers. By the end of the decade, 65 percent of all jobs will require at least some college, and 35 percent a bachelor's degree, according to Anthony Carnevale and his colleagues at the Center on Education and the Workforce at Georgetown University. Their research projects a shortfall of 5 million workers with at least some advanced training. And indeed, in the postrecession recovery, which began in early 2010, 4.6 million jobs have gone to workers with bachelor's degrees and 3.8 million to graduate-degree holders, while those with only a high school diploma account for only 80,000 job placements.[34]

Carnevale and colleagues estimate that degree production would have to increase by roughly 10 percent each year to prevent a shortfall. To achieve the ambitious objectives for educational attainment specified by President Barack Obama in his first address to a joint session of Congress in February 2009—the president envisioned an America that by the end of the present decade would again boast the highest proportion of college graduates in the world—our colleges and universities would have to produce an additional 8.2 million graduates by 2020, over and above the number projected with the current rate of degree production.[35] Another study led by Carnevale and Stephen J. Rose underscored the interrelationship between an "undereducated" society and increasing income inequality: "The undersupply of postsecondary-educated workers has led to two distinct problems: a problem of efficiency and a problem of equity." At issue is both the loss in productivity that comes with a workforce lacking advanced skills and, at the same time, scarcity, which "drives up the cost of postsecondary talent precipitously, exacerbating inequality." The upshot, according to Carnevale, is that "to correct our undersupply and meet our efficiency and equity goals for the economy and for our society, we will need to add an additional 20 million postsecondary-educated workers to the economy by 2025."[36]

### The Persistence of Boutique Production Strategies

Proposals to increase enrollments in the upper echelons of research-grade higher education have typically provoked defensive reactions. Roger Geiger recounts several telling historical episodes: "Too many young men are going to college," Ernest Hopkins, president of Dartmouth, declared in 1922. In this context, Abraham Flexner, founding director of the Institute for Advanced Study, opined that universities had become "service stations for the general public." Flexner also pronounced that American universities had "needlessly cheapened, vulgarized, and mechanized themselves." And to cite but one further example offered by Geiger, when Yale embarked on a capital campaign in 1927, the university sought to reassure stakeholders that the intent was to "make a finer, not a bigger Yale."[37] Expansionist phases, such as the three decades following World War II that have been termed the Golden Age of American higher education, have accordingly been framed as crises of overeducation. As sociologist David Baker explains: "New predictions of a looming overeducation crisis are trotted out with each succeeding wave of educational expansion, such as with the current expansion of graduate education."[38] But to the contention that too many students are enrolling in college, James Lewis Morrill, president of the University of Minnesota from 1945 through 1960, aptly remarked: "Those who so speak are always thinking of the children of someone else, never their own."[39]

The academic gold standard in American higher education represents an immensely successful institutional platform that invariably combines world-class teaching and research with modest levels of enrollment. When it comes to undergraduate education, the scale of this enterprise appears to have been cast in stone by the First Wave. A few figures from some representative liberal arts colleges should be sufficient to evoke the boutique production scale of these schools. During the academic year 2017–2018, total undergraduate enrollment at Swarthmore, for example, was 1,577, and the figures for Bowdoin, Bard, and Williams were 1,816, 1,930, and 2,061, respectively. This comes as no surprise, but many of the leading institutions of the Fourth Wave maintain relatively small undergraduate enrollments as well. A three-to-one student-faculty ratio at Caltech comes by dint of enrollment of 948 undergraduates along with 1,285 graduate students. MIT enrolled 4,602 undergraduate and 6,972 graduate students. From there we begin to scale up to the sort of enrollments one finds at Harvard, where the undergraduate population topped out at 6,699. At its 368th commencement, in May 2019, the university awarded 1,662 baccalaureate degrees. From among 42,749 applicants to the Class of 2022, Harvard College admitted 2,024 prospective students, of which 1,653 matriculated. Although its undergraduate enrollment numbers are par for the Ivy League, Harvard supports one of the larger graduate and professional student populations among the Ivies, which at 15,250 is roughly equivalent to the number of graduate students attending the University of Michigan. Princeton leads the pack among top universities in the 2019 edition of the *U.S. News & World Report* rankings and in fall term 2018 enrolled 5,260 undergraduates but only 2,845 graduate students. (Of course, unlike Harvard and Yale,

Princeton does not have a graduate school of business, law school, or medical school.) Yale enrolled 5,964 undergraduates and 7,469 graduate and professional students. For Stanford those figures are 7,083 and 8,021, respectively, and for Columbia, from a total enrollment of 33,032, undergraduate enrollment was 8,931. Enrollment figures for public research universities are normally far higher than those of their private peer institutions, of course. The entire student body of Harvard College corresponds roughly in number to the total of undergraduate degrees conferred yearly at the University of California, Berkeley, or the number of undergraduates enrolled in the School of Engineering at the University of Texas at Austin. Yet, even these public institutions have not scaled up their enrollment capacities commensurate with either workforce requirements or population growth.

The number of bachelor's degrees awarded by the eight institutions of the Ivy League during the academic year 2016–2017 totaled 15,595, while the top fifty liberal arts colleges awarded 23,074. (We reiterate that ASU awarded 25,974 degrees in academic year 2017–2018, including 7,796 graduate and professional degrees.) During the same academic year, the Ivies rejected 258,355 applicants, while the liberal arts colleges turned away 223,790 or, if we include the military academies, 229,307. This pattern of exclusion is consistent with the trend among leading public universities, which continue to raise standards even while enrollment demand increases. The ratio of California resident freshman applicants to students admitted at UC Berkeley from 1975 to 1995, for example, declined from 77 percent to 39 percent.[40] Institutional data show that between fall semester 1989 and 2018, the ratio of admissions at Berkeley declined from 40 percent to 15 percent. The comparable figures for UCLA show decline from 46.5 percent to 14 percent. The actual numbers present the scenario even more starkly. Of 51,924 resident applicants to Berkeley in fall semester 2018—up from 43,255 five years earlier—only 8,726 were admitted, which means that 43,163 were turned away. At UCLA, 71,570 applied—up from 55,079 five years earlier—but only 8,726 were admitted, which means that 62,844 were excluded. Although the UC system as a whole accepted 76.6 percent of resident freshmen in fall semester 1989, by 2018 the acceptance rate had declined to 59 percent—down from 63 percent five years earlier.[41]

Although there seems to be little reliable data in this context available, we concede the point that the majority of applicants rejected from the Ivy League and other highly selective schools probably end up in some or other highly selective school, even if it turns out not to be their school of first choice. Moreover, the numbers cited for rejected applicants are not for unduplicated individuals. But that is not the point. This objection embodies and perpetuates the conventional focus on the evaluation of individual schools and individual students rather than the de facto system of American higher education. It is essential instead to look at how the system as a whole functions to realize the values of our society. The schools of the Ivy League and other elite universities, which are enormously well resourced from both public and private sources, collectively serve a small slice of the total college-going population. But our society is not made stronger by an academic culture primarily concerned with connecting the students most likely to succeed to schools that boast the most resources while relegating other academically qualified students to a second-order education. In other kinds of markets—let's say the market for designer handbags—whether or not only certain individuals can afford—or "access"—a designer bag does not become a public policy problem. But a designer bag is a private good, whereas quality education is a public good, which means that all of society benefits when individuals access the product. Instead of the present lottery for admission to one of the "best schools" in the estimation of *U.S. News & World Report*, the Fifth Wave represents an alternative model wherein a research-based undergraduate education is available to anyone qualified to access it.[42]

In chapter 1 we considered the inequities associated with admissions policies that purport to be meritocratic from the historical perspectives provided by James Karabel and Joseph Soares, but admissions protocols are even more arbitrary and less equitable when considered from the perspective suggested by Louis Menand. He likens the admissions protocols of highly selective schools to the scouting and scoring processes of major league baseball, wherein subjective processes of evaluation ("sizing up" motivation and personal qualities) vie with data capture across multivariable categories that purport to quantitative rigor (SAT scores and GPAs). He deems the deliberations regarding fairness in college admissions "oversimplified to the point of absurdity." As Menand points out: "There is no single standard for admissions at select colleges because there are so many different buckets to fill. When one applicant displaces an arguably more meritorious applicant, she is almost always displacing an applicant within her own bucket."[43] The "scouting-or-scoring dichotomy" Menand describes provides perspective on the more mundane and pedestrian aspects of a process that has more suitably been deconstructed in terms of the prerogatives of privilege delineated by Karabel and Soares, among others. However, the point here is simply that for the rank and file of academically qualified or even stellar middle-class and socioeconomically disadvantaged students, whose prosperity and well-being are tied to admissions decisions predicated on an inadequate academic infrastructure, the process is not only inequitable but harrowing.

In the mid-twentieth century, high school students from middle-class families who maintained respectable grade point averages could assume with a reasonable degree of certainty the likelihood of admission to the leading public universities of their respective home states. During the 1950s and 1960s, California high school graduates who completed a set of required courses and attained a cumulative 3.0 grade point average qualified for admission to one of the campuses of the University of California. "Eligible students possessed a *right* to enter the university but not necessarily their first-choice campus," Douglass clarifies.[44] The admissions policies of our top-tier institutions may purport to be meritocratic, but a significant proportion of alumni who are graduates of these schools from past decades—many of whom no doubt attribute their personal and professional success in large measure to the caliber of their education—would be summarily turned away under current protocols.

Regardless of the specific numbers one cites, the demands of both equity and prosperity argue that society needs to expand its capacity to produce millions of additional graduates during the next several decades capable of both catalyzing and benefiting from an economy increasingly based on the generation and application of useful knowledge. But when the prevailing academic culture assumes that enrollment growth must come at the expense of reputation and competitive standing, few indeed are the institutions willing to pursue strategies to produce the additional graduates needed to address the problems facing the world. Indeed, scarcity is the brand that our elite universities are selling. The idea that these institutions could exercise their potential to produce millions more highly qualified, workforce-ready, critical thinkers threatens the current business model. To reiterate a crucial point yet again, if leading Fourth Wave research universities deem it appropriate to maintain fixed levels of enrollment while excluding the majority of academically qualified applicants, alternative research-grade academic platforms must emerge that offer broader accessibility to academic excellence.

## Scaling the Fifth Wave: Elite to Mass to Universal

The Fifth Wave may in part be understood as a response to growth and expansion in higher education. The prescient assessments of Trow in this context codified conventional notions of elite, mass, and universal higher education and underscore the disproportionate impact of growth and expansion on the set of major research universities, as noted in chapter 1. In a 1973 report commissioned by the Carnegie Commission on Higher Education, Trow delineated the implications of these processes as well as their interrelatedness and complexity, beginning with the phrase cited earlier in this chapter: "In every advanced society the problems of higher education are problems associated with growth." The balance of the paragraph provides the following elaboration:

> Growth poses a variety of problems for the educational systems that experience it and for the societies that support them. These problems arise in every part of higher education—in its finance; in its government and administration; in its recruitment and selection of students; in its curriculum and forms of instruction; in its recruitment, training, and socialization of staff; in the setting and maintenance of standards; in the forms of examinations and the nature of qualifications awarded; in student housing and job placement; in motivation and morale; in the relation of research to teaching; and in the relation of higher education to the secondary school system on one hand, and to adult education on the other—growth has its impact on every form of activity and manifestation of higher education.[45]

Trow explains that expansion manifests in three different but interrelated ways: (1) in terms of changes in the rates of growth of systems or institutions, (2) in the absolute size of systems or institutions, and (3) in the rates of participation of respective cohorts. Growth is a function of the "broad patterns of development" in higher education in what he termed advanced societies, which he perceived to manifest in three phases of access: elite, mass, and universal. The phases differ both quantitatively and qualitatively.[46]

Access in the elite phase is tightly circumscribed and perceived as a "privilege, either of birth or talent or both." Trow characterizes the elite phase as concerned "primarily with shaping the mind and character of the ruling class, as it prepares students for elite roles in government and the learned professions." Trow correlates its purposes with the objectives of liberal education, which include the "cultivation of aesthetic sensibilities, broad human sympathies, and the capacity for critical and independent judgment."[47] Mass higher education represents participation of respective age cohorts exceeding 15 percent; the universal phase participation exceeding 50 percent. Access in the mass phase is perceived as a "right for those who have certain formal qualifications," and in the universal phase, an obligation for children from the middle and upper middle classes. In the mass phase, priorities shift toward the "transmission of skills for specific technical roles" for a broader elite ("the leading strata of all the technical and economic organizations of the society"). Universal access potentially implicates the entire population, and the "primary concern is to maximize the adaptability of that population to a society whose chief characteristic is rapid social and technological change."[48] In this continuum, as policy scholar Simon Marginson summarizes, "access to higher education shifted from being a privilege in the elite phase to a right in the mass phase and then to an 'obligation' in the universal phase, when higher qualifications become mandatory for full and effective social engagement."[49] The universal phase proposed by Trow corresponds to what some scholars have more recently designated high participation. In 1971 the United States became the first nation in the world to achieve high participation.[50] Marginson explains that inasmuch as Trow intended the term *universal* to refer to participation within a given age cohort above 50 percent, the designation *high participation* is more precise than universal, which suggests 100 percent participation.[51]

Consistent with our observations that each of the five waves comprises both the set of institutions that emerged during a given historical period and contemporary institutions representative of those institutional types, and that institutions from the first four waves continue to operate in parallel, Trow perceived the phases both as distinct historical stages and as "differing constellations of practice that exist alongside each other in the present."[52] The transition from one phase to the next "does *not* necessarily mean that the forms and patterns of the prior phase or phases disappear or are transformed," Trow explains. "On the contrary, the evidence suggests that each phase survives in some institutions and in parts of others while the system as a whole evolves to carry the larger numbers of students and the broader more diverse functions of the next phase." He further observes: "In a mass system, elite institutions may not only survive, but flourish; and elite functions continue to be performed within mass institutions." Because expansion is generally limited to nonelite institutions, highly selective institutions "defend their unique characteristics in the face of the growth and transformation of the system around them."[53]

Transitions between the phases require change in all of the various interrelated aspects of the structures and functions of institutions and systems, including the characteristics and size of institutions and systems; diversity of institutional types; accessibility and selectivity; attitudes toward access and perceptions of function; curricula, modes of instruction, and academic standards; profiles of students and trajectories of their progress; loci of power and decision making; and governance and administrative frameworks.[54] Trow specifies that the three phases represent Weberian ideal types, and indeed his enlistment of the concept suggested the relevance of the ideal-typical method to the schema of five waves. The three phases are thus "abstracted from empirical reality," Trow explains, "and emphasize the functional relationships among the several components of an institutional system common to all advanced industrial societies rather than the unique characteristics of any one." The ideal types elucidate three kinds of problems: functional relationships among constituent aspects of any system; challenges that confront systems in the transition from one phase to the next; and problems that arise in the interface between universities and the economic and political institutions of society.[55]

Of particular relevance to the present assessment: Trow observed that expansion invariably occurs in nonelite institutions. In other words, expansion of accessibility is atypical in research-grade institutions.

Marginson notes that the implications did not elude Trow: "High and growing participation in higher education does not necessarily trigger upward social mobility on a broad scale when social stratification is aligned to vertical institutional segmentation." In this context he quotes Trow: "The establishment of different sectors, reflecting the status hierarchies in the larger society, is a more effective way of using higher education to buttress rather than undermine class structure."[56] More recent studies corroborate the corrosive impact of the correlation between expansion in higher education and social stratification. As one team of researchers frame the dilemma: "The key question about educational expansion is whether it reduces inequality by providing more opportunities for persons from disadvantaged strata or magnifies inequality by expanding opportunities disproportionately for those who are already privileged." Because expansion typically accompanies hierarchical differentiation among institutional types, growth in enrollments generally occurs in less-selective second-tier institutions. Expansion may divert students from first-tier institutions, referring to what we term research-grade institutions.[57] One assessment found that "inequality between any two social strata in the odds of attaining a given level of education persists until the advantaged class reaches the point of saturation."[58] Expansion of higher education in the United States following World War II epitomizes its correlation with stratification, especially insofar as growth has been led by enrollments in less selective or even nonselective institutions such as community colleges and exclusively vocational schools.[59] Among high-participation systems of higher education globally, one team of scholars contend that because "growth of participation is associated with enhanced stratification and intensified competition at key transition points, all else being equal (i.e. without compensatory state policy), the expansion of participation is associated with a secular tendency to greater social inequality in educational outcomes and, through that, social outcomes."[60]

But the Fifth Wave has the potential to transcend the alignment of social stratification and institutional segmentation that these researchers discerned, as well as the host of design limitations associated with each of the three phases identified by Trow and the systems of high participation delineated by Cantwell, Marginson, and Smolentseva. Within seamless sociotechnically integrated academic frameworks, Fifth Wave institutions retain the academic standards and aspirations of the elite phase, which thus provides the sort of comprehensive liberal arts education offered by our nation's leading research universities and selective liberal arts colleges; leverage the expanded accessibility of the mass phase to advance pedagogical innovation to produce adaptive master learners empowered to negotiate the vicissitudes and workforce demands of a knowledge economy driven by perpetual innovation; and utilize the cutting-edge technological enhancement typically associated with the universal phase. As assessed in the case study chapter, the universal phase comprises varied modes, including full-immersion on-campus learning as well as hybrid online learning; online and digital immersion; online and digital immersion delivered at massive scale; and education through experience. The mass phase in the Fifth Wave model does not imply open access or the heedless deployment of MOOCs. Through innovation in delivery, the Fifth Wave will transcend what Trow termed the "tension between the autonomous and popular functions of American colleges and universities," especially insofar as these have been exacerbated by the ongoing transition from the mass toward universal phases of higher education.[61]

## Structural Accretion and Economies of Scale and Scope

"Growth has been the hallmark of American higher education in the past one and one-half centuries," sociologist Neil Smelser observes. But whether rapid or long-term, he points out, growth tracked in quantitative indices such as student enrollments inevitably correlates with qualitative changes that manifest in the social structures of institutions. Expansion in colleges and universities manifests in a process he terms "structural accretion," which he defines as the "incorporation of new functions over time without, however, shedding existing ones (deletion) or splitting into separate organizations." Growth and expansion is driven by new opportunities ("standing still . . . is contrary to the nature of the beast, and contraction is simply an abomination"); "mutual opportunism," referring to the confluence of interests of universities and external agencies, including the dependence of universities on external subsidies; and emulation of prestigious institutions, which we christen "Berkeley envy" or "Harvardization" depending on whether the institution under consideration is either public or private; and organizational inertia. As

Smelser points out, this "accumulation of functions" produces the "multiversity" described by Kerr. He quotes Altbach in this context: "When faced with new situations, traditional institutions either adjust by adding functions without changing their basic character or create new divisions or institutes." The upshot remains that the predominant feature of expansion remains the constant accumulation of functions, in which context Smelser quotes Kerr, who remarked with reference to this sort of inertia, "Change comes more through spawning the new than reforming the old."[62]

The structural changes associated with growth include increases in the size of units; segmentation of units, referring to an increase in the number of identical or similar units; differentiation of units leading to specialization (community colleges as opposed to major research universities, for example); and proliferation ("adding new functions to existing structures"), all of which requires coordination inasmuch as expansion "produces not only larger but also more complex structures with many more moving parts." Moreover, contrary to what he terms simplistic assumptions regarding economies of scale, "increases in scale of all types demand new structures, mechanisms, knowledge, and accompanying financial resources to deal with size and complexity."[63]

Both external restrictions and opportunities determine any element of choice involved in structural changes, Smelser explains, which "ramify in different directions, and express themselves in distinctive anomalies and contradictions, status hierarchies, strategic adaptations, and patterns of competition and conflict." Smelser elaborates regarding the ramifications of cumulative accretion: "The logic is as follows: if you take on a new function, you must add a new structure to perform it (an organized research unit, an administrative division, a special office); if you create a structure you also create a group of people to staff it; and if you create a group, you also create a new constituency, one which, typically, includes as one of its primary interests its own survival and enhancement."[64] But the accretions are nevertheless inevitable and necessary. As Kerr explained: "The three major sources of accretions in the twentieth century have been philanthropic activity among foundations, directed research funding on the part of federal agencies, and investment and collaboration from corporate sources."[65]

Fourth Wave institutions thus readily expand in terms of scope—the accumulation of functions leading to the multifunctionalities associated with the multiversity of Kerr—but paradoxically remain antagonistic both to reorganizing academic frameworks and adjusting scalability to cope with changing enrollments. But the interplay between economies of scale and scope contributes to the academic excellence, accessibility, competitive advantage, and societal impact of Fifth Wave institutions. *Economies of scale* may be defined as the "relative gain in output or saving of costs resulting from the greater efficiency of large-scale processes."[66] According to another basic definition, they are "the factors which make it possible for larger organizations or countries to produce goods or services more cheaply than smaller ones."[67] Economies of scale are achieved when per unit costs of production decrease as the volume of output increases as a consequence of the scale of operations. Diseconomies of scale, however, can occur as enterprises, organizations, and institutions become increasingly complex: "The larger an organization becomes in order to reap economies of scale, the more complex it has to be to manage and run such scale. This complexity incurs a cost, and eventually this cost may come to outweigh the savings gained from greater scale."[68] Economies of scope, by contrast, represent "cost savings which result from the scope (rather than the scale) of the enterprise."[69] *Economies of scope* have been defined as the "relative gain in efficiency or sales that may result from producing, distributing, or marketing a range of products, as opposed to a single product or type of product."[70] By another definition, they are "factors that make it cheaper to produce a range of products together than to produce each one of them on its own." Economies of scale have encouraged corporate gigantism, mass production, and mergers and acquisitions, while economies of scope lead to diversification.[71]

Both economies of scale and scope have been critical to the success of many large firms, Michael Gibbons and colleagues point out, citing the analysis of business historian Alfred Chandler in this context. But analogous dynamics obtain in knowledge production in an academic context, including the crucial interplay between economies of scale and scope: "Economies of scale are the gains made possible by the combination of technology and organisation in which the number of units of production or distribution increases while unit costs fall." What has been termed Big Science exploits the efficiencies of production on an industrial scale, the authors point out, citing the examples of CERN, Brookhaven Laboratories, and the University of California, which manages three national laboratories. All are "large managed research enterprises which can be compared, in terms of people employed, with many large corporations." But both industry and academia exploit economies of scope, which "in contrast, are gains arising from repeatedly configuring the same technologies and skills in different ways to satisfy market demand." Analogies between industry and academia are at once apparent: "Firms seeking economies of scope need continuing access to knowledge of many different kinds and, to acquire the necessary access, they are increasingly drawn into its production." But to the extent that their economies of scale remain derivative of industrial models, efforts to disseminate the outcomes and outputs of research are limited. "As long as universities and government research establishments were relatively isolated from markets, there was little incentive for them to seek outlets for the results of their research beyond their research communities."[72] Among the competitive advantages of large-scale comprehensive Fifth Wave research universities are economies of scope as well as scale that permit increasing diversification, reconfiguration, and transdisciplinary synthesis of knowledge production.

## Scale and Scalability in Research-Grade Universities

We reiterate the question: What constitutes appropriate or optimal scale for a given institution or set of institutions? And to what extent are institutions scalable? Scalability is an important concept in complexity theory,[73] and assessments of scaling in social organizations, referring in this context generally to scaling up, are increasingly common in the literature on social innovation. "Most of what we understand today about scaling up social change has been borrowed from nineteenth-century industrial expansion, twentieth-century pharmaceutical regulation, and twenty-first-century technology startups," according to one assessment. "While there is much that we can learn from these paradigms, they are insufficient for contemporary social innovation. They reflect an old mind-set in which organizations rather than impacts are scaled up, scaling is an imperative, bigger is better, and the purpose of scaling is commercial success."[74]

To begin more broadly, then, what is the meaning and significance of scale—and scaling and scalability—in the present context? According to theoretical physicist Geoffrey West, whose recent book on scale extrapolates from the physical laws governing growth to assess their analogous operation across life forms and various spheres of human endeavor and social organization, offers a succinct definition: the terms simply refer to "how things change with size and the fundamental rules and principles they obey." To glimpse the implications of scaling up, one might begin with the following paragraph:

> *Scaling* simply refers, in its most elemental form, to how a system responds when its size changes. What happens to a city or a company if its size is doubled? Or to a building, an airplane, an economy, or an animal if its size is halved? If the population of a city is doubled, does the resulting city have approximately twice as many roads, twice as much crime, and produce twice as many patents? Do the profits of a company double if its sales double, and does an animal require half as much food if its weight is halved?[75]

All such characteristics scale allometrically, or nonlinearly, West explains: "Nonlinear behavior can simply be thought of as meaning that measurable characteristics of a system generally do not simply double when its size is doubled." As organisms double in size, their metabolic rates scale sublinearly because of economies of scale, which he also terms "systematic savings with increasing size." He elaborates: "Put succinctly, this states that the bigger you are, the less you need per capita (or, in the case of animals, per cell or per gram of tissue) to stay alive." Infrastructure growth in cities scales sublinearly as well, but socioeconomic and cultural determinants scale superlinearly: "Social activity and economic productivity are *systematically* enhanced with increasing size of the population. This systematic value-added bonus as size increases is called *increasing returns to scale* by economists and social scientists." He adds that physicists prefer the "more sexy term *superlinear scaling*."[76]

Whereas West is primarily interested in the quantitative assessment of the structure and dynamics of such social organizations as companies and cities, he cites the numerous qualitative correlates and cumulative advantages to scaling up cities. Despite increased crime, pollution, and disease, scaling up confers both individual and collective benefits that account for the exponential urbanization since the Industrial Revolution. "To summarize: the bigger the city, the greater the social activity, the more opportunities there are, the higher the wages, the more diversity there is, the greater the access to good restaurants, concerts, museums, and educational facilities, and the greater the sense of buzz, excitement, and engagement." In this cosmopolitan milieu, "Successful companies and universities attract the smartest people, resulting in their becoming more successful, thereby attracting even smarter people, leading to even greater success and so on." Among the correlates are more abundant innovation, wealth generation, entrepreneurship, and job creation. West observes: "In this sense cities are prototypically multidimensional, and this is strongly correlated with their superlinear scaling, open-ended growth, and expanding social networks—and a crucial component of their resilience, sustainability, and seeming immortality."[77]

But whereas the "superlinear scaling of cities (and of economies) leads to open-ended growth," West explains, "sublinear scaling in biology leads to bounded growth and a finite life span." And because companies, like organisms, scale sublinearly, most eventually fail. "Companies are surprisingly biological and from an evolutionary perspective their mortality is an important ingredient for generating innovative vitality resulting from 'creative destruction' and 'the survival of the fittest.' Just as all organisms must die in order that the new and novel may blossom, so it is that all companies disappear or morph to allow new innovative variations to flourish." The free market favors the innovation of corporations like Google or Tesla, he points out, rather than the "stagnation of a geriatric IBM or General Motors."[78]

Although the disruptive innovation of a minority of companies grabs headlines, West contends, "most tend to be shortsighted, conservative, and not very supportive of innovative or risky ideas, happy to stay almost entirely with their major successes while the going is good because these 'guarantee' short-term returns." He finds that the relative amount allocated to research and development over bureaucratic and administrative expenses systematically decreases as company size increases and cautions that the pursuit of market share and profits typically correlates with more bureaucratic control accomplished at the expense of innovation. West corroborates Anthony Downs, who observes that, over time, bureaus inevitably develop more formalized systems of rules and regulations, conformity becomes an end in itself, and so does navigation through increasingly complex organizational structures. But— consistent with our claims for institutional innovation in the Fifth Wave—despite the routine, standardization, and inertia imposed by bureaucratization, West underscores that companies that increase their rate of innovation not only survive but also prosper. The point of the Fifth Wave, of course, is not mere survival or stasis but to increase the rate of discovery and innovation. Both companies and universities are actors in the national innovation system, but the multiversities described by Kerr and their counterparts in the Fifth Wave are more appropriately likened to cities, which West terms "prototypically multidimensional." Indeed, because of their role in the advancement of discovery and innovation and their contributions to cultural, economic, and social development, research universities are integral to the fabric of great cities, which, as West puts it, "embody the triumph of innovation over the hegemony of economies of scale."[79]

And, indeed, consistent with the conclusion that economic productivity and innovation increase disproportionally in larger urban agglomerations, universities scale like cities, according to West and colleagues, including Manfred Laubichler, a theoretical biologist and director of the Global Biosocial Complexity Initiative at Arizona State University. A new assessment from a group of scholars that includes West and Laubichler applies scaling analysis to institutions of higher education in the United States to demonstrate that research universities, both public and private, scale systematically in key metrics, including "variation in the level and composition of expenditures, revenues, graduation rates, and estimated economic added value, expressed as functions of total enrollment, our fundamental measure of size." The analysis provides insight into the "basic mechanisms, tradeoffs, and outcomes of university function related to size as societies aim to scale-up total educational outputs." With increased enrollments, research universities "scale superlinearly in revenues and expenditures, i.e., these variables grow more than proportionally with the size of the institution. They diversify into more activities with size, accrue prestige and wealth, becoming increasingly productive in research but expensive for students." The authors elaborate, "Research universities (public and private) scale superlinearly in all activities and sources of revenue, but sacrifice affordability. As they grow larger, they seek to attract increasingly prestigious faculty (as indicated by the superlinear scaling in faculty pay, especially in private universities) and charge higher tuition, also attracting better resourced students. The fact that both research and educational outcomes scale superlinearly suggests that these activities are synergistic." Whereas public research universities exhibit superlinear scaling in "research activities (as measured by expenditures) and research output (as measured by revenue from federal appropriations)," state and community colleges scale sublinearly in terms of revenues and expenditures. In other words, "Size allows them to decrease costs to students and taxpayers more than proportionally."[80]

"The application of scaling theory to social systems reveals important regularities," West and colleagues underscore, "for example, that measures of human creativity increase predictably with city size, and the superadditivity of human interactions in social networks seems to be the driving mechanism."[81] Among the challenges in scaling up the Fifth Wave, consistent with these findings, is the optimization of the structure and dynamics of this subset of major research universities. Institutional designers must thus confront academic platforms shaped by the needs of the nation in the past century as well as administrative frameworks and epistemological presumptions still largely configured according to disciplinary alignments. But the transition toward the complex adaptive knowledge enterprises of the Fifth Wave necessitates an appreciation of the implications of their new scale and scope. As West points out, "Scaling up from the small to the large is often accompanied by an evolution from simplicity to complexity while maintaining basic elements or building blocks of the system unchanged or conserved." He elaborates: "This is familiar in engineering, economies, companies, cities, organisms, and, perhaps most dramatically, evolutionary processes." Thus, there is an urgent need to "understand how to scale organizational structures of increasingly large and complex social organizations such as companies, corporations, cities, and governments, where the underlying principles are typically not well understood because these are continuously evolving complex adaptive systems."[82]

"Larger universities outperform smaller universities, even after correcting for size," according to a study of structural variables associated with the research performance of major research institutions. Variables include the number of publication citations, international co-publications, and university-industry collaborations. The authors conclude that research performance differences among universities stem *mainly* from size, and only secondarily by such factors as age of institution, disciplinary orientation, and country location.

> Larger universities benefit from scale in that they can employ more sophisticated research equipment and run more specialist graduate programs. Scale economies may also exist when collaborating abroad (thanks to specialized international exchange programs as well as visibility), and when collaborating with industry (because of co-investments in specialized laboratories as well as in administrative overheads). Previous research has already shown that the citation impact of universities scales super-linearly with size. Thus, with each doubling of a university's output, the number of citations it receives more than doubles.[83]

Consistent with the findings of Taylor and colleagues, although Fourth Wave research universities vary widely in scale and scope, the largest among them demonstrate that large-scale enrollments and comprehensive curricula are by no means incompatible with world-class knowledge production. The University of Toronto, for example, the largest major research university in Canada and a public AAU member institution, enrolls 67,128 undergraduates and 15,884 graduate students at three urban campuses and reports research expenditures exceeding $1.2 billion annually. The institution consistently ranks topmost among Canadian universities, twenty-eighth globally in the Academic Ranking of World Universities, and twentieth globally in the most recent *Times Higher Education World University Rankings*. Gibbons and colleagues report similar conclusions regarding economies of scope and scale in knowledge production. "The industrialization of science can be described in terms of the adoption of economies of scale, and of industrial management practices."[84]

## The Fifth Wave Anticipates the Sixth Wave

The Fifth Wave addresses challenges associated with continued exponential growth in enrollments among colleges and universities, which,

beginning with the Golden Age of American higher education following World War II,[85] have grown increasingly acute. As previously specified, between 1945 and 1975, growth in undergraduate enrollments, including community colleges, increased fivefold, while enrollments in
graduate schools increased nearly 900 percent.[86] But inasmuch as the
American experience parallels worldwide patterns of growth and expansion, the Fifth Wave model has potential relevance worldwide. According to cross-national analysis of enrollments conducted by sociologists
Evan Schofer and John Meyer, growth in American higher education
typifies a nearly universal hyperexpansion in this sector in the twentieth century that, especially following 1960, in its scale defies conventional
functionalist or conflict and competition explanations. Enrollments
worldwide between 1900 and 2000 increased from 500,000 to 100 million
students, representing growth from a fraction of 1 percent to 20 percent
of respective college-age cohorts, with enrollments in some industrial-
izing countries exceeding 80 percent.[87]

Although the extent of the transformational impact of this extraordinary worldwide growth in educational attainment may in retrospect
be taken for granted, sociologist David Baker reminds us that it has made
higher education an "enduring social institution [that] constructs significant portions of the culture of modern society, rather than merely reproducing it." In terms consonant with structuration: "Not only are
people trained and credentialed through schooling, but the institution
itself changes other social institutions and the entire culture of society."[88]
Schofer and Meyer point to associated institutional processes contributing to this trend, including democratization and expansion of human
rights; momentum of scientific culture and consequent scientization of
society; advent of development planning, with its emphasis on the role
of education in national development; and "expansion of the organizational and institutional structure of the world polity." UNESCO
(United Nations Educational, Scientific, and Cultural Organization) is
cited as emblematic of the institutional frameworks reinforcing and in-
tensifying expansion. As Schofer and Meyer put it: "The postwar shift to
a liberal, rationalist, and developmental model of society generated a
worldwide pattern of increased higher education expansion."[89] Marginson observes that Schofer and Meyer perceived the growth of participa-

tion in terms of a "universal Americanizing script and . . . single global process."[90] Elaboration of the concept of human capital in this context, referring in its most general sense to the measure of the value of the stock of knowledge, skills, and creativity acquired through investment in education and training, superseded then prevalent notions of overeducation precipitating social inefficiencies, and contributed to the expansion as well.[91]

"Knowledge transforms social life, institutions on all scales, and the character of the world," observes Michael Kennedy. We recur to the succinct definition of the knowledge economy proposed by Walter W. Powell and Kaisa Snellman as "production and services based on knowledge-intensive activities that contribute to an accelerated pace of technological and scientific advance as well as equally rapid obsolescence." But with reference to the impacts of knowledge on globalization, Kennedy observes, "not all accounts of transformations attribute terrific significance to knowledge." Fewer still consider the institutional basis of knowledge production nor explicitly recognize the potential of knowledge networks. "Universities themselves are increasingly articulated in global knowledge networks, defining this form of association critical for remaining relevant in the globalizing knowledge-based world," Kennedy elaborates. "These networks change the qualities of the institutions belonging to the network, making them much more open to the global environment of which they are a part." As one example he cites Universitas 21 (U21), an international network of twenty-four research-intensive universities that "empowers its members to share excellence, collaborate across borders, and nurture global knowledge exchange." Its member institutions cooperate to facilitate multinational collaboration on a scale that none could achieve independently or in smaller alliances.[92]

Despite significant cultural, economic, and social variability in different national contexts, universities worldwide exhibit remarkable degrees of isomorphism.[93] Accordingly, new global models for the research university have been posited in tandem with the initialization of the global knowledge economy. J. G. Wissema, professor emeritus of innovation at Delft University of Technology in the Netherlands, for example, proposes the emergence of what he terms the third-generation university, or 3GU: "We distinguish three generations of universities: the medieval, or first-generation university; the Humboldt, or second-generation university; and the third-generation university (3GU)." Writing in 2009, Wissema explains, "The last of these is still in the future; universities are currently in a transition phase and we can see advanced universities moving towards the 3GU model." According to Wissema, third-generation universities exhibit the following seven characteristics: (1) "exploitation of know-how becomes the [chief] objective as universities are seen as the cradle of new entrepreneurial activity"; (2) operation in internationally competitive markets; (3) formation into networks and collaboration with business, industry, and governments; (4) interdisciplinarity ("consilience and creativity as driving forces of similar importance to rational scientific method"); (5) multinationalism and multiculturalism not unlike their medieval antecedents; (6) cosmopolitanism with English as the lingua franca; and (7) independence from state regulation.[94] Inasmuch as the second-generation university appears to be conceived as a conflation of the nineteenth-century German research university and the set of twentieth-century Fourth Wave institutions, the schema lacks precision, but the parallels between the third-generation university and emerging Fifth Wave are obvious.

Baker similarly delineates a model akin to the Fifth Wave that he terms the "super research university," which represents an "intensification of a number of unique qualities of the Western university, resulting in a small but growing number of institutions that have the capacity to generate unprecedented levels of science, technology, and knowledge about human society and the physical universe." He differentiates this usage from more common reference to "world-class universities," which most often denotes position in global rankings. "First and obviously," Baker delineates, "super RUs strive to be ever more research-intensive, not only in science and technology but also in the scientization of disciplines traditionally outside the sciences, such as the now thoroughly scientized study of humans (e.g., behavioral and social sciences)." Such intensification of research requires unprecedented levels of funding. By one estimate, super research universities with medical schools require annual research funding exceeding $1.5 billion. Baker reports that, in 2014, thirty U.S. universities had achieved this level, but none among their European counterparts. Intensification of research correlates with corresponding expectations for research productivity among the faculty as well as increasing complexity of internal academic organization to accommodate new avenues of research specialization. With the new model, the former dominance of individual scholarship has been superseded by a Big Science approach favoring large-scale team collaboration, which to the extent possible is now mirrored by social scientists and humanists. Super research universities conceive their missions as explicitly global rather than local or national and increasingly augment competition with cooperation through knowledge networks comprising peer institutions. Finally, super research universities have come to constitute exemplars for all institutions, regardless of their research intensities.[95]

A decade ago, Baker and two colleagues posited what they termed an Emerging Global Model (EGM) for the research university in transition. In many respects, the Fifth Wave parallels this model as well, which exhibits eight primary characteristics: (1) global mission ("transcending the boundaries of the nation-state . . . and advancing the frontiers of knowledge worldwide"); (2) increasing intensity of knowledge production enlisting scientific approaches throughout the disciplinary spectrum; (3) expansion of faculty roles, which include not only teaching and research but also participation in transdisciplinary, transinstitutional, and transnational networks addressing real-world applications; (4) diversification of financial base to emphasize sponsored research, corporate investment, and technology transfer; (5) collaboration among institutions, and with business and industry and government agencies to advance economic development and knowledge for the public well-being; (6) worldwide recruitment patterns for students, faculty, and administrators; (7) organizational restructuring ("greater internal complexity directed toward research, such as interdisciplinary research centers, integration of research in student training programs, and greater technological infrastructure for discovery"; and (8) collaborative research with governments and nongovernmental organizations worldwide.[96]

Perhaps the most significant departure from the Emerging Global Model is the implicit Fifth Wave tenet that discovery, creativity, and innovation from all disciplinary and transdisciplinary fields and spheres of creative endeavor be valued equally and according to their respective merits. By contrast, Mohrman and colleagues assert that scientific and technological knowledge must be "most prized," with contributions from the social sciences and humanities deemed meritorious according to the extent to which they may be characterized as "increasingly quantitative in methodology and 'scientific' in approach." Mohrman and colleagues appear to acquiesce to the inevitability of a Big Science model throughout academic culture.[97] But the Fifth Wave must endeavor instead to extend the artistic creativity, humanistic and social scientific insight, and the scientific discoveries and technological innovations that the global community will need to draw upon as it negotiates the encroaching complexities of the twenty-first century. In chapter 7 we briefly assess programmatic efforts at reform undertaken in various national contexts that confront the dilemma as to whether to broaden accessibility to higher education because of generalized awareness of the positive societal impacts of well-educated citizens or to advance knowledge production and innovation among an elite cohort of institutions to boost economic development. The imperative to negotiate the implications of accessibility and excellence as well as scale and scalability lies at the heart of this discussion.

## Notes

1. John R. Thelin, *A History of American Higher Education*, 3rd ed. (Baltimore: Johns Hopkins University Press, 2019).

2. Jonathan R. Cole, *The Great American University: Its Rise to Preeminence, Its Indispensable National Role, and Why It Must Be Protected* (New York: Public Affairs, 2009), 134–135. See also John Aubrey Douglass, *The California Idea and American Higher Education: 1850 to the 1960 Master Plan* (Stanford: Stanford University Press, 2000).

3. C. Judson King, *The University of California: Creating, Nurturing, and Maintaining Academic Quality in a Public Research University Setting* (Berkeley: Center for Studies in Higher Education, University of California, Berkeley, 2018), 129–131, 139.

4. King, *University of California*, 124.

5. John Aubrey Douglass, *The Conditions for Admission: Access, Equity, and the Social Contract of Public Universities* (Stanford: Stanford University Press, 2007), 38.

6. King, *University of California*, 137.

7. Douglass, *Conditions for Admission*, 80.

8. King, *University of California*, 135, 137–138. He cites Saul Geiser and Richard C. Atkinson, "Beyond the Master Plan: The Case for Restructuring Baccalaureate Education in California," *California Journal of Politics and Policy* 4, no. 1 (2013): 67–123; fig. 3.

9. Simon Marginson, *The Dream Is Over: The Crisis of Clark Kerr's California Idea of Higher Education* (Oakland: University of California Press, 2016), 3–4.

10. We wish to express our appreciation to policy analyst Kyle Whitman for this comparative analysis.

11. Martin Trow, "Problems in the Transition from Elite to Mass Higher Education" (Berkeley: Carnegie Commission on Higher Education, 1973), 1.

12. Philip G. Altbach, *Global Perspectives on Higher Education* (Baltimore: Johns Hopkins University Press, 2016), 45, 86–87, 150–151.

13. Craig Calhoun, "The University and the Public Good," *Thesis Eleven* 84 (February 2006): 14.

14. David L. Kirp, *Shakespeare, Einstein, and the Bottom Line: The Marketing of Higher Education* (Cambridge, MA: Harvard University Press, 2003), 2.

15. Roger L. Geiger, *Knowledge and Money: Research Universities and the Paradox of the Marketplace* (Stanford: Stanford University Press, 2004), 20.

16. William J. Baumol and William G. Bowen, "On the Performing Arts: The Anatomy of Their Economic Problems," *American Economic Review* 55, no. 1/2 (March 1965): 495–502; William J. Baumol and William G. Bowen, *Performing Arts: The Economic Dilemma* (New York: Twentieth Century Fund, 1966).

17. John V. Lombardi, *How Universities Work* (Baltimore: Johns Hopkins University Press, 2013), 2–10; Paul Duguid, "The Art of Knowing: Social and Tacit Dimensions of Knowledge and the Limits of the Community of Practice," *Information Society* 21 (2005): 112–113, 115n1.

18. David Gardner, "Customization vs. Mass Customization: What Really Matters," *Fast Company* (October 14, 2010).

19. Anthony Grafton, "Can the Colleges Be Saved?" Review of Andrew Delbanco, *College: What It Was, Is, and Should Be* (Princeton, NJ: Princeton University Press, 2012), *New York Review of Books* (May 24, 2012), 24.

20. Michael S. McPherson and Morton Owen Schapiro, "Economic Challenges for Liberal Arts Colleges," in *Distinctively American: The Residential Liberal Arts College*, ed. Steven Koblik and Stephen R. Graubard (New Brunswick, NJ: Transaction, 2000), 49–50.

21. Assessment of the top fifty liberal arts colleges derives from the 2015 and 2019 *U.S. News & World Report* rankings. "US News Best Colleges, National Liberal Arts Colleges," *U.S. News & World Report*, https://www.usnews.com/best-colleges/rankings /national-liberal-arts-colleges?_mode=table.

22. Scott A. Ginder, Janice E. Kelly-Reid, and Farrah B. Mann, *Enrollment and Employees in Postsecondary Institutions, Fall 2017: First Look (Provisional Data)* (Washington, DC: National Center for Education Statistics, 2019), https://nces.ed.gov/pubs2019 /2019021REV.pdf. The document specifies total undergraduate enrollments at Title IV institutions as 17,133,000. With reference to the less than 1 percent figure: excluding the three military schools, 0.94 percent; excluding the military schools but including the next three institutions in the rankings, 0.98 percent; including the military schools, 1.02 percent.

23. According to AAU analysis of IPEDS data, fall 2011 undergraduate enrollment at the sixty member institutions in the United States was 1,129,721. Percentages were calculated based on the total number of undergraduates attending Title IV participating institutions, which in 2011 enrolled 18,497,102. Graduate student enrollment totaled

560,000, which then represented 18.8 percent of the national total. The AAU roster includes two Canadian institutions, enrollments in which were omitted in these calculations. We wish to express our appreciation to AAU policy analysts Josh Trapani and Kimberlee Eberle-Sudre.

24. Carnegie Foundation for the Advancement of Teaching, "Summary Tables: Distribution of institutions and enrollments by classification category, based on IPEDS fall enrollment 2009," http://classifications.carnegiefoundation.org/summary/basic .php; S. A. Ginder and J. E. Kelly-Reid, *Enrollment in Postsecondary Institutions, Fall 2012: First Look (Provisional Data)* (Washington, DC: National Center for Education Statistics, 2013), http://nces.ed.gove/pubsearch. The latter document specifies total undergraduate enrollments at Title IV institutions as 18,236,340. Our tally of fall 2013 enrollments at the 108 RU/VH institutions showed 2,045,667 undergraduates, which represented 11.2 percent of American undergraduates.

25. Ginder, Kelly-Reid, and Mann, *Enrollment and Employees in Postsecondary Institutions, Fall 2017.* Our tally of fall 2017 enrollments at the 115 Carnegie R1—formerly RU/VH—institutions showed 2,465,602 undergraduates, which represented 14.4 percent of total Title IV undergraduate enrollment. Adding R2 institutions, undergraduate enrollment climbed to 3,791,658, or 22.1 percent of total Title IV undergraduate enrollment.

26. National Center for Education Statistics, "Chapter 3: Postsecondary Education," *Digest of Education Statistics: 2017,* https://nces.ed.gov/programs/digest/d17 /ch_3.asp.

27. National Student Clearinghouse Research Center, "Current Term Enrollment— Fall 2017," https://nscresearchcenter.org/current-term-enrollment-estimates-fall-2017/.

28. Christopher Newfield, *The Great Mistake: How We Wrecked Public Universities and How We Can Fix Them* (Baltimore: Johns Hopkins University Press, 2016). He cites Victor E. Ferrall, *Liberal Arts at the Brink* (Cambridge, MA: Harvard University Press, 2011), table 1.1.

29. William B. Rouse, John V. Lombardi, and Diane D. Craig, "Modeling Research Universities: Predicting Probable Futures of Public vs. Private and Large vs. Small Research Universities," *Proceedings of the National Academy of Sciences* 115, no. 50 (December 11, 2018): 12582–12589, www.pnas.org/cgi/doi/10.1073/pnas.18071741115.

30. Barry Bozeman and Daniel Sarewitz, "Public Values and Public Failure in U.S. Science Policy," *Science and Public Policy* 32, no. 2 (2005): 119–136. See also Bozeman and Sarewitz, "Public Value Mapping and Science Policy Evaluation," *Minerva* 49, no. 1 (2011): 1–23.

31. Derrick M. Anderson and Gabel Taggart, "Organizations, Policies, and the Roots of Public Value Failure: The Case of For-Profit Higher Education," *Public Administration Review* 76, no. 5 (September/October 2016): 779–789.

32. Mitchell L. Stevens, "The Changing Ecology of U.S. Higher Education," in *Remaking College: The Changing Ecology of Higher Education,* ed. Michael W. Kirst and Mitchell L. Stevens (Stanford: Stanford University Press, 2015), 4–5.

33. Geiger, *Knowledge and Money,* 19–20.

34. Anthony P. Carnevale, Tamara Jayasundera, and Arten Gulish, "America's Divided Recovery: College Haves and Have-Nots (Washington, DC: Center on Education and the Workforce, Georgetown University, 2016); Carnevale, Nicole Smith, and Jeff Strohl, "Recovery: Job Growth and Education Requirements through 2020" (Washington, DC: Center on Education and the Workforce, Georgetown University, 2014).

35. Anthony P. Carnevale, Nicole Smith, and Jeff Strohl, "Help Wanted: Projections of Jobs and Education Requirements through 2018" (Washington, DC: Georgetown University Center on Education and the Workforce, June 2010), 18; executive summary, 4.

36. Anthony P. Carnevale and Stephen J. Rose, "The Undereducated American" (Washington, DC: Georgetown University Center on Education and the Workforce, June 2011), 1, 8, 10.

37. Roger L. Geiger, "The Ten Generations of American Higher Education," in *Higher Education in the Twenty-First Century: Social, Political, and Economic Challenges,* 4th ed., ed. Michael N. Bastedo, Philip G. Altbach, and Patricia J. Gumport (Baltimore: Johns Hopkins University Press, 2016), 22–23; Roger L. Geiger, *To Advance Knowledge: The Growth of American Research Universities, 1900–1940* (Oxford: Oxford University Press, 1986), 129; Geiger cites Abraham Flexner, *Universities: American, English, German* (Oxford: Oxford University Press, 1930), 44–45.

38. David P. Baker, *The Schooled Society: The Educational Transformation of Global Culture* (Stanford: Stanford University Press, 2014), 125–126.

39. James Morrill is quoted in William G. Bowen, Matthew M. Chingos, and Michael S. McPherson, *Crossing the Finish Line: Completing College at America's Public Universities* (Princeton, NJ: Princeton University Press, 2009), 242.

40. Douglass, *Conditions for Admission,* 127.

41. All figures from University of California, Office of the President, Institutional Research and Academic Planning, https://www.ucop.edu/institutional-research -academic-planning/content-analysis/ug-admissions/ug-data.html.

42. Kyle Whitman, personal correspondence, July 27, 2019. With reference to the fallacies associated with the methodologies of rankings of "best schools," see the famous letter from Gerhard Casper, then president of Stanford University, to James Fallows, then editor of *U.S. News & World Report* (September 23, 1996), http://www.stanford.edu /dept/pres-provost/president/speeches/961206gcfallow.html.

43. Louis Menand, "What Baseball Teaches Us About Measuring Talent," *New Yorker* (April 8, 2019), 88.

44. Douglass, *Conditions for Admission,* 42, 80, 112.

45. Trow, "Problems in the Transition," 1.

46. Trow, "Problems in the Transition," 2, 6–7.

47. Martin Trow, "Reflections on the Transition from Mass to Universal Higher Education," *Daedalus* 99, no. 1 (1970): 2.

48. Trow, "Problems in the Transition," 7–8.

49. Simon Marginson, *The Dream Is Over: The Crisis of Clark Kerr's California Idea of Higher Education* (Oakland: University of California Press, 2016), 28–29.

50. Brendan Cantwell, "Broad Access and Steep Stratification in the First Mass System: High Participation Higher Education in the United States of America," in *High Participation Systems of Higher Education,* ed. Brendan Cantwell, Simon Marginson, and Anna Smolentseva (Oxford: Oxford University Press, 2018), 227.

51. Simon Marginson, "High Participation Systems of Higher Education," in *High Participation Systems of Higher Education,* ed. Brendan Cantwell, Simon Marginson, and Anna Smolentseva (Oxford: Oxford University Press, 2018), 5.

52. Marginson, *The Dream Is Over,* 28–29.

53. Trow, "Problems in the Transition," 18–19, cited in Marginson, *The Dream Is Over,* 28–30.

54. Martin Trow, "Reflections on the Transition from Elite to Mass to Universal Access: Forms and Phases of Higher Education in Modern Societies since WWII," in *International Handbook of Higher Education,* ed. James J. F. Forest and Philip G. Altbach (Dordrecht: Springer, 2007), 244, 252.

55. Trow, "Problems in the Transition," 18–19.

56. Marginson, *The Dream Is Over,* 34; Trow, "Problems in the Transition," 25.

57. Richard Arum, Adam Gamoran, and Yossi Shavit, "More Inclusion Than Diversion: Expansion, Differentiation, and Market Structure in Higher Education," in *Stratification in Higher Education: A Comparative Study,* ed. Yossi Shavit, Richard Arum, and Adam Gamoran (Stanford: Stanford University Press, 2007), 1.

58. Adrian E. Raftery and Michael Hout, "Maximally Maintained Inequality: Expansion, Reform, and Opportunity in Irish Education, 1921–75," *Sociology of Education* 66 (1993): 41–62, cited in Arum, Gamoran, and Shavit, "More Inclusion Than Diversion," 3–4.

59. Josipa Roksa et al., "United States: Changes in Higher Education and Stratification," in *Stratification in Higher Education,* ed. Yossi Shavit, Richard Arum, and Adam Gamoran (Stanford: Stanford University Press, 2007), 165–167.

60. Brendan Cantwell, Simon Marginson, and Anna Smolentseva, "Propositions about High Participation Systems of Higher Education," in *High Participation Systems of Higher Education,* ed. Brendan Cantwell, Simon Marginson, and Anna Smolentseva (Oxford: Oxford University Press, 2018), xxii.

61. Trow, "Reflections on the Transition from Mass to Universal Higher Education," 2.

62. Neil J. Smelser, *Dynamics of the Contemporary University: Growth, Accretion, and Conflict* (Berkeley: University of California Press, 2013), 14; Clark Kerr, *The Uses of the University,* 5th ed. (Cambridge, MA: Harvard University Press, 2001), 1, 102; Philip G. Altbach, "The American Academic Model in Comparative Perspective," in *In Defense of American Higher Education,* ed. Philip G. Altbach, Patricia Gumport, and D. Bruce Johnstone (Baltimore: Johns Hopkins University Press, 2001), 30.

63. Smelser, *Dynamics of the Contemporary University,* 9–12.

64. Smelser, *Dynamics of the Contemporary University,* 12, 20–21.

65. Kerr, *Uses of the University,* 70, quoted in Marginson, *The Dream Is Over,* 204n8.

66. *Oxford English Dictionary,* 3rd ed., online version (June 2008), s.v. "economies of scale."

67. John Black, Nigar Hashimzade, and Gareth Myles, *A Dictionary of Economics* (Oxford: Oxford University Press, 2017), 123.

68. "Economies of Scale and Scope," *The Economist* (October 20, 2008).

69. John C. Panzar and Robert D. Willig, "Economies of Scope," *American Economic Review* 71, no. 2 (May 1981): 268.

70. *Oxford English Dictionary,* 3rd ed., online version (June 2008), s.v. "economies of scope."

71. "Economies of Scale and Scope."

72. Michael Gibbons et al., *The New Production of Knowledge: The Dynamics of Science and Research in Contemporary Societies* (London: Sage, 1994), 51–53.

73. John H. Miller and Scott E. Page, *Complex Adaptive Systems: An Introduction to Computational Models of Social Life* (Princeton, NJ: Princeton University Press, 2007), 85–86.

74. John Gargani and Robert McLean, "Scaling Science," *Stanford Social Innovation Review* 15, no. 4 (Fall 2017): 34–39.

75. Geoffrey West, *Scale: The Universal Laws of Growth, Innovation, Sustainability, and the Pace of Life in Organisms, Cities, Economies, and Companies* (New York: Penguin Press, 2017), 15.

76. West, *Scale,* 18.

77. West, *Scale,* 209–213, 281, 368–369, 409.

78. West, *Scale,* 403.

79. West, *Scale,* 408–410; Anthony Downs, *Inside Bureaucracy* (Boston: Little, Brown, 1967), 8, 18–19.

80. Ryan C. Taylor et al., "The Scalability, Efficiency, and Complexity of Universities and Colleges: A New Lens for Assessing the Higher Education System," arXiv:1910.05470v1 [cs.CY] (October 12, 2019): 1–7.

81. Taylor et al., "Scalability, Efficiency, and Complexity." Taylor and colleagues cite Anthony F. J. van Raan, "Universities Scale Like Cities," *PLOS One* 8, no. 3 (March 2013): 1–14: "As a result of nonlinear interaction in socioeconomic dynamics, an increase of population size of cities (urban agglomerations ranging from about 100,000 to 10,000,000 inhabitants) leads to a disproportional power law scaling of important indicators such as economic productivity and innovation capacity, for instance, the GMP, the Gross Metropolitan Product."

82. West, *Scale,* 16, 24–25.

83. Koen Frenken, Gaston J. Heimeriks, and Jarno Hoekman, "What Drives University Research Performance? An Analysis Using the CWTS Leiden Ranking Data," *Journal of Informetrics* 11, no. 3 (2017): 859–872.

84. Gibbons et al., *New Production of Knowledge,* 52.

85. Louis Menand, "College: The End of the Golden Age," *New York Review of Books* (October 18, 2001).

86. Geiger, "Ten Generations of American Higher Education," 24–25.

87. Evan Schofer and John W. Meyer, "The Worldwide Expansion of Higher Education in the Twentieth Century," *American Sociological Review* 70 (December 2005): 898–920.

88. David P. Baker, *The Schooled Society: The Educational Transformation of Global Culture* (Stanford: Stanford University Press, 2014), 10.

89. Schofer and Meyer, "Worldwide Expansion of Higher Education," 903.

90. Marginson, "High Participation Systems of Higher Education," 17.

91. For the concept of human capital, see Theodore W. Schultz, "Investment in Human Capital," *American Economic Review* 51, no. 1 (March 1961): 1–17. A comprehensive overview is to be found in Gary S. Becker, *Human Capital: A Theoretical and Empirical Analysis, with Special Reference to Education*, 3rd ed. (Chicago: University of Chicago Press, 1993). For economist Paul Romer, human capital is the stock of knowledge and creativity embodied in individuals that, when developed through education, is the factor of production responsible for economic growth. See Romer, "Endogenous Technological Change," *Journal of Political Economy* 98, no. 5, pt. 2 (1990): S71–102.

92. Michael D. Kennedy, *Globalizing Knowledge: Intellectuals, Universities, and Publics in Transformation* (Stanford: Stanford University Press, 2015), 1, 233–235; Walter W. Powell and Kaisa Snellman, "The Knowledge Economy," *Annual Review of Sociology* 30 (2004): 199.

93. John W. Meyer et al., "Higher Education as an Institution," in *Sociology of Higher Education: Contributions and Their Contexts*, ed. Patricia J. Gumport (Baltimore: Johns Hopkins University Press, 2007), 193.

94. J. G. Wissema, *Towards the Third Generation University: Managing the University in Transition* (Cheltenham, UK: Edward Elgar, 2009), 3.

95. Baker, *Schooled Society*, 82–90; 305n2.

96. Kathryn Mohrman, Wanhua Ma, and David Baker, "The Research University in Transition: The Emerging Global Model," *Higher Education Policy* 21, no. 1 (2008): 7.

97. Mohrman, Ma, and Baker, "Research University in Transition," 21–22. See Derek J. de Solla Price, *Little Science, Big Science, and Beyond* (New York: Columbia University Press, 1986).

# FOUR

# Some Historical Perspective on the Fifth Wave

Because the Fifth Wave represents a new phase in the evolution of American higher education, both a historical framework and taxonomy of antecedent institutional types is essential to our understanding of the increasingly complex and still evolving institutional models that have emerged over the course of nearly four centuries in response to the cultural, economic, political, and social challenges that shape our society. To review the main points of the introductory historical discussion in chapter 1, the four preceding waves may be represented in a rough schema by (1) colonial colleges and cohort of colleges founded subsequently during the early republic; (2) state-chartered colleges and universities of the early republic; (3) land-grant colleges and universities that were established as a consequence of the Morrill Act, which was enacted during the Civil War; and (4) the set of major research universities that emerged in the final decades of the nineteenth century. All of these institutional types continue to prosper and evolve in their respective institutional ecologies and design frameworks. Toward the end of the nineteenth century, some of the First Wave colleges—Harvard, Princeton, and Columbia, among them—evolved into major research universities and thus, in the terms of our proposed idiom, transitioned from the First Wave to the Fourth Wave, albeit effectively retaining undergraduate residential liberal arts colleges at the core of their expanded institutions.[1] A number of leading institutions from the Second Wave and Third Wave similarly evolved into major research universities and thus transitioned to the Fourth Wave as well. Seven of the nine colonial colleges, along with Cornell (1865), would come to form the Ivy League, which was officially established as an athletic conference in 1954. Both

William and Mary and Rutgers became public universities, in 1906 and 1945, respectively.

Although First Wave schools that transitioned to the Fourth Wave are products of innovation and evolution from relatively simple to increasingly complex institutional forms, these schools in a sense followed or paralleled a pattern that would be realized without institutional antecedent with the formation of Johns Hopkins University, which was founded in 1876 and represents the prototype for the American research university. The establishment of Stanford University (1885) and the University of Chicago (1892) as research universities without institutional antecedents, following the example of Johns Hopkins, represents the singular variation to the generalized pattern of innovation and evolution. And whereas we speak of innovation and evolution from relatively simple to increasingly complex institutional forms as the mechanism that impels transition from one wave to the next—from the First Wave to the Fourth Wave, as in the case of Harvard University, for example, or from the Third Wave to the Fourth Wave, as in the case of Cornell University or the University of California system—one would ideally expect innovation and evolution to be ongoing within each of the waves. Not all innovation and evolution signals inevitable transition between waves.

We reiterate the point that, in contrast to standard historical accounts,[2] our assessment focuses on the dominant institutional types of colleges and universities and seeks to develop new insight into the dynamics of their structures and functions. Such an analysis is thus at once morphological as well as typological, with the concept of *morphology* referring to the structural attributes of organizations and institutions.[3] And whereas our typology comprises five waves, far more elaborate periodization has been proposed by Roger Geiger, who identifies ten generations in American higher education, over the course of which the character of the endeavor has "perceptibly shifted in each generation, or approximately every thirty years."[4] We reiterate further our proposition that each wave in American higher education has been spearheaded by one or more institutional progenitors, beginning with Harvard College, which set the pattern for the First Wave, followed by the University of Virginia for the Second Wave, Cornell University for the Third Wave, and Johns Hopkins for the Fourth Wave. And not to belabor the obvious but as we contend throughout these chapters, we propose that

Arizona State University be regarded the institutional progenitor of the Fifth Wave. Potential institutional peers in this context include Purdue University, Pennsylvania State University, and the University System of Maryland.

## America's Greek Academies

"One of the remarkable facts of American history is that only six years after their settlement in the Massachusetts wilderness the Puritans established what soon became a reputable college," observes historian George Marsden.[5] When, in 1636, Harvard College welcomed its first class of nine students, presided over by a single master, the entire population of European settlers in the colonies of British America only somewhat exceeded ten thousand.[6] The figure is roughly equivalent to the estimated number of adult male citizens residing within the core urban agglomeration of the Athenian city-state in the fourth century BC.[7] The founding of Harvard within the first decade of settlement in the Massachusetts Bay Colony attests to the social ambitions and cultural aspirations of the Puritan civic and religious leaders, whose academic standards and conception of a liberal education had been formed by their association or familiarity with Oxford and Cambridge. Accordingly, the course of study at Harvard was modeled on that of these venerated institutions.[8] The colonial colleges have been described as our nation's "first enclaves for educating privileged white males . . . in a tightly disciplined Anglo-Saxon educational tradition that was presumed to instill qualifications for leadership in a theocratic community."[9] Indeed, most of the founders of our nation were first-generation college graduates. But inasmuch as instruction in First Wave colleges did not reflect the new intellectual culture of the Scientific Revolution, the limitations of the model would eventually become readily apparent: "The corpus of knowledge transmitted at Harvard College was considered fixed and inquiry after new knowledge was beyond imagining."[10] The curricular focus on classical literatures notwithstanding, however, the objective of "useful knowledge" was already evident in the academic culture of the early American republic and has been attributed in part to the influence of Benjamin Franklin. The intent to "improve the common stock of knowledge" had informed Franklin's intentions for the American Philosophical Society, which he founded in 1743, as well as his plans for the University of Pennsylvania.[11]

What we term the First Wave in American higher education initially comprised nine small colleges that more or less resembled the colleges of Oxford and Cambridge erected amidst the vast wilderness or isolated settlements of the British colonies. Nearly six decades would elapse between the founding of Harvard in 1636 and the College of William and Mary in 1693, followed by a "collegiate school" in Connecticut that would become Yale College in 1701. Historian Jürgen Herbst characterizes these three colleges as "schools of the European Reformation in the New World" established essentially as adjuncts of various authorities and denominations: respectively, Congregationalists and the General Court of the Massachusetts Bay Company, Anglicans and the English crown, and Congregationalists and the governor and councilors of Connecticut. A phrase he quotes from a Puritan commentator in Massachusetts is representative of the motivations of the various founders: Harvard College was founded in order to "advance Learning and perpetuate it to Posterity; dreading to leave an illiterate Ministry to the Churches, when our present Ministers shall lie in the Dust."[12] These schools were founded to transmit a classical curriculum suitable for young Christian gentlemen from propertied families preparing to enter the ministry or the professions. Apart from the classics, their curricula were largely restricted to a set of core subjects including theology, philosophy, history, and the ancient languages.[13] In the Middle Colonies, the College of New Jersey, chartered by Presbyterians in 1746, would become Princeton University in 1896. King's College, chartered by Anglicans in 1754, would become Columbia College in 1784 and Columbia University in 1912. In 1764 Baptists chartered the College of Rhode Island, which would become Brown University.[14] The College of Philadelphia, chartered by Anglicans and Presbyterians, would become the University of Pennsylvania in 1791. Queen's College (1766) would become Rutgers College (1825) and eventually Rutgers, the State University of New Jersey (1917). Dartmouth College was founded in 1769.

Along with the colonial colleges, a number of schools founded during the early Republic—among them, Dickinson College (1783), Williams College (1791), Bowdoin College (1794), and Middlebury College (1800)—would establish the prototype for what has been termed that "distinctively American" institutional type, the residential liberal arts college. Any representative survey of prestigious and highly selective liberal arts colleges would be superfluous, but from among a roster that exceeds two hundred schools, a number founded in the nineteenth century enjoy national or even international reputations.[15] One need only think of Haverford College (1833), Oberlin College (1833), Grinnell College (1846), Swarthmore College (1864), or Bard College (1860). The Seven Sisters—historically women's colleges thus designated with the intent to underscore their affiliation or academic equivalence with the Ivy League—include Barnard College (1889), Bryn Mawr College (1885), Mount Holyoke College (1837), Smith College (1871), and Wellesley College (1870). Whereas these five retain exclusively female undergraduate programs, Vassar College (1861) became co-educational in 1969 and Radcliffe College (1879) merged with Harvard in 1979. Most of these schools retain the relative scale of small First Wave academies to the present day, and the periodic establishment of new schools that conform to the First Wave pattern such as Reed College (1908), Bennington College (1932), Harvey Mudd College (1955), College of the Atlantic (1969), and Olin College (1997) attests to the continued relevance of this institutional model.

Not all First Wave institutions either in the past or present, of course, conform to the image of the highly selective residential liberal arts college that we propound for heuristic purposes. This is the idyllic sense of college as "American pastoral" that Andrew Delbanco concedes only a small fraction of students will ever be privileged to experience.[16] As Steven Koblik, then president of Reed College, points out, liberal arts colleges may be sectarian or nonsectarian, coeducational or single sex, historically black, highly selective or open admissions, local and regional or national, and either strongly theoretical or practical in their orientation. He observes that the residential colleges and honors colleges of many large public universities are modeled on liberal arts colleges and cites the University of California, Santa Cruz, as the prime exemplar of a new university wholly conceived in their image.[17] And whereas our contentions on behalf of the envisioned Fifth Wave focus on the added value of a research-grade environment, William Durden, president emeritus of Dickinson College, points out that liberal arts colleges produce twice the number of students per graduate who eventually complete doctorates in the sciences as other baccalaureate institutions and have pioneered curricular and pedagogical innovations that serve as the basis for the undergraduate experience in the United States.[18] Chemist

Thomas Cech corroborates these points and adds: "Independent research at liberal arts colleges does not approach the leading edge of scientific fields as often as that carried out at research universities but it benefits from highly personal one-on-one interactions between students and faculty mentors, making for an overall experience that often surpasses that at large universities."[19]

The scale of higher education in the colonial period would remain marginal—at the outbreak of the American Revolution, the population of the thirteen colonies would exceed 2.5 million,[20] but by one estimate no more than 750 students were enrolled in the nine colleges then established, a rate of enrollment among respective cohorts of white males of roughly 1 percent.[21] The scale of the First Wave suggests that its societal impact was limited. Estimates place the number of bachelor's degrees awarded by Harvard and Yale in 1721 at fifty. With the colleges that would become Princeton, Columbia, and Penn contributing to degree production, the annual average during the 1760s would become roughly one hundred. The proportion of students attending college in 1800 remained the same as the previously cited 1 percent of the age cohort of white males on the eve of the Revolution. Estimates place the proportion of college graduates at the beginning and end of the century unchanged at roughly eleven per ten thousand. "The intellectual vitality of the colleges from 1760 to 1775 was only faintly echoed in demography," Geiger assesses, with reference to the societal impact of the First Wave. "As a social institution, the colonial colleges never transcended a narrow social base, and the same conditions persisted well into the nineteenth century."[22]

In a sense, the First Wave approximated the relative scope and scale—loosely speaking—of Plato's academy, which, as we subsequently assess in this chapter, enrolled no more than two dozen students at the time of his death in 347 BC. In the twenty-first century, some First Wave colleges retain their seventeenth- or eighteenth-century scope and scale to the present day. "Continuity is evident in individual institutions in which circumstances or self-images of origin and development continue to influence current conditions," as Geiger observes.[23] And because of the sanction of tradition, their unique missions and objectives, and their unassailable prestige in the competitive academic landscape, most liberal arts colleges will elect to continue to evolve within their present institutional category. Some institutions, like the College of William and Mary, transitioned from the First Wave to the Second Wave, beginning with a charter from the Commonwealth of Virginia in 1906. But as we have seen, during the last quarter of the nineteenth century, Harvard and most of its institutional peers in the Ivy League undertook transformation in scope and scale to evolve from First Wave colleges into major research universities that came to assume precedence among the most prominent and influential research universities globally. In terms of their scale and complexity in the evolutionary typology we propose, these latter institutions could be said to have transitioned directly from the First Wave to the Fourth Wave.

None of the First Wave schools were initially universities, as we currently understand them, of course. Even as late as the mid-nineteenth century many institutions may have been termed universities, as Geiger points out, but none merited the designation if by this term one envisions a single academic platform combining a "commitment to the advancement of knowledge through original investigations, corresponding capacity for training advanced scholars, broad coverage of academic fields, including the professions, and incorporation with collegiate education."[24] But colleges and universities formed during given historical periods often evolve in scope and scale and assume the more complex structures and functions of institutions that arose during subsequent waves. Thus, toward the end of the nineteenth century a number of schools that initially defined the First Wave as well as schools from the Second Wave, such as the University of Michigan and University of Virginia, and the Third Wave, such as Cornell University, MIT, and the University of California, evolved into major research universities and, per our idiom, transitioned directly to the Fourth Wave.

Not to belabor the point made in chapter 1, but it is essential to differentiate between the historical and contemporary instantiations of these institutions—and institutional types. The designation First Wave may refer alternately to the historical institutional type—the set of colonial colleges founded prior to the American Revolution—or to an individual school, such as Bowdoin College, at some point in the eighteenth century. But the term First Wave may refer also to the contemporary instantiation of the set of liberal arts colleges in the twenty-first century as well as to Bowdoin College in 2019. Harvard College in the seventeenth century bears little resemblance in scope and scale to the Harvard

University of the Fourth Wave, for example, which began to assume its present contours during the administration of Charles W. Elliot over the course of the four decades following the Civil War. Similarly, the College of New Jersey, founded in 1746, would by the end of the nineteenth century begin to achieve the stature and complexity of a Fourth Wave research university and become Princeton University. Reference to Cornell University might designate the institution during its inception as a land-grant school representative of the Third Wave, but it had evolved by the end of the nineteenth century to become a major research university and constituent of the Fourth Wave.

## Colleges for the New Republic

Following the upheaval of the War for Independence and inspired by the ideals of the Age of Reason, the newly sovereign states took up more systematic efforts to educate their citizens. Geiger terms the academic ideal for this period "republican Christian Enlightenment," which he characterizes as an ethos of "selflessness, patriotism, and virtue" that subordinated theology to the values of the Enlightenment.[25] The small, denominationally affiliated academies of the First Wave, moreover, had proven to be insufficient in both scope and scale. Especially in the South, a heterogeneous array of nonsectarian public colleges and state-chartered universities would be established beginning in the late eighteenth and early nineteenth centuries and constitute the Second Wave in American higher education. Geiger identifies five interrelated factors common to the establishment of the first state or public colleges and universities: "the actions and politics of state legislatures, the aspirations of regions or localities, the interests of religious denominations, the actions of individual entrepreneurs, and preexisting academies." Although this is indeed public higher education, as he points out, conceptions of public and private had not been codified to the extent of our contemporary usages of these terms.[26] And indeed, one must recall that colonial governments issued charters for the colleges of the First Wave.

Beginning with the University of Georgia (1785), University of North Carolina (1789), University of Vermont (1791), University of South Carolina (1801), University of Michigan (1817), and University of Virginia (1819), the Second Wave began to enlarge curricula beyond the classics, philosophy, and theology, in some cases to include agriculture, commerce, engineering, law, medicine, and military science. Although Georgia and North Carolina both vie for recognition as the first state-chartered university,[27] the institution that Thomas Jefferson envisioned is arguably the institutional progenitor of the Second Wave. From its inception, the University of Virginia represented a "new model for American higher education," Roger Geiger contends, citing among its other innovations its explicit embrace of Enlightenment secularism and curriculum that introduced the elective system into American higher education.[28] Many Second Wave schools would subsequently evolve into Fourth Wave research universities. With research expenditures approaching $1.5 billion in FY 2017, the University of Michigan, for example, epitomizes the transition from the Second Wave to the Fourth Wave. State universities established later in the nineteenth century follow this same pattern, including the University of Southern California (1880), University of Texas, Austin (1883), and Georgia Tech (1885). The Second Wave also includes a number of schools established as private technical institutes, including the California Institute of Technology, or Caltech (1891). In the case of schools such as the University of Vermont, University of Wisconsin (1848), University of Minnesota (1851), Michigan State University (1855), University of Maryland (1856), Iowa State University (1858), and MIT (1861), the transition to the Fourth Wave began with their designation as land-grant institutions.

"In 1800 there were twenty-five degree-granting colleges in the United States. By 1820 the number had increased to fifty-two," historian John Thelin observes, aptly concluding, "Higher education would become America's cottage industry."[29] Following 1820, however, the predominance of nonsectarian public colleges would be challenged by the renewed emergence of a multitude of private denominational colleges. Baptists established Colby College, in Maine (1820), for example, and Episcopalians Trinity College, in Connecticut (1826), both of which became leading liberal arts colleges and thus remain squarely situated within the First Wave. Both in terms of number of institutions and total enrollments, private denominational colleges have been termed the characteristic institution of this period.[30] Later in the nineteenth century, Brigham Young University (1875) followed this pattern—as well as a multitude of teachers' colleges, or normal schools. The Second Wave would also witness the establishment of a number of technical schools or technological institutes, both public and private. As Andrew Abbott points out, "America had, in West Point (1802), Rensselaer Polytechnic (1824), Annapolis (1845), MIT (1861), and the Stevens Institute (1870), the rudiments of a separate technical education system."[31] Land-grant status would subsequently be conferred on MIT, which preceded its transition to the Fourth Wave.

Most of the regional colleges, denominational schools, and state-chartered nonsectarian public universities were dedicated almost exclusively to teaching, and the majority that survive continue to operate with this same focus and at relatively the same scale to the present day. However critical these institutions are to the organizational ecology of American higher education, most remain restricted in scope and limited to standardized curricula. We recur to the observation by Philip Altbach in this context that "most of the world's universities are mainly teaching institutions . . . that must look elsewhere to obtain new knowledge and analysis."[32] Policy scholars Hugh Davis Graham and Nancy Diamond paraphrase the assessment of observers of American higher education in this context: "The proliferation of hundreds of state schools and small private sectarian colleges, most of them teaching undergraduate general education, was no pathway to advanced scholarship and scientific excellence."[33]

Slippery Rock University of Pennsylvania, which was established in 1889 as Slippery Rock State Normal School, may be taken as representative of the many regional state colleges that have continued to evolve within the parameters of the Second Wave. In 1926 the school became Slippery Rock State Teachers College and, then, in 1960, Slippery Rock State College. The institution was granted university status in 1983 by the Pennsylvania State System of Higher Education. Despite an expansion of its mission to include some master's degree programs, Slippery Rock remains an accessible and regionally focused Second Wave institution that largely retains its founding mission and objectives. Arizona State University, which in the case study chapter we evaluate as a late-stage Fourth Wave institution on the cusp of evolving into a prototype for the Fifth Wave, similarly began as a late-stage Second Wave institution with its inception as a normal school established by the Thirteenth Territorial Legislature in 1885. With the expansion of sponsored research in the

1980s, however, ASU transitioned from the Second Wave directly to the Fourth Wave.

"The nineteenth century witnessed the transformation from the rudimentary college to the basic framework of the modern American university," Geiger observes. "From institutions that conveyed only textbook knowledge to mostly adolescent boys to panoply of institutions that included advanced and professional studies for young men and women."[34] Among the multitude of heterogeneous institutional types that constitute the Second Wave are community colleges, which in the twentieth century became frequent additions to the Second Wave pattern, representing a new form of mass accessibility to the public institutional model. In our typological assessment, community colleges represent a late-stage iteration of a Second Wave public regional college with a standardized curricular focus. These institutions offered a new form of mass accessibility to the public institutional model. The trend of accessibility has been facilitated by the evolution of technology. Accordingly, California governor Jerry Brown in 2018 proposed that the 115th institution in the community college system serve students statewide exclusively online.

## "Accessible to All, but Especially to the Sons of Toil"

Even without deliberate commitment to engaging a comprehensive base of learners in knowledge acquisition and the discovery process, America's universities fostered indirect knowledge-driven social progress at scale. Social progress, in turn, gave rise to more socially responsive institutions, especially through key policy and legislative interventions.[35] As American society became increasingly diverse and imbued with the utilitarian ethos of the frontier, citizens began to expect more egalitarian access to higher education as well as useful knowledge. Applied research tied to the needs of agriculture and burgeoning industry led to collaboration between colleges and universities and their local regions. In the 1850s, Vermont congressman Justin Morrill argued for federal investment to endow "a college in every State upon a sure and perpetual foundation, accessible to all, but especially to the sons of toil," which is to say, serving the children of farmers and laborers. President Abraham Lincoln signed the Land Grant Act, commonly known as the

Morrill Act, on July 2, 1862, amid a period that witnessed some of the bloodiest confrontations of the Civil War. The legislation led to the formation of the system of land-grant colleges and universities, and many of the schools that emerged as a consequence of the Third Wave became the leading public universities of their respective states.

The social contract implicit in public higher education beginning with the Second Wave—the "profoundly progressive idea that any citizen who met a prescribed set of largely academic conditions would gain entrance to their state university," as John Aubrey Douglass put it—became explicit with the Morrill Act. "To a degree perhaps unmatched by any other single institution in our society or by any other nation in the world, America's public universities were conceived, funded, and developed as tools of socioeconomic engineering," Douglass elaborates, adding that the observation is perhaps "uncomfortable for those who view markets and the rugged individual as the hallmark of the nation's development." The upshot is that the Morrill Act codified the assumption that colleges and universities were to "benefit the individual not as a goal unto themselves but as a means to shape a more progressive and productive society."[36]

With its provisions for the distribution of as many as ninety thousand acres of federal land to each state, the legislation would thus fund the establishment of colleges and universities to provide what was deemed both practical instruction and education in the liberal arts to the children of the working and middle classes. One of the clauses specifies that, for states that accepted the terms of the legislation, the federal government would provide thirty thousand acres of land for each U.S. senator and representative to be used for the "endowment, support, and maintenance of at least one college where the leading object shall be, without excluding other scientific and classical studies, and including military tactics, to teach such branches of learning as are related to agriculture and the mechanic arts, in such manner as the legislatures of the States may respectively prescribe, in order to promote the liberal and practical education of the industrial classes on the several pursuits and professions in life."[37] Thelin explains that the distribution of federal land, widely misunderstood to be "literal gifts of land on which a state government would build a college," in reality constituted incentives for each state to sell distant parcels of land in the West with the obligation to apply profits realized toward the establishment of schools.[38] The funding derived from the sale of federal lands to state governments was intended both to build new colleges and universities and transform existing schools to provide instruction in practical fields.

Some schools were started in concert with this general approach—nearly three dozen land-grant schools were founded within the decade following the enabling legislation. Others evolved as a function of the act—seventeen of them, beginning with Michigan State University (1855), Iowa State University (1858), and the University of Minnesota (1851), had already been established as public colleges or universities but would thereafter be designated land-grant institutions. Historian Allen Nevins offers the following account of the establishment of the land-grant institutions: "Of the institutions benefited by the Morrill land grants, seventeen had been founded (often feebly) before 1862; eighteen more before the end of 1865; and sixteen others before the end of 1870."[39] Although in general usage the designation "land-grant" is often regarded as synonymous with state colleges and universities, a notable few are private, such as the Massachusetts Institute of Technology, which was established in 1861 as a small technical school in the manufacturing center of Boston, or private with public colleges, such as Cornell University, which was founded from whole cloth to advance the utilitarian objectives of the legislation.[40] The University of California (1868) evolved from a single land-grant institution established in Berkeley into the present system of ten campuses, eight of which are land-grant schools. Cornell and the University of California epitomize Third Wave institutions that transitioned to the Fourth Wave.

The diverse and heterogeneous set of colleges and universities that make up the Third Wave have exerted a broad impact disproportionate to their actual number. By one estimate, land-grant institutions have educated one-fifth of all Americans with college degrees.[41] The legislation moreover set a precedent for federal support for higher education, and encouraged state legislatures to provide annual appropriations for universities and colleges.[42] In setting a precedent for federal support, the impact of the legislation would burgeon exponentially following World War II.[43] According to some assessments of American higher education, the global preeminence attained by American research universities in the postwar era is a direct consequence of federal investment, beginning with the seed funding provided to many of the land-grant schools.[44] The system of land-grant universities moreover consolidated the conception of higher education as a public good, which Stephen Gavazzi and Gordon Gee characterize as a covenant—a "bilateral bond that exists between land-grant institutions and the communities they were designed to serve" and the "social conscience of American society and its educational system." Indeed, Gavazzi and Gee go so far as to say that "although not stated explicitly by the creators of the land-grant institutions, the main ideology undergirding this narrative imagines a university that is of the people, by the people, and for the people."[45]

As a consequence of their mandate, the land-grant institutions shaped the research enterprises of the emerging American research universities through an emphasis on scientific inquiry and technological innovation.[46] With the Third Wave we see the first impetus toward applied research in an academic setting, albeit closely tied to agriculture and the needs of local industry, and largely confined to what has been termed "hands-on problem-solving." The legacy of the utilitarian tenets specified in the Morrill Act, epitomized by curricula in the "useful arts" for the "industrial classes"—agriculture, mechanics, mining, and military instruction[47]—would play an important role in the ascendancy of the scientific disciplines and fields of engineering in American research universities.[48] Indeed, economists have correlated the entrepreneurial dimension of the American research university with the utilitarian provisions of the Morrill Act. Nathan Rosenberg points out that because these institutions are comparatively autonomous and operate in a competitive environment devoid of centralized federal authority, most have historically been "heavily beholden to the needs of local industries and to the priorities established by state legislatures." Their attendant economic relevance thus stems from their willingness to accommodate the requirements of agriculture, business, and industry: "America's decentralized higher education system can be fairly described as 'market-driven,' rather than locked into a centralized system in which the reallocation of budgets and personnel is severely restricted by political and bureaucratic considerations, as well as by the constraints of past history."[49]

Among the institutions that were established as a consequence of the Morrill Act, and those previously established that became its beneficiaries, a considerable number emerged in the decades following the Civil

War as research universities. Indeed, in the estimation of some scholars, the land-grant colleges were the "first quasi-research universities in the United States."[50] Of the fifteen institutions singled out by Geiger as foundational to the formation of the American research university,[51] which in our typology represents the Fourth Wave in American higher education, six are land-grant institutions, both public and private: California, Cornell, Illinois, Minnesota, MIT, and Wisconsin. Of the seventy-six land-grant institutions that appear on the roster of the Association of Public and Land-Grant Universities, forty-two, including eight campuses of the University of California system, emerged as major research universities. Twenty land-grant schools, including six University of California campuses, are member institutions of the Association of American Universities (AAU).[52] A second phase of federal investment in higher education began with the Hatch Act of 1887, which provided support for agricultural research, including the operation of agricultural experiment stations generally affiliated with land-grant colleges. The Second Morrill Act of 1890 authorized the establishment of further land-grant institutions and conferral of land-grant status to colleges founded earlier in the century, including the set of schools now termed historically black colleges and universities (HBCUs).[53] The 1890 land-grant system comprises nineteen institutions, including Alabama A&M University, Tuskegee University, and West Virginia State University.

The originating legislation for the land-grant system came only fourteen years prior to the establishment of Johns Hopkins University, in 1876, which would serve as the prototype of the American research university and the Fourth Wave. This set of institutions would thus assume its characteristic structure and contours contemporaneously and in interrelationship with the formation of the land-grant colleges and universities. But the land-grant institutions must themselves be understood as products of the Second Wave. The utilitarian tenets implicit in the state-chartered public colleges and universities of the Second Wave were in a sense codified in the legislation that produced the Third Wave, which in turn would inform the emerging American research university with an orientation conducive to scientific discovery and technological innovation, as well as collaboration with business and industry. And whereas Cornell University has been singled out as the pioneering institutional reification of the ideals of the Morrill Act, the transformation of the

Third Wave into the economic development enterprises that characterize the Fourth Wave began with the embrace of industry that com-
menced with the establishment of MIT, followed by the introduction of
the entrepreneurial dimension into the academic culture of the liberal
arts curriculum at Stanford University in the early twentieth century.[54]
The confluence of the antecedent waves between roughly 1876 and 1915
thus consolidated the institutional type of the Fourth Wave.

### Further Perspective on the Academic Gold Standard

For the purposes of understanding the Fifth Wave it is essential to
realize that the Fourth Wave emerged only very recently during the
modern era, when in the late nineteenth century acceleration in the
growth of scientific knowledge and the imperative for its application to
technological innovation underscored the inadequacies of existing
American colleges and universities, which remained focused primarily
on undergraduate education. Awareness of the scientific rigor of German
universities promulgated by the more than nine thousand Americans
who studied there in the nineteenth century further underscored the
limitations of schools from the first three waves.[55] Just as the German
research university that emerged around 1800 provided institutional accommodation to knowledge production and the burgeoning scientific
culture of the modern era, the Fourth Wave would provide the framework for discovery and innovation in the United States.[56] These patterns
of academic culture coalesced into the new institutional type of the
American research university during the final quarter of the nineteenth
century, when a number of leading institutions from the preceding three
waves, both public and private, sought expansion of function and elaboration of scope to advance research and teaching across a comprehensive spectrum of disciplinary fields. During these decades several new
research-grade universities were built as well from scratch without existing institutional seedlings.

The emergence of a distinct new institutional type must be appreciated as the evolutionary outcome of antecedent models, and in this case
the proximate models may be understood from two interrelated perspectives. Although it is possible to trace the lineage of these institutions in
the West to the British and Continental European universities established in the eleventh or twelfth centuries, and these in turn to the

monastery and cathedral schools of the Middle Ages—or, if one prefers, even more remotely to the academies of classical antiquity[57]—the Fourth Wave for our purposes is both a hybrid of the British and German academic models as well as the institutional descendant of the three prior waves. The colleges of Oxford and Cambridge epitomize the British model, which was elitist and "collegiate," referring to the teaching of undergraduates in residential colleges. The pioneering scientific achievements of the early modern era associated with Oxford and Cambridge notwithstanding, organized research would remain adventitious to the academic culture of the period.[58] The German model, which institutionalized a scientific approach to knowledge production and emphasized advanced graduate study, derives from the founding vision for the University of Berlin, which was established through the influence of the philologist, philosopher, and liberal Prussian minister of education Wilhelm von Humboldt.[59] "The modern German research university," Clark Kerr observed, "beginning with the founding of the University of Berlin in 1809, approached the discovery of truth and knowledge in all fields on the basis of scientific principles, joining the rational and empirical traditions to form the basis of modern scientific research."[60] This scientific approach would inform the modern conception of the humanities, beginning with classical philology, which Chad Wellmon terms the "consummate discipline, exemplifying the virtues of modern science: industriousness, attention to detail, a devotion to method, precision, exactitude, a commitment and facility to open discussion, and a critical disposition."[61]

The fortuitous conflation of the two apparently disparate models in a single institutional framework would uniquely integrate the signature characteristics of two great academic traditions: the "academic cloister of Cardinal Newman," as Kerr characterized it, referring to the cloistered conception of the undergraduate experience held by John Henry Newman, and the more instrumental research orientation of the nineteenth-century German university. "Undergraduate life seeks to follow the British, who have done the best with it, and an historical line that goes back to Plato; the humanists often find their sympathies here," Kerr elaborated. "Graduate life and research follow the Germans, who once did best with them, and an historical line that goes back to Pythagoras; the scientists lend their support to all this."[62] Jonathan Cole corroborates: "If the Germans provided us with a blueprint for advanced research, the British provided us with an outline for organizing undergraduate collegiate education."[63] As Arthur Cohen summarily observed, "Science and research, along with advanced training—the German model—was appended to preexisting institutions that more closely resembled English boarding schools for adolescent boys."[64] As William Clark explains, "At American universities, the undergraduate college remained essentially a descendant of the Oxbridge college, while the graduate schools emerged as a superstructure of German faculties or departments that were added on to the undergraduate college. After the 1870s, the new graduate schools cultivated research, while the college had a traditional pedagogical mission."[65] The American research university would thus become a "new type of institution in the world."[66] Moreover, as Charles W. Eliot, president of Harvard University for four decades beginning in 1869, observed, the new model would be uniquely American: "A university, in any worthy sense of the term, must grow from seed. It cannot be transplanted from England or Germany."[67]

The hybridized model that would define the Fourth Wave—an integrated platform for research and learning in a single institution—remains the basis for the Fifth Wave. But even in its antecedent form, the institution carried within it the potential for new organizational forms—a matter we take up in chapter 6.[68] Humboldt seemed presciently to envision an institution with the capacity to enlarge in scope and scale to embrace manifold functions, which appears to anticipate Kerr's concept of the multiversity—"a whole series of communities and activities held together by a common name, a common governing board, and related purposes"[69]—as well as the growth and expansion through structural accretion that Neil Smelser delineates.[70] This is what Thelin terms the "extension and expansion of the American college" that, through the proliferation of academic departments and eventually specialized research units, led to the "evolution toward a university as a conglomeration of colleges."[71] Moreover, as Wellmon observes, "For Humboldt, the university should not be an institution unto itself; instead, it should be the center of a unified system of education and knowledge production and transmission in which all institutions of knowledge—from elementary and secondary schools to libraries, museums, and academies— functioned as a whole." Consistent with the tenets of the Fifth Wave,

"Humboldt envisioned the university as the center of an ever-expanding media and knowledge ecology."[72]

The prototype for the model of the Fourth Wave research university would be consolidated with the establishment of Johns Hopkins University, which was founded in Baltimore in 1876. In the estimation of historian Edward Shils, the establishment of Johns Hopkins represents "perhaps the single most decisive event in the history of learning in the Western hemisphere," a claim that Geiger deems "extravagant" but not unreasonable.[73] Upon assuming the presidency of Johns Hopkins, former University of California president Daniel Coit Gilman introduced into American higher education the pattern of scientific research and specialized graduate study modeled on the practices of German scientific research institutes and thus an emphasis on the reciprocity of learning and research. Prior to the consolidation of this framework, academic research was deemed "largely adventitious in the scheme of things."[74] As Thelin observes, as late as 1890, American academics "set up their own laboratories, collected their own books and journals, conducted botanical fieldwork, wrote books and tracts, and gathered specimens and artifacts" largely as a "bootleg operation that did not show up in official catalogues . . . and had to be pursued on a piecemeal basis."[75] Apart from the graduate school with "exceptionally high academic standards in what was still a rather new and raw civilization," Kerr lists among the many innovations Johns Hopkins introduced into American higher education a new conception of professional education, especially in medicine; the primacy of the disciplinary-based academic department; research institutes and centers; academic presses; scholarly journals; and the "academic ladder."[76]

Although by wide consensus Johns Hopkins pioneered the model for the American research university, the fifteen institutions delineated by Geiger as formative in the consolidation of the model represent the heterogeneity of the origins of this institutional type. To reiterate the roster cited in chapter 1: five colonial colleges chartered before the American Revolution (Harvard, Yale, Pennsylvania, Princeton, and Columbia); five state universities (Michigan, Wisconsin, Minnesota, Illinois, and California); and five private institutions conceived from their inception as research universities (MIT, Cornell, Johns Hopkins, Stanford, and Chicago). As Geiger elaborates, these universities constitute a unique and differentiated set defined by their interrelationships, both competitive and cooperative; capacity to institutionalize and organize specialized knowledge into academic disciplines; administrative and managerial acumen; and integration of research as a complement to the traditional function of teaching.[77] Whereas our categorization of institutional types may appear to suggest a static conception, our objective rather is to underscore the potential of each type for evolution into the more complex formations of subsequent waves. To consider the Geiger list from the perspective of our typology, five Fourth Wave institutions originated from the First Wave (Harvard, Yale, Pennsylvania, Princeton, and Columbia); the University of Michigan is the sole antecedent from the Second Wave; six are products of the Third Wave (California, Cornell, Illinois, Minnesota, MIT, and Wisconsin); with the remaining three conceived from their inception as Fourth Wave research universities: Johns Hopkins, Stanford, and Chicago.

By 1890 a number of First Wave schools—Harvard, Yale, Princeton, and Columbia, for example—as well as some of the leading state universities, such as the University of Michigan, that had been formed during the Second Wave, were inspired by Johns Hopkins to expand the scope of existing scientific research and graft graduate programs modeled on the academic practices of the German universities onto their residential undergraduate programs. As Thelin remarks of the transition among schools during this period from collegiate to research-grade stature, "Between 1880 and 1890 only a handful of institutions in the United States had legitimate claim to being a 'real university.' Apart from Johns Hopkins, Cornell, Harvard, Clark, and Columbia, the list of serious contenders was slim."[78] Although scientific research institutes had been active throughout Europe for centuries,[79] and academic research was the norm in Germany, there were only pockets of research in the United States. The Lawrence Scientific School at Harvard and the Sheffield Scientific School at Yale were both established in 1847, for example, and as a consequence these institutions led the nation in scientific research. Columbia established the School of Mines in 1864. Along with Johns Hopkins, Geiger holds that Cornell and Harvard, led, respectively, by Andrew Dickson White and Charles W. Eliot, "each in its own way" contributed to the formation of the prototype for this new institutional type. At Harvard, for example, Eliot implemented the elective system developed by

Thomas Jefferson at the University of Virginia, reformed undergraduate education, pioneered graduate programs, and established the Graduate School and the Faculty of Arts and Sciences.[80] "Eliot's reforms are exemplary because of both their content and the extent to which they demonstrated the process of cultural transfer through which German educational ideals found their way into American universities," Louis Menand and colleagues remark, our reference to Jefferson notwithstanding.[81] With their ties to agriculture and industry and inclination toward useful knowledge and technological innovation, the land-grant institutions of the Third Wave had already begun to shape the academic culture of the emerging Fourth Wave.[82] "If any single development had shifted the values in American higher education, it was the remarkable success of Johns Hopkins," observes Geiger. "The 1880s marked the peak influence of German universities, but Hopkins more importantly demonstrated how Germanic research could be incorporated into an American university."[83]

As new research-grade universities built from scratch without existing institutional seedlings, Johns Hopkins, along with Stanford University, established in 1885, and the University of Chicago, in 1890, would prove especially pivotal to the consolidation of the Fourth Wave model. These institutions were conceived as research universities and essentially created through the philanthropic largesse of single individuals: Johns Hopkins through the bequest of the eponymous entrepreneur and railroad magnate and a group of fellow industrialists; Stanford by railroad tycoon Leland Stanford Sr.; and the University of Chicago by oil magnate John D. Rockefeller. The Hopkins bequest of $7 million in 1873—roughly $150 million in 2017 dollars—was intended to be divided evenly between a university and a hospital and at the time represented the largest philanthropic gift in the history of the nation. The Stanford bequest of $20 million in 1885 would be the equivalent of $480 million. And the Rockefeller bequest of $34.7 million in 1890 would be worth $832 million.[84] For the sake of comparison, Michael R. Bloomberg donated $1.8 billion to Johns Hopkins University to fund student financial aid in November 2018. Prior to this, a $600 million gift from Gordon and Betty Moore to Caltech in 2001 remained the largest single gift to a research university during the past half century, followed by two $500 million gifts, to the University of California, San Francisco, and the University of Oregon, from the Helen Diller Foundation in 2017 and Penny and Phil Knight in 2016, respectively.[85]

"Around the world, government funding supports most higher education, but in few other societies do private endowments play the role they do in the United States," Craig Calhoun observes. As a consequence, "the richest universities, in short, are increasingly able to set academic agendas independent of both the government and foundations (though they also get large amounts from each)."[86] "Wealth, like age, does not make a university great," a Harvard admissions brochure from 1963 offered reflectively. "But it helps."[87] And indeed, with an endowment valued in 2017 at $36 billion, diminished from its prerecession peak of $38.4 billion, Harvard remains the most heavily endowed university in the nation and the wealthiest academic institution in the world. Its endowment continues to surpass those of Yale ($27.1 billion), the University of Texas system ($26.5 billion), Stanford ($24.7 billion), and Princeton ($23.8 billion) by a reliably comfortable margin. The combined wealth of the fifteen colleges and universities in Massachusetts with individual endowments exceeding $500 million is valued at more than $70 billion, which amount, the *Chronicle of Higher Education* reports, exceeds the estimated total national wealth of such countries as Sri Lanka, Jordan, and Lithuania.[88] As the economist Ronald G. Ehrenberg aptly remarked, "The magnitude of the endowments that some institutions have is truly mind-boggling."[89]

## Knowledge Production and Perpetual Innovation

"Since its inception in Germany in the early nineteenth century and its reinvention in America later that same century," Wellmon observes, "the research university has been the central institution of knowledge in the West."[90] The locus of that predominance remained in Europe well into the twentieth century, but with the devastation and disruption of World War II and the mobilization of academic research associated with the war effort, the set of American research universities would come to outrank their venerable European counterparts. The Fourth Wave consolidated its global academic preeminence in part as a consequence of unprecedented federal support in the postwar era for scientific research focused primarily on national defense, economic prosperity, and public health.[91] What has been characterized as the "decentralized, pluralistic, and intensely competitive academic marketplace fueled by federal research dollars" encouraged innovation and risk-taking and led a cohort of ambitious universities to emerge as world-class research institutions.[92]

The compact between the federal government and America's research universities was largely defined by Vannevar Bush, the founding director of the newly formed Office of Scientific Research and Development (OSRD) under Presidents Roosevelt and Truman, in the July 1945 policy manifesto *Science—The Endless Frontier: A Report to the President on a Program for Postwar Scientific Research.*[93] The report set forth the terms for postwar federal investment in a national science enterprise facilitated through competitive engagement among a set of elite research universities. What is called the "social contract for science" has been paraphrased thus: "Government promises to fund the basic science that peer reviewers find most worthy of support, and scientists promise that the research will be performed well and honestly and will provide a steady stream of discoveries that can be translated into new products, medicines, or weapons."[94] As Roger Pielke explains, "One of the fundamental assumptions of post-war science policy is that science provides a reservoir or fund of knowledge that can be tapped and applied to national needs."[95] Bush thus envisioned research universities as what he termed "wellsprings of knowledge and understanding" from which "scientists are free to pursue the truth wherever it may lead" and that would provide a "flow of new scientific knowledge to those who can apply it to practical problems in government, in industry, or elsewhere."[96] Implicit in the conception that Bush promulgated is the linear model of innovation, which reinforces the spurious dichotomy between basic and applied research, a matter we take up in chapter 5.

The Manhattan Project had spurred the formation of the system of national laboratories, such as Los Alamos National Laboratory and Lawrence Livermore National Laboratory, and subsequent federal investment led to the establishment of federal agencies such as the National Science Foundation (NSF), National Institutes of Health (NIH), and National Aeronautics and Space Administration (NASA).[97] A significant amount of the research undertaken by academically affiliated scientists and engineers is conducted within the system of national laboratories, which are funded by federal agencies such as the U.S. Department of Energy but administered by industrial contractors or universities.[98] The

ascendency of American research universities as a principal locus for research and development appears in hindsight to have been inevitable,
but funding for research could just as well have been apportioned to industrial laboratories or independent research institutes. But the success
of the Manhattan Project demonstrated the potential and economic benefit of university-based research, and the Bush report consolidated the
formal relationships between the federal government and research universities.[99] The mobilization of the war effort moreover had broad societal implications. "The nation responded to World War II by creating a
national system of innovation, tying together laboratory research, mass
production, battlefield tactics, and boardroom strategies," Gregg Zachary points out. "The scale and rigor of this military-industrial-academic
complex were unprecedented."[100]

The conceptualization of the constellation of interests first identified
by President Dwight D. Eisenhower in his farewell address to the nation
on January 17, 1961, as the "military-industrial complex" would ramify
with the implication of the academic sector by Senator J. William Fulbright, as historian Stuart W. Leslie explains: "The 'golden triangle' of
military agencies, the high-technology industry, and research universities created a new kind of postwar science, one that blurred traditional
distinctions between theory and practice, science and engineering, civil-
ian and military, and classified and unclassified, one that owed its character as well as its contracts to the national security state." The new scientific enterprise of the "Cold War university"—a "university polarized
around the military," as Leslie puts it—would comport with Big Science in what some characterize as a sort of Faustian bargain. As these
institutions became "federalized," so goes the argument, the federaliza-
tion process contributed to the narrowing of their research enterprises
and the bureaucratization of academic science.[101] The focus on science
and technology came at the expense of the social sciences and humanities, an omission that would not be redressed until the 1960s, when the
National Science Foundation began to support the social and behavioral
sciences.[102] A call for the Fifth Wave to reinvent Fourth Wave academic
culture thus presumes negotiation of limitations imposed by the Cold
War university model.

It would be impossible to survey the extent of the transformational
impact that is the outcome of the fundamental discoveries and techno-

logical innovation that may be attributed to the research, development, and education efforts of the set of Fourth Wave research universities. Inasmuch as others have capably assembled vast compendia of these tens of thousands of discoveries and inventions—from lasers to magnetic resonance imaging to global positioning systems to the algorithm for Google searches, as summarized in chapter 4 in our first book—it would be superfluous in the present context to attempt to construct an adequate synopsis.[103] Perpetual innovation enabled by scientific research has spurred economic growth and led to the development of entire new industries.[104] In this context, economist Joel Mokyr underscores the correlation between scientific discovery, technological innovation, and economic growth: "The wider and deeper the epistemic base on which a technique rests, the more likely it is that a technique can be extended and find new applications, product and service quality improved, the production process streamlined, economized, and adapted to changing external circumstances, and the techniques combined with others to form new ones."[105] Indeed, observe economists Partha Dasgupta and Paul A. David, "To say that economic growth in the modern era has been grounded on the exploitation of scientific knowledge is to express a truism."[106] However, the ideas, products, and processes that have improved societal well-being and contributed incalculably to economic growth are not only the outcomes of scientific research and technological innovation but also of creative and scholarly endeavor in the arts, humanities, and social and behavioral sciences. With reference to these latter fields, Cole elaborates: "Scholars in these fields make discoveries all the time," which "often take the form of basic ideas, concepts, theories, and the results of empirical research." Moreover, "Major discoveries in one field quickly diffuse into another—say, from economics to sociology, or from psychology into economics. In short order, powerful concepts move from the initial field to cognate disciplines and from there into the language of everyday life."[107] Implicit in claims for the economic development function of the Fourth Wave is its impact on broad societal development.

An entrepreneurial interrelationship with industry first pioneered by MIT prior to the mid-twentieth century was followed in the second half of the century by an efflorescence of the globalization of research that David Guston terms the "new political economy of academic commercialization."[108] Sheila Slaughter and colleagues have assessed the dimensions of what has been termed "academic capitalism," which in their usage need not refer to any putative corporatization nor subversion of the academy but rather to the acknowledgment of the merits of what we call academic enterprise.[109] With the passage of the Bayh-Dole Act of 1980, which permitted universities to retain intellectual property rights to the ideas, products, and processes developed as a result of federally funded research, growth in patenting and licensing by universities would further promote interaction with industry for commercial development and as a consequence spur economic growth.[110] The legislation consolidated the triple helix of university-industry-government collaboration described by Etzkowitz and colleagues.[111]

Apart from their role in the formation of human capital and facilitation of economic development associated with the commercialization of knowledge, major research universities contribute to the production of knowledge and diffusion of innovation through the formation of regional innovation clusters. Knowledge spillovers from academic research, and especially the start-ups and spin-offs of major research universities, promote the diffusion of innovation, which is facilitated by the agglomeration or clustering of research and development efforts and thus said to be geographically mediated.[112] The most obvious examples of major research universities that spawned regional innovation clusters would be Stanford University and Silicon Valley, and, in Boston, MIT and Route 128.[113] One might also think of the Research Triangle in North Carolina, comprising Duke University; University of North Carolina, Chapel Hill; and North Carolina State University as well as the regional impacts of the University of California, San Diego; University of Texas at Austin; and the University of Rochester and Rochester Institute of Technology.

The influence of market forces on universities, Guston points out, has been viewed with ambivalence and as not altogether benign, inasmuch as critics allege the market's impact on scholarship to be deleterious in its exacerbation of conflicts of interest, altering norms around scholarship, addressing students as consumers, and lowering learning standards. The creation of institutional review boards is evidence of the need felt by many universities to police relationships with market participants and to protect human and animal subjects from exploitation. For institutions to capture the benefits of closer relationships with commercial entities and to cope with the possible negative consequences, Guston argues that they must facilitate the "reflexive study of the interaction of innovation and society."[114]

## A De Facto National University

In our previous book we alluded to the proposition that our nation's leading public research universities could be said collectively to constitute a de facto national university,[115] referring in the American context to the proposed federally chartered seat of learning envisioned by the Philadelphia physician Benjamin Rush and championed by George Washington and James Madison, among other leaders of the founding generation. Although higher education is not discussed per se in the U.S. Constitution, it was a topic of consequence and passion for the architects of the early American republic. During the Constitutional Convention in Philadelphia in 1787, Madison first called for the establishment of a national university and the legislative authority to "offer premiums to encourage the advancement of useful knowledge and discoveries." The scope and purposes of the proposed institution were variously conceived both during initial deliberations and episodically over the course of the century to follow. By consensus it was to be located in the new national capital and charged with two principal functions: graduate education, especially the training of civil servants and government officials, and, more generally, research conducted in the national interest. But the nature of its governance and sources for its funding as well as the enumeration of its curriculum would remain contested.[116] The following overview suggests the rationale for the proposed institution among leaders of the founding generation as well as its continued relevance, which for our purposes is largely symbolic. Although the envisioned national university may now be invoked rhetorically in an effort to summon public resolve to advance discovery and innovation conceived in the national interest, failure to establish the envisioned institution, which may have inspired the concurrent formation of a federal ministry of higher education, has in retrospect fortuitously yielded extraordinary outcomes, setting the course for the decentralized—and highly competitive—configuration of American higher education.[117]

Although by the time debate on the proposal for the establishment of the University of the United States began, Harvard College had already marked its 150th anniversary and the eight other colonial colleges had become esteemed pillars of their respective communities, proponents argued that these existing "seminaries of learning" were not sufficiently capable of providing the breadth and quality of instruction essential for the new nation. Moreover, champions of a federally chartered university argued that such an institution would promote republican values and serve as a unifying force in a still fractious era of starkly differing regional interests. The founders were motivated not solely by their dedication to the ideals of the Age of Reason, Albert Castel contends, or their "conviction that our experiment in republican government could not succeed unless the people and their officials were properly educated." At a moment still rife with sectionalism, he elaborates, some argued that a great national university would "combat divisive tendencies by bringing together at a central seat of learning the choice young men of all the states" to "give to America that unity of purpose and policy which would enable it to fulfill its glorious destiny in the world."[118] Those who held a more narrow conception wanted to confine the scope of a national university to such fields as agriculture, commerce, defense, and navigation, while its potential to promote strong federal government demanded programs in diplomacy, economics, and law. Some scholars envisioned an institution offering a comprehensive curriculum spanning the arts and sciences. But the basis of its governance, sources for funding, enumeration of its curriculum, and, indeed, its very constitutionality would remain perpetually contested.[119] Indeed, the rejection of the proposal, which may have led to the formation of a federal ministry of higher education, has been attributed to its conflict with the doctrine of states' rights.[120]

Amid the intellectual ferment of the American Enlightenment,[121] envisioning a great seat of learning in the new national capital would have seemed essential to the founders, who would have been familiar with British and European institutional models, as well as the model of state control and centralization in systems of higher education, which even today remains the standard framework throughout much of the world.[122] This generation of political leaders would have been familiar with the academies and scientific societies of Great Britain and the Continent, such as the Royal Society of London or the Académie des sciences,[123] and especially institutional antecedents to the prestigious *grandes écoles* in

Paris, which were chartered following the National Convention phase of the French Revolution.[124] Subsequent discussion of proposals for the national university would certainly have been influenced by the formation of the various *grandes écoles*, especially the Institut d'études politiques de Paris, or Sciences Po, established in 1872. Even though they did not explicitly compare a national university to these institutes, proponents likely envisioned a center for scholarship and scientific research of international stature built along the contours of the elite models of the scientific academies and *grandes écoles* across the Atlantic. Nonetheless, as Rosenberg observes, "The fact that Washington, D.C., with its extraordinary archival and library resources, has never become home to a leading research university, in spite of numerous proposals to make it so over the past two centuries . . . is evidence, if further evidence is needed, of a long-standing political aversion to centralizing tendencies in the academic sphere."[125]

George Washington became one of the leading proponents for the formation of a national university. He made it one of the principal causes of his later years, even to the point of setting aside a portion of his own estate toward its establishment. In January 1790, in his first annual message to Congress after having been elected president, he questioned whether the scant number of existing colleges—"seminaries of learning already established"—would be sufficient to meet the needs of the nation:

> Nor am I less persuaded that you will agree with me in the opinion that there is nothing which can better deserve your patronage than the promotion of science and literature. Knowledge is in every country the surest basis of public happiness. Whether this desirable object will be best promoted by affording aids to seminaries of learning already established, by the institution of a national university, or by any other expedient, will be well worthy of a place in the deliberations of the legislature.[126]

In his eighth address to Congress, in January 1796, Washington offered the following assessment:

> I have heretofore proposed to the consideration of Congress the expediency of establishing a national university. . . . Amongst the motives to such an institution, the assimilation of the principles, opinions, and manners of our

countrymen by the common education of a portion of our youth from every quarter well deserves attention. The more homogenous our citizens can be made in these particulars the greater will be our prospect of permanent union; and a primary object of such a national institution should be the education of our youth in the science of government. In a republic what species of knowledge can be equally important and what duty more pressing on its legislature than to patronize a plan for communicating it to those who are to be the future guardians of the liberties of the country?[127]

As the second president of the United States, Thomas Jefferson advocated a constitutional amendment to establish a national university, and failing to garner adequate support, resolved to found the University of Virginia as its surrogate. His successor, James Madison, was likewise unable to unify an increasingly parochial Congress behind the idea. During his presidency, Madison urged the establishment of a national university during four annual addresses. A bill to create such an institution brought before Congress in 1817, for example, was defeated by the House of Representatives.[128] The last of our nation's founders to champion the cause of a national university was President James Monroe. Recognizing the political futility of the cause, he and a group of friends established a private institution along the Potomac, which later became known as George Washington University—a great university, albeit one that historically and in modern times bears little resemblance to the grand vision of its namesake. John Quincy Adams, the final president to champion the cause of a national university, rightly noted the importance of the project to America's national competitiveness, warning that "foreign nations less blessed with that freedom which is power than ourselves are advancing with gigantic strides in the career of public improvements."[129]

Despite the explicit advocacy and staunch support of subsequent presidents, including Grant, Hayes, and Garfield following the Civil War, Congress repeatedly failed to enact the founding legislation.[130] Moreover, the functions envisioned for a national university would, over the course of the nineteenth century, be subsumed by colleges and the scientific schools and technical institutes attached to some of them and, in the final quarter of the century, be superseded by the newly emerging research universities. The Smithsonian Institution, established in 1846 from the immense bequest of British scientist Robert Smithson, largely assumed the function of scientific research. Needless to add that, over time, with the formation of government research agencies and the system of national laboratories, along with think tanks, private research institutes, and the research and development efforts of industry, the functions initially envisioned for the national university were fulfilled by other institutions.[131]

The limitations of the set of schools that constituted the First Wave were apparent to contemporaries concerned with the role of education in the new republic. As one of the initial champions of a federal university, Dr. Benjamin Rush, for example, an associate of John Adams and Thomas Jefferson, sought an institution that would provide a "sort of graduate education to the elites of the various states."[132] In a proposal he published in January 1787, he recommended that its curriculum include "everything connected with government, such as history—the law of nature and nations—the civil law—the municipal laws of our country— and the principles of commerce."[133] In a speech at the University of Pennsylvania in 1795, Rush compared the objective of useful knowledge with the classical curriculum then predominant in the colleges, or "seminaries," of the First Wave. He argued against the persistence of the curriculum taught without "due allowance being made for the different obligations and interests which have been created by time, and the peculiar state of society in a new country, in which the business of the principal part of the inhabitant is to obtain first and foremost means of subsistence." He expressed regret that, rather than offering focus on the "many national duties" associated with the new democracy and "instituting our sons in the Arts most essential to their existence, and in the means of acquiring that kind of knowledge which is connected with the time, the country, and the government in which they live," American colleges compelled students to study Greek and Latin, "two languages which . . . are rarely spoken [and] have ceased to be the vehicles of Science and literature, and which contain no knowledge but that which is to be met with in a more improved and perfect state in modern languages."[134]

Considerable prestige attaches to the designation "national university" in various national contexts. The institutional type remains vital throughout much of the world, where, since the eighteenth century and despite the more recent emulation of America's research universities, the centralized European model of higher education remains the standard framework. In a European context, however, the concept bears little resemblance to the institution envisioned by the founders. Through the bureaucratic efficiency of centralized planning and policymaking, national ministries of higher education determine the admission of cohorts of academically gifted students, mandate institutional specializations, and purport to ensure the equitable allocation of resources. It is noteworthy in this context that many of the most innovative economies in the world today, including Singapore, South Korea, Israel, Switzerland, Australia, and China, all have national universities. Inasmuch as bureaucratic control minimizes competition between institutions, such systems are at variance with the competitive configuration of research-grade education in the United States. As Graham and Diamond elaborate: "The centralized nature of European higher education purchased organizational rationality and bureaucratic efficiency at the expense of competition and innovation." Moreover, "the vertical organization of specialized institutions was poorly designed to respond to the brisk pace of competition that characterized scientific development." Nevertheless, the leading state universities in most national contexts are generally the most prestigious and competitive in terms of admissions, thus setting the standard for advanced education.[135] With the absence of a national university to benchmark academic excellence in the early American republic, the academic gold standard in the United States would fortuitously be set not by a preeminent national institution but rather by the competitive cohort of colleges that would constitute the Ivy League.

To reiterate: The decentralized configuration of American higher education and absence of a federal ministry of higher education would unleash competition between institutions and contribute to this defining attribute of American higher education.[136] A national university "would surely have been the central instrument of Federal government policy regarding higher education in the Union," as Martin Trow elaborates. "Therefore, the defeat . . . was arguably the most important policy decision affecting the role of central government in American higher education, determining or at least conditioning the character of all future Federal government interventions."[137] Higher education in the United States would remain largely the responsibility of the states: "The Tenth

Amendment reserves all powers not delegated to the central government to the states," one assessment explains. "Since education is not explicitly mentioned in the Constitution, the states have taken the lead in this area, with the federal government playing a secondary role."[138] In the absence of a centralized federal agency with this purview, Thelin contends, two foundations—the Carnegie Foundation for the Advancement of Teaching, and the General Education Board, founded by John D. Rockefeller— "assumed the role of a de facto national ministry of education."[139] But, of course, the argument for the emergence of a set of institutions to serve as a de facto national university in the contemporary context is a vastly different proposition.

A mong historical determinants that set the course for this idiosyncratic trajectory were the patterns of settlement in the American colonies, which created on the Eastern seaboard a cluster of distinct and largely autonomous jurisdictions, each of which sought to impose on the new colleges the preferences of local authorities and denominational affiliations. Indeed, Trow explains, "Even after a Federal government emerged in 1789, the Constitution explicitly renounced its authority over education, including higher education, delegating that power to the constituent states." As a consequence, colonial colleges "differed from one another in their origins, links to colonial government, and denominational ties." Moreover, the precedent was set for a plurality of colleges founded "at the initiative or with the encouragement of public authorities and powerful private constituencies."[140]

Apart from the failure to establish a national university, Trow cites two additional interrelated factors especially formative to the subsequent pattern of American higher education: the chartering process for colleges in the American colonies, and the 1819 landmark decision of the U.S. Supreme Court in the Dartmouth College case, which blocked the State of New Hampshire from assuming authority over a private college. Since the founding of the earliest universities in the twelfth and thirteenth centuries in Britain and the Continent, Trow explains, institutions have sought to obtain royal charters. Until a royal charter from King William IV in 1836 permitted the University of London to confer degrees, for example, Oxford and Cambridge had maintained an effective monopoly for this prerogative for seven centuries.[141] But in the seventeenth century on the new continent, charters were merely a "monopoly grant to an institution of the power to grant degrees in a specific colony."[142]

In the case of *The Trustees of Dartmouth College vs. the State of New Hampshire*, the Supreme Court struck a blow against state intervention in higher education. As Trow explains, the state had sought to seize control of the college during a dispute between the president and its board: "New Hampshire maintained that although Dartmouth may have been established in colonial times as a private corporation, it was founded to benefit the people of the state. Consequently, the public, through the state's legislature, deserved and required a voice in the operation of the college." Trow summarizes the decision, which was written by Chief Justice John Marshall: "He wrote that the college was a 'private' rather than a 'civil' corporation, and affirmed the sanctity of the contract (as embodied in the charter) between the state and Dartmouth." Trow elaborates: "After this decision, state control over the whole of higher education was no longer possible. The legal basis for the extraordinary proliferation of privately founded and governed higher education institutions in the United States was now in place." He terms the failure to charter a national university and the success of the Dartmouth College appeal "victories for local initiative and private entrepreneurship." The outcome of the two episodes in his estimation was a "kind of charter for unrestrained individual and group initiative in the creation of colleges of all sizes, shapes, and creeds."[143] This sort of unrestrained initiative is certainly the basis for the "crazy quilt" of American higher education, which in the estimation of Charles Clotfelter includes "fifty of the best universities in the world and five hundred of the worst."[144]

Not to belabor the point, but we underscore in the strongest possible terms that failure to enact legislation that in the eighteenth century could have inspired the concurrent formation of a federal ministry of higher education fortuitously served to set the course for the decentralized—and highly competitive—configuration of American higher education that has been among its greatest assets.[145] Competition has been a major driving force spurring research and development in our nation's research universities. In the twenty-first century, however, collaboration as well as competition between colleges and universities is essential if discovery, creativity, and innovation are to continue to serve the common good. And while the nation is fortunate that no single federally chartered national university was ever established, the well-being of our nation may now well depend on the evolution of a subset of public research universities that collectively assume a societal role that surpasses in scope and scale what the founders envisioned for the single institution. To this extent, the evolving knowledge enterprises this book proposes could arguably be characterized as constituent de facto "national universities," that is, institutions dedicated to knowledge production and research-grade advanced education conceived in service to the nation at an appropriate scale.

Indeed, their significance to the nation might more accurately be designated by their characterization as a league of national *service* universities. We reiterate that this usage is not intended to evoke comparisons to the national service academies, that is, the U.S. Military Academy, in West Point, New York, or the U.S. Naval Academy, in Annapolis, Maryland. Nor is it intended to posit an equivalence between the Fifth Wave and the land-grant colleges and universities that we term the Third Wave, despite their historic service orientation.[146] Most major research universities, both public and private, characterize their missions in terms of the triumvirate of teaching, research, and public service, but the concept of national service universities is intended to bolster the service component associated with the Third Wave and the research orientation associated with the Fourth Wave. The subset of national service universities could be envisioned as comprising differentiated institutional models, but all characterized by common design elements, including scalability, sociotechnical integration, and societal impact. National service universities would operate with a commitment to maximize the scale of public benefit, integrate technology seamlessly into their operational cores, advance teaching and research intended to maximize societal impact, and commit to the production of useful knowledge. A heterogeneous subset of such differentiated institutions—a league of national service universities—inspired with a twenty-first-century vision of egalitarian access and engaged in collaboration with other colleges and universities, business and industry, government agencies and laboratories, and organizations in civil society could realize the aspirations of our nation's founders and integrate academic commitment with an explicit mission of advancing social progress. A league of national service universities could thus be said to constitute the emerging Fifth Wave in American higher education.

### Reinvigorating the American Experiment in Democracy

The emergence of classical Athenian democracy, which informs so many of the norms and values and institutions of contemporary society, has been correlated by a number of scholars with access to knowledge among citizens of the polis. In an account of the genesis of knowledge-based, or epistemic, democracies, classicist Josiah Ober traces Athenian efforts across six generations to harness useful knowledge, which permitted not only the attainment of civic prosperity and competitive advantage among rival city-states but also the growth of effective democratic institutions. He identifies three epistemic processes that advanced learning and innovation as well as effective collective endeavor: (1) the aggregation of dispersed knowledge; (2) the alignment or coordination of citizens with shared values and common knowledge; and (3) the codification of knowledge, which permitted decisions, once taken, to become rules to guide future consensus. The democratic institutions of the Athenians, Ober explains, would prove highly adaptive and thus encourage the sort of institutional innovation that would permit the city-state to flourish at unprecedented levels of prosperity, power, and cultural influence.[147]

The broader epistemological implications of the participatory and deliberative democracy realized by the Athenians remain relevant to the present day. According to Ober, these "lead to defining democracy as the capacity of a public to do things (rather than simply as majority rule), to focusing on the relationship between innovation and learning (not just bargaining and voting), and to designing institutions to aggregate useful knowledge (not merely preferences or interests)."[148] Consistent with this strikingly pragmatist reading of the Athenian polis, contemporary academic culture, which is defined by its values of academic freedom and shared governance, embodies the normative and qualitative characteristics of that ethos. The "democratic advantage" that encouraged rational choice leading to collective action in classical Athens resonates across the centuries as a remote antecedent to the pragmatist advocacy of communicative reason and sustained public debate in the service of actionable knowledge.[149] Indeed, political theorist Hélène Landemore contends that the collective intelligence of citizens produces what she terms "democratic reason," which, consistent with research on cognitive diversity and the wisdom of crowds, buttresses the epistemic argument for democracy.[150]

The extent to which it is possible to interrelate the useful knowledge produced by the epistemic processes and political practices of the Athenians with the emergence of systematic philosophical training remains speculative, but it is tempting to correlate the presence of such institutions as the Academy, founded by Plato in the 380s BC in a grove outside the city walls of Athens, and the Lyceum, founded by his pupil Aristotle, with the development of an epistemic democracy tolerant of diversity and dissent and conducive to personal freedom. And indeed, Ober perceives the free exchange of ideas among Athenians ("effective aggregation of diverse types of knowledge") as essential to the success of the polis.[151] Such a correlation stands in stark contrast to the contemporary misconception of academic culture as an ivory tower. As political theorist Amy Gutmann puts it, "The ideal of a community united solely by the pursuit of knowledge for its own sake may have made more sense where it first flourished: within the Athenian polis, where much work was reserved for resident aliens (metics), slaves, and women, who were excluded from citizenship." Even so, she elaborates, "The purpose of higher learning in Athenian democracy was not wholly non-instrumental, even if it was wholly unspecialized and un-vocational. Knowledge was useful for the polis, or at least for a well-governed polis."[152]

However much the intellectual and cultural accomplishments of classical Athens remain relevant to the present day, their enduring impact is disproportionate to the scale of operations of the philosophical schools. According to the accounts of contemporaries, enrollment in the Academy likely did not exceed two dozen students at the time of Plato's death in 347 BC.[153] Across town, meanwhile, the Lyceum may have subsequently enrolled a roughly equivalent number.[154] But although such numbers seem trifling, by some estimates no more than ten thousand adult male citizens resided within the core urban agglomeration of the Athenian city-state at any point in the fourth century BC.[155] While students of the Academy were typically young men from prosperous families with sufficient means to support their philosophical pursuits, John

Dillon reports that the names of two women appear on the roster at the time of Plato's death: Lastheneia of Mantinea and Axiothea of Phleious. Successors to Plato as scholarch of the Academy, moreover, beginning with his nephew Speussipus, maintained its operations and thus perpetuated its influence for several centuries.[156]

Inasmuch as it is possible to correlate the success of the Athenian experiment in democracy with the aggregation and exchange of knowledge, the implications for our own society in the twenty-first century seem readily apparent. But in a nation with a population of nearly 327 million individuals, the correlation between access to knowledge and the scale of our institutions becomes critical. The Fifth Wave offers the potential for our nation's public research universities to expand enrollment capacity and build an academic infrastructure proportionate to the task of educating to competitive levels of achievement the top third of academically qualified students representative of the socioeconomic and intellectual diversity of our society. To accelerate the evolution of our own society, academic communities must convene with stakeholders to develop new models for a subset of public research universities that combine accessibility with world-class knowledge production and societal impact and that insist upon and leverage the complementarities and synergies between discovery and accessibility.

The imperative that citizens in a democratic society be educated has been integral to our collective identity since first articulated by the founders of our nation. Reaffirming the ideals of the classical Athenian democracy and inspired by the Enlightenment tenet that reason should guide human affairs, John Adams and Thomas Jefferson were representative of leaders of the early republic who expressed the conviction that an educated citizenry is essential to a free society.[157] The corollary assumption that the meritorious will succeed in large measure by dint of educational attainment has similarly shaped the narrative arc of our democratic experiment.[158] Although the challenge of defining the proper role of government in the provision of education remains unresolved to the present day,[159] the perception among the founders that education was critical to the formation of social cohesion and virtuous conduct within the body politic would set the course for the nation to pioneer novel educational frameworks distinct from British and Continental European models.[160] Consistent with its egalitarian principles, the United States led the world in the provision of primary and secondary education beginning in the mid-nineteenth century. And with expectations for a college education becoming the norm by the mid-twentieth century—and increasingly so with the advent of the knowledge economy—advanced educational attainment has become foundational to the success of individuals and the prosperity and competitiveness of the nation.[161]

The pragmatist philosopher John Dewey was foremost among proponents of the proposition that education is integral to democracy. And indeed, he wrote voluminously on the relationship of education to democracy, typified in his contention that "democracy must be born anew every generation, and education is its midwife."[162] But the correlation between democracy and knowledge is hardly an insight of the late modern era. As Ober points out, through the aggregation, alignment, and codification of useful knowledge, Athenians developed effective democratic institutions that encouraged collaboration and innovation among citizens. "The history of Athenian popular government shows that making good use of dispersed knowledge is the original source of democracy's strength."[163] With reference to classical Athens, but expressed in terms that encourage readers to extrapolate to our own experiment in democracy, Ober constructs a compelling argument regarding the interdependence of investment in knowledge and the flourishing of a democratic society: "Democratic conditions of freedom, equality, and dignity promote both rational human capital investments across diverse domains of endeavor *and* the rational disclosure and exchange of useful knowledge that is made more valuable by those investments."[164] In other words, investment in advanced higher education promotes both personal success and public benefit.

As epigraphs to his 2008 book on democracy and knowledge, Ober juxtaposes insights to this effect by John Adams, writing in 1765, more than three decades before he would become the second president of the United States, and the economist Friedrich Hayek. Adams contends that knowledge must be distributed throughout society: "Liberty cannot be preserved without a general knowledge among the people, who have a right, from the frame of their nature, to knowledge." Moreover, "The preservation of the means of knowledge among the lowest ranks is of more importance to the public than all the property of all the rich men in the country." Hayek focuses on access to that distributed knowledge:

"The practical problem [of dispersed knowledge] arises precisely because facts are never so given to a single mind, and because, in consequence, it is necessary that in the solution of the problem knowledge should be used that is dispersed among many people." Indeed, Hayek considers access to knowledge dispersed throughout the collective to be the "central theoretical problem of all social science."[165]

The correlation between educational attainment and a successful democracy has been a cornerstone of political conceptualization in the republic from its outset. Moreover, the earliest formulations express an implicit social compact in public higher education. The Constitution of the Commonwealth of Massachusetts, which was drafted by Adams and ratified in June 1780, would serve as a prototype for the Constitution of the United States. Section 2 of chapter 5 begins as follows: "Wisdom and knowledge, as well as virtue, diffused generally among the body of the people, being necessary for the preservation of their rights and liberties; and as these depend on spreading the opportunities and advantages of education in the various parts of the country, and among the different orders of the people, it shall be the duty of legislatures and magistrates, in all future periods of this commonwealth, to cherish the interests of literature and the sciences, and all seminaries of them." Because the only so-termed seminary in Massachusetts at this time was Harvard College, which had been founded in 1636, the document goes on to specify "especially the university at Cambridge."[166]

The leaders of the founding generation shared a strong sense of the public value of higher education, and it does not seem irrelevant in this context to observe that most were first-generation college graduates. The roster includes John Adams, Samuel Adams, Thomas Jefferson, James Madison, and Benjamin Rush.[167] With reference to these leaders, Susan Mettler notes: "They strongly believed that by encouraging and subsidizing advanced learning, the nation would foster the knowledge, creativity, dynamism, leadership, and skills that would spur economic growth, technological innovation, and social advances." In this context she quotes Benjamin Franklin, who had observed with reference to the establishment of the University of Pennsylvania: "The good Education of Youth has been esteemed by wise Men in all Ages, as the surest Foundation of the Happiness both of private families and of Commonwealth [nations]. Almost all Governments have therefore made it a principal Object of their Attention . . . [to] supply the succeeding Age with Men qualified to serve the Publick with Honour to themselves, and to their Country."[168]

Articulating the tenets of what would become the Second Wave in American higher education, Thomas Jefferson, a graduate of the College of William and Mary, similarly expressed this imperative in the context of his vision for the University of Virginia in 1820: "I know of no safe depository of the ultimate powers of the society, but the people them-selves; and if we think them not enlightened enough to exercise their control with a wholesome discretion, the remedy is not to take it from them, but to inform their discretion by education."[169] In 1786 he had expressed a similar conviction: "I think by far the most important bill in our whole code is that for the diffusion of knowledge among the people. No other sure foundation can be devised for the preservation of freedom and happiness."[170] In a letter to James Madison written the fol-lowing year, Jefferson remarked: "Above all things I hope the education of the common people will be attended to; convinced that on their good sense we may rely with the most security for the preservation of a due degree of liberty."[171] Elsewhere, regarding the necessary correlation be-tween an educated citizenry and the exercise of democracy, Jefferson had observed, "If a nation expects to be ignorant and free, in a state of civilization, it expects what never was and never will be."[172] James Madison, a graduate of the college that would become Princeton, made the same point in 1822 when he wrote, "Knowledge will forever govern ignorance: And a people who mean to be their own governours must arm themselves with the power which knowledge gives."[173]

The conviction that useful knowledge must be distributed through-out society persists in American society. In his State of the Union address on January 11, 1944, President Franklin Roosevelt proposed an economic bill of rights that would include among its recommendations the "right to a good education," which ranked among "economic truths" that had become "self-evident."[174] A few years later, President Harry Truman formed the Commission on Higher Education, which was assigned the task of "examining the functions of higher education in our democracy and the means by which they can best be performed." The report ob-served that the "first and most essential charge upon higher education is that . . . it shall be the carrier of democratic values, ideals, and processes." It enjoined society to provide the "means by which every citizen, youth, and adult is enabled and encouraged to carry his education, formal and informal, as far as his native capacities permit." Among the overarching goals specified by the commission was "education for a fuller realization of democracy in every phase of living." Implicit was the goal of higher education to "liberate and perfect the intrinsic powers of every citizen," which was deemed the "central purpose of democracy."[175] Elsewhere in the report: "It is especially serious that not more of our most talented young people continue their schooling beyond high school in this day when the complexity of life and of our social problems means that we need every bit of trained intelligence we can assemble. The present state of affairs is resulting in far too great a loss of talent—our most precious natural resource."[176] Thelin characterizes the six-volume report "comprehensive and visionary" as well as a "prescient and informed discussion of changes in American society in such matters as demographics, civil rights, social justice, economic opportunity, and the growing belief in access to a college education as an important, perhaps indispensable, passport for navigating citizenship and work in American life of the post–World War II period." Moreover, the report concluded that "free and universal access to education, in terms of the interest, ability, and need of the student, must be a major goal in American education."[177] Still more recently, in his first address to a joint session of Congress in February 2009, President Obama envisioned an America that by the end of the present decade would once again boast the highest proportion of college graduates in the world.[178] Whatever specific numbers one chooses to cite, there seems little disagreement that the demands of both equity and prosperity presume a capacity to produce millions of additional graduates during the next several decades capable of both catalyzing and benefiting from the knowledge economy.

As a committee convened by the National Academies concluded more than a decade ago, "We owe our current prosperity, security, and good health to the investments of past generations, and we are obliged to renew those commitments in education, research, and innovation policies to ensure that the American people continue to benefit from the remarkable opportunities provided by the rapid development of the global economy and its not inconsiderable underpinning in science and technology." Public outcry over inequality in American society represented by the top 1 percent appears to have subsided, yet the polarization and inequality in our society has only increased during the past decade. The National Academies report issues the following caution: "Without a renewed effort to bolster the foundations of our competitiveness, we can expect to lose our privileged position. For the first time in generations the nation's children could face poorer prospects than did their parents and grandparents."[179]

## Notes

1. Steven Koblik, foreword to *Distinctively American: The Residential Liberal Arts Colleges,* ed. Steven Koblik and Stephen R. Graubard (New Brunswick, NJ: Transaction, 2000), xv.

2. For the most comprehensive yet nuanced single-volume compendium, see Roger L. Geiger, *The History of American Higher Education: Learning and Culture from the Founding to World War II* (Princeton, NJ: Princeton University Press, 2015). For an amusing and somewhat more subjective account, see John R. Thelin, *A History of American Higher Education*, 3rd ed. (Baltimore: Johns Hopkins University Press, 2019). And, for the more traditional approach of a bygone era, see, for example, Donald G. Tewksbury, *The Founding of American Colleges and Universities before the Civil War* (New York: Columbia University Press, 1932).

3. We recur to the previously cited (chapter 1, note 27) *Oxford English Dictionary* definition: the term *morphology* broadly refers to "shape, form, external structure or arrangement, especially as an object of study or classification," and more generally to the "history of variation in form." See chapter 6 for further perspective on its usage.

4. Roger L. Geiger, "The Ten Generations of American Higher Education," in *American Higher Education in the Twenty-First Century: Social, Political, and Economic Challenges,* 4th ed., ed. Michael N. Bastedo, Philip G. Altbach, and Patricia J. Gumport (Baltimore: Johns Hopkins University Press, 2016), 3.

5. George M. Marsden, *The Soul of the American University: From Protestant Establishment to Established Nonbelief* (Oxford: Oxford University Press, 1994), 33.

6. Estimates of the population of settlers during this decade vary between ten and twenty thousand, according to David Hackett Fischer. See his *Albion's Seed: Four British Folkways in America* (New York: Oxford University Press, 1989), 16–17, 17n. One estimate places the white population of Massachusetts in 1640 at 7,882 and the total white population of New England at 12,584. See John J. McCusker and Russell R. Menard, *The Economy of British America, 1607–1789*, 2nd ed. (Chapel Hill: University of North Carolina Press, 1991), quoted in Susan B. Carter et al., eds. *Historical Statistics of the United States,* millennial ed., vol. 5 (New York: Cambridge University Press, 2006), 652–654.

7. Mogens H. Hansen, *Polis: An Introduction to the Ancient Greek City-State* (New York: Oxford University Press, 2006), 11–12.

8. Geiger, *History of American Higher Education*, 1.

9. Eugene M. Lang, "Distinctively American: The Liberal Arts College," *Daedalus* 128, no. 1 (Winter 1999): 134.

10. Geiger, *History of American Higher Education*, 3, 80.

11. Jonathan R. Cole, *The Great American University: Its Rise to Preeminence, Its Indispensable National Role, and Why It Must Be Protected* (New York: Public Affairs, 2009), 1, 14, 526n68.

12. Jürgen Herbst, *From Crisis to Crisis: American College Government, 1636–1819* (Cambridge, MA: Harvard University Press, 1982), 1.

13. Caroline Winterer, *The Culture of Classicism: Ancient Greece and Rome in American Intellectual Life, 1780–1910* (Baltimore: Johns Hopkins University Press, 2002).

14. Marsden, *Soul of the American University*, 56–57, 68. Much to the consternation of Thomas Jefferson, Presbyterians would dominate the establishment and governance of schools during the century to follow, vying for influence with Anglicans and Baptists. At least in part to thwart Presbyterian influence, Jefferson expressed his intent to found a nonsectarian institution.

15. Stephen R. Graubard, preface to *Distinctively American: Residential Liberal Arts Colleges*, ed. Steven Koblik and Stephen R. Graubard (New Brunswick, NJ: Transaction, 2000), viii; Koblik, foreword, xv.

16. Andrew Delbanco, *College: What It Was, Is, and Should Be* (Princeton, NJ: Princeton University Press, 2012), 11–12.

17. Koblik, foreword, xvi.

18. William G. Durden, review of *Designing the New American University* by Michael M. Crow and William B. Dabars, *Journal of College and University Law* 42, no. 2 (2016): 556–557.

19. Thomas R. Cech, "Science at Liberal Arts Colleges: A Better Education?," in *Distinctively American: The Residential Liberal Arts Colleges*, ed. Steven Koblik and Stephen R. Graubard (New Brunswick, NJ: Transaction, 2000), 195.

20. According to McCusker and Menard, the white population of the Colonies in 1780 totaled approximately 2,209,949, while the black population totaled approximately 587,905. *Economy of British America, 1607–1789*, quoted in Carter et al., *Historical Statistics of the United States*, 652–654.

21. Geiger, "Ten Generations of American Higher Education," 41–43. Geiger reports that three-quarters of these students attended the four oldest colleges.

22. Geiger, *History of American Higher Education*, 76.

23. Geiger, "Ten Generations of American Higher Education," 37.

24. Geiger, *History of American Higher Education*, 315.

25. Geiger, "Ten Generations of American Higher Education," 41–42.

26. Geiger, *History of American Higher Education*, 110.

27. Thelin, *History of American Higher Education*, 45–46.

28. Geiger, *History of American Higher Education*, 179–182.

29. Thelin, *History of American Higher Education*, 41.

30. Geiger, "Ten Generations of American Higher Education," 46–48.

31. Andrew Abbott, *The System of Professions: An Essay on the Division of Expert Labor* (Chicago: University of Chicago Press, 1988), 205.

32. Philip G. Altbach, *Global Perspectives on Higher Education* (Baltimore: Johns Hopkins University Press, 2016), 86–87.

33. Hugh Davis Graham and Nancy Diamond, *The Rise of American Research Universities: Elites and Challengers in the Postwar Era* (Baltimore: Johns Hopkins University Press, 1997), 11.

34. Roger L. Geiger, "New Themes in the History of Nineteenth-Century Colleges," in *The American College in the Nineteenth Century,* ed. Geiger (Nashville: Vanderbilt University Press, 2000), 1–2.

35. Michael M. Crow and Derrick M. Anderson, "National Service Universities: Fulfilling the Promise of Excellence at Scale in American Higher Education," working paper (Tempe: Office of the President, Arizona State University, 2019), 5.

36. John Aubrey Douglass, *The Conditions for Admission: Access, Equity, and the Social Contract of Public Universities* (Stanford: Stanford University Press, 2007), 6–8.

37. The Morrill Act is officially designated "An Act Donating Public Lands to the Several States and Territories which may Provide Colleges for the Benefit of Agriculture and Mechanic Arts": Act of July 2, 1862, ch.130, 12 Stat. 503, 7 U.S.C., quoted in John R. Thelin, *Essential Documents in the History of American Higher Education* (Baltimore: Johns Hopkins University Press, 2014), 76–79.

38. Thelin, *History of American Higher Education*, 75–77.

39. Allen Nevins, *The State Universities and Democracy* (Urbana: University of Illinois Press, 1962), 26n3, 27, cited in Eugene M. Tobin, "The Modern Evolution of America's Flagship Universities," Appendix A, in *Crossing the Finish Line: Completing College at America's Public Universities,* ed. William G. Bowen, Matthew M. Chingos, and Michael S. McPherson (Princeton, NJ: Princeton University Press, 2009), 320n3.

40. Tobin, "Modern Evolution of America's Flagship Universities," 320.

41. Enrico Moretti, "Estimating the Social Return to Higher Education: Evidence from Longitudinal and Repeated Cross-sectional Data," *Journal of Econometrics* 121 (2004): 190.

42. Thelin, *History of American Higher Education*, 76.

43. Alexandra Oleson and John Voss, eds., introduction to *The Organization of Knowledge in Modern America, 1860–1920* (Baltimore: Johns Hopkins University Press, 1979), xii.

44. A concise discussion of federal support for American higher education is to be found in Richard C. Atkinson and William A. Blanpied, "Research Universities: Core of the U.S. Science and Technology System," *Technology in Society* 30 (2008): 30–48. See also Roger L. Geiger, *Research and Relevant Knowledge: American Research Universities since World War II* (Oxford: Oxford University Press, 1993).

45. Stephen M. Gavazzi and E. Gordon Gee, *Land-Grant Universities for the Future: Higher Education for the Public Good* (Baltimore: Johns Hopkins University Press, 2018).

46. Nathan Rosenberg and Richard R. Nelson, "American Universities and Technical Advance in Industry," *Research Policy* 23, no. 3 (1994): 323–348.

47. Thelin, *History of American Higher Education*, 76. The focus on agriculture, mechanics, mining, and military instruction would lead to the designation A&M in the names of a number of such institutions, Thelin explains.

48. Rosenberg and Nelson, "American Universities and Technical Advance in Industry," 323–348.

49. Nathan Rosenberg, "America's Entrepreneurial Universities," in *The Emergence of Entrepreneurship Policy: Governance, Start-ups, and Growth in the U.S. Knowledge Economy*, ed. David M. Hart (Cambridge: Cambridge University Press, 2003), 113–114, 116.

50. Atkinson and Blanpied, "Research Universities," 33.

51. Roger L. Geiger, *To Advance Knowledge: The Growth of American Research Universities, 1900–1940* (Oxford: Oxford University Press, 1986), 2–3.

52. Association of Public and Land-Grant Universities (APLU), "Land-Grant Heritage," http://www.aplu.org. For a list of member institutions in the Association of American Universities (AAU), comprising sixty-two leading research universities in the United States and Canada, see http://www.aau.edu/about/.

53. Thelin, *History of American Higher Education*, 135. See also Carolyn R. Mahoney, "The 1890 Institutions in African American and American Life," in *Precipice or Crossroads: Where America's Great Public Universities Stand and Where They Are Going Midway through Their Second Century*, ed. Daniel Mark Fogel and Elizabeth Malson-Huddle (Albany: State University of New York Press, 2012), 17–50.

54. Henry Etzkowitz, "Research Groups as Quasi-Firms: The Invention of the Entrepreneurial University," *Research Policy 32* (2003): 110.

55. Louis Menand, *The Metaphysical Club: A Story of Ideas in America* (New York: Farrar, Straus and Giroux, 2001), 256.

56. Chad Wellmon, *Organizing Enlightenment: Information Overload and the Invention of the Modern Research University* (Baltimore: Johns Hopkins University Press, 2015), 3, 13, 22.

57. The classic account of the earliest universities remains Hastings Rashdall, *The Universities of Europe in the Middle Ages* (Oxford: Oxford University Press, 1895). See also Ernst Robert Curtius, *European Literature and the Latin Middle Ages*, trans. Willard R. Trask (1952; Princeton, NJ: Princeton University Press, 2013).

58. Joel Mokyr, *A Culture of Growth: The Origins of the Modern Economy* (Princeton, NJ: Princeton University Press, 2017), 172. Mokyr broadly assesses that European universities of the early modern era were highly conservative guardians of the canon and status quo and "rarely the taproot of intellectual innovation." With reference to the present context, he elaborates: "Even those scientists who started their careers as part of universities escaped them when their fame had risen enough to enable them to find better patronage (Galileo and Newton immediately come to mind)."

59. Wellmon, *Organizing Enlightenment*, 6.

60. Kerr points out that the new model would anticipate the American model of agency-sponsored research. Clark Kerr, *Higher Education Cannot Escape History: Issues for the Twenty-First Century* (Albany: SUNY Press, 1994).

61. Wellmon, *Organizing Enlightenment*, 17. See especially James Turner, *Philology: The Forgotten Origins of the Modern Humanities* (Princeton, NJ: Princeton University Press, 2014).

62. Clark Kerr, *The Uses of the University*, 5th ed. (Cambridge, MA: Harvard University Press, 2001), 1, 13–14. Newman asserts, "It is the diffusion and extension of knowledge rather than the advancement" that defines the "essence" of the university: "If its object were scientific and philosophical discovery, I do not see why a university should have students." John Henry Newman, *The Idea of a University* (1873; Notre Dame: University of Notre Dame Press, 1982), xxxvii. With reference to his conception, Hanna Holborn Gray, president emerita of the University of Chicago, observes: "He proposed an idea of a university founded in a largely traditional conception of the liberal arts with the humanities at their center, one that excluded research, locating the discovery and advancement of knowledge in separate academies and confining the university to the function of teaching." Gray, *Searching for Utopia: Universities and Their Histories* (Berkeley: University of California Press, 2012), 39–40.

63. Cole, *Great American University*, 18.

64. Arthur M. Cohen, *The Shaping of American Higher Education: Emergence and the Growth of the Contemporary System*, 2nd ed. (San Francisco: Jossey-Bass, 2010), 70.

65. William Clark, *Academic Charisma and the Origins of the Research University* (Chicago: University of Chicago Press, 2006), 28.

66. Kerr, *Uses of the University*, 1.

67. Charles W. Eliot, "The New Education: Its Organization," *Atlantic Monthly* 23 (February and March 1869), 203–220, 358–367, quoted in Geiger, *History of American Higher Education*, 315.

68. John F. Padgett and Walter W. Powell, *The Emergence of Organizations and Markets* (Princeton, NJ: Princeton University Press, 2012).

69. Kerr, *Uses of the University*, 1.

70. Neil J. Smelser, *Dynamics of the Contemporary University: Growth, Accretion, and Conflict* (Berkeley: University of California Press, 2013).

71. Thelin, *History of American Higher Education*.

72. Wellmon, *Organizing Enlightenment*, 214.

73. Edward Shils, "The Order of Learning in the United States: The Ascendency of the University," in *The Organization of Knowledge in Modern America, 1860–1920*, ed. Alexandra Oleson and John Voss (Baltimore: Johns Hopkins University Press, 1979), 28–29; Geiger, *To Advance Knowledge*, 7.

74. Roger L. Geiger, "Milking the Sacred Cow: Research and the Quest for Useful Knowledge in the American University since 1920," *Science, Technology, and Human Values* 13, nos. 3 and 4 (summer and fall 1988): 332–334.

75. Thelin, *History of American Higher Education*.

76. Kerr, *Uses of the University*, 10–11.

77. Geiger, *To Advance Knowledge*, 2–3.

78. Thelin, *History of American Higher Education*, 110.

79. Stephen Gaukroger, *The Emergence of a Scientific Culture: Science and the Shaping of Modernity, 1260–1685* (Oxford: Oxford University Press, 2006).

80. Geiger, *History of American Higher Education*, 326, 340.

81. Louis Menand, Paul Reitter, and Chad Wellmon, "General Introduction," *The Rise of the Research University: A Sourcebook* (Chicago: University of Chicago Press, 2017).

82. Rosenberg and Nelson, "American Universities."

83. Geiger, *History of American Higher Education*, 340.

84. John R. Thelin and Richard W. Trollinger, *Philanthropy and American Higher Education* (New York: Palgrave Macmillan, 2014), 19–20.

85. "Major Private Gifts to Higher Education," *Chronicle of Higher Education* (November 18, 2018).

86. Craig Calhoun, "The Public Mission of the Research University," in *Knowledge Matters: The Public Mission of the Research University,* ed. Diana Rhoten and Craig Calhoun (New York: Columbia University Press, 2011), 13; Calhoun, "The University and the Public Good," *Thesis Eleven 84* (February 2006): 28.

87. *Information about Harvard College for Prospective Students* 60 (September 5, 1963), 1–2, quoted in Thelin, *History of American Higher Education*, xxi.

88. "College Endowments Over $500 Million, FY 2017," *Chronicle of Higher Education* (August 19, 2018).

89. Ronald G. Ehrenberg, *Tuition Rising: Why College Costs So Much* (Cambridge, MA: Harvard University Press, 2000), 36.

90. Wellmon, *Organizing Enlightenment*, 6.

91. Atkinson and Blanpied, "Research Universities," 30–48. See also Geiger, *Research and Relevant Knowledge*; Geiger, *Knowledge and Money: Research Universities and the Paradox of the Marketplace* (Stanford: Stanford University Press, 2004).

92. Graham and Diamond, *Rise of American Research Universities*, 9.

93. Vannevar Bush, *Science—The Endless Frontier: A Report to the President on a Program for Postwar Scientific Research* (Washington, DC: U.S. Government Printing Office, 1945).

94. David H. Guston and Kenneth Keniston, "The Social Contract for Science," in *The Fragile Contract: University Science and the Federal Government,* ed. Guston and Keniston (Cambridge, MA: MIT Press, 1994), 1–2.

95. Roger A. Pielke, *The Honest Broker: Making Sense of Science in Policy and Politics* (Cambridge: Cambridge University Press, 2007), 80.

96. Bush, *Science—The Endless Frontier,* 12, quoted in Pielke, *Honest Broker,* 80.

97. Peter J. Westwick, *The National Labs: Science in an American System, 1947–1974* (Cambridge, MA: Harvard University Press, 2003).

98. Atkinson and Blanpied, "Research Universities: Core of the U.S. Science and Technology System," 38.

99. Roger L. Geiger, "Organized Research Units: Their Role in the Development of University Research," *Journal of Higher Education* 61, no. 1 (January/February 1990): 1.

100. G. Pascal Zachary, *Endless Frontier: Vannevar Bush, Engineer of the American Century* (Cambridge, MA: MIT Press, 1999), 225–226.

101. Stuart W. Leslie, *The Cold War and American Science: The Military-Industrial-Academic Complex at MIT and Stanford* (New York: Columbia University Press, 1993), 2. See also Rebecca S. Lowen, *Creating the Cold War University: The Transformation of Stanford* (Berkeley: University of California Press, 1997); and the collection of essays edited by Noam Chomsky, *The Cold War and the University: Toward an Intellectual History of the Postwar Years* (New York: New Press, 1997).

102. Cole, *Great American University*, 100.

103. For a comprehensive overview of the dimensions of academic research, see Cole, *Great American University*, section 2, "Discoveries That Alter Our Lives," 191–342, and his website: http://university-discoveries.com.

104. Don Kash, *Perpetual Innovation: The New World of Competition* (New York: Basic Books, 1989).

105. Joel Mokyr, *The Gifts of Athena: Historical Origins of the Knowledge Economy* (Princeton, NJ: Princeton University Press, 2002), 1–8, 34–35. See also Nathan Rosenberg, *Inside the Black Box: Technology and Economics* (Cambridge: Cambridge University Press, 1982), especially the chapter "How Exogenous Is Science?," 141–159. For additional historical perspective, see Mokyr, *The Lever of Riches: Technological Creativity and Economic Progress* (New York: Oxford University Press, 1992); and Nathan Rosenberg and L. E. Birdzell, *How the West Grew Rich: The Economic Transformation of the Industrial World* (New York: Basic Books, 1986).

106. Partha Dasgupta and Paul A. David, "Toward a New Economics of Science," *Research Policy* 23 (1994): 487.

107. Cole, *Great American University*, 299–300. Cole organizes his survey of important discoveries in the humanities and social and behavioral sciences into five general categories: "concepts related to our decisions and reasoning; values and opinions; culture, economy, and society; ourselves and our sensibilities; and our 'thinking about thinking'—that is, the discoveries made in philosophy, literary theory, and the like" (301).

108. David H. Guston, "Responsible Innovation in the Commercialized University," in *Buying in or Selling Out: The Commercialization of the American Research University*, ed. Donald G. Stein (New Brunswick, NJ: Rutgers University Press, 2004), 162–164.

109. Sheila Slaughter and Larry L. Leslie, *Academic Capitalism: Politics, Policies, and the Entrepreneurial University* (Baltimore: Johns Hopkins University Press, 1997); Sheila Slaughter and Gary Rhoades, *Academic Capitalism and the New Economy: Markets, State, and Higher Education* (Baltimore: Johns Hopkins University Press, 2004). For additional perspective, see Henry Steck, "Corporatization of the University: Seeking Conceptual Clarity," *Annals of the American Academy of Political and Social Science* 585 (2003): 66–83.

110. Officially known as the Patent and Trademark Law Amendments Act (P.L. 96-517), enacted into law in 1980, together with amendments included in P.L. 98-620,

enacted in 1984. Council on Governmental Relations, *The Bayh-Dole Act: A Guide to the Law and Implementing Regulations* (Washington, DC: Council on Governmental Relations, October 1999): 1. David C. Mowery et al., *Ivory Tower and Industrial Innovation: University-Industry Technology Transfer Before and After the Bayh-Dole Act* (Stanford: Stanford University Press, 2004), 2; David C. Mowery et al., "The Growth of Patenting and Licensing by U.S. Universities: An Assessment of the Effects of the Bayh-Dole Act of 1980," *Research Policy* 30 (2000): 99–101.

111. Henry Etzkowitz, *The Triple Helix: University-Industry-Government Innovation in Action* (New York: Routledge, 2008).

112. David B. Audretsch and Maryann P. Feldman, "R&D Spillovers and the Geography of Innovation and Production," *American Economic Review* 86, no. 3 (June 1996): 630–640; Maryann P. Feldman, "The New Economics of Innovation, Spillovers, and Agglomeration: Review of Empirical Studies," *Economics of Innovation and New Technologies* 8 (1999): 5–25.

113. Anna Lee Saxenian, *Regional Advantage: Culture and Competition in Silicon Valley and Route 128* (Cambridge, MA: Harvard University Press, 1994).

114. Guston, "Responsible Innovation in the Commercialized University," 162–164.

115. Michael M. Crow and William B. Dabars, *Designing the New American University* (Baltimore: Johns Hopkins University Press, 2015), 29, 306.

116. George Thomas, *The Founders and the Idea of a National University: Constituting the American Mind* (Cambridge: Cambridge University Press, 2015).

117. Rosenberg, "America's Entrepreneurial Universities." See also Graham and Diamond, *Rise of American Research Universities,* 12–14.

118. Albert Castel, "The Founding Fathers and the Vision of a National University," *History of Education Quarterly* 4, no. 4 (December 1964): 281–282.

119. David Madsen, *The National University: Enduring Dream of the United States* (Detroit: Wayne State University Press, 1966), 10–11, 38–42.

120. Madsen, *National University,* 15–24.

121. Caroline Winterer, *American Enlightenments: Pursuing Happiness in the Age of Reason* (New Haven, CT: Yale University Press, 2016), 23–24.

122. Graham and Diamond, *Rise of American Research Universities,* 12–14.

123. George F. Frick, "The Royal Society in America," in *The Pursuit of Knowledge in the Early American Republic: American Scientific and Learned Societies from Colonial Times to the Civil War,* ed. Alexandra Oleson and Sanborn C. Brown (Baltimore: Johns Hopkins University Press, 1976), 70–83.

124. Roger Hahn, *The Anatomy of a Scientific Institution: The Paris Academy of Sciences, 1666–1803* (Berkeley: University of California Press, 1971).

125. Rosenberg, "America's Entrepreneurial Universities," 114.

126. *The Papers of George Washington,* Presidential Series, vol. 4, *8 September 1789–15 January 1790,* ed. Dorothy Twohig (Charlottesville: University Press of Virginia, 1993), 543–549, accessed in U.S. National Archives, From George Washington to the United States Senate and House of Representatives, 8 January 1790," https://founders.archives.gov/documents/Washington/05-04-02-0361.

127. *The Papers of George Washington,* "From George Washington to United States Congress, 7 December 1796," accessed in National Archives, https://founders.archives .gov/documents/Washington/99-01-02-00063.

128. Thelin, *History of American Higher Education,* 42.

129. Crow and Anderson, "National Service Universities."

130. Thomas, *Founders and the Idea of a National University.*

131. Madsen, *National University,* 57–63, 100, 129.

132. Thomas, *Founders and the Idea of a National University,* 37.

133. Castel, "Founding Fathers and the Vision of a National University," 280.

134. Quoted by Durden, review of *Designing the New American University,* 560–561. Durden cites Harry G. Good, *Benjamin Rush and His Services to American Education* (1916), 235–236.

135. Graham and Diamond, *Rise of American Research Universities,* 12–14: "The European system's greatest strengths lay in its ability to establish and maintain high academic and scholarly standards, to clarify institutional missions and apportion re sources with minimal redundancy, and to coordinate efficiently with the secondary school system in a coherent national screening plan for student selection and training." By contrast, in the United States, "the democratic commitment to provide a high-school education for all citizens pulled standards toward their lowest common denominator."

136. Graham and Diamond, *Rise of American Research Universities,* 9.

137. Martin Trow, "In Praise of Weakness: Chartering, the University of the United States, and Dartmouth College," *Higher Education Policy* 16 (2003): 16.

138. Michael Mumper et al., "The Federal Government and Higher Education," in *American Higher Education in the Twenty-First Century: Social, Political, and Economic Challenges,* 3rd ed., ed. Philip G. Altbach et al. (Baltimore: Johns Hopkins University Press, 2011), 113–138.

139. John R. Thelin and Richard W. Trollinger, *Philanthropy and American Higher Education* (New York: Palgrave Macmillan, 2014), 70.

140. Trow, "In Praise of Weakness," 9–10; Madsen, *National University,* 15–24.

141. Trow, "In Praise of Weakness," 17–21; Sheldon Rothblatt, "Historical and Comparative Remarks on the Federal Principle in Higher Education," *History of Education* 16, no. 3 (1987): 151–180.

142. Trow, "In Praise of Weakness," 10.

143. Trow, "In Praise of Weakness," 9–10, 19–20.

144. Charles T. Clotfelter, *Unequal Colleges in the Age of Disparity* (Cambridge, MA: Harvard University Press, 2017), 15.

145. Trow, "In Praise of Weakness," 17–21; Graham and Diamond, *Rise of American Research Universities,* 14–25.

146. Gavazzi and Gee, *Land-Grant Universities for the Future.*

147. Josiah Ober, *Democracy and Knowledge: Innovation and Learning in Classical Athens* (Princeton, NJ: Princeton University Press, 2008), 26–27.

148. Ober, *Democracy and Knowledge,* 5.

149. Jürgen Habermas, *The Theory of Communicative Action,* vol. 2, *Reason and the Rationalization of Society,* trans. Thomas McCarthy (Cambridge, MA: MIT Press, 1987), 86; see also Richard Rorty, *Philosophy as Cultural Politics: Philosophical Papers,* vol. 4 (Cambridge: Cambridge University Press, 2007), 107.

150. Hélène Landemore, *Democratic Reason: Politics, Collective Intelligence, and the Rule of the Many* (Princeton, NJ: Princeton University Press, 2013). See also the volume edited by Landemore and Jon Elster, *Collective Wisdom: Principles and Mechanisms* (Cambridge: Cambridge University Press, 2012).

151. Josiah Ober, *Political Dissent in Democratic Athens: Intellectual Critics of Popular Rule* (Princeton, NJ: Princeton University Press, 1998); *The Rise and Fall of Classical Greece* (Princeton, NJ: Princeton University Press, 2015), 247.

152. Amy Gutmann, *Democratic Education* (Princeton, NJ: Princeton University Press, 1987).

153. John Dillon, *The Heirs of Plato: A Study of the Old Academy, 347–274 B.C.* (Oxford: Oxford University Press, 2003), 13.

154. John. P. Lynch, *Aristotle's School: A Study of a Greek Educational Institution* (Berkeley: University of California Press, 1972), 83.

155. Hansen, *Polis,* 11–12.

156. Dillon, *Heirs of Plato,* 13, 30–31.

157. Gordon S. Wood, *The Radicalism of the American Revolution* (New York: A. A. Knopf, 1992); Carl J. Richard, *The Founders and the Classics: Greece, Rome, and the American Enlightenment* (Cambridge, MA: Harvard University Press, 1994).

158. Stephen J. McNamee and Robert K. Miller, *The Meritocracy Myth,* 2nd ed. (Lanham: Rowman and Littlefield, 2009), 1–8.

159. Gutmann, *Democratic Education.* See also Mariana Mazzucato, *The Entrepreneurial State: Debunking Public vs. Private Sector Myths* (New York: Public Affairs, 2013).

160. Geiger, *History of American Higher Education,* 90–91.

161. Claudia Goldin and Lawrence F. Katz, *The Race between Education and Technology* (Cambridge, MA: Belknap Press of Harvard University Press, 2008), 29, 130, 247–251.

162. John Dewey, "The Need of an Industrial Education in an Industrial Democracy," *John Dewey: The Middle Works, 1899–1924,* ed. Jo Ann Boydston (Carbondale: Southern Illinois University Press, 1976–1983), 10:139, quoted in Randall S. Hewitt, "Democratic Education: A Deweyan Reminder," *Education and Culture* 22, no. 2 (2006): 43–60. For a full account, see Robert B. Westbrook, *John Dewey and American Democracy* (Ithaca, NY: Cornell University Press, 1991), esp. chap. 6.

163. Ober, *Democracy and Knowledge,* 26–27.

164. Josiah Ober, *Demopolis: Democracy before Liberalism in Theory and Practice* (Cambridge: Cambridge University Press, 2017).

165. John Adams, "A Dissertation on the Canon and Feudal Law" (1765), in *The Works of John Adams,* ed. Charles F. Adams (Boston: Little, Brown, 1851), 13; Friedrich Hayek, "The Use of Knowledge in Society," *American Economic Review* 35, no. 4 (September 1945): 528, 530, both cited by Ober, *Democracy and Knowledge,* 2.

166. See http://www.malegislature.gov/laws/constitution; http://www.harvard.edu/history.

167. Geiger, *History of American Higher Education*, 80.

168. Susanne Mettler, *Degrees of Inequality: How the Politics of Higher Education Sabotaged the American Dream* (New York: Basic Books, 2014), 191, quoting Benjamin Franklin, "Proposals Relating to the Education of Youth in Pensilvania" (1747).

169. Thomas Jefferson to William Charles Jarvis, September 28, 1820, in Thomas Jefferson, *The Writings of Thomas Jefferson*, ed. Paul L. Ford (New York: G. P. Putnam's Sons, 1892–1899), 10:161.

170. Jefferson to George Wythe, Paris, August 13, 1786, in Thomas Jefferson, *The Papers of Thomas Jefferson*, ed. Julian P. Boyd et al. (Princeton, NJ: Princeton University Press, 1950–), 10:243–245, quoted in Jon Meacham, *Thomas Jefferson: The Art of Power* (New York: Random House, 2012), 469.

171. Jefferson to James Madison, December 20, 1787, in Jefferson, *Papers*, 12:442.

172. Jefferson to Charles Yancey, January 6, 1816, cited in William G. Bowen, Martin A. Kurzweil, and Eugene M. Tobin, *Equity and Excellence in American Higher Education* (Charlottesville: University of Virginia Press, 2005), 3; and Richard Hofstadter, *Anti-Intellectualism in American Life* (New York: Knopf, 1970), 300.

173. James Madison to W. T. Barry (August 4, 1822), in James Madison, *The Writings of James Madison*, ed. Gaillard Hunt (New York: G. P. Putnam's Sons, 1900–1910), 9:103.

174. Franklin D. Roosevelt, "State of the Union," January 11, 1944, cited in Goldin and Katz, *Race between Education and Technology*, 247.

175. President's Commission on Higher Education, *Higher Education for American Democracy* (New York: Harper Brothers, 1947), 1:9, quoted in Jason Owen-Smith, *Research Universities and the Public Good: Discovery for an Uncertain Future* (Stanford: Stanford University Press, 2018), 38.

176. President's Commission on Higher Education, *Higher Education for American Democracy*, 1:35–36, quoted in Mettler, *Degrees of Inequality*.

177. Thelin, *Essential Documents in the History of American Higher Education*, 225.

178. Barack Obama, Remarks of President Barack Obama to Joint Session of Congress (February 24, 2009), https://obamawhitehouse.archives.gov/the-press-office/remarks-president-barack-obama-address-joint-session-congress.

179. National Academies Committee on Prospering in the Global Economy of the Twenty-First Century (U.S.), *Rising above the Gathering Storm: Energizing and Employing America for a Brighter Economic Future* (Washington, DC: National Academies Press, 2007), 13.

# FIVE

# Toward a Theoretical and Conceptual Framework for the Fifth Wave

The observation that something may work in theory but not in practice is sometimes reversed with ironic intent. The contrary formulation—more or less to the effect of "Yes, yes, I know it works in practice but does it work in theory?"—underscores the impulse to understand the dynamics at play beneath the surface.[1] To this point, social psychologist Kurt Lewin was apparently known to remark that "sometimes there is nothing more practical than a good theory."[2] Both theories and models begin with simplification and abstraction for heuristic purposes. With reference to their behavioral theory of the firm, for example, economist Richard M. Cyert and political scientist James G. March observed, "The major dilemma in organization theory has been between putting into the theory all the features of organizations we think are relevant and thereby making the theory unmanageable, or pruning the model down to a simple system, thereby making it unrealistic."[3] A similar dilemma confounds explication of the New American University and Fifth Wave models. In this latter context, for example, our usage of the concept of *waves*—which we correlate with the category of *types*—corresponds to the "ideal type" (*Idealtypus*) proposed by Max Weber. And, as Martin Trow explained, Weberian ideal types are "abstracted from empirical reality and emphasize the functional relationships among the several components of an institutional system . . . rather than the unique characteristics of any one."[4] But all of this is just to say that theory has its place in framing the Fifth Wave because, as educational policy scholar Michael Bastedo explains, from resource dependence theory to new institutional theory, "Modern organization theory is built upon the study of colleges and universities."[5]

In this chapter we consider some theoretical and conceptual approaches to framing the Fifth Wave that do not necessarily correspond to the array of more conventional assessments of colleges and universities. In our first book we proposed that the New American University model reconceptualizes the American research university as a complex and adaptive comprehensive knowledge enterprise committed to discovery, creativity, and innovation. We here contend that the Fifth Wave will comprise a league of sociotechnically integrated, scalable, and reflexive complex adaptive knowledge enterprises, designed to complement other institutional types of colleges and universities, all of which will continue to operate in parallel and evolve within their respective design frameworks. Therefore we begin with some perspective on the concept of complex adaptive knowledge enterprises. This discussion is followed by considerations of the relevance of the concepts of Mode 2 knowledge production, sociotechnical integration, responsible innovation, boundary organizations, and sustainable development. Chapter 6 continues in this same vein, considering some theoretical approaches to institutional design and especially the reflexive relationship between knowledge production and its institutional context.

## The Fifth Wave Comprises Complex Adaptive Knowledge Enterprises

The proposition that research universities may be understood as complex adaptive knowledge enterprises draws on the voluminous literature on complexity and complex systems theory and related concepts such as evolution, emergence, nonlinearity, adaptiveness, and resilience. Although there is no generally agreed upon definition of complexity nor a single theory of complex adaptive systems, most readers will be familiar with the terms of the discussion in a general context. Strands of complexity theory have been discerned in late-nineteenth-century commentary on the work of Darwin and Wallace, and the concept of complex systems was first taken up by the scientific community in the 1940s but not widely applied in the social sciences until the 1990s.[6] Only more recently still have complexity theorists taken universities into their purview. Despite the recognition that efforts to frame Fifth Wave universities as complex adaptive knowledge enterprises must inevitably remain provisional, we nevertheless contend that these institutions may be designed to increase the chances that beneficial adaptations emerge as conditions permit. Inherent in the design of Fifth Wave universities is an acknowledgment of the implications of complexity and the recognition that even the best-laid designs will inevitably and immediately be challenged by emerging and evolving conditions over which administration and the faculty have limited control or influence. The design of these institutions may therefore at times have to accommodate and mediate incommensurate and incommensurable missions, goals, and achievements that cannot be managed according to metrics aimed at efficiency or optimization. Education and research are by their nature unruly and emergent. Anyone familiar with the academy can confirm that unexpected and surprising behaviors emerge spontaneously from the interactions of faculty, administrators, and students operating within an internal environment made up of independent schools and departments and an external environment subject to social influences like legislatures and regulatory bodies. In an effort to clarify some of the key concepts associated with complexity in this context, we derive a synopsis from the work of scholars who have laid the foundations for the conceptualization of universities as complex adaptive systems.

The literature on complexity and complex adaptive systems is vast, and each of the associated terms may be defined in various ways. "Complexity theory is an umbrella term that refers to a wide variety of mathematical models of self-organization dynamics in highly interactive and nonhomogeneous systems," according to John Padgett and Walter Powell.[7] *Emergence* is the signal characteristic of complex systems, which, according to John Holland, may be understood to mean simply that the whole is more than the sum of its parts. Complex adaptive systems all involve "great numbers of parts undergoing a kaleidoscopic array of simultaneous interactions" and share the characteristics of *evolution, aggregate behavior,* and *anticipation. Hierarchical organization* is essential to an understanding of complexity theory, Holland explains, inasmuch as the "interactions of emergent properties at various levels [are a] combination of 'top-down' . . . and 'bottom-up' effects." Among the characteristics of complexity that many readers will recognize are "self-organization into patterns, as occurs with flocks of birds or schools of fish; chaotic behaviour where small changes in initial conditions ('the flapping of a butterfly's wings in Argentina') produce large later changes ('a hurricane in the Caribbean'); . . . and adaptive interaction, where interacting agents (as in markets or the Prisoner's Dilemma) modify their strategies in diverse ways as experience accumulates." *Adaptation* for individuals is an integral outcome of education but may refer also to institutional evolution, which, according to Holland, is the aggregate product of interactions between "fit" agents.[8] Because complex systems exhibit emergent behaviors at the collective level that are unpredictable and beyond the influence of leaders, these manifest through the interactions of individual components of the systems. Complex systems are influenced by endogenous and exogenous information and adapt to change through learning or evolutionary processes that enhance fitness.[9]

To understand universities as complex systems, William Rouse begins with the basic distinction between complicated and complex systems. In contrast to complicated systems, which are generally comprehensible because designed according to plans or blueprints and populated by individuals fulfilling prescribed roles, complex systems are outcomes of "practice and precedent" and, like biological systems and human societies, defy comprehension. Among the characteristics Rouse ascribes to complex adaptive systems such as universities are tendencies for nonlinear and dynamic behavior that evade equilibrium and may appear random or chaotic, and adaptation and learning among independent agents leading to conflict or competition, as well as self-organization and emergent behavior.[10]

Extending these insights, Rómulo Pinheiro and Mitchell Young contend that universities should acknowledge and embrace a looser organizational style that promotes the creation of new models as well as the resilience of the institutions and their environment. They contend that universities are complex systems that are nonlinear, dynamic, co-evolutionary and characterized by traits of emergence and self-organization as well as structured by multiple subentities, connections, and linkages. They maintain that leaders of universities have increasingly employed metaphors inspired by physics that insist on optimizing operations through strategic plans driven by management and policy pressures that seek to more tightly couple connections and linkages both intra- and extramurally. Instead, Pinheiro and Young analogize universities to biological assemblages like coral reefs, which function both as actors and environments for other actors. Biological metaphors promote the view that universities are complex systems that adapt continuously in response to internal and external pressures and make room for niches where innovations may flourish.[11]

A biological orientation humbles anyone who tries to impose policies on recalcitrant organizations like universities. Pinheiro and Young assert that viewing universities as complex systems "undermines the idea that policy is an intentional act by the government or the university administration. Complexity means not only that there are multiple actors with fragmented power to act, but also that intentionality is ambiguous." Policy, according to their argument, consists of ambiguous horizontal communications between niches and not directives imposed from on high. Moreover, this approach militates against reductionist or linear analysis of policy proposals because the whole is seen as greater than the sum of its parts. Those who have imbibed the ideology of positivist science or become accustomed to governance as it is traditionally practiced are bound to be disappointed by the ambiguity of complex adaptive systems like universities. Extending the biological metaphor further means that universities must also contend with external competitors who are also constantly adapting to changing conditions by taking advantage of or defining new niches and altering the environment for all.[12]

Although the ability of universities—or any organization for that matter—to impose policy is inevitably constrained, Pinheiro and Young invoke the arguments of Holland, who maintains that emergence "involves patterns of interaction that persist despite a continual turnover in the constituents of the patterns." In other words, "emergence is a pattern" and not a single occurrence, which allows scholars to connect complex systems theory to institutional theory by explaining how institutions like universities can maintain their identities as complex adaptive systems despite continual change among constituents. Sclerotic structures and rigid path dependencies of institutions are unstiffened through the intercession of emergence, which introduces dynamic forces like evolution, agency, and innovative niches into stale academic contexts. Contrary to the stable environments typical of biological evolution, the selection environment of higher education is dynamic in that changing variables by one institution elicit responses from others in ways that reshape the environment itself. As complex adaptive systems, universities must also contend with vertical and horizontal differentiation.

Universities are comfortable pursuing vertical differentiation, which seeks quality or excellence "through rankings, indicator-based management, scoreboards, and excellence initiatives." However, universities have been less willing to embrace horizontal differentiation based on missions. Consequently, universities are simultaneously too complex and not sufficiently differentiated. By adding new functions and units, universities have morphed into the "multiversities" that Clark Kerr described, which do not necessarily always fulfill their missions.[13]

Consistent with our approach, Pinheiro and Young maintain that the current model of higher education does not foster competition on the "input side" by increasing, for instance, the supply of admissions, but seeks only to "meet the output characteristics that allow an institution to be grouped with others that are considered 'world-class.'" This model is thus "driving both comprehensiveness of mission and homogeneity." In their estimation, size instead of variety is a prerequisite for success despite many biological examples where "smaller but more diverse organisms tend to adapt faster, making them more resilient." We contend that schools within the Fifth Wave may operate like independent components of complex systems to offer differentiated opportunities to students that allow them to benefit from the milieu of transdisciplinary collaboration. Since Fifth Wave universities will not supersede those of other waves, we contend that the resilience of the overall system will be enhanced if Fifth Wave universities meet increasing enrollment demand. We are sympathetic to the provocation of Pinheiro and Young that the resilience of higher education benefits from slack, requisite variety, and decoupling, a contention that without explication may inspire opposition from management theorists who promote efficiency and optimization.[14]

Expanding the conceptual framework to include the concept of *resilience* may improve the adaptive capacity of institutions. *Resilience* has been defined as the "capability of a system to maintain its functions and structure in the face of internal and external change and to degrade gracefully when it must." According to Brad Allenby and Jonathan Fink, "Developing enhanced resiliency is a rational strategy when the probability and specifics of a particular challenge are difficult to define."[15] Resilience is especially relevant to complex adaptive systems and has been organized in one assessment according to four basic concepts: "(1) resilience as rebound from trauma and return to equilibrium; (2) resilience as a synonym for robustness; (3) resilience as the opposite of brittleness, i.e., as graceful extensibility when surprise challenges boundaries; (4) resilience as network architectures that can sustain the ability to adapt to future surprises as conditions evolve."[16]

*Slack* represents redundancy and, in the context of higher education, buffers universities against adversity and allows them to withstand, absorb, and respond to shocks. Slack enhances resilience by increasing the range of responses to disruptions. Slack is subject to exogenous conditions like competition, endogenous characteristics like size, and values of actors or groups. *Requisite variety* refers to the "diversity of potential responses" to disruption. Due to bounded rationality, the diversity of people, skills, knowledge, and structure within a system should "match the variety present in the external environment if the organization is to survive and prosper."[17] Fifth Wave universities would accordingly be well advised to avoid overly detailed strategic plans in favor of design aspirations that establish broad policy parameters that inspire academic units to innovate, evolve, and pioneer new niches. In the interest of requisite variety, Fifth Wave universities should resist calls to close schools or departments deemed to underperform by accounting metrics. Underperformance considered from an alternative perspective may provide the variety that sparks innovation and preserves resilience.

Universities have been framed as "organized anarchies" but may more precisely be characterized as "loosely coupled" organizations comprising more or less autonomous and "diverse decentralized stakeholders grouped in intermittent tasks, rather than following organizational hierarchy and line authority."[18] *Decoupling* refers to the tendency of universities to "loosely couple entities where authority is distributed and located downwards." Attempting to increase efficiency and accountability, many universities have tightened coupling "between higher level strategic goals (university/faculty level) and teaching and research activities on the one hand, and amongst teaching and research activities both within and across faculties and departments." Excessively tight coupling decreases diversity and resilience.[19] However, Fifth Wave universities encourage a loosely coupled "school-centric" model that devolves intellectual and entrepreneurial responsibility to the level of colleges and schools and empowers academic units to exercise autonomy and compete for renown and resources not intramurally but to the extent of market limits with peer entities globally.

Universities must acknowledge the importance of slack, requisite variety, and decoupling, Pinheiro and Young maintain, and contend that conceptualization of universities as complex systems precludes the notion that "policy is an intentional act by the government or university administration." Moreover, "Complexity means not only that there are multiple actors with fragmented power to act but also that intentionality is ambiguous." Consistent with this assessment, the Fifth Wave embraces complexity. Toward this end, then, policy scholar Christopher Hood extols the virtues of what he terms *robustness* in this context, referring to the management of universities as complex adaptive systems that maximize resilience through the realization of the following:

> A relatively high degree of slack to provide spare capacity for learning or deployment in crisis; a control framework which focused on input or process rather than measured output in order to avoid building up pressures for misinformation; a personnel management structure which promoted cohesion without punishing unorthodox ideas; a task division structure organized for systemic thinking rather than narrow compartmentalization; and a responsibility structure which made mistakes and errors admissible. Relatively loose coupling and an emphasis on information as a collective asset within the organization would be features of such a design structure.[20]

## The Fifth Wave Institutionalizes "Mode 2" Knowledge Production

An ongoing transition of the longstanding patterns governing traditional academic culture—from an orientation in knowledge production that is primarily disciplinary and analytical toward one that is increasingly transdisciplinary, collaborative, and problem-driven, and that integrates the conventional dichotomy between basic and applied research posited in the conventional and stale linear model of innovation[21]—has been increasingly apparent to participants and observers for decades. The contours of this new approach to knowledge production were systematically characterized by a team of policy scholars and social scientists led by Michael Gibbons in the early 1990s in the following terms: "Knowledge production carried out in the context of application and marked by its transdisciplinarity; heterogeneity; organizational heterarchy and transience; social accountability and reflexivity; and quality control which emphasizes context- and use-dependence."[22] The new approach was termed "Mode 2" and subsequently further characterized as "socially distributed, application-oriented, transdisciplinary, and subject to multiple accountabilities."[23] Although proponents claim that Mode 2 heralds an ongoing transformation in the epistemological, cognitive, and social practices of academic culture increasingly prevalent since the mid-twentieth century, this putative new approach to knowledge production would as characterized ironically restore the foundational platform for science institutionalized during its formative period in the early modern era.[24]

In the account of Gibbons and colleagues, Mode 1 encompasses primarily disciplinary knowledge produced in accord with the scientific—and scientistic—cognitive and social norms that have come increasingly to dominate intellectual culture since the seventeenth century. Mode 1 is said to comprise the "complex of ideas, methods, values, and norms that has grown up to control the diffusion of the Newtonian model to more and more fields of enquiry and ensure its compliance with what is considered sound scientific practice."[25] The disciplinarity governing Mode 1, moreover, must be appreciated in its implication with what Gibbons and colleagues term the "hegemony of theoretical or, at any rate, experimental science . . . and by the autonomy of scientists and their host institutions, the universities."[26] Although chiefly pertaining to science and technology—indeed, Mode 1 is said to be "identical with what is meant by science"—the approach predominates in the social sciences and increasingly in the humanities as well. By contrast, Mode 2 accommodates different patterns of knowledge production and assumes that knowledge is provisional and indeterminate—no longer "self-contained and self-referential . . . but a mixture of theory and practice, abstraction and aggregation, ideas and data."[27]

Among the conceptual problems with the Gibbons schema is that it suggests that Mode 2 knowledge production supersedes Mode 1. Whether intentionally or not, predication of Mode 2 reifies the myth of the linear model of innovation and reinforces the spurious dichotomy between basic and applied research described by Vannevar Bush in his report *Sci-*

*ence: The Endless Frontier.*[28] Indeed, three of the six authors, including Gibbons, revisited the concept nine years after the initial book was published and acknowledged the various critiques. Against allegations that the argument was "either simplistic or banal (or perhaps both)" and lacking in "empirical evidence for the trends it identified (or arguing that these trends were not new)," Helga Nowotny, Peter Scott, and Gibbons defended the conception in part because of the extent to which it had resonated with researchers and policymakers alike.[29]

Despite valid objections from various scholars regarding the dubious periodization of the modes, we nevertheless invoke the concept of Mode 2 as described by Gibbons and colleagues because it offers a useful heuristic in drawing out points essential to the Fifth Wave. Among the most consequential aspects of the envisioned Fifth Wave is its apparent consilience with this emergent paradigm of knowledge production. Indeed, we propose that the tendencies associated with Mode 2 knowledge production are likely to gather further steam with the emergence of the Fifth Wave, inasmuch as the latter represents the culmination of processes and practices that have been gaining momentum in Fourth Wave research universities throughout their ascendency.

This said, we reiterate the point that many of the attributes ascribed to Mode 2 knowledge production constitute the foundational and perpetual intimate dialectic between scientific knowledge and technological innovation.[30] Moreover, American universities, beginning with the land-grant universities of the Third Wave, advanced what was termed applied science and conducted research and development tied to the needs of agriculture and industry.[31] Academic culture suppressed and sought to delegitimate the strong strands of Mode 2 research that were important aspects of the American research enterprise prior to World War II, as Daniel Sarewitz points out. Fourth Wave research universities conducted research and development consistent with Mode 2 work throughout the Cold War but did not acknowledge it as integrative because the connotations were contrary to the valorization of pure research.[32]

The sort of boundary-spanning collaborative engagement between academia, business and industry, and government agencies and laboratories characteristic of Mode 2 is essential to addressing the complex scientific and technological challenges that confront society. Indeed, in the estimation of Gibbons and colleagues, Mode 2 "calls into question the adequacy of familiar knowledge producing institutions, whether universities, government research establishments, or corporate laboratories."[33] Because the university is no longer necessarily the predominant institutional locus of knowledge production, Fourth Wave research universities have already adapted to new levels of engagement with the broad range of knowledge enterprises that constitute the national innovation system.[34] But Fifth Wave research universities more readily facilitate participation in the new mode of knowledge production through the "distributed centres of excellence," or hybrid forums of Mode 2, which coordinate discovery and innovation through what Gibbons and colleagues term the "pluralisation of the elite function."[35] Indeed, Fifth Wave research universities will become key nodes in a network of heterogeneous institutional actors that have operationalized and continue to sustain Mode 2 knowledge production.

A more nuanced explication of Mode 2 knowledge production would be superfluous in the present context, but further consideration of several key terms is essential to an appreciation of their relevance to the framework of the Fifth Wave. The context of application implicit to Mode 2, for example, might be taken to refer to the application of basic research, or the customary methods of applied research or applied science, in the sense of research undertaken to address a specific problem, or, even more narrowly, product development for industry. However, Mode 2 is "different from the process of application by which 'pure' science, generated in theoretical/experimental environments, is 'applied.'"[36] Mode 2 does not apply basic research, a conception that hews to the discredited linear view of science. The concept is predicated on a context of usefulness, as well as what is termed the contextualization and socialization of knowledge: "Such knowledge is intended to be useful to someone, whether in industry or government or society more generally, and this imperative is present from the beginning." Moreover, such knowledge is "always produced under an aspect of continuous negotiation and it will not be produced unless and until the interests of the various actors are included."[37] Mode 2 knowledge production is thus said to evolve through the intensification of contextualization to yield "socially robust knowledge."[38] With reference to this latter concept, Sarewitz explains: "This process of greater inclusion in the scientific endeavor approximates what sociologists of science have termed a transition from reliable knowledge—the product of a closed group of experts with their own set of scientific norms—to socially robust knowledge, where participation of diverse interests leads to results that satisfy everyone."[39] Indeed, as Sheila Jasanoff points out, such robustness is a function of its embeddedness in society.[40]

The context of application is intrinsic to the transdisciplinarity that is the signal attribute of the new production of knowledge under the Fifth Wave. Indeed, the principal distinction between the two approaches may be their relation to the predominant disciplinary demarcation governing academic culture in the modern era. In Mode 2, "Discoveries lie outside the confines of any particular discipline and practitioners need not return to it for validation." Although the taxonomy of disciplinarity is notoriously elusive, transdisciplinarity is generally distinguished from interdisciplinarity by its transinstitutional scope, that is, knowledge production construed as co-production between the academy and extramural actors, including business, industry, and government.[41] But transdisciplinarity requires more than collaboration among diverse teams of specialists, and the consensus that guides enquiry must in Mode 2 evolve according to its context of application. Both the production and dissemination of new knowledge is unlikely to be confined to disciplinary boundaries: "Because the solution comprises both empirical and theoretical components it is undeniably a contribution to knowledge, though not necessarily disciplinary knowledge." Such enquiry is thus said to be dynamic, in the sense that knowledge production advances through its interaction with a sequence of "problem contexts." Subsequent diffusion of new knowledge likely occurs as practitioners confront new problem contexts.[42]

Inasmuch as the scientific culture of the modern era evolved reflexively within the institutional context of research universities, as Chad Wellmon points out, knowledge production is organized and legitimated disciplinarily as well as institutionally dependent.[43] The Fourth Wave has perpetuated the disciplinarity of Mode 1 knowledge production and, through increasing specialization, further fragmented the contemporary approach to knowledge. By contrast, Mode 2—especially as operationalized in the Fifth Wave—demands transdisciplinarity, the implications of which we assess more fully in chapter 6. Gibbons and colleagues term this shift in the "bureaucratic ethos" of the institution the "least tangible but perhaps the most important." As against the "remorseless specialization that has led universities to abandon most moral and cultural claims transcending the accumulation of intellectual and professional expertise," Mode 2 encourages accountability and social reflexivity, and because it is conceived in the context of application, no longer exclusively prioritizes the pursuit of the unknown and the isolation and analysis of increasingly specialized disciplinary knowledge. The new approach legitimates knowledge that is the product of assimilation, synthesis, implementation, and application,[44] and thus accords with patterns of technological development that are the product of recombinant innovation, which refers to the combination or recombination of existing ideas, products, and processes.[45] Indeed, the reorganization of academic frameworks to accommodate transdisciplinary knowledge production is the hallmark of the New American University and the Fifth Wave.[46]

Mode 2 contravenes the standard linear model of knowledge production, which, according to Gibbons and colleagues, evolves in three stages and favors stabilization: "Specialisation born in a discipline first takes root in institutions and then becomes professionalized."[47] However, because the university no longer functions as the sole locus of knowledge production, the criteria for the evaluation of quality in transdisciplinary research have become social, political, and economic, as well as disciplinary.[48] Knowledge that is the product of this new mode does not necessarily require legitimation ("quality control") through conventional patterns of institutionalization, nor especially strict disciplinary peer review.[49] Because Mode 2 knowledge production is socially distributed, interaction among various sites of knowledge production offers new avenues for collaboration. Such socially distributed knowledge production is indifferent to its institutional context and stands in stark contrast to the conventional pipeline model. Jasanoff approaches the dilemma from the perspective of the governance of science and the imperative to advance science in the public interest: "The problem is how to institutionalize polycentric, interactive, and multipartite processes of knowledge-making within institutions that have worked for decades at keeping expert knowledge away from the vagaries of populism and politics."[50]

Some sense of this expanded relationship is captured in the concept of *trans-science* expounded in a prescient 1972 article by physicist Alvin Weinberg. As Sarewitz explains, "Weinberg observed that society would increasingly be calling upon science to understand and address the complex problems of modernity—many of which, of course, could be traced back to science and technology." But with the recognition that such problems could not be resolved by science alone, Weinberg proposed the category of trans-science. Sarewitz elaborates: "If traditional sciences aim for precise and reliable knowledge about natural phenomena, trans-science pursues realities that are contingent or in flux. . . . This means that the objects and phenomena studied by trans-science are never absolute but instead are variable, imprecise, uncertain—and thus always potentially subject to interpretation and debate."[51]

Because Mode 2 knowledge production occurs in contexts of application, the sociotechnically integrated institutional platforms of the Fifth Wave permit the operationalization of use-inspired research that must increasingly address complex and intractable problems. In contrast to the operations of "normal science" described by Thomas Kuhn, Mode 2 knowledge production corresponds to what Silvio Funtowicz and Jerome Ravetz somewhat misleadingly term "post-normal" science, which is inevitably fraught with uncertainty and contested values and thus demands the "extended peer review" of stakeholders as well as scientists. This perspective becomes essential when "facts are uncertain, values in dispute, stakes high, and decisions urgent," as Ravetz explains,[52] and no less critical if research and scholarship are to address "wicked" problems, which planning theorists Horst Rittel and Melvin Webber describe as defying definitive formulation and resolution.[53] Jasanoff proposes the alternative designations "socially relevant" or "sociotechnical,"[54] which are consistent with the sociotechnical integration of Fifth Wave knowledge enterprises subsequently assessed in this chapter.

Consistent with discovery and innovation facilitated by Fifth Wave institutions, Mode 2 is characterized by heterogeneity and diversity, which apply both to the multi- and transdisciplinary approaches of researchers and practitioners, as well as to the socially distributed transinstitutional linkages and plurality of sites of knowledge production. Heterogeneity is to be found in the nature of the new knowledge itself, which advances through the "simultaneous differentiation, at these sites, of fields and areas of study into finer and finer specialties, the recombination and reconfiguration [of which] form the bases for new forms of useful knowledge." Such knowledge, in characteristic postmodern fashion, arises from a "mixture of theory and practice, abstraction and aggregation, ideas and data."[55]

Organizational structure itself in Mode 2 is characterized as postbureaucratic and heterarchic, in contradistinction to the hierarchic configuration of Fourth Wave academic culture. Complex adaptive systems may be characterized as heterarchic networks.[56] Heterarchies are nonhierarchical and tend to self-organize and exhibit distributed accountability and decentralization of authority: "Heterarchy represents a mode of organizing that is neither market nor hierarchy: whereas hierarchies involve relations of dependence and markets involve relations of independence, heterarchies involve relations of interdependence," according to one assessment. "As the term suggests, heterarchies are characterized by minimal hierarchy and organizational heterogeneity."[57] With horizontal rather than vertical relations and multiple loci of expertise and accountability, such dynamic and boundary-spanning organizational forms have been likened to "trading zones." In the context considered by physicist Peter Galison, trading zones represent disciplinary or theoretical subcultures that coordinate the exchange of ideas through the cultivation of mutually comprehensible pidgins, or creoles. In postbureaucratic organizations, trading zones "structure coordination across boundaries" in response to demands for speed and flexibility under conditions marked by uncertainty.[58]

The consolidation of Mode 2 knowledge production in Fifth Wave knowledge enterprises promotes integrative problem-driven collaborative research that transcends the facile dichotomy between basic and applied research posited in the standard linear model of innovation, which, to reiterate a point made in chapter 1, represents the conviction that technological innovation is a process that begins with fundamental research but requires subsequent research oriented toward specific problems that may eventually lead to the development of products and services appropriate to the market.[59] Ben Shneiderman succinctly contrasts these respective modes: basic, or fundamental, research is "curiosity driven . . . employs reductionist models . . . searches for universal

principles . . . and relies on simplification and idealizations"; applied research is "mission driven . . . looks for practical solutions and guidelines . . . examines complex interactions between multiple variables . . .
and uses realistic (rather than idealized) scenarios." The Fifth Wave
facilitates what Shneiderman calls the "ABC Principle," which refers to
applied and basic combined, or, alternatively, achieving breakthrough
collaborations. Quite simply, as he puts it: "Combining applied and basic research produces higher impact research, compared to doing them
separately." Shneiderman moreover advocates the corollary principle
that "blending the methods of science, engineering, and design produces
higher impact research, compared to working separately." This precept
he designates the "SED Principle."[60] This sort of integrative approach
corresponds to research that, in the idiom of the New American University, is use-inspired, which we considered in chapter 1 in terms of the
"Quadrant Model of Scientific Research" proposed by Donald Stokes.
His effort to reveal the limitations of the standard binary opposition between basic and applied research led him to champion the approach to
research undertaken by Louis Pasteur, who favored "basic research that
seeks to extend the frontiers of understanding but is also inspired by
considerations of use."[61] By building on the accomplishments of the
Fourth Wave, the Fifth Wave seeks to ameliorate problems by invoking
the spirit of Pasteur's quadrant.

In terms of the scale of higher education, Gibbons and colleagues
correlate the transition to Mode 2 knowledge production with what they
term the "progressive massification" of higher education. The team identifies concurrent shifts in academic culture that correspond to the expansion in scope and scale that accompanies the emergence of Mode 2
knowledge production.[62] Mode 2 both depends on and contributes to
this massification, which came in the wake of the nearly universal
"hyper-expansion" of higher education in the twentieth century, especially following 1960, assessed by Evan Schofer and John W. Meyer.[63] The
Fifth Wave parallels patterns of the Mode 2 transformation, beginning
with the expansion in scope and scale that accompanies its diversification of functions. As Gibbons and colleagues explain, "As a result the
distinction between an institution's core and its periphery has become
less clear."[64] In some sense the diversification of functions parallels the
characteristics ascribed to the "multiversity" defined by Clark Kerr in the

1960s as "a whole series of communities and activities held together by a common name, a common governing board, and related purposes."[65] Although the integration of teaching, research, and public service has been a hallmark of Fourth Wave research universities, growth in the diversification of functions promises to expand the scope and scale of these operations in the Fifth Wave.

Not surprisingly, Gibbons and colleagues correlate the expansion of higher education with the transformation of the social profile of student populations: "Students are no longer predominantly male and drawn from the upper middle and professional classes; nor are they destined to fill elite positions in society and the economy."[66] Such expansion has been ongoing, of course, as is apparent in the growth in undergraduate and graduate enrollments and diversification in the demographic profile of students attending colleges and universities during the decades following World War II.[67] The Fifth Wave, however, employs deliberate measures to maximize the extent of the democratization of academic communities drawn from the broadest possible spectrum representative of the socioeconomic and intellectual diversity of the nation and global community.

Consistent with the objectives of students from diverse socioeconomic backgrounds, the Gibbons team maintains that the arts and sciences no longer dominate curricula: "These core subjects have been overlaid by layers of professional education."[68] The potential for graduates in any field to achieve professional success, however, depends on their capacity to become adaptive master learners as envisioned in the Fifth Wave. And a balanced and integrated liberal arts education is a prerequisite to becoming someone who can learn from and adapt to constant change. Although Fifth Wave institutions will enthusiastically advance increasingly varied curricular options for professional education, the liberal arts curriculum remains the foundational core and—an important point often missed or dismissed peremptorily in discussions of workforce development— includes the natural sciences as well as the arts, humanities, and social sciences. Policy makers seeking only economic returns on public investment in colleges and universities as well as proponents of efficiency and thrift frame higher education in narrowly utilitarian terms as workforce development, but, even for schools that prioritize workforce preparation, students are invariably shortchanged by misguided efforts to dismiss, demote, or demean the liberal arts.

Given the importance of scientific discovery and technological innovation to our national competitiveness, the Fifth Wave seeks to maximize the quantitative, scientific, and technological literacy of all students. But the resolution of the complex challenges that confront society depends on more than science and technology, as policy makers in developing economies discovered when efforts to build research-grade institutions focused exclusively on these disciplines invariably fell short of expectations. The exclusion of the humanities and social sciences has hampered efforts to produce qualified graduates and desired societal outcomes because education restricted to science and technology does not provide the breadth of instruction in ethics and values offered by the full spectrum of the liberal arts. The Fifth Wave thus responds to the concerns expressed in a report from the American Academy of Arts and Sciences, which observed, "At the very moment when China and some European nations are seeking to replicate our model of broad education in the humanities, social sciences, and natural sciences—as a stimulus to innovation and a source of social cohesion—we are instead narrowing our focus and abandoning our sense of what education has been and should continue to be—our sense of what makes America great."[69]

As a consequence of expanding enrollments, Gibbons and colleagues perceive still unresolved tensions between teaching and research: "The product of elite institutions is seen to be knowledge in the form of scientific publications and technological devices rather than trained young minds."[70] The authors correlate this expansion with growth in problem-oriented research, referring to the shift in emphasis from the fundamental disciplinary inquiry associated with Mode 1 to transdisciplinary problem solving oriented toward application that is characteristic of Mode 2 knowledge production. But whereas these scholars attribute this shift in part to budgetary constraints imposed by funding agencies and operating costs associated with expanded enrollments, Fifth Wave frameworks accommodate both fundamental research and integrative problem-driven collaborative research that transcends the spurious dichotomy between basic and applied research, as well as expanded enrollments that are an outcome of accessibility to academically qualified students at the requisite scale.

The decline of primary knowledge production accompanying Mode 2 has further critical epistemological implications: "The emphasis in many fields has switched from primary production of data and ideas to their configuration in novel patterns and dissemination to different contexts." Although Gibbons and colleagues cite the accessibility of knowledge through ubiquitous information technologies and the escalating costs of research as primary factors in this shift ("works of synthesis are cheaper to produce"), from an epistemological perspective the decline in producing new data and ideas arguably signals a more expansive conception of knowledge. The embrace of a "mixture of theory and practice, abstraction and aggregation, ideas and data" legitimates knowledge that is necessarily provisional and indeterminate as well as collaborative and contingent. The configuration of new knowledge based on applications to real-world problems—as well as the reconfiguration of existing knowledge—is often the source of innovation and comparative advantage. By concentrating on addressing problems through transformational inquiry, such an approach is more likely to be transdisciplinary and transinstitutional—produced in collaboration with business, industry, and government.[71]

The Mode 2 approach to knowledge production institutionalized in the Fifth Wave is inherently collaborative and concerned with contexts of application. In its concern with the resolution of problems and intent that inquiry be transformational, the Fifth Wave accords with the pragmatist orientation addressed in our earlier book. Pragmatism is more concerned with the successful resolution of problems than the abstract truth criterion of knowledge, and, as propounded by John Dewey, seeks actionable knowledge exercised in a particular context, time, and place in response to real-world problems.[72] Moreover, because the Mode 2 shift is inherently collaborative, it accords with the pragmatist notion that knowledge is inherently social and the product of negotiation and consensus—the process that Jürgen Habermas terms "communicative rationality."[73]

The filiopietism, or excessive veneration of tradition, associated with the disciplinary guilds of medieval universities that still dominates knowledge production in the Fourth Wave informs the self-governance of the academy to the present day, which exacerbates tendencies toward a lack of accountability in the evaluation of social outcomes. In the estimation of Gibbons and colleagues, the Mode 2 shift, including growth in the heterogeneity of institutional types associated with Mode 2, diminishes the autonomy of universities, which heretofore had operated "largely as self-contained and self-referential." Diminished autonomy, however, is favorably construed as a "broadening of accountability." The transition is marked as well by the decline of the peer-review process as the dominant mode of legitimation ("primary quality control").[74] Peer review has traditionally served a "gatekeeping function" within academic culture: "*Sub specie academicus*, academic excellence, is validated by the process of peer review," writes J. Britt Holbrook. Academic excellence thus legitimated, however, he points out, is regrettably "often inversely proportional to societal relevance."[75]

The skepticism of Gibbons and colleagues toward learning technologies represents a departure from the concordance between Mode 2 knowledge production and its correlation with the Fifth Wave. Envisioning the transformation of undergraduate education—"for the better, if new technology encourages independent learning; for the worse, if it creates an alienating anti-humane environment or leads to mechanistic forms of learning"—the authors fear the erosion of the integration of teaching and research, which "may grow apart because technology-assisted teaching needs to be highly structured, while research will deal increasingly with indeterminate knowledge." Their ambivalence may no doubt be attributed to the timeframe of the assessment, which precedes much of the recent innovation and successful implementation of digital technologies that offer the potential for adaptive, interactive, personalized learning at an infinite scale. Inasmuch as the Fifth Wave will comprise sociotechnically integrated, scalable, complex adaptive knowledge enterprises, per our discussion of sociotechnical integration, the new institutional model aligns with the digital revolution, which promises not only pedagogical innovation but also performance enhancement and cost containment.[76]

Although for many scholars the concept of co-production as it is variously defined in what is generally termed the field of science and technology studies overshadows discussion of Mode 2 knowledge production, the latter concept nevertheless provides valuable perspective in the present context. In the words of William James, we seek to "unstiffen" the theory of Mode 2 and set it to work in new ways. And although the present chapter is not the place to arbitrate among various theories of knowledge production, we sketch the advent of the theory of co-production in this context with reference to an article by Clark Miller and Carina Wyborn, who describe the development of the concept. Miller and Wyborn point out that Elinor Ostrom, the Nobel Prize–winning economist, invoked the concept of co-production while working in the field of public administration in the 1970s. For Ostrom, co-production describes the provision of public services that are "distributed throughout society, with citizens working in collaboration with public institutions, not something that government agencies did solely on behalf of or for society." Ostrom thus contends that governments cannot provide services without the participation of citizens.[77] We concur and extend her logic to Fifth Wave universities, which cannot educate students without the participation of citizens.

Another strand in developing the concept of co-production, according to Miller and Wyborn, came with the empirical turn in the sociology of science inspired by Kuhn in *The Structure of Scientific Revolutions*.[78] Following in Kuhn's footsteps, science and technology studies scholars rejected the sequestration of science from the social contexts in which it is was created. Jasanoff thus terms co-production the "simultaneous production of knowledge and social order" and maintains that science is as much the "product of politics and power as of research."[79] According to Jasanoff:

> Co-production is shorthand for the proposition that the ways in which we know and represent the world (both nature and society) are inseparable from the ways in which we choose to live in it. Knowledge and its material embodiments are at once products of social work and constitutive of forms of social life; society cannot function without knowledge any more than knowledge can exist without appropriate social supports. Scientific knowledge, in particular, is not a transcendent mirror of reality. It both embeds and is embedded in social practices, identities, norms, conventions, discourses, instruments and institutions—in short, in all the building blocks of what we term the social. The same can be said even more forcefully of technology.[80]

Building on Jasanoff's definition, David Guston observes that boundary organizations are involved in co-production through their facilitation of collaboration between scientists and nonscientists and the creation of the "combined scientific and social order through the generation of boundary objects and standardized packages."[81] We return to the concept of boundary objects and organizations later in this chapter. Fifth Wave universities could similarly be said both to produce knowledge and be constituted by it. Indeed, knowledge for Fifth Wave universities is not a "transcendent mirror of reality" restricted to academic culture but is embedded in the "social practices, identities, norms, conventions, discourses, instruments and institutions" of society.[82] Of course, Richard Rorty, from his neopragmatist perspective, would similarly express skepticism regarding the conception of knowledge as the mirror of nature.[83] The concept of co-production in this sense operationalizes the pragmatist insight that knowledge and action are interdependent. This, then, would be to argue that the concept of Mode 2 science is not incompatible with co-production.

## The Fifth Wave Strives for Sociotechnical Integration

The Fifth Wave comprises a set of institutions that integrate technology seamlessly into their operational cores to advance the production of useful knowledge and maximize societal impact. Sociotechnical integration assumes the integration of social, ethical, and cultural concerns into the process of knowledge production, especially but not exclusively limited to scientific discovery and technological innovation.[84] A sociotechnical assessment builds on a nuanced conception of the role of technological innovation in our knowledge-based society. Although technology generally refers to physical artifacts and processes, generally in the sense of the application of scientific understanding—the "assemblage of practices and components . . . and entire collection of devices and engineering practices available to a culture," as W. Brian Arthur puts it— the concept more broadly represents "any means to fulfill a human purpose. . . . As a means, a technology may be a method or process or device: a particular speech recognition algorithm, or a filtration process in chemical engineering, or a diesel engine."[85] Daniel Sarewitz and Richard Nelson thus offer a definition of technology as "any practice with a standardized, controllable, replicable core that successfully achieves what it aims to do."[86] According to Nathan Rosenberg, "Technology is itself a body of knowledge about certain classes of events and activities. . . . It is a knowledge of techniques, methods, and designs that work, and that work in certain ways and with certain consequences, even when one cannot explain exactly why."[87] Joel Mokyr observes: "Simply put, technology is knowledge, even if not all knowledge is technological." But technology is useful knowledge, a condition specified alike by Benjamin Franklin and Simon Kuznets. In this context Mokyr underscores the distinction between what he terms propositional and prescriptive knowledge, which is analogous to the historical distinction between *episteme* and *techne*, and corresponds to contemporary distinctions between science and technology as well as the co-production of fundamental and applied knowledge. Propositional knowledge in his usage may thus be termed knowledge "what," referring to beliefs about natural phenomena, whereas prescriptive knowledge corresponds to knowledge "how," or knowledge of techniques.[88]

In contrast to explicit knowledge—that is, the codified principles of science and technology—tacit knowledge represents the practical understanding of "how things are done," which is to say, the "know-how" underpinning the development of a given technology. The significance of the tacit dimension varies by sector and over time, wherein innovation proceeds in accord with respective technological paradigms. Each sector is thus defined by a technological paradigm, which co-evolves through its component technologies, industrial infrastructure, and supporting institutions, especially universities.[89] Accordingly, whereas technology has been construed as "applied knowledge embedded in tools, equipment, and facilities" but also "work methods, practices and processes, and the design of products and services," technology is also "'know-how' in contrast to the 'know-why' that characterizes science."[90] Sarewitz and Nelson define "know-how" as "knowledge, some articulated and some tacit, that guides the actions of skilled agents who aim to achieve a particular practical objective." It thus follows that the "state of know-how defines best practice in an arena of human activity."[91] Elsewhere Nelson defines the term as the "wide range of techniques and understandings human societies have acquired over the years that enable them to meet their wants." Know-how is "multifaceted and variegated, and stored in different places and forms," he explains. And although some of it is "relatively well articulated 'how it is done' knowledge," much is "embodied in particular human skills, as contrasted with 'blueprint-like' know-how." Moreover, he continues, "it is important to recognize the variety of particular skills involved, and that effective performance is a group achievement."[92] But there is an institutional sense of technology that comports with an understanding of the concept as a body of knowledge or set of practices.

Although the foundations of organized science in the West may be traced to the Middle Ages and even antiquity, the emergence of scientific culture in the early modern era is inextricably interrelated with its institutional accommodation and disciplinary legitimation within academic frameworks, beginning with the emergence of the German research university at the outset of the nineteenth century. Thus Wellmon identifies the modern research university as the principal "technology of the Enlightenment"—in the "same historical lineage of technologies that extends from the invention of writing and the codex to the printing press and the modern scientific lab." Endowed with uncontested "epistemic authority," universities claimed and were granted the prerogative to legitimate knowledge deemed sufficiently "scientific." This new technology provided an "institutional response" to the proliferation of knowledge unleashed in the wake of the Scientific Revolution and Enlightenment. Indeed, the research university facilitated the emergence of the modern era through its "organization of the Enlightenment," which the new academic culture accomplished by institutionalizing science and partitioning knowledge into disciplines. Because the scientific culture of the modern era would shape the research university—and vice versa—knowledge production itself would become institutionally dependent. Indeed, by the end of the nineteenth century, the research university had become the "consummate technology for organizing knowledge."[93] Inasmuch as the modern—and contemporary—research university could thus be termed an institutional technology, recourse to the lexicon of technological innovation is both necessary and appropriate.

"The modern German research university," writes Kerr, "approached the discovery of truth and knowledge in all fields on the basis of scientific principles, joining the rational and empirical traditions to form the basis of modern scientific research."[94] Although the concept *Wissenschaft* encompasses more than science—Louis Menand parses the term as "pure learning, the ideal of knowledge for its own sake"[95]—claims to knowledge invariably sought and continue to seek scientific status. As Gibbons and colleagues put the matter, "A history of knowledge production since the seventeenth century could be written in terms of the efforts of the proponents of previously non-scientific forms of knowledge production to gain recognition as scientific."[96] As Stephen Gaukroger observes, the new scientific culture is one in which "cognitive values generally become subordinated to scientific ones, and where, correspondingly, science is expected to provide an archetypal path to cognitive success not just for scientific disciplines but for any discipline with cognitive aspirations, such as theology, metaphysics, political theory, political economy, law, and history."[97]

Inasmuch as the research university may be framed as a technology, and one may thus liken the evolution of the institutional type to technological innovation, the desideratum of sociotechnical integration is integral to an understanding of the emergence of the Fifth Wave. Although sociotechnical integration assumes the integration of social, ethical, and cultural concerns into the process of knowledge production, according to Erik Fisher and colleagues, the *societal* aspect of the concept can simply denote the contextual dimension of knowledge, while *technical* refers to the content of knowledge as practiced by any given form of specialized expertise: "The societal context can encompass cultural, ethical, political, environmental, linguistic, epistemological, axiological, and numerous other value dimensions." Moreover, sociotechnical integration is "generally characterized by the reciprocal and productive combination of opposing, diverging, or previously segregated contextual dimensions of expert practices," which must "confront challenges arising from differences in language, practice, values, power, and other potential sources of 'incommensurability,' 'incongruence,' or 'discordancy.'" Because the objective requires collaboration, the integrative process "seeks to work deliberatively, explicitly, and reflectively across various conceived and constructed socio-technical divides."[98]

Because the concept of sociotechnical integration could well be freighted with dystopian connotations, its implications warrant further explication. Whereas we have long since moved past the conception of technology as mere artifacts or machines, Brad Allenby and Daniel Sarewitz point out, a more complex understanding of what is at stake requires us to appreciate that technology "emerges from social systems and thus necessarily reflects, internalizes, and often changes power relations and cultural assumptions." Further, "technological systems are now as complex, pervasive, and incomprehensible as natural systems." Moreover, "social systems are in reality techno-social systems that impose certain orders of behavior on our lives about which we have little choice, and that . . . lock in paths of dependency that make a mockery of human agency." To wit, Allenby and Sarewitz enjoin us to "decarbonize the global energy system."[99]

Systems theory has been integral to the conceptualization of complex sociotechnical systems. Indeed, systems approaches, including operations research, systems analysis, systems dynamics, and systems engineering, have defined problem solving since World War II.[100] The concept of an open system, coined by the pioneering systems theorist Ludwig von Bertalanffy, is central to the objective of a unified transdisciplinary science. According to Sytse Strijbos, the approach seeks to negotiate the reductionist impulse in Western scientific culture and "transcend the Cartesian program and the study of the world as an assemblage of parts that can be broken apart and analyzed separately."[101] But the human predisposition toward the simple and straightforward impedes engagement with complex, nondecomposable, and nonlinear systems, according to design theorists Donald Norman and Pieter Jan Stappers, who explain that complex sociotechnical systems comprise interdependent components devoid of modularity and characterized by nonlinear causal relations governed by feedback loops: "Feedback changes the behavior of the system, making it impossible to understand the whole through each of its parts," which likely presumes emergent behavior. Indeed, "the interrelationships among the components can be more important than the components themselves."[102]

Because transdisciplinary collaboration is implicit in sociotechnical integration, it becomes imperative to transcend the "gulf of mutual incomprehension" between the "two cultures" diagnosed by C. P. Snow in his seminal 1959 Cambridge lecture—the sciences on the one hand, which in his usage refer to the natural sciences, mathematics, and sometimes engineering, and, on the other hand, the humanities and, by extension, the social sciences.[103] Accordingly, Guston characterizes sociotechnical integration as the "creation of opportunities, in both research and training, for substantive interchange across the 'two cultures' divide that is aimed at long-term reflective capacity building."[104] Collaborative sociotechnical integration, however, is differentiated from other multidisciplinary research by "explicit recognition by the domain experts of the societal contexts in which their work is conducted and in which it will be applied." In other words, it requires scientific practitioners to be reflexive. Consequently, "Successful integration demonstrably changes technical practice, modifying it both formally and tacitly."[105]

### Frameworks for Responsible Innovation

Sociotechnical integration is integral to the principles and objectives of responsible innovation—the ongoing efforts to realize approaches to the governance (whether through self-governance or through formal regulation) of scientific discovery and technological innovation that, despite inevitable uncertainties and possible ambiguities, attempts to coordinate and facilitate robust and accountable societal outcomes. Emerging science and innovation often fall into an "institutional void" with limited oversight or governance. Jack Stilgoe, Richard Owen, and Phil Macnaghten thus define *responsible innovation* simply as "taking care of the future through collective stewardship of science and innovation in the present."[106] The imperative for responsible innovation begins with the acknowledgment that science and innovation have produced not only "understanding, knowledge, and value (economic, social, or otherwise), but also questions, dilemmas, and unintended (and sometimes undesirable) impacts." Thus, in the "absence of certainty, evidence, and understanding . . . the appropriate (and proportionate) oversight and stewardship of the processes of science and innovation . . . becomes a central challenge for responsible innovation." If the intent is more nuanced than the negotiation of risk and maximization of economic and social benefit, it is imperative to establish a consistent and broadly accepted framework for responsible innovation, which presumes "far wider, systemic reconfiguration, and indeed a significant culture change in this regard."[107]

Stilgoe, Owen, and Macnaghten identify four dimensions of responsible innovation: anticipation, reflexivity, inclusion, and responsiveness. *Anticipation* involves thinking systematically about resilience, pursuing innovation, and influencing "agendas for socially-robust risk research." Although *reflexivity* has multiple connotations, the authors argue for "institutional reflexivity," which "means holding a mirror up to one's own activities, commitments and assumptions, being aware of the limits of knowledge and being mindful that a particular framing of an issue may not be universally held." *Inclusion* refers to diversifying governance. Although scholars dispute the conditions and assumptions under which inclusion can or should be conducted, it raises issues related to the legitimate exercise of power. *Responsiveness* alludes to the need to retain the ability to shape the development of innovations while recognizing the limits of knowledge and control.[108] Owen and colleagues point out that anticipation, reflexivity, inclusion, and responsiveness build upon the foundations of responsible innovation: technology assessment, "upstream" engagement, and anticipatory governance. Yet application of such intent is largely limited at present to codes of conduct and formal review processes: "There are currently few, if any, examples of a systematic and institutionally-embedded framework that integrates and iteratively applies all four dimensions together in and around the processes of science and innovation." In this context the authors call for what has been termed "institutional reflexivity."[109] Because the Fifth Wave aspires to comprise sociotechnically integrated, scalable, complex adaptive knowledge enterprises, the imperative for its institutions to serve as frameworks for responsible innovation becomes readily apparent.

The imperative for the institutional accommodation of sociotechnical integration comports with the recognition that the process manifests at various levels of analysis in both scope and scale. Micro-level implications of the concept refer to its impact on individuals; meso-level to group dynamics and organizational settings; and more global macro-level implications to the structural underpinnings of collaboration, including its institutional context. Micro-level applications are often embedded, as when artists and humanities scholars join scientists and technologists. More broadly, the macro-level application of the concept suggests the potential for reciprocal and transdisciplinary collaboration among scholars and practitioners across the spectrum of disciplines and interdisciplinary fields.[110]

Sociotechnical integration is moreover either implicit or explicit in a number of collaborative approaches to research identified by Fisher and colleagues that are delineated in their respective literatures as scholarly engagement; ethical, legal, and social implications or aspects (ELSI or ELSA); laboratory studies; team science; applied ethics; technology assessment; inter- and transdisciplinarity; and public engagement. Fisher and colleagues, however, choose to define collaborative sociotechnical integration as distinct from all of these insofar as its approach seeks to transform scientific and technical practice. Collaborative sociotechnical integration is in this sense, they argue, central to such approaches as responsible research and innovation; anticipatory governance; reflexive governance; and convergence work: "These visions concern the explicit integration of societal considerations into scientific and technical practices as knowledge systems and technological trajectories evolve."[111]

Inasmuch as one may liken the evolution of the research university to technological innovation, further insight on path dependency and entrenchment in technological innovation could offer additional perspective on the emergence of Fifth Wave knowledge enterprises. The Collingridge dilemma, articulated by David Collingridge in 1980, has become a point of reference for discussions of technology assessment and, in the present context, assumes relevance to our contention that structural inertia and corresponding design limitations constrain Fourth Wave institutions:

> The social consequences of a technology cannot be predicted early in the life of the technology. By the time undesirable consequences are discovered, however, the technology is often so much part of the whole economic and social fabric that its control is extremely difficult. This is the dilemma of control. When change is easy, the need for it cannot be foreseen; when the need for change is apparent, change has become expensive, difficult, and time consuming.[112]

By one assessment, the dilemma of control thus poses an "intractable double bind [that] stymies efforts to exert societal control over technology."[113] Another interpretation, however, underscores that Collingridge did not envision the dilemma as historically invariant nor intend to imply inevitable technological determinism. Entrenchment nevertheless threatens to stifle innovation: "After technologies have been developed and diffused, different types . . . can constitute a complex nexus of various dependencies." With such entrenchment comes a form of technological determinism, as the technology "stays and evolves on the path like a train on a track."[114]

The regulation and control of technologies has historically taken the forms of indirect public engagement or formal governance, Fisher, Roop L. Mahajan, and Carl Mitcham explain. By contrast, what has been termed "midstream modulation" of technology offers the potential for "governance from within."[115] Because responsiveness to societal aspirations and values is a critical aspect of responsible innovation, sociotechnically integrated institutions would evaluate research and development programs accordingly: "Building responsiveness into research prioritization can support productivity, contribute to more socially robust outcomes, and possibly even enhance national competitiveness," according to one assessment.[116] Indeed, "institutionalizing responsiveness" has been cited as one of the key emerging aspects of responsible innovation, which assumes the "integration and institutionalization of established mechanisms of reflection, anticipation, and inclusive deliberation."[117]

## Fifth Wave Universities and Boundary Organizations

Cooperation and collaboration among heterogeneous actors in complex research settings may be advanced through an understanding of what Susan Leigh Star and James Griesemer call, in a much-cited 1989 article, "boundary objects." They are referring in a broad sense to information, including such constructs as concepts, models, and systems, but also concrete entities such as patents and contracts that "inhabit several intersecting social worlds . . . and satisfy the informational requirements of each of them." Boundary objects retain their identities despite being used for different purposes by participants on both sides of boundaries. Such objects are "both adaptable to different viewpoints yet robust enough to maintain identity across them." Although their meaning may vary according to the divergent perspectives of respective constituents, their structure remains sufficiently robust to retain a common identity. As a case study of the implications of such heterogeneity in a research setting, Star and Griesemer examine the interactions among scientists, curators, amateur naturalists, patrons, and administrators in the formation of the Museum of Vertebrate Zoology at the University of California, Berkeley. "Science requires cooperation—to create common understandings, ensure reliability across domains, and gather information that retains its integrity across time, space, and local contingencies," the authors explain. But the attainment of a "mutual *modus operandi*" demands that participants "translate, negotiate, debate, triangulate, and simplify in order to work together."[118]

Boundary objects thus occupy a position between different social spheres yet retain their identities even as individuals use them for their own specific purposes. The interpretative flexibility of boundary objects is illustrated by patents, Guston explains: "A patent on research results can be used by a scientist to establish priority or for commercial gain. It can simultaneously be used by a politician to measure the productivity of research. In some cases, entire organizations can serve as boundary objects, as did many of the public interest organizations created by scientists in midcentury to facilitate political goals while protecting scientific ones."[119] In a subsequent article published in 2010, Star bemoaned that the interpretative flexibility associated with boundary objects had been extended beyond the carefully crafted definition that she and Griesemer had derived.[120] Nevertheless, it is precisely this interpretative flexibility that permits participants with varied perspectives to assess boundary objects in ways that are useful for individual purposes but robust enough to withstand inconsistent understandings. Interpretative flexibility facilitates compromise as well as cooperation and collaboration.

Scholars have thus extended the logic of boundary objects to organizations. And indeed, as Guston points out, organizations can serve as boundary objects. According to Guston, boundary organizations provide a "space for the creation and use of boundary objects or standardized packages, or a combined scientific and social order; the collaborative participation of principals and agents, or scientists and non-scientists; and the mooring to mutual interests and distinct lines of accountability." He terms them "two-faced entities" that accommodate actors who, "Janus-like," operate at the "boundary between politics and science." Accordingly, boundary organizations are sites of co-production.[121] Guston invokes the Office of Technology Assessment (OTA) as the quintessential example of a boundary organization. Before the 104th Congress withdrew funding for the agency in 1995, the OTA had for more than two decades produced objective and authoritative analysis of issues related to science and technology for members and committees of the U.S. Congress. Guston contends: "As a politically neutral organization, OTA . . . internalized partisan differences, negotiated them for each study, and produced in its studies a boundary object . . . that either party (or any of several congressional committees) could use for its own purposes."[122] Crucially for Guston, the OTA was accountable to both political parties.

Because universities as a whole are not bound by the same kind of accountability to other organizations as the OTA, their status as boundary organizations in the strict sense defined by Guston is equivocal.

In contrast to Guston's conception of boundary organizations, which he derived from his empirical analysis of the OTA and other organizations, John Parker and Beatrice Crona extend the criteria that Guston specifies to develop the concept of university-based boundary organizations.[123] Universities straddle many physical, political, and intellectual boundaries. Boundary-spanning organizations and collaborations have been addressed by scholars in many ways, including those discussed above by Gibbons and colleagues in relation to Mode 2. Boundary organizations as identified by Guston and described above serve some of the same functions but operate according to different mechanisms than other boundary-spanning organizations. It is likely that all boundary organizations are subsumed under the broader category of boundary-spanning organizations, but not vice versa. The university-based boundary organizations defined by Parker and Crona and described below are a subset of boundary-spanning organizations, but it is not clear if they meet the definition of boundary organizations as identified by Guston. Although the parameter of different types of organizations may be disputed, we believe that Fifth Wave universities provide some of few places where societies can identify, monitor, research, and mediate important social issues that straddle boundaries.

Parker and Crona refer to the criteria of boundary organizations identified by Guston as theoretical assumptions, which does not acknowledge the empirical basis of the criteria. The first criterion challenged by Parker and Crona is that boundary organizations act as agents to only two principals. While this criterion held for applied research institutions, where the boundary organization construct was originally developed, it does not pertain to most universities, for two reasons. First, no clear lines of demarcation separate science and policy in university-based boundary organizations. They are "hybrid spaces" that have ties to both politics and industry. Second, university-based boundary organizations often address more than two principals. Parker and Crona adopt a stakeholder approach that facilitates analysis of "complex arrays of constituencies" and permits analysis of the influence of each stakeholder on the activities and direction of the boundary organization.

The second criterion relates to the accountability between university-based boundary organizations and stakeholders. Because rewards and expectations within universities are not monolithic, they "can become decoupled both between and within university administrations and academic departments." As a result, accountability to stakeholders may be "skewed," allowing some stakeholders to exercise disproportionate influence. The third criterion amended relates to the conflicting or incommensurable needs of stakeholders. Guston found that boundary organizations could reconcile the demands of their principals. However, if demands are incommensurable, then reconciliation is not possible. As an example, in the context of university-based boundary organizations, Parker and Crona cite expectations associated with peer review. If one stakeholder expects peer review to be "effective (thorough and accurate)" and another imagines it to be "efficient (expeditious)," then the expectations are incommensurable, and a choice must be made in lieu of negotiating reconciliation. As choices accumulate, the research agenda, social milieu, and organizational structure of university-based boundary organizations are affected.[124]

As a case study of university-based boundary organizations, Parker and Crona investigate the formation and development of the Decision Center for a Desert City (DCDC) at Arizona State University. DCDC was "explicitly designed as a boundary organization" situated within ASU, which the authors identify as a New American University that "aspires to be a boundary organization writ large." The relevance of the concept in this context is its emphasis on the application of transdisciplinary knowledge production and social embeddedness. But the authors concede potential pitfalls by identifying four "management tensions" that arose between DCDC and its stakeholders: degrees of interdisciplinarity, rates of production, differences between basic and applied knowledge production, and decision latitude.[125]

Inasmuch as Parker and Crona consider DCDC as a case study of university-based boundary organizations, a brief digression from the theoretical might bring further insight. DCDC seeks to develop a framework for the transdisciplinary production of evidence-supported strategies to advance the transition to urban water sustainability in the Colorado River Basin. The integrated research, education, and outreach efforts of the center have produced a network of scientists, students, and stakeholders who envision the advancement of societal transformation through the development of regional urban water systems in the Colorado River Basin that are "resilient to climate change and generate equitable social and economic benefits while providing a range of ecosystem services." A research unit of the Julie Ann Wrigley Global Institute of Sustainability (GIOS), DCDC was first established in 2004 with an investment from the U.S. National Science Foundation (NSF) through the Decision Making under Uncertainty (DMUU) program. Further NSF investment, which totals approximately $18 million, has permitted ASU to expand the parameters of research beyond central Arizona to include cities dependent upon water from the Colorado River in Colorado, Nevada, and California.[126]

DCDC co-produces climate, water, and decision research to bridge the boundaries between scientists and policy makers. From the outset, DCDC was conceived to operationalize the strategic insights of the boundary organization construct in the context of water sustainability and adaptation to urban climate change.[127] Inasmuch as key features of boundary organizations include accountability to both science and policy communities and participation of actors from multiple communities as well as professional mediators,[128] research has sought to understand and improve the function of this particular instantiation of a university-based boundary organization as well as to develop lessons useful for similar efforts. The operationalization of the center illustrates how universities can advance place-based and use-inspired initiatives to more effectively link knowledge with decision making for positive social impact.[129]

This process not only creates new knowledge but enables productive dialogue among academic scientists and a wide range of other stakeholders including city managers, farmers, environmentalists, and Native American communities to improve regional water sustainability. Scientists and stakeholders cooperatively develop knowledge and tools such as models, simulations, scenarios, and computer decision support systems. The primary boundary object in the case of DCDC was a water balance model called WaterSim, which estimates water supply and demand for the Phoenix Metropolitan Area. The model was developed to bridge a specific gap in science and policy, that is, the need for knowledge to inform regional water sustainability planning, incorporating the plausible impacts of climate change at multiple temporal and spatial scales. This need was not sufficiently addressed by the many individual water management agencies, each of which was understandably focused on their own service territory and customer base. Nor was this need filled by state or federal agencies, which tended to focus on larger spatial scales and broader policy issues. WaterSim was developed using a participatory modeling approach. Scientists from the university-based boundary organization worked with stakeholders from the water management community to design the model, cooperatively selecting and negotiating the data sources, model calculations, spatial extent, time scale, outcome metrics, and visualizations. Through an iterative process, the model was refined and redesigned based on stakeholder feedback to enhance the scientific credibility, improve its relevance to decision making, and to increase the legitimacy of the model to multiple stakeholder groups. By opening the "black box" of modeling for critique and improvement, the university-based boundary organization and stakeholders co-developed the boundary object. As a result, the immersive visualization, modeling, and simulation of three-dimensional complex multivariate data via the ASU Decision Theater allow scientists and stakeholders to engage with peers around the world.[130]

A retrospective assessment of research associated with decision making under uncertainty conducted by DCDC underscored the significance of empirical research and decision-support tools to improve understanding of decision making and the identification of alternative pathways related to climate change. The assessment moreover confirmed that iterative interactions associated with boundary activities among scientists and policy makers improve university-based boundary organizations and promote the formation of social networks and collaborative learning.[131] Parker and Crona propose what they term a Landscape of Tensions (LOT) model that depicts how the position of DCDC "meandered" relative to the boundaries between it and its stakeholders over time. Course corrections were required as the DCDC coped with the shifting structures, changing research emphases, facilitating boundary objects, and the challenges of interdisciplinarity.[132] The Landscape of Tensions model illustrates the fraught institutional environment that Fifth Wave universities will have to negotiate as they evolve into nested university-based boundary organizations that produce useful interdisciplinary knowledge at scale and with the velocity required to respond to society's problems.

Arizona State University's Decision Theater (DT) exemplifies the characteristics of boundary organizations as identified in the relevant literature. The Decision Theater collaborates with community stakeholders and researchers to build computational models and convene diverse groups of decision makers across academia, government, and industry to explore alternative futures. The computational models integrate machine learning and predictive analytics to digest structured and unstructured data presented in the DT Drum, which immerses participants in a data-rich environment by presenting interactive models across seven panoramic HD monitors in a 270-degree display. The data informatics and complex systems thinking inherent in the process encourage stakeholders to understand how multiple social systems interact to reveal the large-scale implications of research findings. To this end, DT collaborates with university faculty, industry experts, practitioners, and policymakers to examine the legitimacy, relevance, credibility, and usability of its models. A participatory approach framework maps the landscapes of interrelated systems and, through iterative analysis and narrative development, encourages engagement and co-production to facilitate more informed decision making. Consistent with the convergence paradigm advanced by the NSF, the integration of stakeholders as co-creators exemplifies the transdisciplinary approach of the initiative. Since 2016 DT has advanced Achieve60AZ, a community-based initiative to increase educational attainment for all Arizonans. In a state where postsecondary attainment for adults ages twenty-five to sixty-four is currently 35 percent, including associate's, bachelor's, and graduate degrees, the overarching goal of this effort is to reach 60 percent postsecondary attainment by 2030. The Arizona Board of Regents (ABOR) is a leading member of the Achieve60AZ Alliance.[133]

An understanding of research universities as boundary organizations writ large, which in turn create and sustain subsidiary boundary organizations such as colleges, schools, and research centers, may be derived from Parker and Crona. But Fifth Wave universities must also realize, as Guston points out, that the "primary task of the university—the creation and dissemination of new knowledge—has normative dimensions." He thus theorizes the formation of interstitial entities that he terms Centers for Responsible Innovation (CRI), which imbue knowledge production with a normative commitment. The imperative for this normative dimension assumes the premise that, despite threats to their hegemony from new information technologies, major research universities will remain in the "business of knowledge-based innovation for at least several generations." Moreover, this set of institutions will continue to market new knowledge, conceding, as he puts it, that the academy has been commercialized at least since the land-grant universities first consolidated ties with industry. As Guston reminds us, "Knowledge-based innovation has normative dimensions that science policy confronts only marginally or in ad hoc ways."[134]

The influence of market forces on universities, Guston points out, has been viewed with ambivalence and as not altogether benign, inasmuch as critics allege its impact on scholarship to be deleterious. Market forces are alleged to exacerbate conflicts of interest, alter norms of scholarship, reconstitute students as consumers, and debase learning standards. The creation of institutional review boards is evidence of the perception that universities must police relationships with market participants to protect human and animal subjects from exploitation. Inasmuch as the postwar era witnessed the globalization of research and what Guston terms the "new political economy of academic commercialization," he advocates the formation of CRIs to capture the benefits of closer relationships with business and industry and address the need to cope with possible negative consequences through the "reflexive study of the interaction of innovation and society." For Guston, CRIs would also broker interdisciplinary education by acting as boundary organizations that provide the "collaborative assurance" needed to facilitate cooperation between scientists and others in pursuing mutually beneficial ends. In an environment increasingly dominated by commercial forces, the mission of CRIs would be to institutionalize responsible innovation at research universities.[135]

### Frameworks for Sustainable Development

Implicit in the conceptualization of the Fifth Wave as a framework for responsible innovation is its role in advancing sustainable development. The concept was initially framed by the questions posed in the 1972 report commissioned by the Club of Rome, *The Limits to Growth*—

"How much population growth and development, how much modification of natural systems, how much resource extraction and consumption, and how much waste generation can the earth sustain without provoking regional or even global catastrophe?"[136] But a point of departure for the contemporary discussion of sustainable development remains the widely cited Brundtland Commission definition presented to the United Nations (UN) General Assembly in 1987: "Development that meets the needs of the present without compromising the ability of future generations to meet their own needs." The commission is credited with reorienting the discussion from scientific research on the environment to the interdependence of nature and emergent social goals, underscoring the possibility of reconciling environmental concerns with the objectives of development.[137] According to David G. Victor, the commission's report introduced the concept of sustainable development, stating that it "argued that boosting the economy, protecting natural resources, and ensuring social justice are not conflicting but interwoven and complementary goals."[138]

The concept assumed even greater prominence after the UN adopted the eight Millennium Development Goals (MDG) in 2000: (1) to eradicate extreme poverty and hunger; (2) to achieve universal primary education; (3) to promote gender equality and empower women; (4) to reduce child mortality; (5) to improve maternal health; (6) to combat HIV/AIDS, malaria, and other diseases; (7) to ensure environmental sustainability; and (8) to develop a global partnership for development. Fifteen years later, the UN released a report describing uneven progress toward attaining the MDGs. Although significant progress was made in reducing suffering and enhancing well-being, important but more intractable problems remained: gender inequality hampered the prospects of women; large gaps between the poor and rich and between rural and urban areas meant that children living in the poorest households in developing countries were more likely to be stunted; climate change and degradation of the environment continued to afflict the poor disproportionately; displacement caused by wars and conflicts impeded human development; and 800 million people continued to suffer from hunger.[139]

But some believe that progress has been made despite and not because of the MDGs. Victor deprecates the consensus-driven approach adopted by the UN and contends that it has "spawned overspecialized and largely meaningless checklists and targets."[140] Yet despite such critique of the initial goals, in 2015 the UN introduced seventeen Sustainable Development Goals (SDGs): (1) No Poverty; (2) Zero Hunger; (3) Good Health and Well-Being; (4) Quality Education; (5) Gender Equality; (6) Clean Water and Sanitation; (7) Affordable and Clean Energy; (8) Decent Work and Economic Growth; (9) Industry, Innovation, and Infrastructure; (10) Reduced Inequalities; (11) Sustainable Cities and Communities; (12) Responsible Consumption and Production; (13) Climate Action; (14) Life Below Water; (15) Life on Land; (16) Peace, Justice, and Strong Institutions; and (17) Partnerships for the Goals.[141]

Since 1972 the concept of sustainable development has become increasingly contested, as commentators have noted inherent contradictions among its various objectives. Some maintain that the "proliferation of definitions has limited the concept's credibility."[142] Others contend that whereas the intent was to address global challenges, the concept is invoked increasingly only to promote focus on local and project-level problems: "No clear definition of sustainable development exists to guide politicians in solving challenges at the global or regional levels."[143] Inasmuch as the concept has been reinterpreted frequently to address conflicting relationships between social, economic, and environmental factors, some question whether it continues to be useful at all. For others, sustainable development matters precisely because it is contested and challenges researchers and policy makers to enter into debate and formulate compromises.[144]

Just as significant factions within the American electorate and their elected officials deny anthropogenic climate change and favor economic growth and jobs over protecting the environment, many nations inevitably interpret the ambiguities contained in the popular definition of sustainable development offered by the Brundtland Commission in ways that support their perceived interests. As Jennifer Elliott points out, whereas developed countries are more likely to advocate conserving resources to protect the environment, developing countries generally favor exploiting natural resources to boost economic development. Further, many commentators are concerned about striking an equitable balance between the intergenerational needs of current citizens against those yet unborn as well as maintaining intragenerational fairness between the young and senior citizens.[145]

What is not at issue is that the earth is falling increasingly under the influence of a single, dominant life form.[146] And as we previously put it, that this life form, notable for its ability to learn, reason, innovate, communicate, plan, predict, and organize its activities, nonetheless exhibits serious limitations in all these same areas. Although improvements in our standard of living and quality of life over the past 150 years are generally outcomes of the scientific discovery and technological innovation that originated in the libraries, laboratories, and classrooms of our research universities, prima facie evidence is abundant that the present model is not working.[147] Two decades ago, for example, Peter Vitousek and colleagues offered a synopsis of the human domination of the ecosystem in the following terms: "Between one-third and one-half of the land surface has been transformed by human action; the carbon dioxide concentration in the atmosphere has increased by nearly 30 percent since the beginning of the Industrial Revolution; more atmospheric nitrogen is fixed by humanity than by all natural terrestrial sources combined; more than half of all accessible surface fresh water is put to use by humanity; and about one-quarter of the bird species on Earth have been driven to extinction."[148] Humankind is earth's unruly tenant, as Jane Lubchenco eloquently put it,[149] and among more recent confirmations that the model is not working—should one feel the need for yet another reality check—are the conclusions of the special report of the Intergovernmental Panel on Climate Change (IPCC), *Global Warming of 1.5° C.*[150] "Over and over we've gotten scientific wake-up calls, and over and over we've hit the snooze button," Bill McKibben observes with reference to the "very grim forecast" of the report. "If we keep doing that, climate change will no longer be a problem, because calling something a problem implies there's still a solution."[151]

In our previous book, we lamented that neither the Constitution of the United States nor the principles of capitalism formulated contemporaneously with the Industrial Revolution by Adam Smith in the *Wealth of Nations* acknowledged limits on the ability of humanity to exploit natural resources indefinitely.[152] Although sustainable development is a concept essential to the survival of our species, its definition is varied and even resisted or rejected by significant numbers. It is therefore incumbent on Fifth Wave universities to advance transdisciplinary teaching and research about sustainable development as well as to convene and mediate relevant and allied transdisciplinary conversations. Accordingly, they must assume a role in identifying and acknowledging contradictions in contested discussions and attempt to resolve or reconcile tensions if possible, or in managing the tensions if the contradictions are irreducible. David Cash and colleagues analyzed several efforts to create knowledge intended to encourage sustainable development. In order for knowledge to be useful in this context they propose that it must be credible, salient, and legitimate. Credibility looks at the trustworthiness of knowledge: Is it accurate, complete, and reliable? Salience asks whether knowledge is relevant: Is it responsive to the type and scale of the problem at hand? Legitimacy assesses whether knowledge is fair and just: Have those who will be affected by the knowledge participated in its generation and given consent? Knowledge generated by Fifth Wave universities must pass this tripartite test.[153]

The challenges posed by sustainable development are indeed global, but solutions will be implemented at the local level, where Fifth Wave universities can generate useful knowledge and facilitate conversations. Fifth Wave universities must conduct research to gain more knowledge and participate in conversations that address the shortcomings in the ways that sustainable development has been framed to date. Fifth Wave universities are in a position to mediate the type of informal political dialogue that Victor contends is the "process through which priorities are shaped and agreed upon."[154] In fact, the political stalemate in Washington over climate change provides opportunities for Fifth Wave universities to promote local responses to global problems. By partnering with local governments, Fifth Wave universities may help create responses to global problems at the local level that are reproducible. Because Fifth Wave universities are embedded in both local and virtual communities, as articulated in the design aspirations of the New American University, they must serve and assume responsibility for social, economic, and environmental outcomes of those communities.

The changing definitions of sustainable development are a consequence of constantly shifting conceptions of the environment and development.[155] In addition, the continuing and acrimonious debates regarding sustainable development have reflexively influenced conversations about both environment and development.[156] Therefore, it is not surprising that sustainable development does not have a stable meaning that is accepted by all factions. But Fifth Wave universities cannot avoid the debates by taking refuge in academic neutrality nor recur to Newtonian and Cartesian models that promote "reductionist thinking and mechanistic interpretation" that interferes with knowledge construed as action.[157] Instead, sustainable development—regardless of the definition used—requires interdisciplinary and transdisciplinary approaches to assess, monitor, and influence systems at the local and global levels. Fifth Wave universities must participate in the conversations as partners with an optimistic, pluralistic, and melioristic orientation in an effort to mediate the dictates of economic individualism on the one hand and the limitations of the natural systems of the earth on the other to forestall the potential ruinous long-term detriment of all.[158]

Fifth Wave universities may be among the only institutions in society that are positioned to facilitate the conversations that are needed to govern the strongly held and often incommensurate positions of opposing groups. Since they are firmly embedded in local cultures, Fifth Wave universities are in a better position than earlier waves to resist the mimetic impulse that entices other universities to emulate the approaches of venerated institutions that may nevertheless be inappropriate to local needs. Fifth Wave universities can tailor methods to fit their unique conditions. Or, better yet, because Fifth Wave universities encourage experimentation that pushes the envelope of the normative culture and skirts the coercive bureaucracy that tends to infect the set of dominant institutions, they may be ideally positioned to advance discovery, creativity, and innovation. As communities of pragmatists who believe that ideas facilitate action and that knowledge must adjust to changing circumstances, the academic communities of Fifth Wave universities must become participants in the development of what has been termed sustainability knowledge. According to Thad Miller, Tischa A. Muñoz-Erickson, and Charles L. Redman, characteristics of sustainability knowledge include "social robustness, recognition of system complexity and uncertainty, acknowledgement of multiple ways of knowing, and the incorporation of normative and ethical premises," and its implementation would demand reflexive academic frameworks committed to epistemological pluralism.[159] This is consistent with the development of ecological design intelligence, which, sustainability scholar David Orr explains, represents the capacity to "recognize limits, get the scale of things right, and calibrate human purposes and natural constraints and do so with grace and economy." Attainment of this sort of ecological literacy among faculty and students alike, Orr contends, may require "nothing less than the redesign of education itself."[160]

## Notes

1. David C. Lane, "It Works in Practice but Does It Work in Theory?" *Systems Research and Behavioral Science* 23 (2006): 565–570. Apt in this context is the well-known aphorism attributed to the pioneering nuclear physicist Lord Ernest Rutherford to the effect that "a theory that you can't explain to a bartender is probably no damn good." Quoted by Geoffrey West, *Scale: The Universal Laws of Growth, Innovation, Sustainability, and the Pace of Life in Organisms, Cities, Economies, and Companies* (New York: Penguin Press, 2017), 450.

2. Kurt Lewin, *Field Theory in Social Science: Selected Theoretical Papers* (London: Tavistock, 1952), 169, quoted by Ben Shneiderman, *The New ABCs of Research: Achieving Breakthrough Collaborations* (Oxford: Oxford University Press, 2016), 17.

3. Richard M. Cyert and James G. March, "Models in a Behavioral Theory of the Firm," *Behavioral Science* 4, no. 2 (April 1959): 81–95, quoted in Kathleen Manning, *Organizational Theory in Higher Education* (New York: Routledge, 2013).

4. Martin Trow, "Problems in the Transition from Elite to Mass Higher Education" (Berkeley: Carnegie Commission on Higher Education, 1973), 18. For a discussion of Weber's usage of the concept of the "ideal type," see note 31 in chapter 1 of this volume.

5. Michael N. Bastedo, "Organizing Higher Education: A Manifesto," in *The Organization of Higher Education: Managing Colleges for a New Era*, ed. Michael N. Bastedo (Baltimore: Johns Hopkins University Press, 2012), 3.

6. David Byrne and Gill Callaghan, *Complexity Theory and the Social Sciences: The State of the Art* (London: Routledge, 2014); John Urry, "The Complexity Turn," *Theory, Culture, and Society* 22, no. 5 (2005): 2.

7. John F. Padgett and Walter W. Powell, *The Emergence of Organizations and Markets* (Princeton, NJ: Princeton University Press, 2012), 1–2.

8. John H. Holland, *Complexity: A Very Short Introduction* (Oxford: Oxford University Press, 2014), 5–6; Holland, "Complex Adaptive Systems," *Daedalus* 121, no. 1 (1992): 19.

9. Melanie Mitchell, *Complexity: A Guided Tour* (Oxford: Oxford University Press, 2009), 12–14.

10. William B. Rouse, *Universities as Complex Enterprises: How Academia Works, Why It Works These Ways, and Where the University Enterprise Is Headed* (Hoboken, NJ: John Wiley and Sons, 2016), 6. Rouse cites R. Poli, "A Note on the Difference between Complicated and Complex Social Systems," *Cadmus* 2, no. 1 (2013): 142–147.

11. Rómulo Pinheiro and Mitchell Young, "The University as an Adaptive Resilient Organization: A Complex Systems Perspective," in *Theory and Method in Higher Edu-*

*cation Research*, vol. 3, ed. Jeroen Huisman and Malcolm Tight (Bingley, UK: Emerald Group, 2017), 119–136.

12. Pinheiro and Young, "University as an Adaptive Resilient Organization," 121.

13. Pinheiro and Young, "University as an Adaptive Resilient Organization," 122–124. The authors quote John H. Holland, *Emergence: From Chaos to Order* (New York: Addison-Wesley, 1998), 7.

14. Pinheiro and Young, "University as an Adaptive Resilient Organization," 125–126.

15. Braden Allenby and Jonathan Fink, "Toward Inherently Secure and Resilient Societies," *Science* 309 (August 12, 2005), 1034–1036.

16. David D. Woods, "Four Concepts for Resilience and the Implications for the Future of Resilience Engineering," *Reliability Engineering and System Safety* 141 (2015): 5–9.

17. Pinheiro and Young, "University as an Adaptive Resilient Organization," 126–129.

18. Michael D. Cohen, James G. March, and Johan P. Olsen, "A Garbage Can Model of Organizational Choice," *Administrative Science Quarterly* 17, no. 1 (1972): 1; J. Douglas Orton and Karl E. Weick, "Loosely Coupled Systems: A Reconceptualization," *Academy of Management Review* 15, no. 2 (April 1990).

19. Pinheiro and Young, "University as an Adaptive Resilient Organization," 129–130.

20. Christopher Hood, "A Public Management for All Seasons?" *Public Administration* 69, no. 1 (1991): 15, quoted in Pinheiro and Young, "University as an Adaptive Resilient Organization," 132.

21. Shneiderman, *New ABCs of Research*.

22. Michael Gibbons et al., *The New Production of Knowledge: The Dynamics of Science and Research in Contemporary Societies* (London: Sage, 1994), 167.

23. Helga Nowotny, Peter Scott, and Michael Gibbons, "Mode 2 Revisited: The New Production of Knowledge," *Minerva* 41 (2003): 179.

24. Henry Etzkowitz, *The Triple Helix: University-Industry-Government Innovation in Action* (New York: Routledge, 2008), 141–142. As Etzkowitz puts it, "Paradoxically, the so-called mode 2 interdisciplinary research, with both theoretical and practical applications, is the original format of science from its institutionalization in the seventeenth century."

25. Gibbons et al., *New Production of Knowledge*, 2, 167.

26. Nowotny, Scott, and Gibbons, "Mode 2 Revisited," 179.

27. Gibbons et al., *New Production of Knowledge*, 2–3, 79–81.

28. G. Pascal Zachary, *Endless Frontier: Vannevar Bush, Engineer of the American Century* (Cambridge, MA: MIT Press, 1999).

29. Nowotny, Scott, and Gibbons, "Mode 2 Revisited," 179.

30. Harvey Brooks, "The Relationship between Science and Technology," *Research Policy* 23 (1994): 477–486.

31. Nathan Rosenberg and Richard R. Nelson, "American Universities and Technical Advance in Industry," *Research Policy* 23, no. 3 (1994): 323–348.

32. Daniel Sarewitz, personal correspondence, May 14, 2018. See, for example, Stuart W. Leslie, *The Cold War and American Science: The Military-Industrial-Academic Complex at MIT and Stanford* (New York: Columbia University Press, 1993).

33. Gibbons et al., *New Production of Knowledge*, 1.

34. Richard R. Nelson, "National Innovation Systems: A Retrospective on a Study," *Industrial and Corporate Change* 1, no. 2 (1992): 347–374; Richard R. Nelson and Nathan Rosenberg, "Technical Innovation and National Systems," in *National Innovation Systems: A Comparative Analysis*, ed. Richard R. Nelson (Oxford: Oxford University Press, 1993), 1–21.

35. Gibbons et al., *New Production of Knowledge*, 145–147.

36. Nowotny, Scott, and Gibbons, "Mode 2 Revisited," 186.

37. Gibbons et al., *New Production of Knowledge*, 3–4.

38. Helga Nowotny, Peter Scott, and Michael Gibbons, *Rethinking Science: Knowledge and the Public in an Age of Uncertainty* (Cambridge: Polity Press, 2001), 166–178.

39. Daniel Sarewitz, "Animals and Beggars: Imaginative Numbers in the Real World," in *Science, Philosophy, and Sustainability: The End of the Cartesian Dream*, ed. Ângela Guimarães Pereira and Silvio Funtowicz (London: Routledge, 2015): 137–138.

40. Sheila Jasanoff, "Technologies of Humility: Citizen Participation in Governing Science," *Minerva* 41 (2003): 235.

41. Robert Frodeman, *Sustainable Knowledge: A Theory of Interdisciplinarity* (Basingstoke, UK: Palgrave Macmillan, 2014).

42. Gibbons et al., *New Production of Knowledge*, 4–5.

43. Chad Wellmon, *Organizing Enlightenment: Information Overload and the Invention of the Modern Research University* (Baltimore: Johns Hopkins University Press, 2015), 22.

44. Richard R. Nelson et al., "How Medical Know-How Progresses," *Research Policy* 40 (2010): 1339–1344.

45. W. Brian Arthur, *The Nature of Technology: What It Is and How It Evolves* (New York: Free Press, 2009), 21.

46. See especially Michael M. Crow and William B. Dabars, *Designing the New American University* (Baltimore: Johns Hopkins University Press, 2015), chapter 5, and chapter 6 in the present book.

47. Gibbons et al., *New Production of Knowledge*, 140.

48. Peter Weingart, "A Short History of Knowledge Formations," in *The Oxford Handbook of Interdisciplinarity*, ed. Robert Frodeman, Julie Thompson Klein, and Carl Mitcham (Oxford: Oxford University Press, 2010), 12.

49. For a discussion of the impetus toward transdisciplinary peer review, see J. Britt Holbrook, "Peer Review," in *The Oxford Handbook of Interdisciplinarity*, ed. Robert Frodeman, Julie Thompson Klein, and Carl Mitcham (Oxford: Oxford University Press, 2010), 321–332.

50. Jasanoff, "Technologies of Humility," 235.

51. Alvin M. Weinberg, "Science and Trans-Science," *Minerva* 10, no. 2 (April 1972): 209–222, cited in Daniel Sarewitz, "Saving Science," *The New Atlantis: A Journal of Technology and Society* 49 (Spring/Summer 2016): 5–40.

52. Thomas S. Kuhn, *The Structure of Scientific Revolutions,* 50th anniv. ed. (1962; Chicago: University of Chicago Press, 2012); Silvio O. Funtowicz and Jerome R. Ravetz, "Three Types of Risk Assessment and the Emergence of Post-Normal Science," in *Social Theories of Risk,* ed. Sheldon Krimsky and D. Golding (New York: Praeger, 1992), 251–273, cited in Jasanoff, "Technologies of Humility," 232–233.

53. Horst W. J. Rittel and Melvin W. Webber, "Dilemmas in a General Theory of Planning," *Policy Sciences* 4, no. 2 (June 1973): 155–169.

54. Jasanoff, "Technologies of Humility," 232–233.

55. Gibbons et al., *New Production of Knowledge,* 2–3, 6, 81, 96–98.

56. Rouse, *Universities as Complex Enterprises.*

57. Monique Girard and David Stark, "Distributing Intelligence and Organizing Diversity in New Media Projects," *Environment and Planning* 34 (2002): 1927–1949.

58. Peter Galison, *Image and Logic: A Material Culture of Physics* (Chicago: University of Chicago Press, 1997), 48. For assessment of the context relevant to Mode 2 knowledge production, see Katherine C. Kellogg, Wanda J. Orlikowski, and JoAnne Yates, "Life in the Trading Zone: Structuring Coordination across Boundaries in Postbureaucratic Organizations," *Organization Science* 17, no. 1 (2006): 22–44.

59. Venkatesh Narayanamurti and Toluwalogo Odumosu, *Cycles of Invention and Discovery: Rethinking the Endless Frontier* (Cambridge, MA: Harvard University Press, 2016), 27–30.

60. Shneiderman, *New ABCs of Research,* 1–2; 15–20.

61. Donald E. Stokes, *Pasteur's Quadrant: Basic Science and Technological Innovation* (Washington, DC: Brookings Institution Press, 1997), 72–75.

62. Gibbons et al., *New Production of Knowledge,* 70–89. Chapter 3 is titled "Massification of Research and Education."

63. Evan Schofer and John W. Meyer, "The Worldwide Expansion of Higher Education in the Twentieth Century," *American Sociological Review* 70 (December 2005): 898–920.

64. Gibbons et al., *New Production of Knowledge,* 76–77.

65. Clark Kerr, *The Uses of the University,* 5th ed. (1963; Cambridge, MA: Harvard University Press, 2001), 1.

66. Gibbons et al., *New Production of Knowledge,* 74, 77.

67. Roger L. Geiger. "The Ten Generations of American Higher Education," in *American Higher Education in the Twenty-First Century: Social, Political, and Economic Challenges,* 4th ed., ed. Michael N. Bastedo, Philip G. Altbach, and Patricia J. Gumport (Baltimore: Johns Hopkins University Press, 2016), 24–25.

68. Gibbons et al., *New Production of Knowledge,* 77.

69. American Academy of Arts and Sciences, *The Heart of the Matter: The Humanities and Social Sciences For A Vibrant, Competitive, and Secure Nation* (Cambridge, MA: American Academy of Arts and Sciences, 2013), 10.

70. Gibbons et al., *New Production of Knowledge*, 78.

71. Gibbons et al., *New Production of Knowledge*, 79, 81, 122.

72. John J. Stuhr, *Pragmatism, Postmodernism, and the Future of Philosophy* (New York: Routledge, 2002), 129, 154–155.

73. Jürgen Habermas, *The Theory of Communicative Action,* vol. 2, *Reason and the Rationalization of Society,* trans. Thomas McCarthy (Cambridge, MA: MIT Press, 1987), 86; Habermas, "Postscript," in *Habermas and Pragmatism,* eds. Mitchell Adoulafia, Myra Bookman, and Catherine Kemp (London: Routledge, 2002), 227.

74. Gibbons et al., *New Production of Knowledge*, 8, 79.

75. J. Britt Holbrook, "Peer Review," in *The Oxford Handbook of Interdisciplinarity,* ed. Robert Frodeman, Julie Thompson Klein, and Carl Mitcham (Oxford: Oxford University Press, 2010), 321.

76. See, for example, Erik Brynjolfsson and Andrew McAfee, *The Second Machine Age: Work, Progress, and Prosperity in a Time of Brilliant Technologies* (New York: W. W. Norton, 2014), 7, 91; Nicole Howard, *The Book: The Life Story of a Technology* (Baltimore: Johns Hopkins University Press, 2009).

77. Clark A. Miller and Carina Wyborn, "Co-production in Global Sustainability: Histories and Theories," *Environmental Science and Policy* (2018): 1.

78. Kuhn, *Structure of Scientific Revolutions*.

79. Sheila Jasanoff, "Beyond Epistemology: Relativism and Engagement in the Politics of Science," *Social Studies of Science* 26, no. 2 (1996): 393–418. Miller and Wyborn cite as evidence of the broad applicability of the concept the observation by Steven Shapin and Simon Shaffer: "Solutions to the problem of knowledge are solutions to the problem of social order." See Shapin and Shaffer, *Leviathan and the Air-Pump: Hobbes, Boyle, and the Experimental Life* (Princeton, NJ: Princeton University Press, 1985), 332.

80. Sheila Jasanoff, "The Idiom of Co-production," in *States of Knowledge: The Co-production of Science and Social Order,* ed. Sheila Jasanoff (London: Routledge, 2004): 3–4.

81. David H. Guston, "Boundary Organizations in Environmental Policy and Science: An Introduction," *Science, Technology & Human Values* 26, no. 4 (2001): 401.

82. Jasanoff, "Idiom of Co-production," 3–4. For a related discussion, see Massimiano Bucchi and Federico Neresini, "Science and Public Participation," in *The Handbook of Science and Technology Studies,* 3rd ed., ed. Edward J. Hackett et al. (Cambridge, MA: MIT Press, 2008), 799–840.

83. Richard Rorty, *Philosophy and the Mirror of Nature*, 30th anniv. ed. (1979; Princeton, NJ: Princeton University Press, 2009).

84. Erik Fisher et al., "Mapping the Integrative Field: Taking Stock of Sociotechnical Collaborations," *Journal of Responsible Innovation* 2, no. 1 (2015): 40–41.

85. Arthur, *Nature of Technology*, 28.

86. Daniel Sarewitz and Richard R. Nelson, "Progress in Know-How: Its Origins and Limits," *Innovations: Technology, Governance, and Globalization* 3, no. 1 (Winter 2008): 105.

87. Nathan Rosenberg, *Inside the Black Box: Technology and Economics* (Cambridge: Cambridge University Press, 1982). See especially chapter 7, "How Exogenous Is Science?," 141–159.

88. Joel Mokyr, *The Gifts of Athena: Historical Origins of the Knowledge Economy* (Princeton, NJ: Princeton University Press, 2002), 2–4, 3n1, 13–18; Mokyr cites Simon Kuznets, *Economic Growth and Structure* (New York: W. W. Norton, 1965).

89. Richard R. Nelson, "The Simple Economics of Basic Scientific Research," *Journal of Political Economy* 67, no. 3 (June 1959): 297–306.

90. Suleiman K. Kassicieh and H. Raymond Radosevich, *From Lab to Market: Commercialization of Public Sector Technology* (New York: Plenum Press, 1994), 127.

91. Sarewitz and Nelson, "Progress in Know-How," 101.

92. Richard R. Nelson, "On the Uneven Evolution of Human Know-How," *Research Policy* 32 (2003): 909–910.

93. Wellmon, *Organizing Enlightenment*, 3–4, 13, 22. Wellmon characterizes the imposition of disciplinary culture in the research university as a response to "pervasive Enlightenment anxiety about information overload" (4).

94. Clark Kerr, *Higher Education Cannot Escape History: Issues for the Twenty-First Century* (Albany: SUNY Press, 1994).

95. Louis Menand, *The Metaphysical Club: A Story of Ideas in America* (New York: Farrar, Straus, and Giroux, 2001), 256.

96. Gibbons et al., *New Production of Knowledge*, 2.

97. Stephen Gaukroger, *The Natural and the Human: Science and the Shaping of Modernity, 1739–1841* (Oxford: Oxford University Press, 2016). Gaukroger reminds us that historians of science trace the emergence of scientific culture in the West to the thirteenth century.

98. Fisher et al., "Mapping the Integrative Field," 40–41.

99. Braden Allenby and Daniel Sarewitz, *The Techno-Human Condition* (Cambridge, MA: MIT Press, 2013), 32.

100. Roger E. Levien, "RAND, IIASA, and the Conduct of Systems Analysis," in *Systems, Experts, and Computers: The Systems Approach to Management and Engineering, World War II and After,* Agatha C. Hughes and Thomas P. Hughes (Cambridge, MA: MIT Press, 2000), 46, cited in D. J. Huppatz, "Revisiting Herbert Simon's 'Science of Design.'" *Design Issues* 31, no. 2 (2015): 31.

101. Sytse Strijbos, "Systems Thinking," in *The Oxford Handbook of Interdisciplinarity,* 2nd ed., ed. Robert Frodeman, Julie Thompson Klein, and Roberto C. S. Pacheco (Oxford: Oxford University Press, 2017), 291–292.

102. Donald A. Norman and Pieter Jan Stappers, "Design X: Complex Sociotechnical Systems," *She Ji: Journal of Design, Economics, and Innovation* 1, no. 2 (Winter 2015): 87–89.

103. C. P. Snow, *The Two Cultures and the Scientific Revolution* (Cambridge: Cambridge University Press, 1960), 2–4, 12. In a retrospective assessment published four years after the lecture as "A Second Look," Stefan Collini explains, Snow attempted to remedy the oversimplification of his initial dichotomization between the sciences and humanities with the introduction of the social sciences as a third category. Collini, introduction to C. P. Snow, *The Two Cultures* (Cambridge: Cambridge University Press, 1998), liv–lv.

104. David H. Guston, "Understanding Anticipatory Governance," *Social Studies of Science* 44, no. 2 (2014): 226.

105. Hannot Rodríguez, Erik Fisher, and Daan Schuurbiers, "Integrating Science and Society in European Framework Programmes: Trends in Project-Level Solicitations," *Research Policy* 42, no. 5 (2013): 1126–1137; Erik Fisher and Genevieve Maricle, "Higher-Level Responsiveness? Sociotechnical integration within US and UK Nanotechnology Research Priority Setting," *Science and Public Policy* 42 (2015): 72–85, cited in Fisher et al., "Mapping the Integrative Field," 42.

106. Jack Stilgoe, Richard Owen, and Phil Macnaghten, "Developing a Framework for Responsible innovation," *Research Policy* 42, no. 9 (2013): 1569–1570. See also David H. Guston et al., "Responsible Innovation: Motivations for a New Journal," *Journal of Responsible Innovation* 1, no. 1 (2014): 1–8; and Brian Wynne, "Public Uptake of Science: A Case for Institutional Reflexivity," *Public Understanding of Science* 2, no. 4 (1993): 321–337, cited by Richard Owen et al., "A Framework for Responsible Innovation," in *Responsible Innovation: Managing the Responsible Emergence of Science and Innovation in Society*, ed. Richard Owen, John Bessant, and Maggy Heintz (Chichester: John Wiley and Sons, 2013).

107. Owen et al., "Framework for Responsible Innovation," 27–29, 38.

108. Stilgoe, Owen, and Macnaghten, "Developing a Framework for Responsible Innovation," 1570–1572.

109. Owen et al., "Framework for Responsible Innovation," 27–29, 38.

110. Katy Börner et al., "A Multi-Level Systems Perspective for the Science of Team Science," *Science of Translational Medicine* 2, no. 49 (September 15, 2010): 1–5.

111. Fisher et al., "Mapping the Integrative Field," 40.

112. David Collingridge, *The Social Control of Technology* (New York: St. Martin's Press, 1980), 11.

113. Stephen Hilgartner, Barbara Prainsack, and J. Benjamin Hurlbut, "Ethics as Governance in Genomics and Beyond," in *The Handbook of Science and Technology Studies*, 4th ed., ed. Ulrike Felt et al. (Cambridge, MA: MIT Press, 2017), 826.

114. Wolfgang Liebert and Jan C. Schmidt, "Collingridge's Dilemma and Technoscience: An Attempt to Provide a Clarification from the Perspective of the Philosophy of Science," *Poiesis Prax* 7 (2010): 57, 57n4.

115. Erik Fisher, Roop L. Mahajan, and Carl Mitcham, "Midstream Modulation of Technology: Governance from Within," *Bulletin of Science, Technology, and Society* 26, no. 6 (December 2006): 485–496.

116. Fisher and Maricle, "Higher-Level Responsiveness?," 72–85.

117. Richard Owen, Philip Macnaghten, and Jack Stilgoe, "Responsible Research and Innovation: From Science in Society to Science for Society, with Society," *Science and Public Policy* 39 (2012): 751–760, cited in Fisher and Maricle, "Higher-Level Responsiveness?," 73.

118. Susan Leigh Star and James R. Griesemer, "Institutional Ecology, Translations, and Boundary Objects: Amateurs and Professionals in Berkeley's Museum of Vertebrate Zoology, 1907–39," *Social Studies of Science* 19, no. 3 (1989): 387–389, 393.

119. Guston, "Boundary Organizations," 403. See also Guston, "Stabilizing the Boundary between U.S. Politics and Science: The Rôle of the Office of Technology Transfer as a Boundary Organization," *Social Studies of Science* 29, no. 1 (February 1999): 81–111. Guston cites Kelly Moore, "Organizing Integrity: American Science and the Creation of Public Interest Organizations, 1955–1975," *American Journal of Sociology* 101, no. 6 (1996): 1592–1627.

120. Susan Leigh Star, "This Is Not a Boundary Object: Reflections on the Origin of a Concept," *Science, Technology, & Human Values* 35, no. 5 (2010): 601–617.

121. Guston, "Stabilizing the Boundary," 87, 90, 93, 105–106.

122. Guston, "Boundary Organizations," 403.

123. John Parker and Beatrice Crona, "On Being All Things to All People: Boundary Organizations and the Contemporary Research University," *Social Studies of Science* 42, no. 2 (2012): 262–289.

124. Parker and Crona, "On Being All Things to All People," 265–267.

125. Parker and Crona, "On Being All Things to All People," 267, 285n4, 270–273.

126. David D. White, "Decision Center for a Desert City: Strategic Management Plan, 2015–2019" (Tempe: Global Institute of Sustainability, Arizona State University, 2015), 1–20.

127. David D. White, E. A. Corley, and M. S. White, "Water Managers' Perceptions of the Science-Policy Interface in Phoenix, Arizona: Implications for an Emerging Boundary Organization," *Society and Natural Resources* 21, no. 3 (2008): 230–243.

128. Guston, "Boundary Organizations," 399–408.

129. Ray Quay, Kelli L. Larson, and M. S. White, "Enhancing Water Sustainability through University-Policy Collaborations: Experiences and Lessons from Researchers and Decision-Makers," *Water Resources Impact* 15, no. 2 (2013): 17–19.

130. David D. White et al., "Credibility, Salience, and Legitimacy of Boundary Objects: Water Managers' Assessment of a Simulation Model in an Immersive Decision Theater," *Science and Public Policy* 37, no. 3 (2010): 219–232.

131. Kelli L. Larson et al., "Decision-Making under Uncertainty for Water Sustainability and Urban Climate Change Adaptation," *Sustainability* 7 (2015): 14761–14784, DOI: 10.3390/su71114761. See also David D. White et al. "Water Management Decision Makers' Evaluations of Uncertainty in a Decision Support System: The Case of WaterSim in the Decision Theater," *Journal of Environmental Planning and Management* 58, no. 4 (2015): 616–630, DOI: 10.1080/09640568.2013.875892.

132. Parker and Crona, "On Being All Things to All People," 273–283.

133. Margaret Hinrichs and Erik Johnston, "The Creation of Inclusive Governance Infrastructures through Participatory Agenda Setting," manuscript submitted for publication (2019).

134. David H. Guston, "Responsible Innovation in the Commercialized University," in *Buying in or Selling Out: The Commercialization of the American Research University*, ed. Donald G. Stein (New Brunswick, NJ: Rutgers University Press, 2004), 162–164.

135. Guston, "Responsible Innovation," 162–164, 168, 170.

136. Donella H. Meadows et al., *The Limits to Growth: A Report for the Club of Rome's Project on the Predicament of Mankind* (New York: Universe, 1972). The Club of Rome first convened in 1968 to "foster understanding of the varied but interdependent components—economic, political, natural, and social—that make up the global system in which we all live" (9).

137. World Commission on Environment and Development (WCED), "Our Common Future," accessed on May 4, 2018. http://www.un-documents.net/our-common-future.pdf. See also World Commission on Environment and Development, *Our Common Future* (Oxford: Oxford University Press, 1987). Convened by the United Nations in 1983, the WCED is also known as the Brundtland Commission, after its chairman, Gro Harlem Brundtland, then prime minister of Norway.

138. David G. Victor, "Recovering Sustainable Development," *Foreign Affairs* 85, no. 1 (January/February 2006): 91.

139. United Nations, "The Millennium Development Goals Report 2015," accessed on May 4, 2018, http://www.un.org/millenniumgoals/2015_MDG_Report/pdf/MDG%202015%20rev%20(July%201).pdf.

140. Victor, "Recovering Sustainable Development," 92–94.

141. United Nations, "Sustainable Development Goals," accessed on May 14, 2018, https://www.un.org/sustinabledevelopment/sustinable-developoment-goals/.

142. Ivan Bolis, Sandra N. Morioka, and Laerte I. Sznelwar, "When Sustainable Development Risks Losing Its Meaning: Delimiting the Concept with a Comprehensive Literature Review and Conceptual Model," *Journal of Cleaner Production* 83 (2014): 7.

143. Erling Holden, Kristin Linnerud, and David Banister, "Sustainable Development: Our Common Future Revisited," *Global Environmental Change* 26 (2014): 130.

144. Jennifer A. Elliott, *An Introduction to Sustainable Development* (New York: Routledge, 2012): 8.

145. Elliott, *Introduction to Sustainable Development*, 8.

146. Will Steffen, Paul J. Crutzen, and John R. McNeill, "The Anthropocene: Are Humans Now Overwhelming the Great Forces of Nature?" *Ambio* 36, no. 8 (December 2007): 614–621.

147. Crow and Dabars, *Designing the New American University*, 228–229.

148. Peter M. Vitousek et al., "Human Domination of Earth's Ecosystems," *Science* 277, no. 5325 (1997): 494.

149. Jane Lubchenco, "Entering the Century of the Environment: A New Social Contract for Science," *Science* 279 (1998): 491–497, http://www.sciencemag.org/cgi/content/full/279/5350/491.

150. Intergovernmental Panel on Climate Change (IPCC), *Global Warming of 1.5° C: An IPCC Special Report on the Impacts of Global Warming of 1.5° C above Pre-industrial Levels and Related Global Greenhouse Gas Emission Pathways,* ed. V. Masson-Delmotte et al. (Geneva: World Meteorological Organization, 2018).

151. Bill McKibben, "A Very Grim Forecast," *New York Review of Books* (November 22, 2018).

152. Crow and Dabars, *Designing the New American University,* 225–229.

153. David W. Cash et al., "Knowledge Systems for Sustainable Development," *Proceedings of the National Academy of Sciences* 100, no. 14 (2003): 8086–8091.

154. David G. Victor, "Seeking Sustainability: Cities, Countryside, Wilderness," *Population and Development Review* 32, no. 1 (2006): 205.

155. Paul Warde, *The Invention of Sustainability: Nature and Destiny, c. 1500–1870* (Cambridge: Cambridge University Press, 2018).

156. Elliott, *Introduction to Sustainable Development,* 14.

157. Rodrigo Lozano, Kim Ceulemans, Mar Alonso-Almeida, Donald Huisingh, Francisco J. Lozano, Tom Waas, Wim Lambrechts, Rebeka Lukman, and Jean Hugé, "A Review of Commitment and Implementation of Sustainable Development in Higher Education: Results from a Worldwide Survey," *Journal of Cleaner Production* 108 (2015): 3.

158. Crow and Dabars, *Designing the New American University,* 218, 227.

159. Thaddeus R. Miller, Tischa A. Muñoz-Erickson, and Charles L. Redman, "Transforming Knowledge for Sustainability: Towards Adaptive Academic Institutions," *International Journal of Sustainability in Higher Education* 12, no. 2 (2011): 177.

160. David W. Orr, *Earth in Mind: On Education, Environment, and the Human Prospect* (Washington, DC: Island Press, 2004), 1–2.

# SIX

# Designing Fifth Wave Knowledge Enterprises

Issues of organizational change and institutional design converge with particular resonance in any assessment of the evolution of the American research university. Organizational change may be understood as either an implicit evolutionary process or, conversely, the product of explicit and deliberate intervention or design—or, as is more often the case, some combination thereof. "When we observe organizational change in the short run, and particularly at a moment of large and rapid shifts, we see environmental forces molding organizations through the mediation of human minds," the polymath Herbert Simon observed in his seminal analysis of organizational innovation.[1] It is in this latter sense—or even the sense that through intervention it is possible to force evolution—that we approach institutional innovation in the Fifth Wave. Accordingly, Helga Nowotny, Peter Scott, and Michael Gibbons observe, "The creative act lies just as much in the capacity to mobilize and manage . . . a range of theoretical perspectives and practical methodologies, their 'external' orchestration, as in the development of new theories or conceptualizations, or the refinement of research methods, the 'internal' dynamics of scientific creativity."[2] A theoretical appreciation of the challenges associated with the "external orchestration" of academic frameworks—institutional innovation or the design process—thus encapsulates the scope of this chapter.

And whereas innovation—like design—has often been narrowly construed to refer primarily to product development in industry, the term has more recently come to designate any "reconfiguration of elements into a more productive combination." According to economist Henry Etzkowitz, this new conception of innovation may thus refer to the "restructuring and enhancement of the organizational arrangements and incentives that foster innovation," which is a process he terms the "innovation of innovation."[3] The design process for the Fifth Wave engages this broader sense of design. This is what architect Ann Pendleton-Jullian and organizational theorist John Seely Brown term design "unbound from thingness." The upshot is expressed in the following terms: "When people think of design, it is usually as problem solving that results in the making of things." However, "Not all problems to be solved result in . . . things that have material solidity. Many of the most important problems have to do with systems and models that are not physical, or they are wicked, meaning that they do not lend themselves to solutions at all." Among the wicked challenges that Pendleton-Jullian and Brown enumerate— overpopulation, water shortages, climate change, geopolitical conflicts—is education. "To work in and on these problems requires more than fiddling with things in contexts," the authors observe. "It requires that we work on the contexts themselves."[4]

Design of this sort provides a framework for emergence in a "white water world." Unbound design seeks to define a new tool set for a world that is "rapidly changing, increasingly interconnected, and where, because of this increasing interconnectivity, everything is more contingent on everything else happening around it." The authors characterize this as a white water world because in "white-water river kayaking, navigation—often survival—depends upon understanding how to skill up for dynamic contexts in which things change and emerge without respite." Design of this sort—an "offspring of complexity science"—must be at once visionary, in the sense that design envisions the future; optimistic, although skeptically so, because design must be "grounded through the test of theory hitting the real world" where it serves to "translate and mediate change"; and opportunistic to the extent that entrepreneurialism is essential to negotiate change at appropriate scale. Design of this sort requires an "ontological shift—a different way of being in the world"—which accommodates its radical contingency. But what it conveys is *agency*, which in this sense of the word the *Oxford English Dictionary* defines as the "ability to act or exert power; active working or operation; action or intervention producing a particular effect; means, instrumentality, mediation."[5] The imagination is a "special form of agency," Pendleton-Jullian and Brown observe, that, through its productive entanglement with creativity, becomes instrumentalized as the pragmatic imagination. Consistent with the tenets of American pragmatism expounded by Charles Peirce and William James and John Dewey considered in previous chapters, the pragmatic imagination as conceived by Pendleton-Jullian and Brown perceives thought and action as indivisible and reciprocal: "The imagination provides vision and intention, often with the novelty needed to move us forward," Pendleton-Jullian and Brown explain. But it is the "cues and constraints of context" that "instrumentalize the imagination toward pragmatic action." The pragmatic imagination is moreover agnostic, as the authors observe, in the sense that it may be used "ambidextrously," which is to say by the arts, humanities, and social sciences on the one hand and the natural sciences and technological fields on the other.[6]

The Fifth Wave builds on the bedrock of the Fourth Wave—epistemologically, administratively, and socially—but institutional innovation need not be merely "planned incremental improvement on what already exists," as John Padgett and Walter Powell observe. Because this book purports to be about the emergence—and especially the design—of a hypothetical new institutional type, it might more precisely correspond to what Padgett and Powell term a study in the "historical emergence of organizational novelty." They state, "Organizational genesis does not mean virgin birth. All new organizational forms, no matter how radically new, are combinations and permutations of what was there before. Transformations are what make them novel. Evolution, therefore, is not teleological progress toward some ahistorical . . . ideal. It is a thick and tangled bush of branchings, recombinations, transformations, and sequential path-dependent trajectories, just as Darwin said it was." Contemporary academic culture thus offers "many theories about how to choose alternatives, once these swim into our field of vision," as Padgett and Powell put it. "But our theories have little to say about the invention of new alternatives in the first place. New ideas, new practices, new organizational forms, new people must enter from off the stage of our imaginary before our analyses can begin."[7] With reference to the emergence of novel organizational forms, Padgett elsewhere observes, "Explaining choices, once alternatives exist, has not proven difficult for the social sciences. Explaining the discovery of alternatives is slightly more difficult, since the search space outside of current alternatives is sometimes not well defined. Explaining the emergence of true novelty, before alternatives even exist to be found, is the real challenge."[8]

Padgett and Powell address economic organizations but contend that their approach applies to political organizations as well. Because universities have inevitably been involved in political processes and are increasingly becoming economic actors, we extrapolate their insights to the wave model of university development.[9] Because the Fifth Wave builds on the bedrock of the Fourth Wave, the design process must evaluate new alternatives with reference to the persistence of the status quo and the potential for novel forms of academic organization and even new institutional types. Pendleton-Jullian and Brown turn to the poet and philosopher Paul Valéry for insight in this context: "Invention depends on two processes," Valéry observed. "The first generates a collection of alternatives, the other chooses, recognizing what is desirable and appears important among that produced by the first." It is this latter capacity that is critical to the design process—"the facility of the second in recognizing the value in what has been presented, and seizing upon it."[10]

## The Organization of Inquiry to Fulfill Its Proper Function

Recognition of the imperative for more optimal institutional design to facilitate inquiry is hardly novel, having been implicit in the quest of modern science since its advent as an organized activity in the seventeenth century to create a "community well designed for the attainment of epistemic goals," as philosopher Philip Kitcher has observed. This objective highlights the contingent situatedness of knowledge production—that the seemingly self-evident question, "How should inquiry be organized so as to fulfill its proper function?"—is inevitably dependent on one or another institutional context.[11] Organized science, moreover, is a "group activity carried on by limited and fallible men," as the historian A. Hunter Dupree so eloquently put it, adding that "much of their effectiveness stems from their organization and the continuity and flexibility of their institutional arrangements."[12] Appreciation of the significance of optimal institutional design for the attainment of epistemic goals is also deepened through historical and theoretical perspective, including the approaches characterized as social epistemology, which assess the social dimensions of knowledge and belief.[13]

Whether evaluated from the perspective of the set of major research universities, system of government agencies and federal laboratories, or the research and development efforts of industry, knowledge production is dependent on its institutional context and thus facilitated by more optimal institutional arrangements. Although knowledge production is increasingly collaborative across these sectors, the set of Fourth Wave research universities predominate among institutional actors that constitute the national innovation system.[14] But an institution as complex as the American research university must continuously evolve to keep pace with changing cultural, economic, political, and social circumstances and the proliferation of new knowledge.[15] Nevertheless the assumption in academic culture persists that institutional frameworks have somehow always and inevitably been optimally configured to facilitate discovery, creativity, and innovation. But knowledge production is a collaborative endeavor and thus socially constructed and historically contingent[16]—"in part a product of the activity, context, and culture in which it is developed and used"[17]—and thus path-dependent, which is to say, shaped by previous sequences of decisions.[18] The concept of path dependence underscores the extent to which historical contingencies determine institutional evolution. As Mitchell Stevens and Benjamin Gebre-Medhin explain: "Past shapes present by providing the organizational contexts within which action may be taken at any given point in time; by providing the identities of groups which are or are not allowed to take certain kinds of actions; and by defining what individuals and groups may even conceive as possible in particular places and times."[19] Knowledge production may be understood as a product of the reflexive relationship between *structure*, referring to the institutional matrix of the university, and *agency*, referring to the scholarship, inventiveness, and creativity of the academic community, which process Anthony Giddens terms *structuration*.[20] The institutional context of knowledge production constitutes its historical a priori, which, as Ian Hacking explains, functions something like the paradigms of normal science described by Thomas Kuhn. At the very least, "the historical *a priori* points at conditions on the possibilities of knowledge."[21]

But the implications of this interdependence are too often dismissed as adventitious to discovery and innovation and minimized as merely perfunctory administrative contingencies: "In a society that attaches particular value to 'abstract knowledge,'" organizational theorists John Seely Brown and Paul Duguid observe, "the details of practice have come to be seen as nonessential, unimportant, and easily developed once the relevant abstractions have been grasped."[22] Institutional design in our usage thus refers to such details of practice and the imperative for deliberation and consensus that determines the structures—and hence functions—of knowledge enterprises such as research universities. In contrast to standard historical accounts of American higher education, we reiterate that our assessment seeks to develop an understanding of structure and function in the successive waves of institutional types. Such an analysis is at once morphological and typological rather than primarily historical, with the concept of morphology referring to the structural attributes of organizations and institutions. Of course, even a concept as seemingly fixed as structure may be regarded as relative. "Structure is itself a deceptive reality," Andrew Abbott reminds us. "Although fixed for the purpose of analysis, it perpetually changes, in myriad little ways, and must eventually be regarded as changed in kind, even though sudden shifts in it cannot be discerned." The upshot, according to Abbott: "There is a sense in which structure is simply our conventional name for things that change more slowly than other things."[23]

The recognition that knowledge is a construct has been variously formulated since antiquity and was reinforced by Kant, who redefined our appreciation of the interdependence of mind and world.[24] More recently the construction of knowledge has been elucidated in terms of constructivist epistemology and, when epistemic evaluation is explicitly social or interpersonal, social epistemology. Then again, "epistemology without history is blind," as Kitcher puts it, and from this premise it follows that human understanding is enriched through an account of the contingencies of its production.[25] But contemporary academic culture nevertheless valorizes the notion of discovery, as if within an organizational context knowledge were not invariably "conceived and constructed out of an organization's own values, routines, and operating assumptions, both explicit and hidden," as Clark Miller and Tischa Muñoz-Erickson contend. One might thus as readily conceive of knowledge production as designing knowledge or, in an organizational context, the design and operation of knowledge systems, referring to the "organizational practices and routines that make, validate, communicate, and apply knowledge." Miller and Muñoz-Erickson point out that knowledge systems determine what questions are asked and which are not and, when asked, how the questions are framed and evaluated. Because knowledge claims that organizations evaluate are premised on "uncertain propositions whose relationship to truth cannot be easily or directly ascertained," an appreciation of the conditions of knowledge production assumes greater significance. In this context, Miller and Muñoz-Erickson offer a litany of catastrophes and debacles associated with failures in knowledge systems, ranging from Pearl Harbor to Three Mile Island to the space shuttle *Challenger*, and, more recently, the futile efforts to identify weapons of mass destruction in Iraq, ballot recounts in Florida following the 2000 presidential election, and the terrorist attacks on September 11, 2001. As if these were not enough, their survey continues with the responses to Hurricanes Katrina and Sandy, the 2008 financial meltdown, the Deepwater Horizon oil spill, and the rancorous ongoing contention about climate change.[26]

We see that it is incumbent on institutions to refine and modulate frameworks to comport with the reflexive and contingent nature of knowledge and more fully facilitate transdisciplinary knowledge production undertaken in a context of application. The imperative to recalibrate and redefine academic organization and processes, including administrative, epistemological, and social alignments, assumes increasing urgency. "New forms of knowledge production are putting existing institutional structures and procedures under strain," Michael Gibbons and colleagues observe, with reference to Mode 2 knowledge production. Therefore, these institutions "require new and radical transformations." In chapter 5 we correlated the Fifth Wave with the new mode of knowledge production, which is "carried out in the context of application and marked by its transdisciplinarity; heterogeneity; organizational heterarchy and transience; social accountability and reflexivity; and quality control which emphasizes context- and use-dependence." Consistent with the proposition that the imperative for the Fifth Wave arises due to design constraints inherent in the Fourth Wave, the emergence of Mode 2 "calls into question the adequacy of familiar knowledge producing institutions, whether universities, government research establishments, or corporate laboratories."[27]

## Organizational Change: Evolutionary Process and the Science of Design

Two contrasting conceptualizations of organizational change are evolutionary models, which focus on change construed in terms of adaptation and the dynamics of competition for resources in complex and competitive organizational ecologies, and the alternative perspective that maintains that change is predominantly the product of deliberate intervention.[28] Technological innovation has been modeled as an evolutionary process,[29] and, by extrapolation, institutional innovation may be similarly understood. As Frederick Brooks clarifies, with reference to this usage of *evolutionary* in a design context: "*Evolution* is used loosely here. The model is evolutionary in that both the understanding of the problem and the development of the solution are incrementally generated and incrementally evaluated."[30] Policy scholars Derrick Anderson and Andrew Whitford offer further perspective on the distinction between the two approaches: "While evolutionary theories of organizational change contend that transformation comes about through responses to environmental stimuli, institutional design perspectives hold that change can embody purposeful maximization of preferences and human values."[31] "The natural selection model . . . posits that environmental factors select those organizational characteristics that best fit the environment," sociologists Howard Aldrich and Jeffrey Pfeffer explain. "A complementary model, variously called a political economy model, a dependence exchange approach, and a resource dependence model, argues for greater attention to internal organizational political decision-making processes and also for the perspective that organizations seek to manage or strategically adapt to their environments."[32] Organizational change may moreover transcend incremental and cumulative change: "Punctuated equilibrium theory depicts organizations as evolving through relatively long periods of stability (equilibrium periods) in their basic patterns of activity that are punctuated by relatively short bursts of fundamental change (revolutionary periods)." In this conception, "revolutionary periods substantively disrupt established activity patterns and install the basis for new equilibrium periods."[33]

By contrast, Simon views institutional change as distinctly the product of deliberate intervention, which he terms the "science of design."

In the series of lectures that formed the basis of *The Sciences of the Artificial*, Simon underscores the essential dichotomy between natural science, referring to "knowledge about natural objects and phenomena," and "artificial science"—artifacts that are human-made as opposed to natural. Whereas the natural sciences are concerned with how things are, as he put it, the artificial sciences address how things "ought to be in order to *attain goals*, and to *function*." He thus terms knowledge of the realization of ideas, products, and processes the science of design. Moreover, "Everyone designs who devises courses of action aimed at changing existing situations into preferred ones." In this context, Simon emphasizes a critical distinction: "Artificial things can be characterized in terms of functions, goals, adaptation." And with reference to function and purpose, Simon remarks: "Fulfillment of purpose or adaptation to a goal involves a relation among three terms: the purpose or goal, the character of the artifact, and the environment in which the artifact performs."[34] Simon thus establishes the theoretical basis for conceptualizing institutional design as a process of deliberate intervention that seeks to improve form in that which we construct in whatever context.

"The central theme of design is the conception and planning of the artificial," design theorist Richard Buchanan paraphrases Simon.[35] But Simon moreover asserts that design is a process properly understood as scientific problem solving. What is novel in this conception is the supposition that scientific method could appropriately be applied in the various contexts here at stake—administrative, epistemological, and social. "Problem solving is often described as a search through a vast maze of possibilities. . . . Successful problem solving involves searching the maze selectively and reducing it to manageable proportions." Thus: "Problem solving requires *selective* trial and error." Within the space of two paragraphs he reiterates: "From the most blundering to the most insightful, [problem solving] involves nothing more than varying mixtures of trial and error and selectivity." Discovery is thus the upshot of the process: "The test that something has been discovered is that something new has emerged that could not have been predicted with certainty and that the new thing has value or interest of some kind."[36]

Because his expansive conception of design led Simon to designate as artifice the totality of our cultural production—from the most rudimentary tools to the "strings of artifacts called 'symbols' that we receive through eyes and ears in the form of written and spoken language"—he underscores its contingency on design to the extent that he would contend that "in large part, the proper study of mankind is the science of design, not only as the professional component of a technical education but as a core discipline for every liberally educated man."[37] Indeed, Simon's conceptualization of design may be regarded as part of his broader effort to unify the social sciences through the scientific method and quantitative assessment as the bases of problem solving.[38] Accordingly, Buchanan argues for the reconceptualization of design as what he terms a "liberal art of technological culture," restoring to design a broader sense of the concept as both architectonic and integrative—*architectonic* because design is constructive and *integrative* because design must integrate theory and practice.[39]

The reference to design as a "liberal art of technological culture" moreover restores to technology a sense of the concept apart from "things and machines" that arose during the Industrial Revolution. "Most people continue to think of technology in terms of its product rather than its form as a discipline of systematic thinking," Buchanan explains. Accordingly, design produces plans: "The plan is an argument, reflecting the deliberations of designers and their efforts to integrate knowledge in new ways, suited to specific circumstances and needs." He thus calls for design as a "new discipline of practical reasoning and argumentation," deliberation directed toward "overcoming the limitations of mere verbal or symbolic argument—the separation of words and things, or theory and practice." As a new liberal art, he expects design to challenge notions of what we deem impossible, which, after all, may only reflect the limitations of our imaginations.[40]

Consistent with the sense of design posited by Simon, the field has come increasingly to conceive of its purposes as problem solving oriented toward processes rather than the production of artifacts, thus transcending the artisanal conception of design epitomized by the Bauhaus model.[41] This more expansive—as well as socially ameliorative—conception is sometimes termed "design thinking," which claims the intent to plan and improve processes, systems, and organizations.[42] Accordingly, design theorist Bruce Mau conceives of change in terms of "designing systems, designing organizations, and designing organisms." Change at this scale requires the exploration of what he terms "design economies," wherein the "patterns that emerge reveal complexity, integrated thinking across disciplines, and unprecedented interconnectivity."[43] "New conceptions of design now define its charter as the development of systems rather than individual artifacts," Prasad Boradkar observes. "New design thinking emphasizes concerns of social equity and environmental responsibility, pushing design's purview beyond its historical fixation on form. It is now also commonly recognized that design alone cannot solve these problems in isolation. The sheer wickedness and complexity of these issues warrants engagement with other disciplines."[44]

Design thinking operationalized in a Fifth Wave context has the potential to address the "wicked" problems characterized by Horst Rittel and Melvin Webber in their seminal 1973 paper. With the concept borrowed from philosopher Karl Popper, Rittel and Webber delineated ten properties of wickedness in problems, beginning with their indeterminacy. Rittel and Webber propose that wicked problems defy definitive formulation and resolution and are fraught with uncertainty and contested value.[45] Buchanan argues that indeterminacy and wickedness are inevitable in design because "design has no special subject matter of its own apart from what a designer conceives it to be." As a consequence, the "subject matter of design is potentially *universal* in scope, because design may be applied to any area of human experience." Moreover, design thinking demands a transdisciplinary approach because it recognizes the "impossibility of relying on any one of the sciences (natural, social, or humanistic) for adequate solutions to what are the inherently *wicked problems*." Buchanan explains: "Designers are exploring concrete integrations of knowledge that will combine theory with practice for new productive purposes."[46]

An appreciation of the four broad domains of design in contemporary theory and practice suggests the extent of its ambitions. According to Buchanan, these include symbolic and visual communications; material objects; activities and organized services; and complex systems or environments for living, working, playing, and learning. The key point in this context is that "argument in design thinking moves toward the concrete interplay and interconnection of signs, things, actions, and thoughts." Apart from systems engineering, architecture, and urban planning, Buchanan specifies a context applicable to academic administration in the Fifth Wave, the role of design in the "functional analysis of the parts of complex wholes and their subsequent integration in hierarchies."[47]

Research universities operate in complex and competitive organizational ecologies, and because public administration may be regarded as a design science, following Simon's delineation of the artificial sciences, administrators and policy scholars alike are empowered with the potential to contribute to the evolution of these institutions, and especially the calibration of their alignments with the external environment of public organizations and governing systems. All organizations are public, as Barry Bozeman reminds us,[48] and through the exercise of public administration as a design science, scholars and practitioners alike may promote both the effectiveness of these institutions and the public interest.[49] Designs of public universities were initially legalistic, bureaucratic, and faculty-centric—as opposed to client- or student-centric. Subject to conserver models of organizational behavior, universities thus exhibited only minimal rates of adaptation and change over long periods of time. Consistent with the call for a "new public administration" that is a legacy of the Minnowbrook Conference convened by the Maxwell School of Citizenship and Public Affairs of Syracuse University fifty years ago, the intent in rethinking the frameworks of Fourth Wave institutions is to reconceptualize their design principles to facilitate the flexibility, change-orientation, system responsivity, client centricity, transdisciplinarity, and adaptivity essential to the Fifth Wave.[50]

## Inertia and Isomorphism Impede Institutional Innovation

"Academics have a marvelous sense of fertilization," Jonathan Cole remarks. "We are experts at gestation and early development; we know about maturation and full expansion; but we refuse to confront death and dying." Cole is referring to organizational inertia, which impedes organizational change, nowhere more insidiously than in the American research university. "Once something is in place, it is very difficult to get rid of it." He concludes: "The academic way of death for outdated or redundant programs and entities is traditionally through atrophy at a Darwinian pace."[51] Policy scholar Burton Clark turned to Émile Durkheim for an assessment of the broader context for this sort of inertia. Education, Durkheim observed, is a "collection of practices and institutions that have been organized slowly in the course of time, which are comparable with all other social institutions and which express them, and which, therefore, can no more be changed at will than the structure of society itself."[52] With reference to resistance to innovation, Neil Smelser observes, "Faculties appear to have cultivated the art of resistance commensurate with their levels of intelligence and ingenuity." In this context he quotes John Kay regarding his experiences with the committee system at Oxford during his efforts to establish the Said Business School. Kay identified "eight oars of indecision: deferral, referral, procedural objection, 'the wider picture,' evasion, ambiguity, precedent, and denial." Quips Smelser: "Perhaps he could have discovered even more than eight had he not been constrained by the metaphor of the rowing shell."[53] As Richard Nelson and Sidney Winter observed in this context: "We think of organizations as being typically much better at the tasks of self-maintenance in a constant environment than they are at major change, and much better at changing in the direction of 'more of the same' than they are at any other kind of change."[54]

Bureaucratic patterns and the replication of isomorphic organizational formations hamper innovation and encourage the ossification of academic culture. Resistance to novel institutional arrangements exacerbates the tendencies toward routine, standardization, and inertia that have been identified as hallmarks of bureaucratization.[55] But the bureaucratic mind-set pejoratively associated with large impersonal public agencies that perform standardized and repetitive tasks is not normally conducive to discovery, creativity, and innovation. Filiopietism, or the excessive veneration of tradition, moreover encourages adherence to historical models long after their relevance or usefulness has diminished.[56] Of course, this should come as no surprise inasmuch as universities are "deeply conservative organizations that bear the obvious hallmark of their medieval origins and their many purposes," as sociologist Jason Owen-Smith has observed.[57] "Change and innovation have been consistent fixtures of higher education since its inception, even though artifacts and rituals that celebrate continuity and tradition pervade college and university campuses," educational theorists William Tierney and Michael Lanford observe. Nevertheless, "Within academe an authoritative explanation of innovation has proven elusive."[58]

Isomorphism describes the paradoxical tendency for organizations and institutions operating within given sectors to emulate one another and become increasingly homogeneous but not necessarily more efficient. As sociologists Paul DiMaggio and Walter Powell contend, the outcome of the competition for power and legitimacy that produces dominant organizational models is not differentiation but isomorphic conformity because the "major factors that organizations must take into account are other organizations." But inasmuch as institutions succumb to coercive, mimetic, and normative pressures, isomorphism may be an entirely rational response. Coercion may arise from governmental regulation, for example. Mimetic isomorphism, or isomorphic modeling, describes efforts by organizations to model themselves on competitors to achieve legitimacy. Professionalization produces normative modeling. The struggle for professional legitimation produces a "pool of almost interchangeable individuals who occupy similar positions across a range of organizations and possess a similarity of orientation and disposition that may override variations in tradition . . . that might otherwise shape organizational behavior."[59]

Among the more insidious implications of isomorphic replication is the tendency of organizations to respond "relatively slowly to the occurrence of threats and opportunities in their environments," according to sociologists Michael Hannan and John Freeman. At issue is the "responsiveness of the structure to designed changes. How quickly can an organization be reorganized?"[60] Also of concern is the character and quality of knowledge production itself, the epistemological parameters of which are inevitably shaped by the contours of their administrative and social frameworks. Knowledge production constrained by isomorphic academic organization and the replication of homologous institutional structures is unlikely to produce the variation and diversity essential to discovery and innovation. In the face of entrenched isomorphic homogeneity within the set of Fourth Wave research universities, the Fifth Wave encourages differentiation and heterogeneity among institutions.

As simultaneously epistemological, administrative, and sociocultural modes of organization,[61] academic disciplines contribute to isomorphism in knowledge production. Despite skepticism regarding the strictures of disciplinary hegemony, disciplinary acculturation and the correlation between academic disciplines and departments remain remarkably consistent with historical patterns established primarily in the late nineteenth century.[62] "The academic disciplines effectively monopolize (or attempt to monopolize) the production of knowledge in their fields," observes Louis Menand, "and they monopolize the production of knowledge producers as well." Disciplinary guilds in effect became primarily accountable only to themselves, he contends. "Since it is the system that ratifies the product—ipso facto, no one outside the community of experts is qualified to rate the value of the work produced within it—the most important function of the system is not the production of knowledge. It is the reproduction of the system."[63] This sort of reproduction of the system is manifest in every aspect of our academic practices, including the curriculum. John Lombardi, former president of the Louisiana State University system, suggests two of the sources of this isomorphism. "The similarity of college curricula comes from the twin power of competition and regulation," he observes. "Competition ensures that each college and university offers much the same curriculum to a common marketplace of students and parents seeking equivalent products." Further, "Regulation reinforces this standardization of content through accreditation, a process that encourages or coerces colleges and universities to deliver remarkably similar undergraduate programs."[64]

Isomorphism contributes to the persistence or reproduction of suboptimal organizational structures. In this context, Walter Powell poses the following questions: "How are practices and structures perpetuated over time, particularly in circumstances where utilitarian calculations would suggest they are dysfunctional? Why are practices reproduced when superior options are available? Why are less-than-optimal arrangements sustained, even in the face of opposition?" Powell posits cogent explanations consistent with contentions on behalf of the imperative for the Fifth Wave, including the following: "Persistence may not depend upon active agency because a particular practice or structure is so embedded in a network of practices and procedures that change in any one aspect requires changes in many other elements." Moreover: "Social patterns may also reproduce themselves without active intervention when practices and structures come to be taken for granted, hence they are not questioned or compared against alternatives." And yet further: "Organizational procedures and forms may persevere because of path-dependent patterns of development in which initial choices preclude future options, including those that would have been more effective in the long run." And finally: "Success is frequently the enemy of experimentation and leads to competency traps—circumstances in which favorable performance with an inferior procedure or technology leads an organization to accumulate additional experience with it, thus keeping knowledge of a more advantageous procedure or technology too limited to make it rewarding to use."[65]

## Organizational Contexts That Facilitate Knowledge Production

Organizational contexts may either frustrate or facilitate knowledge production, philosophers Scott Cook and John Seely Brown point out, extrapolating from an insight derived from José Ortega y Gasset. Organizational *knowledge* is generally construed as some subset of knowledge that certain individuals possess, which Cook and Brown thus term the "epistemology of possession." By contrast, organizational *knowing* may be characterized as the "epistemology of practice." Knowing implies dynamic engagement and comports with the pragmatist tenet that knowledge implies action: "The pragmatist perspective takes a primary concern not with 'knowledge,' which is seen as abstract and static, but with 'knowing,' which is understood as . . . dynamic human action." Organizational knowing thus refers to the "coordinated activities of individuals and groups in doing their 'real work' as informed by a particular organizational or group context." Because organizational knowledge and organizational knowing are complementary and mutually enabling, their interplay is likened to a "generative dance" that advances organizational innovation. In positing a dialectical relationship between the epistemologies of possession and practice, Cook and Brown invoke John Dewey and the process he termed "productive inquiry." The concept is framed thus: "It is *inquiry* because what motivates us to action is in some sense a query: a problem, a question, a provocative insight, or a troublesome situation. It is *productive* because it aims to produce (to make) an answer, solution, or resolution." Productive inquiry is thus facilitated, or "afforded," by appropriate organizational contexts: "Harnessing innovation calls for organizational and technological infrastructures that support the interplay of knowledge and knowing."[66]

The transinstitutional dimension of the Fifth Wave is ideally represented in the triple helix model of innovation described by economist Henry Etzkowitz. The triple helix of collaboration between academic, industry, and government partners comprises intersecting knowledge networks that leverage input from diverse multidisciplinary perspectives.[67] But organizational theorists contend that the value of stocks of knowledge is diminishing and that the knowledge base must be continually replenished through participation in relevant flows of knowledge.[68] Indeed, theoretical discussions of organizational design tend to overlook less obvious models that may be heuristically relevant to an understanding of the Fifth Wave. Knowledge networks and knowledge-centric social formations, including invisible colleges, communities of practice, epistemic communities, and firms construed as knowledge-centric organizations, represent viable models for the sort of transdisciplinary collaborative engagement that characterizes Fifth Wave institutions.

Correspondence among intellectuals and scholars during the seventeenth and eighteenth centuries produced the celebrated transatlantic Republic of Letters, which, along with the printed word in books and periodicals, facilitated the circulation of ideas during the Enlightenment.[69] The Republic of Letters was envisioned as a "realm with no boundaries and no inequalities other than those determined by talent," writes the historian Robert Darnton. "Read through the correspondence of Voltaire, Rousseau, Franklin, and Jefferson—each filling about fifty volumes—and you can watch the Republic of Letters in operation." Darnton speaks of the "faith in the power of knowledge" of the era epitomized in the exchange of letters between Jefferson and Madison, respectively, in Paris and Philadelphia. Among their topics was the American Constitution.[70] The concept of invisible colleges—an important historical model for what today we term knowledge networks—derives from this period and refers to any informal collaborative engagement of scholars and scientists from any number of disciplinary perspectives focused on similar or related problems. Joel Mokyr explains the relevance of the concept thus: "The blossoming of open science and the emergence of invisible colleges—that is, informal scholarly communities spanning different countries, within which seventeenth-century scholars and scientists kept close and detailed correspondences with each other—compounded these advances."[71] In a sense, invisible colleges represent a historical prototype for the academic leagues that Cole envisions.[72] The metaphor is attributed to the pioneering chemist and natural philosopher Robert Boyle, who coined the term with reference to his peers in the Royal Society of London.[73] Prior to the institutionalization of organized research in universities, the formation of such institutions as the Royal Society and Académie des sciences was critical to scientific and scholarly exchange, which circulated in learned journals that first appeared during the early modern period as well as informally in the salons of the era.[74]

Communities of practice and epistemic communities are essentially knowledge-based social networks.[75] The recognition that firms may be understood as knowledge-centric is implied by their correlation with academic, and especially scientific, research groups.[76] Indeed, firms have been modeled as epistemic communities wherein competitive advantage is a function of collaborative contextual conceptualization of intellectual capital, both explicit and tacit.[77] As organizational theorist David J. Teece characterizes the role of communication in this context: "The essence of the firm is its ability to create, transfer, assemble, integrate, and exploit knowledge assets."[78]

The process of design, or the design process, offers the potential for colleges and universities transitioning to the Fifth Wave to reconceptualize their missions and goals and restructure and recalibrate their organization, operations, and standard operating procedures to more productively advance discovery, creativity, and innovation. Such reconceptualization offers the potential to reveal or create new paradigms for knowledge production and application. Novel transdisciplinary configurations represent institutional experiments that can recalibrate the course of inquiry and enhance the application of research. If academic infrastructure calibrated to the disciplinary orientation of the Fourth Wave proves inadequate to the resolution of large-scale challenges, new units conducive to Fifth Wave approaches must be purpose-built. This is not to suggest that Fourth Wave universities have invariably been constrained in the reorganization of academic frameworks. At a number of major research universities, including Harvard, Columbia, and Stanford, the interdisciplinary ethos has not only taken hold in new large-scale initiatives but has also been expressed architectonically in new buildings designed to facilitate multi- and interdisciplinary collaboration. Inherent design constraints, however, could be termed "teleonomic failures," with *teleonomy* defined by the *Oxford English Dictionary* as the "property common to all living systems of being organized toward the attainment of ends." The applicability of a concept that refers to apparent purpose and goal-directedness in the structures and functions of organisms seems appropriate in this context. Novel aggregations in their inceptions may simply represent best-guess strategic amalgamations, but such reconfigurations offer the potential to lead to unexpected discoveries through serendipity.[79]

The organizational frameworks of the Fifth Wave are sufficiently fluid, flexible, resilient, and capacious to accommodate myriad alternative forms of academic organization including a number of those posited by historian David Staley, who in his recent book, *Alternative Universities,* takes up a challenge issued by British higher education theorist Ronald Barnett to reimagine the contemporary university. "All systems of higher education across the world are moving inexorably in the direction of the marketised university," Barnett contends, alternately terming these forms of organization corporate and bureaucratic. As a consequence, "Ideas of the university in the public domain are hopelessly impoverished." To counter this purported inevitability, Staley points out, Barnett calls for a "new poetics of the university" and envisions a number of speculative academic utopias that he specifies must nevertheless be feasible to implement ("feasible utopias"). Staley himself envisions as many as ten such forms of academic organization, including what he terms the "platform university," which he likens to the Athenian agora because its organization would derive spontaneously and organically; micro-colleges, each consisting of a single professor with twenty students; humanities think tanks, which bring those disciplines to bear on issues of concern to business and industry and governments; nomadic universities, which consist of a sequence of apprenticeships in various local cultures; interface universities, which explore the potential of cognition hybridized with artificial intelligence; the university of the body, which recognizes that cognition is a corporeal process; institutes for advanced play, which explore the role of creativity and imagination in knowledge production; polymath universities, where every student majors in three disparate fields; and the university of the future, where the curriculum straddles pure and applied "futuring." This sort of thought experiment ("concept universities") is an exercise in speculative design, Staley points out, citing the approach advocated by design theorists Anthony Dunne and Fiona Raby. Indeed, design becomes speculative and a form of critique when it envisions alternative futures preferable to the present.[80]

### Fifth Wave Knowledge Production Is Transdisciplinary

Transdisciplinarity is the overarching attribute of Mode 2 knowledge production as well as the dominant organizing principle of institutional design in Fifth Wave knowledge enterprises. A committee of the National Research Council characterizes transdisciplinarity as research that "aims to deeply integrate and also transcend disciplinary approaches to generate fundamentally new conceptual frameworks, theories, models, and applications."[81] An editorial in *Science* framed the imperative for the transdisciplinary collaboration characteristic of the Fifth Wave more than a decade ago: "The time is upon us to recognize that the new frontier is the interface, wherever it remains unexplored. . . . In the years to come, innovators will need to jettison the security of familiar tools, ideas, and specialties as they forge new partnerships."[82] The Fifth Wave seeks to facilitate the expansion of the "seamless web of cognitive influence among the individual disciplines" that for Cole is the hallmark of great universities.[83]

Although the taxonomy of interdisciplinarity remains contested, our usage of the term connotes knowledge production construed as integrative—transcending the spurious dichotomy between research characterized as either fundamental or applied—as well as collaborative, which thus may include researchers from multiple disciplines as well as from outside the academy. The Fifth Wave approach to transdisciplinarity is consistent with its explication by Gibbons and colleagues: "Knowledge which emerges from a particular context of application with its own distinct theoretical structures, research methods, and modes of practice, but which may not be locatable on the prevailing disciplinary map."[84] Moreover, it follows an understanding of the concept as transinstitutional, that is, knowledge production construed as co-production by actors beyond the academy.[85] And because the university is no longer regarded as the sole locus of knowledge production, the criteria for the evaluation of quality in transdisciplinary research become social, political, and economic, as well as disciplinary.[86] Collaboration across transdisciplinary, transinstitutional, and transnational frameworks maximizes the potential to advance knowledge production and innovation in real time and at the scale necessary for the attainment of desired social and economic outcomes.

The sort of effective inter- and transdisciplinary collaboration characteristic of the Fifth Wave requires optimally configured institutional frameworks as well as an academic culture oriented toward innovation. Despite broad consensus regarding the imperative for such collaboration, however, disciplinary acculturation continues to shape successive generations of scientists, scholars, and practitioners, while the traditional correlation between disciplines and departments persists as the basis for academic organization. Even as interdisciplinary collaboration flourishes in contemporary academic practice, persistent disciplinary partitioning represents one of the most pernicious design limitations to the further evolution of knowledge production in the American research university.

Entrenchment in discipline-based departments mirrors an academic culture that prizes individualism over teamwork and the discovery of specialized knowledge over problem-based collaboration. Because Fourth Wave academic culture places a premium on the discovery of new knowledge by individual scientists, less prestige attaches to applied, problem-based collaborative endeavors. The same is true for collaborative execution of projects that advance knowledge through assimilation, synthesis, implementation, and application.[87] Similarly inimical in this context is the assumption that research and scholarship are primarily solitary endeavors and that optimal outcomes inevitably emerge from the amalgamation of individual contributions. As Cook and Brown frame the dilemma: "Not every action by a human collective can be meaningfully or usefully reduced to an account of actions taken by the individuals in them."[88] Academic culture valorizes individual attainment over team collaboration, but, without strategic coordination, the ad hoc aggregation of individual endeavors often fails to transcend the inevitable limitations of an isolated investigator.

The interdisciplinary collaboration characteristic of the Fifth Wave sometimes follows patterns of technological development that are the product of recombinant innovation, which refers to the combination or recombination of existing ideas, products, and processes.[89] Recent analysis of nearly 18 million scientific papers confirms the extent to which new knowledge derives from novel insights into existing knowledge. According to Brian Uzzi and colleagues, "The highest-impact science is primarily grounded in exceptionally conventional combinations of prior work yet simultaneously features an intrusion of unusual combinations." Their assessment suggests that the interdisciplinary collaboration characteristic of team research is especially conducive to innovation and impact: "Teams are 37.7 percent more likely than solo authors to insert novel combinations into familiar knowledge domains."[90] The imperative for the restructuring of academic organization to accommodate the interdisciplinary collaboration characteristic of the Fifth Wave is further attested to by the rapid growth in the percentage of publications contributed by two or more authors.[91] Across all scientific fields, single-author research papers have declined from 30 percent in 1981 to 11 percent in 2012. In some fields, scientific papers now average five authors.[92] In 2013, teams authored 90 percent of papers in science and engineering journals.[93] Although coauthored contributions need not be interdisciplinary, assessments of coauthorship patterns attest to increasing heterogeneity in disciplinary affiliation.[94]

Fifth Wave knowledge production requires the sort of collaborative discovery, creativity, and innovation undertaken by researchers and practitioners from across the spectrum of disciplinary and interdisciplinary fields. "Team research leads to higher quality outcomes and higher impact, compared to individual research," Ben Shneiderman contends. "Teams often produce higher quality research than an individual can because they bring complementary knowledge, skills, and attitudes, take on more ambitious projects, apply diverse research methods, and have larger networks."[95] Although research teams sometimes comprise researchers from within a single disciplinary field,[96] the essential precondition for the majority of effective team endeavors is interdisciplinary collaboration. Indeed, with the exception of research conducted by the sort of singular polymaths whose expertise spans multiple disciplines, interdisciplinary research must generally be construed as research conducted by a team. Conversely, team collaboration is in most instances inevitably interdisciplinary.[97] Research teams representing pluralities of disciplinary perspectives have been conceptualized as interdependent constituent agents that exhibit in their aggregate behavior the characteristics of complex adaptive systems, including nonlinearity, self-organization, and emergence.[98] The distributed cognition inherent in epistemic cultures posited by Karin Knorr Cetina as well as the crowd-sourcing and "cognitive surplus" described by Clay Shirky are relevant in this context.[99]

Recognition of the potential for enhanced productivity and creativity inherent in scientific teamwork is hardly novel,[100] but recent explication has further elucidated still more nuanced appreciation of its operations. The coordination of effort by team practitioners facilitates opportunities for the transmission of tacit knowledge and the application of existing knowledge. Collaborative engagement leverages the tacit dimension to knowledge production, referring in the context of scientific discovery and technological innovation to the exchange of inherent practical understanding of given research problems and methods and associated technologies based on direct experience. Whereas explicit knowledge is readily standardized, codified, and diffused, tacit knowledge is more effectively transmitted through the direct interpersonal communication characteristic of teams.[101] The cognitive diversity characteristic of teams, moreover, correlates with enhanced performance and outcomes.[102]

Among the questions to the Committee on the Science of Team Science in the National Research Council report *Enhancing the Effectiveness of Team Science* is: "What types of organizational structures, policies, practices, and resources are needed to promote effective team science in academic institutions, research centers, industry, and other settings?"[103] A decade earlier, the National Academies report *Facilitating Interdisciplinary Research* emphasized the essential correlation between interdisciplinary collaboration and applied research initiatives that depend for their effectiveness on team efforts. The recommendations of the report prove especially pertinent to institutional design efforts to accommodate the transdisciplinarity critical to Fifth Wave universities, which, consistent with Mode 2 knowledge production, span academic, industry, and government contexts. The report underscores the imperative to "stimulate new modes of inquiry and break down the conceptual and institutional barriers to interdisciplinary research that could yield significant benefits to science and society." Standard operating procedure in industrial and government laboratories, interdisciplinary collaboration in academic settings is essential to applied research initiatives that depend for their effectiveness on team efforts to address intractable challenges on the scale of global climate change and destruction of ecosystems. Such large-scale initiatives comprise "scientists, engineers, social scientists, and humanists . . . addressing complex problems that must be attacked simultaneously with deep knowledge from different perspectives." The report contends that there can be "no question about the productivity and effectiveness of research teams formed of partners with diverse expertise" and recommends "substantial alteration of the traditional academic structures or even replacement with new structures and models to reduce barriers" to interdisciplinary collaboration.[104]

New frameworks are essential because "prevailing academic cultures and structures tend to replicate existing areas of expertise, reward individual effort rather than collaborative work, limit hiring input to a single department in a single school or college, and limit incentives and rewards for interdisciplinary and collaborative work." The report points out that academic careers have historically been forged along disciplinary lines, which define social organization to such an extent that interdisciplinarians often find recognition among peers difficult. No less challenging is recognition by professional associations, business and industry, and most importantly, federal agencies, which in the estimation of the committee remain focused on disciplinary endeavor. Consistent with its call for new structural models, the report underscores the importance of supportive institutional policies: "Whatever their structure, interdisciplinary projects flourish in an environment that allows researchers to communicate, share ideas, and collaborate across disciplines."[105]

Because what has been termed "deep knowledge integration" is among the principal challenges that confront science teams,[106] the concept of convergence is especially relevant in this context. Convergence refers to the increasing integration of the life sciences, physical sciences, mathematical and computational sciences, and fields of engineering, as well as the behavioral and social sciences and arts and humanities. As formulated by a committee convened by the National Research Council, convergence is an approach to research that engenders "comprehensive synthetic frameworks that merge areas of knowledge from multiple fields to address specific challenges." The development of partnerships requisite to scientific investigation is essential to the integration of important "subsets of expertise."[107] An earlier National Science Foundation assessment accordingly considered the unification of scientific disciplines and convergence of technologies with reference to the integration and synergistic recombination of the four domains of nanoscience and nanotechnology; biotechnology and biomedicine, including genetic engineering; information technology, including advanced computing and communications; and, cognitive science, including cognitive neuroscience—collectively termed "NBIC," that is, "nano-bio-info-cogno."[108]

Consistent with the Fifth Wave objective of integrative research that transcends the spurious dichotomy between the categories of fundamental and applied, researchers and administrators from ten research universities formed the HIBAR Research Alliance (HRA) in 2017 to enhance fundamental research excellence in service to society and catalyze the emergence of an academic culture that yields more effective HIBAR research, referring to what is termed "highly integrative basic and responsive" research. HIBAR research transcends the standard linear model of innovation, which, to reiterate a point made in previous chapters, represents the conviction that technological innovation is a process that begins with fundamental research but requires subsequent reorientation toward specific problems that may eventually lead to the development of products and services appropriate to the market.[109] The council guiding the HRA specifies its intent to promote research that integrates basic and applied research in *all four* of the following key ways: (1) the impetus for discovery *with* the intent to solve problems; (2) traditional research *with* creative design; (3) university scientists and scholars working *with* experts and practitioners from business, industry, and government agencies; and (4) long-term objectives *with* a strong sense of urgency. The simultaneous integration of all four of these aspects is not readily accomplished, but the outcomes of research conducted in this manner are extremely generative, which is to say, broadly applicable; thoughtful, visionary, and creative; explanatory, that is, providing valuable understanding; use-inspired, that is, motivated and informed by societal concerns; engaged, that is, conducted in partnership with society; and practical, that is, motivated by the intent to solve practical problems with an appropriate sense of urgency. Although the term HIBAR is fairly new, the approach claims a venerable provenance associated with both what Donald Stokes termed Pasteur's quadrant and the use-inspired basic research of the New American University model.[110]

Because HIBAR research has decreased in recent decades due to the decline of long-term research in industry, the HRA council contends that universities should compensate by expanding their commitment to this approach while improving fundamental research excellence. This will require, among other things, widespread institutional support. Accordingly, the council has called for universities to strive to increase the number of HIBAR projects from an estimated one in twenty at present to one in five within ten years. Transformative collective change in academic culture sufficient to accomplish this objective will require the realization of a critical mass of researchers at major research institutions. Institutional recalibration in this context may be achieved through the effort of distributed networks of cooperating teams, which represent multilevel initiatives for organizational change conceptualized as community-based forms of organization, or what are termed "C-forms." This sort of community architecture is defined by its "(1) fluid, informal peripheral boundaries of membership; (2) significant incorporation of voluntary labor; (3) information-based product output; and (4) significantly open sharing of knowledge." The mobilization of volunteers across the globe to address complex projects in this manner has been likened to the coordination of volunteer effort that produced the initial iteration of the *Oxford English Dictionary* in 1857 and, more recently, the Linux operating system, which was realized in 1991 through the collective efforts of individuals worldwide.[111] Consistent with this approach, members of the academic communities of the ten founding member institutions have formed collaborative action groups to consider recommendations concerning academic incentive structures, relations with funding agencies, dissemination of best practices, and the discovery of new HIBAR research opportunities.[112] Importantly, involvement in these action groups is restricted neither to the founding universities of the HIBAR Research Alliance, nor to university participants.[113] Further, the dissemination of the findings of the alliance will be a collaborative effort undertaken with numerous organizations with compatible interests, including the Association of Public and Land-grant Universities (APLU), Government-University-Industry Research Roundtable (GUIRR), National Academies, and National Academy of Inventors.[114]

## The Trajectory toward Intellectual Bilingualism

Despite its allegiance to Mode 1 disciplinary entrenchment, the academic culture of the Fourth Wave American research university has reluctantly accommodated the groundswell of interdisciplinary, and, more recently, transdisciplinary knowledge production characteristic of Mode 2, which will remain the task of the Fifth Wave to fully institutionalize. Although an entry for the term *interdisciplinarity* did not appear until the second edition of the *Oxford English Dictionary* in 1937, the Social Science Research Council had already expressed its intent in 1934 to prioritize focus on the "inter-discipline or interstitial."[115] In addition, recognition of the potential for enhanced productivity and creativity inherent in the collaboration among disciplines characteristic of scientific teamwork preceded by decades the theoretical explication of interdisciplinarity during the first international conference on the topic at the University of Nice in September 1970, which was organized by the Centre for Educational Research and Innovation (CERI) in collaboration with the Organisation for Economic Co-operation and Development (OECD).[116]

Reconfiguration of academic organization to accommodate interdisciplinarity in the social sciences was evident as early as 1924, with the formation of the Maxwell School of Citizenship and Public Affairs at Syracuse University, which had been established to offer graduate professional education in public administration and international relations and graduate degrees in the social sciences, including political science, economics, and history. A number of institutions conceived novel organizational configurations in the humanities during the 1930s, including Princeton University and Columbia University. In 1941, the University of Chicago formed the acclaimed Committee on Social Thought, instituted by then president Robert M. Hutchins, which promoted broad study in the humanities as well as the social sciences. Since then, numerous programmatic efforts by colleges and universities to establish interdisciplinary programs, reconfigure academic departments, or revise curricula to foster interdisciplinary approaches have met with mixed success. The Program in Modern Thought and Literature at Stanford University, established in 1960, served as a prototype for numerous programs in the humanities that would crop up amid the interdisciplinary ferment of the 1960s and 1970s.

An adequate historical assessment of interdisciplinary momentum in scientific and technological fields lies outside the scope of the present discussion, but an appreciation for antecedents to the contemporary shift to Mode 2 knowledge production in the Fifth Wave could arguably begin with the formation of large-scale multidisciplinary research and development efforts associated with the growth in federal investment in scientific research during World War II. These initiatives included the MIT Radiation Laboratory, active between 1940 and 1945; the Manhattan Project, active between 1942 and 1946; followed by the development of the system of national laboratories, where the "pursuit of large multidisciplinary programs put a premium on . . . the team approach."[117] Basic scientific research conducted in contexts of technological application— the industrial research and development operations at AT&T Bell Labs in the mid-twentieth century, for example[118]—encouraged disciplinary integration and collaborative endeavor. "Team research is the source of some of the great breakthroughs of all time, such as the 1947 invention of the transistor," Shneiderman observes. "It took the complementary skills of an applied researcher, Walter Brattain, a basic researcher in quantum theory, John Bardeen, and the solid-state physicist William Shockley."[119]

But as the central nodes of an integrative discovery and commercialization network, research universities have served as the key institutional actors in the national system of innovation, a concept that embraces the economic, political, and social institutions relevant to knowledge production.[120] The growth in organized research units (ORUs)—interdisciplinary research centers and institutes established by universities to advance basic and applied research distinct from basic academic departments—following World War II has been integral to the ascent to global dominance of the postwar American scientific research enterprise.[121] The impetus toward interdisciplinary collaboration has, by one estimate, led to the establishment of nearly three thousand research centers presently active at twenty-five leading major research universities.[122]

More recently, differentiated institutional configurations explicitly conceived to span disciplinary boundaries attest to the potential for alternative academic platforms to advance collaborative engagement. An interdisciplinary think tank modeled on the Institute for Advanced Study in Princeton, the Zentrum für interdisziplinäre Forschung (ZiF), or Center for Interdisciplinary Research, for example, serves as the nucleus of Universität Bielefeld in Germany, which was established in 1969 and conceived interdisciplinarily from its inception.[123] To cite but a single example of an independent interdisciplinary research institute spanning the natural and social sciences, the Santa Fe Institute, established in 1984, has brought together a community of scholars that has produced groundbreaking theoretical approaches to the study of complex adaptive systems. In the twenty-first century, a number of major research institutions, including University College London, have sought to reconfigure their research enterprises based on transdisciplinary "grand challenge" themes.

The flexible academic frameworks of the Fifth Wave have the potential to accommodate the novel epistemological reconfigurations of postmodern knowledge production, which threatens to destabilize the analytical constructs and pretense to certainty associated with our academic culture. Antidisciplinarity, for example, refers to academic output that transcends Simon's categories of natural and artificial and is generated without reference to disciplinary categorization. As Joichi Ito, director of the MIT Media Lab, put it: "Antidisciplinary research is akin to the famous observation by mathematician Stanislaw Ulam that the study of nonlinear physics is like the study of 'non-elephant animals,'" the upshot being that antidisciplinarity is "all about the non-elephant animals." Alternatively, he proposes that knowledge could be conceptualized as a sheet of white paper peppered with small black dots, each of which represents an academic discipline: "The massive amount of white space between the dots represents antidisciplinary space."[124] The proposition that knowledge production may emanate from this negative ground suggests the need for new approaches to understanding our world. Although we may be "empowered by the tools of the Enlightenment," according to inventor and computer scientist Danny Hillis, in this post-modern era we have entered the Age of Entanglement. For Hillis, the digitization of knowledge is simply a manifestation of residual "Enlightenment exuberance." He contends that computers are the "cathedrals of the Enlightenment, the ultimate expression of logical deterministic control." But our very technological mastery now threatens to bring us into an equivocal relationship to the products of our own ingenuity: "Instead of being masters of our creations, we have learned to bargain with them, cajoling and guiding them in the general direction of our goals." Our knowledge—the "currency of the Enlightenment"—has wrought a second nature: "We have built our own jungle, and it has a life of its own." What he terms the final blow to the Enlightenment will come when artificial intelligence permits "our machines to surpass us, to shape the world and themselves in ways that we never could have imagined." But what he terms this "brave new world" offers new opportunities, beginning with the implications of the recognition that the duality between humanity and nature is illusory: "We can no longer see ourselves as separate from the natural world—or our technology—but as a part of them, integrated, codependent, and entangled." Whereas in the wake of the Enlightenment, "progress was analytic and came from taking things apart," for example, "progress in the Age of Entanglement is synthetic and comes from putting things together. Instead of classifying organisms, we construct them. Instead of discovering new worlds, we create them." If we are indeed "governed neither by the mysteries of nature or the logic of science, but by the magic of their entanglement," then we must seek new ways of understanding this new reality.[125]

If indeed we are to navigate the negative ground of antidisciplinarity, we must first chart a map and perhaps devise an appropriate compass. Toward this end, designer and architect Neri Oxman, a faculty member in the MIT Media Lab, proposes a model for academic output and creative expression that she terms the "Krebs cycle of creativity" (KCC). A term borrowed from biochemistry, the Krebs cycle refers to the metabolic pathway or sequence of reactions through which organisms generate energy. Oxman seeks to represent the antidisciplinary hypothesis, which holds that disciplinary boundaries are illusory because knowledge is wholly entangled, with a map for creative exploration comprising four domains, or modalities: (1) science, (2) engineering, (3) design, and (4) art. The goal, as she formulates it, is to "establish a tentative, yet holistic, cartography of the interrelation between these domains, where one realm can incite (r)evolution inside another, and where a single individual or project can reside in multiple domains." She derives her model from fellow designer John Maeda, who correlated specialized missions with each of the quadrants: science correlates with exploration, engineering with invention, design with communication, and art with expression. Oxman posits a dynamic relationship between these interrelated and complementary domains that is analogous to the metabolic pathway of the Krebs cycle, which, through the oxidation of nutrients, perpetually produces chemical energy. "In this analogy, the four modalities of human creativity—science, engineering, design, and art—replace the carbon compounds of the Krebs cycle. Each of the modalities (or compounds) produces currency by transferring into another." With reference to the conversions: science converts information into knowledge; engineering converts scientific knowledge into utility; design converts utility into behavior; art questions behavior and converts it back into new perceptions. At this Cinderella moment, as she puts it, "new perception inspires new scientific exploration" and "all silos coalesce (back) into the Pangea of information." In this "quantum entanglement," particles can only be discerned en masse. "If Enlightenment was the salad, Entanglement is the soup."[126]

Ito proposes that the Krebs cycle of creativity represents a suitable model for rethinking academic practice. He calls for academic institutions everywhere to follow the example of MITx and edX and make knowledge freely available online. He recommends interaction and collaboration both within academia and across all sectors to "create a vehicle for the exchange of ideas that allows all those working in the antidisciplinary space . . . to challenge existing academic silos." Among his other recommendations: a "new antidisciplinary journal with an open collaborative model of interaction" that might bypass the strictures of the formal peer-review system to tackle the grand challenges that confront humanity at this juncture. The dynamic of the status quo, he points out, is "learning more and more about less and less" and a hyperspecialization that obstructs collaboration and occludes communication.[127] The Fifth Wave certainly accords with these recommendations and seeks to facilitate fluid movement between the domains of creative expression charted by Oxman as well as their entanglement.

Although it is our intention to suggest an approach to institutional design that may be globally applicable among major research institutions, the restructuring of academic organization to facilitate the transition toward the Fifth Wave is a process that in each case must necessarily be approached as sui generis. The sequence of deliberations and decisions associated with the design process cannot readily be codified into a lexicon of tactics and strategies generally applicable to other institutional contexts. And while the potential of such traits of Mode 2 knowledge production as transdisciplinarity appear to be validated by increasingly broad advocacy within academic culture, the modus operandi of Mode 1 remains the epistemological, social, and administrative foundation of Fourth Wave research universities. The fundamental challenge remains for institutions to advance discovery, creativity, and innovation, and through these processes produce students who are adaptive master learners empowered to integrate a broad array of interrelated disciplines and negotiate the changing workforce demands of the knowledge economy.

The inter- and transdisciplinary reconfiguration of knowledge production characteristic of the Fifth Wave consolidates and gives institutional expression to currents in intellectual culture evident across the past several centuries. But if the Fifth Wave is to advance collaborative innovation, the debate must engage a broad community of disciplines as well as the wisdom and expertise developed in commerce, industry, and government. The maintenance of strict disciplinary boundaries still prevalent in the Fourth Wave undermines the impetus to initiate conversations with those outside one's own sphere of disciplinary expertise. Scientists, scholars, and practitioners from disparate domains of knowledge must cultivate "interlanguages" intelligible to other disciplines—not unlike the pidgins or creoles through which different subcultures negotiate trading zones.[128] Stefan Collini aptly frames this imperative as the "intellectual equivalent of bilingualism," which he defines as a "capacity not only to exercise the language of our respective specialisms, but also to attend to, learn from, and eventually contribute to, wider cultural conversations."[129] Our collective survival as a species may be contingent on our capacity to collaborate across disciplinary boundaries, which assumes the continued evolution of knowledge enterprises optimally designed to foster mutual intelligibility among academic disciplines and interdisciplinary fields.

## Notes

1. Herbert A. Simon, *Administrative Behavior: A Study of the Decision-Making Processes in Administrative Organizations*, 4th ed. (New York: Free Press, 1997), 360.

2. Helga Nowotny, Peter Scott, and Michael Gibbons, "Mode 2 Revisited: The New Production of Knowledge," *Minerva* 41 (2003): 186.

3. Henry Etzkowitz, *The Triple Helix: University-Industry-Government Innovation in Action* (New York: Routledge, 2008), 4.

4. Ann M. Pendleton-Jullian and John Seely Brown, *Design Unbound: Designing for Emergence in a White Water World* (Cambridge, MA: MIT Press, 2018), 1:43.

5. *Oxford English Dictionary (OED)*, 3rd ed. (Oxford: Oxford University Press, 2012), online version accessed May 2018, s.v. "agency."

6. Pendleton-Jullian and Brown, *Design Unbound*, 1:vi, 26; 2:437, 439.

7. John F. Padgett and Walter W. Powell, *The Emergence of Organizations and Markets* (Princeton, NJ: Princeton University Press, 2012), 1–2.

8. John F. Padgett, "Evolvability of Organizations and Institutions," in *Complexity and Evolution: Toward a New Synthesis for Economics*, ed. David Wilson, Jr. and Alan Kirman (Cambridge, MA: MIT Press, 2016), 190–191.

9. Padgett and Powell, *The Emergence of Organizations and Markets*, 1–2.

10. Pendleton-Jullian and Brown, *Design Unbound*, 1:75.

11. Philip Kitcher, *Science, Truth, and Democracy* (Oxford: Oxford University Press, 2001), 109, 113.

12. A. Hunter Dupree, *Science in the Federal Government: A History of Policies and Activities to 1940* (Baltimore: Johns Hopkins University Press, 1986), 9.

13. Alvin I. Goldman, *Knowledge in a Social World* (Oxford: Clarendon Press, 1999); Alvin I. Goldman, "A Guide to Social Epistemology," in *Social Epistemology: Essential Readings*, ed. Alvin I. Goldman and Dennis Whitcomb (Oxford: Oxford University Press, 2011).

14. David C. Mowery and Nathan Rosenberg, "The U.S. National Innovation System," in *National Innovation Systems: A Comparative Analysis*, ed. Richard R. Nelson (Oxford: Oxford University Press, 1993), 29–75.

15. Alan Wilson, *Knowledge Power: Interdisciplinary Education for a Complex World* (London: Routledge, 2010).

16. Goldman, *Knowledge in a Social World*.

17. John Seely Brown, Allan Collins, and Paul Duguid, "Situated Cognition and the Culture of Learning," *Educational Researcher* 18, no. 1 (January–February 1989): 33.

18. Mark S. Peacock, "Path Dependence in the Production of Scientific Knowledge," *Social Epistemology* 23, no. 2 (2009): 105–124.

19. Mitchell L. Stevens and Benjamin Gebre-Medhin, "Association, Service, Market: Higher Education in American Political Development," *Annual Review of Sociology* 42 (2016): 131–132.

20. Anthony Giddens, *The Constitution of Society: Outline of the Theory of Structuration* (Berkeley: University of California Press, 1984).

21. Ian Hacking, *Historical Ontology* (Cambridge, MA: Harvard University Press, 2002), 5. See Thomas S. Kuhn, *The Structure of Scientific Revolutions*, 50th anniv. ed. (1962; Chicago: University of Chicago Press, 2012).

22. John Seely Brown and Paul Duguid, "Organizational Learning and Communities-of-Practice: Toward a Unified View of Working, Learning, and Innovation," *Organization Science* 2, no. 1 (1991): 40.

23. Andrew Abbott, *The System of Professions: An Essay on the Division of Expert Labor* (Chicago: University of Chicago Press, 1988), 321.

24. Richard Rorty, "Philosophy as a Transitional Genre," in *Pragmatism, Critique, Judgment: Essays for Richard J. Bernstein*, ed. Seyla Benhabib and Nancy Fraser (Cambridge, MA: MIT Press, 2004), 3–28.

25. Philip Kitcher, "Epistemology without History Is Blind," *Erkenntnis* 75, no. 3 (2011): 505–524.

26. Clark A. Miller and Tischa A. Muñoz-Erickson, *The Rightful Place of Science: Designing Knowledge* (Tempe, AZ: Consortium for Science, Policy & Outcomes, 2018), 2–4.

27. Michael Gibbons et al., *The New Production of Knowledge: The Dynamics of Science and Research in Contemporary Societies* (London: Sage, 1994), 1, 140, 167.

28. See, for example, Michael T. Hannan and John Freeman, "The Population Ecology of Organizations," *American Journal of Sociology* 82, no. 5 (1977): 929–964; Michael T. Hannan and John Freeman, *Organizational Ecology* (Cambridge, MA: Harvard University Press, 1989). For introductory overviews of organizational change, see W. Warner Burke, *Organization Change: Theory and Practice*, 4th ed. (Los Angeles: Sage, 2014) and Christiane Demers, *Organizational Change Theories: A Synthesis* (Los Angeles: Sage, 2007).

29. John Ziman, ed., *Technological Innovation as an Evolutionary Process* (Cambridge: Cambridge University Press, 2000).

30. Frederick P. Brooks, *The Design of Design: Essays from a Computer Scientist* (Boston: Addison-Wesley, 2010), 53.

31. Derrick M. Anderson and Andrew Whitford, "The Institutional Design Frontiers of Publicness and University Performance," *Public Administration Review* 76, no. 5 (September/October 2016): 753.

32. Howard E. Aldrich and Jeffrey Pfeffer, "Environments of Organizations," *Annual Review of Sociology* 2 (1976): 79–105.

33. Elaine Romanelli and Michael L. Tushman, "Organizational Transformation as Punctuated Equilibrium," *Academy of Management Journal* 37, no. 5 (1994): 1141–1166; see also C. J. G. Gersick, "Revolutionary Change Theories: A Multilevel Exploration of

the Punctuated Equilibrium Paradigm," *Academy of Management Review* 16, no. 1: 10–36; Karl E. Weick and Robert E. Quinn, "Organizational Change and Development," *Annual Review of Psychology* 50 (1999): 361–386.

34. Herbert A. Simon, *The Sciences of the Artificial,* 3rd ed. (1966; Cambridge, MA: MIT Press, 1996), 3, 5, 111.

35. Richard Buchanan, "Myth and Maturity: Toward a New Order in the Decade of Design," *Design Issues* 6, no. 2 (1990), 78, quoted by Prasad Boradkar, "Design as Problem Solving," in *The Oxford Handbook of Interdisciplinarity*, ed. Robert Frodeman, Julie Thompson Klein, and Carl Mitcham (Oxford: Oxford University Press, 2010), 273.

36. Simon, *Sciences of the Artificial*, 54, 106, 195.

37. Simon, *Sciences of the Artificial*, 2, 138.

38. Daniel J. Huppatz, "Revisiting Herbert Simon's 'Science of Design,'" *Design Issues* 31, no. 2 (Spring 2015): 29. Although the conception of design as scientific problem solving proposed by Simon remains seminal to contemporary theory, Huppatz points out that some early proponents of his approach came to perceive it as technocratic and lament its apparent "repression of judgment, intuition, experience, and social interaction." According to one critic, "For Simon the key to design lies in translating substantive decisions about goals and values into technical decisions about efficiency." Frank Fischer, *Technocracy and the Politics of Expertise* (Los Angeles: Sage, 1990), 288, quoted by Huppatz, "Revisiting Herbert Simon's 'Science of Design,'" 37.

39. Richard Buchanan, "Wicked Problems in Design Thinking," *Design Issues* 8, no. 2 (Spring 1992): 6, 19–21. Buchanan elaborates: "Throughout Western culture, the liberal arts have similarly been described as 'architectonic' because of their integrative capacity" (6n3).

40. Buchanan, "Wicked Problems in Design Thinking," 6, 19–21.

41. Huppatz, "Revisiting Herbert Simon's 'Science of Design,'" 29, 35.

42. "A competent designer can always improve upon last year's new widget, but an interdisciplinary team of skilled design thinkers is in a position to tackle more complex problems," observes Tim Brown. For an overview of design thinking, see his *Change by Design: How Design Thinking Transforms Organizations and Inspires Innovation* (New York: Harper Collins, 2009), 6–7.

43. Bruce Mau and Jennifer Leonard, *Massive Change* (London: Phaidon Press, 2004), 16–17.

44. Prasad Boradkar, "Design as Problem Solving," in *The Oxford Handbook of Interdisciplinarity*, ed. Robert Frodeman, Julie Thompson Klein, and Carl Mitcham (Oxford: Oxford University Press, 2010), 274.

45. Horst W. J. Rittel and Melvin W. Webber, "Dilemmas in a General Theory of Planning," *Policy Sciences* 4, no. 2 (June 1973): 155–169.

46. Buchanan, "Wicked Problems in Design Thinking," 14–17, 20–21.

47. Buchanan, "Wicked Problems in Design Thinking," 9–10.

48. Barry Bozeman, *All Organizations Are Public: Comparing Public and Private Organizations* (Washington, DC: Beard Books, 2004).

49. Ralph F. Shangraw and Michael M. Crow, "Public Administration as a Design Science," *International Journal of Public Administration* 21, no. 6–8 (1998): 1059–1077.

50. Michael M. Crow and Ralph F. Shangraw, "Revisiting 'Public Administration as a Design Science' for the Twenty-First Century Public University," *Public Administration Review* 76, no. 2 (2016): 762–763.

51. Jonathan R. Cole, *The Great American University: Its Rise to Preeminence, Its Indispensable National Role, and Why It Must Be Protected* (New York: Public Affairs, 2009), 67.

52. Émile Durkheim, *Education and Society*, trans. Sherwood D. Fox (1922; Glencoe, IL: Free Press, 1956), 65, quoted in Burton R. Clark, "Development of the Sociology of Higher Education," in *Sociology of Higher Education: Contributions and Their Contexts*, ed. Patricia J. Gumport (Baltimore: Johns Hopkins University Press, 2007), 5.

53. Neil Smelser, *Dynamics of the Contemporary University: Growth, Accretion, and Conflict* (Berkeley: University of California Press, 2013), 14.

54. Richard R. Nelson and Sidney G. Winter, *An Evolutionary Theory of Economic Change* (Cambridge, MA: Belknap Press of Harvard University Press, 1984), 9–10.

55. Anthony Downs, *Inside Bureaucracy* (Boston: Little, Brown, 1967), 8.

56. Michael M. Crow and William B. Dabars, *Designing the New American University* (Baltimore: Johns Hopkins University Press, 2015), 116–117.

57. Jason Owen-Smith, *Research Universities and the Public Good: Discovery for an Uncertain Future* (Stanford: Stanford University Press, 2018), 31.

58. William G. Tierney and Michael Lanford, "Conceptualizing Innovation in Higher Education," in *Higher Education: Handbook of Theory and Research*, vol. 31, ed. M. B. Paulsen (New York: Springer, 2016), 1–3.

59. Paul J. DiMaggio and Walter W. Powell, "The Iron Cage Revisited: Institutional Isomorphism and Collective Rationality in Organizational Fields," *American Sociological Review* 48, no. 2 (1983): 147–149, 150–152.

60. Michael T. Hannan and John Freeman, "Structural Inertia and Organizational Change," *American Sociological Review* 49 (April 1984): 151.

61. Immanuel Wallerstein, "Anthropology, Sociology, and Other Dubious Disciplines," *Current Anthropology* 44, no. 4 (August–October 2003): 453–465.

62. Andrew Abbott, *Chaos of Disciplines* (Chicago: University of Chicago Press, 2001), 126–128.

63. Louis Menand, *The Marketplace of Ideas: Reform and Resistance in the American University* (New York: W. W. Norton, 2010), 105.

64. John V. Lombardi, *How Universities Work* (Baltimore: Johns Hopkins University Press, 2013), 47, quoted in David J. Staley, *Alternative Universities: Speculative Design for Innovation in Higher Education* (Baltimore: Johns Hopkins University Press, 2019), 12–21.

65. Walter W. Powell, "Expanding the Scope of Institutional Analysis," in *The New Institutionalism in Organizational Analysis*, ed. Walter W. Powell and Paul J. DiMaggio (Chicago: University of Chicago Press, 1991), 183, 190–193. For the final quotation, Powell

cites Barbara Levitt and James G. March, "Organizational Learning," *Annual Review of Sociology* 14 (1988): 319–340.

66. Scott D. N. Cook and John Seely Brown, "Bridging Epistemologies: The Generative Dance between Organizational Knowledge and Organizational Knowing," *Organization Science* 10, no. 4 (July–August 1999): 383, 386–388. Italics appear in the original. With reference to the discussion in chapter 5, the "epistemology of possession" roughly corresponds to what Joel Mokyr terms "propositional knowledge," while the "epistemology of practice" is somewhat analogous to "prescriptive knowledge." These usages thus correspond to what Mokyr identifies as the distinction between knowledge "what," referring to beliefs about natural phenomena, and knowledge "how," referring to techniques. In as sense these follow the distinction between *episteme* and *techne*. See Joel Mokyr, *The Gifts of Athena: Historical Origins of the Knowledge Economy* (Princeton, NJ: Princeton University Press, 2002), 4.

67. Henry Etzkowitz, *The Triple Helix: University-Industry-Government Innovation in Action* (New York: Routledge, 2008).

68. John Hagel, John Seely Brown, and Lang Davison, *The Power of Pull: How Small Moves, Smartly Made, Can Set Big Things in Motion* (New York: Basic Books, 2010), 7, 11, 73.

69. Caroline Winterer, *American Enlightenments: Pursuing Happiness in the Age of Reason* (New Haven, CT: Yale University Press, 2016). See also Dena Goodman, *The Republic of Letters: A Cultural History of the French Enlightenment* (Ithaca, NY: Cornell University Press, 1996).

70. Robert Darnton, "Google and the Future of Books," *New York Review of Books* (February 12, 2009).

71. Mokyr, *Gifts of Athena*, 56.

72. Jonathan R. Cole, *Toward a More Perfect University* (New York: Public Affairs, 2016), 171–183.

73. Derek J. de Solla Price, *Little Science, Big Science, and Beyond* (1963; New York: Columbia University Press, 1986).

74. Roger Hahn, *The Anatomy of a Scientific Institution: The Paris Academy of Sciences, 1666–1803* (Berkeley: University of California Press, 1971).

75. Etienne Wenger, *Communities of Practice: Learning, Meaning, and Identity* (Cambridge: Cambridge University Press, 1998); Hugh T. Miller and Charles J. Fox, "The Epistemic Community," *Administration and Society* 32, no. 6 (2001): 668–685.

76. Henry Etzkowitz, "Research Groups as Quasi-Firms: The Invention of the Entrepreneurial University," *Research Policy* 32 (2003): 109–121.

77. Lars Håkanson, "The Firm as an Epistemic Community: The Knowledge-Based View Revisited," *Industrial and Corporate Change* 19, no. 6 (2010): 1801–1828.

78. David J. Teece, "Knowledge and Competence as Strategic Assets," in *Handbook on Knowledge Management,* ed. C. W. Holsapple (Berlin: Springer Verlag, 2003), 1:149.

79. Robert K. Merton and Elinor Barber, *The Travels and Adventures of Serendipity: A Study in Sociological Semantics and the Sociology of Science* (Princeton, NJ: Princeton University Press, 2004).

80. Staley, *Alternative Universities*, 12–21; Ronald Barnett, *Imagining the University* (London: Routledge, 2013), 1, 13; Anthony Dunne and Fiona Raby, *Speculative Everything: Design, Fiction, and Social Dreaming* (Cambridge, MA: MIT Press, 2013), 9, 33–36.

81. National Research Council, *Enhancing the Effectiveness of Team Science*, ed. Nancy J. Cooke and Margaret L. Hilton (Washington, DC: National Academies Press, 2015), 5–6.

82. F. C. Kafatos and T. Eisner, "Unification in the Century of Biology," *Science* 303 (February 27, 2004): 1257.

83. Cole, *The Great American University*, 5.

84. Gibbons et al., *New Production of Knowledge*, 168.

85. Robert Frodeman, *Sustainable Knowledge: A Theory of Interdisciplinarity* (Basingstoke, UK: Palgrave Macmillan, 2014), 16.

86. Peter Weingart, "A Short History of Knowledge Formations," in *The Oxford Handbook of Interdisciplinarity*, ed. Robert Frodeman, Julie Thompson Klein, and Carl Mitcham (Oxford: Oxford University Press, 2010), 12.

87. Richard R. Nelson et al., "How Medical Know-how Progresses," *Research Policy* 40 (2010): 1339–1344.

88. Cook and Brown, "Bridging Epistemologies," 399n8.

89. W. Brian Arthur, *The Nature of Technology: What It Is and How It Evolves* (New York: Free Press, 2009), 21, 122, the latter cited in Erik Brynjolfsson and Andrew McAfee, *The Second Machine Age: Work, Progress, and Prosperity in a Time of Brilliant Technologies* (New York: W. W. Norton, 2014), 79.

90. Brian Uzzi et al., "Atypical Combinations and Scientific Impact," *Science* 342 (October 25, 2013): 468.

91. Stefan Wuchty, Benjamin F. Jones, and Brian Uzzi, "The Increasing Dominance of Teams in Production of Knowledge," *Science* 316 (May 18, 2007): 1036–1039.

92. Paul Voosen, "Microbiology Leaves the Solo Author Behind," *Chronicle of Higher Education* (November 11, 2013).

93. National Research Council, *Enhancing the Effectiveness of Team Science*, 19.

94. Alan L. Porter et al., "Measuring Researcher Interdisciplinarity," *Scientometrics* 72, no. 1 (2007): 117–147.

95. Ben Shneiderman, *The New ABCs of Research: Achieving Breakthrough Collaborations* (Oxford: Oxford University Press, 2016), 157–158.

96. Kara L. Hall et al., "Moving the Science of Team Science Forward: Collaboration and Creativity," *American Journal of Preventive Medicine* 35 (2008): S243–S249.

97. Stephen M. Fiore, "Interdisciplinarity as Teamwork: How the Science of Teams Can Inform Team Science," *Small Group Research* 39, no. 3 (2008): 251.

98. John H. Miller and Scott E. Page, *Complex Adaptive Systems: An Introduction to Computational Models of Social Life* (Princeton, NJ: Princeton University Press, 2007); S. W. J. Kozlowski and K. J. Klein, "A Multilevel Approach to Theory and Research in Organizations: Contextual, Temporal, and Emergent Processes," in K. J. Klein and S. W. J. Kozlowski, eds., *Multilevel Theory, Research, and Methods in Organizations:*

*Foundations, Extensions, and New Directions* (San Francisco: Jossey-Bass, 2000), cited in National Research Council, *Enhancing the Effectiveness of Team Science*, 54.

99. Karin Knorr Cetina, *Epistemic Cultures: How the Sciences Make Knowledge* (Cambridge, MA: Harvard University Press, 1999); Clay Shirky, *Cognitive Surplus: Creativity and Generosity in a Connected Age* (New York: Penguin, 2010).

100. George P. Bush and Lowell H. Hattery, "Teamwork and Creativity in Research," *Administrative Science Quarterly* 1, no. 3 (December 1956): 361–372.

101. Eric Von Hippel, "Sticky Information and the Locus of Problem Solving: Implications for Innovation," *Management Science* 40, no. 4 (1994): 429–439.

102. Lu Hong and Scott E. Page, "Groups of Diverse Problem-Solvers Can Outperform Groups of High-Ability Problem Solvers," *Proceedings of the National Academy of Sciences* 101, no. 46 (2004): 16385–16389.

103. National Research Council, *Enhancing the Effectiveness of Team Science*, 3

104. National Academies Committee on Facilitating Interdisciplinary Research (CFIR) and Committee on Science, Engineering, and Public Policy (COSEPUP), *Facilitating Interdisciplinary Research* (Washington, DC: National Academies Press, 2005), ix, xi, 17.

105. National Academies CFIR and COSEPUP, *Facilitating Interdisciplinary Research,* ix–xi, 1–6, 149–170.

106. National Research Council, *Enhancing the Effectiveness of Team Science*, 5.

107. National Research Council, *Convergence: Facilitating Transdisciplinary Integration of Life Sciences, Physical Sciences, Engineering, and Beyond* (Washington, DC: National Academies Press, 2014), 17.

108. M. C. Roco and W. S. Bainbridge, eds., *Converging Technologies for Improving Human Performance: Nanotechnology, Biotechnology, Information Technology, and Cognitive Science* (Washington, DC: National Science Foundation, 2002).

109. Venkatesh Narayanamurti and Toluwalogo Odumosu, *Cycles of Invention and Discovery: Rethinking the Endless Frontier* (Cambridge, MA: Harvard University Press, 2016), 27–30.

110. Donald E. Stokes, *Pasteur's Quadrant: Basic Science and Technological Innovation* (Washington, DC: Brookings Institution Press, 1997), 72–75.

111. Marc-David Seidel et al., "The Distributed Network of Cooperating Teams (DNCT): A Multi-Level Initiative for Organizational Change" (August 6, 2017), DOI: 10.14288/1.0354236; Marc-David Seidel and Katherine J. Stewart, "An Initial Description of the C-Form," *Communities and Organization: Research in the Sociology of Organizations* 33 (2011): 37–72.

112. HIBAR Research Alliance, "The HIBAR Research Alliance for Greater University Research Impact" (December 11, 2018), https://hibar-research.org. Alliance member institutions are Arizona State University; Brandeis University; University of British Columbia; University of California, Davis; University of California, Los Angeles; University of California, San Diego; University of Idaho; University of Maryland; University of South Florida; and Washington State University.

113. See www.hibar-research.org, accessed July 11, 2019.

114. Lorne Whitehead, Scott Slovic, and Janet Nelson, "Reinvigorating HIBAR Research for the Twenty-First Century: Enhancing Fundamental Research Excellence in Service to Society," *Technology and Innovation: Journal of the National Academy of Inventors* (in press).

115. Abbott, *Chaos of Disciplines*, 131–132.

116. Bush and Hattery, "Teamwork and Creativity in Research," 361–372; Léo Apostel et al., eds., *Interdisciplinarity: Problems of Teaching and Research in Universities* (Paris: Organisation for Economic Co-operation and Development/Center for Educational Research and Innovation, 1972).

117. Peter J. Westwick, *The National Labs: Science in an American System, 1947–1974* (Cambridge, MA: Harvard University Press, 2003), 28, 65.

118. Daniel Sarewitz, "Saving Science," *The New Atlantis: A Journal of Technology and Society* 49 (Spring/Summer 2016): 5–40.

119. Shneiderman, *New ABCs of Research*, 157.

120. Michael M. Crow and Barry Bozeman, *Limited by Design: R&D Laboratories in the U.S. National Innovation System* (New York: Columbia University Press, 1998).

121. Roger L. Geiger, "Organized Research Units: Their Role in the Development of University Research," *Journal of Higher Education* 61, no. 1 (January/February 1990): 1–19.

122. Jerry A. Jacobs, *In Defense of Disciplines: Interdisciplinarity and Specialization in the Research University* (Chicago: University of Chicago Press, 2013), 91.

123. Ipke Wachsmuth, "ZiF (Zentrum für interdisziplinäre Forschung/Center for Interdisciplinary Research)," in *The Oxford Handbook of Interdisciplinarity*, ed. Robert Frodeman, Julie Thompson Klein, and Carl Mitcham (Oxford: Oxford University Press, 2010), 292–293.

124. Joichi Ito, "Design and Science: Can Design Advance Science, and Can Science Advance Design?" *Journal of Design and Science* (November 21, 2017).

125. W. Daniel Hillis, "The Enlightenment Is Dead, Long Live the Entanglement," *Journal of Design and Science* (February 22, 2016), DOI: 10.21428/1a042043.

126. Neri Oxman, "Age of Entanglement," *Journal of Design and Science* (January 23, 2016).

127. Ito, "Design and Science."

128. Peter Galison, *Image and Logic: A Material Culture of Physics* (Chicago: University of Chicago Press, 1997), 48.

129. Stefan Collini, introduction to C. P. Snow, *The Two Cultures* (Cambridge: Cambridge University Press, 1998), viii.

# SEVEN

# Some Comparative Perspective on Accessibility and Excellence

The same nexus of socioeconomic, cultural, and demographic determinants that prompts the emergence of the Fifth Wave in the United States has brought reform efforts in higher education to the forefront of policy discussions throughout the world. It is essential, however, to underscore the distinction between government initiatives that as a primary goal seek to advance research output and knowledge production, which to some extent generally seek to emulate the structures and operations of the set of American research universities, and those intended to expand access to greater proportions of respective populations. From the standpoint of the Fifth Wave, to reiterate the point yet again, mere access to standardized forms of instruction decoupled from discovery and knowledge production will not deliver desired societal outcomes. As Philip G. Altbach explains, "Most of the world's universities are mainly teaching institutions (in developing countries virtually all are in this category) that must look elsewhere to obtain new knowledge and analysis." He underscores that the "rest of the system lies on the periphery of the research centers."[1] In China and Russia, for example, state-sponsored quality assurance and academic excellence initiatives aim primarily at the formation of sets of globally competitive research universities designed to bolster innovation and economic development, which have been characterized, respectively, as the Chinese and Russian Ivy Leagues.[2] But in many emerging economies, the transition from the elite to the mass to the universal phases of higher education that Martin Trow delineates, the imperative to accommodate the hyperexpansion of student cohorts that Evan Schofer and John Meyer document, and the attendant patterns of "massification" that Michael Gibbons and colleagues identify inevitably compete with intentions to develop research-grade academic platforms.[3] As economist Martin Carnoy and a group of colleagues put it: "The effort to establish 'world-class' universities, particularly in China and Russia . . . is partly driven by national states wanting to emulate the United States' innovation and technology-led growth and partly by the ideological value in their own countries of having such universities."[4]

"Mass higher education had become the international norm by the end of the twentieth century," Altbach observes, although many industrialized nations report enrollments exceeding half of age cohorts. Initiatives to address this imperative have in some instances been compelled by government decree: "In many countries, mass higher education has been forced on universities," Altbach explains. "In much of Europe, access is guaranteed by law or tradition to students who successfully complete their secondary-school examinations; growing numbers passed these examinations and chose to enter the universities. Governments in general did not, however, provide the funding needed to support a quality education for all these students, and as a result, the conditions of study have deteriorated."[5]

Simon Marginson perceives three tendencies in higher education globally that interrelate according to national contexts: "The first tendency is mass-scale growth, or 'massification'; the second is the intensification of competition between institutions and the adoption of business-like features, marketization, under the influence of neoliberal policies; the third is the partial global integration and convergence between national systems, or globalization." Ambivalence regarding the implications of globalization and marketization within academic culture sometimes outweighs determination to address growth in participation, he points out, but "massification is monumental in scale and the most universal of the three tendencies." National systems of higher education that enroll more than 50 percent of respective age cohorts are termed high participation systems by Marginson and colleagues Brendan Cantwell and Anna Smolentseva, which corresponds to the designation *universal* by Trow, who had termed participation beyond 15 percent *mass* higher education and participation beyond 50 percent *universal*.[6]

Programmatic efforts at reform thus inevitably confront the dilemma of whether to undertake systemic efforts to broaden accessibility because of generalized awareness of the positive societal impacts of well-educated citizens or to advance knowledge production and innovation among an elite cohort of institutions to boost economic development.[7] The advancement of research and development operationalized within the framework of comprehensive knowledge production that includes the liberal arts, however, predominantly correlates to the elite phase of higher education that Trow described.[8] In effect, this amounts to reinvigorating research-intensive academic platforms or, where none particularly exist, establishing the conditions for discovery and innovation de novo.

The reinvigoration—or construction from scratch—of research-grade academic platforms invariably begins with the emulation of the structures, operations, and practices of the set of American research universities. This approach stems in large part from the perception that this set of institutions represents a uniquely successful model, which, because it integrates undergraduate and graduate education with knowledge production and research and development, contributes to societal advancement, economic growth, and national competitiveness. From the perspectives of ruling elites, the United States offers what by general consensus is held to be the definitive model for higher education, which, in a global context, implicitly refers to the set of Fourth Wave research universities. Replication of the academic culture of this set of heterogeneous institutions is not easily accomplished by fiat, however. Efforts to derive a "blueprint for greatness" require a nuanced appreciation of the structure and dynamics of the American model, as Jonathan Cole points out,[9] and could easily falter if in some cases participants from diverse national cultures are not sufficiently attuned to the competitive basis of innovation.[10]

The United States is hardly unique among nations in confronting the need to reconcile the frameworks of the elite, mass, and universal phases of higher education coupled with the imperative to advance knowledge production and innovation. But the Fifth Wave model is unique in its potential to offer accessibility to world-class research-grade platforms at a scale commensurate to enrollment demand coupled with research agendas dedicated to desired societal outcomes. As we underscore throughout these chapters, the same competitive ecosystem that forged the Fourth Wave constitutes the matrix for the emergence of the Fifth Wave. What distinguishes the Fifth Wave model is its capacity to simultaneously promote knowledge production and innovation and equitably disseminate it to a significant proportion of citizens. Moreover, Fifth Wave institutional innovation offers the prospect of differentiation and diversification among institutions because it is undertaken through autonomous self-determination among universities rather than imposed top-down by government fiat. Fifth Wave institutions, moreover, operate within the context of an integrated national innovation system spanning academia, business and industry, and government, perennial debate regarding the appropriate role of the latter notwithstanding.[11]

## Reform Initiatives in the BRICS Nations

The dilemma whether to undertake systemic efforts to broaden accessibility or to advance knowledge production and innovation among an elite cohort of institutions to boost economic development is nowhere more starkly evident than in the BRIC nations, referring to Brazil, Russia, India, and China. With the more recent addition of South Africa to the roster, these nations are alternatively termed the BRICS and, in either case, are often grouped together to describe economies that have undergone rapid economic development alongside relative growth in regional political strength. Altbach terms their academic systems transitional and observes that only Russia among them possesses what he deems a mature system of higher education at the same time that it seeks to achieve international prominence academically. With the possible exception of China, in his estimation, the BRICS remain "peripheral in the global knowledge system."[12]

Each of the BRICS nations is attempting to balance the development of world-class research universities with the manifold challenges of expanding enrollments. "Although the BRICs are acutely aware of their new role in the global economy, their governments must negotiate complex political demands at home, including ensuring domestic economic growth, social mobility, and political participation," Carnoy and colleagues observe. "Because more and better higher education is perceived by the public to be positively associated with all these elements of a developed society, BRIC governments' focus on their university systems has become an important part of their domestic economic and social policy." Accordingly, "A key change taking place in the BRIC countries . . . is the *increasing differentiation* between the 'mass' universities and colleges, which absorb the vast majority of students in the BRIC countries, and the 'elite' universities, which, particularly in China and Russia, are being pushed to become 'world-class' research-type universities and serve a relatively limited group of students." With reference to what the authors term the "world-class university phenomenon," they observe: "China and Russia tend to be much more interested in creating 'world-class' universities in a direct way, systematically increasing resources to a chosen few universities, while focusing other higher education institutions' attention on enrollment expansion."[13]

Leaving aside consideration of the conditions essential to knowledge production and innovation, a glimpse of the extent of reform measures focused on increasing broad accessibility in the BRICS nations during the past several decades attests to the worldwide transition from the mass to the universal phases of higher education. "More than a third of the world's tertiary education systems enroll more than 50 per cent of young people after they leave secondary school, with roughly a third or so of the age cohort entering degree-level-programmes," Marginson reports.[14] As emblematic of the scale that these top-down reform efforts must confront, Carnoy and colleagues offer the following assessment: "Forty million: that is the number of young people who have graduated from universities and other four- or five-year higher education institutions in the BRICs from 2005 to 2010, equal to the population of California, yet only a fraction of the number who will graduate in the decade of the 2010s. This impressive figure is the result of the huge leap in college enrollment in the past twenty years outside the developed countries and particularly in the BRICs."[15] Worldwide enrollment in institutions of higher education has more than doubled since 1990, according to economists Ian Goldin and Chris Kutarna, from less than 14 percent to 33 percent in 2014. By their estimate, the global population of living recipients of university degrees exceeds the total number of degrees ever granted prior to 1980. Moreover, 25 to 50 million additional degree recipients are presently added to this roster with each passing year.[16] In some societies, Craig Calhoun points out, this growth has been fueled by the "postwar dream of widespread social mobility, prosperity for all, economic development led by science and technology, and the democratic participation of an educated citizenry that would recognize its stake in the existing order and resist the extremism of left or right."[17]

All of the BRICS appear in the QS World University top fifty ranking of systems of higher education but struggle to compete against their American, British, and Western European counterparts. Sequentially, from strongest to weakest, China is eighth, Brazil is twenty-second, India is twenty-fourth, Russia is twenty-sixth, and South Africa is thirtieth. Such rankings vary according to methodologies and measures of performance and an alternate evaluation orders these national systems quite differently. The Universitas 21 top fifty ranking of systems of higher education places sequentially, from strongest to weakest, China twenty-ninth, South Africa thirty-fourth, Russia thirty-fifth, Brazil fortieth, and India forty-ninth.[18] Whereas at one time the designation "world-class" attached to an institution to some extent on the basis of subjective factors such as reputation, the development of comprehensive international comparisons to evaluate quantifiable metrics has lent rigor to the process. Jamil Salmi, former education coordinator for the World Bank, proposes that there are no more than between thirty and fifty legitimately world-class universities globally. But there is "no universal recipe or magic formula for making a world-class university [because] national contexts and institutional models vary widely."[19] However, it is no coincidence that the Academic Ranking of World Universities (ARWU) developed by Shanghai Jiao Tong University is among the most authoritative and widely cited. The benchmarking of leading Chinese universities against world-class counterparts led to the publication of the rankings beginning in 2003. The ARWU differs from others because its methodology focuses on scientific research output and thus implicitly on the potential for innovation.[20]

Before we look more closely at reform initiatives in Russia and China, we now briefly survey some initiatives that illustrate the conventional recourse to one of two options: either the enrollment capacity approach, in which governments promote economic development and societal well-being through the implementation of initiatives designed to boost systemic capacity and accessibility, or, conversely, programmatic efforts to promote the formation of sets of world-class research universities dedicated primarily to discovery and innovation. The former approach has predominated in Great Britain, beginning as early as the nineteenth century, and was taken up with renewed resolve in England in the 1960s with the publication of the Robbins Report. Efforts to promote innovation and economic growth through the formation of sets of world-class research universities have, by contrast, more recently been undertaken in France and Germany and among the BRICS nations, especially China and Russia.

## Robbins and Expansion of Scale in British Higher Education

With institutions such as Oxford, Cambridge, University College London, King's College London, and Imperial College London forming the bulwark of a longstanding world-class configuration of research-grade excellence, Britain during the twentieth century focused reform efforts on broadening accessibility. With reference to the decades following World War II, Michael Shattock observes, "Policy drivers varied at different points over the period depending on changing political, economic, and structural contexts but two stand out consistently over the whole period: the increasing demand for places in higher education and the implications of financing the expansion."[21] Policy makers addressed the imperative for greater accessibility through phases of structural reform intended to promote the rapid expansion of enrollment capacity— initially during the 1960s and then again in the 1990s—which together brought about a fivefold increase in rates of enrollment.[22]

In 1961, the British government commissioned a committee under the leadership of economist Lionel Robbins to evaluate higher education and issue recommendations for improvements to the system. Based on the recommendations of the Robbins Report,[23] published in 1963, measures were undertaken to expand access and improve the overall quality and prominence of the various categories of institutions, thus attempting to minimize the disparities between Oxbridge and the balance of colleges and universities. According to committee member Claus Moser, the committee created its own Golden Rule, which became known as the Robbins principle: "Higher education should be available to all those suited by ability and attainment, and who wish to attend."[24]

In the decades following World War II, awareness of the correlation between scientific and technical education—the latter referring to what was then termed applied science as well as vocational training for industry and commerce—and economic growth brought focus to the inadequacies of the existing system.[25] Despite enrollment demand among academically qualified students far exceeding the supply of available slots, Robbins and colleagues found that no more than 4 percent of potential students then entered university degree programs, with only 1 percent of female and 3 percent of male students identified as working class enrolling.[26] Despite the conventional wisdom that increased enrollment undermines quality, the report recommended expansion of the system, which in part would be accomplished through the establishment of new institutions and conversion of existing categories such as the civic colleges and technical colleges—which were then designated colleges of advanced technology, or CATs—into full universities. The initiatives set precedents for legislation in the late 1980s and early 1990s to promote what was termed massification and culminated in various government policies to embrace marketization, wherein more autonomous institutions compete for increasingly limited government resources.[27]

"The early 1960s saw the biggest transformation of English higher education of the past hundred years," observes David Willetts, former UK minister of state for universities.[28] The reform efforts appear especially transformational when considered against the relative historical stasis of British higher education. Until a royal charter from King William IV established the University of London, which in 1836 conjoined University College London with King's College London, founded, respectively, in 1826 and 1829, Oxford and Cambridge had maintained an effective monopoly.[29] "After the Oxbridge monopoly was broken in the 1830s," Willetts explains, "England saw the creation of colleges with diverse missions including delivering education and training to meet the needs of the local economy." However, "Many of these new institutions were denounced at the time just as alternative providers are now because they were seen as threats to the established model of a university." He elaborates: "The Oxbridge model commands such prestige that it has proved hard to sustain a sense of diverse university missions—instead almost all of England's higher educational institutions aim for the prestige which comes from academic research and the rituals associated with it."[30] Indeed, Trow contends that Robbins had only reinforced the pattern of an "inverted pyramid" in British higher education, with the continued dominance of the elite institutions at the top.[31]

Concern over accessibility preceded the Robbins Report by more than a century, however, and contributed to the formation of the University of London as well as institutional innovation leading to the proliferation of institutional types that, not unlike the successive waves in American higher education, operate in parallel. As early as 1851, provincial towns and industrial centers such as Manchester had begun to establish civic colleges conceived to impart skills to sustain and build upon the technological advances of the Industrial Revolution. Although some critics contend that these schools were chartered only to emulate the academic cultures and standards of the ancient universities, referring to Oxford and Cambridge, curricula were focused on applied practice rather than theory and research.[32] Early in the twentieth century, new civic colleges—colloquially referred to as "red brick universities," or "red bricks," and roughly equivalent to state universities in the United States—were established through the efforts and funding of large industrial cities.[33] Much of their contribution stemmed from their embeddedness in local communities and accessibility.[34] Thereafter, by some assessments, Oxford and Cambridge began to embrace an impartial admissions model once subverted by claims of social prerogative. The civics assumed full university status prior to the Robbins Report and likely influenced the committee's understanding of how to expand and improve higher education. These municipal institutions stimulated the government to expand access through the national grant system but also promoted research tailored to the knowledge economy. Nevertheless, the civic universities could not satisfy the projected enrollment demand specified in the report.[35]

The report recommended the conversion of colleges of advanced technology into what have been termed the "plate glass universities," referring to their characteristic midcentury façades of plate glass reinforced by steel and concrete. The recommendation stemmed from concern over the existing lack of institutional autonomy, power to set academic qualifications, and authority to award degrees.[36] With the intent to harness research to both industrial and social needs, Robbins not only expanded accessibility but also encouraged a comprehensive education that, by the assessment of one contemporary, would promote social advancement: "This is not an attempt to add a gloss of wider culture to the technologist, but to develop in him a sense of his own contribution to society and its culture."[37] The pronouncement may have been influenced by the 1959 Cambridge lecture and subsequent volume by

C. P. Snow, *The Two Cultures*, in which one of Britain's leading public intellectuals lamented the pernicious influence of the cultural schism between the sciences and the humanities and social sciences that had produced a "gulf of mutual incomprehension" between two polarized camps that had "almost ceased to communicate at all."[38]

The 1960s were deemed the binary phase of British higher education because, parallel to the traditional university sector, a second tier was established, comprising roughly thirty polytechnic institutions.[39] Robbins himself expressed skepticism regarding the binary system, which he feared would only exacerbate the perception of hierarchy in British higher education. Shattock observes: "Robbins argued that one rationale for a unitary policy was simply that the prestige of a university career and degree was such as to render most alternatives decidedly second best."[40] Yet, whereas in 1960 less than 5 percent of the population was enrolled in higher education, by 1969 that number rose to 14 percent, with two-thirds of that percentage enrolled in polytechnics.[41] The expansion of higher education through the newly chartered plate glass universities and recently founded polytechnics helped mitigate demand for enrollment at research-grade universities, but another development that came only thirty years after Robbins expanded accessibility to a greater and even more diverse demographic.

The Education Reform Act of 1988 freed the polytechnics from local authority control and the Further and Higher Education Act of 1992 created the so-called new universities, or post-1992 universities, which among other initiatives chartered thirty-eight polytechnics as full universities. Although the incorporation of the polytechnics as universities meant the dissolution of the binary system, some scholars point out that "in practice a hierarchy of prestige remained within the reformed system."[42] The new universities promoted unconventional curricula, including alternating practical on-the-job experience with academic coursework, modular degrees, and continuing education for "mature" students over the age of twenty-one.[43] The incorporation of polytechnics as universities marked their social reconceptualization, which increased enrollments, especially among women and minority populations. The gross enrollment ratio of students attending tertiary education rose from 23 percent in 1988 to a peak of 60 percent in 1999.[44] From another perspective, in the six years beginning in 1988, the enrollment rate increased from 15 percent to 32 percent.[45] Consistent with the numerical standard posited by Trow, Britain entered the mass phase of higher education starting with the 1988 and 1992 acts.[46]

## "A Mega-University outside Paris to Rival the Silicon Valley"

Prominent among programmatic efforts undertaken to promote economic development and education through the advancement of world-class research universities dedicated primarily to discovery and innovation is the Université Paris-Saclay, which is a new federal research university and industry cluster outside of Paris that has been characterized as a "mega-university to rival Silicon Valley."[47] The Université Paris-Saclay represents a complex of nineteen autonomous institutions—three universities, nine *grandes écoles*, and components of seven national research institutions—that has been under development since 2008 on the Plateau de Saclay near Paris. Formally incorporated in 2015, the new federated research university enrolls 65,000 students, including 6,000 doctoral students, with academic staff and research professionals exceeding 10,000. According to founding director Dominique Vernay, the intent is for Paris-Saclay to attain rank as the "top university in continental Europe."[48] The Paris-Saclay Foundation, the body charged with development of the complex, intends for the innovation district to compete with and outperform other top clusters—most notably Stanford University and Silicon Valley in California, and Harvard University, MIT, and Route 128 in Boston.[49] Initial government funding for Paris-Saclay totaled 1 billion euros from a 22 billion euro stimulus package in 2010, allocated in accordance with the 2007 educational platform of former French president Nicholas Sarkozy, which shifted power from national research agencies to universities.[50]

Whereas American research universities integrate undergraduate and graduate instruction with research and development operations, Continental European states historically maintain parallel and differentiated research sectors that centralize basic R&D functions in designated research institutes that compete with universities.[51] The most acclaimed of these institutions are the Max Planck Society (MPS) in Germany and, in France, the Centre national de la recherche scientifique (CNRS), the largest national funding agency for basic research in

Europe, which encompasses a network of ten institutions staffed by 32,000 researchers, engineers, and technicians.[52] Whereas Germany equitably spreads projects between societies such as Max Planck and the Helmholtz and Leibniz Associations, France focuses the major share of research in CNRS. The next most significant French public research institution, the Atomic Energy and Alternative Energies Commission, has less than a fifth of the relative contribution to research of CNRS, based on an adjusted article count metric widely used to show research productivity.[53]

According to critics, however, structural inefficiencies plague French efforts to improve higher education and research excellence. Although the French government has attempted to refocus research into universities through the formation of the innovation cluster, research management remains concentrated in CNRS. By some assessments, French universities lack the experience to manage large-scale research projects despite assistance from CNRS. Others say the Paris-Saclay innovation hub remains merely aspirational until proven otherwise, currently lacking a reasonable timeline, adequate financial resources, and fundamental infrastructure to sustain the specified desideratum. Sarkozy has termed Paris-Saclay a "mosaic of institutions, each highly prestigious, but badly coordinated among themselves and separated by artificial institutional barriers [that are] totally obsolete in an era of global scientific competition." The government accepts that cross-institutional research promotes research excellence, but some argue that the top-down approach provided by the main grant program imposed impossibly short deadlines that likely will result in uneven progress.[54]

Catherine Paradeise characterizes the French system of higher education since World War II as a "double dualism between research and teaching, as well as between elite and accessible higher education institutions." She elaborates: "Its three subsystems—universities, *grandes écoles*, and research organizations—developed interdependently, as the weaknesses of each justified the existence of the others. Over time, each specific legal public status has consolidated the identity, relative power, and social status of each subset." Paradeise traces two waves of reform of higher education in France since 1980. The first she describes as the "incremental wave," spanning the period from 1981 to 2006, during which the tripartite system of French higher education was forced to confront massification. Decreasing funding and the "increasingly dramatic disintegration and dispersion of public resources" exacerbated problems associated with a spike in enrollments. A wave of more radical reforms, spanning the period from 2006 to 2012, followed on the previous wave. She perceives a continuing tug of war between those who want to centralize authority in the national educational bureaucracy and those who advocate devolving more authority to local institutions. Paris-Saclay was inserted into this fraught political environment by law. Nevertheless, Paradeise maintains that Paris-Saclay is the "most impressive of the projects fostered by the reforms" because it provides a "good test as to how the implementation of reforms has resisted" research policies that many believe are not responsive to the needs of the country.[55]

The ambition for Paris-Saclay to become one of the top twenty universities in the world has led to a number of further dilemmas, according to Paradeise. Conflicts have arisen between what she terms "arrogant *grandes écoles* and defensive universities," which fear that their best students will opt for *grandes écoles*, while the latter are concerned their prestigious reputations will suffer by association with universities. In response, Paris-Saclay has constructed a "complex governance model that establishes common ground while preserving the assets of its individual members." Nevertheless, one of the *grandes écoles* asserted control over assets in a manner that interfered with carefully crafted compromises and ultimately led to sanctions. The unfortunate event reduced trust among the other parties and interfered with efforts to improve the governance model. Paradeise concedes that the ambitious project represented by Paris-Saclay may not be sustainable.[56]

The dilemma of whether to focus reform efforts on broader accessibility or the advancement of world-class knowledge production has occupied German policy makers as well. Although Germany retains the strongest system of higher education in Continental Europe, it has undertaken a multifaceted so-termed modernization initiative in order to compete with Anglophone institutions, which overwhelmingly dominate global rankings of top universities. Prior to 2005, official policy had deemed that all publicly funded universities, which encompass virtually the entire system, would be tuition-free and relatively equitable in quality and reputation. Collectively, the system was dependable, but policy makers realized the necessity to challenge the status quo and, abandoning their longstanding egalitarian approach, create what has been termed a German Ivy League to compete against top-ranking world universities. Accordingly, the German Universities Excellence Initiative was introduced to reinvigorate institutions and inspire the interuniversity competition characteristic of research-grade American higher education.[57] The initiative began in 2006 as an eleven-year, 4.6 billion euro program—at the time the equivalent of 5 billion USD—to raise top-performing universities in Germany to the levels of prestige of Oxbridge and the Ivy League.[58]

German universities occupy an administrative status not unlike their public American counterparts in the sense that German states, not the federal government, are responsible for their oversight and funding. The federal government implemented various funding initiatives through the second half of the twentieth century, but, pursuant to the constitution, federal subsidies and monies were restricted to project-based research. The Excellence Initiative drastically expanded the role of the federal government. According to the terms of an agreement reached following eighteen months of negotiation, beginning in 2006 the federal government would proportionally disburse 75 percent of respective budgets, while state governments would allocate the balance over a five-year period. Prospective participants were instructed to propose "ambitious overall objectives, particularly innovative approaches to research and training, and a convincing strategic vision for the long-term institutional development." Funding streams would be available for institutions with graduate schools to strengthen doctoral training and for the formation of excellence clusters to advance collaborative research and cross-disciplinary cooperation among universities and industry and with research institutes such as the Max Planck Society, which formerly had been largely isolated from university partners.[59] By some assessments, however, the focus on the formation of specialized elite institutions controverts the Humboldtian model that integrates research with teaching.[60]

## Initiatives to Advance Economic Prosperity and Social Development

In remarks from the Great Hall of the People in Beijing coinciding with the centennial of Tsinghua University in 2011, Hu Jintao, then president of the People's Republic of China, underscored the critical role of the nation's universities in advancing economic prosperity and social development. But, according to Robert Rhoads and colleagues, "China's leaders expect their universities to assume standing among the elite universities of the world—the Harvards, Oxfords, and Stanfords—at the same time they hold them accountable for assisting in China's economic and social transformation." Accordingly, complementary government initiatives known as Projects 211 and 985 were conceived with the intent to build a set of world-class research universities in China.[61]

Projects 211 and 985 have radically increased government expenditures to a set of state universities in order to advance scholarly productivity and develop world-class R&D capabilities. Project 211 was initiated in 1995 to advance the international competitiveness of approximately one hundred universities through funding increases intended to mobilize research capacity, especially in the fields of science and technology. The Project 211 universities were allotted additional funding of $20 billion to improve research productivity. Project 985 was instituted in 1998 as a complement to Project 211 to advance the academic excellence of the C9 League, China's nine top-performing universities, which are often termed the Chinese Ivy League. In 2004, the government expanded the program to include an additional thirty universities to further increase national R&D productivity. Although implementation of Project 211 ended in the early 2000s, when taken collectively with its sister project, Project 985, the results indicate significant improvement relative to other national initiatives. Beijing's success in instituting Projects 211 and 985 would further internationalize the Chinese higher education system, in an effort to prepare it to compete with the leading global research universities.[62]

According to Rhoads and colleagues, the well-funded national initiatives reflect China's shift, beginning in the 1980s, toward increased marketization, deregulation, and privatization. For colleges and universities, marketization meant the implementation of tuition and fees, reliance on market strategies, and increased competition among institutions. Deregulation meant decreased national funding—except for the roughly one hundred universities selected for the complementary initiatives—and increasing autonomy. Privatization corresponded with the neoliberal conviction regarding private sources of revenue, but only imperfectly because of the continued administrative role of the central government. Among other trends shaping higher education in China, Rhoads and colleagues further observe massification and correlate the participation rate to the mass level described by Trow. Whereas in 1990 less than 5 percent of respective age cohorts were enrolled in institutions of higher education, by 2009 World Bank data indicated a 25 percent rate of participation.[63]

Marketization inspired China to attempt to realize the integral role of higher education in advancing its participation in the knowledge economy, and, not unlike Russia's de facto overhaul of its system of higher education, the initiatives attest to China's determination to compete among the leading Western universities, which historically have dominated international ranking tables. China's commitment to transforming its research universities is certain to prove exemplary to other nations similarly attempting to advance institutional innovation. These policies arguably surpass the efforts of other nations, as manifested in impressive increases in expenditures and successful coordination between the Ministry of Education and universities. As envisioned in the Chinese initiatives, an equitable balance between cooperation among institutions and competition for government funding is intended to spur innovation as well as increase institutional rankings internationally, reminiscent of the competitive interrelationships that federal investment spurred among American research universities following World War II.

These initiatives supported concurrent exponential enrollment increases at Chinese universities beginning in the 1990s. Over the course of the decade between 2000 and 2010, the number of Chinese graduates quadrupled to about 8 million per year. By 2020, China expects that it will have almost 195 million graduates of tertiary education—comparatively, the United States projects 120 million.[64] To sustain access and maintain superior-quality education, the Ministry of Education announced the World Class 2.0 initiative in 2015, creating a framework for expanded international collaboration, suggesting that a strategy of international cooperation inevitably promotes internal systemic improvements. The improved performance in university rankings amplifies China's potential to raise six of its nine most prestigious universities to the top-fifteen rank globally.

The institutional innovation undertaken by Shanghai Jiao Tong University (SJTU), frequently termed the MIT of China and a member institution of the preeminent C9 League, epitomizes China's global academic ambitions. SJTU administrators recognized the imperative to embrace change in institutional culture in order to better compete internationally. SJTU president Jie Zhang explains that the university is "moving from knowledge transfer to knowledge creation and from instruction-centered teaching to student-centered teaching." The approach follows a new innovation-centric strategic vision, which includes the engagement of outstanding researchers committed to interdisciplinary research to broaden the impact of knowledge production on society. Beginning in 2007, SJTU implemented three distinct career tracks (teaching, research, and tenure) for faculty members and merged two disparate tenure systems. Subsequently, the university has produced tangible results by doubling its annual revenues, which tripled competitive research income, and bringing the social sciences at SJTU into the fold of R&D, which likely increased from five to sixteen the number of disciplines ranked by Thomson Reuters *Essential Science Indicators* among the global top 1 percent.[65] SJTU serves as a model for universities globally that aspire to achieve research excellence to address both local and global challenges.

China outpaces its BRICS counterparts in global rankings, and the consistent rise in rankings of C9 institutions suggests that Chinese universities are successfully aligning their administrative directives with national goals of competing against the world's top universities. The synchronization between state efforts and institutions to alter academic cultures has contributed to unprecedented systemic improvements. China has moreover demonstrated that government involvement in higher education reform has contributed to the operationalization of a new class of research universities. Perhaps as a consequence of central government control over research prerogatives expressly oriented toward applications integral to high-tech industrial growth and national security, China appears to be outpacing the United States in the race to develop artificial intelligence.

### Project 5/100: Russia's Effort to Launch an Ivy League

In post-Soviet Russia, reform in higher education has been exemplified by what is termed Project 5/100, which represents an ambitious effort by the national government to invest in a set of research universities to achieve global competitiveness in academic excellence and research in order to advance innovation and catalyze economic growth.[66] "The Russian government wants to have its own world-class universities," observes Igor Fedyukin, director for policy studies at the New Economic School in Moscow. "But first it must introduce the concept of differentiation to Russian higher education, and make clear that not all universities are quite equal. This point might seem self-evident to a U.S. reader, but in Russia—as in many European countries—the egalitarian tradition is deeply rooted."[67]

The breakup of the Soviet Union in 1991 provided the impetus for reform in higher education. In the newly created Russian Federation, Moscow attempted to address the perceived inefficiencies of the Soviet era through reforms in curricula, advancement of institutional autonomy, massification and diversification, and the introduction of tuition fees.[68] Russian president Vladimir Putin most likely saw the initial reforms as lacking impact on its economy because, despite liberalization in this sector, Russia continued to lag behind in quality assurance standards among the member countries of the Organisation for Economic Co-operation and Development (OECD). Consequently, from 2012 to 2013, the Russian government implemented a number of regulatory and legislative provisions to better align the sector with a globalized knowledge economy. With a presidential decree signed in May 2012, Putin created the framework for a new academic excellence initiative known as Project 5/100, which spearheaded his initiatives and drastically increased state investment in R&D funding streams from which universities would be able to acquire support through grants.[69]

The primary objective of Project 5/100 is to leverage at least five Russian universities into the top one hundred list in global university rankings. Participating institutions are encouraged to adopt differentiated strategic development programs, maximize their societal impact, and catalyze economic development through the formation of innovation clusters between the academic sector and industry focused on R&D. The initiative has attempted to prompt increased collaboration between institutions and the private sector, both domestically and internationally, as well as efforts to coordinate research with the Russian Academy of Sciences.[70] As envisioned in the provisions of Project 5/100, the distribution of funding on a competitive basis is intended to spur innovation as well as increase institutional rankings internationally, reminiscent of the outcomes associated with the competitive interrelationships among American universities following World War II and a departure from the historical centralization of research in the Russian Academy of Sciences, which retains its Soviet-era preeminence.

Russia's policies compare favorably with the efforts of other nations, as evinced in impressive increases in expenditures and the implementation of measures to strengthen the research capacities of universities as part of the broader effort to advance innovation through the integration of higher education and industry. Policy makers have realized the potential of world-class institutions to sustain economic growth following the transition to a market economy with the formation of the Russian Federation. The Skolkovo Institute of Science and Technology (Skoltech), for example, which is the centerpiece of the Skolkovo Innovation Center on the outskirts of Moscow, was originally proposed by Dmitry Medvedev in 2009 when he served as president of the Russian Federation during the interregnum between the terms of Vladimir Putin. The Skolkovo Innovation Center concentrates on what are termed five presidential high-tech sectors: energy, information technologies, telecommunications, biomedical, and nuclear research.

Skoltech solidified partnerships with prominent international corporations—for example, Siemens, Microsoft, Boeing, Intel, Johnson & Johnson, Cisco, and IBM—to catalyze knowledge production between academia and industry, and drew inevitable comparison to Silicon Valley.[71] The day after it was created, Skoltech signed what was termed a trilateral agreement with MIT and the Skolkovo Foundation to advance education, research, and entrepreneurship programs. Research universities, of course, constitute the hubs of notable government-initiated innovation clusters worldwide. In Saudi Arabia, for example, King Abdullah University of Science and Technology (KAUST) is a key node in the King Abdullah Economic City (KAEC), and, in South Korea, KAIST, which was formed in 1971 as the Korea Advanced Institute of Science and Technology, is the hub of the surrounding Daedeok Innopolis.[72] In an effort to become globally competitive, other emerging economies have undertaken similar initiatives with varying degrees of success. But in some instances, efforts have been restricted to opportunistic technical fixes intended primarily to boost rankings rather than performance.

The founding president of Skoltech, Edward Crawley, who served from 2011 to 2016, was a member of the faculty at MIT when appointed. In 2013, Crawley and two colleagues published a paper that applied the CDIO Syllabus to analyze Skoltech.[73] The syllabus is a component of the CDIO Initiative, the initialism referring to the terms "conceive, design, implement, and operate," which is a pedagogical framework conceived at MIT to advance undergraduate engineering education.[74] During their application of the syllabus to Skoltech, Crawley and his colleagues interacted with thirty-eight stakeholders to define learning outcomes that would enable Skoltech to become a university "organized around innovation" that could represent a prototype for a new model of higher education. But Nadir Kinossian and Kevin Morgan conclude that the strategy of "development by decree" is seriously flawed. Efforts by the state to impose modernization from above through mega-projects, including innovation clusters like Skoltech, are doomed to disappointment because the "political system fails to create favorable institutional conditions for modernization; the economic system is beset by deeply embedded structural problems; and the regional policy apparatus is torn between the goals of spatial equalization and spatial agglomeration."[75] Innovation is unlikely to flourish in an environment of authoritarian rule.

By one assessment, structural barriers in Russian higher education pose daunting challenges to the implementation of Project 5/100. These include the preeminence of the Russian Academy of Sciences ("concentration of money and talent"); the restricted focus of many universities; the relative absence of research and academic professionals at the peak of their careers owing to the economic recession of the 1990s ("mid-career talent gap"); top-down administrative cultures that discourage bottom-up academic enterprise; and the lack of fluency and publication in English, the global academic lingua franca.[76] Structural change is moreover hampered by the challenges associated with organizational restructuring and the formation of institutional identities in the wake of prior academic excellence initiatives. In 2005, an initiative encouraged a select number of regional institutions to merge into what are designated federal universities. Some of these newly merged universities and other high-performing institutions in 2008–2011 sought designation as national research universities in an effort to obtain increased federal funding and more comprehensive integration of teaching and research.

Subsequently, a significant proportion of these federal and national re-search universities successfully bid to participate in Project 5/100 with the objective of becoming leading institutions globally.[77]

While the institutions participating in the initiative are all very different, each tends to be focused on the objective of preeminence within Russia and prominence internationally in a single particular field. Although the selection process for Project 5/100 institutions has relied on measures of the global competitiveness of individual academic departments, assuming an interdisciplinary approach to research could improve overall performance, advance rankings internationally, and encourage enrollment by international students.[78] The intention of the government to promote world-class academic excellence has thus pressured a broad range of institutions that do not compete academically among the most prestigious institutions but are nonetheless integral to the overall educational ecosystem to undertake institutional advancement measures not only to increase recruitment numbers but to revitalize regional economies. Despite such challenges, Russia has been able to strengthen specialized institutions that focus on particular disciplines to compete on the world stage. The specialized Moscow Institute of Physics and Technology, for example, a Project 5/100 institution, joined Moscow State University and St. Petersburg State University in the *Times Higher Education* 2016 rankings of the top one hundred universities in the world.[79]

These relative gains in global rankings must be juxtaposed with the lack of a systemic plan apart from Project 5/100, which only provides financial incentives for universities to improve their status in rankings. Moscow has consistently allocated greater funding since the advent of Project 5/100, but as an administrator from one of the premier national research universities acknowledges, "Such pressure [to increase institutional rankings] may distort institutions' long-term goals of creating new knowledge if they are too focused on making a quick impact in rankings indicators." The Ministry of Education and Science strategically chose institutions across Russia to participate in Project 5/100 to promote increased access to research-grade academic platforms rather than following precedent by centralizing funding in Moscow and St. Petersburg, the historical hubs of Russian economic power and academic excellence. The preoccupation with rankings, however, may distract from a focus on innovation to boost economic growth and hamper efforts to develop regional innovation clusters.[80]

Inasmuch as the methodologies of assessments such as *Times Higher Education World University Rankings* and *QS World University Rankings* typically apportion 20 percent to research output measured by the number of citations per faculty member in journals indexed by Thomson Reuters or Scopus, the pressure to publish is a notoriously flawed indicator of productivity and impact.[81] Directly linking government allocation of higher education funding to rankings moreover exacerbates the potential for academic corruption. Because funding of institutions in Russia is tied to performance in world rankings, faculty sometimes assume an opportunistic approach to publishing by submitting academic work to predatory pay-to-publish journals, which are sometimes mistakenly indexed by academic databases and thus counted by authoritative ranking organizations, allowing institutions to manipulate ranking status.[82]

The potential for corruption is not limited to publication. Not dependent on Project 5/100 participation, public universities in Russia receive state funding calculated according to enrollment numbers as well as tuition and fees. Inasmuch as student attrition would threaten both sources, the funding model potentially compromises academic excellence and quality assurance standards. According to one assessment: "If [universities] expelled underachieving students, the university would lose a substantial part of its budget, which might lead to a decline in its research activities and the laying off of professors and staff."[83] Moreover, the pervasive scale of cheating and plagiarism at Russian universities would suggest that current excellence initiatives do not necessarily address academic integrity.[84]

The United States and Russia face comparable challenges in providing access to advanced world-class higher education to a broader range of citizens. As of 2010, the United States had 6,673 students per 100,000 residents enrolled in higher education, roughly the same ratio of students in Russia enrolled in tertiary education: 6,599 students per 100,000 of the population.[85] But although the issue of access to research-grade higher education is paralleled in the United States by a growing and increasingly diverse population, Russia interestingly faces population decline, even as the demand for superior higher education increases. With the creation of academic excellence initiatives such as Project 5/100, however, the seemingly existential threat posed to Russian universities by a declining population resulting in decreased enrollments has had the residual effect of increasing Russia's position in the world as an emerging academic and research and development powerhouse. And despite the host of challenges that confront these institutions, Russian universities have been seeing positive results in the international rankings.

Much of the success of leading universities worldwide has been attributed to emulation of American research universities. "The apparent thinking is that a few more excellent universities based on the U.S. model will help each of these nations produce the skilled talent to develop their own new technology, [which] in turn, they argue, would contribute to rapid economic growth nationally," Carnoy and colleagues contend.[86] But although the United States is considered the prototypical high-participation system, as Marginson observes, it is erroneous to assume that "massification follows a single track and that the worldwide tendency towards HPS is a process of Americanization."[87] Aspiration to realize a whole-cloth adaptation of the conventional model as undertaken by many emerging economies has obvious limitations. In the United States, the relevance of an otherwise highly successful model for a significant proportion of academically qualified students is limited by lack of accessibility. And the impact of world-leading discovery and innovation sometimes falls short of its potential because of indifference to its outcomes.

The contours of the dilemma that limited accessibility to academic excellence poses to the United States reaffirms the imperative for the new model for a subset of public research universities, which offers broader access to research-grade education. The New American University model is "American" in the sense that it was developed to respond to the needs of the United States, but its integration of three foundational design components is relevant to institutions and nations worldwide: academic platforms committed to discovery and knowledge production that link pedagogy with research; broad accessibility to students from highly diverse demographic and socioeconomic backgrounds; and an institutional commitment to maximizing societal impact. The advancement of subsets of major public research universities that accelerate positive social outcomes through the seamless integration of world-class knowledge production with a commitment to accessibility to the broadest possible demographic representative of the socioeconomic and intellectual diversity of societies worldwide has global applicability. If the Fifth Wave is the New American University writ large, then perhaps its application to different national contexts might suggest the potential for the emergence of a Sixth Wave of global mega-research universities and successive waves yet to be imagined.

## Notes

1. Philip G. Altbach, *Global Perspectives on Higher Education* (Baltimore: Johns Hopkins University Press, 2016), 29, 86–87.

2. "Chinese Ivy League," *China Daily* (October 21, 2009); Igor Fedyukin, "Russia's Ivy League," *RBTH (Rossiyskaya Gazeta)* (August 25, 2010).

3. Martin Trow, "Problems in the Transition from Elite to Mass Higher Education" (Berkeley: Carnegie Commission on Higher Education, 1973), 1–8; Evan Schofer and John W. Meyer, "The Worldwide Expansion of Higher Education in the Twentieth Century," *American Sociological Review* 70 (December 2005): 898–920; Michael Gibbons et al., *The New Production of Knowledge: The Dynamics of Science and Research in Contemporary Societies* (London: Sage, 1994), 70–89.

4. Martin Carnoy et al., *University Expansion in a Changing Global Economy: Triumph of the BRICs?* (Stanford: Stanford University Press, 2013), 15.

5. Altbach, *Global Perspectives on Higher Education*, 29, 45–46.

6. Simon Marginson, "High Participation Systems of Higher Education," in *High Participation Systems of Higher Education*, ed. Brendan Cantwell, Simon Marginson, and Anna Smolentseva (Oxford: Oxford University Press, 2018), 3.

7. Walter W. McMahon, *Higher Learning, Greater Good: The Private and Social Benefits of Higher Education* (Baltimore: Johns Hopkins University Press, 2009).

8. Trow, "Problems in the Transition from Elite to Mass Higher Education," 1–8.

9. Jonathan R. Cole, *The Great American University: Its Rise to Preeminence, Its Indispensable National Role, and Why It Must Be Protected* (New York: Public Affairs, 2009), 2.

10. Richard C. Atkinson and William A. Blanpied, "Research Universities: Core of the U.S. Science and Technology System," *Technology in Society* 30 (2008): 41–43.

11. Mariana Mazzucato, *The Entrepreneurial State: Debunking Public vs. Private Sector Myths* (New York: Public Affairs, 2013).

12. Altbach, *Global Perspectives on Higher Education*, 102; personal correspondence, January 23, 2019.

13. Carnoy et al., *University Expansion in a Changing Global Economy*, 2, 7, 24. Emphasis in original.

14. Marginson, "High Participation Systems of Higher Education," 4.

15. Carnoy et al., *University Expansion in a Changing Global Economy*, 34.

16. Ian Goldin and Chris Kutarna, *The Age of Discovery: Navigating the Risks and Rewards of our New Renaissance* (New York: St. Martin's Press, 2016), 82.

17. Craig Calhoun, "The Public Mission of the Research University," in *Knowledge Matters: The Public Mission of the Research University*, ed. Diana Rhoten and Craig Calhoun (New York: Columbia University Press, 2011), 13.

18. "QS Higher Education System Strength 2016," *QS*, http://www.topuniversities .com/system-strength-rankings/2016; "U21 Ranking of National Higher Education Systems 2019," https://universitas21.com/sites/default/files/2019-04/Full%20Report%20and %20Cover.pdf.

19. Jamil Salmi, *The Challenge of Establishing World-Class Universities* (Washington, DC: World Bank, 2009), 6, 12, cited in Robert A. Rhoads et al., *China's Rising Research Universities: A New Era of Global Ambition* (Baltimore: Johns Hopkins University Press, 2014), 22.

20. Nian Cai Liu, "The Story of Academic Ranking of World Universities," *International Higher Education* 54 (Winter 2009): 2–3.

21. Michael Shattock, *Making Policy in British Higher Education, 1945–2011* (London: Open University Press, 2012), 1.

22. Vikki Boliver, "Expansion, Differentiation, and the Persistence of Social Class Inequalities in British Higher Education," *Higher Education* 61, no. 3 (2011): 230.

23. UK Committee on Higher Education, *Higher Education: Report of the Committee Appointed by the Prime Minister under the Chairmanship of Lord Robbins, 1961–63* (London: HM's Stationery Office, 1963), hereafter cited simply as the Robbins Report.

24. Claus Moser, "The Report," in *Shaping Higher Education: Fifty Years after Robbins*, ed. Nicholas Barr (London: London School of Economics, 2014), 27.

25. Peter Venables, "Technical Education in Great Britain: Second Thoughts on the Robbins Report," *International Review of Education* 11, no. 2 (1965): 151.

26. Nicholas Barr and Howard Glennerster, preface to *Shaping Higher Education: Fifty Years after Robbins*, ed. Nicholas Barr (London: London School of Economics, 2014), xvii–xviii.

27. Richard Layard, "What Was the World Like Then? The Context in 1963," in *Shaping Higher Education: Fifty Years after Robbins*, ed. Nicholas Barr (London: London School of Economics, 2014), 14.

28. David Willetts, *A University Education* (Oxford: Oxford University Press, 2017), 40.

29. Although many colleges and seminaries had obviously operated apart from Oxford and Cambridge prior to the nineteenth century, the royal charter that permitted the University of London to confer degrees would secure its claim to be the third-oldest university in the realm and must be understood in this administrative context. Negley Harte, *The University of London, 1836–1986* (London: Athlone Press, 1986).

30. Willetts, *University Education*, 35.

31. Martin Trow, "Robbins: A Question of Size," *Universities Quarterly* 18 (1963): 136–152, cited in Shattock, *Making Policy in British Higher Education*, 270.

32. Sarah V. Barnes, "England's Civic Universities and the Triumph of the Oxbridge Ideal," *History of Education Quarterly* 36, no. 3 (1996): 272.

33. Michael Shattock, "United Kingdom," in *International Handbook of Higher Education*, ed. James J. F. Forest and Philip G. Altbach (Dordrecht: Springer, 2006), 1020–1021.

34. John Morgan, "How the Redbrick Universities Created British Higher Education," *Times Higher Education* (November 12, 2015).

35. Barnes, "England's Civic Universities," 292.

36. Robbins Report, 131.

37. E. G. Edwards, "Colleges of Advanced Technology in Britain," *Nature* 199, no. 4899 (1963): 1134, 1136, doi:10.1038/1991131a0.

38. C. P. Snow, *The Two Cultures and the Scientific Revolution* (Cambridge: Cambridge University Press, 1960), 2–4, 12.

39. Boliver, "Expansion, Differentiation, and the Persistence of Social Class Inequalities," 232.

40. Shattock, *Making Policy in British Higher Education*, 85.

41. UK University Grants Commission, *Statistics of Education 1970* (London: HMSO, 1973).

42. Sin Yi Cheung and Muriel Egerton, "Great Britain: Higher Education Expansion and Reform—Changing Educational Inequalities," in *Stratification in Higher Education: A Comparative Study*, ed. Yossi Shavit, Richard Arum, and Adam Gamoran (Stanford: Stanford University Press, 2007): 195–219.

43. Barry James, "New Names Ennoble U.K. Polytechnics," *New York Times* (October 8, 1992).

44. UNESCO, Institute of Statistics. The Gross Enrollment Ratio is the number of students enrolled at the tertiary level as a percentage of the population of the age group that officially corresponds to that level in the United Kingdom.

45. UK Department of Education, *Education and Training for the 21st Century* (London, 1991); U.K. Department for Education and Skills, *Higher Education: A New Framework* (London, 1991); Boliver, "Expansion, Differentiation, and the Persistence of Social Class Inequalities," 233.

46. Cheung and Egerton, "Great Britain: Higher Education Expansion and Reform," 199.

47. Jean-Claude Thoenig, "Why France Is Building a Mega-University at Paris-Saclay to Rival Silicon Valley," *The Conversation* (May 27, 2015).

48. Oliver Staley, "Nations Chasing Harvard Merge Colleges to Ascend Rankings," *Bloomberg* (March 13, 2014).

49. Anna Lee Saxenian, *Regional Advantage: Culture and Competition in Silicon Valley and Route 128* (Cambridge, MA: Harvard University Press, 1994). See also Bruce Katz and Julie Wagner, *The Rise of Innovation Districts: A New Geography of Innovation in America* (Washington, DC: Brookings Institution, 2014).

50. Declan Butler, "French Research Wins Huge Cash Boost," *Nature* 464, no. 838 (2009), doi:10.1038/462838a. See also Jack Grove, "Paris-Saclay: A Mega-University with Ambitions to Match," *Times Higher Education* (April 9, 2015).

51. Atkinson and Blanpied, "Research Universities," 41–43.

52. "Nature Index: Ten Institutions that Dominated Science in 2015," *Nature* (April 20, 2016).

53. Joseph Parilla and Marek Gootman, "Paris Bets Big on Science and Technology with New Mega-University," *Brookings* (May 11, 2016).

54. Declan Butler, "Paris Plans Science in the Suburbs," *Nature* 467, no. 897 (2010): doi: 10.1038/467897a.

55. Catherine Paradeise, "How Effective Have Reform Policies Been in Redesigning the French Higher Education and Research System?," in *Universities and the Production of Elites: Discourses, Policies, and Strategies of Excellence and Stratification in Higher Education,* ed. Roland Bloch et al. (London: Palgrave Macmillan, 2018): 104, 108, 110, 120.

56. Paradeise, "How Effective Have Reform Policies Been," 121–122.

57. Gretchen Vogel, "A German Ivy League Takes Shape," *Science* 314, no. 5798 (2006): 400, http://www.jstor.org/stable/20031550.

58. Anton Geyer, "The German Excellence Initiative," in *Promoting Research Excellence: New Approaches to Funding* (Paris: OECD, 2014), 146–149, http://dx.doi.org/10.1787/9789264207462-en.

59. Geyer, "The German Excellence Initiative," 146–149; Quirin Schiermeier, "Germany's Science Hubs Win in Major Research Revamp," *Nature* 530, no. 7588 (2016): 18–19.

60. Manuela Boatcă, "Catching Up with the (New) West: The German Excellence Initiative, Area Studies, and the Reproduction of Inequality," *Human Architecture* 10, no. 1 (2012): 21; Gretchen Vogel, "Max Planck Accused of Hobbling Universities," *Science* 319, no. 5862 (2008): 396, DOI: 10.1126/science.319.5862.396.

61. Rhoads et al., *China's Rising Research Universities,* 4.

62. Rhoads et al., *China's Rising Research Universities,* 12; Suthathip Yaisawarng and Ying Chu Ng, "The Impact of Higher Education Reform on Research Performance of Chinese Universities," *China Economic Review* 31, no. 1 (2013): 94–105; Qingnan Xiong, Duanhong Zhang, and Hong Liu, "Governance Reform at China's '985 Project' Universities," *Chinese Education and Society* 44, no. 5 (2011): 31–40.

63. Rhoads et al., *China's Rising Research Universities,* 12–16.

64. Keith Bradsher, "Next Made-in-China Boom: College Graduates," *New York Times* (January 16, 2013).

65. Jie Zhang, "Chinese University Reform in Three Steps," *Nature* 514 (2014): 295–297.

66. Anna Smolentseva et al., "Stratification by the State and the Market: High Participation Higher Education in Russia," in *High Participation Systems of Higher Education,* ed. Brendan Cantwell, Simon Marginson, and Anna Smolentseva (Oxford: Oxford University Press, 2018), 315–319.

67. Fedyukin, "Russia's Ivy League."

68. Tatiana Gounko and William Smale, "Modernization of Russian Higher Education: Exploring Paths of Influence," *Compare: A Journal of Comparative Education* 37, no. 4 (2007): 533–548, accessed December 16, 2015, doi: 10.1080/03057920701366358.

69. Kremlin, "Executive Order on Implementing State Policy in Science and Education," President of Russia, May 7, 2012, accessed October 16, 2015, http://en.kremlin

.ru/events/president/news/15236. The Kremlin announced that it would initially increase funding for state research foundations to 25 billion rubles as well as increase spending on R&D to 1.77 percent of GDP.

70. Oleg Alekseev, "First Steps of Russian Universities to Top-100 Global University Rankings," *Higher Education in Russia and Beyond* 1, no. 1 (2014): 6, http://herb.hse.ru/data/2014/05/30/1325398755/1HERB_01_Spring.pdf.

71. Nadir Kinossian and Kevin Morgan, "Development by Decree: The Limits of Authoritarian Modernization in the Russian Federation," *International Journal of Urban and Regional Research* 38, no. 5 (2014): 1685.

72. C. Judson King, *The University of California: Creating, Nurturing, and Maintaining Academic Quality in a Public Research University Setting* (Berkeley: Center for Studies in Higher Education, University of California, Berkeley, 2018), 124.

73. Edward F. Crawley, Kristina Edström, and Tanya Stanko, "Educating Engineers for Research-based Innovation: Creating the Learning Outcomes Framework," in *Proceedings of the 9th International CDIO Conference, Cambridge, MA* (2013).

74. Edward F. Crawley, "The CDIO Syllabus: A Statement of Goals for Undergraduate Engineering Education," Department of Aeronautics and Astronautics, Massachusetts Institute of Technology (2001).

75. Kinossian and Morgan, "Development by Decree," 1678, 1689.

76. Alex Usher, "Structural Barriers to Russian Success in Global University Rankings," *Higher Education in Russia and Beyond* 2, no. 4 (2015): 13–14.

77. Smolentseva et al., "Stratification by the State and the Market," 315–319.

78. Alexander Povalko, "Push for the Top," *Times Higher Education* (December 5, 2014), https://www.timeshighereducation.com/world-university-rankings/2015/brics-and-emerging-economies/analysis/push-for-the-top; Marat Safiullin, Mikhail Savelichev, and Elena Smolnikova, "Higher Education Institutions on the Way towards Multidisciplinarity," *Higher Education in Russia and Beyond* 1, no. 1 (2014): 18–20, accessed January 9, 2016, http://herb.hse.ru/data/2014/05/30/1325398755/1HERB_01_Spring.pdf.

79. Maria Yudkevich, "The Pros and Cons of Russia's Project 5-100," *Times Higher Education* (December 2, 2015).

80. Yudkevich, "Pros and Cons of Russia's Project 5-100."

81. Daniel Sarewitz, "The Pressure to Publish Pushes Down Quality," *Nature* 533, no. 147 (May 12, 2016), DOI:10.1038/533147a.

82. Jeffrey Beall, "Essential Information about Predatory Publishers and Journals," *Higher Education in Russia and Beyond* 1, no. 7 (2016): 8.

83. Elena Denisova-Schmidt, Elvira Leontyeva, and Yaroslav Prytula, "Corruption at Universities Is a Common Disease for Russia and Ukraine," Cambridge, MA: Harvard University, Edmond J. Safra Center for Ethics, June 17, 2014.

84. Igor Chirikov, "The Mystery of Russian Students: Poor Learning Experience, High Satisfaction," *Higher Education in Russia and Beyond* 1, no. 3 (2015): 10–11.

85. Carnoy et al., *University Expansion in a Changing Global Economy,* table 2.1, 37.

86. Carnoy et al., *University Expansion in a Changing Global Economy,* 15.

87. Marginson, "High Participation Systems of Higher Education," 229.

CONCLUSION

# Toward Frameworks for Universal Learning

Various translations of excerpts from what is termed the Ephebic Oath of the Athenian city-state, which was administered to young Athenians about to undertake the duties of citizenship and military service, appear chiseled in stone in public buildings throughout the world.[1] One variant is found in the foyer of the Maxwell School of Citizenship and Public Affairs at Syracuse University: "We will ever strive for the ideals and sacred things of the city, both alone and with many; we will unceasingly seek to quicken the sense of public duty. We will revere and obey the city's laws; we will transmit this city not only not less, but greater, better, and more beautiful than it was transmitted to us." The excerpt captures less the sense of obedience to authority or the obligations of civic duty than it expresses the privilege of participation in the public sphere of a democratic society. The emergence of the classical Athenian democracy has been correlated with access to knowledge, as we have previously assessed, citing the concept of the knowledge-based or epistemic democracy.[2] Amy Gutmann reminds us that the point, of course, was for knowledge to be useful: "The purpose of higher learning in Athenian democracy was not wholly non-instrumental, even if it was wholly unspecialized and un-vocational. Knowledge was useful for the polis, or at least for a well-governed polis."[3]

The conviction expressed by leaders of the founding generation of our nation that in order for a democracy to function its citizens must be well educated requires reaffirmation. Inasmuch as access to knowledge underpins the societal objectives of a pluralistic democracy, accessibility to academic milieus underpinned by knowledge production must be at the core of evolving institutional models. The Fifth Wave research university is accordingly envisioned as an institution defined by its alignment with public values as well as service to the public interest. And indeed, this conception is consistent with the characterization of the university by Gerard Delanty as the "paradigmatic institution of the public sphere and of modernity more generally."[4] Modernity itself is a contested and variously interpreted concept,[5] but to the extent that it is possible to correlate the modern era with the values and ideals of the Enlightenment, which Steven Pinker delineates as reason, science, humanism, and progress,[6] the research university exemplifies that commitment. As Hannah Holborn Gray, president emerita of the University of Chicago, observed, the institution envisioned by Wilhelm von Humboldt has from the outset been predicated on "academic freedom for professor and student alike, so that the goal of intellectual creativity, the following of rigorous investigation and analysis wherever these might lead, could be fully encouraged and realized."[7]

To this commitment to discovery, creativity, and innovation the Fifth Wave would endeavor to add dedication to the public interest. As Barry Bozeman reminds us, the public interest "refers to the outcomes best serving the long-run survival and well-being of a social collective construed as a public." But Bozeman cites Dewey to point out that the public interest "cannot be known in any important sense in the absence of social inquiry and public discussion and debate."[8] And indeed, this is consistent with the pragmatist tenet that knowledge is a product of negotiation and consensus and in order to become actionable must be exercised in a particular context, time, and place in response to real-world problems.[9] Accordingly, the Fifth Wave will endeavor to bring its intellectual resources to the public sphere and facilitate dialogue among citizens. As Seth Moglen points out, universities are uniquely positioned to initiate substantive discussion regarding the complex challenges that confront our nation and the global community in a manner that is "nonreductive, open to competing viewpoints, respectful of difference, and capable of drawing on diverse sources of knowledge." We concur with his proposition that universities explicitly proclaim democratic missions and exercise their prerogative to promote diversity and expand the public sphere with the intent to become "engines for democracy."[10] Recent calls for heterodoxy in the academy presume a commitment to intellectual and ideological pluralism

as well as open access, permeable boundaries, and constructive disagreement.[11]

The Fifth Wave will strive to embody the normative and qualitative
characteristics of the democratic ethos. Indeed, the pluralistic, multicul-
tural, and cosmopolitan milieu of major universities constitutes a mi-
crocosm of the ideal democratic society that one might envision. But any
assessment of the present moment in our society cannot overlook the
rancor and polarization that has defined our politics nor the animosity
directed at academic culture. Pundits proclaim a crisis in American
higher education. Accounts of disruption, dysfunction, and demise
abound. Skyrocketing tuition and student debt grab headlines while
screeds decrying liberal bias in the academy reinforce skepticism toward
what has increasingly been framed as a dubious enterprise. The vitriol
has become so commonplace that it would be superfluous to cobble together even a representative compilation.[12] Contempt for expertise and
professional standards threatens to render our democracy dysfunctional.
"Democracy itself can enter a death spiral that presents an immediate
danger of decay either into rule by the mob or toward elitist technocracy," Tom Nichols cautions. "Both are authoritarian outcomes."[13] And
as Robert Kagan reminds us, "Authoritarianism has reemerged as the
greatest threat to the liberal democratic world."[14] Postmodern skepticism
of truth claims notwithstanding, reason itself has been under assault and
science under siege. "Contemporary democracy is not the deliberative
self-governing polity of informed free citizens envisioned by modern Enlightenment thinkers," observes Yaron Ezrahi.[15]

If the Fifth Wave is to be held to account, it must assume primary responsibility for sustaining reason, science, humanism, and progress—
the ideals that have defined our nation from the outset—along with what
Pinker terms that "great Enlightenment experiment, American constitutional democracy with its checks on government power."[16] And because
democracies are inherently epistemic, as we considered in chapter 4,
knowledge is the "foundation for democratic governance," as Clark
Miller points out.[17] The implications of what has been termed the epistemic case for democracy are consistent with Fifth Wave academic culture and begin with the supposition that there may be wisdom in the
collective, which has been variously assessed in terms of collective intelligence, cognitive diversity, or the wisdom of crowds. Political theorist

Hélène Landemore contends that the collective intelligence of informed citizens produces what she terms "democratic reason," which, not all that unlike the emergent intelligence of social insects modeled in complexity theory, "might in fact be distinct from individual reason writ large."[18]

Policy scholar Sheila Jasanoff calls for democratic societies to reimagine and reinvent their patterns of governance. If citizens are to "construct shared social commitments," she contends, democracy must be an exercise in "reasoning together to plan futures which all can see as serving their needs and interests."[19] It is no coincidence that pragmatism, with its insistence on the indivisibility of thought and action and emphasis on the practical application of knowledge within the context of social practice, is a product of the ferment of our democracy.[20] This again is the socially robust knowledge that is a product of its increasing contextualization across academia, business and industry, government agencies and laboratories, and organizations in civil society, which also draws from the currents of the broader cultural Zeitgeist.[21]

Insofar as democracy is an epistemic process, and our vocabularies are contingent, then, the Fifth Wave must commit itself to imagining and constructing a better world through the accommodation of the literary culture that Richard Rorty envisions alongside the culture of science and the scientific approach to knowledge that has dominated academic culture since the Enlightenment. This again is a world where "intellectuals will have given up the idea that there is a standard against which the products of the human imagination can be measured other than their social utility, as this utility is judged by a maximally free, leisured, and tolerant global community."[22] As Daniel Sarewitz observes, if our aspirations, interests, and views of human purpose are not to be narrow, "then we must find purpose through a never-ending process of expanding the limits of our imagination about the kinds of worlds that we could, and should, aspire to." Sarewitz characterizes this desideratum as "democratic imagination."[23] It is precisely this sort of democratic imagination that must serve as a guiding principle of academic culture if our colleges and universities are to contribute to the restoration and reinvigoration of our democracy.

"All significant policy prescriptions presuppose a theory, a political theory, of the proper role of government in education," Amy Gutmann, president of the University of Pennsylvania, contends. "When the theory remains implicit, we cannot adequately judge its principles or the policy prescriptions that flow from them."[24] In this context, we reiterate one final time that when the exclusion of the majority of academically qualified applicants from the excellence of a research-grade university education becomes de facto national policy, the consequences are pernicious and ethically unacceptable. The imperative is to ensure that far more students have access to research-grade academic platforms that deliver robust and competitive world-class educations commensurate with the demands of the knowledge economy. Discovery and innovation, moreover, must be conducted with reference to concern for societal outcomes and the equitable distribution of the benefits of research and development. Disregard of the socioeconomic challenges faced by most Americans threatens to impede the capacity of these institutions to contribute decisively and consistently to the collective. Richard Nelson considers the urgency of this imperative in an assessment of how little has changed since he first surveyed some of the challenges that confronted our society more than four decades ago:

> Why was it that a country that recently had accomplished the truly remarkable feat of sending a man to the moon and bringing him back to earth safely, had wiped out scourges like infantile paralysis, and more generally had achieved an historically unprecedented standard of living for the middle class, for some reason seemed unable to provide an effective education for ghetto kids, halt or significantly slow down the rising cost of medical care, keep the air and water clean, or cut down on the incidence of drug addiction and drug-related crime?[25]

Following the death in 1820 of George III, who had reigned as king of Great Britain and Ireland for more than half a century, his personal collection of 65,000 printed books and manuscripts and roughly 19,000 pamphlets was acquired by the British Museum and is today housed in the British Library in what is termed the King's Library Tower. The George III collection, which has been described as among the most comprehensive assembled during the Enlightenment, constitutes the best efforts of that era to represent the breadth of human knowledge.[26] Attempts to quantify the proliferation of knowledge in our own era reveal only that, in its aggregate, its rate is exponential. Four decades ago, Buckminster Fuller, for example, proposed the "knowledge-doubling curve," which when plotted on a graph appears as a J-curve that represented his estimate of the acceleration of the growth of new knowledge. Using some measure of texts in print in 1980 as proxy for knowledge, Fuller estimated that, historically, knowledge had doubled every century until the twentieth, when it began to double every eighteen months in some fields, as exponential growth replaced mere linear growth. By some estimates, knowledge is now doubling every twelve hours. Whatever estimates one chooses to believe, the proliferation of knowledge at present defies quantification and makes broad accessibility to advanced levels of higher education especially imperative. But, as we have argued, accessibility is a function of the structure of our knowledge enterprises. Thus: "You never change things by fighting the existing reality," as Fuller once remarked. "To change something build a new model that makes the existing model obsolete."[27]

In 1865, marking the advent of the Third Wave in higher education, Ezra Cornell proclaimed, "I would found an institution where any person can find instruction in any study." This, of course, became enshrined as the motto of Cornell University. At the end of the nineteenth century, James Burrill Angell, who served as president of the University of Michigan from 1871 to 1909, expressed the similar conviction—formulated in the gender-specific locution of a bygone era—that the university should provide an "uncommon education for the common man." In the first quarter of the twenty-first century, a confluence of factors permits us to glimpse an era when the aspirations of Cornell and Angell may yet transcend mere rhetoric. As with other periods of rapid social change, this new era of human enterprise invites us to consider our social values and aspirations, which inform how we go about designing, managing, and evaluating organizations and institutions. If our nation is to prosper in the decades ahead, then, a subset of public research universities must take up the challenge to evolve in scope and scale to promote accessibility to world-class knowledge production to a demographic representative of the socioeconomic and intellectual diversity of our nation, constituting the vanguard of a league of colleges and universities committed to service to the nation that may more accurately be characterized as national service universities. We reiterate that at issue is not the education of students who graduate from the top 5 or 10 percent of their high school classes but rather the imperative to educate to internationally competitive levels of achievement the top quarter or third of respective age cohorts and through universal learning to provide opportunities for lifelong learning to more than half the population of the United States. Frameworks for universal learning will permit individuals, regardless of their socioeconomic status or life situation, to gain the knowledge and skills to thrive and be empowered to freely shape their own intellectual development and self-determined creative and professional pursuits.[28] As frameworks for universal learning, Fifth Wave universities would seek to serve any learner from any socioeconomic background at any stage of work and learning through broad accessibility to world-class knowledge production.

## Notes

1. John Wilson Taylor, "The Athenian Ephebic Oath," *Classical Journal* 13, no. 7 (April 1918): 495–501.

2. Josiah Ober, *Democracy and Knowledge: Innovation and Learning in Classical Athens* (Princeton, NJ: Princeton University Press, 2008), 26–27.

3. Amy Gutmann, *Democratic Education* (Princeton, NJ: Princeton University Press, 1987), 186n26.

4. Gerard Delanty, "The Sociology of the University and Higher Education: The Consequences of Globalization," in *The Sage Handbook of Sociology*, ed. Craig Calhoun, Chris Rojek, and Bryan Turner (London: Sage, 2005), 530, cited in Craig Calhoun, "The University and the Public Good," *Thesis Eleven* 84 (February 2006): 10.

5. See, for example, Anthony Giddens, *The Consequences of Modernity* (Cambridge: Polity, 1990); Charles Taylor, "Two Theories of Modernity," *Public Culture* 11, no. 1 (1999): 153–174.

6. Steven Pinker, *Enlightenment Now: The Case for Reason, Science, Humanism, and Progress* (New York: Viking, 2018).

7. Hanna Holborn Gray, *Searching for Utopia: Universities and Their Histories* (Berkeley: University of California Press, 2012), 39–40.

8. Barry Bozeman, *Public Values and Public Interest: Counterbalancing Economic Individualism* (Washington, DC: Georgetown University Press, 2007), 13.

9. John J. Stuhr, *Pragmatism, Postmodernism, and the Future of Philosophy* (New York: Routledge, 2002), 129, 154–155.

10. Seth Moglen, "Sharing Knowledge, Practicing Democracy: A Vision for the Twenty-First Century University," in *Education, Justice, and Democracy*, ed. Danielle Allen and Rob Reich (Chicago: University of Chicago Press, 2013), 267–268.

11. Greg Lukianoff and Jonathan Haidt, *The Coddling of the American Mind: How Good Intentions and Bad Ideas Are Setting Up a Generation for Failure* (New York: Penguin Press, 2018).

12. See, for example, Richard Arum and Josipa Roksa, *Academically Adrift: Limited Learning on College Campuses* (Chicago, University of Chicago Press, 2010); Bryan Caplan, *The Case against Education: Why the Education System Is a Waste of Time and Money* (Princeton, NJ: Princeton University Press, 2018); and Kevin Carey, *The End of College: Creating the Future of Learning and the University of Everywhere* (New York: Riverhead Books, 2015).

13. Tom Nichols, *The Death of Expertise: The Campaign against Established Knowledge and Why It Matters* (Oxford: Oxford University Press, 2017).

14. Robert Kagan, "The Strongmen Strike Back," *Washington Post* (March 14, 2019).

15. Yaron Ezrahi, *Imagined Democracies: Necessary Political Fictions* (Cambridge: Cambridge University Press, 2012).

16. Pinker, *Enlightenment Now*, 200.

17. Clark A. Miller, "Knowledge and Democracy: The Epistemics of Self-Governance," in *Science and Democracy: Making Knowledge and Making Power in the Biosciences and Beyond*, ed. Stephen Hilgartner, Clark A. Miller, and Rob Hagendijk (New York: Routledge, 2015), 201.

18. Hélène E. Landemore, *Democratic Reason: Politics, Collective Intelligence, and the Rule of the Many* (Princeton, NJ: Princeton University Press, 2013); Hélène E. Landemore, "Why the Many Are Smarter Than the Few and Why It Matters," *Journal of Public Deliberation* 8, no. 1 (2012): 1–12. See also the volume edited by Landemore and Jon Elster, *Collective Wisdom: Principles and Mechanisms* (Cambridge: Cambridge University Press, 2012).

19. Sheila Jasanoff, *Science and Public Reason* (London: Routledge, 2012), 1.

20. Richard J. Bernstein, *The Pragmatic Turn* (Cambridge: Polity, 2010).

21. Helga Nowotny, Peter Scott, and Michael Gibbons, *Rethinking Science: Knowledge and the Public in an Age of Uncertainty* (Cambridge: Polity Press, 2001).

22. Richard Rorty, "Philosophy as a Transitional Genre," in *Pragmatism, Critique, Judgment: Essays for Richard J. Bernstein*, ed. Seyla Benhabib and Nancy Fraser (Cambridge, MA: MIT Press, 2004), 27.

23. Daniel Sarewitz, "Animals and Beggars: Imaginative Numbers in the Real World," in *Science, Philosophy, and Sustainability: The End of the Cartesian Dream*, ed. Ângela Guimarães Pereira and Silvio Funtowicz (London: Routledge, 2015): 144–145.

24. Amy Gutmann, *Democratic Education* (Princeton, NJ: Princeton University Press, 1987), 6.

25. Richard R. Nelson, "The Moon and the Ghetto Revisited," *Science and Public Policy* 38, no. 9 (November 2011): 681.

26. John Brooke, "The Library of King George III," *Yale University Library Gazette* 52, no. 1 (July 1977): 33–45.

27. R. Buckminster Fuller, *Critical Path* (New York: St. Martin's Press, 1981), 329–331.

28. Michael M. Crow, Derrick M. Anderson, Jacqueline Smith, and Luke Tate, "Universal Learning as a New Aspiration for Higher Education," working paper (Tempe: Office of the President, Arizona State University, 2019).

# SELECTED BIBLIOGRAPHY

Abbott, Andrew. *Chaos of Disciplines.* Chicago: University of Chicago Press, 2001.

Abbott, Andrew. *The System of Professions: An Essay on the Division of Expert Labor.* Chicago: University of Chicago Press, 1988.

Abrams, M. H. "What's the Use of Theorizing About the Arts?" In *In Search of Literary Theory.* Edited by Morton W. Bloomfield, 52–54. Ithaca, NY: Cornell University Press, 1972.

Adams, John. "A Dissertation on the Canon and Feudal Law" (1765). In *The Works of John Adams.* Edited by Charles F. Adams. Boston: Little, Brown, 1851.

Aldrich, Howard E., and Jeffrey Pfeffer. "Environments of Organizations." *Annual Review of Sociology* 2 (1976): 79–105.

Allen, Danielle, and Rob Reich, eds. *Education, Justice, and Democracy.* Chicago: University of Chicago Press, 2013.

Allenby, Braden, and Jonathan Fink. "Toward Inherently Secure and Resilient Societies." *Science* 309 (August 12, 2005), 1034–1036.

Allenby, Braden, and Daniel Sarewitz. *The Techno-Human Condition.* Cambridge, MA: MIT Press, 2013.

Altbach, Philip G. "The American Academic Model in Comparative Perspective." In *In Defense of American Higher Education.* Edited by Philip G. Altbach, Patricia Gumport, and D. Bruce Johnstone, 11–37. Baltimore: Johns Hopkins University Press, 2001.

Altbach, Philip G. *Global Perspectives on Higher Education.* Baltimore: Johns Hopkins University Press, 2016.

American Academy of Arts and Sciences. *The Heart of the Matter: The Humanities and Social Sciences For A Vibrant, Competitive, and Secure Nation.* Cambridge, MA: American Academy of Arts and Sciences, 2013.

American Academy of Arts and Sciences. *Public Research Universities: Recommitting to Lincoln's Vision: An Educational Compact for the Twenty-First Century.* Cambridge, MA: American Academy of Arts and Sciences, 2016.

Anderson, Derrick M., and Gabel Taggart. "Organizations, Policies, and the Roots of Public Value Failure: The Case of For-Profit Higher Education." *Public Administration Review* 76, no. 5 (September/October 2016): 779–789.

Anderson, Derrick M., and Andrew Whitford. "The Institutional Design Frontiers of Publicness and University Performance." *Public Administration Review* 76, no. 5 (September/October 2016): 753–755.

Apostel, Léo, Guy Berger, Asa Briggs, and Guy Michaud, eds. *Interdisciplinarity: Problems of Teaching and Research in Universities.* Paris: Organisation for Economic Cooperation and Development, 1972.

Arthur, W. Brian. *The Nature of Technology: What It Is and How It Evolves.* New York: Free Press, 2009.

Arthur, W. Brian. "Positive Feedbacks in the Economy." *Scientific American* 262, no. 2 (1990): 92–99.

Arum, Richard, Adam Gamoran, and Yossi Shavit. "More Inclusion Than Diversion: Expansion, Differentiation, and Market Structure in Higher Education." In *Stratification in Higher Education: A Comparative Study.* Edited by Yossi Shavit, Richard Arum, and Adam Gamoran, 1–35. Stanford: Stanford University Press, 2007.

Arum, Richard, and Josipa Roksa. *Academically Adrift: Limited Learning on College Campuses.* Chicago: University of Chicago Press, 2010.

Atkinson, Richard C., and William A. Blanpied. "Research Universities: Core of the U.S. Science and Technology System." *Technology in Society* 30 (2008): 30–48.

Audretsch, David B., and Maryann P. Feldman. "R&D Spillovers and the Geography of Innovation and Production." *American Economic Review* 86, no. 3 (June 1996): 630–640.

Baker, David P. *The Schooled Society: The Educational Transformation of Global Culture.* Stanford: Stanford University Press, 2014.

Barnett, Ronald. *Imagining the University.* London: Routledge, 2013.

Barnes, Sarah V. "England's Civic Universities and the Triumph of the Oxbridge Ideal." *History of Education Quarterly* 36, no. 3 (1996): 271–305.

Bastedo, Michael N. "Organizing Higher Education: A Manifesto." In *The Organization of Higher Education: Managing Colleges for a New Era.* Edited by Michael N. Bastedo, 3–17. Baltimore: Johns Hopkins University Press, 2012.

Bastedo, Michael N., ed. *The Organization of Higher Education: Managing Colleges for a New Era.* Baltimore: Johns Hopkins University Press, 2012.

Baumol, William J. *The Cost Disease: Why Computers Get Cheaper and Health Care Doesn't.* New Haven, CT: Yale University Press, 2012.

Baumol, William J., and William G. Bowen. "On the Performing Arts: The Anatomy of Their Economic Problems." *American Economic Review* 55, no. 1/2 (March 1965): 495–502.

Baumol, William J., and William G. Bowen. *Performing Arts: The Economic Dilemma.* New York: Twentieth Century Fund, 1966.

Becker, Gary S. *Human Capital: A Theoretical and Empirical Analysis, with Special Reference to Education*, 3rd ed. Chicago: University of Chicago Press, 1993.

Bernstein, Richard J. *The Pragmatic Turn.* Cambridge: Polity Press, 2010.

Blumenstyk, Goldie. *American Higher Education in Crisis? What Everyone Needs to Know.* Oxford: Oxford University Press, 2015.

Bok, Derek. *Universities in the Marketplace: The Commercialization of Higher Education.* Princeton, NJ: Princeton University Press, 2004.

Boliver, Vikki. "Expansion, Differentiation, and the Persistence of Social Class Inequalities in British Higher Education." *Higher Education* 61, no. 3 (2011): 229–242.

Boradkar, Prasad. "Design as Problem Solving." In *The Oxford Handbook of Interdisciplinarity.* Edited by Robert Frodeman, Julie Thompson Klein, and Carl Mitcham, 273–287. Oxford: Oxford University Press, 2010.

Börner, Katy, Noshir Contractor, Holly J. Falk-Krzesinski, Stephen M. Fiore, Kara L. Hall, Joann Keyton, Bonnie Spring, Daniel Stokols, William Trochim, Brian Uzzi. "A Multi-Level Systems Perspective for the Science of Team Science." *Science of Translational Medicine* 2, no. 49 (September 15, 2010): 1–5.

Bound, John, and Sarah Turner. "Collegiate Attainment: Understanding Degree Completion." NBER Report 2010, no. 4. Cambridge, MA: National Bureau of Economic Research, 2010.

Bourdieu, Pierre. "The Forms of Capital." In *Handbook for Theory and Research in the Sociology of Education.* Edited by John G. Richardson, 241–258. Westport, CT: Greenwood Press, 1986.

Bourdieu, Pierre. *Homo Academicus.* Translated by Peter Collier. Stanford: Stanford University Press, 1988.

Bowen, William G., Matthew M. Chingos, and Michael S. McPherson. *Crossing the Finish Line: Completing College at America's Public Universities.* Princeton, NJ: Princeton University Press, 2009.

Bowen, William G., Martin A. Kurzweil, and Eugene M. Tobin. *Equity and Excellence in American Higher Education.* Charlottesville: University of Virginia Press, 2006.

Boyer Commission on Educating Undergraduates in the Research University. "Reinventing Undergraduate Education: A Blueprint for America's Research Universities." Stony Brook: State University of New York, 1998.

Bozeman, Barry. *All Organizations Are Public: Comparing Public and Private Organizations.* Washington, DC: Beard Books, 2004.

Bozeman, Barry. *Public Values and Public Interest: Counterbalancing Economic Individualism.* Washington, DC: Georgetown University Press, 2007.

Bozeman, Barry, and Daniel Sarewitz. "Public Value Mapping and Science Policy Evaluation." *Minerva* 49, no. 1 (2011): 1–23.

Bozeman, Barry, and Daniel Sarewitz. "Public Values and Public Failure in U.S. Science Policy." *Science and Public Policy* 32, no. 2 (2005): 119–136.

Brint, Steven G., and Jerome Karabel. *The Diverted Dream: Community Colleges and the Promise of Educational Opportunity in America, 1900–1985.* Oxford: Oxford University Press, 1989.

Brooke, John. "The Library of King George III." *Yale University Library Gazette* 52, no. 1 (July 1977): 33–45.

Brooks, David. "The Education Gap." *New York Times* (September 25, 2005).

Brooks, David. "What the Working Class Is Still Trying to Tell Us." *New York Times* (November 8, 2018).

Brooks, Frederick P. *The Design of Design: Essays from a Computer Scientist.* Boston: Addison-Wesley, 2010.

Brooks, Harvey. "The Relationship between Science and Technology." *Research Policy* 23 (1994): 477–486.

Brown, John Seely, Allan Collins, and Paul Duguid. "Situated Cognition and the Culture of Learning." *Educational Researcher* 18, no. 1 (January–February 1989): 32–42.

Brown, John Seely, and Paul Duguid. "Knowledge and Organization: A Social-Practice Perspective." *Organizational Science* 12, no. 2 (March–April 2001): 198–213.

Brown, John Seely, and Paul Duguid. "Organizational Learning and Communities-of-Practice: Toward a Unified View of Working, Learning, and Innovation." *Organization Science* 2, no. 1 (1991): 40–57.

Brown, Tim. *Change by Design: How Design Thinking Transforms Organizations and Inspires Innovation.* New York: Harper Collins, 2009.

Bruun, Hans Henrik. *Science, Values, and Politics in Max Weber's Methodology*. London: Routledge, 2016.

Brynjolfsson, Erik, and Andrew McAfee. *The Second Machine Age: Work, Progress, and Prosperity in a Time of Brilliant Technologies*. New York: W. W. Norton, 2014.

Bucchi, Massimiano, and Federico Neresini. "Science and Public Participation." In *The Handbook of Science and Technology Studies*, 3rd ed. Edited by Edward J. Hackett et al., 799–840. Cambridge, MA: MIT Press, 2008.

Buchanan, Richard. "Myth and Maturity: Toward a New Order in the Decade of Design." *Design Issues* 6, no. 2 (1990): 75–85.

Buchanan, Richard. "Wicked Problems in Design Thinking." *Design Issues* 8, no. 2 (Spring 1992): 5–21.

Burke, W. Warner. *Organization Change: Theory and Practice*, 4th ed. Los Angeles: Sage, 2014.

Bush, George P., and Lowell H. Hattery. "Teamwork and Creativity in Research." *Administrative Science Quarterly* 1, no. 3 (December 1956): 361–372.

Bush, Vannevar. *Science—The Endless Frontier: A Report to the President on a Program for Postwar Scientific Research*. Washington, DC: U.S. Government Printing Office, 1945.

Byrne, David, and Gill Callaghan. *Complexity Theory and the Social Sciences: The State of the Art*. London: Routledge, 2014.

Cahalan, Margaret, and Laura Perna. *Indicators of Higher Education Equity in the United States: 45-Year Trend Report*. Washington, DC: Pell Institute for the Study of Opportunity in Higher Education, 2015.

Cahalan, Margaret, Laura W. Perna, Mika Yamashita, J. Wright, and Sureima Santillan. *Indicators of Higher Education Equity in the United States: 2018 Historical Trend Report*. Washington, DC: Pell Institute for the Study of Opportunity in Higher Education, 2018.

Calhoun, Craig. "The Public Mission of the Research University." In *Knowledge Matters: The Public Mission of the Research University*. Edited by Diana Rhoten and Craig Calhoun, 1–33. New York: Columbia University Press, 2011.

Calhoun, Craig. "The University and the Public Good." *Thesis Eleven* 84 (February 2006): 7–43.

Calinescu, Matei. *Five Faces of Modernity: Modernism, Avant-Garde, Decadence, Kitsch, Postmodernism*. Durham, NC: Duke University Press, 1987.

Cantwell, Brendan. "Broad Access and Steep Stratification in the First Mass System: High Participation Higher Education in the United States of America." In *High Participation Systems of Higher Education*. Edited by Brendan Cantwell, Simon Marginson, and Anna Smolentseva, 227–265. Oxford: Oxford University Press, 2018.

Cantwell, Brendan, and Simon Marginson. "Vertical Stratification." In *High Participation Systems of Higher Education*. Edited by Brendan Cantwell, Simon Marginson, and Anna Smolentseva, 125–149. Oxford: Oxford University Press, 2018.

Cantwell, Brendan, Simon Marginson, and Anna Smolentseva. *High Participation Systems of Higher Education*. Oxford: Oxford University Press, 2018.

Caplan, Bryan. *The Case against Education: Why the Education System Is a Waste of Time and Money*. Princeton, NJ: Princeton University Press, 2018.

Carey, Kevin. "Americans Think We Have the World's Best Colleges." *New York Times* (June 28, 2014).

Carey, Kevin. *The End of College: Creating the Future of Learning and the University of Everywhere.* New York: Riverhead Books, 2015.

Carnevale, Anthony P., Tamara Jayasundera, and Arten Gulish. "America's Divided Recovery: College Haves and Have-Nots." Washington, DC: Center on Education and the Workforce, Georgetown University, 2016.

Carnevale, Anthony, and Stephen Rose. "The Economy Goes to College: The Hidden Promise of Higher Education in the Post-Industrial Service Economy." Washington, DC: Georgetown University Center for Education and the Workforce, 2015.

Carnevale, Anthony P., and Stephen J. Rose. "The Undereducated American." Washington, DC: Georgetown University Center on Education and the Workforce, June 2011.

Carnevale, Anthony P., Nicole Smith, and Jeff Strohl. "Help Wanted: Projections of Jobs and Education Requirements through 2018." Washington, DC: Georgetown University Center on Education and the Workforce, June 2010.

Carnevale, Anthony P., Nicole Smith, and Jeff Strohl. "Recovery: Job Growth and Education Requirements through 2020." Washington, DC: Georgetown University Center on Education and the Workforce, 2014.

Carnoy, Martin, Prashant Loyalka, Maria Dobryakova, Rafiq Dossani, Froumin, Isak Froumin, Katherine Jandhyala Kuhns, and Rong Wang. *University Expansion in a Changing Global Economy: Triumph of the BRICs?* Stanford: Stanford University Press, 2013.

Carter, Susan B., et al., eds. *Historical Statistics of the United States,* millennial ed. Vol. 5. New York: Cambridge University Press, 2006.

Cash, David W., William C. Clark, Frank Alcock, Nancy M. Dickson, Noelle Eckley, David H. Guston, Jill Jäger, and Ronald B. Mitchell. "Knowledge Systems for Sustainable Development." *Proceedings of the National Academy of Sciences* 100, no. 14 (2003): 8086–8091.

Cass, Oren. *The Once and Future Worker: A Vision for the Renewal of Work in America.* New York: Encounter, 2018.

Castel, Albert. "The Founding Fathers and the Vision of a National University." *History of Education Quarterly* 4, no. 4 (December 1964): 280–302.

Caws, Peter J. "Design for a University." *Daedalus* 99, no. 1 (Winter 1970): 84–107.

Cech, Thomas R. "Science at Liberal Arts Colleges: A Better Education?" In *Distinctively American: The Residential Liberal Arts Colleges.* Edited by Steven Koblik and Stephen R. Graubard, 195–216. New Brunswick, NJ: Transaction, 2000.

Chetty, Raj, John N. Friedman, Emmanuel Saez, Nicholas Turner, and Danny Yagan. "Mobility Report Cards: The Role of Colleges in Intergenerational Mobility." NBER Working Paper no. 23618. Cambridge, MA: National Bureau of Economic Research, January 2017.

Cheung, Sin Yi, and Muriel Egerton. "Great Britain: Higher Education Expansion and Reform—Changing Educational Inequalities." In *Stratification in Higher Education: A Comparative Study.* Edited by Yossi Shavit, Richard Arum, and Adam Gamoran, 195–219. Stanford: Stanford University Press, 2007.

Chomsky, Noam. *The Cold War and the University: Toward an Intellectual History of the Postwar Years.* New York: New Press, 1997.

Christensen, Clayton M., and Henry J. Eyring. *The Innovative University: Changing the DNA of Higher Education from the Inside Out.* San Francisco: Jossey-Bass, 2011.

Christensen, Clayton M., Michael B. Horn, Louis Caldera, and Louis Soares. "Disrupting College: How Disruptive Innovation Can Deliver Quality and Affordability to Postsecondary Education." Washington, DC: Center for American Progress, February 2011.

Clark, Burton R. *Creating Entrepreneurial Universities: Organizational Pathways of Transformation*. Oxford: Elsevier, 1998.

Clark, Burton R. "Development of the Sociology of Higher Education." In *Sociology of Higher Education: Contributions and Their Contexts*. Edited by Patricia J. Gumport, 3–16. Baltimore: Johns Hopkins University Press, 2007.

Clark, Burton R. "The Entrepreneurial University: Demand and Response." *Tertiary Education and Management* 4, no. 1 (1998): 5–16.

Clark, William. *Academic Charisma and the Origins of the Research University*. Chicago: University of Chicago Press, 2006.

Clotfelter, Charles T. *Unequal Colleges in the Age of Disparity*. Cambridge, MA: Harvard University Press, 2017.

Cohen, Arthur M. *The Shaping of American Higher Education: Emergence and the Growth of the Contemporary System,* 2nd ed. San Francisco: Jossey-Bass, 2010.

Cohen, Michael D., James G. March, and Johan P. Olsen. "A Garbage Can Model of Organizational Choice." *Administrative Science Quarterly* 17, no. 1 (1972): 1–25.

Cole, Jonathan R. *The Great American University: Its Rise to Preeminence, Its Indispensable National Role, and Why It Must Be Protected*. New York: Public Affairs, 2009.

Cole, Jonathan R. *Toward a More Perfect University*. New York: Public Affairs, 2016.

Collingridge, David. *The Social Control of Technology*. New York: St. Martin's Press, 1980.

Collini, Stefan. Introduction to C. P. Snow, *The Two Cultures*. Cambridge: Cambridge University Press, 1998.

Collins, Randall. "Credential Inflation and the Future of Universities." In *The Future of the City of Intellect*. Edited by Steven Brint, 23–46. Stanford: Stanford University Press, 2002.

Cook, Scott D. N., and John Seely Brown. "Bridging Epistemologies: The Generative Dance between Organizational Knowledge and Organizational Knowing." *Organization Science* 10, no. 4 (July–August 1999): 381–400.

Craig, Ryan. *College Disrupted: The Great Unbundling of Higher Education*. New York: Palgrave Macmillan, 2014.

Crow, Michael M. "None Dare Call It Hubris: The Limits of Knowledge." *Issues in Science and Technology* 23, no. 2 (Winter 2007): 29–32.

Crow, Michael M., and Derrick M. Anderson. "From Agency to Enterprise: Arizona State University and a New Institutional Paradigm for American Higher Education." Working Paper. Tempe: Office of the President, Arizona State University, 2018.

Crow, Michael M., and Derrick M. Anderson. "National Service Universities: Fulfilling the Promise of Excellence at Scale in American Higher Education." Working Paper. Tempe: Office of the President, Arizona State University, 2019.

Crow, Michael M., Derrick M. Anderson, Jacqueline Smith, and Luke Tate. "Universal Learning as a New Aspiration for Higher Education." Working Paper. Tempe: Office of the President, Arizona State University, 2019.

Crow, Michael M., and Barry Bozeman. *Limited by Design: R&D Laboratories in the U.S. National Innovation System*. New York: Columbia University Press, 1998.

Crow, Michael M., and William B. Dabars. *Designing the New American University*. Baltimore: Johns Hopkins University Press, 2015.

Crow, Michael M., and William B. Dabars. "Interdisciplinarity and the Institutional Context of Knowledge in the American Research University." In *The Oxford Handbook of Interdisciplinarity*, 2nd ed. Edited by Robert Frodeman, Julie Thompson Klein, and Roberto Carlos Dos Santos Pacheco, 471–484. Oxford: Oxford University Press, 2017.

Crow, Michael M., and William B. Dabars. "Interdisciplinarity as a Design Problem: Toward Mutual Intelligibility among Academic Disciplines in the American Research University." In *Enhancing Communication and Collaboration in Interdisciplinary Research*. Edited by Michael O'Rourke, Stephen Crowley, Sanford D. Eigenbrode, and J. D. Wulfhorst, 294–322. Los Angeles: Sage, 2013.

Crow, Michael M., and William B. Dabars. "University-Based Research and Economic Development: The Morrill Act and the Emergence of the American Research University." In *Precipice or Crossroads: Where America's Great Public Universities Stand and Where They Are Going Midway Through Their Second Century*. Edited by Daniel Mark Fogel and Elizabeth Malson-Huddle, 119–158. Albany: State University of New York Press, 2012.

Crow, Michael M., and Ralph F. Shangraw. "Revisiting 'Public Administration as a Design Science' for the Twenty-First Century Public University." *Public Administration Review* 76, no. 5 (2016): 762–763.

Crow, Michael M., Kyle Whitman, and Derrick M. Anderson. "Rethinking Academic Entrepreneurship: University Governance and the Emergence of the Academic Enterprise." *Public Administration Review* (in press), https://onlinelibrary.wiley.com/doi/abs/10.1111/puar.13069.

Curtius, Ernst Robert. *European Literature and the Latin Middle Ages*. Translated by Willard R. Trask. Princeton, NJ: Princeton University Press, 2013. Originally published 1952.

Cyert, Richard M., and James G. March. "Models in a Behavioral Theory of the Firm." *Behavioral Science* 4, no. 2 (April 1959): 81–95.

Darnton, Robert. "Google and the Future of Books." *New York Review of Books* (February 12, 2009).

Dasgupta, Partha, and Paul A. David. "Toward a New Economics of Science." *Research Policy* 23 (1994): 487–521.

Delanty, Gerard. "The Sociology of the University and Higher Education: The Consequences of Globalization." In *The Sage Handbook of Sociology*. Edited by Craig Calhoun, Chris Rojek, and Bryan Turner, 530–545. London: Sage, 2005.

Delbanco, Andrew. *College: What It Was, Is, and Should Be*. Princeton, NJ: Princeton University Press, 2012.

Demers, Christiane. *Organizational Change Theories: A Synthesis*. Los Angeles: Sage, 2007.

Dewey, John. "The Need of an Industrial Education in an Industrial Democracy." *John Dewey: The Middle Works, 1899–1924*. Vol. 10. Edited by Jo Ann Boydston, 137–143. Carbondale: Southern Illinois University Press, 1976–1983.

Dillon, John. *The Heirs of Plato: A Study of the Old Academy (347–274 B.C.).* Oxford: Oxford University Press, 2003.

DiMaggio, Paul J., and Walter W. Powell. "The Iron Cage Revisited: Institutional Isomorphism and Collective Rationality in Organizational Fields." *American Sociological Review* 48, no. 2 (April 1983): 147–160.

Donmoyer, Robert. "Take My Paradigm . . . Please! The Legacy of Kuhn's Construct in Educational Research." *International Journal of Qualitative Studies in Education* 19, no. 1 (2006): 11–34.

Douglass, John Aubrey. *The California Idea and American Higher Education: 1850 to the 1960 Master Plan.* Stanford: Stanford University Press, 2000.

Douglass, John Aubrey. *The Conditions for Admission: Access, Equity, and the Social Contract of Public Universities.* Stanford: Stanford University Press, 2007.

Downs, Anthony. *Inside Bureaucracy.* RAND Corporation Research Study. Boston: Little, Brown, 1967.

Dreier, Peter, and Richard D. Kahlenberg. "Making Top Colleges Less Aristocratic and More Meritocratic." *New York Times* (September 12, 2014).

Duguid, Paul. "The Art of Knowing: Social and Tacit Dimensions of Knowledge and the Limits of the Community of Practice." *Information Society* 21 (2005): 109–118.

Dunne, Anthony, and Fiona Raby. *Speculative Everything: Design, Fiction, and Social Dreaming.* Cambridge, MA: MIT Press, 2013.

Dupree, A. Hunter. *Science in the Federal Government: A History of Policies and Activities to 1940.* Baltimore: Johns Hopkins University Press, 1986.

Durden, William G. Review of *Designing the New American University,* by Michael M. Crow and William B. Dabars. *Journal of College and University Law* 42, no. 2 (2016): 553–564.

Durkheim, Émile. *Education and Society.* Translated by Sherwood D. Fox. Glencoe, IL: Free Press, 1956). First published 1922.

Edsall, Thomas B. "The Reproduction of Privilege." *New York Times* (March 12, 2012).

Edwards, E. G. "Colleges of Advanced Technology in Britain." *Nature* 199, no. 4899 (1963): DOI:10.1038/1991131a0.

Ehrenberg, Ronald G. *Tuition Rising: Why College Costs So Much.* Cambridge, MA: Harvard University Press, 2000.

Eliot, Charles W. "The New Education: Its Organization." *Atlantic Monthly* 23 (February and March 1869), 203–220, 358–367.

Elliott, Jennifer A. *An Introduction to Sustainable Development.* New York: Routledge, 2012.

Etzkowitz, Henry. "Entrepreneurial Scientists and Entrepreneurial Universities in American Academic Science." *Minerva* 21 (1983): 1–21.

Etzkowitz, Henry. "Research Groups as Quasi-firms: The Invention of the Entrepreneurial University." *Research Policy* 32 (2003): 109–121.

Etzkowitz, Henry. *The Triple Helix: University-Industry-Government Innovation in Action.* New York: Routledge, 2008.

Ezrahi, Yaron. *Imagined Democracies: Necessary Political Fictions.* Cambridge: Cambridge University Press, 2012.

Felt, Ulrike, Rayvon Fouché, Clark A. Miller, and Laurel Smith-Doerr, eds. *The Handbook of Science and Technology Studies,* 4th ed. Cambridge, MA: MIT Press, 2017.

Ferrari, Bernard T., and Phillip H. Phan. "Universities and the Conglomerate Challenge." *McKinsey Quarterly* (September 2018) 116–119.

Fethke, Gary C., and Andrew J. Policano. *Public No More: A New Path to Excellence for America's Public Universities.* Stanford: Stanford University Press, 2012.

Fiore, Stephen M. "Interdisciplinarity as Teamwork: How the Science of Teams Can Inform Team Science." *Small Group Research* 39, no. 3 (2008): 251–277.

Fischer, David Hackett. *Albion's Seed: Four British Folkways in America.* New York: Oxford University Press, 1989.

Fischer, Frank. *Technocracy and the Politics of Expertise.* Los Angeles: Sage, 1990.

Fisher, Erik, and Genevieve Maricle. "Higher-Level Responsiveness? Sociotechnical integration within US and UK Nanotechnology Research Priority Setting." *Science and Public Policy* 42 (2015): 72–85.

Fisher, Erik, Roop L. Mahajan, and Carl Mitcham. "Midstream Modulation of Technology: Governance from Within." *Bulletin of Science, Technology, and Society* 26, no. 6 (December 2006): 485–496.

Fisher, Erik, Michael O'Rourke, Robert Evans, Eric B. Kennedy, Michael E. Gorman, and Thomas P. Seager. "Mapping the Integrative Field: Taking Stock of Sociotechnical Collaborations." *Journal of Responsible Innovation* 2, no. 1 (2015): 39–61.

Fogel, Daniel Mark. "Challenges to Equilibrium: The Place of the Arts and Humanities in Public Research Universities." In *Precipice or Crossroads: Where America's Great Public Universities Stand and Where They Are Going Midway through Their Second Century.* Edited by Daniel Mark Fogel and Elizabeth Malson-Huddle, 241–257. Albany: State University of New York Press, 2012.

Forest, James J. F., and Philip G. Altbach, eds. *International Handbook of Higher Education.* Dordrecht: Springer, 2006.

Foucault, Michel. *Power/Knowledge: Selected Interviews and Other Writings, 1972–1977.* New York: Pantheon, 1980.

Frick, George F. "The Royal Society in America." In *The Pursuit of Knowledge in the Early American Republic: American Scientific and Learned Societies from Colonial Times to the Civil War.* Edited by Alexandra Oleson and Sanborn C. Brown, 70–83. Baltimore: Johns Hopkins University Press, 1976.

Frodeman, Robert. *Sustainable Knowledge: A Theory of Interdisciplinarity.* Basingstoke, UK: Palgrave Macmillan, 2014.

Frodeman, Robert, Julie Thompson Klein, and Carl Mitcham, eds. *The Oxford Handbook of Interdisciplinarity.* Oxford: Oxford University Press, 2010.

Frodeman, Robert, Julie Thompson Klein, and Roberto C. S. Pacheco, eds. *The Oxford Handbook of Interdisciplinarity,* 2nd ed. Oxford: Oxford University Press, 2017.

Fuller, R. Buckminster. *Critical Path.* New York: St. Martin's Press, 1981.

Funtowicz, Silvio O., and Jerome R. Ravetz. "Three Types of Risk Assessment and the Emergence of Post-Normal Science." In *Social Theories of Risk.* Edited by Sheldon Krimsky and D. Golding, 251–273. New York: Praeger, 1992.

Galison, Peter. *Image and Logic: A Material Culture of Physics.* Chicago: University of Chicago Press, 1997.

Gardner, Howard. *Frames of Mind: The Theory of Multiple Intelligences.* New York: Basic Books, 1983.

Gardner, Howard. *Multiple Intelligences: New Horizons.* New York: Basic Books, 1993.

Gargani, John, and Robert McLean. "Scaling Science." *Stanford Social Innovation Review* 15, no. 4 (Fall 2017): 34–39.

Gaukroger, Stephen. *The Emergence of a Scientific Culture: Science and the Shaping of Modernity, 1260–1685.* Oxford: Oxford University Press, 2006.

Gaukroger, Stephen. *The Natural and the Human: Science and the Shaping of Modernity, 1739–1841.* Oxford: Oxford University Press, 2016.

Gavazzi, Stephen M., and E. Gordon Gee. *Land-Grant Universities for the Future: Higher Education for the Public Good.* Baltimore: Johns Hopkins University Press, 2018.

Geiger, Roger L. *The History of American Higher Education: Learning and Culture from the Founding to World War II.* Princeton, NJ: Princeton University Press, 2015.

Geiger, Roger L. *Knowledge and Money: Research Universities and the Paradox of the Marketplace.* Stanford: Stanford University Press, 2004.

Geiger, Roger L. "Milking the Sacred Cow: Research and the Quest for Useful Knowledge in the American University since 1920." *Science, Technology, and Human Values* 13, nos. 3 and 4 (summer and fall 1988): 332–348.

Geiger, Roger L. "New Themes in the History of Nineteenth-Century Colleges." In *The American College in the Nineteenth Century.* Edited by Roger L. Geiger, 1–36. Nashville: Vanderbilt University Press, 2000.

Geiger, Roger L. "Organized Research Units: Their Role in the Development of the Research University." *Journal of Higher Education* 61, no. 1 (January/February 1990): 1–19.

Geiger, Roger L. *Research and Relevant Knowledge: American Research Universities since World War II.* Oxford: Oxford University Press, 1993.

Geiger, Roger L. "Science, Universities, and National Defense, 1945–1970." *Osiris* 2nd series, 1992, no. 7: 26–48.

Geiger, Roger L. "The Ten Generations of American Higher Education." In *American Higher Education in the Twenty-First Century: Social, Political, and Economic Challenges,* 4th ed. Edited by Michael N. Bastedo, Philip G. Altbach, and Patricia J. Gumport, 3–34. Baltimore: Johns Hopkins University Press, 2016.

Geiger, Roger L. *To Advance Knowledge: The Growth of American Research Universities, 1900–1940.* Oxford: Oxford University Press, 1986.

Geiser, Saul, and Richard C. Atkinson. "Beyond the Master Plan: The Case for Restructuring Baccalaureate Education in California." *California Journal of Politics and Policy* 4, no. 1 (2013): 67–123.

Gersick, C. J. G. "Revolutionary Change Theories: A Multilevel Exploration of the Punctuated Equilibrium Paradigm." *Academy of Management Review* 16, no. 1 (1991): 10–36.

Gibbons, Michael, Camille Limoges, Helga Nowotny, Simon Schwartzman, Peter Scott, and Martin Trow. *The New Production of Knowledge: The Dynamics of Science and Research in Contemporary Societies.* London: Sage, 1994.

Giddens, Anthony. *The Consequences of Modernity.* Cambridge: Polity, 1990.

Giddens, Anthony. *The Constitution of Society: Outline of the Theory of Structuration.* Berkeley: University of California Press, 1984.

Girard, Monique, and David Stark. "Distributing Intelligence and Organizing Diversity in New Media Projects." *Environment and Planning* 34 (2002): 1927–1949.

Godfrey-Smith, Peter. *Theory and Reality: An Introduction to the Philosophy of Science.* Chicago: University of Chicago Press, 2003.

Golden, Daniel. *The Price of Admission: How America's Ruling Class Buys Its Way into Elite Colleges—and Who Gets Left outside the Gates*. New York: Random House, 2006.

Goldin, Claudia, and Lawrence F. Katz. *The Race between Education and Technology*. Cambridge, MA: Belknap Press of Harvard University Press, 2008.

Goldin, Ian, and Chris Kutarna. *The Age of Discovery: Navigating the Risks and Rewards of our New Renaissance*. New York: St. Martin's Press, 2016.

Goldman, Alvin I. "A Guide to Social Epistemology." In *Social Epistemology: Essential Readings*. Edited by Alvin I. Goldman and Dennis Whitcomb, 11–37. Oxford: Oxford University Press, 2011.

Goldman, Alvin I. *Knowledge in a Social World*. Oxford: Oxford University Press, 1999.

Goodman, Dena. *The Republic of Letters: A Cultural History of the French Enlightenment*. Ithaca, NY: Cornell University Press, 1996.

Gordon, Robert J. "The Demise of U.S. Economic Growth: Restatement, Rebuttal, and Reflections." NBER Working Paper 19895. Cambridge, MA: National Bureau of Economic Research, February 2014.

Gordon, Robert J. "The Great Stagnation of American Education." *New York Times* (September 7, 2013).

Gordon, Robert J. *The Rise and Fall of American Growth: The U.S. Standard of Living since the Civil War*. Princeton, NJ: Princeton University Press, 2016.

Grafton, Anthony. "Can the Colleges Be Saved?" Review of *College: What It Was, Is, and Should Be*, by Andrew Delbanco (Princeton, NJ: Princeton University Press, 2012). *New York Review of Books* (May 24, 2012).

Graham, Hugh Davis, and Nancy Diamond. *The Rise of American Research Universities: Elites and Challengers in the Postwar Era*. Baltimore: Johns Hopkins University Press, 1997.

Grant, Malcolm. "The Future of the University of London: A Discussion Paper from the Provost of University College London." (March 2005).

Graubard, Stephen R. Preface to *Distinctively American: The Residential Liberal Arts Colleges*. Edited by Steven Koblik and Stephen R. Graubard, vii–xiv. New Brunswick, NJ: Transaction, 2000.

Grawe, Nathan D. *Demographics and the Demand for Higher Education*. Baltimore: Johns Hopkins University, 2018.

Gray, Hanna Holborn. *Searching for Utopia: Universities and Their Histories*. Berkeley: University of California Press, 2012.

Gumport, Patricia J., ed. *Sociology of Higher Education: Contributions and Their Contexts*. Baltimore: Johns Hopkins University Press, 2007.

Guston, David H. "Boundary Organizations in Environmental Policy and Science: An Introduction." *Science, Technology, & Human Values* 26, no. 4 (2001): 399–408.

Guston, David H. "Responsible Innovation in the Commercialized University." In *Buying In or Selling Out: The Commercialization of the American Research University*. Edited by Donald G. Stein, 161–174. New Brunswick, NJ: Rutgers University Press, 2004.

Guston, David H. "Stabilizing the Boundary Between U.S. Politics and Science: The Rôle of the Office of Technology Transfer as a Boundary Organization." *Social Studies of Science* 29, no. 1 (February 1999): 81–111.

Guston, David H. "Understanding Anticipatory Governance." *Social Studies of Science* 44, no. 2 (2014): 218–242.

Guston, David H., Erik Fisher, Armin Grunwald, Richard Owen, Tsjalling Swierstra, and Simone van der Burg. "Responsible Innovation: Motivations for a New Journal." *Journal of Responsible Innovation* 1, no. 1 (2014): 1–8.

Guston, David H., Lori Hidinger, and Daniel Sarewitz. "IF/IS: The Institute for the Future of Innovation in Society." Working paper. Tempe, AZ: School for the Future of Innovation in Society, Arizona State University, 2018.

Guston, David H., and Kenneth Keniston. "The Social Contract for Science." In *The Fragile Contract: University Science and the Federal Government*. Edited by David H. Guston and Kenneth Keniston, 1–41. Cambridge, MA: MIT Press, 1994.

Gutmann, Amy. *Democratic Education*. Princeton, NJ: Princeton University Press, 1987.

Habermas, Jürgen. "Postscript." In *Habermas and Pragmatism*. Edited by Mitchell Adoulafia, Myra Bookman, and Catherine Kemp. London: Routledge, 2002.

Habermas, Jürgen. *The Theory of Communicative Action*. Vol. 2, *Reason and the Rationalization of Society*. Translated by Thomas McCarthy. Cambridge, MA: MIT Press, 1987.

Hacking, Ian. *Historical Ontology*. Cambridge, MA: Harvard University Press, 2002.

Hacking, Ian. "Introductory Essay." In *The Structure of Scientific Revolutions*. 50th anniv. ed. By Thomas S. Kuhn, vii–xxxvii. Chicago: University of Chicago Press, 1996. First published 1962.

Hagel, John, John Seely Brown, and Lang Davison. *The Power of Pull: How Small Moves, Smartly Made, Can Set Big Things in Motion*. New York: Basic Books, 2010.

Hahn, Roger. *The Anatomy of a Scientific Institution: The Paris Academy of Sciences, 1666–1803*. Berkeley: University of California Press, 1971.

Håkanson, Lars. "The Firm as an Epistemic Community: The Knowledge-Based View Revisited." *Industrial and Corporate Change* 19, no. 6 (2010): 1801–1828.

Hall, Kara L., et al. "Moving the Science of Team Science Forward: Collaboration and Creativity." *American Journal of Preventive Medicine* 35, 2S (2008): S243–S249.

Hancock, Dawson R., and Bob Algozzine. *Doing Case Study Research: A Practical Guide for Beginning Researchers*. New York: Teachers College Press, 2011.

Hannan, Michael T., and John Freeman. *Organizational Ecology*. Cambridge, MA: Harvard University Press, 1989.

Hannan, Michael T., and John Freeman. "The Population Ecology of Organizations." *American Journal of Sociology* 82, no. 5 (1977): 929–964.

Hannan, Michael T., and John Freeman. "Structural Inertia and Organizational Change." *American Sociological Review* 49 (April 1984): 149–164.

Hansen, Mogens H. *Polis: An Introduction to the Ancient Greek City-State*. Oxford: Oxford University Press, 2006.

Hardin, Garrett. "The Tragedy of the Commons." *Science* 162, no. 3859 (December 13, 1968): 1243–1248.

Hart, David M., ed. *The Emergence of Entrepreneurship Policy: Governance, Start-Ups, and Growth in the U.S. Knowledge Economy*. Cambridge: Cambridge University Press, 2003.

Harte, Negley. *The University of London, 1836–1986*. London: Athlone Press, 1986.

Hawkins, John J., and W. James Jacob. Introduction to *The New Flagship University: Changing the Paradigm from Global Ranking to National Relevancy.* Edited by John Aubrey Douglass, xi–xii. London: Palgrave Macmillan, 2016.

Heller, Donald E. "State Support of Higher Education: Past, Present, and Future." In *Privatization and Public Universities.* Edited by Douglas M. Priest and Edward P. St. John, 11–37. Bloomington: Indiana University Press, 2006.

Herbst, Jürgen. *From Crisis to Crisis: American College Government, 1636–1819.* Cambridge, MA: Harvard University Press, 1982.

Hess, Charlotte, and Elinor Ostrom, eds. *Understanding Knowledge as a Commons: From Theory to Practice.* Cambridge, MA: MIT Press, 2007.

Hewitt, Randall S. "Democratic Education: A Deweyan Reminder." *Education and Culture* 22, no. 2 (2006): 43–60.

HIBAR Research Alliance. "The HIBAR Research Alliance for Greater University Research Impact" (December 11, 2018), Lorne Whitehead, ed. Working paper. University of British Columbia.

Hilgartner, Stephen, Barbara Prainsack, and J. Benjamin Hurlbut. "Ethics as Governance in Genomics and Beyond." In *The Handbook of Science and Technology Studies,* 4th ed. Edited by Ulrike Felt, Rayvon Fouché, Clark A. Miller, and Laurel Smith-Doerr, 823–851. Cambridge, MA: MIT Press, 2017.

Hillis, W. Daniel. "The Enlightenment Is Dead, Long Live the Entanglement." *Journal of Design and Science* (February 22, 2016). DOI: 10.21428/1a042043.

Hirsch, Fred. *Social Limits to Growth.* Cambridge, MA: Harvard University Press, 1976.

Hofstadter, Richard. *Anti-Intellectualism in American Life.* New York: Knopf, 1970.

Holden, Erling, Kristin Linnerud, and David Banister. "Sustainable Development: Our Common Future Revisited." *Global Environmental Change* 26 (2014): 130–139.

Holbrook, J. Britt. "Peer Review." In *The Oxford Handbook of Interdisciplinarity,* ed. Robert Frodeman, Julie Thompson Klein, and Carl Mitcham, 321–332. Oxford: Oxford University Press, 2010.

Holland, John H. "Complex Adaptive Systems." *Daedalus* 121, no. 1 (1992): 17–30.

Holland, John H. *Complexity: A Very Short Introduction.* Oxford: Oxford University Press, 2014.

Holland, John H. *Emergence: From Chaos to Order.* New York: Addison-Wesley, 1998.

Hong, Lu, and Scott E. Page. "Groups of Diverse Problem-Solvers Can Outperform Groups of High-Ability Problem Solvers." *Proceedings of the National Academy of Sciences* 101, no. 46 (2004): 16385–16389.

Hood, Christopher. "A Public Management for All Seasons?" *Public Administration* 69, no. 1 (1991): 3–19.

Howard, Nicole. *The Book: The Life Story of a Technology.* Baltimore: Johns Hopkins University Press, 2009.

Huppatz, D. J. "Revisiting Herbert Simon's 'Science of Design.'" *Design Issues* 31, no. 2 (2015): 29–40.

Intergovernmental Panel on Climate Change (IPCC). *Global Warming of 1.5° C: An IPCC Special Report on the Impacts of Global Warming of 1.5° C above Pre-industrial Levels and Related Global Greenhouse Gas Emission Pathways.* Edited by V. Masson-Delmotte et al. Geneva: World Meteorological Organization, 2018.

Ito, Joichi. "Design and Science: Can Design Advance Science, and Can Science Advance Design?" *Journal of Design and Science* (November 21, 2017), DOI.10.21428/f4c68887.

Jacobs, Jerry A. *In Defense of Disciplines: Interdisciplinarity and Specialization in the Research University*. Chicago: University of Chicago Press, 2013.

Jasanoff, Sheila. "Beyond Epistemology: Relativism and Engagement in the Politics of Science." *Social Studies of Science* 26, no. 2 (1996): 393–418.

Jasanoff, Sheila. "The Idiom of Co-production." In *States of Knowledge: The Co-production of Science and Social Order*. Edited by Sheila Jasanoff, 1–12. London: Routledge, 2004.

Jasanoff, Sheila. *Science and Public Reason*. London: Routledge, 2012.

Jasanoff, Sheila. "Technologies of Humility: Citizen Participation in Governing Science." *Minerva* 41 (2003): 223–244.

Jefferson, Thomas. *The Papers of Thomas Jefferson*. Edited by Julian P. Boyd et al. Princeton, NJ: Princeton University Press, 1950–.

Jefferson, Thomas. *The Writings of Thomas Jefferson*. Edited by Paul L. Ford. New York: G. P. Putnam's Sons, 1892–1899.

Jonas, Hans. *The Imperative of Responsibility: In Search of an Ethics for the Technological Age*. Chicago: University of Chicago Press, 1984.

Jørgensen, Torben Beck, and Barry Bozeman. "Public Values: An Inventory." *Administration and Society* 39, no. 3 (May 2007): 354–381.

Kafatos, F. C., and T. Eisner. "Unification in the Century of Biology." *Science* 303 (February 27, 2004): 1257.

Kagan, Robert. "The Strongmen Strike Back." *Washington Post* (March 14, 2019).

Kahlenberg, Richard D. *Rewarding Strivers: Helping Low-Income Students Succeed in College*. New York: Century Foundation, 2010.

Kamenetz, Anya. *DIY U: Edupunks, Edupreneurs, and the Coming Transformation of Higher Education*. White River Junction, VT: Chelsea Green, 2010.

Kania, John, and Mark Kramer. "Collective Impact." *Stanford Social Innovation Review* (Winter 2011): 36–41.

Karabel, Jerome. *The Chosen: The Hidden History of Admission and Exclusion at Harvard, Yale, and Princeton*. Boston: Houghton Mifflin, 2005.

Kash, Don E. Perpetual Innovation: *The New World of Competition*. New York: Basic Books, 1989.

Kassicieh, Suleiman K., and H. Raymond Radosevich. *From Lab to Market: Commercialization of Public Sector Technology*. New York: Plenum Press, 1994.

Katz, Bruce, and Julie Wagner. *The Rise of Innovation Districts: A New Geography of Innovation in America*. Washington, DC: Brookings Institution, 2014.

Katz, Daniel, and Robert L. Kahn. *The Social Psychology of Organizations*. New York: Wiley, 1966.

Kellogg, Katherine C., Wanda J. Orlikowski, and JoAnne Yates. "Life in the Trading Zone: Structuring Coordination across Boundaries in Postbureaucratic Organizations." *Organization Science* 17, no. 1 (2006): 22–44.

Kennedy, Michael D. *Globalizing Knowledge: Intellectuals, Universities, and Publics in Transformation*. Stanford: Stanford University Press, 2015.

Kerr, Clark. *Higher Education Cannot Escape History: Issues for the Twenty-First Century*. Albany: SUNY Press, 1994.

Kerr, Clark. *The Uses of the University*, 5th ed. Cambridge, MA: Harvard University Press, 2001. First published 1963.

Kerr, Clark. "*The Uses of the University* Two Decades Later: Postscript 1982." *Change* 14 (October 1982): 23–31.

King, C. Judson. *The University of California: Creating, Nurturing, and Maintaining Academic Quality in a Public Research University Setting.* Berkeley: Center for Studies in Higher Education, University of California, Berkeley, 2018.

Kirp, David L. *Shakespeare, Einstein, and the Bottom Line: The Marketing of Higher Education.* Cambridge, MA: Harvard University Press, 2003.

Kirst, Michael W., and Mitchell L. Stevens, eds. *Remaking College: The Changing Ecology of Higher Education.* Stanford: Stanford University Press, 2015.

Kitcher, Philip. "Epistemology without History Is Blind." *Erkenntnis* 75, no. 3 (2011): 505–524.

Kitcher, Philip. *Science, Truth, and Democracy.* Oxford: Oxford University Press, 2001.

Knorr Cetina, Karin. *Epistemic Cultures: How the Sciences Make Knowledge.* Cambridge, MA: Harvard University Press, 1999.

Koblik, Steven. Foreword to *Distinctively American: The Residential Liberal Arts Colleges.* Edited by Steven Koblik and Stephen R. Graubard, xv–xvi. New Brunswick, NJ: Transaction, 2000.

Kozlowski, S. W. J., and K. J. Klein. "A Multilevel Approach to Theory and Research in Organizations: Contextual, Temporal, and Emergent Processes." In *Multilevel Theory, Research, and Methods in Organizations: Foundations, Extensions, and New Directions.* Edited by K. J. Klein and S. W. J. Kozlowski, 3–90. San Francisco: Jossey-Bass, 2000.

Kuhn, Thomas S. *The Structure of Scientific Revolutions*, 50th anniv. ed. Chicago: University of Chicago Press, 2012. First published 1962.

Kuznets, Simon. *Economic Growth and Structure.* New York: W. W. Norton, 1965.

Labaree, David F. *A Perfect Mess: The Unlikely Ascendency of American Higher Education.* Chicago: University of Chicago Press, 2017.

Lakatos, Imre. *The Methodology of Scientific Research Programmes: Philosophical Papers*, Vol. 1. Cambridge: Cambridge University Press, 1978.

Landemore, Hélène. *Democratic Reason: Politics, Collective Intelligence, and the Rule of the Many.* Princeton, NJ: Princeton University Press, 2013.

Landemore, Hélène. "Why the Many Are Smarter Than the Few and Why It Matters." *Journal of Public Deliberation* 8, no. 1 (2012): 1–12.

Landemore, Hélène, and Jon Elster, eds. *Collective Wisdom: Principles and Mechanisms.* Cambridge: Cambridge University Press, 2012.

Lane, David C. "It Works in Practice but Does It Work in Theory?" *Systems Research and Behavioral Science* 23 (2006): 565–570.

Lang, Eugene M. "Distinctively American: The Liberal Arts College." *Daedalus* 128, no. 1 (Winter 1999): 133–150.

Larson, Kelli L. et al. "Decision-Making under Uncertainty for Water Sustainability and Urban Climate Change Adaptation." *Sustainability* 7 (2015): 14761–14/84. DOI: 10.3390/su71114/61.

Leonhardt, David. "Top Colleges Largely for the Elite." *New York Times* (May 25, 2011).

Leslie, Stuart W. *The Cold War and American Science: The Military-Industrial-Academic Complex at MIT and Stanford.* New York: Columbia University Press, 1993.

Levien, Roger E. "RAND, IIASA, and the Conduct of Systems Analysis." In *Systems, Experts, and Computers: The Systems Approach to Management and Engineering, World War II and After.* Edited by Agatha C. Hughes and Thomas P. Hughes. Cambridge, MA: MIT Press, 2000.

Levitt, Barbara, and James G. March. "Organizational Learning." *Annual Review of Sociology* 14 (March 1988): 319–340.

Lewin, Kurt. *Field Theory in Social Science: Selected Theoretical Papers.* London: Tavistock, 1952.

Liebert, Wolfgang, and Jan C. Schmidt. "Collingridge's Dilemma and Technoscience: An Attempt to Provide a Clarification from the Perspective of the Philosophy of Science." *Poiesis Prax* 7 (2010): 55–71.

Lightman, Alan, Daniel Sarewitz, and Christina Desser, eds. *Living with the Genie: Essays on Technology and the Quest for Human Mastery.* Washington, DC: Island Press, 2003.

Liu, Nian Cai. "The Story of Academic Ranking of World Universities." *International Higher Education* 54 (Winter 2009): 2–3.

Lombardi, John V. *How Universities Work.* Baltimore: Johns Hopkins University Press, 2013.

Lowen, Rebecca S. *Creating the Cold War University: The Transformation of Stanford.* Berkeley: University of California Press, 1997.

Lozano, Rodrigo, Kim Ceulemans, Mar Alonso-Almeida, Donald Huisingh, Francisco J. Lozano, Tom Waas, Wim Lambrechts, Rebeka Lukman, and Jean Hugé. "A Review of Commitment and Implementation of Sustainable Development in Higher Education: Results from a Worldwide Survey." *Journal of Cleaner Production* 108 (2015): 1–18.

Lubchenco, Jane. "Entering the Century of the Environment: A New Social Contract for Science." *Science* 279 (1998): 491–497.

Lukianoff, Greg, and Jonathan Haidt. *The Coddling of the American Mind: How Good Intentions and Bad Ideas Are Setting Up a Generation for Failure.* New York: Penguin Press, 2018.

Lynch, John. P. *Aristotle's School: A Study of a Greek Educational Institution.* Berkeley: University of California Press, 1972.

Macfarlane, Bruce, and Ming Cheng. "Communism, Universalism, and Disinterestedness: Reexamining Contemporary Support among Academics for Merton's Scientific Norms." *Journal of Academic Ethics* 6 (2008): 67–78.

Madison, James. *The Writings of James Madison.* Edited by Gaillard Hunt. New York: G. P. Putnam's Sons, 1900–1910.

Madsen, David. *The National University: Enduring Dream of the United States.* Detroit: Wayne State University Press, 1966.

Mahoney, Carolyn R. "The 1890 Institutions in African American and American Life." In *Precipice or Crossroads: Where America's Great Public Universities Stand and Where They Are Going Midway through Their Second Century.* Edited by Daniel Mark Fogel and Elizabeth Malson-Huddle. Albany: State University of New York Press, 2012.

Manning, Kathleen. *Organizational Theory in Higher Education.* New York: Routledge, 2013.

Marcus, Jon. "More High School Grads Than Ever Are Going to College, but One in Five Will Quit." *Hechinger Report* (July 5, 2018).

Marginson, Simon. *The Dream Is Over: The Crisis of Clark Kerr's California Idea of Higher Education.* Oakland: University of California Press, 2016.

Marginson, Simon. "High Participation Systems of Higher Education." In *High Participation Systems of Higher Education.* Edited by Brendan Cantwell, Simon Marginson, and Anna Smolentseva, 3–38. Oxford: Oxford University Press, 2018.

Marginson, Simon. "Public/Private in Higher Education: A Synthesis of Economic and Political Approaches." *Studies in Higher Education* 43, no. 2 (2018): 322–337.

Marsden, George M. *The Soul of the American University: From Protestant Establishment to Established Nonbelief.* Oxford: Oxford University Press, 1994.

Mau, Bruce, and Jennifer Leonard. *Massive Change.* London: Phaidon Press, 2004.

Mazzucato, Mariana. *The Entrepreneurial State: Debunking Public vs. Private Sector Myths.* New York: Public Affairs, 2013.

McCusker, John J., and Russell R. Menard. *The Economy of British America, 1607–1789,* 2nd ed. Chapel Hill: University of North Carolina Press, 1991.

McKibben, Bill. "A Very Grim Forecast." *New York Review of Books* (November 22, 2018).

McMahon, Walter W. *Higher Learning, Greater Good: The Private and Social Benefits of Higher Education.* Baltimore: Johns Hopkins University Press, 2009.

McNamee, Stephen J., and Robert K. Miller. *The Meritocracy Myth,* 2nd ed. Lanham, MD: Rowman and Littlefield, 2009.

McPherson, Michael S., and Morton Owen Schapiro. "Economic Challenges for Liberal Arts Colleges." In *Distinctively American: The Residential Liberal Arts College.* Edited by Steven Koblik and Stephen R. Graubard, 47–76. New Brunswick, NJ: Transaction, 2000.

McPherson, Peter, et al. "Competitiveness of Public Research Universities and Consequences for the Country: Recommendations for Change." NASULGC Discussion Paper. Washington, DC: Association of Public and Land-Grant Universities, 2009.

Meacham, Jon. *Thomas Jefferson: The Art of Power.* New York: Random House, 2012.

Meadows, Donella H., Dennis L. Meadows, Jørgen Randers, and William W. Behrens. *The Limits to Growth: A Report for the Club of Rome's Project on the Predicament of Mankind.* New York: Universe, 1972.

Menand, Louis. "College: The End of the Golden Age." *New York Review of Books* (October 18, 2001).

Menand, Louis. *The Marketplace of Ideas: Reform and Resistance in the American University.* New York: W. W. Norton, 2010.

Menand, Louis. *The Metaphysical Club: A Story of Ideas in America.* New York: Farrar, Straus and Giroux, 2001.

Menand, Louis. "What Baseball Teaches Us About Measuring Talent." *New Yorker* (April 8, 2019): 85–89.

Menand, Louis, Paul Reitter, and Chad Wellmon, eds. *The Rise of the Research University: A Sourcebook.* Chicago: University of Chicago Press, 2017.

Merton, Robert K. *On the Shoulders of Giants: A Shandean Postscript.* Chicago: University of Chicago Press, 1993.

Merton, Robert K. *Sociology of Science and Sociology as Science.* Edited by Craig Calhoun. New York: Columbia University Press, 2010.

Merton, Robert K. *The Sociology of Science: Theoretical and Empirical Investigations.* Chicago: University of Chicago Press, 1973.

Merton, Robert K., and Elinor Barber. *The Travels and Adventures of Serendipity: A Study in Sociological Semantics and the Sociology of Science.* Princeton, NJ: Princeton University Press, 2004.

Mettler, Suzanne. *Degrees of Inequality: How the Politics of Higher Education Sabotaged the American Dream.* New York: Basic Books, 2014.

Meyer, John W. "The Effects of Education as an Institution." *American Sociological Review* 83, no. 1 (July 1977): 55–77.

Meyer, John W., Francisco O. Ramirez, David John Frank, and Evan Schofer. "Higher Education as an Institution." In *Sociology of Higher Education: Contributions and Their Contexts.* Edited by Patricia J. Gumport, 188–220. Baltimore: Johns Hopkins University Press, 2007.

Miller, Clark A. "Knowledge and Democracy: The Epistemics of Self-Governance." In *Science and Democracy: Making Knowledge and Making Power in the Biosciences and Beyond.* Edited by Stephen Hilgartner, Clark A. Miller, and Rob Hagendijk, 198–219. New York: Routledge, 2015.

Miller, Clark A., and Tischa A. Muñoz-Erickson. *The Rightful Place of Science: Designing Knowledge.* Tempe, AZ: Consortium for Science, Policy & Outcomes, 2018.

Miller, Clark A., and Carina Wyborn. "Co-production in Global Sustainability: Histories and Theories." *Environmental Science and Policy* (2018), https://doi.org/10.1016/j.envsci.2018.01.016.

Miller, Hugh T., and Charles J. Fox. "The Epistemic Community." *Administration and Society* 32, no. 6 (2001): 668–685.

Miller, John H., and Scott E. Page. *Complex Adaptive Systems: An Introduction to Computational Models of Social Life.* Princeton, NJ: Princeton University Press, 2007.

Miller, Thaddeus R., Tischa A. Muñoz-Erickson, and Charles L. Redman. "Transforming Knowledge for Sustainability: Towards Adaptive Academic Institutions." *International Journal of Sustainability in Higher Education* 12, no. 2 (2011): 177–192.

Miller, Thaddeus R., Arnim Wiek, Daniel Sarewitz, John Robinson, Lennart Olsson, David Kriebel, and Derk Loorbach. "The Future of Sustainability Science: A Solutions-Oriented Research Agenda." *Sustainability Science* 9 (2014): 239–246.

Mitchell, Melanie. *Complexity: A Guided Tour.* Oxford: Oxford University Press, 2009.

Mitchell, Michael, Michael Leachman, and Kathleen Masterson. "A Lost Decade in Higher Education Funding: State Cuts Have Driven Up Tuition and Reduced Quality." Washington, DC: Center on Budget and Policy Priorities, August 2017.

Mitchell, Michael et al. "Unkept Promises: State Cuts to Higher Education Threaten Access and Equity." Washington, DC: Center on Budget and Policy Priorities, 2018.

Moglen, Seth. "Sharing Knowledge, Practicing Democracy: A Vision for the Twenty-First Century University." In *Education, Justice, and Democracy.* Edited by Danielle Allen and Rob Reich, 267–284. Chicago: University of Chicago Press, 2013.

Mohrman, Kathryn, Wanhua Ma, and David Baker. "The Research University in Transition: The Emerging Global Model." *Higher Education Policy* 21, no. 1 (2008): 5–27.

Mokyr, Joel. *A Culture of Growth: The Origins of the Modern Economy.* Princeton, NJ: Princeton University Press, 2017.

Mokyr, Joel. *The Gifts of Athena: Historical Origins of the Knowledge Economy.* Princeton, NJ: Princeton University Press, 2002.

Mokyr, Joel. *The Lever of Riches: Technological Creativity and Economic Progress.* Oxford: Oxford University Press, 1990.

Moore, Kelly. "Organizing Integrity: American Science and the Creation of Public Interest Organizations, 1955–1975." *American Journal of Sociology* 101, no. 6 (1996): 1592–1627.

Moretti, Enrico. "Estimating the Social Return to Higher Education: Evidence from Longitudinal and Repeated Cross-sectional Data." *Journal of Econometrics* 121 (2004): 175–212.

Mowery, David C., and Nathan Rosenberg. "The U.S. National Innovation System." In *National Innovation Systems: A Comparative Analysis.* Edited by Richard R. Nelson, 29–75. Oxford: Oxford University Press, 1993.

Mowery, David C., Richard R. Nelson, Bhaven N. Sampat, and Arvids A. Ziedonis. "The Growth of Patenting and Licensing by U.S. Universities: An Assessment of the Effects of the Bayh-Dole Act of 1980." *Research Policy* 30 (2000): 99–119.

Mowery, David C., Richard R. Nelson, Bhaven N. Sampat, and Arvids A. Ziedonis. *Ivory Tower and Industrial Innovation: University-Industry Technology Transfer Before and After the Bayh-Dole Act.* Stanford: Stanford University Press, 2004.

Mumper, Michael, Lawrence E. Gladieux, Jacqueline E. King, and Melanie E. Corrigan. "The Federal Government and Higher Education." In *American Higher Education in the Twenty-First Century: Social, Political, and Economic Challenges*, 3rd ed. Edited by Philip G. Altbach et al., 113–138. Baltimore: Johns Hopkins University Press, 2011.

Narayanamurti, Venkatesh, and Toluwalogo Odumosu. *Cycles of Invention and Discovery: Rethinking the Endless Frontier.* Cambridge, MA: Harvard University Press, 2016.

National Academies. *Rising above the Gathering Storm: Energizing and Employing American for a Brighter Economic Future.* Washington, DC: National Academies Press, 2007.

National Academies. *Rising above the Gathering Storm Revisited: Rapidly Approaching Category 5.* Washington, DC: National Academies Press, 2010.

National Academies Committee on Facilitating Interdisciplinary Research (CFIR) and Committee on Science, Engineering, and Public Policy (COSEPUP). *Facilitating Interdisciplinary Research.* Washington, DC: National Academies Press, 2005.

National Academies Committee on Prospering in the Global Economy of the Twenty-First Century. *Capitalizing on Investments in Science and Technology.* Washington, DC: National Academies Press, 1999.

National Research Council. *Convergence: Facilitating Transdisciplinary Integration of Life Sciences, Physical Sciences, Engineering, and Beyond.* Washington, DC: National Academies Press, 2014.

National Research Council. *Enhancing the Effectiveness of Team Science.* Edited by Nancy J. Cooke and Margaret L. Hilton. Washington, DC: National Academies Press, 2015.

National Research Council. *Research Universities and the Future of America: Ten Breakthrough Actions Vital to Our Nation's Prosperity and Security.* Washington, DC: National Academies Press, 2012.

*Nature.* "Nature Index: Ten Institutions that Dominated Science in 2015" (April 20, 2016).

Nelson, Richard R. "The Moon and the Ghetto Revisited." *Science and Public Policy* 38, no. 9 (November 2011): 681–690.

Nelson, Richard R. "National Innovation Systems: A Retrospective on a Study." *Industrial and Corporate Change* 1, no. 2 (1992): 347–374.

Nelson, Richard R. "On the Uneven Evolution of Human Know-How." *Research Policy* 32 (2003): 909–922.

Nelson, Richard R. "The Simple Economics of Basic Scientific Research." *Journal of Political Economy* 67, no. 3 (June 1959): 297–306.

Nelson, Richard R., Kristin Buterbaugh, Marcel Perl, and Annetine Gelijns. "How Medical Know-How Progresses." *Research Policy* 40 (2011): 1339–1344.

Nelson, Richard R., and Nathan Rosenberg. "Technical Innovation and National Systems." In *National Innovation Systems: A Comparative Analysis.* Edited by Richard R. Nelson, 1–21. Oxford: Oxford University Press, 1993.

Nelson, Richard R., and Sidney G. Winter. *An Evolutionary Theory of Economic Change.* Cambridge, MA: Belknap Press of Harvard University Press, 1984.

Nevins, Allen. *The State Universities and Democracy.* Urbana: University of Illinois Press, 1962.

Newfield, Christopher. "The End of the American Funding Model: What Comes Next?" *American Literature* 82, no. 3 (September 2010): 611–635.

Newfield, Christopher. *The Great Mistake: How We Wrecked Public Universities and How We Can Fix Them.* Baltimore: Johns Hopkins University Press, 2016.

Newfield, Christopher. *Unmaking the Public University: The Forty-Year Assault on the Middle Class.* Cambridge, MA: Harvard University Press, 2008.

Newfield, Christopher. "What Is New about the New American University?" *Los Angeles Review of Books* (April 5, 2015).

Newman, John Henry. *The Idea of a University.* Notre Dame, IN: University of Notre Dame Press, 1982. Reprint of the edition published by Longmans, Green, and Company, 1873.

Nichols, Tom. *The Death of Expertise: The Campaign against Established Knowledge and Why It Matters.* Oxford: Oxford University Press, 2017.

Niosi, Jorge, Paolo Saviotti, Bertrand Bellon, and Michael M. Crow. "National Systems of Innovation: In Search of a Workable Concept." *Technology in Society* 15 (1993): 207–227.

Norman, Donald A., and Pieter Jan Stappers. "Design X: Complex Sociotechnical Systems." *She Ji: Journal of Design, Economics, and Innovation* 1, no. 2 (Winter 2015): 83–106.

Nowotny, Helga, Peter Scott, and Michael Gibbons. "Mode 2 Revisited: The New Production of Knowledge." *Minerva* 41 (2003): 179–194.

Nowotny, Helga, Peter Scott, and Michael Gibbons. *Rethinking Science: Knowledge and the Public in an Age of Uncertainty.* Cambridge: Polity Press, 2001.

Ober, Josiah. *Democracy and Knowledge: Innovation and Learning in Classical Athens.* Princeton, NJ: Princeton University Press, 2008.

Ober, Josiah. *Demopolis: Democracy before Liberalism in Theory and Practice.* Cambridge: Cambridge University Press, 2017.

Ober, Josiah. *Political Dissent in Democratic Athens: Intellectual Critics of Popular Rule.* Princeton, NJ: Princeton University Press, 1998.

Ober, Josiah. *The Rise and Fall of Classical Greece.* Princeton, NJ: Princeton University Press, 2015.

Oleson, Alexandra, and John Voss, eds. *The Organization of Knowledge in Modern America, 1860–1920.* Baltimore: Johns Hopkins University Press, 1979.

Orr, David W. *Earth in Mind: On Education, Environment, and the Human Prospect.* Washington, DC: Island Press, 2004.

Ostrom, Elinor. *Governing the Commons: The Evolution of Institutions for Collective Action.* Cambridge: Cambridge University Press, 1990.

Ostrom, Elinor, and Charlotte Hess. "A Framework for Analyzing the Knowledge Commons." In *Understanding Knowledge as a Commons: From Theory to Practice.* Edited by Charlotte Hess and Elinor Ostrom, 41–81. Cambridge, MA: MIT Press, 2007.

Owen, Richard, Philip Macnaghten, and Jack Stilgoe. "Responsible Research and Innovation: From Science in Society to Science for Society, with Society." *Science and Public Policy* 39 (2012): 751–760.

Owen, Richard, Jack Stilgoe, Phil Macnaghten, Mike Gorman, Erik Fisher, and David Guston. "A Framework for Responsible Innovation." In *Responsible Innovation: Managing the Responsible Emergence of Science and Innovation in Society.* Edited by Richard Owen, John Bessant, and Maggy Heintz, 27–50. Chichester: John Wiley and Sons, 2013.

Owen-Smith, Jason. *Research Universities and the Public Good: Discovery for an Uncertain Future.* Stanford: Stanford University Press, 2018.

Oxman, Neri. "Age of Entanglement." *Journal of Design and Science* (January 23, 2016).

Padgett, John F. "Evolvability of Organizations and Institutions." In *Complexity and Evolution: Toward a New Synthesis for Economics.* Edited by David Wilson, Jr. and Alan Kirman, 185–199. Cambridge, MA: MIT Press, 2016.

Padgett, John F., and Walter W. Powell. *The Emergence of Organizations and Markets.* Princeton, NJ: Princeton University Press, 2012.

Panzar, John C., and Robert D. Willig. "Economies of Scope." *American Economic Review* 71, no. 2 (May 1981): 268–272.

Paradeise, Catherine. "How Effective Have Reform Policies Been in Redesigning the French Higher Education and Research System?" In *Universities and the Production of Elites: Discourses, Policies, and Strategies of Excellence and Stratification in Higher Education.* Edited by Roland Bloch, Alexander Mitterle, Catherine Paradeise, and Tobias Peter, 103–125. London: Palgrave Macmillan, 2018.

Parker, John, and Beatrice Crona. "On Being All Things to All People: Boundary Organizations and the Contemporary Research University." *Social Studies of Science* 42, no. 2 (2012): 262–289.

Peacock, Mark S. "Path Dependence in the Production of Scientific Knowledge." *Social Epistemology* 23, no. 2 (2009): 105–124.

Pendleton-Jullian, Ann M., and John Seely Brown. *Design Unbound: Designing for Emergence in a White Water World.* Cambridge, MA: MIT Press, 2018. 2 vols.

Pielke, Roger A. *The Honest Broker: Making Sense of Science in Policy and Politics.* Cambridge: Cambridge University Press, 2007.

Piketty, Thomas. *Capital in the Twenty-First Century.* Translated by Arthur Goldhammer. Cambridge, MA: Belknap Press of Harvard University Press, 2014.

Pinheiro, Rómulo, and Mitchell Young. "The University as an Adaptive Resilient Organization: A Complex Systems Perspective." In *Theory and Method in Higher Education Research.* Vol. 3. Edited by Jeroen Huisman and Malcolm Tight, 119–136. Bingley, UK: Emerald Group, 2017.

Pinker, Steven. *Enlightenment Now: The Case for Reason, Science, Humanism, and Progress.* New York: Viking, 2018.

Polanyi, Michael. "The Republic of Science." *Minerva* 1, no. 1 (1962): 54–73.

Poli, R. "A Note on the Difference between Complicated and Complex Social Systems." *Cadmus* 2, no. 1 (2013): 142–147.

Porter, Alan L., et al. "Measuring Researcher Interdisciplinarity." *Scientometrics* 72, no. 1 (2007): 117–147.

Powell, Walter W. "Expanding the Scope of Institutional Analysis." In *The New Institutionalism in Organizational Analysis.* Edited by Walter W. Powell and Paul J. DiMaggio, 183–203. Chicago: University of Chicago Press, 1991.

Powell, Walter W., and Paul J. DiMaggio, eds. *The New Institutionalism in Organizational Analysis.* Chicago: University of Chicago Press, 1991.

Powell, Walter W., and Kaisa Snellman. "The Knowledge Economy." *Annual Review of Sociology* 30 (2004): 199–220.

Press, Eyal, and Jennifer Washburn. "The Kept University." *Atlantic Monthly* 285, no. 3 (March 2000): 39–54.

Price, Derek J. de Solla. *Little Science, Big Science, and Beyond.* New York: Columbia University Press, 1986. First published 1963.

Raftery, Adrian E., and Michael Hout. "Maximally Maintained Inequality: Expansion, Reform, and Opportunity in Irish Education, 1921–75." *Sociology of Education* 66 (1993): 41–62.

Rashdall, Hastings. *The Universities of Europe in the Middle Ages.* Oxford: Oxford University Press, 1895.

Readings, Bill. *The University in Ruins.* Cambridge, MA: Harvard University Press, 1996.

Rhoads, Robert A., Xiaoyang Wang, Xiaoguang Shi, and Yongcai Chang. *China's Rising Research Universities: A New Era of Global Ambition.* Baltimore: Johns Hopkins University Press, 2014.

Rhodes, Frank H. T. *The Creation of the Future: The Role of the American University.* Ithaca, NY: Cornell University Press, 2001.

Richard, Carl J. *The Founders and the Classics: Greece, Rome, and the American Enlightenment.* Cambridge, MA: Harvard University Press, 1994.

Rittel, Horst W. J., and Melvin W. Webber. "Dilemmas in a General Theory of Planning." *Policy Sciences* 4, no. 2 (June 1973): 155–169.

Roco, M. C., and W. S. Bainbridge, eds. *Converging Technologies for Improving Human Performance: Nanotechnology, Biotechnology, Information Technology, and Cognitive Science.* Washington, DC: National Science Foundation, 2002.

Rodríguez, Hannot, Erik Fisher, and Daan Schuurbiers. "Integrating Science and Society in European Framework Programmes: Trends in Project-Level Solicitations." *Research Policy* 42, no. 5 (2013): 1126–1137.

Rogers, E. M. *The Diffusion of Innovations.* New York: Free Press, 2003.

Roksa, Josipa, Eric Grodsky, Richard Arum, and Adam Gamoran. "United States: Changes in Higher Education and Stratification." In *Stratification in Higher Education: A Comparative Study.* Edited by Yossi Shavit, Richard Arum, and Adam Gamoran, 165–191. Stanford: Stanford University Press, 2007.

Romanelli, Elaine, and Michael L. Tushman. "Organizational Transformation as Punctuated Equilibrium." *Academy of Management Journal* 37, no. 5 (1994): 1141–1166.

Romer, Paul M. "Endogenous Technological Change." *Journal of Political Economy* 98, no. 5, pt. 2 (1990): S71–102.

Rorty, Richard. *Philosophy and the Mirror of Nature.* 30th anniv. ed. Princeton, NJ: Princeton University Press, 2009. Originally published 1979.

Rorty, Richard. *Philosophy as Cultural Politics: Philosophical Papers.* Vol. 4. Cambridge: Cambridge University Press, 2007.

Rorty, Richard. "Philosophy as a Transitional Genre." In *Pragmatism, Critique, Judgment: Essays for Richard J. Bernstein.* Edited by Seyla Benhabib and Nancy Fraser, 3–28. Cambridge, MA: MIT Press, 2004.

Rosenberg, Nathan. "America's Entrepreneurial Universities." In *The Emergence of Entrepreneurship Policy: Governance, Start-Ups, and Growth in the U.S. Knowledge Economy.* Edited by David M. Hart, 113–137. Cambridge: Cambridge University Press, 2003.

Rosenberg, Nathan. *Inside the Black Box: Technology and Economics.* Cambridge: Cambridge University Press, 1982.

Rosenberg, Nathan, and L. E. Birdzell. *How the West Grew Rich: The Economic Transformation of the Industrial World.* New York: Basic Books, 1986.

Rosenberg, Nathan, and Richard R. Nelson. "American Universities and Technical Advance in Industry." *Research Policy* 23, no. 3 (1994): 323–348.

Rothblatt, Sheldon. "Historical and Comparative Remarks on the Federal Principle in Higher Education." *History of Education* 16, no. 3 (1987): 151–180.

Rouse, William B. *Universities as Complex Enterprises: How Academia Works, Why It Works These Ways, and Where the University Enterprise Is Headed.* Hoboken, NJ: John Wiley, 2016.

Rouse, William B., John V. Lombardi, and Diane D. Craig. "Modeling Research Universities: Predicting Probable Futures of Public vs. Private and Large vs. Small Research Universities." *Proceedings of the National Academy of Sciences* 115, no. 50 (December 11, 2018): 12582–12589.

Saez, Emmanuel, and Gabriel Zucman. "Wealth Inequality in the United States since 1913: Evidence from Capitalized Income Tax Data" *Quarterly Journal of Economics* 131, no. 2 (May 2016): 519–578.

Salmi, Jamil. *The Challenge of Establishing World-Class Universities.* Washington, DC: World Bank, 2009.

Samuels, Robert. *Why Public Higher Education Should Be Free: How to Decrease Cost and Increase Quality at American Universities.* New Brunswick, NJ: Rutgers University Press, 2013.

Samuelson, Paul A. "The Pure Theory of Public Expenditures," *Review of Economics and Statistics* 36, no. 4 (1954): 387–389.

Sarewitz, Daniel. "Animals and Beggars: Imaginative Numbers in the Real World." In *Science, Philosophy, and Sustainability: The End of the Cartesian Dream.* Edited by Ângela Guimarães Pereira and Silvio Funtowicz, 135–146. London: Routledge, 2015.

Sarewitz, Daniel. *Frontiers of Illusion: Science, Technology, and the Politics of Progress.* Philadelphia: Temple University Press, 1996.

Sarewitz, Daniel. "Saving Science." *The New Atlantis: A Journal of Technology and Society* 49 (Spring/Summer 2016): 5–40.

Sarewitz, Daniel, and Richard R. Nelson. "Progress in Know-How: Its Origins and Limits." *Innovations: Technology, Governance, and Globalization* 3, no. 1 (Winter 2008): 101–117.

Saxenian, Anna Lee. *Regional Advantage: Culture and Competition in Silicon Valley and Route 128.* Cambridge, MA: Harvard University Press, 1994.

Schlosser, Peter. "Global Futures Initiative: Outline of Concept and Draft of Charter." December 14, 2017.

Schofer, Evan, and John W. Meyer. "The Worldwide Expansion of Higher Education in the Twentieth Century." *American Sociological Review* 70 (December 2005): 898–920.

Schultz, Theodore W. "Investment in Human Capital." *American Economic Review* 51, no. 1 (March 1961): 1–17.

Schumpeter, Joseph A. *The Theory of Economic Development.* Cambridge, MA: Harvard University Press, 1934.

Seidel, Marc-David, and Katherine J. Stewart. "An Initial Description of the C-Form." *Communities and Organization: Research in the Sociology of Organizations* 33 (2011): 37–72.

Seidel, Marc-David, Lorne Whitehead, Michele Mossman, and Creso Sá. "The Distributed Network of Cooperating Teams (DNCT): A Multi-Level Initiative for Organizational Change" (August 6, 2017), University of British Columbia Faculty Research and Publications. DOI: 10.14288/1.0354236.

Selingo, Jeffrey J. *College Unbound: The Future of Higher Education and What It Means for Students.* New York: Houghton Mifflin Harcourt, 2013.

Selingo, Jeffrey, Kevin Carey, Hilary Pennington, Rachel Fishman, and Iris Palmer. "The Next Generation University." Washington, DC: New America, 2013.

Shangraw, Ralph F., and Michael M. Crow. "Public Administration as a Design Science." *International Journal of Public Administration* 21, no. 6–8 (1998): 1059–1077.

Shapin, Steven, and Simon Shaffer. *Leviathan and the Air-Pump: Hobbes, Boyle, and the Experimental Life.* Princeton, NJ: Princeton University Press, 1985.

Shattock, Michael. *Making Policy in British Higher Education, 1945–2011.* London: Open University Press, 2012.

Shavit, Yossi, Richard Arum, and Adam Gamoran, eds. *Stratification in Higher Education: A Comparative Study.* Stanford: Stanford University Press, 2007.

Shelley, Mary. *Frankenstein: Annotated for Scientists, Engineers, and Creators of All Kinds.* Edited by David H. Guston, Ed Finn, and Jason Scott Robert. Cambridge, MA: MIT Press, 2017.

Shils, Edward. "The Order of Learning in the United States: The Ascendency of the University." In *The Organization of Knowledge in Modern America, 1860–1920.* Edited by Alexandra Oleson and John Voss. Baltimore: Johns Hopkins University Press, 1979.

Shirky, Clay. *Cognitive Surplus: Creativity and Generosity in a Connected Age.* New York: Penguin, 2010.

Shneiderman, Ben. *The New ABCs of Research: Achieving Breakthrough Collaborations.* Oxford: Oxford University Press, 2016.

Simon, Herbert A. *Administrative Behavior: A Study of the Decision-Making Processes in Administrative Organizations,* 4th ed. New York: Free Press, 1997. First published in 1946.

Simon, Herbert A. *Reason in Human Affairs.* Stanford: Stanford University Press, 1983.

Simon, Herbert A. *The Sciences of the Artificial,* 3rd ed. Cambridge, MA: MIT Press, 1996. First published 1966.

Slaughter, Sheila, and Larry L. Leslie. *Academic Capitalism: Politics, Policies, and the Entrepreneurial University.* Baltimore: Johns Hopkins University Press, 1997.

Slaughter, Sheila, and Gary Rhoades. *Academic Capitalism and the New Economy: Markets, State, and Higher Education.* Baltimore: Johns Hopkins University Press, 2004.

Smelser, Neil J. *Dynamics of the Contemporary University: Growth, Accretion, and Conflict.* Berkeley: University of California Press, 2013.

Smolentseva, Anna, Isak Froumin, David L. Konstantinovskiy, and Mikhail Lisyutkin. "Stratification by the State and the Market: High Participation Higher Education in Russia." In *High Participation Systems of Higher Education.* Edited by Brendan Cantwell, Simon Marginson, and Anna Smolentseva, 295–332. Oxford: Oxford University Press, 2018.

Snow, C. P. *The Two Cultures and the Scientific Revolution.* Cambridge: Cambridge University Press, 1960.

Soares, Joseph A. *The Power of Privilege: Yale and America's Elite Colleges.* Stanford: Stanford University Press, 2007.

Staley, David J. *Alternative Universities: Speculative Design for Innovation in Higher Education.* Baltimore: Johns Hopkins, 2019.

Stanley, Jason. *Know How.* Oxford: Oxford University Press, 2011.

Star, Susan Leigh. "This Is Not a Boundary Object: Reflections on the Origin of a Concept." *Science, Technology, & Human Values* 35, no. 5 (2010): 601–617.

Star, Susan Leigh, and James R. Griesemer. "Institutional Ecology, 'Translations' and Boundary Objects: Amateurs and Professionals in Berkeley's Museum of Vertebrate Zoology, 1907–39." *Social Studies of Science* 19, no. 3 (1989): 387–420.

Steck, Henry. "Corporatization of the University: Seeking Conceptual Clarity." *Annals of the American Academy of Political and Social Science* 585 (2003): 66–83.

Steffen, Will, Paul J. Crutzen, and John R. McNeill. "The Anthropocene: Are Humans Now Overwhelming the Great Forces of Nature?" *Ambio* 36, no. 8 (December 2007): 614–621.

Stevens, Mitchell L. "The Changing Ecology of U.S. Higher Education." In *Remaking College: The Changing Ecology of Higher Education.* Edited by Michael W. Kirst and Mitchell L. Stevens, 1–15. Stanford: Stanford University Press, 2015.

Stevens, Mitchell L., and Benjamin Gebre-Medhin. "Association, Service, Market: Higher Education in American Political Development." *Annual Review of Sociology* 42 (2016): 121–142.

Stiglitz, Joseph E. "Knowledge as a Global Public Good." In *Global Public Goods: International Cooperation in the Twenty-First Century.* Edited by Inge Kaul, Isabelle Grunberg, and Marc Stern, 308–325. Oxford: Oxford University Press, 1999.

Stokes, Donald E. *Pasteur's Quadrant: Basic Science and Technological Innovation.* Washington, DC: Brookings Institution Press, 1997.

Strijbos, Sytse. "Systems Thinking." In *The Oxford Handbook of Interdisciplinarity,* 2nd ed. Edited by Robert Frodeman, Julie Thompson Klein, and Roberto C. S. Pacheco, 291–302. Oxford: Oxford University Press, 2017.

Stuhr, John J. *Pragmatism, Postmodernism, and the Future of Philosophy.* New York: Routledge, 2002.

Taylor, Charles. "Two Theories of Modernity." *Public Culture* 11, no. 1 (1999): 153–174.

Taylor, John Wilson. "The Athenian Ephebic Oath." *Classical Journal* 13, no. 7 (April 1918): 495–501.

Taylor, Ryan C., Xiaofan Liang, Manfred D. Laubichler, Geoffrey B. West, Christopher P. Kempes, and Marion Dumas. "The Scalability, Efficiency, and Complexity of Universities and Colleges: A New Lens for Assessing the Higher Education System." arXiv:1910.05470v1 [cs.CY] (October 12, 2019): 1–15.

Teece, David J. "Knowledge and Competence as Strategic Assets." In *Handbook on Knowledge Management.* Vol. 1. Edited by C. W. Holsapple, 129–152. Berlin: Springer Verlag, 2003.

Tewksbury, Donald G. *The Founding of American Colleges and Universities before the Civil War.* New York: Columbia University Press, 1932.

Thelin, John R. *Essential Documents in the History of American Higher Education.* Baltimore: Johns Hopkins University Press, 2014.

Thelin, John R. *A History of American Higher Education.* 3rd ed. Baltimore: Johns Hopkins University Press, 2019.

Thelin, John R., and Richard W. Trollinger. *Philanthropy and American Higher Education.* New York: Palgrave Macmillan, 2014.

Thomas, George. *The Founders and the Idea of a National University: Constituting the American Mind.* Cambridge: Cambridge University Press, 2015.

Tierney, William G., and Michael Lanford. "Conceptualizing Innovation in Higher Education." In *Higher Education: Handbook of Theory and Research.* Vol. 31. Edited by M. B. Paulsen, 1–40. New York: Springer, 2016.

Tobin, Eugene M. "The Modern Evolution of America's Flagship Universities." Appendix A of *Crossing the Finish Line: Completing College at America's Public Universities.* Edited by William G. Bowen, Matthew M. Chingos, and Michael S. McPherson. Princeton, NJ: Princeton University Press, 2009.

Toma, J. Douglas. "Institutional Strategy: Positioning for Prestige." In *The Organization of Higher Education: Managing Colleges for a New Era.* Edited by Michael N. Bastedo, 118–159. Baltimore: Johns Hopkins University Press, 2012.

Trow, Martin. "In Praise of Weakness: Chartering, the University of the United States, and Dartmouth College." *Higher Education Policy* 16 (2003): 9–26.

Trow, Martin. "Problems in the Transition from Elite to Mass Higher Education." Berkeley: Carnegie Commission on Higher Education, 1973.

Trow, Martin. "Reflections on the Transition from Elite to Mass to Universal Access: Forms and Phases of Higher Education in Modern Societies since WWII." In *International Handbook of Higher Education.* Edited by James J. F. Forest and Philip G. Altbach, 243–280. Dordrecht: Springer, 2007.

Trow, Martin. "Reflections on the Transition from Mass to Universal Higher Education." *Daedalus* 99, no. 1 (Winter 1970): 1–42.

Trow, Martin. "Robbins: A Question of Size." *Universities Quarterly* 18 (1963): 136–152.

Tucker, Christopher, and Bhaven Sampat. "Laboratory-Based Innovation in the American National Innovation System." In *Limited by Design: R&D Laboratories in the U.S. National Innovation System.* Edited by Michael M. Crow and Barry Bozeman, 41–72. New York: Columbia University Press, 1998.

Turner, James. *Philology: The Forgotten Origins of the Modern Humanities.* Princeton, NJ: Princeton University Press, 2014.

Urry, John. "The Complexity Turn." *Theory, Culture, and Society* 22, no. 5 (2005): 1–14.

Uzzi, Brian, Satyam Mukherjee, Michael Stringer, and Ben Jones. "Atypical Combinations and Scientific Impact." *Science* 342 (October 25, 2013): 468–472.

Veysey, Laurence R. *The Emergence of the American University.* Chicago: University of Chicago Press, 1965.

Victor, David G. "Recovering Sustainable Development." *Foreign Affairs* 85, no. 1 (January/February 2006): 91–103.

Victor, David G. "Seeking Sustainability: Cities, Countryside, Wilderness." *Population and Development Review* 32, no. 1 (2006): 203–206.

Vitousek, Peter M., Harold A. Mooney, Jane Lubchenco, and Jerry M. Melillo. "Human Domination of Earth's Ecosystems." *Science* 277, no. 5325 (1997): 494–499.

Von Hippel, Eric. "Sticky Information and the Locus of Problem Solving: Implications for Innovation." *Management Science* 40 (1994): 429–439.

Voosen, Paul. "Microbiology Leaves the Solo Author Behind." *Chronicle of Higher Education* (November 11, 2013).

Wallerstein, Immanuel. "Anthropology, Sociology, and Other Dubious Disciplines." *Current Anthropology* 44, no. 4 (August–October 2003): 453–465.

Walsh, Taylor. *Unlocking the Gates: How and Why Leading Universities Are Opening Up Access to Their Courses.* Princeton, NJ: Princeton University Press, 2010.

Warde, Paul. *The Invention of Sustainability: Nature and Destiny, c. 1500–1870.* Cambridge: Cambridge University Press, 2018.

Weber, Max. "Objectivity in Social Science and Social Policy." [1904]. In *The Methodology of the Social Sciences.* Edited and translated by Edward A. Shils and Henry A. Finch. London: Routledge, 2011.

Weick, Karl E., and Robert E. Quinn. "Organizational Change and Development." *Annual Review of Psychology* 50 (1999): 361–386.

Weinberg, Alvin M. "The Axiology of Science." *American Scientist* 58, no. 6 (November–December 1970): 612–617.

Weinberg, Alvin M. "Science and Trans-Science." *Minerva* 10, no. 2 (April 1972): 209–222.

Weingart, Peter. "A Short History of Knowledge Formations." In *The Oxford Handbook of Interdisciplinarity.* Edited by Robert Frodeman, Julie Thompson Klein, and Carl Mitcham, 3–14. Oxford: Oxford University Press, 2010.

Wellmon, Chad. *Organizing Enlightenment: Information Overload and the Invention of the Modern Research University.* Baltimore: Johns Hopkins University Press, 2015.

Wenger, Etienne. *Communities of Practice: Learning, Meaning, and Identity.* Cambridge: Cambridge University Press, 1998.

West, Geoffrey. *Scale: The Universal Laws of Growth, Innovation, Sustainability, and the Pace of Life in Organisms, Cities, Economies, and Companies.* New York: Penguin Press, 2017.

Westbrook, Robert B. *John Dewey and American Democracy*. Ithaca, NY: Cornell University Press, 1991.

Westwick, Peter J. *The National Labs: Science in an American System, 1947–1974*. Cambridge, MA: Harvard University Press, 2003.

Whitehead, Lorne, Scott Slovic, and Janet Nelson. "Reinvigorating HIBAR Research for the Twenty-First Century: Enhancing Fundamental Research Excellence in Service to Society." *Technology and Innovation: Journal of the National Academy of Inventors* (in press).

Willetts, David. *A University Education*. Oxford: Oxford University Press, 2017.

Wilson, Alan. *Knowledge Power: Interdisciplinary Education for a Complex World*. London: Routledge, 2010.

Wilson, James Q. *Bureaucracy: What Government Agencies Do and Why They Do It*. New York: Basic Books, 1989.

Winterer, Caroline. *American Enlightenments: Pursuing Happiness in the Age of Reason*. New Haven, CT: Yale University Press, 2016.

Winterer, Caroline. *The Culture of Classicism: Ancient Greece and Rome in American Intellectual Life, 1780–1910*. Baltimore: Johns Hopkins University Press, 2002.

Wissema, J. G. *Towards the Third Generation University: Managing the University in Transition*. Cheltenham, UK: Edward Elgar, 2009.

Wood, Gordon S. *The Radicalism of the American Revolution*. New York: A. A. Knopf, 1992.

Woods, David D. "Four Concepts for Resilience and the Implications for the Future of Resilience Engineering." *Reliability Engineering and System Safety* 141 (2015): 5–9.

World Commission on Environment and Development. *Our Common Future*. Oxford: Oxford University Press, 1987.

Wuchty, Stefan, Benjamin F. Jones, and Brian Uzzi. "The Increasing Dominance of Teams in the Production of Knowledge." *Science* 316 (May 18, 2007): 1036–1039.

Wynne, Brian. "Public Uptake of Science: A Case for Institutional Reflexivity." *Public Understanding of Science* 2, no. 4 (1993): 321–337.

Yin, Robert K. *Case Study Research and Applications: Design and Methods*. Los Angeles: Sage, 2018.

Zachary, G. Pascal. *Endless Frontier: Vannevar Bush, Engineer of the American Century*. Cambridge, MA: MIT Press, 1999.

Zhang, Jie. "Chinese University Reform in Three Steps." *Nature* 514 (2014): 295–297.

Ziman, John. "Commentary." Special issue. *Minerva* 38 (2000): 21–25.

Ziman, John, ed. *Technological Innovation as an Evolutionary Process*. Cambridge: Cambridge University Press, 2000.

Zucman, Gabriel. "Global Wealth Inequality." Working Paper 25462. Cambridge, MA: National Bureau of Economic Research, January 2019.

# INDEX

References to figures are in *italics*.

AAU. *See* Association of American
Universities
Abbott, Andrew, 51, 52, 256, 357
Abrams, M. H., 59
academia. *See* academic community
(communities)
academic community (communities), 49–50,
59–60, 81, 86n26, 355–356, 423; academic
enterprise, correlation with, 132–133;
Arizona State University, xi–xii, 27,
102–103, 124–125, 169, 210; ASU charter
statement, 126–127; as democratic, 421–422;
historical, 86n26; as inherently transdisciplinary, 383–384; Mertonian norms, 49–50;
multiversity and, 81
academic culture (Fourth Wave), 39–41,
48–52, 54–56, 60–61, 70–72, 270, 307–321;
academic freedom, 49–50, 282, 421;
CUDOS norms, 49–50; democratic values,
49, 282–289, 420–426; "endless frontier" as
myth, 56; linear model of innovation, 269,
308–309; meritocratic presumptions of, 40,
62, 72, 78, 222; Mertonian norms, 49–50;
"republic of science," 55–56; science,
epistemic authority of, 50–51, 262–263,
311–312, 323–324; "twelve core foundational
values," 49–50. *See also* scientific culture
academic departments, 27, 50–51, 264–265;
Arizona State University (design process),
148–157, 164–169; disciplinary correlation,
50–51; German academic model, 50–51,
263–264, 264–265; interdisciplinary
reconfiguration, 107–108, 122–123, 129,
149–157, 164–169, 378–380; Johns Hopkins
University, 265
academic disciplines. *See* disciplinarity;
interdisciplinarity; transdisciplinarity
academic enterprise, 7–8, 10, 70, 78–79,
130–143, 143–148; academic capitalism in,
272; academic commercialization in,
271–272; Arizona State University, 105, 128,

139–143; bureaucratic agencies, in, 107,
130–148; complex adaptive knowledge
enterprises and, 29, 102, 301–307; design
aspiration, 127–128; versus corporate
university, 134–135, 199n51, 271–272
academic freedom, 49–50, 51, 282, 421;
German academic culture and, 14, 136–137,
262–265, 266–267, 421. *See also* German
academic model; University of Berlin
"academic marketplace." *See* higher
education, American, decentralization of
academic models. *See specific entries*
academic organization. *See* design,
institutional
Academic Ranking of World Universities
(ARWU), 46, 90n91, 125–126, 197n34, 397,
407–408. See also rankings of colleges and
universities
academic tradition. *See* filiopietism; tradition,
academic
accessibility, vii–viii, 1–4, 61–70, 70–73;
discovery and knowledge production, 3, 8,
38–39, 69–70, 77–78, 392; egalitarian
presumptions of, 10, 17–18, 30, 40, 71–72,
211–212, 257–262, 281–285; versus excellence,
61–70, 70–73, 194; family income, correlation
with, 1–3, 42–43, 61–70, 73–77, 89n78, 207–210;
Ivy League, 66–68, 212–214, 215, 219–221,
241–242n23; meritocratic presumptions of,
40, 62, 72, 78, 222; Morrill Act and, 107–108;
national imperative, vii–viii; Pell Grant
program, impact of, 69, 117–118, 143–144, 146,
188–189, 209–210; segmentation, vertical,
38–39; socioeconomic mobility, vii–viii,
41–43, 44–45, 61–70, 73–77, 137; stratification,
38–39. *See also* admissions; Arizona State
University; University Innovation Alliance
Adams, John, 277, 284, 285–286
adaptation (adaptivity), institutional. *See*
complex adaptive knowledge enterprises;
design, institutional; organizational change

457